California
HMH SCIENCE DIMENSIONS™

Grade 7

Watch the cover come alive as you adjust factors for plant growth.
Download the HMH Science Dimensions AR app available on Android or iOS devices.

This Write-In Book belongs to

_____

Teacher/Room

_____

Houghton Mifflin Harcourt™

Consulting Authors

Michael A. DiSpezio

Global Educator
North Falmouth, Massachusetts

Michael DiSpezio has authored many HMH instructional programs for Science and Mathematics. He has also authored numerous trade books and multimedia programs on various topics and hosted dozens of studio and location broadcasts for various organizations in the United States and worldwide. Most recently, he has been working with educators to provide strategies for implementing the Next Generation Science Standards, particularly the Science and Engineering Practices, Crosscutting Concepts, and the use of Evidence Notebooks. To all his projects, he brings his extensive background in science, his expertise in classroom teaching at the elementary, middle, and high school levels, and his deep experience in producing interactive and engaging instructional materials.

Marjorie Frank

Science Writer and Content-Area Reading Specialist
Brooklyn, New York

An educator and linguist by training, a writer and poet by nature, Marjorie Frank has authored and designed a generation of instructional materials in all subject areas, including past HMH Science programs. Her other credits include authoring science issues of an award-winning children's magazine, writing game-based digital assessments, developing blended learning materials for young children, and serving as instructional designer and coauthor of pioneering school-to-work software. In addition, she has served on the adjunct faculty of Hunter, Manhattan, and Brooklyn Colleges, teaching courses in science methods, literacy, and writing. For *California HMH Science Dimensions™*, she has guided the development of our K–2 strands and our approach to making connections between NGSS and Common Core ELA/literacy standards.

Acknowledgments

Cover credits: (plant) ©HMH; (Earth at night) ©Nastco/iStock/Getty Images Plus/Getty Images.

Section Header Master Art: (machinations) ©DNY59/E+/Getty Images; (rivers on top of Greenland ice sheet) ©Maria-José Viñas, NASA Earth Science News Team; (human cells, illustration) ©Sebastian Kaulitzki/Science Photo Library/Corbis; (waves) ©Alfred Pasieka/Science Source

Copyright © 2020 by Houghton Mifflin Harcourt Publishing Company

All rights reserved. No part of this work may be reproduced or transmitted in any form or by any means, electronic or mechanical, including photocopying or recording, or by any information storage or retrieval system, without the prior written permission of the copyright owner unless such copying is expressly permitted by federal copyright law. Requests for permission to make copies of any part of the work should be submitted through our Permissions website at https://customercare.hmhco.com/contactus/Permissions.html or mailed to Houghton Mifflin Harcourt Publishing Company, Attn: Intellectual Property Licensing, 9400 Southpark Center Loop, Orlando, Florida 32819-8647.

Printed in the U.S.A.

ISBN 978-1-328-91486-6

8 9 10 0877 27 26 25 24 23 22 21 20 19

4500777272 A B C D E F G

If you have received these materials as examination copies free of charge, Houghton Mifflin Harcourt Publishing Company retains title to the materials and they may not be resold. Resale of examination copies is strictly prohibited.

Possession of this publication in print format does not entitle users to convert this publication, or any portion of it, into electronic format.

Michael R. Heithaus, PhD

Dean, College of Arts, Sciences & Education
Professor, Department of Biological Sciences
Florida International University
Miami, Florida

Mike Heithaus joined the FIU Biology Department in 2003 and has served as Director of the Marine Sciences Program and Executive Director of the School of Environment, Arts, and Society, which brings together the natural and social sciences and humanities to develop solutions to today's environmental challenges. He now serves as Dean of the College of Arts, Sciences & Education. His research focuses on predator-prey interactions and the ecological importance of large marine species. He has helped to guide the development of Life Science content in *California HMH Science Dimensions™*, with a focus on strategies for teaching challenging content as well as the science and engineering practices of analyzing data and using computational thinking.

Bernadine Okoro

Access and Equity Consultant

S.T.E.M. Learning Advocate & Consultant
Washington, DC

Bernadine Okoro is a chemical engineer by training and a playwright, novelist, director, and actress by nature. Okoro went from working with patents and biotechnology to teaching in K–12 classrooms. A 12-year science educator and Albert Einstein Distinguished Fellow, Okoro was one of the original authors of the Next Generation Science Standards. As a member of the Diversity and Equity Team, her focus on Alternative Education and Community Schools and on Integrating Social-Emotional Learning and Brain-Based Learning into NGSS is the vehicle she uses as a pathway to support underserved groups from elementary school to adult education. An article and book reviewer for NSTA and other educational publishing companies, Okoro currently works as a S.T.E.M. Learning Advocate & Consultant.

Cary I. Sneider, PhD

Associate Research Professor
Portland State University
Portland, Oregon

While studying astrophysics at Harvard, Cary Sneider volunteered to teach in an Upward Bound program and discovered his real calling as a science teacher. After teaching middle and high school science in Maine, California, Costa Rica, and Micronesia, he settled for nearly three decades at Lawrence Hall of Science in Berkeley, California, where he developed skills in curriculum development and teacher education. Over his career, Cary directed more than 20 federal, state, and foundation grant projects and was a writing team leader for the Next Generation Science Standards. He has been instrumental in ensuring *California HMH Science Dimensions™* meets the high expectations of the NGSS and provides an effective three-dimensional learning experience for all students.

Program Advisors

Paul D. Asimow, PhD
Eleanor and John R. McMillan Professor of Geology and Geochemistry
California Institute of Technology
Pasadena, California

Joanne Bourgeois
Professor Emerita
Earth & Space Sciences
University of Washington
Seattle, WA

Dr. Eileen Cashman
Professor
Humboldt State University
Arcata, California

Elizabeth A. De Stasio, PhD
Raymond J. Herzog Professor of Science
Lawrence University
Appleton, Wisconsin

Perry Donham, PhD
Lecturer
Boston University
Boston, Massachusetts

Shila Garg, PhD
Emerita Professor of Physics
Former Dean of Faculty & Provost
The College of Wooster
Wooster, Ohio

Tatiana A. Krivosheev, PhD
Professor of Physics
Clayton State University
Morrow, Georgia

Mark B. Moldwin, PhD
Professor of Space Sciences and Engineering
University of Michigan
Ann Arbor, Michigan

Ross H. Nehm
Stony Brook University (SUNY)
Stony Brook, NY

Kelly Y. Neiles, PhD
Assistant Professor of Chemistry
St. Mary's College of Maryland
St. Mary's City, Maryland

John Nielsen-Gammon, PhD
Regents Professor
Department of Atmospheric Sciences
Texas A&M University
College Station, Texas

Dr. Sten Odenwald
Astronomer
NASA Goddard Spaceflight Center
Greenbelt, Maryland

Bruce W. Schafer
Executive Director
Oregon Robotics Tournament & Outreach Program
Beaverton, Oregon

Barry A. Van Deman
President and CEO
Museum of Life and Science
Durham, North Carolina

Kim Withers, PhD
Assistant Professor
Texas A&M University-Corpus Christi
Corpus Christi, Texas

Adam D. Woods, PhD
Professor
California State University, Fullerton
Fullerton, California

English Development Advisors

Mercy D. Momary
Local District Northwest
Los Angeles, California

Michelle Sullivan
Balboa Elementary
San Diego, California

Classroom Reviewers & Hands-On Activities Advisors

Julie Arreola
Sun Valley Magnet School
Los Angeles, California

Pamela Bluestein
Sycamore Canyon School
Newbury Park, California

Andrea Brown
HLPUSD Science & STEAM TOSA
Hacienda Heights, California

Stephanie Greene
Science Department Chair
Sun Valley Magnet School
Sun Valley, California

Rana Mujtaba Khan
Will Rogers High School
Van Nuys, California

Suzanne Kirkhope
Willow Elementary and Round Meadow Elementary
Agoura Hills, California

George Kwong
Schafer Park Elementary
Hayward, California

Imelda Madrid
Bassett St. Elementary School
Lake Balboa, California

Susana Martinez O'Brien
Diocese of San Diego
San Diego, California

Craig Moss
Mt. Gleason Middle School
Sunland, California

Isabel Souto
Schafer Park Elementary
Hayward, California

Emily R.C.G. Williams
South Pasadena Middle School
South Pasadena, California

Contents

UNIT 1 Science and Engineering — 1

Lesson 1 • Science, Engineering, and Resource Use are Related 4
    Hands-On Lab Investigate the Influence of Decisions on Resource Use 11
    People in Science Shreyas Sundaram, Electrical Engineer 17

Lesson 2 • Engineer It: Using the Engineering Design Process 22
    Hands-On Lab Design a Bicycle Helmet Model 30
    Careers in Engineering Civil Engineering 37

Unit Review 43
ENGINEER IT Unit Performance Task 47

UNIT 2 The Structure of Matter — 49

Lesson 1 • Patterns Can Be Observed in Organisms and Nonliving Things 52
    Hands-On Lab Model Particles in Objects 63
    People in Engineering Gianluca Cusatis, Civil Engineer 65

Lesson 2 • Matter Exists in Different States 70
    Hands-On Lab Observe States of Matter 73

Lesson 3 • Changes of State Are Caused by Changes in Thermal Energy 84
    Hands-On Lab Investigate a Change of State 87
    Careers in Science Forensics 99

Lesson 4 • Organisms and Nonliving Things Are Made of Atoms 104
    Hands-On Lab Model Molecules 114

Unit Review 127
Unit Performance Task 131

Contents

UNIT 3 Chemical Processes   133

Lesson 1 • Matter Changes Identity in Chemical Reactions 136
  Hands-On Lab Observe Substances Before and After a Change 147

Lesson 2 • Chemical Equations Model Chemical Reactions 154
  Hands-On Lab Observe a Chemical Reaction 163

Lesson 3 • Engineer It: Using Thermal Energy in a Device 174
  Hands-On Lab Choose a Chemical Process 185
  People in Science   Fritz Haber and Carl Bosch, Chemists 189

Lesson 4 • Synthetic Materials Are Made from Natural Resources 194
  Hands-On Lab Make a Synthetic Material 208
  Careers in Engineering   Biomass Engineer 213

Unit Review 219
  ENGINEER IT Unit Performance Task 223

This is a crystal of progesterone, an important hormone in the human body. It can be synthetically produced from plant materials using a series of chemical reactions known as the Marker Degradation.

Contents

UNIT 4 Matter and Energy in Organisms and Rock — 225

Lesson 1 • The Flow of Energy Drives the Cycling of Matter in Organisms 228
- Hands-On Lab Investigate Decomposition 238

Lesson 2 • Chemical Reactions Provide Energy for Cells 248
- Hands-On Lab Investigate the Effect of Sunlight on *Elodea* 254

Lesson 3 • The Flow of Energy Drives Weathering, Erosion, and Deposition 266
- Hands-On Lab Model Erosion and Deposition 277

Lesson 4 • The Flow of Energy Drives the Rock Cycle 284
- Hands-On Lab Model Crystal Formation 289

Unit Review 309

ENGINEER IT Unit Performance Task 313

Mountain goats feed and play on the rocky peaks formed by Earth's processes.

vii

Contents

UNIT 5 Earth's Resources and Ecosystems — 315

Lesson 1 • The Movement of Earth's Plates Affects Earth's Surface 318
   Hands-On Lab Model the Movement of Continents 330
   People in Science Doug Gibbons, Research Scientist Engineer 335

Lesson 2 • Natural Resources Are Distributed Unevenly 340
   Hands-On Lab Model Recharge and Withdrawal in an Aquifer 353

Lesson 3 • Resource Availability Affects Organisms 360
   Hands-On Lab Investigate Effects of Limited Resources 371

Lesson 4 • Patterns Can Be Observed in Interactions between Organisms 382
   Hands-On Lab Simulate Feeding Relationships 386

Lesson 5 • The Flow of Energy Drives the Cycling of Matter in Ecosystems 400
   Hands-On Lab Model Energy Flow in an Ecosystem 405
   People in Science Charles Elton, Ecologist 411

Unit Review 417

ENGINEER IT Unit Performance Task 421

We depend on forests for many resources, including paper, furniture, medicines, and biofuels.

Contents

UNIT 6 Earth's Surface and Society — 423

Lesson 1 • Geologic Processes Change Earth's Surface 426
- Hands-On Lab Analyze Visual Evidence 436

Lesson 2 • Natural Hazards Disrupt Earth's Surface 444
- Hands-On Lab Assess Building Sites Near a Volcano 455

Lesson 3 • Some Natural Hazards Can Be Predicted and Mitigated ... 466
- Hands-On Lab Predict a Landslide 470

Lesson 4 • Human Use of Synthetic Materials Affects Earth's Surface ... 492
- Hands-On Lab Sort Synthetic Materials Using Properties 509
- Careers in Engineering Materials Engineer 511

Unit Review 517

ENGINEER IT Unit Performance Task 521

UNIT 7 Biodiversity and Ecosystem Dynamics — 523

Lesson 1 • Biodiversity Indicates Ecosystem Health 526
- Hands-On Lab Measure Biodiversity 530
- Careers in Science Restoration Ecologist 539

Lesson 2 • Ecosystems Can Stabilize in Response to Change 544
- Hands-On Lab Identify Factors That Influence a Population Change ... 554
- People in Science Rodolfo Dirzo, Terrestrial Ecologist 557

Lesson 3 • Engineer It: Maintaining Biodiversity and Ecosystem Services ... 562
- Hands-On Lab Model Habitat Fragmentation 572
- Careers in Science Ecotourism 583

Unit Review 589

ENGINEER IT Unit Performance Task 593

ix

Claims, Evidence, and Reasoning

Constructing an Argument

Constructing a strong argument is useful in science and engineering and in everyday life. A strong argument has three parts: a claim, evidence, and reasoning. Scientists and engineers use claims-evidence-reasoning arguments to communicate their explanations and solutions to others and to challenge or debate the conclusions of other scientists and engineers. The words *argue* and *argument* do not mean that scientists or engineers are fighting about something. Instead, this is a way to support a claim using evidence. Argumentation is a calm and rational way for people to examine all the facts and come to the best conclusion.

A **claim** is a statement that answers the question "What do you know?" A claim is a statement of your understanding of a phenomenon, answer to a question, or solution to a problem. A claim states what you think is true based on the information you have.

Evidence is any data that are related to your claim and answer the question "How do you know that?" These data may be from your own experiments and observations, reports by scientists or engineers, or other reliable data. Arguments made in science and engineering should be supported by empirical evidence. Empirical evidence is evidence that comes from observation or experiment.

Evidence used to support a claim should also be relevant and sufficient. Relevant evidence is evidence that is about the claim, and not about something else. Evidence is sufficient when there is enough evidence to fully support the claim.

Reasoning is the use of logical, analytical thought to form conclusions or inferences. Reasoning answers the question "Why does your evidence support your claim?" So, reasoning explains the relationship between your evidence and your claim. Reasoning might include a scientific law or principle that helps explain the relationship between the evidence and the claim.

Here is an example of a claims-evidence-reasoning argument.

Claim	Ice melts faster in the sun than it does in the shade.
Evidence	Two ice cubes of the same size were each placed in a plastic dish. One dish was placed on a wooden bench in the sun and one was placed on a different part of the same bench in the shade. The ice cube in the sun melted in 14 minutes and 32 seconds. The ice cube in the shade melted in 18 minutes and 15 seconds.
Reasoning	This experiment was designed so that the only variable that was different in the set-up of the two ice cubes was whether they were in the shade or in the sun. Because the ice cube in the sun melted almost 4 minutes faster than the one in the shade, this is sufficient evidence to say that ice melts faster in the sun than it does in the shade.

To summarize, a strong argument:

- presents a claim that is clear, logical, and well-defended
- supports the claim with empirical evidence that is sufficient and relevant
- includes reasons that make sense and are presented in a logical order

Constructing Your Own Argument

Now construct your own argument by recording a claim, evidence, and reasoning. With your teacher's permission, you can do an investigation to answer a question you have about how the world works. Or you can construct your argument based on observations you have already made about the world.

Claim	
Evidence	
Reasoning	

For more information on claims, evidence, and reasoning, see the online **English Language Arts Handbook.**

Safety Preview

Whether you are in the lab or in the field, you are responsible for your own safety and the safety of others. To fulfill these responsibilities and avoid accidents, be aware of the safety of your classmates as well as your own safety at all times. Take your lab work and fieldwork seriously, and behave appropriately. Elements of safety to keep in mind are shown below and on the following pages.

Safety in the Lab

- [ ] Be sure you understand the materials, your procedure, and the safety rules before you start an investigation in the lab.
- [ ] Know where to find and how to use fire extinguishers, eyewash stations, shower stations, and emergency power shutoffs.
- [ ] Use proper safety equipment. Always wear personal protective equipment, such as eye protection and gloves, when setting up labs, during labs, and when cleaning up.
- [ ] Do not begin until your teacher has told you to start. Follow directions.
- [ ] Keep the lab neat and uncluttered. Clean up when you are finished. Report all spills to your teacher immediately. Watch for slip/fall and trip/fall hazards.
- [ ] If you or another student are injured in any way, tell your teacher immediately, even if the injury seems minor.
- [ ] Do not take any food or drink into the lab. Never take any chemicals out of the lab.

Safety in the Field

- [ ] Be sure you understand the goal of your fieldwork and the proper way to carry out the investigation before you begin fieldwork.
- [ ] Use proper safety equipment and personal protective equipment, such as eye protection, that suits the terrain and the weather.
- [ ] Follow directions, including appropriate safety procedures as provided by your teacher.
- [ ] Do not approach or touch wild animals. Do not touch plants unless instructed by your teacher to do so. Leave natural areas as you found them.
- [ ] Stay with your group.
- [ ] Use proper accident procedures, and let your teacher know about a hazard in the environment or an accident immediately, even if the hazard or accident seems minor.

Safety Symbols

To highlight specific types of precautions, the following symbols are used throughout the lab program. Remember that no matter what safety symbols you see within each lab, all safety rules should be followed at all times.

Dress Code

- Wear safety goggles (or safety glasses as appropriate for the activity) at all times in the lab as directed. If chemicals get into your eye, flush your eyes immediately for a minimum of 15 minutes.
- Do not wear contact lenses in the lab.
- Do not look directly at the sun or any intense light source or laser.
- Wear appropriate protective non-latex gloves as directed.
- Wear an apron or lab coat at all times in the lab as directed.
- Tie back long hair, secure loose clothing, and remove loose jewelry. Remove acrylic nails when working with active flames.
- Do not wear open-toed shoes, sandals, or canvas shoes in the lab.

Glassware and Sharp Object Safety

- Do not use chipped or cracked glassware.
- Use heat-resistant glassware for heating or storing hot materials.
- Notify your teacher immediately if a piece of glass breaks.
- Use extreme care when handling any sharp or pointed instruments.
- Do not cut an object while holding the object unsupported in your hands. Place the object on a suitable cutting surface, and always cut in a direction away from your body.

Chemical Safety

- If a chemical gets on your skin, on your clothing, or in your eyes, rinse it immediately for a minimum of 15 minutes (using the shower, faucet, or eyewash station), and alert your teacher.
- Do not clean up spilled chemicals unless your teacher directs you to do so.
- Do not inhale any gas or vapor unless directed to do so by your teacher. If you are instructed to note the odor of a substance, wave the fumes toward your nose with your hand. This is called wafting. Never put your nose close to the source of the odor.
- Handle materials that emit vapors or gases in a well-ventilated area.
- Keep your hands away from your face while you are working on any activity.

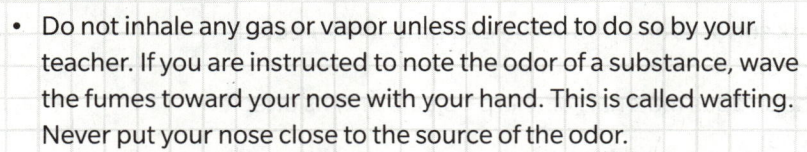

Safety Symbols, continued

Electrical Safety

- Do not use equipment with frayed electrical cords or loose plugs.
- Do not use electrical equipment near water or when clothing or hands are wet.
- Hold the plug housing when you plug in or unplug equipment. Do not pull on the cord.
- Use only GFI-protected electrical receptacles.

Heating and Fire Safety

- Be aware of any source of flames, sparks, or heat (such as flames, heating coils, or hot plates) before working with any flammable substances.
- Know the location of the lab's fire extinguisher and fire-safety blankets.
- Know your school's fire-evacuation routes.
- If your clothing catches on fire, walk to the lab shower to put out the fire. Do not run.
- Never leave a hot plate unattended while it is turned on or while it is cooling.
- Use tongs or appropriately insulated holders when handling heated objects.
- Allow all equipment to cool before storing it.

Plant and Animal Safety

- Do not eat any part of a plant.
- Do not pick any wild plant unless your teacher instructs you to do so.
- Handle animals only as your teacher directs.
- Treat animals carefully and respectfully.
- Wash your hands throughly with soap and water after handling any plant or animal.

Cleanup

- Clean all work surfaces and protective equipment as directed by your teacher.
- Dispose of hazardous materials or sharp objects only as directed by your teacher.
- Wash your hands throughly with soap and water before you leave the lab or after any activity.

Name: _____   Date: _____

Student Safety Quiz

Circle the letter of the BEST answer.

1. Before starting an investigation or lab procedure, you should
   A. try an experiment of your own
   B. open all containers and packages
   C. read all directions and make sure you understand them
   D. handle all the equipment to become familiar with it

2. At the end of any activity you should
   A. wash your hands thoroughly with soap and water before leaving the lab
   B. cover your face with your hands
   C. put on your safety goggles
   D. leave hot plates switched on

3. If you get hurt or injured in any way, you should
   A. tell your teacher immediately
   B. find bandages or a first aid kit
   C. go to your principal's office
   D. get help after you finish the lab

4. If your glassware is chipped or broken, you should
   A. use it only for solid materials
   B. give it to your teacher for recycling or disposal
   C. put it back into the storage cabinet
   D. increase the damage so that it is obvious

5. If you have unused chemicals after finishing a procedure, you should
   A. pour them down a sink or drain
   B. mix them all together in a bucket
   C. put them back into their original containers
   D. dispose of them as directed by your teacher

6. If electrical equipment has a frayed cord, you should
   A. unplug the equipment by pulling the cord
   B. let the cord hang over the side of a counter or table
   C. tell your teacher about the problem immediately
   D. wrap tape around the cord to repair it

7. If you need to determine the odor of a chemical or a solution, you should
   A. use your hand to bring fumes from the container to your nose
   B. bring the container under your nose and inhale deeply
   C. tell your teacher immediately
   D. use odor-sensing equipment

8. When working with materials that might fly into the air and hurt someone's eye, you should wear
   A. goggles
   B. an apron
   C. gloves
   D. a hat

9. Before doing experiments involving a heat source, you should know the location of the
   A. door
   B. window
   C. fire extinguisher
   D. overhead lights

10. If you get chemicals in your eye you should
    A. wash your hands immediately
    B. put the lid back on the chemical container
    C. wait to see if your eye becomes irritated
    D. use the eyewash station right away, for a minimum of 15 minutes

Go online to view the Lab Safety Handbook for additional information.

UNIT 1

Science and Engineering

How do humans explore and design our world?

Unit Project	2
Lesson 1 Science, Engineering, and Resource Use Are Related	4
Lesson 2 Engineer It: Using the Engineering Design Process	22
Unit Review	43
Unit Performance Task	47

Many communities around the world face housing shortages. One of the goals of the CalEarth SuperAdobe project is to provide affordable and sustainable housing to these communities.

You Solve It How Can You Design a Ship to Carry Cargo?

Design container ships for different purposes, including carrying a large volume of cargo, traveling the fastest, being the most fuel efficient, and having the least environmental impact.

Go online and complete the You Solve It to explore ways to solve a real-world problem.

UNIT 1 PROJECT

Develop a Solution

Waste management issues affect parks, schools, and businesses.

A. Look at the photo. On a separate sheet of paper, write down as many different questions as you can about the photo.

B. Discuss With your class or a partner, share your questions. Record any additional questions generated in your discussion. Then choose the most important questions from the list that are related to addressing and solving a problem in your community or school. Write them below.

C. Choose a problem in your school or community to research. Here's a list of problems you can consider:

Food Allergies   Bullying
Garbage and Waste   Accessibility
Food and Snack Options   Transportation
Extracurricular Activities

D. Use the information above, along with your research, to develop a solution to the issue you chose to address.

Discuss the next steps for your Unit Project with your teacher and go online to download the Unit Project Worksheet.

Unit 1 Science and Engineering

UNIT 1

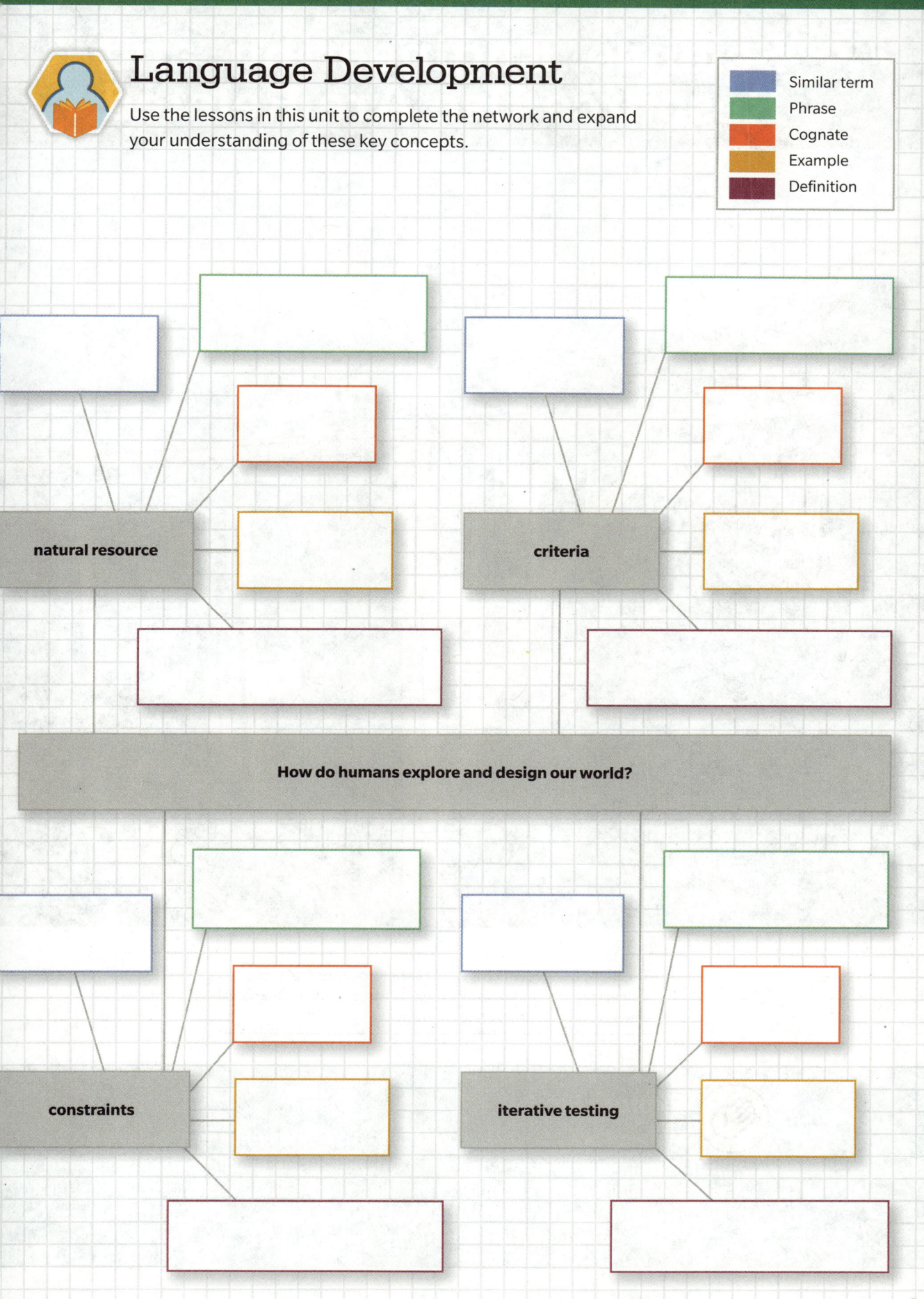

Language Development

Use the lessons in this unit to complete the network and expand your understanding of these key concepts.

- Similar term
- Phrase
- Cognate
- Example
- Definition

natural resource

criteria

How do humans explore and design our world?

constraints

iterative testing

Unit 1 Science and Engineering 3

LESSON 1
Science, Engineering, and Resource Use Are Related

The Bixby Bridge, which is built of reinforced concrete, spans a steep canyon cut by Bixby Creek. The bridge offers dramatic views along California State Highway 1.

Explore First

Mining Clay Mix several beads into a ball of clay. Flatten the clay onto a small paper plate so it is about 3 cm thick. Try to get all the beads back out without moving or changing the shape of the clay. How does this constraint influence your mining method? Do you think minerals in Earth's crust can be mined without disrupting the land, soil, or plants?

Go online to view the digital version of the Hands-On Lab for this lesson and to download additional lab resources.

CAN YOU EXPLAIN IT?

How could this construction boom in China be related to this flood in Indonesia?

As the human population increases, cities such as Chongqing, China are growing rapidly. As buildings, roads, and bridges are built, the demand for concrete skyrockets.

This is one of thousands of flooded homes along the Bengawan Solo River in Indonesia. Flooding in the region has increased due to sand mining activities along the banks of the river.

1. Chongqing is over 4,000 km from this flooded area in Indonesia. How might these two places be related?

2. How does each image relate to society's needs? Explain your answer.

EVIDENCE NOTEBOOK As you explore this lesson, gather evidence to help explain how a construction boom in China could relate to flooding in Indonesia.

Lesson 1 Science, Engineering, and Resource Use Are Related 5

EXPLORATION 1

Relating Natural Resources to Science and Engineering

Natural Resources and Society

All societies depend on natural resources for food, water, materials, and energy. A **natural resource** is any natural material or energy source that humans use. Examples include water, oil, minerals, plants, sunlight, wind, and animals. Societies use resources as a way of building wealth by mining, harvesting, and trading the resources with one another. It may be hard to imagine how products such as plastic or concrete come from nature. These kinds of products are made by processing natural resources.

Nonrenewable resources, such as sand, coal, and oil, are used more quickly than they can form. *Renewable resources* are replaceable in a relatively short time period. Plants are examples of renewable resources because they grow relatively quickly. Sunlight and wind are continually available as sources of energy, so they are also called renewable resources.

3. **Discuss** Could an object, tool, or structure be made without the use of a natural resource? Explain your answer.

Products Made Using Sand, a Nonrenewable Natural Resource

Silica, found in sand, is a major ingredient of glass, used for everything from windows to phone screens.

Without sand, concrete would not be available to make roads, sidewalks, bridges, or buildings.

Electronic devices contain silicon microchips made from the silica found in sand.

The Distribution of Natural Resources

Natural resources are part of the Earth system, which includes the hydrosphere, biosphere, geosphere, and atmosphere. For example, the water we drink comes from the hydrosphere. Food is part of the biosphere. Minerals are obtained from the geosphere. The air we breathe is in the atmosphere.

Most natural resources are concentrated in specific locations on Earth. The natural processes that lead to the formation or growth of a resource may occur only in specific locations under certain conditions. Citrus fruits grow best in warm, rainy climates. Coal forms in swamp environments. Sand forms as certain rocks are broken down into tiny pieces. Both sand and coal are formed by geologic processes that can take place over millions of years. One major factor that affects how accessible a resource is to people is location. For example, it is easier to mine sand from a beach than from the bottom of a deep lake.

Ecosystems and Ecosystem Services

An *ecosystem* is a community of organisms and the nonliving components in their environment. Natural processes in healthy, functioning ecosystems result in clean air and water, fertile soil, and other *ecosystem services* that benefit humans. Ecosystem services also include shade, recreation, the pollination of plants, and pest control. These services are essential to human societies and economies. For example, wetland ecosystems can prevent severe flooding when heavy rains occur.

Humans alter ecosystems to obtain and use natural resources. When native plants are removed to plant crops or mine minerals, the biodiversity of the ecosystem is negatively affected. This is because the number of plants—and any organisms depending on those plants—would decrease. *Biodiversity* refers to the number and variety of organisms in an ecosystem. Ecosystem processes and services are weakened or destroyed as biodiversity decreases. Humans also build over ecosystems. For example, covering wetland soils with asphalt and concrete makes the ground *impervious*, which means the ground cannot absorb water. Rainwater ends up collecting and flowing over the surface instead of soaking into the ground. This decreases the ability of the wetland to provide the ecosystem service of flood prevention.

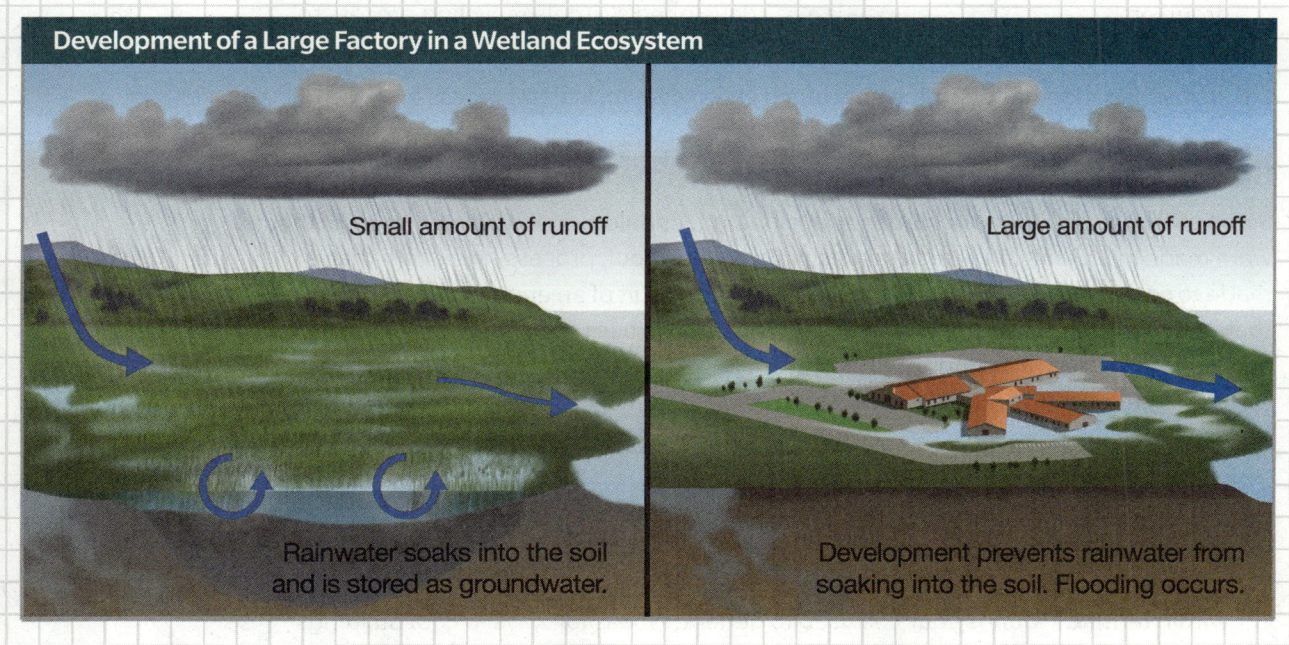

Development of a Large Factory in a Wetland Ecosystem

Small amount of runoff

Rainwater soaks into the soil and is stored as groundwater.

Large amount of runoff

Development prevents rainwater from soaking into the soil. Flooding occurs.

4. **Engineer It** The development of this factory resulted in frequent floods in the area, mostly due to the addition of impervious surfaces. The owners of the factory want to make changes to prevent future flooding. Help the owners brainstorm solutions for the flooding problem. Choose one solution and describe how you could test it.

The Roles of Scientists and Engineers in Society

Through science, we learn how the world works. *Science* is the practice of asking questions and developing explanations about how things work in both the natural world and the designed world. People are not only curious about how the world works, but they want to address needs and solve problems. This is why engineers exist. *Engineering* is the practice of defining problems and developing solutions for those problems. Society's needs and desires have a major influence on scientific investigations, engineering, and the development of technology.

Scientists and engineers work together. Scientists use tools developed by engineers to investigate the world. Engineers use scientific knowledge while they solve problems. For example, scientists might discover a natural compound that kills infectious microbes, but the scientists would need to work with engineers to develop a way to manufacture medicine from this natural compound.

5. Complete the following description to differentiate between scientists and engineers.

    A community was facing a problem with excessive waste from paper products. A group of ~~scientists~~ / **engineers** developed a simple recycling process to help solve the problem. A group of **scientists** / ~~engineers~~ then conducted an investigation to determine how much energy the recycling process took.

Science, Engineering, and Technology

Some of the first evidence of humans developing technology includes cutting tools that were made over 3 million years ago. *Technology* is any tool, process, or system that is made to solve a problem. Technology is usually the result of an engineering solution—that is, technology is developed to address a need. The use of technology in engineering and science has led to important discoveries about the natural world and led to the development of entire industries and engineered systems.

Ask Science and Engineering Questions

6. **Discuss** Scientists discovered that large termite mounds maintain an interior temperature that is cooler than the outside temperature. The cooling process within termite mounds could be used to generate ideas for ways to cool buildings in hot weather. With a partner, identify one question scientists might ask about this phenomenon to understand it. Then identify one question that engineers might ask to address the need for cooling buildings.

Unit 1 Science and Engineering

EXPLORATION 2

Describing Natural Resource Use

Resource Use Can Be Modeled as a Life Cycle

Each natural resource has a unique life cycle, beginning when it is grown or extracted and ending when it is thrown away. However, its story may continue if the resource is reused or recycled. For example, rocks containing aluminum are extracted from Earth's crust. The aluminum is separated from the rock by a series of chemical processes. The aluminum is then transported to factories to make products such as soda cans and aluminum foil. Products are transported to stores, sold to consumers, used, and then thrown away, recycled, or reused. Just as a rock does not look like a soda can, a raw natural resource does not always resemble the final product.

7. **Language SmArts | Draw** Identify a tool or object you use in school and think about its life cycle, from a natural resource to the final product. Draw a diagram of your object's life cycle and label each stage.

Obtaining Resources

A natural resource's life cycle begins when the resource is obtained. Natural resources can be collected, mined, or harvested in many ways. For example, fresh water is pumped for drinking. Lettuce is grown for food. Sand, gravel, and limestone are mined to make concrete. The sun's energy is collected and used to generate electrical energy.

Obtaining Natural Resources

drinking water extraction

sand mining

solar energy collection

vegetable farming

Production

While some resources can be used directly, others must be processed to make them usable. Production, or manufacturing, involves modifying a resource from its original state. Processing raw materials requires energy and technologies such as tools, equipment, and manufacturing processes. For example, vegetables are harvested, washed, and packaged. Water, cement, gravel, and sand are combined in large mixers to produce concrete. Fresh water is often filtered and treated to remove harmful substances and microbes, which makes it safe to drink. Once a product is made, it is prepared for distribution.

Concrete is a mixture of cement, which is a binder, water, sand, and a mix of fine and coarse pebbles called aggregate.

Distribution

After a product is made, it is distributed to the user or consumer. For example, concrete is used in the construction of buildings and roadways, so concrete is distributed to construction sites. Sometimes, the raw materials to make concrete are sent to construction sites and the concrete is produced on site. Drinking water is another resource that must be distributed. Water pumped from its source can go through treatment plants, reservoirs, and underground pipes before being used by a household. Drinking water is also bottled and distributed to stores for purchase. Some products must be transported long distances to get to consumers. Often, there are many steps involved in the supply chain that distributes a product to its users.

8. The city of Dubai is surrounded by desert sand, but it imports sand from Australia for construction. This is because the wind-blasted desert sand surrounding Dubai is too smooth to be used to make construction materials. Nearby marine sands were once used but the supply is now exhausted. How do you think Dubai's need for construction sand affects Australian societies? How might it affect Australian ecosystems?

These tall skyscrapers in Dubai include glass and concrete, both of which require large amounts of sand to make.

Hands-On Lab
Investigate the Influence of Decisions on Resource Use

With a partner, use the table to model scenarios in which two people share a limited resource. Each person chooses a low, medium, or high rate of use. Depending on their choices, each person will get a different benefit level, with 1 being the lowest benefit and 10 being the highest benefit. For example, if Person 1 chooses a low rate of resource use and Person 2 chooses a medium rate, you look at the first row and second column, which contains the numbers 1 and 9. The benefit level is 1 for Person 1 and 9 for Person 2.

Procedure

STEP 1 You and your partner live in a place with a limited supply of water to use each month. What are some ways you will need use the water?

STEP 2 Model at least five scenarios with different combinations of each person's rate of use. For each scenario, record the rate of use and benefit levels for each person.

		Person 2	
Person 1	**Low**	**Medium**	**High**
Low	1 / 1	1 / 9	1 / 10
Medium	9 / 1	8 / 8	3 / 9
High	10 / 1	9 / 3	4 / 4

Analysis

STEP 3 What patterns do you observe from your results?

STEP 4 Does one person's choice affect the benefit the other person gets? Use evidence from your results to explain.

STEP 5 How does this model demonstrate the consequences of making choices about resource use?

Consumer Use

A product's life cycle includes its use by consumers. As the human population rapidly increases, so does the need for food, water, and shelter. Consumer use of technology such as cell phones and computers also increases. More roads, bridges, and buildings are constructed as well. Consumer preferences also drive the life cycle of different natural resources. For example, the demand for fruits and vegetables that are blemish-free means that growers will likely not have a market for fruits and vegetables that are slightly misshapen but otherwise perfectly edible.

Examples of Consumer Use of Natural Resources

Clean drinking water is a natural resource that is essential to a healthy life.

Concrete is a critical building material that is used for buildings as well as recreation areas, such as this skate park.

Solar panels similar to the ones on this boat reduce society's dependence on fossil fuels as an energy source.

Produce from farms provides food. Fresh fruits and vegetables are processed less than packaged foods.

EVIDENCE NOTEBOOK

9. How are the construction and technology industries driving the demand for sand? Record your evidence.

Disposal

There are several ways products can be handled after consumers use them. For example, plastic bags from a grocery store can be discarded by throwing them into the trash. They can be reused by taking them back to the store, or they can be recycled to make different plastic products. Concrete from an old building can be reused to make new concrete or other products. Recycled paper can be processed to make cereal boxes, paper towel rolls, and many other products.

10. Look back at your life-cycle steps and diagram from earlier in the lesson. How would reusing or recycling the product change the product's life cycle and the demand on resources used to make the product?

Do the Math
Analyze Land Reclamation in Singapore

To address the growing population of the city state of Singapore, engineers have increased the island's land area using sand and other aggregate materials.

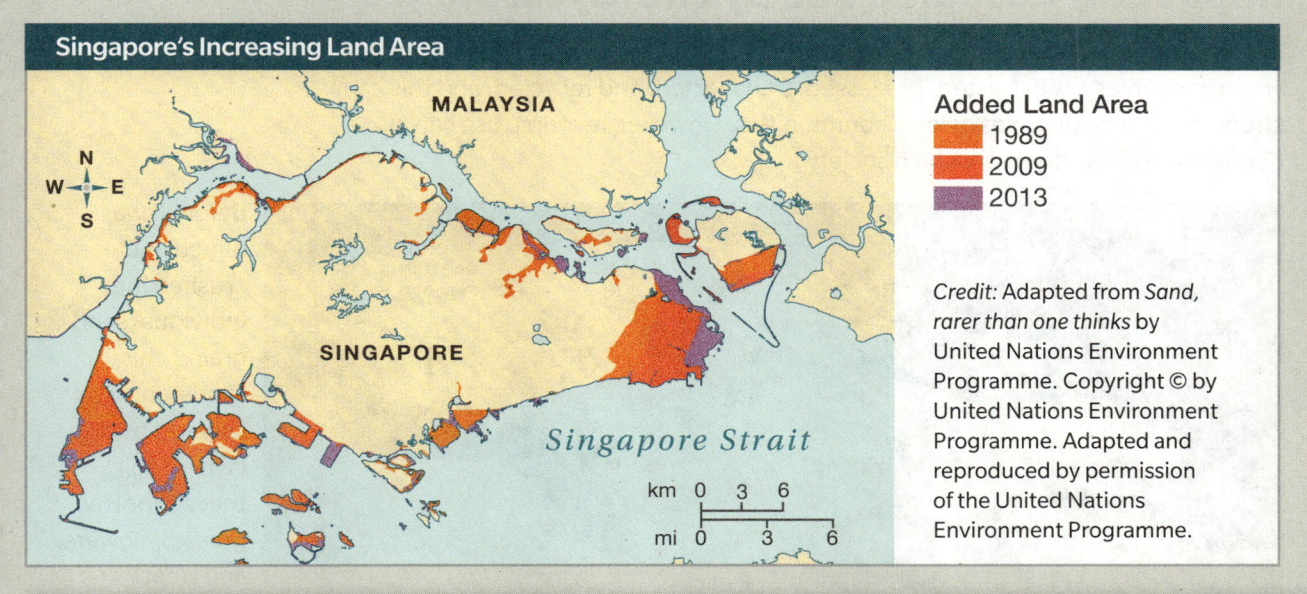

Singapore's Increasing Land Area

Added Land Area
- 1989
- 2009
- 2013

Credit: Adapted from *Sand, rarer than one thinks* by United Nations Environment Programme. Copyright © by United Nations Environment Programme. Adapted and reproduced by permission of the United Nations Environment Programme.

11. In 1989, the total land area of Singapore was 626.4 km². By 2013, it was 716.5 km². By how many square kilometers did Singapore grow from 1989 to 2013?

12. Calculate the percentage increase in land from 1989 to 2013. First, take the amount of added land over that time period and divide it by the original land area in 1989. Then, multiply by 100%.

13. Discuss Much of the sand used to increase Singapore's land area has been imported from other countries. Some sand has been dredged from the surrounding ocean floor, and some artificial sand has been made by crushing rock. With a partner, develop a scientific question regarding Singapore's use of sand.

EXPLORATION 3

Describing the Impacts of Resource Use

Impacts of Resource Use by Life-Cycle Stages

Natural resource use affects society in positive and negative ways. Jobs are created where resources are extracted, processed, transported, and recycled, and this can strengthen the economies of local communities. However, resource use can also damage the ecosystems on which society relies.

Before it was mined and crushed into individual sand grains, this sandstone was covered by a layer of soil that supported grasses, flowers, and trees.

14. Many organisms, such as birds, deer, and bees, depended on the vegetation and soil that was removed to mine sandstone here. Their populations have decreased dramatically since the mining operation started. How might the decrease in these populations affect humans? Explain your reasoning.

Obtaining Resources

Ecosystems are affected by the way resources are obtained. An area sustains physical damage such as erosion and the loss of vegetation when it is cleared to extract or harvest resources. Pollution caused by fuel spills and improperly stored waste can contaminate soil and water sources. Erosion can physically remove organisms. These negative impacts can decrease the biodiversity of ecosystems. When sand is mined from a river bottom, water can flow faster and erode the river's banks. Flooding can also occur, further disrupting the river ecosystem and any people who depend on or live near the river. In some countries, mining companies are required to follow strict laws that help control the damage that mining may cause. Careful selection of where to mine sand can reduce damage and allow time for affected ecosystems to recover from mining activities.

Production

Processing resources to make usable products requires energy and other resources. Fossil fuels are often burned to provide energy to processing facilities. Therefore, the production phase of a resource's life cycle can have negative impacts on the environment. Fossil fuels are nonrenewable and cause pollution when they are burned. The waste from processing resources must be properly handled to ensure that it does not pollute the soil, water, or air.

The Trans-Alaska pipeline transports crude oil from northern Alaska to refineries in Valdez, in southern Alaska.

Distribution

The impacts of resource distribution can negatively affect ecosystems and the people who depend on those ecosystems. Roads and other infrastructure built to transport resources divide habitats and disrupt migration patterns. Ships carrying consumer goods can cause changes to aquatic ecosystems. However, distributing natural resources is often necessary. For example, clean drinking water is a resource that is not equally distributed on Earth. Having better access to clean drinking water improves the health of individuals and raises the overall living standards in the society.

Consumer Use

As the human population increases, the need for resources increases. The negative effects of resource use can include depletion of nonrenewable resources and pollution. For example, coal is burned to provide energy, but this process pollutes the environment. Coal is also a nonrenewable resource. Wind turbines are a cleaner energy resource. However, producing and installing them requires changes to the environment, and using them can injure and kill birds.

Societies must weigh the advantages and disadvantages of resource use. This may involve a choice between renewable and nonrenewable resources. Additionally, consumers might choose to use products that take less energy or fewer resources to make, or they may choose to reduce their use of resources.

Urban Development in Shenzhen, Guangdong, China

As the population in this city grows, consumers use more resources for building and transportation.

1985

2016

15. As cities grow, why does the need for sand increase? Select all that apply.

   A. Technologies, such as solar panels and computers, are in higher demand.
   B. More roads must be constructed for transportation.
   C. More buildings must be constructed for homes and offices.
   D. More people require water and food.

Disposal

Discarding materials can have negative impacts on ecosystems. Discarded materials end up in landfills, where they may take hundreds or thousands of years to decompose. Discarded materials can also introduce pollutants into soil and water if the materials are not stored properly. Increased use and disposal of products by consumers increases demand for landfill space.

Recycling and reusing products reduces the demand on natural resources because fewer new products have to be made. Recycling and reusing products also reduces the demand for landfill space.

16. **Discuss** Compare and contrast ways to reuse and recycle a consumer product.

Old concrete is crushed into fine particles in order to be recycled to make new concrete items.

> **EVIDENCE NOTEBOOK**
> 17. Describe the effects of using sand on both society and on ecosystems. Record your evidence.

Describe the Effects of Using a Resource

18. Humans depend on ecosystems for ecosystem services and resources. For example, this river ecosystem provides water, fish, and a place to swim. The forest ecosystem provides wood, shade, and erosion control. Choose a resource and describe the possible effects of its use on society and on ecosystems throughout its life cycle.

TAKE IT FURTHER

Continue Your Exploration

Name: _____ Date: _____

Check out the path below or go online to choose one of the other paths shown.

People in Science → • Frac-Sand Mining
• Hands-On Labs
• Propose Your Own Path
→ *Go online to choose one of these other paths*

Shreyas Sundaram

Shreyas Sundaram was interested in science, engineering, and mathematics at an early age. He lived in India until age 10, when he moved to Canada. He earned degrees in computer engineering and electrical engineering.

Dr. Sundaram researches the design and resilience of national economies, power grids, ecosystems, and networks such as the Internet. *Resilience* is the ability of a system to function when it is being overused or disrupted.

Shreyas Sundaram (at left) and his PhD student Ashish Hota work together on Dr. Sundaram's prospect theory project.

Modeling Human Behavior

Several models have been developed to help predict what people will do in a given situation. Prospect theory describes how people make decisions when the likelihood of certain outcomes is known and the risks and rewards of each outcome are defined. For example, imagine this choice.

- **Option 1:** You are guaranteed to receive $5.
- **Option 2:** You have a 50% chance of receiving $10, and a 50% chance of receiving no money.

Which option would you choose? Not everyone will choose the same option, and most decisions will be based on how much a person values the money.

Game theory studies the ways in which one person's behavior and choices affect another's. Dr. Sundaram applies prospect and game theory to study how people use large-scale shared resources. He theorizes that while using shared resources, people may make decisions in their own best interest, even if it hurts the entire group. Shared resources such as forests, hiking trails, roads, and fresh air are used by everyone. The way that some people use shared resources affects other people's ability to use them. For example, a factory that produces a lot of air pollution affects the air quality for everyone in the community. According to prospect theory, the more people value something, the less likely they are to risk losing it. People who value a shared resource are less likely to

Lesson 1 Science, Engineering, and Resource Use Are Related   17

TAKE IT FURTHER

Continue Your Exploration

use it in a way that might harm or destroy it. People who value clean air may be more likely to use public transportation than to drive their own cars. Dr. Sundaram and others have shown that people's values have an effect on resource use. For example, people may value the freedom of driving their own vehicle over air quality.

1. Which of the following do you think would be a better situation? Use evidence from the graph to support your answer.
   - **Situation 1:** Everyone in a community values a forest a moderate amount.
   - **Situation 2:** 50% of people highly value the forest and 50% of people do not value the forest.

Relationship between How Much People Value and Consume a Resource

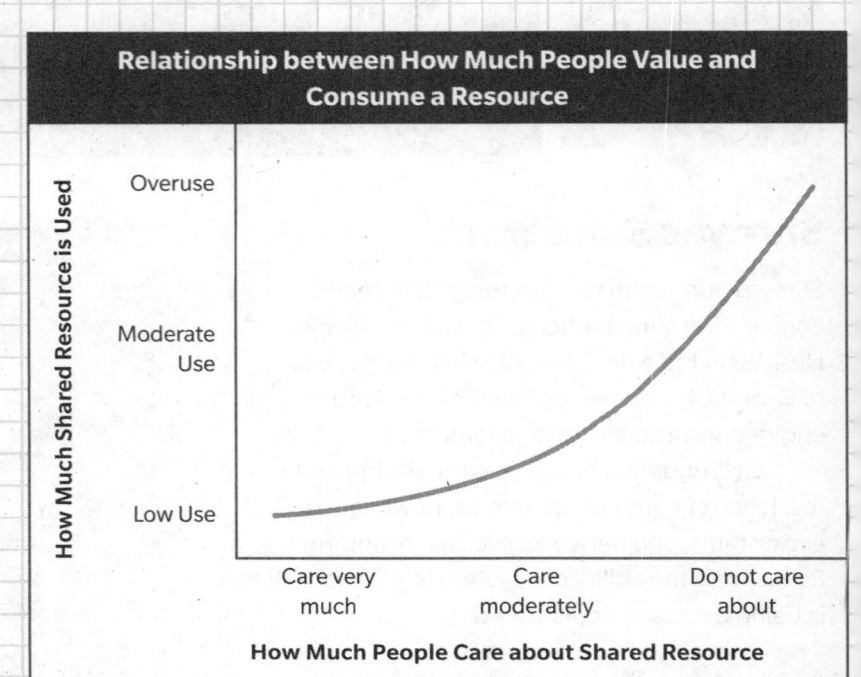

Credit: Adapted from "Fragility of the Commons under Prospect-Theoretic Risk Attitudes," doi.org/10.1016/j.geb.2016.06.003, from *Games and Economic Behavior*, Volume 98 by Ashish R. Hota et al. Copyright © 2016 Elsevier. Adapted and reproduced by permission of Elsevier.

2. Why is it important for scientists to understand how and why a population might use a shared resource?

3. How might a shared resource be protected from overuse? Use an example of a shared resource in your answer.

4. **Collaborate** Research a resource that has been overused in the past or is currently being overused. Present a poster to the class that describes the resource, how it has been used in the past and by whom, and goals for managing the use of the resource in the future. Explain why education can help manage the use of shared resources.

LESSON 1 SELF-CHECK

Can You Explain It?

Name: _____   Date: _____

How could this construction boom in China be related to this flood in Indonesia?

EVIDENCE NOTEBOOK
Refer to the notes in your Evidence Notebook to help you construct an explanation for how a construction boom in China could relate to flooding in Indonesia.

1. State your claim. Make sure your claim fully explains the relationship between the construction boom in Chonqing, China, and the flooding near this river in Indonesia.

2. Summarize the evidence you have gathered to support your claim and explain your reasoning.

Lesson 1 Science, Engineering, and Resource Use Are Related   19

LESSON 1 SELF-CHECK

Checkpoints

Answer the following questions to check your understanding of the lesson.

Use the photo to answer Questions 3–4.

3. Sand is mined from this location in order to make concrete. Growing cities use large amounts of concrete to construct buildings and roads. Which of the following is something an engineer might ask about sand mining and concrete use?

   A. What is an alternative material?

   B. What is the cost of concrete as compared to the alternative material?

   C. How does the strength and durability of concrete compare to the strength and durability of the alternative material?

   D. Why are cities growing so quickly?

   E. What impacts does sand mining have on the biodiversity of a beach ecosystem?

4. People catch fish in this aquatic ecosystem and sell the fish to make a living. Why might these people be concerned about sand mining here? Select all that apply.

   A. Sand mining disturbs the habitats of the fish.

   B. Sand mining brings more fish into the area.

   C. Sand mining kills and drives away predators of the fish.

   D. Sand mining kills and drives away the organisms fish eat.

Use the photo to answer Questions 5–7.

5. Silicon is needed to make digital camera sensors such as the one shown. Silicon is obtained from silica, a mineral found in sand. Order the steps below to describe the life cycle of silica as a resource. The first and last steps are done for you.

   _1_ Sand is extracted from an environment by mining.

   ___ People buy cameras and use them.

   ___ The silica in the sand is processed to obtain silicon.

   ___ Digital camera sensors are made and put into digital cameras.

   ___ Digital cameras are distributed to stores for purchase.

   _6_ The camera stops working, and its parts are recycled.

6. Consumer demand for digital cameras is related to sand mining. As consumer demand increases, the amount of sand mined _increases_ / decreases / stays the same.

7. Scientists use technology to _ask questions_ / solve problems about the world. Engineers develop and use technology in order to ask questions / _solve problems_ to address the needs of society.

Unit 1 Science and Engineering

LESSON 1 SELF-CHECK

Interactive Review

Complete this section to review the main concepts of the lesson.

Natural resources and ecosystem services are needed by humans. Scientists work to explain the world, while engineers work to solve problems.

A. Describe how both a scientist and an engineer could contribute to reducing the use of a nonrenewable resource.

The life cycle of a natural resource can include obtaining the resource, and resource production, distribution, consumer use, and disposal.

B. Identify one resource you use, and describe its life cycle.

Resource use affects both the environment and people. The effects can be positive and negative.

C. How would a solution allowing humans to grow more food crops on less land benefit humans and ecosystems?

Lesson 1 Science, Engineering, and Resource Use Are Related **21**

LESSON 2 | ENGINEER IT
Using the Engineering Design Process

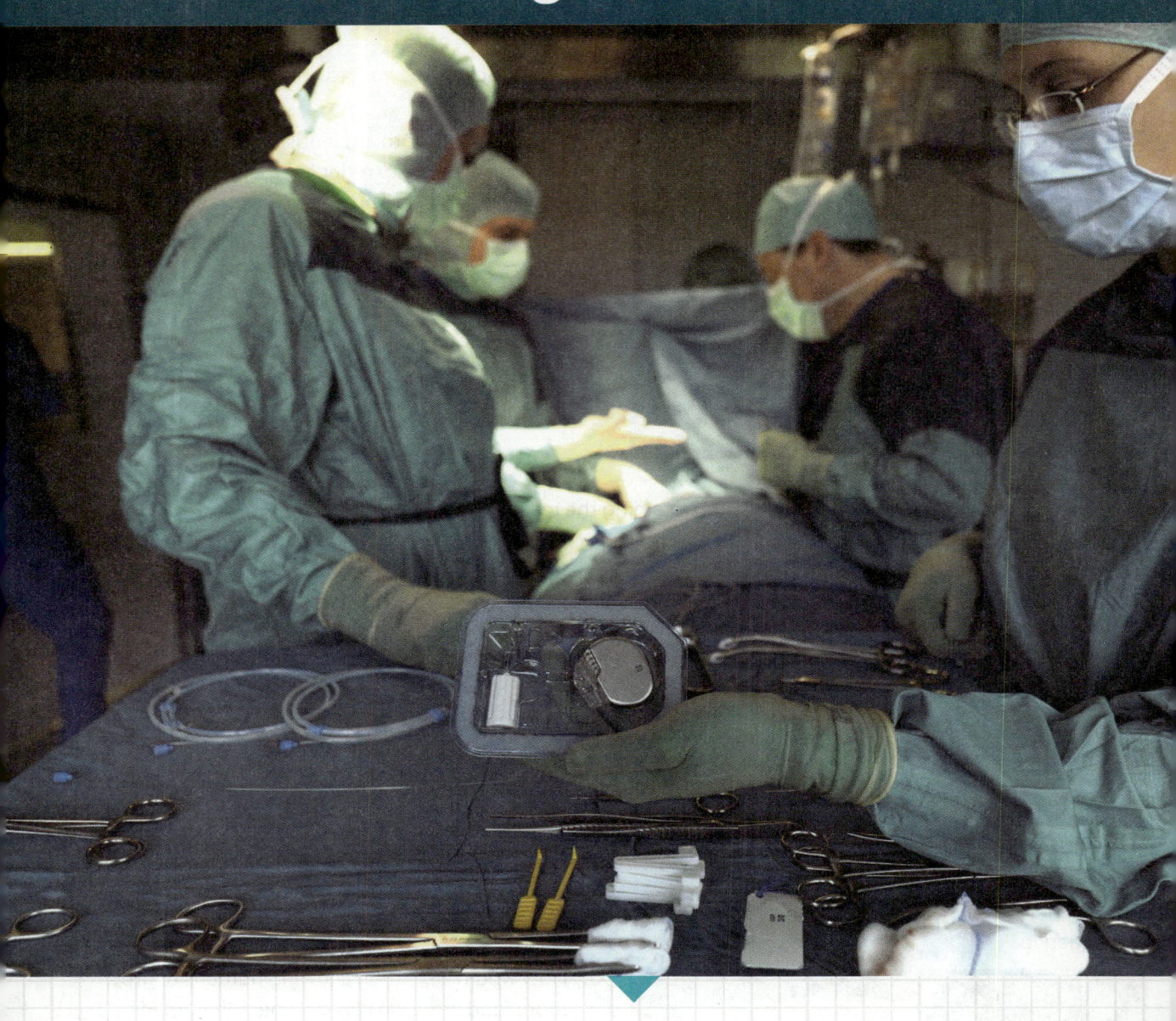

The function of the artificial heart pacemaker remains the same since the first one was developed in the 1920s, but its design has changed significantly since then.

Explore First

Modeling a Cargo Boat How might construction materials affect an engineering solution? Build a boat out of a sheet of paper and an identically-sized sheet of aluminum foil. Place both boats in a tub of water. Slowly add pennies or other similar-sized weights to both boats. What do you observe as more weight is added to each boat?

Go online to view the digital version of the Hands-On Lab for this lesson and to download additional lab resources.

CAN YOU EXPLAIN IT?

How is engineering related to this Plastic Bottle Village?

Builder Robert Bezeau addressed several engineering problems with one solution by developing the "Plastic Bottle Village" in Panama. This open wall shows how the plastic bottles are arranged within the walls. The walls of the finished homes will be plastered to insulate them further.

1. What problems do you think the plastic bottles embedded in these walls are intended to solve?

2. The Plastic Bottle Village is built on an island off the coast of Panama. Do you think this design solution could be used in other locations? Explain your answer. What advantages are there to using old plastic bottles as building materials? Are there disadvantages? Explain your answer.

EVIDENCE NOTEBOOK As you explore this lesson, gather evidence to help you explain how engineering is related to this Plastic Bottle Village.

Lesson 2 Engineer It: Using the Engineering Design Process   23

EXPLORATION 1

Developing Engineering Solutions

You use many engineered objects and processes every day. Each of them was designed and built to help with a need. Cell phone cases and roller coasters are very different devices. However, they are both developed using engineering design processes. Designing useful tools, devices, objects, processes, and systems requires careful planning, testing, and manufacturing. The engineering design process has many steps. Although there is not a fixed order of steps, the processes engineers use to design a cell phone case and a roller coaster are very similar.

Explore Online

This chimp uses a stick to collect stinging ants from an ant colony so she can eat large numbers of them quickly.

3. **Language SmArts | Discuss** Together with a partner, look at the photo of the chimpanzee eating ants from a stick. Chimps, unlike humans, are limited to using nearby natural materials to make tools to gather the stinging ants. In your own words, state the design problem faced by the chimp.

Every Solution Begins with a Design Problem

Engineers solve problems. In order to design a solution, engineers must start with a clearly stated problem. In engineering, the word *problem* does not mean that something is wrong. Instead, an engineering design problem is a statement that defines what solution is needed. The design problem must be stated in a way that describes what the solution needs to do and how it needs to do it. The problem does not have to be complicated for an engineered solution to work. The chimpanzees in the photo are not engineers, but they do have something in common with engineers. They are faced with a problem they need to solve.

The Engineering Design Process

Engineering design has much in common with scientific practices. However, its purpose is different from that of scientific inquiry. The engineering design process involves defining and solving problems or meeting needs. Engineers must first define the design problem. They must identify features and qualities that a successful solution must have. Then they continue on in the engineering design process, which is shown in the diagram. Engineers do not always follow the design process steps in order. For example, it is common for engineers to go back and redefine the problem for which they've brainstormed several possible solutions. It is also common for design changes to be made after testing proposed solutions.

An Outline of the Engineering Design Process

Testing and data analysis are parts of the engineering design process. Developing the best solution to a problem is based on analyzing data that indicate how well each design solution works.

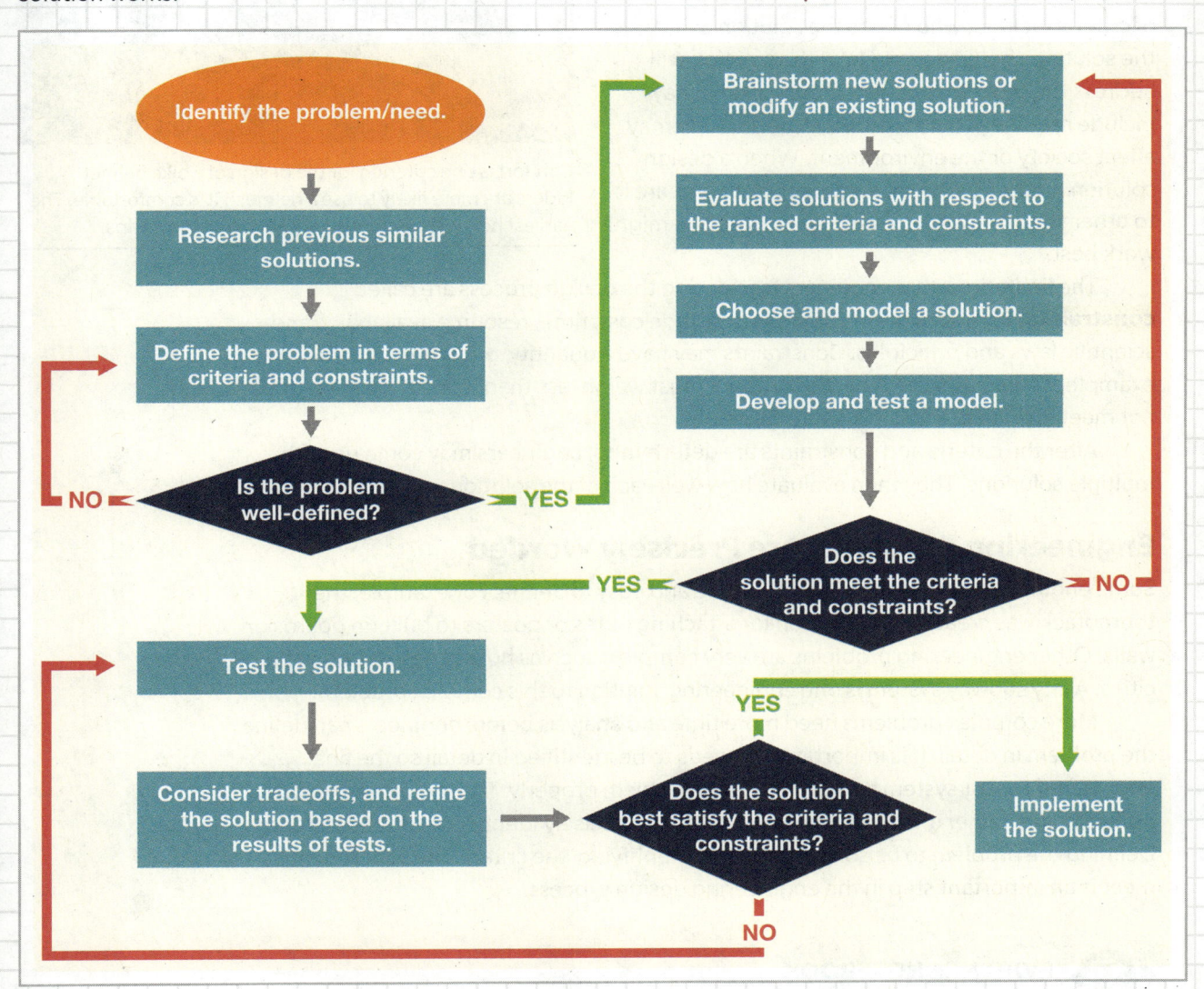

```
Identify the problem/need.
        ↓
Research previous similar solutions.
        ↓
Define the problem in terms of criteria and constraints.
        ↓
Is the problem well-defined?
   NO → (back to Define)
   YES → Brainstorm new solutions or modify an existing solution.
            ↓
        Evaluate solutions with respect to the ranked criteria and constraints.
            ↓
        Choose and model a solution.
            ↓
        Develop and test a model.
            ↓
        Does the solution meet the criteria and constraints?
            NO → (back to Brainstorm)
            YES → Test the solution.
                    ↓
                  Consider tradeoffs, and refine the solution based on the results of tests.
                    ↓
                  Does the solution best satisfy the criteria and constraints?
                    NO → (back to Test the solution)
                    YES → Implement the solution.
```

Lesson 2 Engineer It: Using the Engineering Design Process

Identify Needs or Desires

An engineered solution begins with a need or desire for a solution. That desire or need may come from individuals, groups, or society.

Solutions to a need for a safe and more comfortable way for people with Type I diabetes to take insulin, or a desire or preference for a cell phone with a better camera, are the foundations of the engineering design process. Precisely identifying and defining the problem that needs solving is a first step to building its solution.

Define Engineering Problems

The **criteria** of a design problem are the features or qualities the solution should have. Examples of criteria include: who needs the solution, what the solution should do, and how the solution will address the problem or need. Other criteria may include requirements about ways the solution may affect society or the environment. When a design solution meets all criteria, engineers can compare it to other solutions and evaluate which solution might work best.

Comfort is one criterion for the design of a bike helmet. Riders are more likely to use a helmet if it is comfortable. The earliest helmets were made of padded leather strips.

The limitations that engineers face during the design process are called **constraints.** Some common constraints include cost, time, resource availability, and scientific laws and principles. Constraints may have a quantity, or numerical value. For example, a law may state that "the product must weigh less than 95 g." If a design does not meet the constraints, it is not acceptable.

After the criteria and constraints are determined, engineers may come up with multiple solutions. They then evaluate how well each of the solutions solves the problem.

Engineering Problems Are Precisely Worded

Some engineering problems are very simple and easy to define. For example, the thumbtack was created as a solution for attaching notes or posters to bulletin boards or walls. Other engineering problems are very complex, such as how to get around in busy cities. A city subway system is one engineering solution to this complex problem.

More complex problems need more time and analysis before engineers can define the problem in detail. It is important for needs to be identified in detail so the final engineered tool or system solves the design problem properly. The more complex the problem, the longer it will likely take engineers to precisely identify needs and criteria. Defining the problem to be solved by clearly identifying the criteria the solution must meet is an important step in the engineering design process.

> **EVIDENCE NOTEBOOK**
> 4. What needs are addressed by using old plastic bottles as building materials? Are they the needs of individuals, a group of people, or an entire society? Record your evidence.

Case Study: Bicycle Helmets

The idea of using a head covering to protect a bicyclist during a fall began more than a hundred years ago, due to concerns about head injuries to riders. As more people began to ride bikes, more head injuries from falls occurred. It was a long time before helmets began to look like the ones you wear today. One of the earliest designs was made of simple strips of leather stitched together. While this design was light and comfortable to wear, it offered little protection to the rider. Bike riders also used motorcycle helmets, mountain climbing helmets, and construction hardhats. However, none of these helmets were designed specifically for the type of fall a bicyclist might have.

More and more injuries occurred for two main reasons: more people were cycling, and riders were either not wearing helmets or were wearing helmets not designed for biking. Society needed a safety tool to help bicyclists protect their heads in falls from their bikes. A helmet designed specifically for biking conditions needed to be designed to provide protection.

Components of a Bicycle Helmet

The components of bicycle helmets are designed to meet the following criteria: reducing the impact forces to a rider's skull from a fall or collision, keeping the helmet secure on the wearer's head, and being lightweight and comfortable. Many components have changed over time due to changes in legal requirements and new scientific research.

- The shiny, flat covering on the outside of the helmet reduces the frictional forces on the helmet that would occur if the expanded polystyrene shell were bare. The smooth covering reduces the possibility of the soft polystyrene interior snagging on a rough surface and causing a severe neck injury.

- The expanded polystyrene shell provides protection by absorbing the energy of an impact. The foamy material absorbs the kinetic energy of the impact, collapses, and may crack. It also cushions the head from the sudden acceleration change that would happen if the skull were in direct contact with a hard surface such as asphalt or cement.

- Fitting pads work along with the straps to keep the helmet stable on the rider's head.

- A helmet that moves or falls off during a collision does not protect. Adjustable straps are needed for a good fit.

Do the Math
Calculate the Amount of Material Needed

When determining the manufacturing cost of a design, one of the most important factors is the price and amount of materials that are needed to build it.

The airbag helmet was developed by design students Anna Haupt and Terese Alstin. It is made of nylon fabric that inflates when sensors in the collar detect a fall. Anna is showing how the collar is worn.

5. It takes a 1.5 m length of 137 cm-wide fabric to make the collar of an airbag helmet. The manufacturer is making 250 special-order collars. One morning, a technician finds they have only 65% of the length of fabric they need to make the collars. How many more meters of fabric are needed to be able to make all 250 collars? Show your work.

Brainstorm, Develop, and Test Solutions

When it came to developing a bike helmet, many designs were looked at and tested. Some ideas worked. Some did not. The process of identifying which designs work and which do not is similar for all engineering design challenges.

After a design problem is defined, a team comes up with as many solutions as possible. Some ideas may seem silly. However, starting off with many solution ideas is better than starting with only one idea. Each idea is compared to see how well it meets the criteria and constraints of the problem. The ideas that meet the criteria and constraints the best are kept. The other ideas are set aside. The most promising ideas are then rated. The rating is based on how well parts of each design meet the criteria and constraints. This rating step is helpful because some parts of a solution might be very successful. Other parts of the same solution might not solve the problem as well. If no single design idea addresses the problem well, the best features of each design may be combined into one best idea.

Unit 1 Science and Engineering

Consider Tradeoffs

To work within the constraints of a design problem, engineers often make tradeoffs. A *tradeoff* is the act of giving up one design feature in order to keep another, more desirable one. A tradeoff may also be agreeing that a given criterion is not as highly rated as another criterion. For example, keeping costs low is important in any design project. However, using stronger, more expensive materials means the product is less likely to break and will last longer. For modern bike helmets, a light bike helmet design was preferred over a thicker, full-face-covering design. Even though a thicker helmet that covers the face offers more protection, cyclists would be less likely to wear such a helmet because it would be heavier. Therefore, maximum protection was traded for a lighter design that more people would be more likely to wear. For this bike helmet design, the criterion that the helmet is comfortable is more important than the criterion that the helmet offers the maximum protection to the rider.

This spork design includes a cutting edge along one of the fork prongs and a spoon on the other end.

This spork design has a combination of a spoon and fork in one and a traditional full handle.

6. Sometimes, the best parts of different solutions can be combined to create a solution that is better than any solutions that came before it. Is making design tradeoffs the same as, or different from, the practice of combining the best parts of different solutions? Explain your answer.

Optimize Solutions

After proposed solutions are selected and tested, the solution that performs the best in tests is chosen. Additional tests are done with this possible solution. A test model of the best solution is built, and tests are carried out on this model. Design improvements are made to the model as a result of repeated, controlled tests. For example, after repeated tests, the many-layered design of bicycle helmets was identified as the best way to protect bicyclists from head injury. Tests continued on helmet solutions to maximize bicyclists' safety. Tests were done to identify the density of foam that absorbs energy the best during a fall. Based on the test results, changes were made again to the helmet design. Its overall performance was improved due to this additional testing.

Design testing that is repeated many times is called **iterative testing.** The iterative design process involves testing, analyzing, and refining a product, system, or process based on test results. During the iterative design process, changes are made to the most recent version of the design based on test results. The purpose of the iterative design process is to improve the quality and usefulness of a design. The results of iterative tests help engineers develop the best solution possible.

> **EVIDENCE NOTEBOOK**
> 7. Would it be better to start the design process for plastic bottle homes by working with one building design idea or with four different building design ideas? Record your evidence.

Hands-On Lab
Design a Bicycle Helmet Model

Design and test a bicycle helmet model based on specific criteria and constraints.

Criteria are the features a design solution should have. *Constraints* are the limits designers have to work within and can be thought of as the "must haves" of a design solution.

MATERIALS
- aluminum foil
- bubble wrap with small bubbles
- duct tape or reinforced strapping tape
- egg (raw)
- flexible foam sheeting
- newspaper
- paperboard strips
- scissors
- string or yarn

Procedure and Analysis

STEP 1 The table on the next page is a decision matrix. A *decision matrix* helps engineers determine which design solutions best fit the criteria and constraints of the problem. Review and discuss the criteria listed in the decision matrix. Add at least two more criteria that you would like your bicycle helmet model to have. Add at least one more constraint.

STEP 2 In the 2nd column, rate each criterion from 1–3, depending on how important you think it is. Use 1 to represent "not very important," 2 to represent "somewhat important," and 3 to represent "very important."

STEP 3 Brainstorm design solutions. Choose two of your solutions to evaluate using the decision matrix. Describe these solutions.

Design A:

Design B:

STEP 4 In the table, evaluate Design A. For each criterion, the design can be rated 1 out of 3, 2 out of 3, or 3 out of 3. Constraints should be rated as either "yes" (it will meet the criterion) or "no" (it will not and should be rejected). Total the number of points. Next, evaluate Design B.

STEP 5 Total the points for each design. A decision matrix is a good way to compare different designs and determine which best fit the criteria and constraints of the problem, but it does not make the decision for you. If you favor a design that did not get the maximum number of points, there may be a criterion you are using that is not listed. If so, redefine the problem by adding this criterion to your matrix.

STEP 6 Decide which is the best solution, and explain your reasoning.

Criteria	Rating (1–3)	Design A	Design B
The helmet protects the egg from cracking when dropped from a height of 1.5 m.			
The helmet is as small as possible, no more than twice the width of the egg.			
The egg can easily be placed in the helmet and removed.			
Total Points for Each Design			

Constraints		Design A	Design B
Use only the materials provided		Yes / No	Yes / No
		Yes / No	Yes / No
		Yes / No	Yes / No

STEP 7 Test the model by dropping your helmet (open side up) with a raw egg inside. Describe the effects on the egg.

STEP 8 A large chicken egg weighs about 56.7 g. A human head weighs about 4.5 kg. In what ways is an egg a good model for a human head in this test? How is an egg not a good model? Explain your answers.

Define a Real-Life Design Problem

A working fire alarm can double the chances of surviving a house fire. Fire alarms generally attach to a ceiling. As a result, they can be hard to reach. Their loud, shrill sound can be very annoying, especially when the cause is burnt toast. However, these annoying aspects are actually important to the design. Because smoke rises, an alarm should be located high on a wall or ceiling to quickly and reliably detect smoke. The piercing sound may be needed to wake up sleeping people during a fire. The location and types of sound that are most effective have been determined by many years of research, testing, and analysis.

8. It is important to define the criteria and constraints of a design problem to come up with a successful solution. Choose whether the following points are criteria or constraints. Place a check mark in the correct column.

Fire alarms are designed specifically to sound shrill and annoying. Lives may depend on a fire alarm's alerting people in the event of a fire.

Requirements	Criterion	Constraint
According to a government regulation, the alarm must produce a signal of at least 65 decibels at a distance of 10 feet.		
The battery compartment should be easy to open.		
The alarm should have a signal for alerting users that the battery is low.		
The alarm should weigh less than 225 g (about 9 oz).		
For safety, lithium ion batteries cannot be used. Only larger 9V batteries may be used.		
The design should have as few moving parts as possible.		

9. **Write** Add one other criterion or constraint that would be appropriate for a fire alarm design. Compare your criterion or constraint with a partner's.

_____
_____
_____
_____

Unit 1 Science and Engineering

EXPLORATION 2

Comparing Engineering and Science Practices

Science and engineering are related to one another. However, they have different purposes. Science asks questions about phenomena and how the universe works, then attempts to develop explanations based on evidence. Engineering is the systematic practice of solving problems with designed solutions. New technologies are developed when engineers use scientific knowledge to develop solutions to problems.

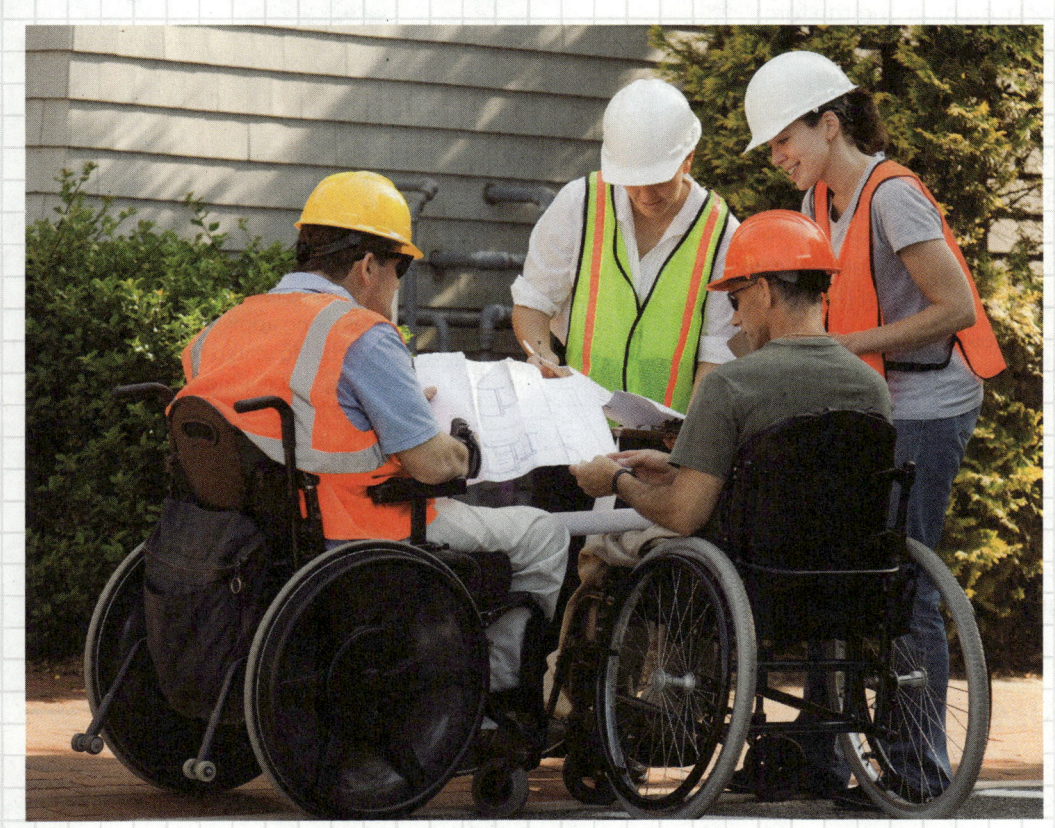

Buildings, roads, bridges, and parks are designed to meet people's needs and solve community problems. Teams of engineers and others combine their practical experience with knowledge of mathematics and science. This team is discussing engineering drawings at a construction site.

Investigations in Science and Engineering

Science and engineering practices involve investigations. In science, the purpose of investigations is to explore phenomena and learn about how and why things work the way they do. In engineering, the purpose of investigations is to define and solve problems. Both science and engineering use investigative processes that depend on the results of tests and data analysis.

10. Read each of the following questions and decide whether it most likely would be asked by a _scientist_ or by an _engineer_. Write your answer beside the question.

   A. What tectonic processes lead to the formation of sandstone? _____

   B. What is the most effective glass thickness for a small greenhouse? _____

   C. What fuel-to-air ratio in a car engine produces the most power? _____

   D. What type of drill is the best to use for a sand mining operation? _____

   E. What is the minimum diameter of wire needed for a 150,000-volt transmission line? _____

Ask Questions and Define Problems

Scientists ask questions and seek answers in a systematic way. Engineers define a problem and look for a solution in a systematic way. For example, consider an investigation of *tensile strength*, the amount of force that a material can tolerate before it breaks. As a measured mass is added below the strip of material, the force exerted on the material increases. The material will stretch and eventually break. The amount of stretching and the force needed to cause a break depend on the property of the material known as tensile strength.

A tensile strength test could be used to investigate a science question, such as how the chemical properties of a material relate to its ability to withstand being pulled out of shape. The same test could be used to solve an engineering question, such as what material could be used to manufacture a part that must stretch less than 1% of its length when a certain-sized load is applied to it.

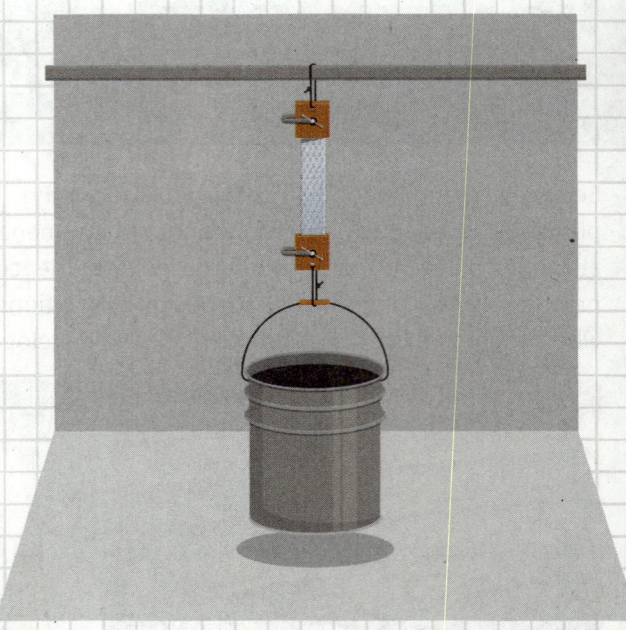

Tensile tests are commonly used to test how a material will react to pulling forces (forces being applied in tension). Here, a strip of bubble packaging is being tested to see how well the material withstands pulling and tearing.

> **EVIDENCE NOTEBOOK**
>
> **11.** What types of questions might be useful to ask about materials when designing a home for the plastic bottle village? Record your evidence.

Develop and Use Models

In a scientific investigation, a model might be used to make a prediction. For example, a mathematical model might predict how a new material will stretch, based on its chemical composition and its physical structure. A computer model of the atmosphere could forecast weather and climate changes. A physical model can show how atoms form molecules. Models are designed to account for many variables that affect the real life object or phenomenon, but models cannot account for all variables. These differences are considered when analyzing data generated by the model.

Engineers also use models, but in a different way. Engineering models are generally built to test a solution to a problem or to determine whether a proposed solution will work. Models known as *prototypes* are often used to test a design. Prototypes are physical models. They are used to communicate ideas about design solutions to other people. Prototypes are also tested to improve the design of the solution. They can also be a smaller model of the object or a component of a larger object. For example, a prototype of a bridge part might be built and tested to find out whether it can withstand forces without stretching or breaking.

Plan and Carry Out Investigations

In a scientific investigation, planning means asking a question and determining a way to investigate the question that will result in data that could help answer the question. For example, a scientist may ask how chemical structure affects tensile strength and then test materials with different chemical structures to measure the tensile strength of each material. In an engineering investigation, planning means clearly defining a need and the criteria and constraints of the solution. For example, an engineer defines a need for an inexpensive packing material that does not stretch more than a certain amount under a specific load. During the planning process, it is determined whether the material is too expensive to be used in the solution. The engineer will only test materials that meet the cost constraints.

Strength testing of models is an important part of many engineering design projects.

Use Mathematical and Computational Thinking

Being able to apply prior knowledge to novel situations that can arise during investigations is an important skill for scientists and engineers to have. So is the ability to break a problem down into smaller parts and organize and analyze data.

Analyze and Interpret Data

The results of tests are useful because they can provide answers to questions or solutions to problems. Results of tests often include measurements that provide data. These data are analyzed then evaluated to help answer the question or solve the problem. For example, data from a tensile strength study can be analyzed and evaluated by plotting the data on a graph. Graphing data like these allows an engineer to compare the amount of mass supported by the part to how much the material stretched.

12. **Do the Math** In the first part of the graph, the steep curve indicates elastic deformation of the material. If the weight is removed now, it will return to its original shape. Notice how the curve levels out toward the right. This indicates plastic deformation. Applying this much force to the material changes the its structure and causes it to stretch permanently. The point at which the deformation changes from elastic to plastic is called the *yield point*.

Evaluate the graph. What would happen to the material if 2,000 g were applied and removed?

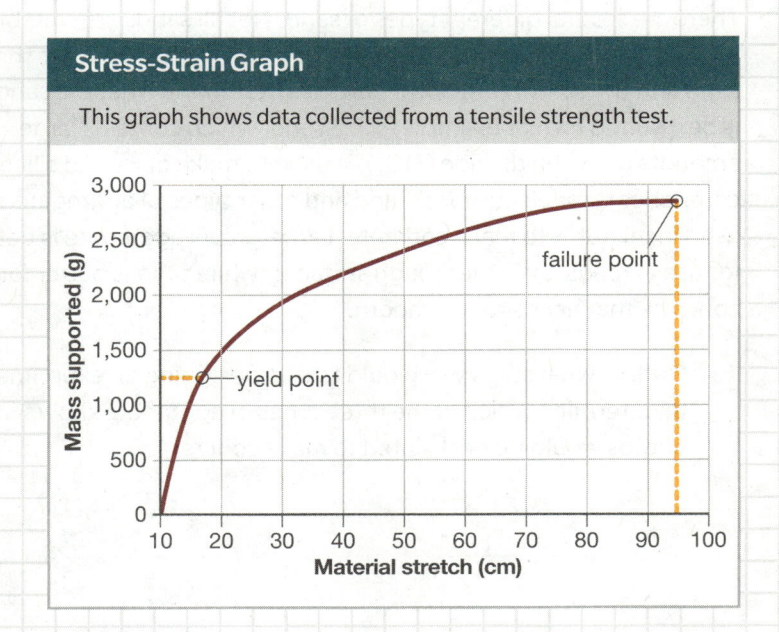

Stress-Strain Graph

This graph shows data collected from a tensile strength test.

Lesson 2 Engineer It: Using the Engineering Design Process **35**

Construct Explanations and Design Solutions

Scientists use data to develop explanations of why or how something occurs. For example, they may relate the yield point of a material to its structure in order to explain how chemical bonds affect stretching. Engineers use data to design solutions. The yield point of a material determines how it can be used in an application where a force might cause a part to stretch.

Engage in Argument from Evidence

Both scientists and engineers make arguments based on analyzed data. When the word *argument* is used this way, it does not necessarily mean that there is disagreement among people. Instead, an argument is a statement that explains something based on reason and evidence. Data are used to support the argument. Data show how the results match predictions or meet criteria and constraints.

Communicate Information

After results of an investigation or test are evaluated, they must be communicated clearly if they are to be useful to other scientists and engineers. Data communication means clearly stating the results of the investigation, arguing that the results provide an explanation or solution, and supporting the conclusion with evidence. Other people should be able to use the communicated information to repeat the investigation and obtain the same results.

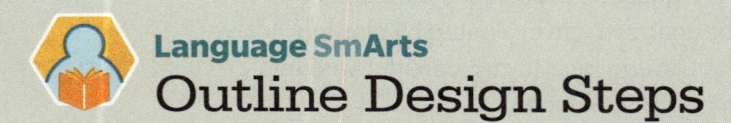

Language SmArts
Outline Design Steps

There are several different types of sand. Not all sands are suitable for the same applications. The types of minerals that make up the sand and the size of the sand's particles determine what the sand is best suited for. For example, silica sand, which contains large amounts of silicon dioxide (SiO_2), is used to make glass and silicon components for electronics. Sand and other types of aggregate are used in mixtures to make concrete. Large-gravel aggregate is better for use in roads and other rough surfaces, while sand is better for concrete that needs to be smooth.

gravel

desert sand

River sand

13. Outline what steps you would take in designing an experiment to determine which of the three types of aggregate shown in the photos would be best suited to make concrete.

_____
_____
_____
_____
_____
_____
_____

TAKE IT FURTHER

Continue Your Exploration

Name: _____ Date: _____

Check out the path below or go online to choose one of the other paths shown.

Careers in Engineering

- Earliest Examples of Technology
- Hands-On Labs
- Propose Your Own Path

Go online to choose one of these other paths.

Notice the structures that have been built in your town, such as roads, bridges, and buildings. Civil and mechanical engineers work on those structures. *Civil engineers* design and maintain public facilities, including roads, buildings, railroads, and airports. *Mechanical engineers* design machines, such as elevators, that are used in these facilities. Civil engineers who work on improving and restoring natural systems (such as rivers, seashores, and forests) are called *environmental engineers*.

Civil Engineering

Civil engineers are involved at every step of construction projects. They oversee project design and construction and maintain the project once it is complete. They use all the tools and steps of the engineering process from determining the engineering problem, defining its criteria and constraints, brainstorming new ideas, modeling and testing the ideas, to working on the final design. Then they supervise the construction. There are many roles within civil engineering. Some of these include architectural, structural, and environmental engineering. Civil engineers also develop transportation systems and manage water resources.

Engineers from the Army Corps of Engineers inspect and secure a levee built across a roadway during a flood.

Lesson 2 Engineer It: Using the Engineering Design Process

TAKE IT FURTHER

Continue Your Exploration

Army Corps of Engineers

While many people think of the army as being involved in military activities only, the Army Corps of Engineers includes units that are trained for nonmilitary responses as well. Natural disasters can occur anywhere in the world. The U.S. Army Corps of Engineers has teams of engineers who respond to disasters in the United States and elsewhere. These teams are made up of engineers and other specialists who have the training and knowledge to deal with the effects of hurricanes, floods, earthquakes, and other natural disturbances that disrupt communities. Each team includes engineers who can lead missions, such as removing debris so that traffic can begin to move, providing emergency power, and assessing bridges and other structures to determine whether they are safe. The Army Corps of Engineers also helps perform search-and-rescue operations during disasters. They help find survivors who may be trapped and unable to reach safety on their own. Army Corps of Engineers team members include electrical, civil, transportation, structural, and hydrological engineers.

1. Which of these activities would likely include the work of civil engineers? Choose all that apply.
   A. designing a new sports stadium
   B. testing concrete formulas to be used in a parking garage
   C. brainstorming improvements to plastics used in making toys
   D. rebuilding severely eroded banks of a river to reduce flooding

2. Which of these activities would most likely be carried out by a civil engineer who specializes in environmental engineering?
   A. testing steel beams for a large bridge
   B. brainstorming ways to prevent landslides on steep slopes
   C. designing a new system for unloading cargo from rail cars
   D. developing a robot to search for survivors of natural disasters

3. Explain why a response team that provides help after an earthquake would benefit from including civil engineers.

4. **Collaborate** Identify one or more natural disasters in which engineers were involved in a community's recovery. Identify the roles that engineers had in restoring the functions of the community.

LESSON 2 SELF-CHECK

Can You Explain It?

Name: _____   Date: _____

How is engineering related to this Plastic Bottle Village?

EVIDENCE NOTEBOOK
Refer to the notes in your Evidence Notebook to help you construct an explanation for how engineering is related to this Plastic Bottle Village.

1. State your claim. Make sure your claim fully explains how engineering is related to this Plastic Bottle Village.

2. Summarize the evidence you have gathered to support your claim and explain your reasoning.

LESSON 2 SELF-CHECK

Checkpoints

Answer the following questions to check your understanding of the lesson.

Use the photograph to answer Questions 3 and 4.

3. Which of the items shown in the photo were developed using engineering design processes to develop a solution to a problem? Choose all that apply.
   A. computer
   B. coffee cup
   C. table
   D. pen

4. Match items shown in the photo with the problem statement they were most likely designed to address. Write the name of the object after each statement.

   A. Made of a type of ceramic that reduces the loss of thermal energy from a hot liquid over time. _____

   B. Writes clearly on paper without smudging or leaking ink. _____

   C. Portable loudspeakers that minimize sound leakage _____.

Use the photograph to answer Questions 5 and 6.

5. An engineer proposes that a newly developed chemical could be sprayed from aircraft to slow the rate of burning in a forest fire. What is the next step the engineer is likely to take to develop a solution to fighting forest fires?
   A. Test a number of similar chemicals.
   B. Spray and compare the effectiveness of each tested chemical to water.
   C. Add the chemical to all aircraft spray tanks.
   D. Design a spray system for the chemical.

6. Scientists and engineers study the effects of fires. Identify which of these questions would most likely be asked by a scientist, an engineer, or both. Write S for scientist, E for engineer, or B for both.
   A. Which materials are best for fighting fires? _____
   B. How does turbulence above a fire affect aircraft that drop water on a fire? _____
   C. What percent of fires have natural causes? _____
   D. How does the type of terrain affect the path of fires? _____

LESSON 2 SELF-CHECK

Interactive Review

Complete this interactive study guide to review the lesson.

The engineering design process identifies a problem and then proposes, tests, and optimizes a solution to that problem.

A. Explain why testing a solution based on the criteria and constraints of the design problem is a key part of the engineering design process.

Science and engineering are related fields, but they have different goals and purposes.

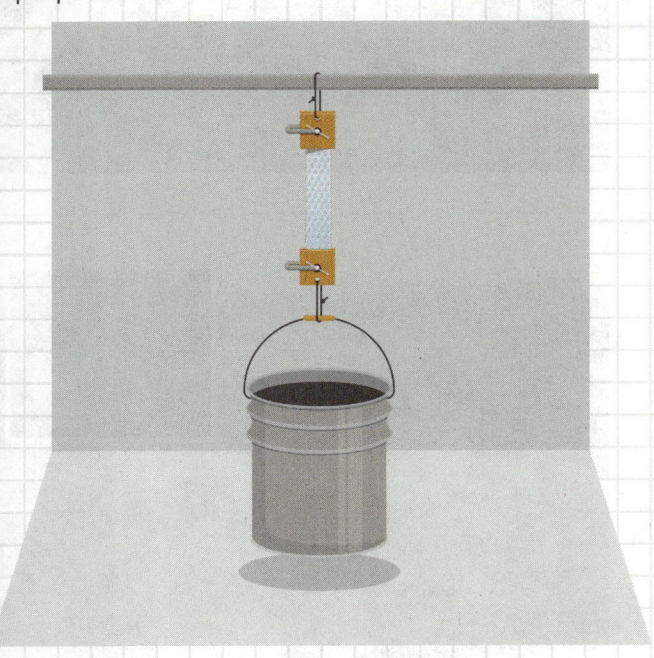

B. Models are important tools for both scientists and engineers. How do scientists and engineers differ in the way that they use models in their areas of study?

Lesson 2 Engineer It: Using the Engineering Design Process

UNIT 1 CONNECTIONS

Choose one of the activities to explore how this unit connects to other topics.

☐ People in Science

Nader Khalili Imagine living in a home that you built yourself out of affordable and easily-available resources. What would it look like? Would it stand up to the elements? Would it be comfortable? Nader Khalili was an Iranian-born architect who designed such homes, with the intent that they would be easy to construct. His design uses soil-filled sandbags and barbed wire to build stable, well insulated homes. The thick, curved walls are so stable they are earthquake resistant.

Research the use of this home design to help house war refugees and the homeless. Identify the features of the design that make it suitable for such uses.

☐ Health Connection

Cholera Today Cholera, an often deadly intestinal infection, has long plagued societies. In 1854 in London, England, cases of cholera were linked to water pumps that were near sources of fecal waste. Water and sewage infrastructure in London were redeveloped as a result of these outbreaks. Today, the World Health Organization estimates there are roughly 1.4 to 4.0 million cases of cholera per year, resulting in 21,000 to 143,000 deaths worldwide.

Research a cholera outbreak and make a presentation about the causes of the epidemic. Describe how society and technology could prevent future outbreaks.

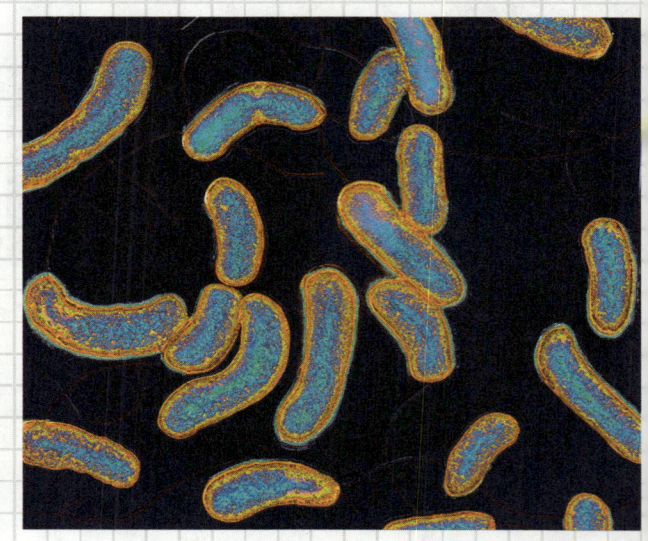

☐ Technology Connection

Biomimicry Biomimetics, or biomimicry, is the imitation of nature to solve human problems. Studying nature can help produce better human-made technologies and structures. In a recent example, scientists studied the ability of geckos to climb smooth surfaces. This phenomenon inspired NASA to develop a material with small synthetic hairs that allow it to remain sticky after many uses.

Research another nature-inspired technology. Use the research to create a poster, visual display, or electronic image that explains the technology. Present your findings to the class.

UNIT 1 REVIEW

Name: _____ Date: _____

Complete this review to check your understanding of the unit.

Use the image of different wind turbine designs to answer Questions 1–2.

1. Wind is an important renewable energy resource. These wind turbine designs were developed by ~~scientists~~ / **engineers** in order to harness wind power in different environments. Each design has its own advantages and disadvantages. **Scientists** / ~~Engineers~~ investigated each type of wind turbine to answer questions about how the turbines affect migrating birds.

2. Using wind energy lessens air pollution and **benefits** / ~~harms~~ ecosystems.

Vertical Axis   Horizontal Axis   Vertical Axis

Use the graph to answer Questions 3–5.

3. *Diporeia* is a shrimp-like organism that is native to Lake Michigan. The quagga mussel was introduced to this aquatic ecosystem by humans in the late 1980s. As the graph shows, the *Diporeia* population ~~increased~~ / **decreased** as the mussel population **increased** / ~~decreased~~.

Populations of Lake Michigan Aquatic Organisms

4. Lake whitefish depend on *Diporeia* for food. Which of the following likely happened to the lake whitefish population over the time period shown on the graph?

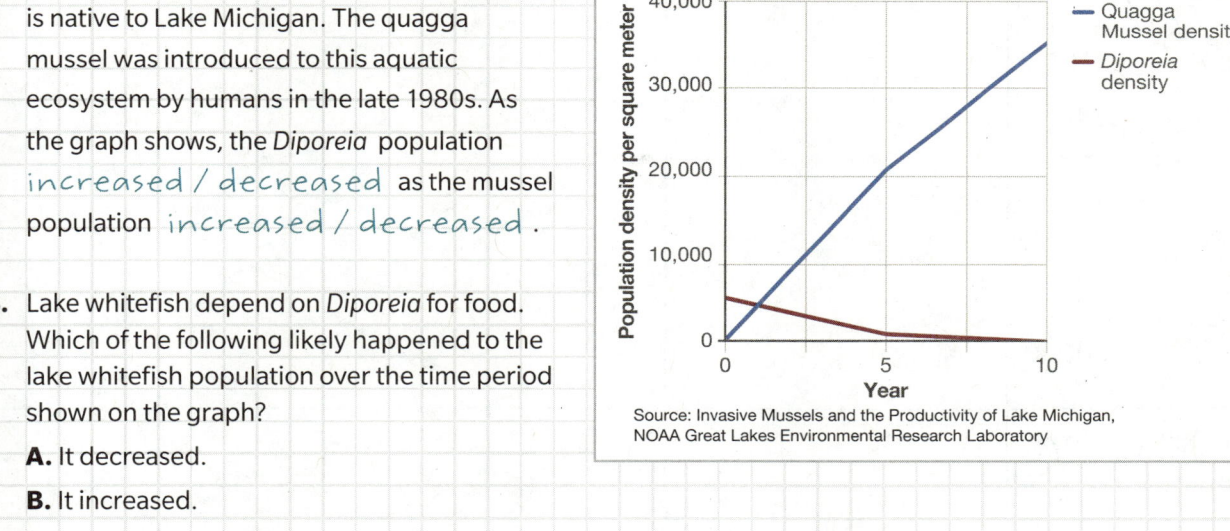

   A. It decreased.

   B. It increased.

   C. It stayed the same.

5. **Scientists** / ~~Engineers~~ collected the data shown in the graph to answer the question "Is there a relationship between quagga mussel and *Diporeia* populations?" Together, scientists and engineers are working on understanding this relationship in order to solve problems related to the decline in the *Diporeia* population.

Unit 1 Science and Engineering   43

UNIT 1 REVIEW

6. Complete the table by providing at least one example of how these engineering and science topics relate to each big concept.

Engineering and science	Energy and matter	Stability and change	Cause and effect
Natural resources	Natural resources are used to generate energy and to make materials. It takes energy to gather and produce resources and even to recycle them. Matter is conserved in a natural resource's life cycle.		
Impacts of resource use			
Technology			

44   Unit 1 Review

UNIT 1 REVIEW

Name: _____   Date: _____

Use the diagram of the life cycle of a pencil to answer Questions 7–9.

The Pencil Production Process

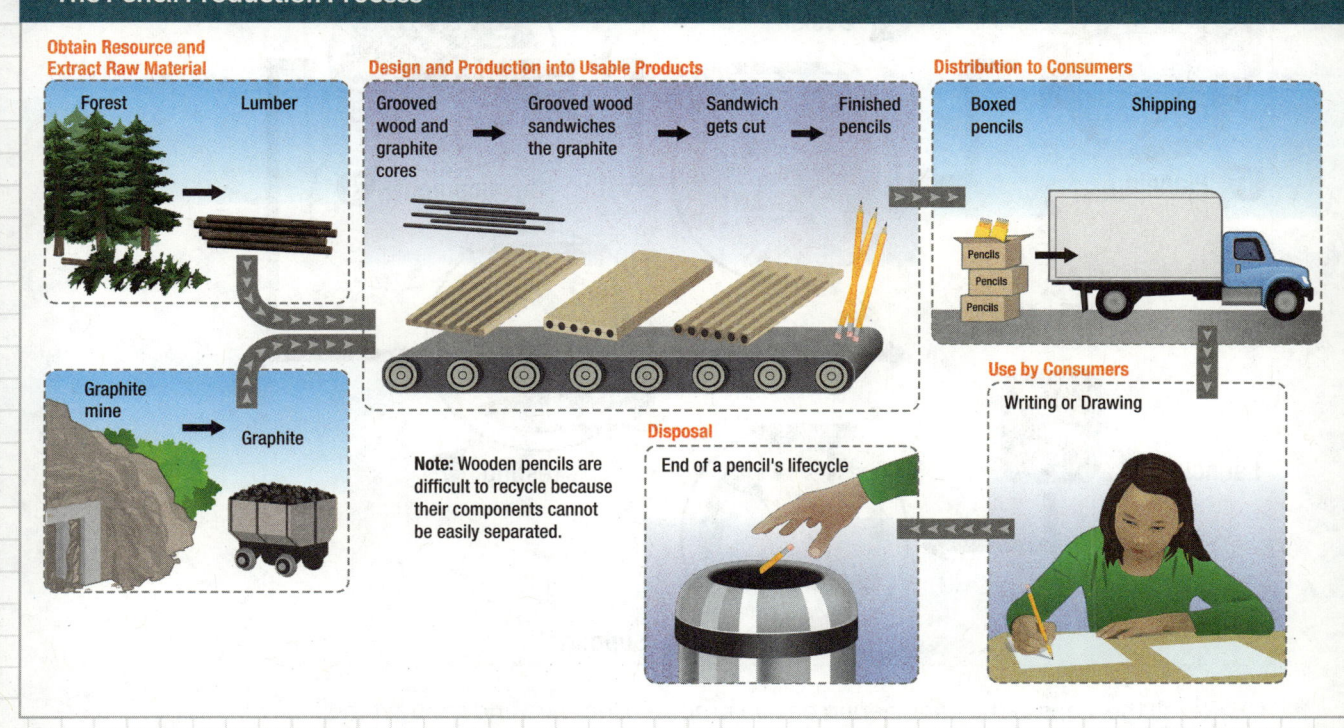

Obtain Resource and Extract Raw Material
- Forest → Lumber
- Graphite mine → Graphite

Design and Production into Usable Products
- Grooved wood and graphite cores → Grooved wood sandwiches the graphite → Sandwich gets cut → Finished pencils

Distribution to Consumers
- Boxed pencils → Shipping

Use by Consumers
- Writing or Drawing

Disposal
- End of a pencil's lifecycle

Note: Wooden pencils are difficult to recycle because their components cannot be easily separated.

7. Identify one effect each step of the pencil's life cycle may have on society or the environment.

8. What are the inputs of the production stage? What are the outputs? How would a decrease in the outputs of the forest or graphite mine affect the production stage's inputs and outputs?

9. The pencil is a device that has been improved over time through the engineering design process. How do a pencil's design features satisfy the criteria and constraints for a writing tool? How could the design be improved?

Unit 1 Science and Engineering   45

UNIT 1 REVIEW

Use the diagram of the web design process to answer Questions 10–12.

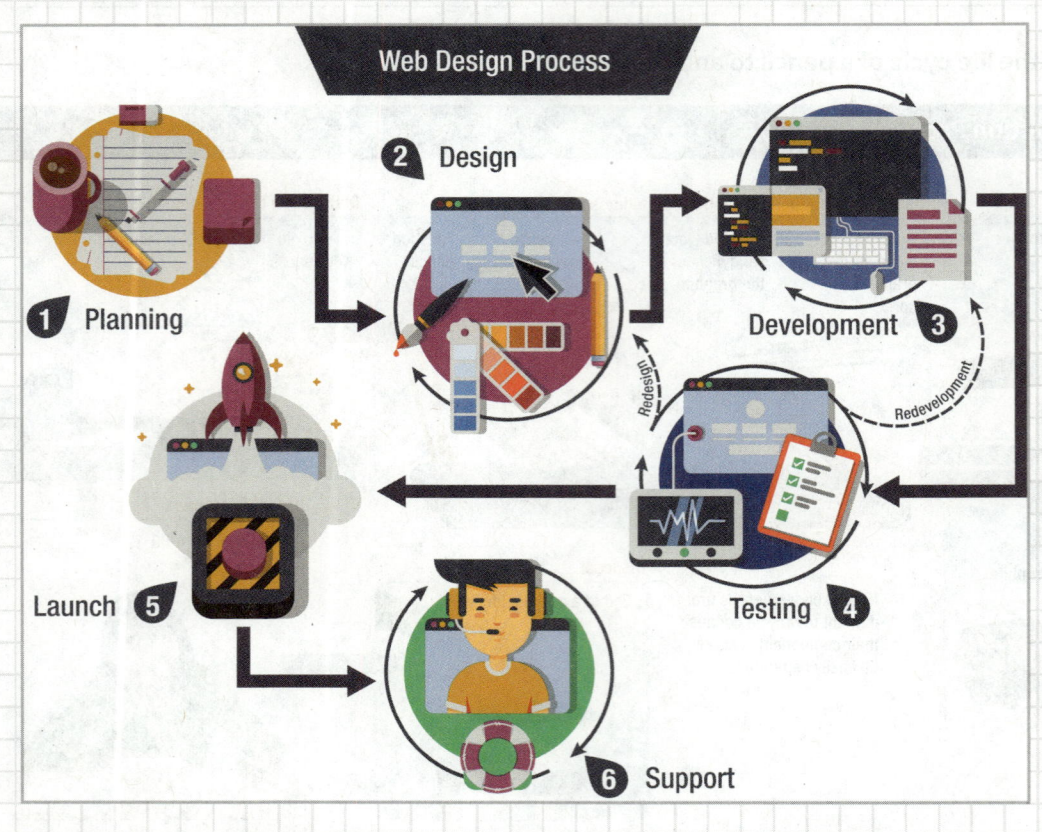

Web Design Process

1. Planning
2. Design
3. Development
4. Testing
5. Launch
6. Support

(Redesign / Redevelopment)

10. Recall the steps of the engineering design process. Compare and contrast the similarities and differences between the stages of the web design process and the engineering design process.

11. At what stage in the web design process are web designers most likely to return to planning with feedback for design improvement? What stage of the web design process most closely resembles the stage of the engineering design process at which the solution is implemented?

12. The engineering design process and the web design process both require the design teams to return to earlier stages and incorporate changes along the way. Why do these design processes involve multiple iterations of the design solution?

UNIT 1 PERFORMANCE TASK

Name: _____ Date: _____

Which is the better water filtering solution for a village?

The water supply for a village in a developing nation is not safe to drink due to bacterial contamination. Your team has been asked to evaluate two purification systems to provide drinkable water. Identify and recommend which design best solves the problem.

Gravity filter

Filter straws

In this design, gravity pulls water from a large clay tank through filters with tiny pores that remove bacteria. This design can be used to provide enough clean water for a family.

These tubes contain fibers that trap bacteria as water passes through. This design allows individuals to drink freely using suction as clean water passes through the fibers.

The steps below will help guide your research and develop your recommendation.

Engineer It

1. **Define the Problem** Write a statement defining the problem you have been asked to solve. What are the criteria and constraints involved in selecting a water filtration method?

Unit 1 Science and Engineering   **47**

UNIT 1 PERFORMANCE TASK

Engineer It

2. **Conduct Research** Identify possible societal and environmental consequences of each design solution. Describe the strengths and weaknesses of the solutions based on these factors.

3. **Evaluate Data** Analyze each design's ability to meet the criteria and constraints of the problem. Is one solution more useful than the other? Which purification method will help the most people in the community?

4. **Identify and Recommend a Solution** Make a recommendation based on your research. Which design do you think the town should use? Explain your reasoning.

5. **Communicate** Present your decision to the community. Your argument should use evidence that supports the design that best meets the specified criteria and constraints. You should also describe the strengths and weaknesses of the design. Describe a situation where the alternate solution may be more useful.

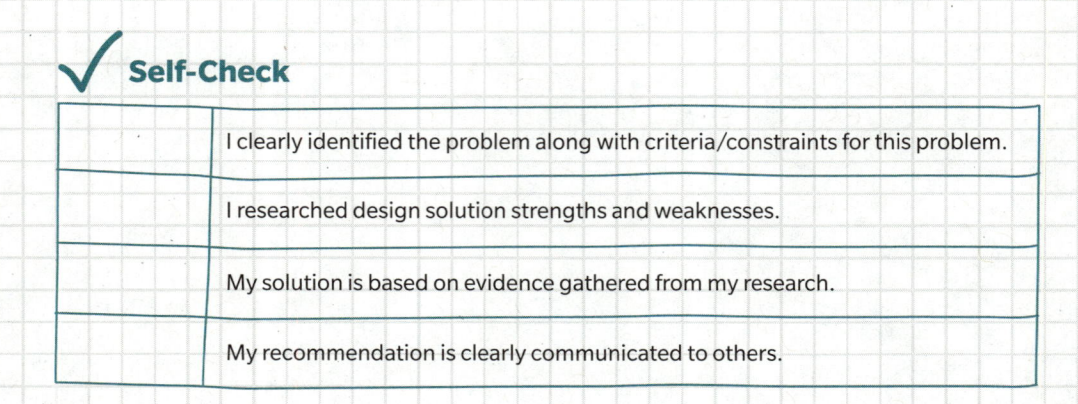

✓ Self-Check

	I clearly identified the problem along with criteria/constraints for this problem.
	I researched design solution strengths and weaknesses.
	My solution is based on evidence gathered from my research.
	My recommendation is clearly communicated to others.

UNIT 2

The Structure of Matter

How are the properties of matter related to its particles?

Unit Project	50
Lesson 1 Patterns Can Be Observed in Organisms and Nonliving Things	52
Lesson 2 Matter Exists in Different States	70
Lesson 3 Changes of State Are Caused By Changes in Thermal Energy	84
Lesson 4 Organisms and Nonliving Things Are Made of Atoms	104
Unit Review	127
Unit Performance Task	131

Hot gases and molten rock from beneath Earth's surface ooze from Kīlhauea, a volcano in Hawaii.

You Solve It How Can You Make a Synthetic Magnet?
Design cow magnets by selecting different combinations of metals, shapes, and sizes. Test your magnets to see which ones meet the given criteria.

Go online and complete the You Solve It to explore ways to solve a real-world problem.

49

UNIT 2 PROJECT

Explore Disappearing Arctic Sea Ice

Large portions of ice in both arctic regions of Earth are disappearing at alarming rates.

A. Look at the photo. On a separate sheet of paper, write down as many different questions as you can about the photo.

B. Discuss With your class or a partner, share your questions. Record any additional questions generated in your discussion. Then choose the most important questions from the list that are related to disappearing arctic sea ice. Write them below.

C. Identify technologies that contribute to the disappearing arctic sea ice. The following are some examples.

cruise ships
cars
coal power plants
commercial ranching

D. Use the information above to develop a plan for protecting disappearing arctic sea ice.

Discuss the next steps for your Unit Project with your teacher and go online to download the Unit Project Worksheet.

UNIT 2

Language Development

Use the lessons in this unit to complete the network and expand your understanding of these key concepts.

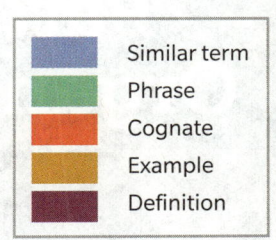

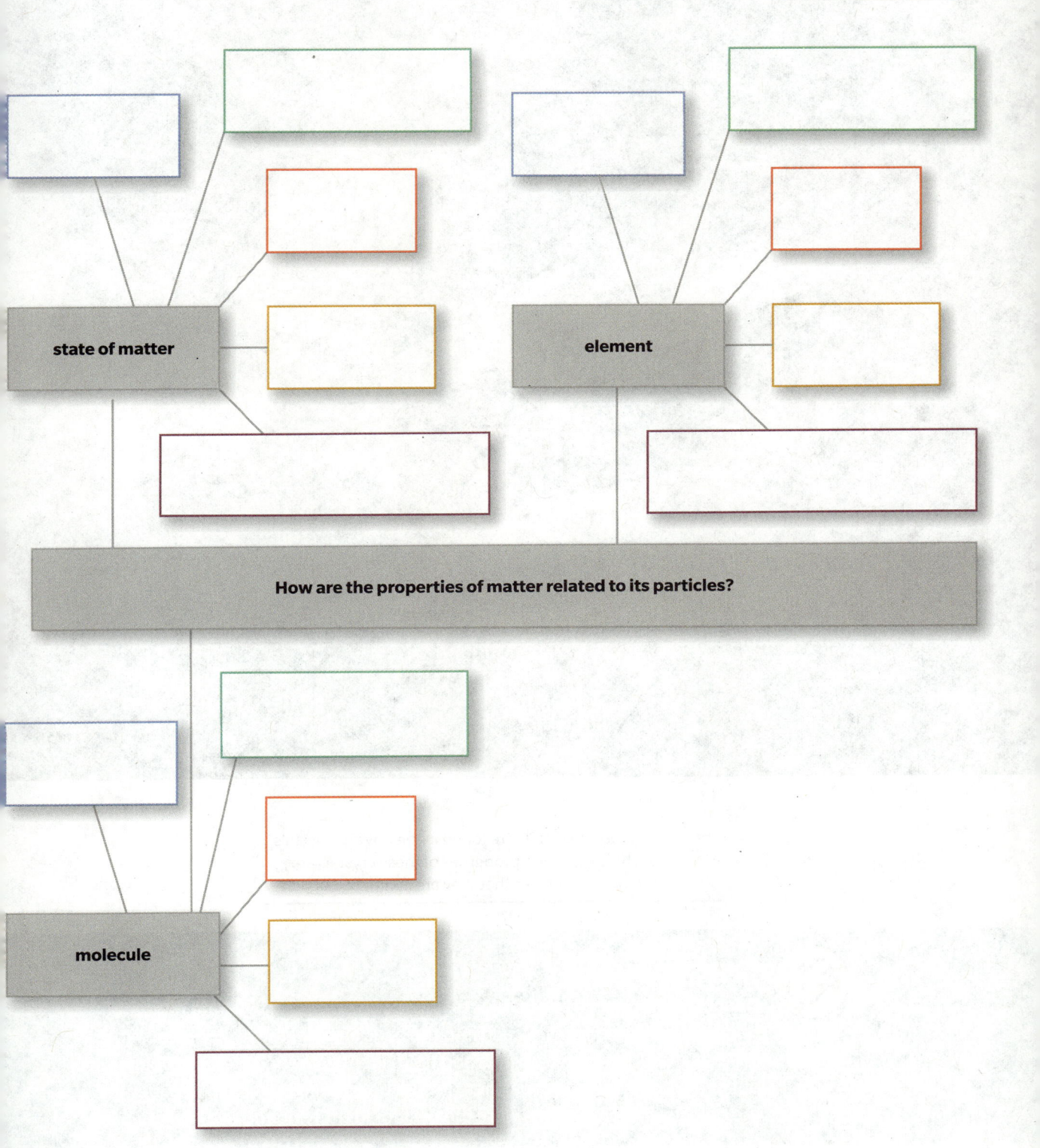

- Similar term
- Phrase
- Cognate
- Example
- Definition

state of matter

element

How are the properties of matter related to its particles?

molecule

Unit 2 The Structure of Matter

LESSON 1

Patterns Can Be Observed in Organisms and Nonliving Things

Enormous gypsum crystals are found in the Cave of Crystals in Mexico. The shapes and properties of these crystals are determined by the particles that they are composed of.

Explore First

Describing Properties of Objects Place two objects in separate bags and trade bags with a partner. Reach into the bags and feel the two objects. Write down features of the two objects and try to identify them. Take both objects out of the bags. With your partner, discuss how well you were able to identify the objects. Which features were the best for identifying the two objects?

Unit 2 The Structure of Matter

Go online to view the digital version of the Hands-On Lab for this lesson and to download additional lab resources.

CAN YOU EXPLAIN IT?

Why do people choose wool as a material for warm clothing?

Wool is a type of fiber that comes from the coats of sheep and other animals. The first photo shows a sheep with a full coat of wool. The second photo shows clothing made from sheep's wool. Clothing such as jackets, socks, and scarves are often made from wool.

1. Humans make all sorts of objects and devices with many different purposes and made up of many different materials. How do people decide which materials to use for a specific purpose?

EVIDENCE NOTEBOOK As you explore the lesson, consider the reasons why wool is used to make warm clothing.

Lesson 1 Patterns Can Be Observed in Organisms and Nonliving Things 53

EXPLORATION 1

Observing Patterns in Matter

Think about everything around you during your day. Your shirt, your desk at school, the water you wash your hands with, and the air blowing through your hair all have something in common. They are all matter. Matter is a word used to describe physical things. Most things you can see or feel are matter.

A basketball is made of matter.

The light and heat that makes up fire are not matter.

2. A basketball is very different from a fire. What are some differences that might make a basketball matter, while light from a fire is not matter?

Matter

All matter, including basketballs and water, shares two properties. **Matter** is anything that has mass and volume. **Mass** is a measure of the amount of matter an object contains. **Volume** is a measure of how much space an object takes up. Both living and nonliving things are matter. Your body, a tiny ant, and the rocks and soil in a garden are all matter. Some things that you cannot see are also matter. Air is matter. It takes up space inside a basketball and its mass can be measured. However, the actual flame that you see in a fire is a combination of light and heat. Neither light nor heat has mass or takes up space. Because light and heat do not have mass or take up space, they are not matter.

3. **Discuss** Which of the following are matter? Select all that apply.

   A. light from the sun
   B. milk in a carton
   C. heat from a candle
   D. the sound of thunder
   E. a pebble on a beach

Everything that takes up space and has mass is matter. Even the air, which you cannot see, is matter.

54 Unit 2 The Structure of Matter

Patterns and Categories in Matter

Many different patterns can be observed in matter. Samples of matter may have the same color, hardness, or smell. Some matter is liquid while some is solid or a gas. Looking for patterns in matter allows you to identify when two samples of matter share characteristics. If two samples show enough similar patterns, they could even be the same material. Recognizing patterns also allows you to categorize matter.

Placing things into categories can make them easier to interpret. Think about the grocery store. There is a section for fruits and vegetables, one for frozen food, and one for baked goods. Without these categories, going shopping would take you a lot longer. Some matter makes up living organisms and some makes up nonliving objects. Some objects that contain matter are made by humans and some occur naturally.

Language SmArts
Categorize Matter

4. In the first table, list at least three different patterns that you see in the matter in this photo. Identify objects that exhibit each of these patterns. In the second table, use your observations of patterns in matter to sort the objects into the categories *Living* and *Human Made*.

Pattern	Things That Exhibit the Pattern
white color	

Living	Human Made

EVIDENCE NOTEBOOK

5. Alpacas live on cold mountains and have coats similar to sheep. What patterns do you notice about these animals? Record your evidence.

Lesson 1 Patterns Can Be Observed in Organisms and Nonliving Things   55

Ecosystems and Water Distribution

Nile Delta

Nile River

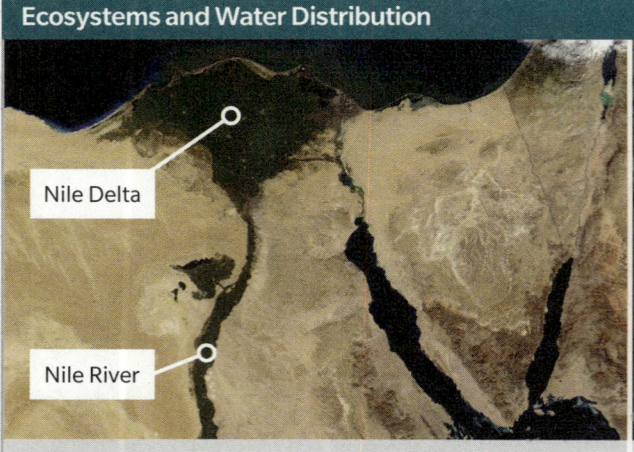

This satellite photo shows the area around the Nile River and its delta.

The lighter patches of sand are drier areas, while the darker patches are wet areas closer to the river.

6. What patterns do you notice in the plant growth shown in these two photos?

Patterns in Resource Distribution

In addition to the patterns between different samples of matter, there are patterns in the distribution of matter. These affect how living organisms interact with their environments. For example, all living things use water, so the distribution of water affects ecosystems. The distribution of water follows patterns, such as water flowing to lower areas. More living things will be in areas where more fresh water is available. Rainforests are dense with life compared to drier areas such as deserts. Droughts and human activity can affect the distribution of water, which then will affect ecosystems.

This rainforest has an abundant supply of water.

Observe Patterns in the World

Recognizing patterns can help scientists develop explanations of how the world works. They can then test these explanations to determine how specific patterns arise.

7. What are some questions that you could ask in order to determine more about why bears are drawn to rivers that salmon migrate through?

A bear catches salmon to eat in a river.

56   Unit 2 The Structure of Matter

EXPLORATION 2

Analyzing Properties of Matter

Suppose you are playing a guessing game. You need to describe an object so someone can guess its identity. You might describe its size or weight, but the person guessing would likely need to know other properties of the object to guess what it is.

8. **Discuss** Identify three differences between the objects that you can see in the photo.

Notice how light reflects differently from the rock and the bell. Luster is a property that describes how light reflects off of and interacts with a substance.

Properties of Matter

Some patterns that you can identify matter with can be studied and formalized. An example of this was Fredrich Mohs' study of minerals in the early 1800s. After noticing patterns in how hard different samples were, Mohs developed a definition for *hardness* and the Mohs hardness scale. Mohs identified a property of matter.

Properties of matter are specific characteristics that matter exhibits. The mass of an object and the amount of space it takes up are both properties of that object. Other properties of matter can include how it looks, feels, or reacts to other matter. By observing patterns in matter, scientists can identify consistent properties. Properties of matter can be used to identify a sample of matter. They can also be used to tell the difference between two similar samples. For example, quartz and calcite are both white minerals. To correctly identify these minerals you must test other properties. Quartz has a much higher hardness than calcite, and calcite will bubble when acid is placed on it.

Physical Properties

Physical properties are properties that can be observed without changing the identity of a sample of matter. You can see the color of a ball. You can measure the ball's mass. If you physically change a sample, its physical properties will change, but the identity of the sample will not. If you were to rip a piece of paper in half, it would change the mass, volume, and shape of the paper, but it would still be paper. If you were to take a piece of wood and use sand paper to make it smooth it would change the texture, but still be wood. Some other physical properties include thermal conductivity and flexibility. For instance, wool does not transfer heat well, allowing warm objects to stay warm. It is also flexible and can be bent into many shapes without breaking.

Lesson 1 Patterns Can Be Observed in Organisms and Nonliving Things

9. Some matter that undergoes changes to its physical properties can appear very different afterwards. You could crumple a can or melt ice. When wood burns, do you think its physical properties are simply changing or is something else happening to the wood? Explain your reasoning.

When wood burns, it turns to ash and energy is released.

Chemical Properties

Chemical properties are very different from physical properties. Just looking at or feeling an object will not tell you its chemical properties. A chemical property can only be identified during a chemical reaction or after one has taken place. An easy chemical property to observe is a substance's flammability, or the ability of a substance to burn. When a substance burns, it undergoes a chemical reaction and the identity of the substance changes. Wood can become ash, smoke, and carbon dioxide.

Some of the most easily observable chemical properties are a substance's ability to react with various other substances. Have you ever left apple slices out on the counter? The inside of an apple turns brown due to a reaction with oxygen. A piece of iron rusting is also a reaction with oxygen. The inside of an apple and iron both have the chemical property that they react with oxygen. Chemical properties govern how different substances will react with other substances.

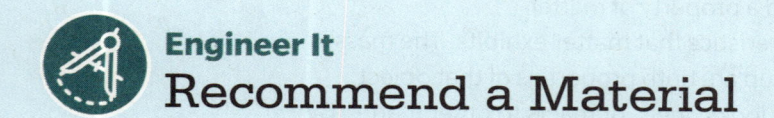

Engineer It
Recommend a Material

Electric conductivity, a physical property, is a measure of how well a material will transmit electric charges. Reactivity, a chemical property, refers to how likely a material is to undergo a chemical reaction. Knowing these two properties can allow you to choose what type of matter works best in a specific situation.

Material	Electric Conductivity	Reactivity
Gold	High	Low
Aluminum	Medium	Medium
Sodium	Low	High

10. If you were making an electric device and needed a piece that would easily transmit an electric charge and also not react with other materials, what material would you choose? Explain your choice.

58 Unit 2 The Structure of Matter

11. Label the following properties as either physical or chemical. Write a P next to physical properties and a C next to chemical properties.
    A. thermal conductivity—the rate thermal energy spreads through a substance _____
    B. flammability—the ability of a substance to burn _____
    C. magnetic attraction—whether a substance is pulled by a magnet _____
    D. melting point—the temperature at which a solid changes to a liquid _____
    E. reactivity with oxygen—the ability of a substance to chemically react with oxygen _____

Caves and Ecosystems

Limestone is a sedimentary rock that is formed primarily of calcium carbonate. Limestone is soluble in water. This solubility causes caves to form when water flows through large limestone deposits.

Some species of bat live in caves. They sleep hanging upside down from the ceiling of the caves.

Many species of cavefish are blind. Eyesight is not necessary to survive in their natural habitat, which is without light.

12. How would bats be affected if limestone were not easily dissolved by water?
    A. They would have fewer areas to use as shelter.
    B. Their food supply would diminish.
    C. They would be found in different areas around the world.

Lesson 1 Patterns Can Be Observed in Organisms and Nonliving Things   59

Properties of Natural Resources

The chemical properties of limestone shape the type of ecosystem that develops around it. Limestone caves often form as the limestone dissolves in water. These caves become habitats for organisms that would not be able to live in the area if these caves did not exist. The makeup of ecosystems are based on the properties of matter in the area. Animals that live in the arctic tend to be white in color; they blend in with the snow that accumulates in that location. Fish have evolved gills and are able to breathe underwater.

Humans also interact with their environments based on the properties of matter that make it up. Farms tend to be in areas with nutrient-rich soil and flat land. Many cities are built on the coast or on rivers to make shipping easier. The types of rocks and soil in an area can determine whether or not basements are built in an area. When the properties of resources in an area change, human society is forced to change as well.

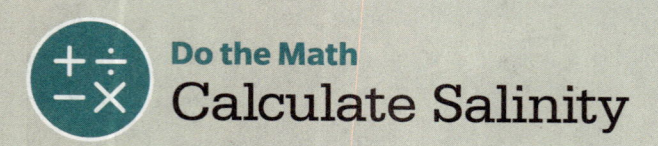

Do the Math
Calculate Salinity

Like pure substances, mixtures of different substances also have properties. Salinity is a property of matter that describes the salt content of a liquid mixture. Salinity is calculated by dividing the mass of salt in grams (g) by the volume of water in milliliters (ml) that the salt is dissolved in. That result is multiplied by 1000 to give salinity in parts per thousand (ppt). A salinity of 40.0 ppt would mean that if you took 1000 ml of a solution and evaporated all the water away, you would be left with 40 g of salt.

13. Calculate the salinity of the liquids in the table.

$$\frac{\text{mass of salt (g)}}{\text{volume of water (ml)}} \times 1000 = \text{salinity (ppt)}$$

Sample Solution	Mass of Salt	Volume of Water	Salinity (ppt)
A	27 g	1000 ml	
B	15 g	850 ml	
C	94 g	2355 ml	
D	119 g	324 ml	

14. You are designing artificial plasma. The plasma must have a salinity between 30 ppt and 40 ppt. Which of the sample solutions from the table above fit this requirement?

EVIDENCE NOTEBOOK

15. Wool is often used to make cold-weather clothing. What are some properties of wool that make it a good coat for sheep and good for making clothing out of? Record your evidence.

EXPLORATION 3

Modeling Matter

Consider a thought experiment in which you tear a piece of paper in half. Then tear it in half again and then again. How many times could you continue this? Either you divide this piece of paper in half forever or you reach a point where it could no longer be divided in half and still be considered paper.

16. Do you think matter is continuous or made of tiny particles? Explain your answer and cite evidence from your life experiences.

17. Do you think water can be split into pieces? An electrolysis device uses electricity to separate water into oxygen and hydrogen. When separated, the oxygen always takes up about half as much space as the hydrogen. What might this tell you about the materials that make up water?

Evidence for the Particle Theory of Matter

Throughout history, philosophers and mathematicians have proposed many different models of matter. One hypothesis was that large pieces of matter were made up of many tiny particles.

During electrolysis, water is separated into oxygen and hydrogen. The two gases are collected in separate tubes.

Electrolysis of Water

The first convincing evidence for the particle theory of matter was discovered in 1803. That year, John Dalton separated some pure substances, including water, into their components. Dalton realized that when these pure substances were separated into their components, they always separated into the same ratios. This supported the idea that matter was made of building blocks that always combined in specific ways.

Lesson 1 Patterns Can Be Observed in Organisms and Nonliving Things

Brownian Motion

In the late 1820s, Robert Brown was studying the pollen of different plants by suspending pollen in water and looking at it under a microscope. During his research, he noticed that the pollen was moving. Brown decided to test if this motion only occurred with pollen. He did further experiments by placing different crushed materials in water and he saw the same random motion. This motion is now known as Brownian motion. There were several hypotheses for why these tiny, inanimate objects would move. One idea that seemed to explain the behavior well was that this motion was caused by microscopic particles colliding with the pollen.

18. How do the observations of Brownian motion help to reinforce or weaken the hypothesis that matter is made up of tiny particles?

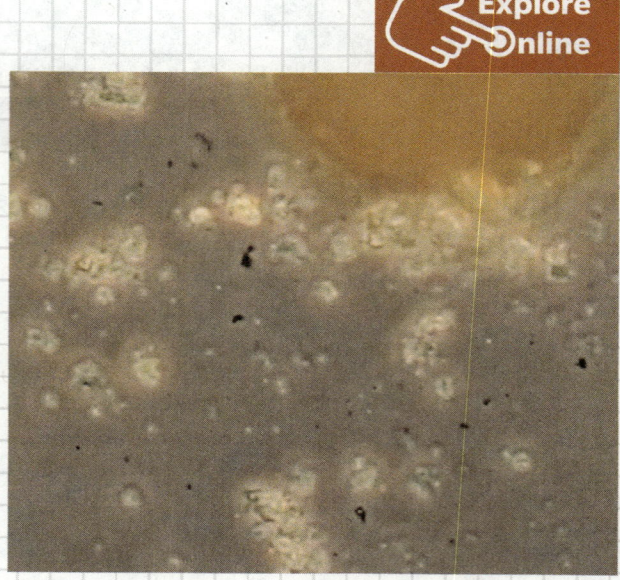

Particles of pollen suspended in water tend to move in random directions. This motion is called Brownian motion.

Evidence from New Technologies

New technologies have only provided more evidence for a particle theory of matter. In the 1980s, a very powerful microscope known as a scanning tunneling microscope was invented. Microscopes such as these have been able to generate images of individual particles of matter. Mass spectrometers are tools that can be used to determine the ratios of particles that make up a sample of matter. Mass spectrometers have also provided evidence that matter is made of particles. These new technologies provide direct evidence that further confirms ideas from hundreds of years ago.

19. If matter is made of many tiny particles, why does it seem to be continuous? Why doesn't water seem to behave like sand?

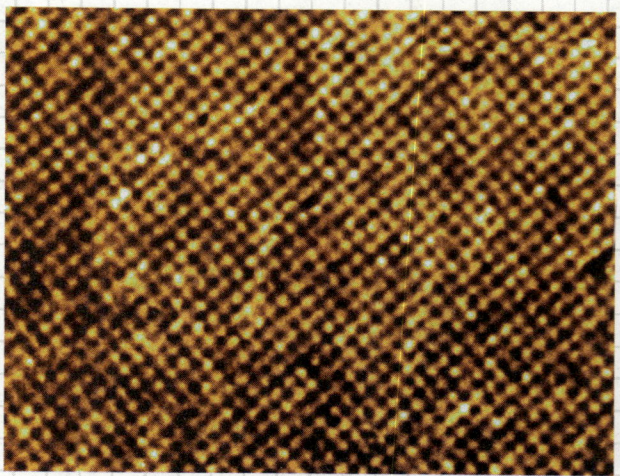

By using a scanning tunneling microscope, scientists are able to generate images of these gold particles.

Hands-On Lab
Model Particles in Objects

Use a variety of materials to develop several ways to model the particles that make up matter. Though all matter is made up of particles, different samples of matter still behave differently. Experiment with several ways to model different varieties of matter.

MATERIALS
- bags, plastic
- building blocks
- clay
- marbles
- paper
- pom poms, craft
- scissors
- straws
- string

Procedure

STEP 1 Pick a solid object in the room. Use the supplied materials to develop a model of the particles that make up that object.

STEP 2 Use the supplied materials to develop a model of the particles that make up a liquid, such as water.

STEP 3 Describe how you modeled the particles that make up the solid and the liquid. What similarities and differences were there in your two models? How are those related to the properties of the solid and the liquid?

STEP 4 Draw When table salt is separated into its components, equal parts sodium and chlorine are produced. Develop a model of salt that indicates the particles that it is made up of. Then, draw a diagram that also indicates the particles that make up table salt.

Lesson 1 Patterns Can Be Observed in Organisms and Nonliving Things

STEP 5 From your experience modeling particles, what are some conclusions you can draw?

Use Models to Understand How Particles Affect Properties

Does a house made out of wood have different properties than a house made out of mud? The properties of an object are affected by the particles it is made of. An object's color, mass, and density are just a few of the properties that are defined by its particles. Density is a measure of the mass of an object compared to how much space it takes up. The equation to calculate density is mass divided by volume.

20. Which of the following would cause mercury to be denser than water? Choose all that apply.
    A. the particles that make it up have more mass
    B. the particles that make it up are closer together
    C. the particles that make it up move around faster
    D. the particles that make it up are a darker color

Mercury is a metal that is in the liquid state at room temperature.

21. How do you think a substance's properties are affected by the properties of the particles the substance is composed of?

64 Unit 2 The Structure of Matter

TAKE IT FURTHER

Continue Your Exploration

Name: _____ Date: _____

Check out the path below or go online to choose one of the other paths shown.

People in Science & Engineering
- Exploring Properties of Matter
- Hands-On Labs
- Propose Your Own Path

Go online to choose one of these other paths.

Gianluca Cusatis, Civil Engineer

Gianluca Cusatis is a Civil and Environmental Engineering professor at Northwestern University. He is originally from Italy, where he earned his PhD. in Structural Engineering. Cusatis teaches structural and civil engineering courses, and researches how different materials behave. A large focus of Cusatis' work is modeling materials using computers. Recently, Cusatis has researched materials that could be used for construction on Mars.

The idea of living on another planet has intrigued people for years, but many problems need to be solved before anyone can do it. One big problem with settling other planets is that astronauts will not have access to building materials normally used on Earth. People build many things out of concrete. Houses, sidewalks, and roads all use it. However, to make concrete, you need water, which is hard to get on planets like Mars. Cusatis and his PhD students conducted experiments and used computer modeling to explore ways to make concrete with materials found on Mars.

Gianluca Cusatis has designed concrete that could be manufactured on Mars.

Cusatis' team realized that to make concrete on Mars, astronauts would need to use something other than water. They looked at the materials known to exist on Mars and realized that sulfur could be used instead. Sulfur is very abundant on Mars, and melting sulfur into a liquid allowed Cusatis' team to make concrete. Once this was determined, it was just a matter of determining the right recipe to make a useful concrete. Cusatis' team used computer models and physical tests to find a useful concrete recipe. What Cusatis' team ended up making was a recyclable construction material strong enough to withstand the impact of a meteorite. Their work takes us one step closer to making dreams of living on Mars a reality.

Lesson 1 Patterns Can Be Observed in Organisms and Nonliving Things

TAKE IT FURTHER

Continue Your Exploration

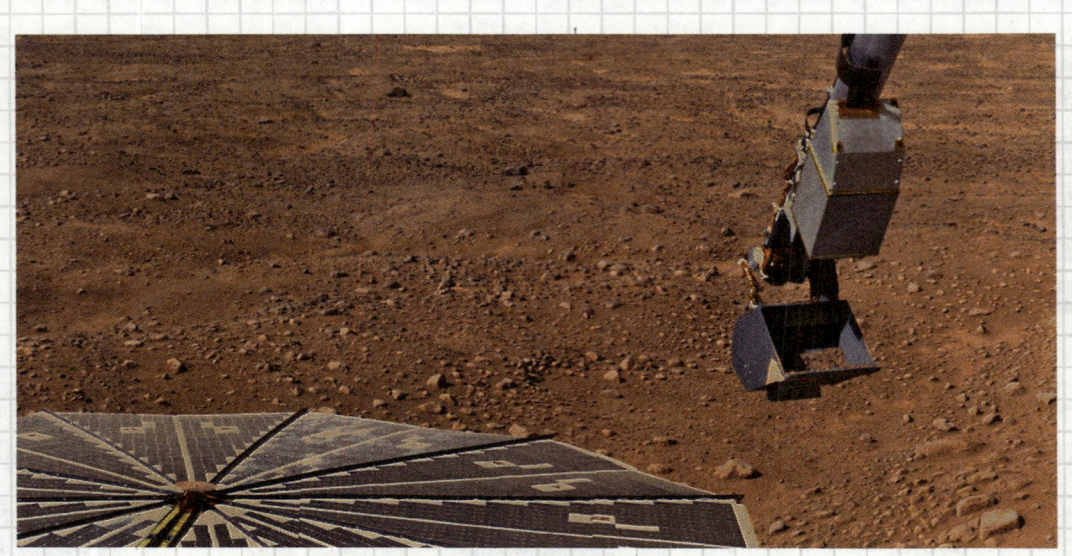

Scientists have been able to determine the types of matter present on Mars using instruments built into the Mars rovers and observations from telescopes.

1. Concrete is made up of three main components, water, aggregate (rocks), and cement, which is a powder. When the powder and water mix, they make a paste that hardens around the rock to form concrete. Why is concrete so useful in construction? Choose all that apply.

   A. It is easy to make and use.
   B. It lasts a long time.
   C. It is light and easy to move.
   D. It is fire resistant.

2. The waterless concrete Dr. Cusatis and his students developed is made using molten sulfur instead of water. Why would this concrete be useful on Mars?

3. Why might computer simulations be used to test the properties of different types of concrete? What would be the advantages of modeling these situations over making each type of concrete and then testing them?

4. **Collaborate** Think about resources that would be available on the moon. What obstacles would have to be overcome to live on the moon? What are some other technologies or materials that might need to be replaced if people wanted to settle Earth's moon?

LESSON 1 SELF-CHECK

Can You Explain It?

Name: _____ Date: _____

Why do people choose wool as a material for warm clothing?

EVIDENCE NOTEBOOK
Refer to the notes in your Evidence Notebook to help you construct an explanation for why we use wool to make clothing.

1. State your claim. Make sure your claim fully explains why wool is chosen as a clothing material.

2. Summarize the evidence you have gathered to support your claim and explain your reasoning.

Lesson 1 Patterns Can Be Observed in Organisms and Nonliving Things

LESSON 1 SELF-CHECK

Checkpoints

Answer the following questions to check your understanding of the lesson.

Use the photo to answer Questions 3–4.

3. Which of the following features of the sulfur crystals are evidence that sulfur is composed of matter? Choose all that apply.
   A. It is yellow.
   B. It takes up space.
   C. It is visible.
   D. It has mass.

4. Which of the following properties of a mineral, such as sulfur, would help you identify it? Choose all that apply.
   A. hardness
   B. size
   C. color
   D. luster

Use the photo to answer Question 5.

5. The rocks in this photo are red. This is a *chemical / physical* property of the rocks. The red color of the rocks was caused by oxidation and rust. The ability of a sample of matter to rust is a *chemical / physical* property.

6. Which of the following would happen to the particles when you break a rock in half?
   A. Particles at the break would be destroyed.
   B. Particles at the break would detach from one another.
   C. All of the particles would be rearranged into new particles.
   D. New particles would be formed at the break.

Unit 2 The Structure of Matter

LESSON 1 SELF-CHECK

Interactive Review

Complete this section to review the main concepts of the lesson.

Patterns of matter can be observed in both living and nonliving things.

A. How do patterns in different samples of matter help us categorize and study matter?

Properties of matter can be used to categorize and identify objects and substances. Matter has both physical and chemical properties.

B. Describe the differences between a chemical property and a physical property.

All matter is made up of very small particles. Before technology was developed to see particles, scientists still concluded that they existed.

C. Explain how the idea that matter is made up of particles is supported by a piece of evidence.

Lesson 1 Patterns Can Be Observed in Organisms and Nonliving Things **69**

LESSON 2

Matter Exists in Different States

Solid water provides an icy home to these penguins. They are also comfortable swimming in the liquid ocean water.

✋ Explore First

Identifying States of Matter What makes an object a liquid, a solid, or a gas? Make a list of liquids, solids, and gases that you interact with daily. Make a list of the properties that all of the solids share. Do the same for liquids and gases.

70 Unit 2 The Structure of Matter

CAN YOU EXPLAIN IT?

How do the three forms of bromine differ from each other?

This container holds a single substance in three different forms at the same time. The light orange haze, the reddish-orange pool, and the bar are all forms of the element bromine.

1. Describe the differences in the three forms of bromine shown in the picture.

2. What could be the reason for these differences?

EVIDENCE NOTEBOOK As you explore the lesson, gather evidence to help explain the differences you see in the three forms of bromine.

Lesson 2 Matter Exists in Different States **71**

EXPLORATION 1

Observing Properties of Matter

Most of the matter around you is in one of three *states*, also known as *phases* of matter—solid, liquid, or gas. Each state can be described by the physical properties of volume and shape. You can observe shape by looking carefully at a material. There are many ways to measure volume, the amount of space matter takes up. For example, you might use a graduated cylinder to measure the volume of a liquid. To classify matter as a solid, liquid, or gas, you need to observe how the volume and shape of the sample can change.

3. Think of the solids and liquids that you encounter every day. In what ways are solids and liquids similar? In what ways are they different?

Liquid aluminum is poured into molds to make solid bars.

4. Why can the liquid metal be poured into a block-shaped mold? Describe what happens to the shape and volume of the liquid metal.

72   Unit 2 The Structure of Matter

Hands-On Lab
Observe States of Matter

Observe the shapes of a solid and liquid in different containers. Investigate how the volume of a solid, liquid, and gas may change and explain how the properties of each state of matter differ.

MATERIALS
- marbles, 16 mm (3), in clear plastic cup
- plastic syringe with cap, disposable, needleless
- water in clear plastic cup

Procedure and Analysis

STEP 1 Draw 10 mL of air into the syringe. Record the initial volume in the table below.

STEP 2 Tighten the cap onto the end of the syringe, if one is available. Alternatively, you can press your finger against the end of the syringe to act as a cap. Push in the plunger. Record the final volume and any other observations. SAFETY NOTE: Always point the tip safely away from others when pushing in the plunger.

STEP 3 Observe the shape of the marbles in the cup. Remove the plunger and place the marbles in the syringe. Then replace the plunger so the bottom of the plunger touches the top of the marbles. Record the volume and observations.

STEP 4 Tighten the cap. Push in the plunger. Record the volume and observations.

STEP 5 Observe the shape of the water in the cup. Remove the marbles from the syringe and replace the plunger. Then draw 10 mL of water into the syringe. Record the volume and observations.

STEP 6 Tighten the cap. Push in the plunger. Record the volume and observations.

	Observations		
	Gas (air)	Solid (marbles)	Liquid (water)
Initial shape	not visible		
Shape in syringe	not visible		
Initial volume			
Final volume			
Additional observations			

Lesson 2 Matter Exists in Different States

STEP 7 **Do the Math** How much did the volume of the samples change when you pushed in the plunger? Based on your results for the volume of air, what might you conclude about the shape of air in the syringe? Explain.

STEP 8 Which patterns did you observe that would help you classify any sample of matter as a solid, liquid, or gas? Compare the observations that you made for the solid, liquid, and gas samples of matter. Write *can* or *cannot* to make each statement true.

Gases ____can____ change shape and ____can____ change volume.
Liquids ____can____ change shape and ____cannot____ change volume.
Solids ____cannot____ change shape and ____cannot____ change volume.

Solids, liquids, and gases can be classified by whether or not their shape and volume can change. A **solid** is the state of matter in which the volume and shape of a substance are fixed. A **liquid** is the state of matter that has a fixed volume, but can change shape. A **gas** is the state of matter that can change both shape and volume. Liquids and gases take the shape of their container, while solids have a definite shape. Liquids and solids have constant volumes, while a gas can take up different amounts of space.

EVIDENCE NOTEBOOK
5. How do your observations of solids, liquids, and gases help you describe the differences in the three forms of bromine? Record your evidence.

Engineer It

Identify Patterns in Shape and Volume

6. Properties of matter affect how people handle different states of matter. Look at the tank of the truck in the photo. This tank is designed to carry propane gas. Why is this tank design useful for transporting a gas? Considering the volume and shape properties of each state of matter, how might the container on a truck carrying a liquid or solid be designed differently?

Unit 2 The Structure of Matter

EXPLORATION 2

Explaining States of Matter

Particles of Matter

All matter is made of tiny, moving particles. For any given substance, its solid, liquid, and gas forms are made up of the same kinds of particles. For example, water in any state is made up of the same type of particles. When water exists as a gas, the particles spread out. When water exists as a solid, the particles are arranged into a more structured pattern and cannot easily be rearranged.

In each state of matter, the particles that make up a substance move differently. Particles are generally attracted toward one another. When particles are not moving very much, the attractive forces between particles hold them close to one another. When particles are moving a lot, these attractive forces cannot hold the particles together and they spread out. A substance's state of matter depends on the motions of its particles.

The hardened, black lava and the flowing, red lava are both made of the same kinds of particles.

7. What states of rock can you see in the photo?

8. Discuss Think about the properties you have observed for solids, liquids, and gases. How might the arrangement and motion of the particles in each state result in these properties? Together with a partner or small group, describe or draw how you would model the particles of one substance as a solid, a liquid, and a gas.

Model Particles in Solids, Liquids, and Gases

Kinetic energy is the energy of motion. The kinetic energy of an object depends on its mass and speed. A moving car's kinetic energy increases as its speed increases.

The particles that make up matter also have kinetic energy. In all states of matter, even solids, the particles are in constant motion. However, the particles move in different ways in each state. As the motion of the particles increases, their kinetic energy also increases. Look at each model below to see how the particle spacing and motion differs in each state of matter.

9. Write *gas*, *liquid*, or *solid* to label the state that each model shows.

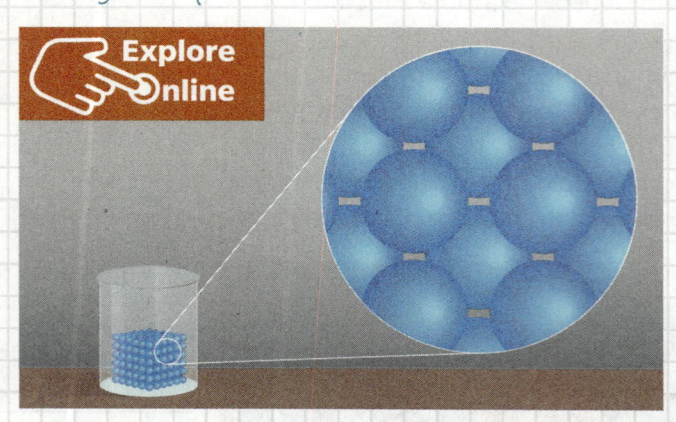

Particles are closely spaced and in contact with each other in a structured pattern. Particles vibrate in place without changing their positions in the structure.

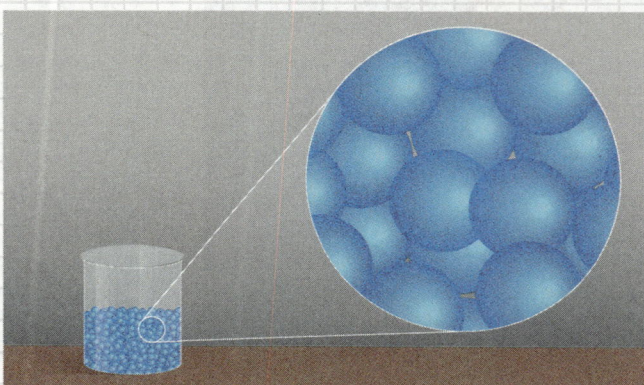

_____

Particles are closely spaced and in contact with each other. Particles move past and around each other, so they change relative positions as they move.

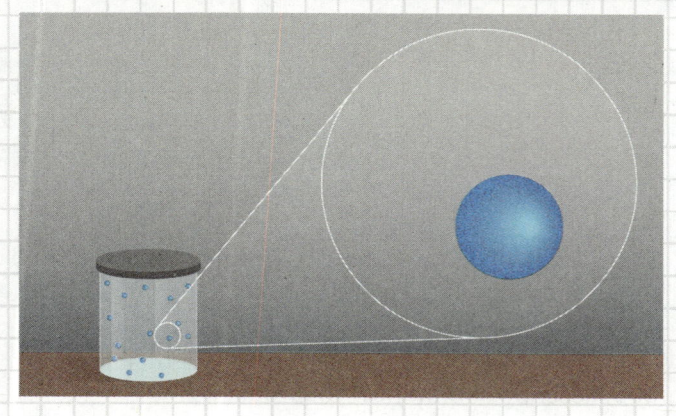

_____

Particles are spaced far apart and only occasionally collide with each other. Particles change position relative to each other constantly because they are moving quickly.

_____

> **EVIDENCE NOTEBOOK**
> **10.** How do kinetic energy, particle motion, and particle attraction help explain the differences in the forms of bromine? Record your evidence.

76 Unit 2 The Structure of Matter

11. **Language SmArts** Use what you have observed and learned about each state of matter to describe the characteristics of a solid, liquid, and gas. Write *yes* or *no* to complete the table.

	Characteristics	Solid	Liquid	Gas
Shape	fixed shape			no
	shape changes to fit container			
Volume	fixed volume	yes		
	volume changes to fit container			
Particle motion	vibrate in place		no	
	slide past each other, change position			
	move freely, change position			
Kinetic energy	has a low kinetic energy			
	has a medium kinetic energy	no	yes	no
	has a high kinetic energy			

12. Attractions between particles hold the particles of liquids and solids close together. Why is the attraction that particles have for each other not enough to keep gas particles close together?

13. Use what you have learned about particle attraction and kinetic energy. Write *increases* or *decreases* to label each arrow.

kinetic energy _____ →

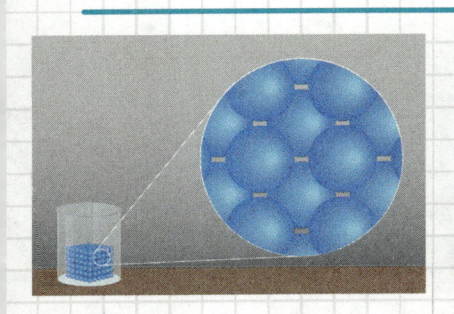

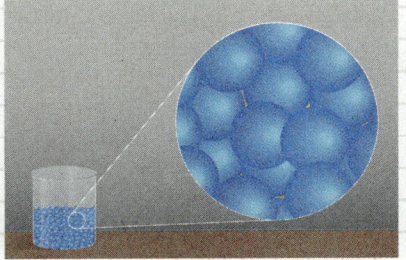

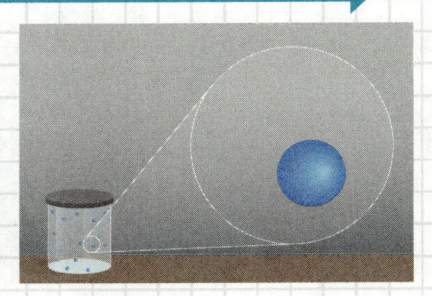

← influence of particle attraction _____

Lesson 2 Matter Exists in Different States **77**

Particles in Motion

The particles in matter are always moving, which means that the particles have kinetic energy. In a gas, the particles of a substance are far apart, move in all directions, and constantly change their relative locations. The attraction between particles has the least influence on gas particles because they have the most kinetic energy. In a liquid, the kinetic energy is less. The influence of particle attraction is greater in a liquid than in a gas. This means that liquid particles can change position, but stay close together. Particles in a solid are held close together and can only vibrate in one position. These particles vibrate in position because they have the least kinetic energy, and so they are most influenced by particle attraction.

Make Analogies for Particles in Motion

14. Consider what you know about the motion and spacing of the particles in each state of matter. How can the illustrations of people watching a movie, getting concessions, and walking outside be used as models for different states of matter? Explain which group best represents the particles in a solid, liquid, and gas.

_____
_____
_____
_____
_____
_____
_____

15. Act Together as a group, act out a scenario to model how the arrangement of particles differs between solids, liquids, and gases.

TAKE IT FURTHER

Continue Your Exploration

Name: _____ Date: _____

Check out the path below or go online to choose one of the other paths shown.

- **Why Does Ice Float?**
- Plasma—A Fourth State of Matter
- Hands-On Labs
- Propose Your Own Path

Go online to choose one of these other paths.

Most Liquids and Solids

Particles that make up solids have attractions to each other that hold the particles very close in fixed positions. Particles in liquids have more kinetic energy, so they are able to move around more, but they are still held very close. In most substances, the particles in a liquid state are a bit farther apart than they are in a solid state. Because liquid particles are not packed as tightly together, the liquid state of a substance takes up more space than the same mass of the solid state. This difference in density means that a piece of solid will generally sink to the bottom of a liquid of the same substance.

A solid cube of oil sinks to the bottom of liquid oil. The solid is denser than the liquid.

Ice floats in liquid water. Unlike most materials, the solid is less dense than the liquid.

1. Why are most substances denser in the solid state than in the liquid state?
   A. Particles in a solid are smaller.
   B. Particles in a solid have more mass.
   C. Particles in a solid have no kinetic energy.
   D. Particles in a solid tend to be arranged into a smaller space.

Lesson 2 Matter Exists in Different States **79**

TAKE IT FURTHER

Continue Your Exploration

Liquid and Solid Water

Water does not follow the predicted pattern of density that is found in most other substances. Remember, the ice cube floats in water, while the oil cube sinks in oil. If the solid ice were denser than liquid water, it would sink. But it does not sink, which means that ice is less dense than liquid water.

As with other substances, the water particles vibrate in place in ice and slip past one another in liquid water. Ice is similar to many solids because water particles are arranged in a specific pattern that repeats throughout ice. However, this pattern differs from the pattern of particles in most solids because the spacing between water particles in ice is greater than the spacing between water particles in liquid water. As a result, fewer water particles in ice are packed into the same amount of space compared to liquid water. So, ice is less dense than liquid water.

2. These two particle models show water particles in ice and in liquid water. Write _solid water_ or _liquid water_ to label the models.

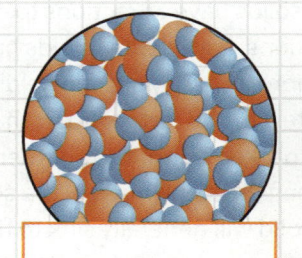

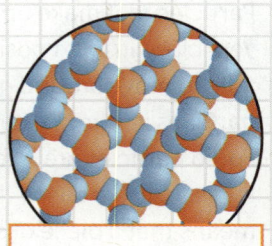

Water on Earth

The lower density of ice compared to liquid water does not only mean that ice cubes float in your water cup. This property of water is important for life on Earth because both liquid water and ice are part of Earth's hydrosphere. The hydrosphere, which contains all the water on Earth's surface, is an essential part of the Earth system. It interacts with the atmosphere and biosphere in many ways. For example, large pieces of floating ice provide penguins, polar bears, and walruses with a resting place as they look for food in the ocean.

3. Think about what happens in the hydrosphere and biosphere when ice forms at the top of a lake? What might happen instead if ice were denser than liquid water?

4. **Collaborate** With a partner, discuss your ideas about what would happen to an icy lake in the winter if ice were denser than liquid water. Come to an agreement about what would happen and draw a model of the lake with ice that is denser than liquid water. Then share your ideas and model with the class.

LESSON 2 SELF-CHECK

Can You Explain It?

Name: _____   Date: _____

How do the three forms of bromine differ from each other?

EVIDENCE NOTEBOOK
Refer to the notes in your Evidence Notebook to help you construct an explanation for the differences seen in the three forms of bromine.

1. State your claim. Make sure your claim fully explains why the three forms of bromine are different.

2. Summarize the evidence you have gathered to support your claim and explain your reasoning.

Lesson 2 Matter Exists in Different States

LESSON 2 SELF-CHECK

Checkpoints

Answer the following questions to check your understanding of the lesson.

Use the photo to answer Questions 3–4.

3. Write *shape* or *volume* to complete each sentence.

   The photo demonstrates that liquids can change _____.

   The _____ of the spilled milk is the same as the _____ of the milk that was in the glass to start.

4. Why does the milk flow out of the glass and spread out into a thin puddle rather than staying in the glass or spreading out more across the floor?

   A. The particles can break apart but cannot move.

   B. The particles can slide past each other, but attractions hold them close together.

   C. The particles cannot move, but they can grow in size.

Use the photo to answer Questions 5–7.

5. How can the volume of gas in the balloons be greater than the volume of the cylinder used to fill them?

   A. A gas has a fixed shape.

   B. A gas expands to fill its container.

   C. The volume of the container does not depend on the gas.

6. How can the properties of the particles in a gas explain why the volume of the balloons is greater than the volume of the container?

   A. The gas particles are bigger in the balloons.

   B. The distance between the gas particles is greater in the balloons.

   C. The gas particles are locked in place in the cylinder, but can move in any direction inside the balloons.

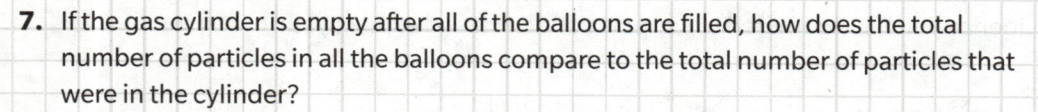

7. If the gas cylinder is empty after all of the balloons are filled, how does the total number of particles in all the balloons compare to the total number of particles that were in the cylinder?

   A. There are more particles in the balloons than were in the cylinder.

   B. There are fewer particles in the balloons than were in the cylinder.

   C. The number of particles in the balloons is the same as the number of particles that was in the cylinder.

8. A student drew a model showing particles that are close together in a regular pattern. Which sample has the student most likely drawn a model of?

   A. a bar of gold

   B. molten aluminum

   C. an air sample

   D. water vapor

Unit 2 The Structure of Matter

LESSON 2 SELF-CHECK

Interactive Review

Complete this section to review the main concepts of the lesson.

Solids, liquids, and gases can be classified by their abilities to change their shapes and volumes.

A. What properties do liquids share with solids? What properties do liquids share with gases?

Differences in particle energy, particle motion, and particle arrangement explain the observed differences in the properties of solids, liquids, and gases.

B. Complete the chart to describe differences in a solid, a liquid, and a gas.

	Solid	Liquid	Gas
Particle arrangement			
Particle motion			
Particle energy			

Lesson 2 Matter Exists in Different States

LESSON 3

Changes of State Are Caused by Changes in Thermal Energy

As outdoor temperatures rise, icebergs may start to melt.

Explore First

Categorizing State of Matter Changes What causes matter to change state? With a partner, make a list of at least eight instances of matter changing state. Sort the state changes by what they have in common. What are some common features of state changes?

84 Unit 2 The Structure of Matter

Go online to view the digital version of the Hands-On Lab for this lesson and to download additional lab resources.

CAN YOU EXPLAIN IT?

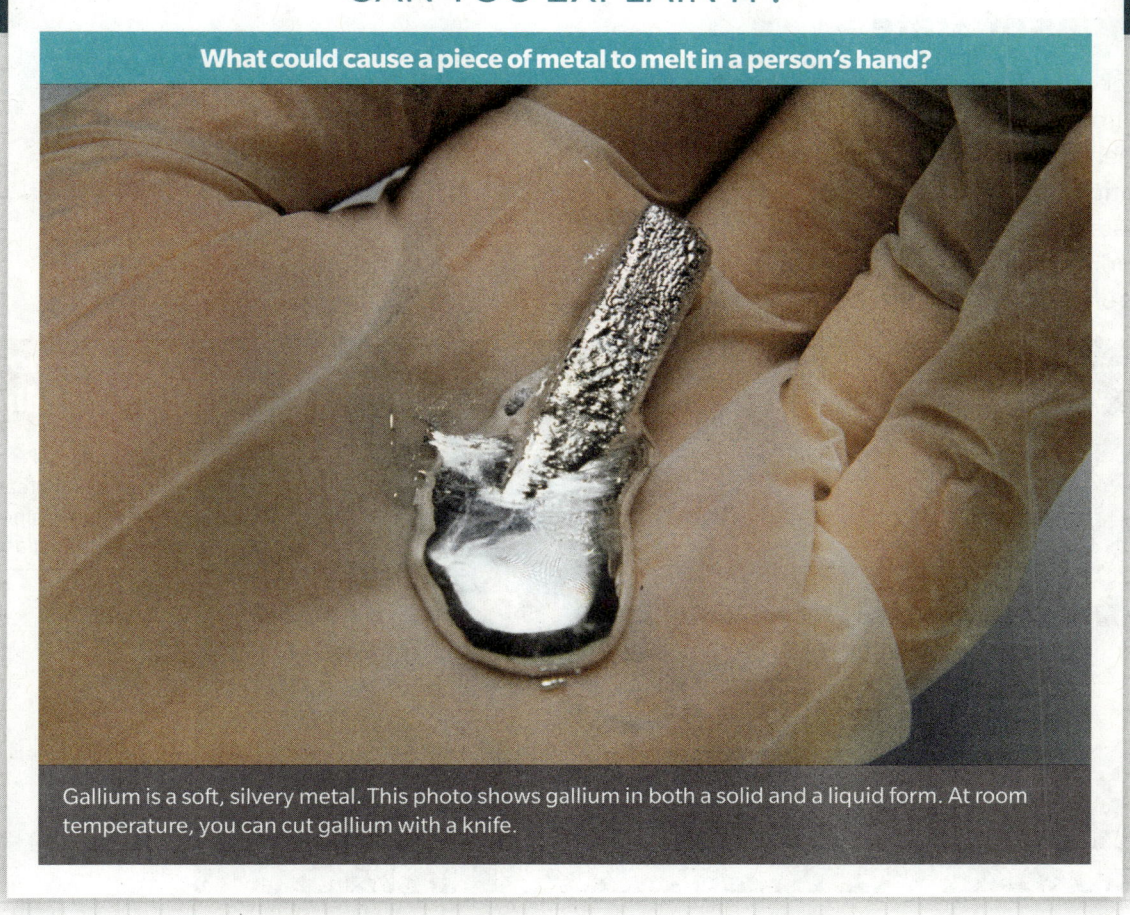

What could cause a piece of metal to melt in a person's hand?

Gallium is a soft, silvery metal. This photo shows gallium in both a solid and a liquid form. At room temperature, you can cut gallium with a knife.

1. Think about some times you have seen a substance melting. What explanation can you suggest for how the gallium could melt in someone's hand?

EVIDENCE NOTEBOOK As you explore the lesson, gather evidence to help explain how a piece of metal could melt in someone's hand.

Lesson 3 Changes of State Are Caused by Changes in Thermal Energy · 85

EXPLORATION 1

Analyzing How Energy Influences a Change of State

Changes of State

All matter can exist in three common states, or phases—solid, liquid, and gas—and can change from one state to another. The process by which matter changes from one state to another is called a **change of state**. A change of state is a physical change, because the identity of a substance is the same regardless of the state it is in. For example, water is still water whether in an ice cube or after the ice melts into liquid water.

During a change of state, matter is neither created nor destroyed and the same number of particles make up a substance before and after a change of state.

Explore Online

A professional glassworker creates a vase by changing the shape of the glass.

2. **Discuss** Together with a partner, determine the change of state that is shown in the photo. What observations led to your conclusion?

3. Think about what takes place when the change of state shown in the photo occurs. How does that change relate to the chemical identity and physical properties of glass?

86   Unit 2 The Structure of Matter

Hands-On Lab
Investigate a Change of State

Predict ways in which you can make a change of state happen more quickly as an ice cube melts. Then plan and carry out an investigation to test your predictions.

MATERIALS
- cups, clear plastic
- ice cubes, small (4)
- paper towels

Procedure

STEP 1 Work with a partner or small group to list ways that you might make an ice cube melt faster than it would melt if you left it sitting in a cup on your desk. You may only use items in your classroom.

STEP 2 For your investigation, choose three of the methods your group discussed. Write each method in the table.

STEP 3 Gather the ice cubes. Place one ice cube in a cup on your desk. Use the methods you chose in Step 2 to melt the other three ice cubes.

STEP 4 Observe the ice cubes until one of them melts completely.

STEP 5 Record your observations in the table.

What did you do?	What were the results?
ice cube in a cup, on desk	

Lesson 3 Changes of State Are Caused by Changes in Thermal Energy

Analysis

STEP 6 Circle the best word to complete each sentence.

In this activity, energy was added / removed to make the ice cube melt faster.

The ice cube that received the most / least energy melted fastest.

STEP 7 Describe two actions that are different from what you did in this activity that might make the ice melt more quickly. Explain your reasoning.

EVIDENCE NOTEBOOK
4. How does energy relate to the question of how a piece of metal might melt in someone's hand? Record your evidence.

Identify a Change of State

5. This glass of ice water shows two changes of state happening:
- The solid ice in the glass is melting to form liquid water.
- Water vapor in the air is changing to liquid water on the surface of the glass.

Write gaining or losing to complete each sentence.

The ice is melting in the glass because it is _____ energy as it changes from solid to liquid.

Water drops form on the surface of the glass because water vapor is _____ energy as it changes from gas to liquid.

88 Unit 2 The Structure of Matter

EXPLORATION 2

Modeling the Addition of Thermal Energy to a Substance

Energy Gain and Change of State

Each particle in a substance is moving in some way, so each particle has *kinetic energy*. **Thermal energy** is the total kinetic energy of all the particles in a substance. Adding thermal energy to a substance increases the kinetic energy. This increase in kinetic energy means the particles move faster. **Temperature** is a measure of the average kinetic energy of the particles.

6. **Discuss** Explain what is happening to the movement and kinetic energy of the water particles shown in the photo.

A flame adds energy to the water in this flask. As a result, the water temperature increases.

Change of State: Solid to Liquid

Adding enough thermal energy to a substance can cause a change of state to occur. The change of state from a solid to a liquid is called *melting*. When energy is added to an ice cube, the ice particles begin to vibrate more as energy is absorbed. Eventually, the solid ice melts and becomes liquid water. The temperature at which melting begins is called the *melting point*. Every substance has a specific melting point. This melting point will always be the same for that substance under the same conditions no matter the amount of the substance. The temperature at which ice melts and becomes liquid water is 0 °C at sea level.

Change of State: Liquid to Gas

If enough energy is added to a liquid, the liquid will turn into a gas. A change of state from a liquid to a gas is called *evaporation*. Water in a gas state is called water vapor. Adding thermal energy to liquid water particles causes them to move more. When enough energy is added, the water changes to the gas state, forming bubbles, as the liquid water turns to water vapor. This process is called *boiling*. Boiling and evaporation both involve the same change of state: liquid to gas. The difference is the location of the change. Evaporation takes place at the surface of the liquid and can occur over a wide range of temperatures. Boiling occurs throughout the entire liquid and takes place at a specific temperature. Each substance has its own *boiling point*, the temperature at which the substance begins to boil. The boiling point of water is 100 °C at sea level.

7. Write *melting, evaporation,* or *boiling* to label each photo.

Lesson 3 Changes of State Are Caused by Changes in Thermal Energy

Change of State from Solid to Liquid

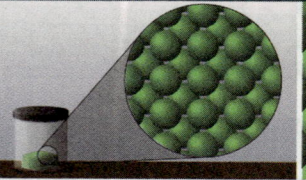

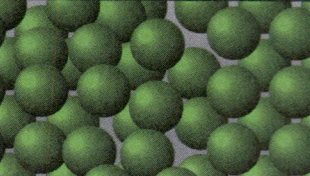

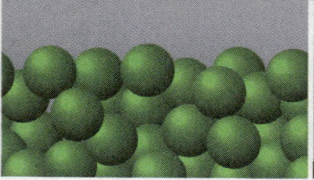

The particles of a solid vibrate in place, held together by forces of attraction. Particles in a liquid remain close, but they have more kinetic energy, and they have more freedom of movement.

Change of State from Liquid to Gas

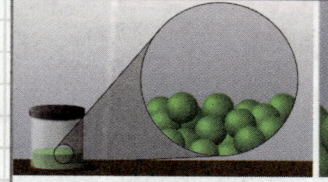

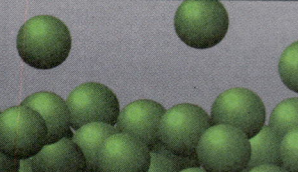

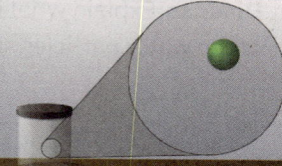

The particles in a gas have enough energy to overcome attractive forces, so they move about freely.

8. Describe the relationship between thermal energy and change of state. Write *solid, liquid,* or *gas* to complete each sentence.

   If enough thermal energy is added to a liquid, it will change to a _____.

   If enough thermal energy is added to a _____, it will change to a liquid.

Energy Gain and Particle Motion

The particles of a solid are held together by strong forces of attraction. These forces hold the particles of a solid in a definite shape. As thermal energy is added to a solid, the kinetic energy of its particles increases. The particles vibrate faster until they can move more freely and slide around each other, and the substance becomes a liquid. This freedom of movement allows a liquid to flow and take the shape of its container.

When thermal energy is added to a liquid, its particle movement increases until the particles have enough energy to overcome the attractive forces. They completely break away from each other, and the substance becomes a gas. The movement of the gas particles not only allows the gas to take the shape of its container, but the gas particles will also move about and fill the entire space within its container.

Do the Math
Analyze Temperature During a Change of State

Think about warming a piece of ice. The ice gains energy and its temperature rises as the motion of the particles increases. The rise in temperature causes the ice to melt and eventually causes the resulting liquid water to boil. This is true for water just as it is true for any substance. What would the graph of temperature change over time look like?

You might think that the temperature would steadily increase as energy is added to a substance at a constant rate, but that is not the case. The graph actually shows two time periods where the temperature does not change even though energy is being added. The first time period corresponds to the temperature at which the solid is changing to a liquid, or melting. The second time period corresponds to the temperature at which the substance is changing to a gas, or boiling. The horizontal lines indicate that, during these times, energy transferred to the particles contributes to changing the state of the substance, instead of raising the substance's temperature.

9. Which statements correctly describe what is happening during the two flat-line periods in the graph? Select all that apply.
   A. Between points A and B, the solid substance is changing to a liquid.
   B. Between points A and B, the substance is losing energy.
   C. Between points C and D, the liquid substance is changing to a gas.
   D. Between points C and D, the substance is gaining energy.

Changing the State of a Substance

This graph shows how the temperature of a substance changes as thermal energy is added at a constant rate.

10. You are warming a pot of ice. Explain what happens to the temperature when the water reaches its melting point and boiling point.

EVIDENCE NOTEBOOK

11. How might melting point and a change in the kinetic energy of particles help to explain why a piece of metal could melt in someone's hand? Record your evidence.

Classify and Explain a Change of State

Snow is made up of frozen water in the form of ice. As the temperature increases, the snow begins to melt and run off as liquid water.

12. What changes might occur as sunlight shines on snow? Select all that apply.

    A. Liquid water that forms as the snow melts will flow downhill.

    B. The snow will get warmer and change into a large chunk of ice.

    C. The snow quickly warms up and may begin to boil.

    D. The temperature of the snow will slowly increase.

13. **Engineer It** Some towns depend on water from snow that falls high up in the mountains, melts, and flows down the mountain. Some years, spring comes early and the snow begins to melt earlier than usual. What is one problem of early water runoff that engineers might be asked to solve? What criteria and constraints might need to be considered for concerns such as materials, space, and cost?

_____
_____
_____
_____
_____
_____
_____
_____
_____
_____

EXPLORATION 3

Modeling the Removal of Thermal Energy from a Substance

Energy Loss and Change of State

You now know that when enough energy is added to a substance, it can change state. But what happens when a substance loses energy? Think about what happens when you put water in a freezer. The temperature of the liquid water is warmer than the temperature inside the freezer. As a result, energy from the water is lost to the air inside the freezer and the water particles slow down. When enough energy is lost, the attractive forces between the water particles hold them in a regular pattern, and the particles can only vibrate. The liquid water changes to solid ice.

In the winter, ice forms on this lake. The ice starts to form on the water closest to shore.

Over the course of the winter, the lake continues to freeze. Eventually, most of the lake is covered in ice.

14. The photos show the process of a lake freezing in the winter. Why does the lake water change to ice in the winter? Include the gain or loss of energy in your explanation.

Lesson 3 Changes of State Are Caused by Changes in Thermal Energy   93

Change of State: Gas to Liquid

A gas changes state and becomes a liquid when the gas particles lose enough thermal energy. The process of a gas changing state to a liquid is called *condensation*. A common example of condensation is when liquid water droplets form on the outside of a glass of ice water. Water vapor from the air condenses and becomes liquid water on the cold surface of the glass of ice water.

Change of State: Liquid to Solid

The process in which a liquid changes to a solid is called *freezing*. Many people think that freezing means liquid water turning into ice, but freezing is the term used to describe any change from a liquid state to a solid state.

Think again about water placed in a freezer. The liquid water freezes to become solid ice. The temperature at which water freezes is its *freezing point*. The freezing point of a substance is the same as its melting point. In other words, a liquid substance that has a freezing point of 20 °C will not only freeze at 20 °C, but if the substance were a solid, it would also begin to melt at 20 °C.

15. Write *freezing* or *condensation* to label each photo.

a dripping faucet on a cold day

a window on a cold day

your breath in cold air

94   Unit 2 The Structure of Matter

Change of State from Liquid to Solid

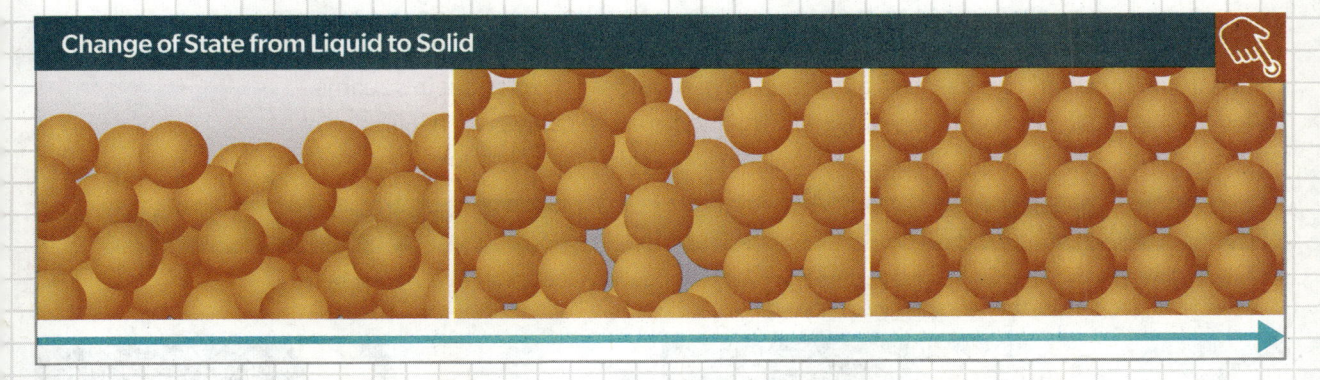

16. The process being modeled is condensation / **freezing** .

    As the particles **slow down** / speed up , particle attraction forces hold them in a regular pattern.

    This causes the particles to lock into the fixed arrangement of a liquid / **solid** .

    The change in particle motion happens because of a(n) increase / **decrease** in the particles' kinetic energy.

Energy Loss and Particle Motion Decreases

As the temperature of a substance decreases, the motion of its particles also changes and these changes affect the properties of the substance. The particles in a gas have a high amount of energy and move very fast. As thermal energy decreases, particle motion slows, allowing the attractive forces between particles to pull the particles closer together. The gas will become a liquid. If temperatures continue to decrease, the attraction between particles eventually overcomes the energy of their motion. The particles are then locked into the fixed arrangement of a solid.

17. **Language SmArts | Draw** In the space below or on a piece of paper, finish the drawing to show what happens to the particles in a substance when a gas becomes a liquid. Add a caption to describe what happens to the particles' motion and energy during this change of state.

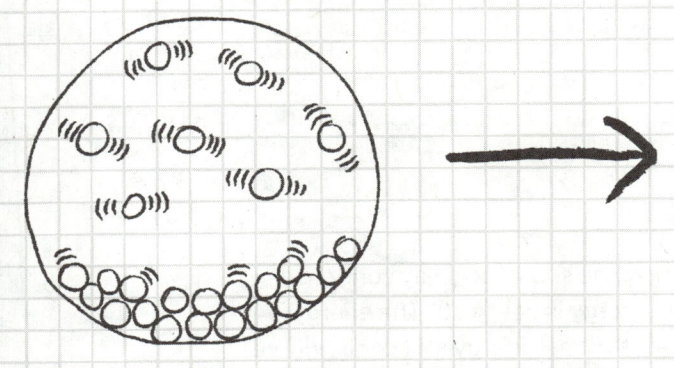

Gas particles are far apart and moving quickly above the surface of the liquid because gas particles have enough energy to overcome particle attraction.

Lesson 3 Changes of State Are Caused by Changes in Thermal Energy

Analyze Changes of State

Lava is liquid rock that comes out of a volcano. Lava sometimes comes out in streams, called lava flows, that travel slowly downhill. The temperature of lava when it first erupts can vary between 700 °C–1,200 °C. As the lava flows, it slowly cools.

Lava Flowing Into the Ocean

As lava flows downhill, it sometimes reaches a body of water, such as the ocean. These two photos show what happens as the lava spills into the water.

time →

18. What change of state do you see happening in the photos?

   _____
   _____
   _____
   _____
   _____
   _____
   _____

19. What evidence do you see in the photos to support your answer?

   _____
   _____
   _____
   _____
   _____
   _____

20. When thermal energy is removed from a substance, the substance may condense or freeze. But when something loses energy, that energy is not "lost." The energy is transferred to something else. When the lava loses thermal energy as it cools, where is the energy going? Select all that apply.

   A. The thermal energy is transferred from the lava to the air.
   B. The thermal energy is transferred from the lava to the ground.
   C. The thermal energy is transferred from the lava to the water.
   D. The thermal energy is held within the solid rock that forms.

Unit 2 The Structure of Matter

EXPLORATION 4

Evaluating How Pressure Can Affect Changes of State

Pressure

As gas particles move freely, they collide with surfaces around them. The gas particles have kinetic energy, and their collisions with surfaces produce a force. These collisions produce a force spread out over an area, known as **pressure**.

In the morning, this bike rider gets ready to go for a long bike ride. As part of getting ready, she checks the tire pressure.

The bike rider finishes her ride in the afternoon. She checks the tire pressure again.

21. The tire pressure changed between morning and afternoon. In the afternoon, the tire pressure was ~~less~~ / *greater* than the tire pressure in the morning. This change in pressure is caused by a *warmer* / ~~cooler~~ temperature of the air in the tires compared to morning. As the temperature increases, the kinetic energy of the gas particles *increases* / ~~decreases~~.

Elevation and Air Pressure

You might not think about the pressure that air puts on your body, but it is always present. Gas particles in the atmosphere exert pressure on everything, including you.

The diagram shows that as you move toward a higher elevation, there are not as many air particles to collide with a surface. As a result, at higher elevations, the air pressure is lower. Air at lower elevations contains a greater number of air particles in a given volume, resulting in a greater number of particle collisions with the ground and other surfaces. Therefore, lower elevations have greater air pressure.

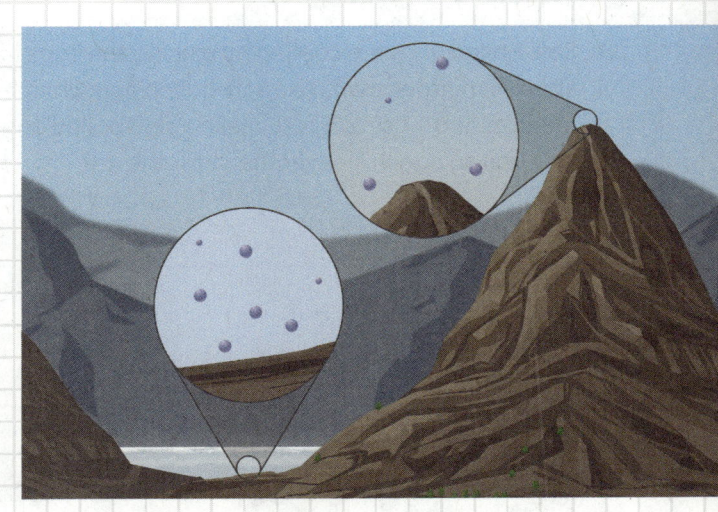

The air at lower elevations contains more particles in a given volume than air at higher elevations.

Lesson 3 Changes of State Are Caused by Changes in Thermal Energy

Pressure and Changes of State

Even if the kinetic energy of particles does not change, a change of state can occur when there is a change in pressure. The relationship between a change in pressure and a change of state is especially noticeable for the changes that occur between the liquid and gas states.

If you increase the pressure on a substance, its particles are brought closer to each other. When this happens to a gas, attractive forces may be strong enough to hold the particles close together, and the gas can condense into a liquid.

When the pressure on a substance is decreased, particles can move farther apart from each other. Fewer collisions occur, putting less force on the particles. With less force acting on the particles, it takes less energy for a liquid to change into a gas. With less air pressure on the surface of a liquid, particles can move from the liquid state to the gas state with less energy than that change would require at a higher pressure.

Boiling Point of Water at Different Elevations

Location	Elevation (meters above sea level)	Pressure (in atmospheres)	Boiling point of water (°C)
San Francisco, CA	sea level	1.0	100.0
Denver, CO	1,609	0.82	95.0
Quito, Ecuador	2,850	0.71	90.0
Mount Everest	8,848	0.31	76.5

22. **Discuss** Water boils at 100 °C in San Francisco, which is at sea level. But as you can see in the table, the boiling point of water varies at other locations. Consider this scenario: You are at sea level and you have some liquid water at 80 °C. What would happen to the water if it was suddenly transported to an elevation of 8,848 meters above sea level? Work with a group to explain what would happen and why. Include the relationship of pressure, energy, and changes of state in your explanation.

Determine the Effect of Pressure on a Change of State

23. Soft-boiled eggs are cooked by placing the eggs in boiling water. In Denver, it takes about 4 minutes to make a soft-boiled egg whereas at sea level, it takes about 3 minutes and 11 seconds to make a soft-boiled egg. Why does it take more time to soft-boil an egg in Denver than at sea level?

Unit 2 The Structure of Matter

TAKE IT FURTHER

Continue Your Exploration

Name: _____ Date: _____

Check out the path below or go online to choose one of the other paths shown.

Careers in Science

- Freezing Point Depression
- Hands-On Labs
- Propose Your Own Path

Go online to choose one of these other paths.

Forensics

A scientist who analyzes evidence and presents data in a court of law is called a forensic scientist. Forensic scientists apply scientific knowledge and procedures to criminal investigations. They may analyze clues from crime scenes or accident scenes. Forensic scientists are able to help solve crimes using scientific analysis.

Evidence is collected at a crime scene. Just looking at an item may not tell an investigator much. However, an expert in a crime lab can learn more from a detailed analysis of the evidence.

1. Which of the following processes would a forensic scientist use? Select all that apply.

    A. analyzing fragments to determine what they are made of
    B. analyzing paint flecks to determine the color and chemical makeup
    C. determining the identity of a person based on a shoe print
    D. identifying a substance that was found on a fiber
    E. determining whether liquids found are the same or different

Lesson 3 Changes of State Are Caused by Changes in Thermal Energy

TAKE IT FURTHER

Continue Your Exploration

Analyzing the Evidence

Gas chromatography (GC) is a method used to identify certain chemicals. A tiny bit of a sample is dissolved in a liquid called the solvent and the liquid is then injected into a chamber where the sample is heated until it becomes a gas. The gas travels through a long, thin tube. The different chemicals that make up the sample travel at different rates because of their different properties. A sensor detects when a chemical passes and records the time. The scientist can identify each chemical by the amount of time it takes to pass through the gas chromatograph.

Scientists can use GC to make sure that the chemical composition of a product is correct, to identify pollutants, or to identify unknown substances in a crime scene sample.

2. Which statement best describes the process that happens in the heated sample chamber of a gas chromatograph?

   A. The sample melts and becomes a gas.
   B. The sample boils and becomes a gas.
   C. The sample condenses and becomes a gas.

When using gas chromatography to identify an unknown sample, a scientist first prepares a standard that contains known chemicals. The standard is analyzed to see how long it takes those chemicals to go through the gas chromatograph. By comparing the results for the unknown sample with a standard of known chemicals, the identity of the unknown sample can be determined.

A forensic scientist has been asked to examine a fiber from the scene of a fire. Gas chromatography was used to identify an oil, which is composed of a mixture of different chemicals, found on the fiber. The analysis of the sample is shown in the chromatogram. From the results, the scientist determined that the sample was linseed oil. Linseed oil is commonly used as paint thinner and is very flammable.

Chromatogram of the Evidence Sample

The different peaks are used to identify the solvent, substances in the sample, and their amounts.

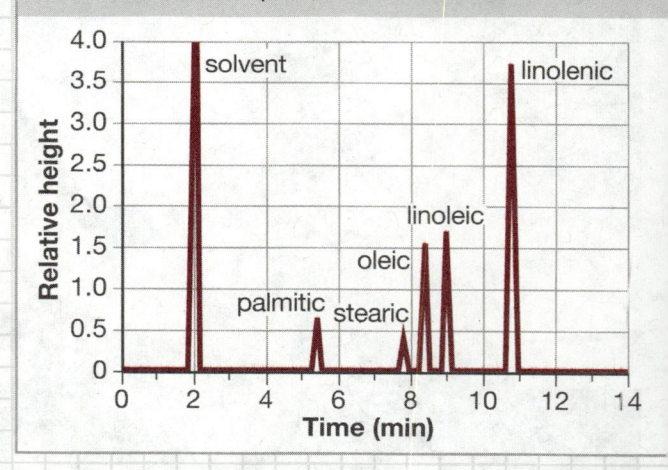

3. How might knowing that the material on the fiber was paint thinner help an investigator solve a crime?

4. **Collaborate** Work with a partner to put together a brief presentation for the class about how forensic scientists use chemical analysis to help solve crimes. Use some kind of technology in your presentation to support your idea, such as presentation software, a video link, or digital photos.

LESSON 3 SELF-CHECK

Can You Explain It?

Name: _____   Date: _____

What could cause a piece of metal to melt in a person's hand?

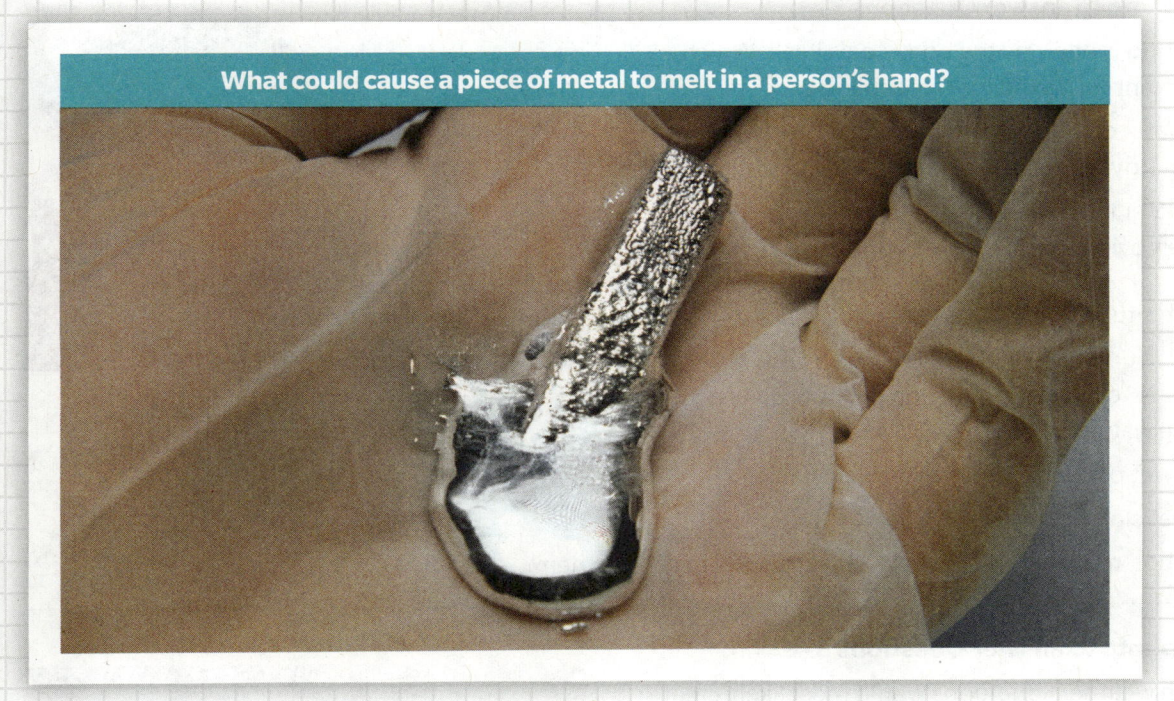

EVIDENCE NOTEBOOK
Refer to the notes in your Evidence Notebook to help you construct an explanation for what could cause a piece of metal to melt in someone's hand.

1. State your claim. Make sure your claim fully explains how the gallium could melt in a person's hand.

2. Summarize the evidence you have gathered to support your claim and explain your reasoning.

Lesson 3 Changes of State Are Caused by Changes in Thermal Energy

LESSON 3 SELF-CHECK

Checkpoints

Answer the following questions to check your understanding of the lesson.

Use the photo to answer Questions 3–4.

3. Sweating is one way the body cools itself. Which statement best explains this cooling process?
   A. Water condenses on the skin, adding thermal energy to the body.
   B. Water from the body evaporates from the skin, removing thermal energy from the body.

4. Which situation models a process similar to sweating? Select all that apply.
   A. water droplets forming on the outside of a glass of ice water
   B. a wet bandana around the neck of hiker
   C. wet clothes hanging on a clothes line
   D. a hot, moist towel placed on sore muscles to soothe them

Use the photo to answer Questions 5–6.

5. Which weather conditions would most likely create the fog as shown in the photo?
   A. rapidly cooling air that is low in water vapor
   B. rapidly cooling air that is high in water vapor
   C. rapidly warming air that is low in water vapor
   D. rapidly warming air that is high in water vapor

6. Clouds and fog form under similar conditions. Air pressure at higher altitudes affects the formation of clouds. As air rises, the reduced pressure allows the air to expand and cool until water vapor evaporates / freezes / condenses into water droplets that form the clouds.

7. As snow slowly melts in the sunshine, what is happening to the particles of water that make up the snow? Select all that apply.
   A. Particles are gaining energy.
   B. Particle motion is decreasing.
   C. Particle motion is increasing.

102 Unit 2 The Structure of Matter

LESSON 3 SELF-CHECK

Interactive Review

Complete this section to review the main concepts of the lesson.

A change of state is the change of a substance from one physical state to another, such as from a liquid to a solid.

A. Explain whether the identity of a substance changes during a change of state. Give an example.

A change of state can occur when thermal energy is added to a substance.

B. Describe the change in motion and kinetic energy of the particles as thermal energy is added to a liquid. Which change of state might happen?

A change of state can occur when thermal energy is removed from a substance.

C. Describe the change in motion and kinetic energy of the particles as thermal energy is removed from a liquid. Which change of state might happen?

Changes in pressure can affect changes of state.

D. Explain why liquid particles at a high pressure would need more energy to change to a gas than liquid particles at a low pressure.

Lesson 3 Changes of State Are Caused by Changes in Thermal Energy **103**

LESSON 4

Organisms and Nonliving Things Are Made of Atoms

Penguins, grass, water, and all other matter are all made up of different types of particles.

Explore First

Building Objects Use crafting materials to make two objects. Use the same materials in both of your objects, but try and make the two objects as different as possible. What are some of they ways that you were able to make your two objects different?

104 Unit 2 The Structure of Matter

CAN YOU EXPLAIN IT?

Why can objects made of the same materials have different properties?

Propane is a natural gas that is used as a fuel. It is often burned to cook food or heat water. Despite being an invisible gas, propane is composed of many of the same types of matter as humans. Around 90% of the types of matter in humans is also in propane. Both contain hydrogen, carbon, and oxygen.

1. What are some of the major differences between humans and propane?

2. Both humans and propane are mostly composed of the same types of matter. Why might humans and propane have different properties?

EVIDENCE NOTEBOOK As you explore the lesson, gather evidence to help explain how objects made of the same materials can have different properties.

Lesson 4 Organisms and Nonliving Things Are Made of Atoms

EXPLORATION 1

Analyzing Particles of Matter

Think about the materials that you see every day. Some materials can be separated physically into their parts. For instance, you can filter sand out of water or melt rocks in order to separate metals from the rock.

Some substances cannot be physically separated into parts because all the particles have the same properties. Physically separating pure water will just give you two volumes of water. Many of these substances can only be separated into components by chemically changing the substance.

Sugar particles can be physically separated out of sugar cane.

3. Do you think that every substance can be separated physically or chemically into other substances? Explain your answer.

Elements

Even though water cannot be physically separated, running electricity through water causes a chemical change that breaks the water down into oxygen and hydrogen. Chemical changes such as this can break down many pure substances into their components, but there are some pure substances that cannot be separated physically or chemically. An **element** is a substance that cannot be separated into simpler substances by chemical changes. Elements are the building blocks of all other substances. Both oxygen and hydrogen are elements. Currently, 118 elements are known and each element has a one, two, or three letter symbol associated with it. For instance, carbon is represented by the symbol C. Most objects that you see are made up of combinations of these elements. For example, a humans and propane gas both contain large amounts of oxygen, hydrogen, and carbon. On the other hand, a diamond is made of pure carbon.

106 Unit 2 The Structure of Matter

Properties of Elements

Each element has a unique set of physical and chemical properties. Oxygen is very different from copper. Carbon is very different from either oxygen or copper. Some elements may have similar colors or similar densities, or they may react in similar ways, but no two elements have the exact same set of properties. Copper and silver can both conduct electricity. They are also both malleable and can be used to make jewelry, but they have different colors and densities.

> **EVIDENCE NOTEBOOK**
> 4. All matter is composed of atoms of various elements. What are the elements that make up both humans and propane? Record your evidence.

5. An element cannot be broken down into other substances by chemical or physical means. But you can still split a sample of an element into smaller pieces. For example, a piece of aluminum foil can be cut in half and then in half again, and all of the pieces will still be aluminum. What do you think would eventually happen if you could continue dividing that piece of aluminum foil?

Types of Particles

All matter is made up of particles. However, as you have seen when modeling matter, not all particles behave in the same way. There are two main types of particles: atoms and molecules. Atoms are the building blocks of matter. Every piece of matter that you interact with is composed of atoms. Sometimes atoms can be connected together to form extended structures of atoms, such as crystals or metals.

Molecules are another type of particle that composes matter. Molecules are composed of atoms that are bonded together to form a new particle. These bonded atoms behave as a single particle that has its own unique set of properties.

Water particles are actually molecules. These molecules are made up of oxygen and hydrogen atoms.

Lesson 4 Organisms and Nonliving Things Are Made of Atoms

Atoms

Although an element cannot be broken down into other substances, a sample of the element can be divided into smaller pieces. An **atom** is the smallest unit of an element that has the chemical identity of that element. Atoms of the same elements have the same chemical properties and behave similarly. Iron atoms found on a meteorite will behave the same way as iron atoms pulled up from the bottom of the ocean.

Each element has its own chemical and physical properties due to the properties of its atoms. Every object that you see is made up of a huge number of atoms. Atoms are so tiny that they cannot be seen with an optical microscope. Even the most advanced microscopes can barely detect individual atoms.

This image shows individual atoms on the surface of a piece of silicon. The image was made using data from a scanning tunneling microscope.

Do the Math
Model the Scale of an Atom

Atoms are very tiny objects. It is difficult to even imagine how small they are, so people use models to describe atoms. The largest atoms measure less than one nanometer in diameter. A nanometer is one one-billionth of a meter. If matter were expanded so that an atom could barely be seen, your body would be big enough to reach from Philadelphia, Pennsylvania, to Miami, Florida.

6. Each iron atom has a mass of about 9×10^{-23} grams. Even a small grain of iron has an incredible number of atoms in it—about 1×10^{18} atoms in one grain. Which of these is most similar to the number of atoms in a grain of iron?

   A. the number of people in a large stadium; about 1×10^5
   B. the number of people on Earth; about 1×10^{10}
   C. the number of meters between Earth and the star Vega; about 2.4×10^{17}

One of the tiny grains of iron shown has a mass of about 0.9 mg, or 9×10^{-4} grams.

7. This stadium can hold 100,000, or 1×10^5, people. The number of atoms in a grain of iron is about 1×10^{18}. Would you need 1×10^{10} or 1×10^{13} stadiums to hold the same number of people as the number of atoms in a grain of iron? Explain your answer.

Unit 2 The Structure of Matter

Molecules

A **molecule** is two or more atoms held together by chemical bonds. A *chemical bond* is the attractive force that holds atoms together. For example, an oxygen molecule contains two oxygen atoms connected by a chemical bond. Molecules are particles of matter. They can range in size from two atoms to thousands of atoms. The wide variety of matter that you see is a result of the ways different atoms can combine. Because there are so many molecules, there are names for many of them. Three oxygen atoms form a molecule known as ozone. All ozone molecules have the same properties.

Compounds

In some molecules, such as an oxygen molecule, all the atoms are the same type of atom. This type of molecule makes up certain elements. Elements are pure substances made entirely of the same type of atom.

Other molecules are made up of two or more different types of atoms. These molecules make up a type of matter called a compound. A **compound** is a substance made up of two or more different types of atoms joined by chemical bonds.

Compounds can be broken down into simpler substances and those substances always form in a fixed ratio. For example, water always has two hydrogen atoms for every one oxygen atom. Each particle of water is a molecule because it is made up of two or more atoms held together by bonds. Water is also a compound because the water particle is made up of more than one type of atom, specifically hydrogen and oxygen.

8. Circle the molecules that are also compounds.

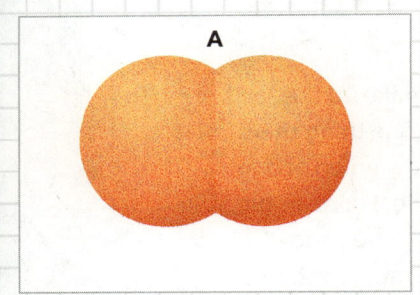

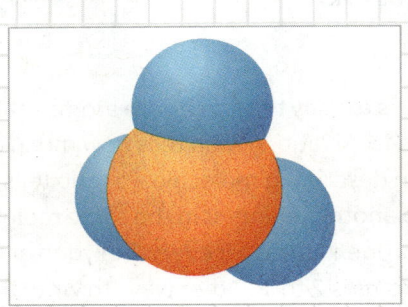

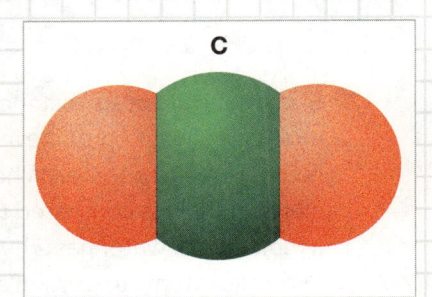

A

B

C

9. Which statements are true about molecules and compounds? Select all that apply.
    A. Molecules are made of one atom and compounds are made of two or more atoms.
    B. Some molecules are also compounds.
    C. Molecules are always composed of two or more elements.
    D. Compounds are always composed of two or more elements.

> **EVIDENCE NOTEBOOK**
> 10. What are some ways that the same types of atoms could be present in two different samples when the two samples have different properties? Record your evidence.

11. Draw A sodium atom joined with a chlorine atom forms the compound sodium chloride. Sodium chloride has properties that are different from the properties of sodium or chlorine alone. In a similar way, a compound word is the joining together of two different words. The word *dog* joined with the word *house* forms the compound word *doghouse*. The word *doghouse* has a different meaning compared to the meanings of the words *dog* or *house* alone.

Write two more compound words that are formed by joining two words and then draw a picture to show the meaning of your new compound words.

sodium atom + chlorine atom = sodium chloride

dog + house = doghouse

Word 1	Word 2	Compound Word	Drawing

Do the Math
Identify Ratios

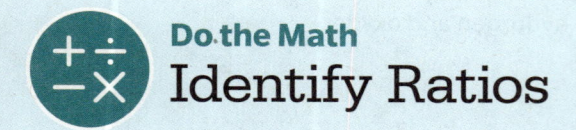

12. Each molecule of a substance is exactly the same. The atoms that make up the molecule always combine in a fixed ratio. A ratio tells how much of one thing there is compared to another. When describing molecules, a ratio tells how much of one element there is compared to another element in the same molecule. For example, a molecule of water has 2 hydrogen atoms for every 1 oxygen atom. The ratio of hydrogen atoms to oxygen atoms is 2 to 1. Other ways to write the ratio are 2:1 and $\frac{2}{1}$.

For the statements below, write the correct ratio for the molecules described.

- sulfur
- oxygen
- nitrogen

A. For every molecule of sulfur dioxide, the ratio of sulfur atoms to oxygen atoms is 1: _____ .

B. In a molecule of nitrogen dioxide, the ratio of nitrogen atoms to oxygen atoms is _____ : 2.

C. For every molecule of nitrous oxide, the ratio of nitrogen atoms to oxygen atoms is: $\frac{}{1}$.

D. In a molecule of sulfur trioxide, the ratio of sulfur atoms to oxygen atoms is _____ : _____ .

110 Unit 2 The Structure of Matter

Pure Substances

When understanding the properties of elements and compounds, it is useful to look at how they behave as pure substances. A **pure substance** is a sample of matter that has specific chemical and physical properties, such as appearance, melting point, and reactivity. A pure substance will always be made of the same matter. A sample of atoms or molecules of one element is a pure substance. A sample of molecules of a compound is a pure substance. The particles in pure substances can be atoms or molecules as long as the matter is consistent throughout the entire substance. The properties of an element or compound can be measured when you have a pure sample.

13. The particle structure of three pure substances are modeled below. Observe the arrangement of the atoms. Record your observations in the table.

Pure substance	Particle structure	Observations
chlorine	Cl–Cl	
hydrogen	H–H	
hydrogen chloride	H–Cl	

Compare Models of Elements and Compounds

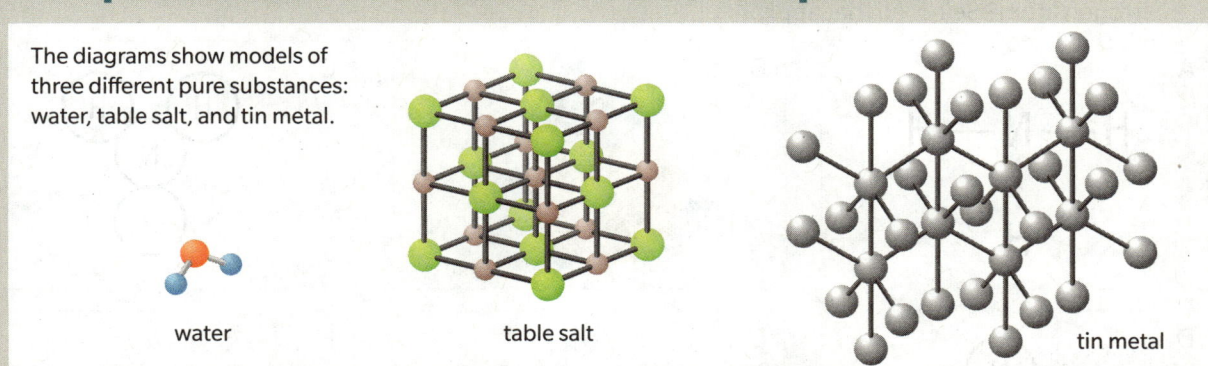

The diagrams show models of three different pure substances: water, table salt, and tin metal.

water   table salt   tin metal

14. Water, table salt, and tin are all pure substances. Which of these pure substances are compounds? Explain your reasoning.

_____
_____
_____

Lesson 4 Organisms and Nonliving Things Are Made of Atoms

EXPLORATION 2

Modeling Molecules

Molecules are extremely small. A water molecule, for instance, is about 3×10^{-10} m (0.0000000003 m) in diameter, which is very much smaller than the period at the end of this sentence. The structure of matter at the atomic and molecular levels is too small to observe directly. So what do scientists do when they want to study these structures? They develop and use models of atoms and molecules. Scientists use models to help them understand the real world and how it works. Models can help people learn about and visualize things they cannot see directly.

Examples of Molecular Models

These diagrams show three different molecules modeled in different ways.

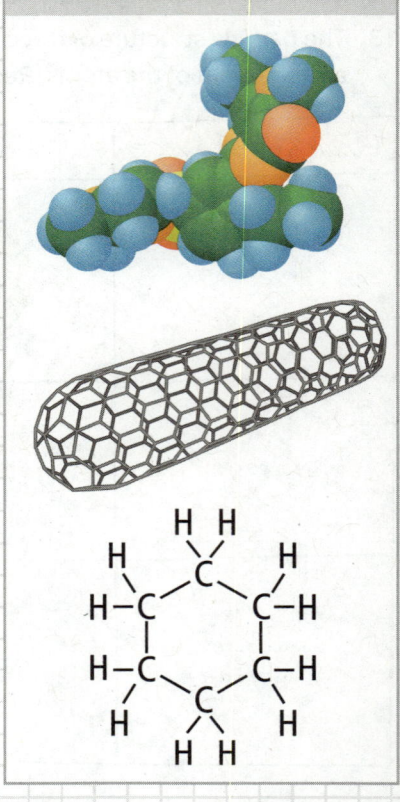

15. There are many different types of models. The diagrams to the right show some different ways to model molecules. How are the models alike? How are they different?

16. Molecules are atoms held together by attractive forces. Which of these diagrams could be a way to model a simple molecule of three hydrogen atoms joined to a nitrogen atom? Select all that apply.

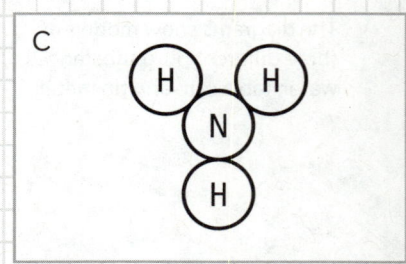

A, B, 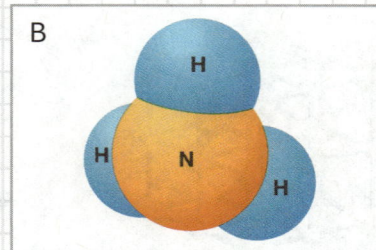 C, D, 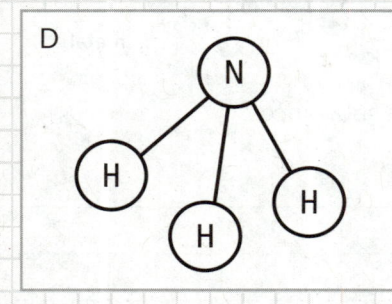 E, 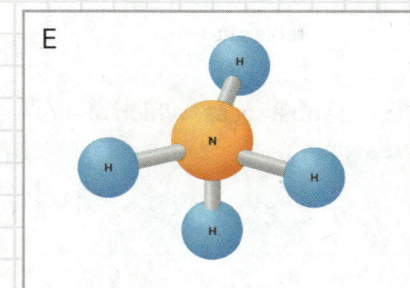 F

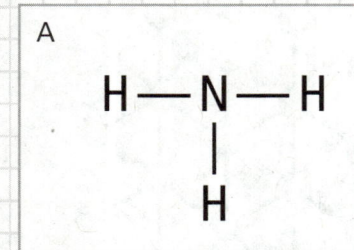

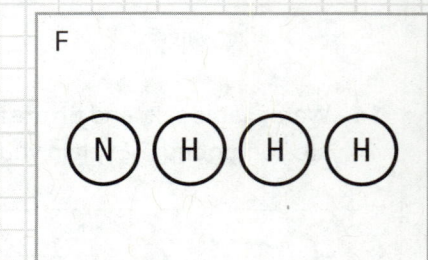

112 Unit 2 The Structure of Matter

Models of Simple Molecules

There are many different ways to model molecules. A model of the simplest molecule would show just two atoms joined together. The atoms could be the same, such as in hydrogen, which has two hydrogen atoms. Or the atoms could be different, such as in a molecule of carbon monoxide, which is made up of one carbon atom and one oxygen atom. Other models could show three or more atoms.

Molecules are groups of atoms joined together by chemical bonds. In some models, you may see the chemical bonds represented by lines or sticks. But a chemical bond is not a physical thing. It is the attractive force that holds atoms together. Some models do not show anything at all to represent chemical bonds. They may instead show two atoms—perhaps modeled by two spheres—that touch each other.

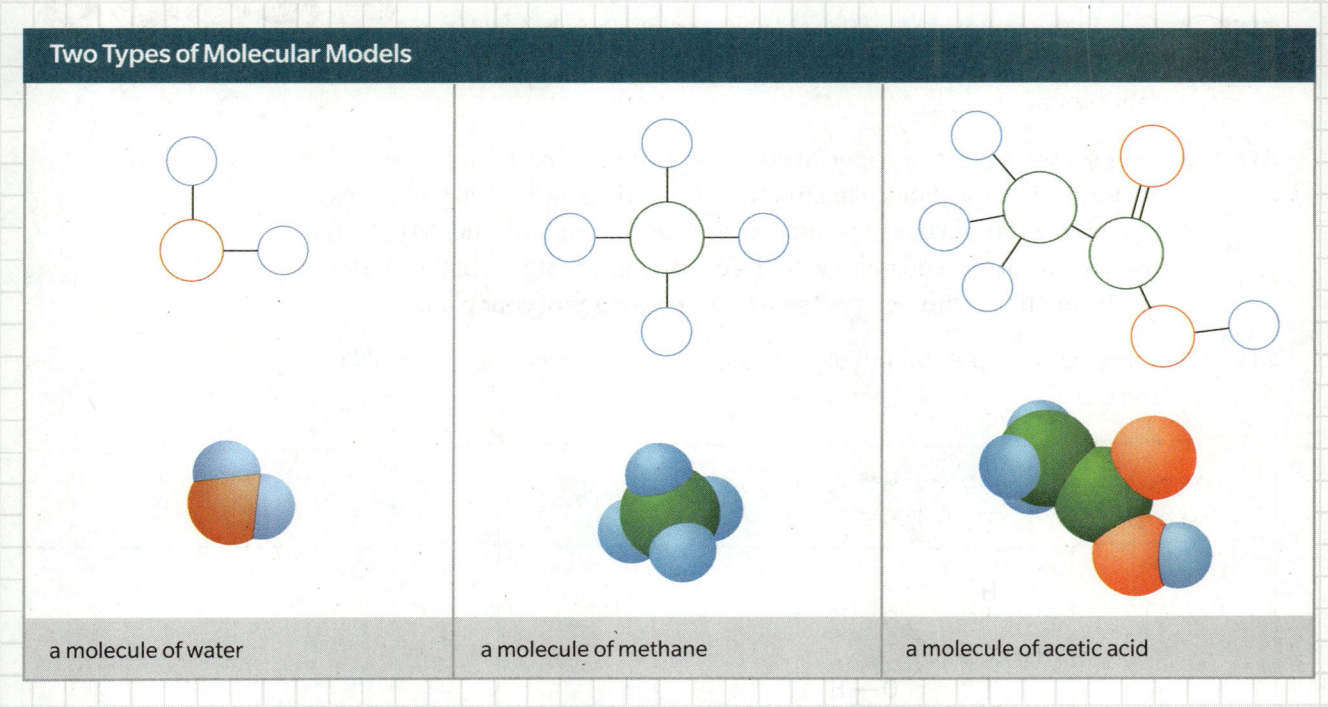

Two Types of Molecular Models

| a molecule of water | a molecule of methane | a molecule of acetic acid |

17. The diagrams show two different ways that water, methane, and acetic acid can be modeled. Look closely at each type of model. Explain what each type of model shows best.

Lesson 4 Organisms and Nonliving Things Are Made of Atoms

Hands-On Lab
Model Molecules

Observe two compounds that are made of only carbon, hydrogen, and oxygen atoms. Plan and carry out an investigation to explore how models of each molecule can explain why the compounds have different properties.

MATERIALS
- acetic acid
- clay
- isopropyl alcohol
- toothpicks

Procedure

STEP 1 Look at the samples of acetic acid and isopropyl alcohol. What properties can you observe? Record your observations in the table below.

STEP 2 On a separate piece of paper, make a plan to build a model of each molecule. Use the molecular structures from the table to help you. Think about how you can use the materials provided by your teacher to build the models. What can you make with the clay to represent part of the models? What can the toothpicks represent? Write the steps of your plan.

STEP 3 Carry out your plan for building the models. Then draw what you built in the table.

Compound Name	Molecule Structure	Observations	Draw Your Model
Acetic Acid	H-C(H)(H)-C(=O)-O-H		
Isopropyl Alcohol	H-C(H)(H)-C(H)(O-H)-C(H)(H)-H		

114 Unit 2 The Structure of Matter

Analysis

STEP 4 How are the structures of acetic acid and isopropyl alcohol similar? How are they different?

STEP 5 Why do you think acetic acid and isopropyl alcohol have different properties? Use the models you developed to help you explain.

Models of Complex Molecules

A simple molecule may contain a few atoms bonded together. A complex molecule may contain thousands of atoms. The atoms in complex molecules often form a repeating pattern. A repeating unit can be formed by a single type of atom or two or more different types of atoms. Most of the molecules that make up living things are complex molecules based around carbon. Complex molecules like these are possible because carbon atoms are able to form very stable bonds with each other.

Some plastics, such as the PVC plastic in these chairs, contain thousands of carbon, hydrogen, and chlorine atoms joined together in long chains.

This model shows how a molecule of the plastic polyvinyl chloride (PVC) is made up of repeating units of carbon, hydrogen, and chlorine atoms.

18. This model is another way to show the structure of a molecule of PVC. Circle the unit that repeats.

Lesson 4 Organisms and Nonliving Things Are Made of Atoms **115**

19. Observe the diamond photo and its molecular structure diagram. Describe the repeating unit in the structure.

The Structure of the Diamond Substance

You may be familiar with diamonds as a precious gemstone. It is also one of the hardest natural materials on Earth. Diamond can be used to cut through other very hard materials, such as rock.

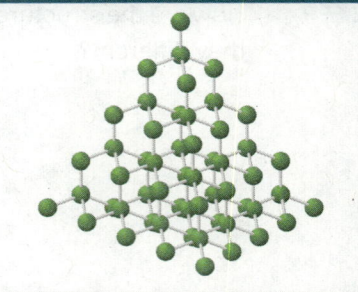

Diamond is a pure carbon substance. There is a repeating structure in a diamond, even though the atoms are all the same.

Extended Structures

Some solid elements and compounds are not composed of particles that are single atoms or individual molecules. Instead, they are made of extended structures. Extended structures are made up of repeating subunits of atoms. These subunits do not form individual particles in the same way that molecules do. Some extended structures, such as those in diamonds, are also crystals. *Crystals* are extended structures with a repeating structure of atoms. These structures define many of a crystal's properties.

Some elements occur as extended structures made of one type of atom. For example, aluminum has an extended structure. Aluminum atoms form a repeating subunit that makes the substance consistent throughout.

Some compounds also have extended structures made up of more than one type of atom. Similar to molecules, the atoms that make up these extended structures also come in constant ratios. Sodium chloride, or table salt, is a compound that has extended structures. A repeating structure of sodium and chlorine atoms makes it consistent throughout the substance.

20. Draw lines to match each statement to the model it describes.

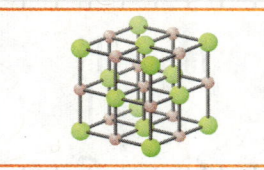

Table sugar is a molecule made up of carbon, hydrogen, and oxygen atoms arranged as two rings joined together.

Silver metal is an extended structure made up of atoms of silver arranged in a regular pattern.

Table salt is an extended structure made up of sodium and chlorine atoms arranged in a repeating pattern.

Language SmArts
Evaluate Molecule Models

Deoxyribonucleic acid (DNA) is a molecule that contains genetic information. DNA is found in all living things. DNA is a *macromolecule*, or large molecule, that is made up of many smaller molecules.

The diagram shows two models to help you analyze the structure of DNA.

- The model on the left looks something like a curved ladder. The blue "ribbon" represents a sugar-phosphate backbone of smaller molecules that forms the structure of the DNA. Each of the four colored "bars" represents a different type of smaller molecule. This model shows how the smaller molecules are connected within the DNA macromolecule.

- The model on the right also shows the overall spiral structure of DNA, but it shows the individual atoms rather than showing types of molecules.

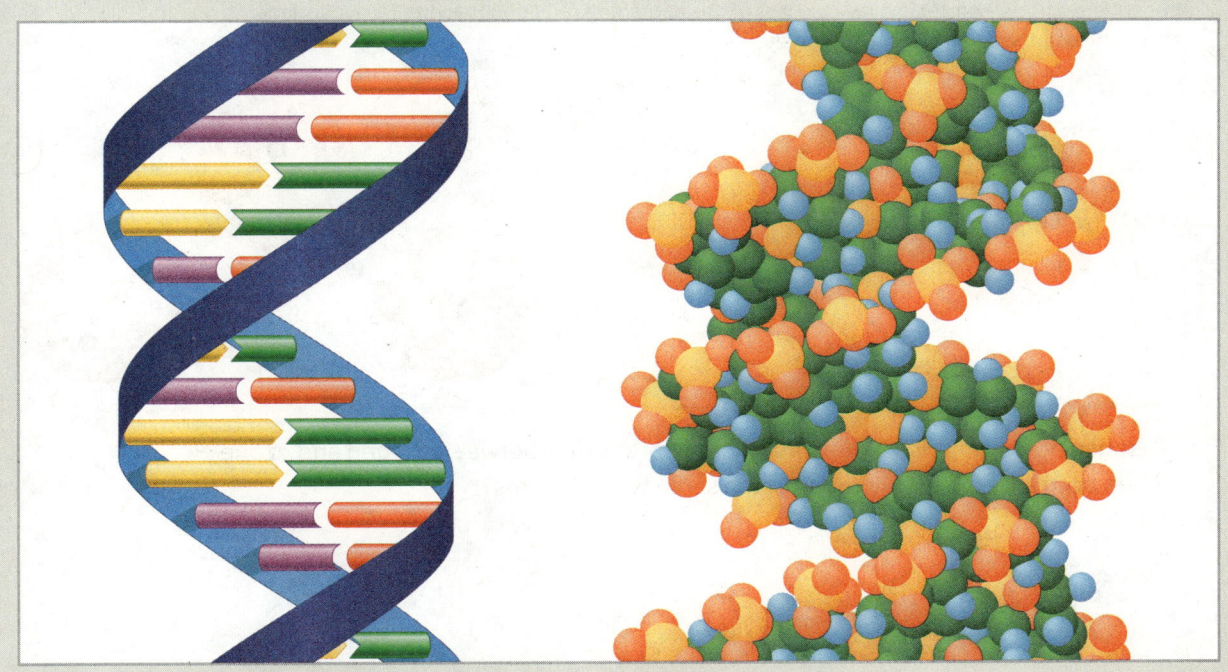

Both models show a section of DNA. The models use color to distinguish the various parts of the structure of DNA, but they show the DNA differently. The model on the left shows how smaller molecules within the DNA macromolecule are connected. The model on the right shows individual atoms.

21. If you are interested in finding patterns in the way the smaller molecules bond to make up DNA, which model would be most helpful?

The model on the *left / right* shows the atoms that make up the smaller molecules. It shows the detailed shape of the entire section of DNA, but molecules are not clearly seen. The model on the *left / right* shows how smaller molecules within the DNA are bonded to each other. It shows the order and relative position of the smaller molecules and the general shape of the DNA.

The model on the *left / right* is best for finding patterns in the way the smaller molecules bond.

EXPLORATION 3

Relating the Identity and Structure of Matter to Its Properties

Many of the physical and chemical properties that you observe come from the particles that make up the matter around you. The vast majority of the matter you interact with is composed of molecules or extended structures. The makeup and structure of those molecules and extended structures affect their properties. These properties impact how ecosystems and humans interact with substances. Atoms of the same elements can form molecules necessary for life as well as molecules that are toxic to living things.

Molecular Structure of Oxygen and Ozone

Both oxygen gas and ozone are made up of only oxygen atoms—but they are completely different substances. Both occur in the atmosphere and are important for life on Earth. Humans and animals need to breathe oxygen gas to live. Ozone absorbs ultraviolet radiation. Its presence in the atmosphere acts as a protective layer so less of this damaging radiation reaches Earth's surface. Ozone can also be used to sterilize drinking water.

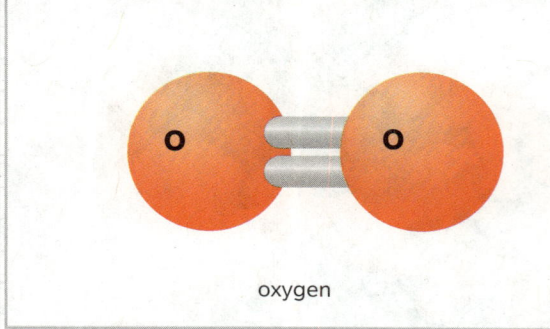

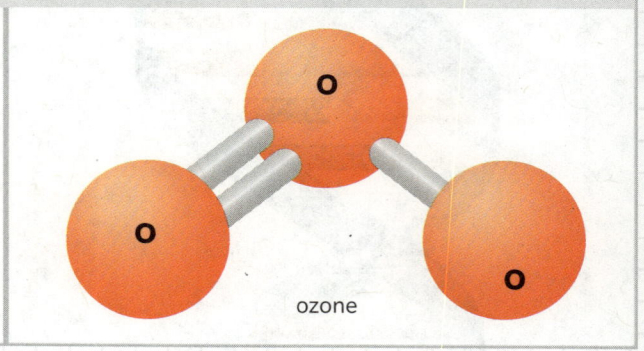

oxygen

ozone

22. Discuss What might explain differences in properties between oxygen and ozone when both substances are made of the same type of atoms?

Differences in Composition

The type and number of the atoms that make up a molecule or extended structure affect the properties of that matter. For instance, when even a single atom is different between molecules, they may behave very differently. A single oxygen atom is known as monoxide, a toxic gas that is poisonous to humans. Two oxygen atoms bonded together form an oxygen molecule, which humans need to survive. Three oxygen atoms bonded together form ozone, a gas that absorbs ultraviolet radiation in the atmosphere. The particles that make up a sample of matter greatly affect the properties of that matter.

> **EVIDENCE NOTEBOOK**
> **23.** How might differences in the combinations of atoms change the properties of carbon, oxygen, and hydrogen? Record your evidence.

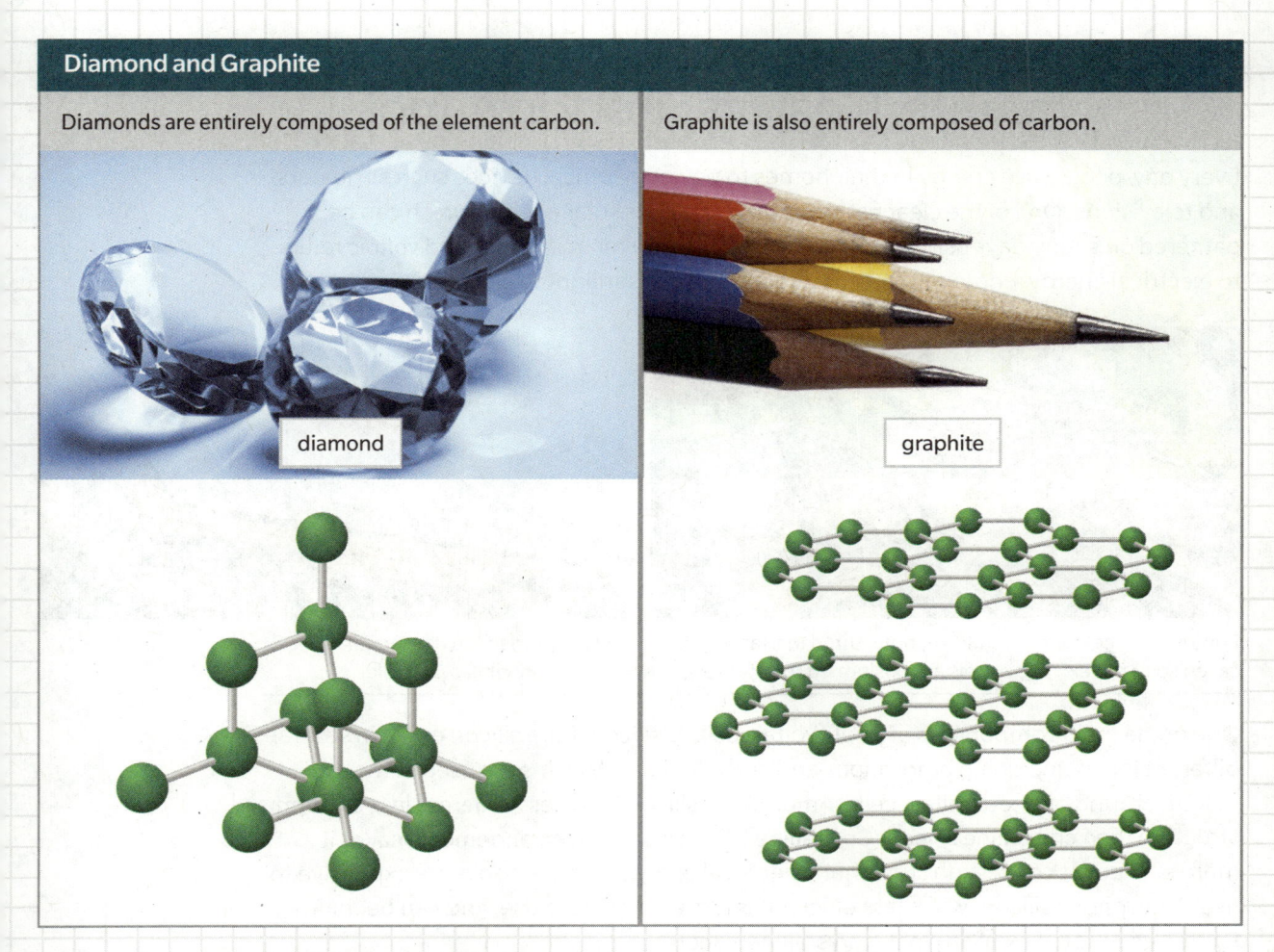

Diamond and Graphite

Diamonds are entirely composed of the element carbon.

diamond

Graphite is also entirely composed of carbon.

graphite

24. Diamond and graphite are both pure carbon. They are both pure substances made of carbon atoms, but the atoms are arranged in different ways. Diamonds are one of the hardest substances on Earth. Graphite is very soft and will easily break apart. What is it about the structure of graphite that might explain its properties?

  A. The layered structure of graphite causes the bonds between atoms to strengthen.

  B. Graphite is soft because its structure causes the individual atoms to bend.

  C. The layered structure of graphite allows the layers to slide past each other.

  D. Graphite breaks apart easily because its atoms are dark in color.

Differences in Structure

The way that atoms connect to one another affects the properties of matter. This is easy to observe in some extended structures. Diamonds and the graphite in your pencil are both entirely composed of carbon. Graphite is one of the softest materials and diamonds are one of the hardest. In graphite, the carbon atoms are loosely connected into sheets, leading to the flaky nature of graphite. In diamonds, extreme temperatures and pressure force the carbon atoms to bond in a rigid, ordered structure that gives a diamond its incredible hardness.

Molecules can also have different structures, even when they are made of atoms of the same elements. Propadiene and propyne are composed of the same combination of atoms, but have different structures. They have different melting and boiling points.

Engineer It
Evaluate Cost vs. Performance

Every day, people use energy in their homes to power electrical devices such as heaters and televisions. One of the cleanest sources of energy is solar energy, which can be gathered on sunny days using photovoltaic cells. *Photo* refers to light, and *voltaic* refers to electrical energy. Photovoltaic cells directly convert sunlight to electrical energy.

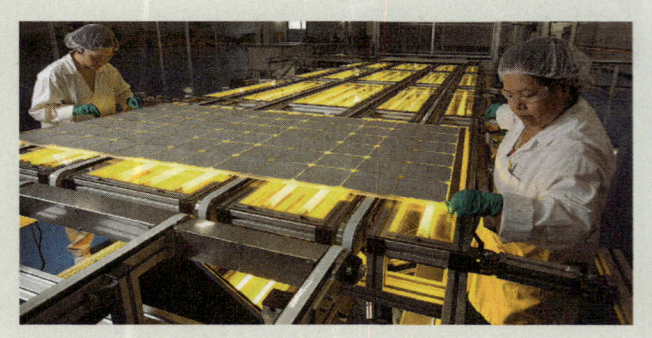

Photovoltaic cells are carefully manufactured in a factory. Then they are formed into larger frames called solar panels. The panels are positioned to capture as much direct sunlight as possible.

One of the main components of photovoltaic cells is silicon. Pure silicon exists in several different forms, including amorphous and crystalline. Both forms are used in the manufacturing of photovoltaic cells. Amorphous silicon has a less ordered, less uniform structure than crystalline silicon. Crystalline silicon's ordered arrangement makes it more efficient at converting sunlight to electrical energy, but it is also more expensive to use. Amorphous silicon, while less efficient, is less expensive to use, and can be thinner, lighter, and more flexible than the crystalline silicon.

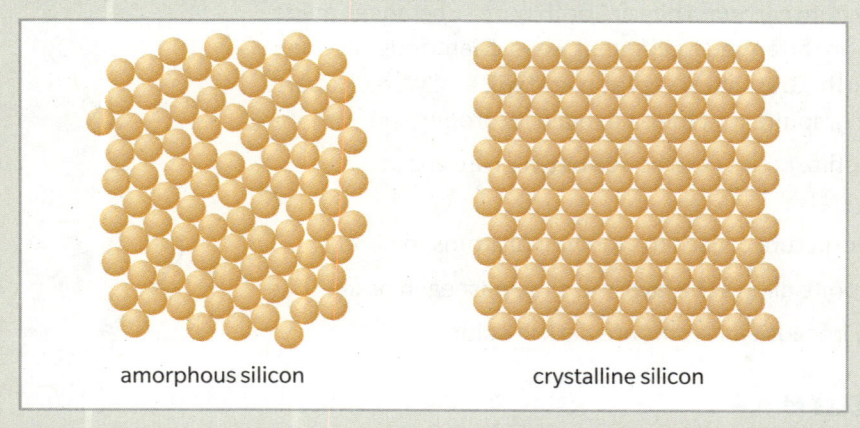

amorphous silicon   crystalline silicon

25. Assess the pros and cons of using crystalline silicon and amorphous silicon to manufacture photovoltaic cells. Which material would be used if the main criterion was keeping the cost of materials as low as possible? Which material would be used if the main criterion was getting the best performance from the material? Explain your reasoning.

_____
_____
_____
_____
_____

120   Unit 2   The Structure of Matter

TAKE IT FURTHER

Continue Your Exploration

Name: Date:

Check out the path below or go online to choose one of the other paths shown.

People in Science
- Molecules and Your Sense of Smell
- Hands-On Labs
- Propose Your Own Path

Go online to choose one of these other paths.

Joseph Proust, Chemist

In the 18th century and early 19th century, French chemist Joseph Proust worked and taught in France and Spain. He is best known for his work on what is called the law of definite proportions. This law states that a pure chemical compound always contains the same elements in exactly the same proportions by mass. Although many scientists assumed this to be true, it was Proust who first gathered evidence to support it.

Suppose you have a sample of sodium chloride, or table salt. You determine that the sample consists of 39% by mass of the element sodium and 61% by mass of the element chlorine, a ratio of 39% sodium to 61% chlorine. This proportion is true not only for this sample of sodium chloride, but for all samples of sodium chloride. No matter where this pure substance is found, this proportion holds true.

The Law of Definite Proportions

As shown in the top row, 10.00 g of lead reacts with 1.55 g of sulfur to produce 11.55 g of lead sulfide. If you only add more sulfur (middle row) or only add more lead (bottom row), you will still end up with exactly 11.55 g of lead sulfide with the added substance left over. The compound always contains the same elements in exactly the same proportion.

10.00 g of lead + 1.55 g of sulfur → 11.55 g of lead sulfide

10.00 g of lead + 3.00 g of sulfur → 11.55 g of lead sulfide + 1.45 g of sulfur (leftovers)

18.00 g of lead + 1.55 g of sulfur → 11.55 g of lead sulfide + 8.00 g of lead (leftovers)

Lesson 4 Organisms and Nonliving Things Are Made of Atoms

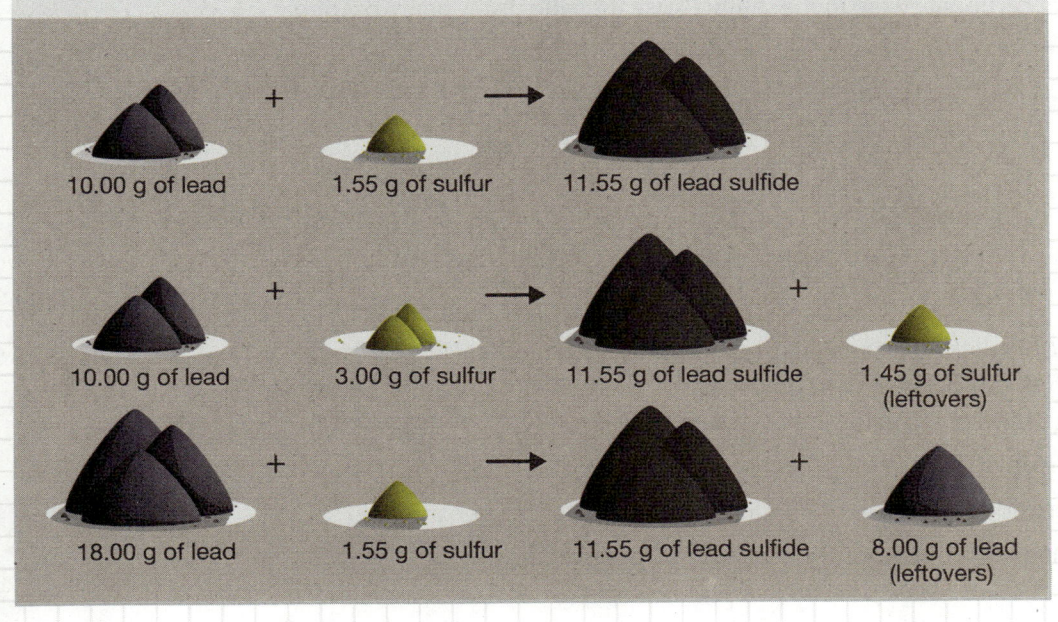

TAKE IT FURTHER

Continue Your Exploration

1. Why is Proust's law of definite proportions important? Why is it important to know the ratios in which elements combine to make different substances?

Copper Carbonate

Through investigation, Proust showed that copper carbonate always has 5.3 parts copper to 4 parts oxygen to 1 part carbon. In other words, the ratio of copper to oxygen to carbon is 5.3 : 4 : 1. The picture shows that in a 103 g sample of copper carbonate, there is 53 g of copper, 40 g of oxygen, and 10 g of carbon.

103 g of copper carbonate → 53 g of copper + 40 g of oxygen + 10 g of carbon

2. In a sample of copper carbonate, how much copper and oxygen would there be for 5 g of carbon? Use the ratio of copper to oxygen to carbon.

3. A sample of copper carbonate was found to contain 15.9 g of copper. How many grams of copper carbonate were in the sample? Use the ratio of copper to oxygen to carbon.

4. **Collaborate** Work with a partner. An oxygen atom is 16 times heavier than a hydrogen atom. A carbon atom is 12 times heavier than a hydrogen atom. Determine the mass ratios of two of the following pure substances:
   - Water is made up of 2 hydrogen atoms and 1 oxygen atom.
   - Hydrogen peroxide is made up of 2 hydrogen atoms and 2 oxygen atoms.
   - Methane is made up of 1 carbon atom and 4 hydrogen atoms.

122 Unit 2 The Structure of Matter

LESSON 4 SELF-CHECK

Can You Explain It?

Name: _____   Date: _____

Why can objects made of the same materials have different properties?

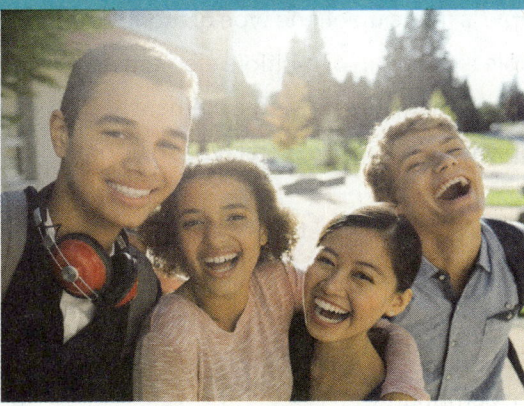

EVIDENCE NOTEBOOK
Refer to the notes in your Evidence Notebook to help you construct an explanation for how the objects made of the same materials can have different properties.

1. State your claim. Make sure your claim fully explains how humans and propane can be made of many of the same materials.

2. Summarize the evidence you have gathered to support your claim and explain your reasoning.

Lesson 4 Organisms and Nonliving Things Are Made of Atoms   **123**

LESSON 4 SELF-CHECK

Checkpoints

Answer the following questions to check your understanding of the lesson.

3. You have a sample of a substance that you cannot physically separate into components. You also cannot chemically separate that substance into components. Which of the following are true about your sample? Choose all that apply.

    A. The sample is made up of one type of atom.

    B. The sample is made up of multiple elements.

    C. The sample is made up of a single element.

    D. The sample is made up of several types of atoms.

Use the diagram to answer Questions 4–5.

4. Which of the following can be observed from the model of water? Select all that apply.

    A. Water is a molecule.

    B. Water is a compound.

    C. Water is made up of three types of atoms.

5. Another way to model water is with letters and lines is like this: H–O–H. What is one way that these two models are different?

    A. They show different types and numbers of atoms.

    B. The atoms are connected in a different order.

    C. The chemical bonds are represented differently.

    D. One model clearly shows a repeating pattern.

Use the models to answer Question 6.

6. Based on the models of these structures, white phosphorus is a(n) *simple molecule* / extended structure.
    Red phosphorus is a(n) *simple molecule* / extended structure.
    Both are examples of a(n) compound / *element*.

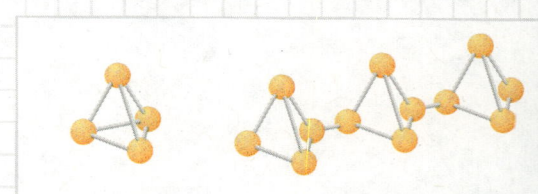

    white phosphorus   red phosphorus

7. The structure of carbon tetrachloride, CCl_4, is similar to the structure of carbon tetrabromide, CBr_4. Both molecules have four atoms connected to a central carbon atom. Does that mean the two substances have the same properties?

    A. Yes, because molecules with similar structures must have the same properties.

    B. Yes, because the carbon atom determines the properties of both substances.

    C. No, because the types of atoms in a molecule and its structure both influence the properties of a substance.

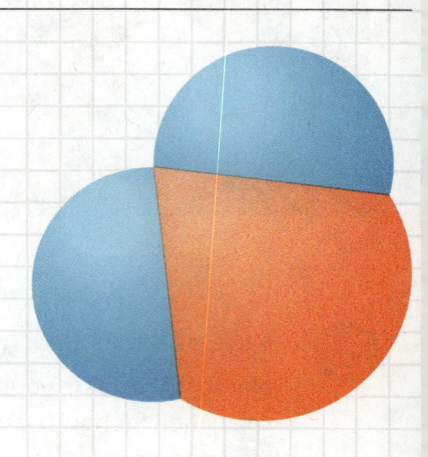

LESSON 4 SELF-CHECK

Interactive Review

Complete this section to review the main concepts of the lesson.

Atoms make up all matter. Some matter is made of individual atoms, and some matter is made of atoms arranged in molecules.

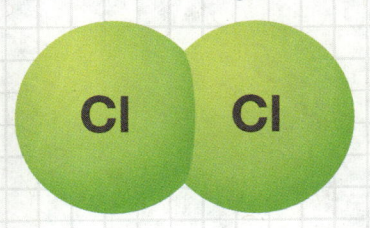

A. How are atoms molecules, compounds, and pure substances related?

Models can be used to study simple molecules, complex molecules, and extended structures.

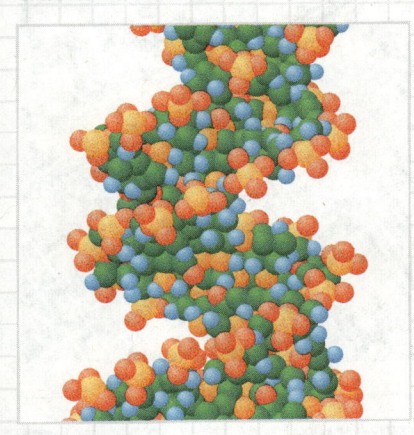

B. What do models of molecules and extended structures show?

The properties of pure substances are directly influenced by their structures.

C. What is the relationship between the structure of a substance and the properties of a substance? Explain.

Lesson 4 Organisms and Nonliving Things Are Made of Atoms 125

UNIT 2 CONNECTIONS

Choose one of the activities to explore how this unit connects to other topics.

☐ People in Science

Dorothy Hodgkin, Chemist Dorothy Hodgkin was born in 1910 and first became interested in chemistry at age ten. She eventually attended Sommerville College of Oxford University where she researched X-ray crystallography. She continued her research at Cambridge, where she earned her PhD. Hodgkin was a pioneer of crystallography and studied the structure of biomolecules. She identified the three-dimensional structures of many molecules, including insulin in 1969. Hodgkin was awarded the Nobel Prize in Chemistry in 1964 for her work.

Research how three-dimensional models of molecules were developed and Dorothy Hodgkin's influence on the field.

☐ Technology Connection

Silicon Valley Silicon Valley is the region in the San Francisco Bay Area where a large number of tech companies are based and many technological innovations are developed. Its name comes from the fact that the element silicon is a key component of computer chips.

Research how silicon is obtained and why its physical properties make it useful for the computer industry. Create a presentation highlighting silicon's properties and give examples of how it is used in electronic devices.

☐ Art Connection

Working with Wax Not all "paintings" are made with paints. Some artists practice hot wax painting, also known as encaustic painting. This technique gives paintings unique characteristics quite different from traditional oil or latex paintings. It was often used for Coptic Egyptian mummy portraits.

Research encaustic painting. Describe the materials used and how artists utilize a change of state to create their artwork. Prepare a visual display and verbal presentation that describes the technique of encaustic painting. Provide several example images to share in your presentation.

An encaustic painting on the mummy of Marco Antinous.

UNIT 2 REVIEW

Name: _____ Date: _____

Complete this review to check your understanding of the unit.

Use the diagram to answer Questions 1 and 2.

1. Air is / ~~is not~~ a pure substance because it is made up of a single / **more than one** type of matter.

2. Which of the following components of air is a compound?
   A. carbon dioxide
   B. oxygen
   C. nitrogen
   D. argon

Atmospheric Composition

This pie chart shows the composition of the air in Earth's atmosphere.

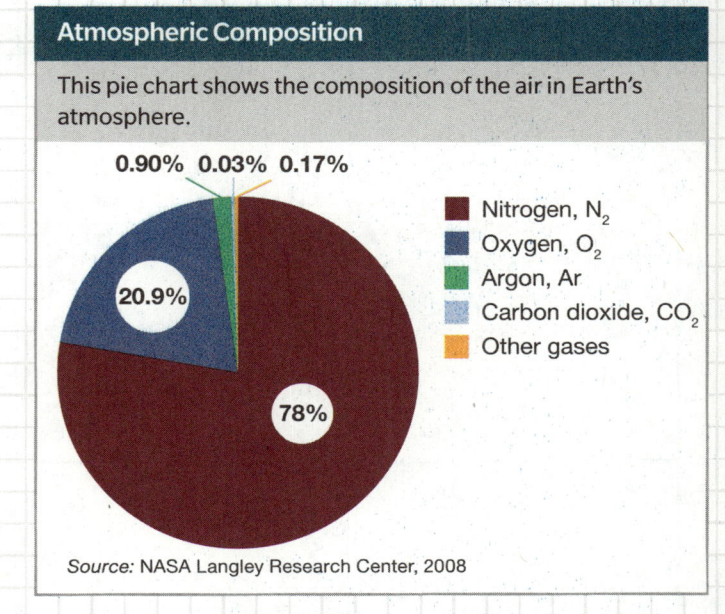

0.90% 0.03% 0.17%

20.9%

78%

- Nitrogen, N_2
- Oxygen, O_2
- Argon, Ar
- Carbon dioxide, CO_2
- Other gases

Source: NASA Langley Research Center, 2008

3. A molecule of carbon dioxide is made up of a carbon atom and two oxygen atoms. Which of the following models represents carbon dioxide?

   A.   B. 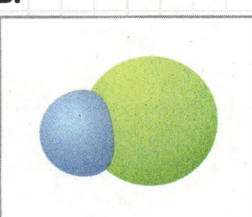   C.    D.

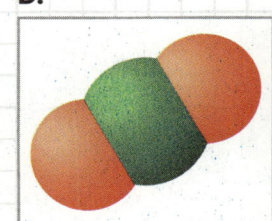

These are images of wet paper towels placed on a bag of room temperature water and a bag of hot water. Use the images to answer Questions 4 and 5.

4. The water molecules that are warmed by the hot water are moving **faster** / ~~slower~~ than the water molecules on the room temperature water bag.

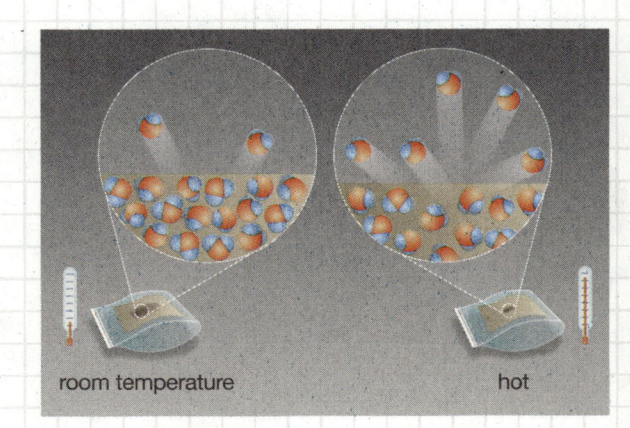

5. From which paper towel do you expect the water to evaporate first?
   A. the room temperature paper towel, because the molecules are moving slower
   B. the heated paper towel, because the molecules are moving faster
   C. water will evaporate from both paper towels at the same time because higher temperatures do not affect the water molecules
   D. water will not evaporate from either paper towel

room temperature   hot

Unit 2 The Structure of Matter **127**

UNIT 2 REVIEW

6. Complete the table by providing at least one example of how each category of matter relates to each big concept.

Matter	Scale	Structure	Everyday example
atom	the smallest unit of an element that has the chemical identity of that element		
molecule			
compound			
extended structures			

128 Unit 2 Review

UNIT 2 REVIEW

Name: _____   Date: _____

Use the images of sodium and silver to answer Questions 7–10.

Pure sodium, Na, and pure silver, Ag, appear similar when they are in their solid forms. When sodium is added to water, an explosive reaction occurs. However, no reaction occurs when pure silver is placed in water.

sodium

sodium in water

silver

silver in water

7. Describe the physical properties of sodium and silver.

8. Describe the chemical properties of sodium and silver. Why is silver often used to make eating utensils?

9. Sodium and silver are both pure elements. If the sodium atoms were bonded to other atoms to form a compound, would you expect that compound to behave the same as sodium? Explain your answer.

10. Compare sodium and silver before and after they are placed in water. Has a new substance been produced in each case?

Unit 2 The Structure of Matter   129

UNIT 2 REVIEW

Complete this review to check your understanding of the unit.
Use the graph to answer Questions 11–14.

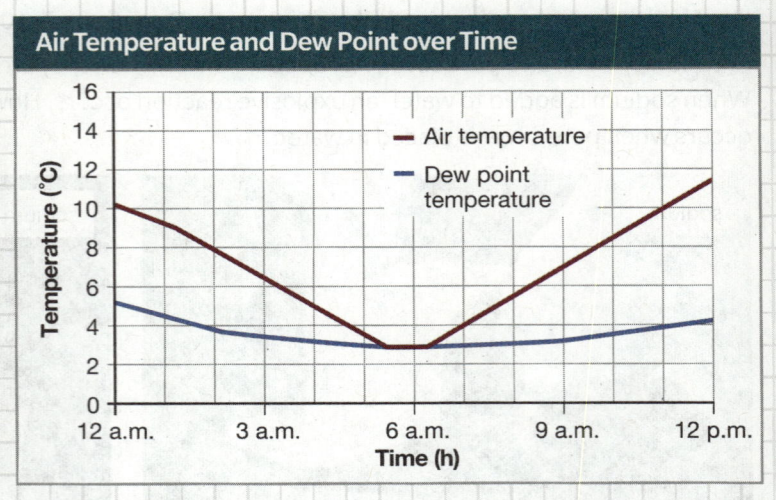

Air Temperature and Dew Point over Time

11. Dew forms when the air temperature is low enough for water in the air to condense on outdoor surfaces. At what time would you expect to see dew, according to the graph? Explain your answer.

12. What would you expect to happen if the temperature dropped to below freezing after 6:00 a.m.? Explain your answer.

13. In terms of thermal and kinetic energy, describe how water vapor forms when dew evaporates.

14. In terms of thermal and kinetic energy, describe how water droplets form on a blade of grass.

UNIT 2 PERFORMANCE TASK

Name: Date:

Molecular Clues!

Scientists use their knowledge of matter's structure and properties to develop new technologies and processes. Gel electrophoresis is a method used to study proteins and other large molecules. It enables scientists to separate these complex molecules based on their sizes and can be used in many different scientific fields, including forensics and medicine.

Research gel electrophoresis. Describe the technique and how it works, provide examples of when it is used, and design a model to demonstrate this useful technology. Then prepare a presentation that highlights your findings.

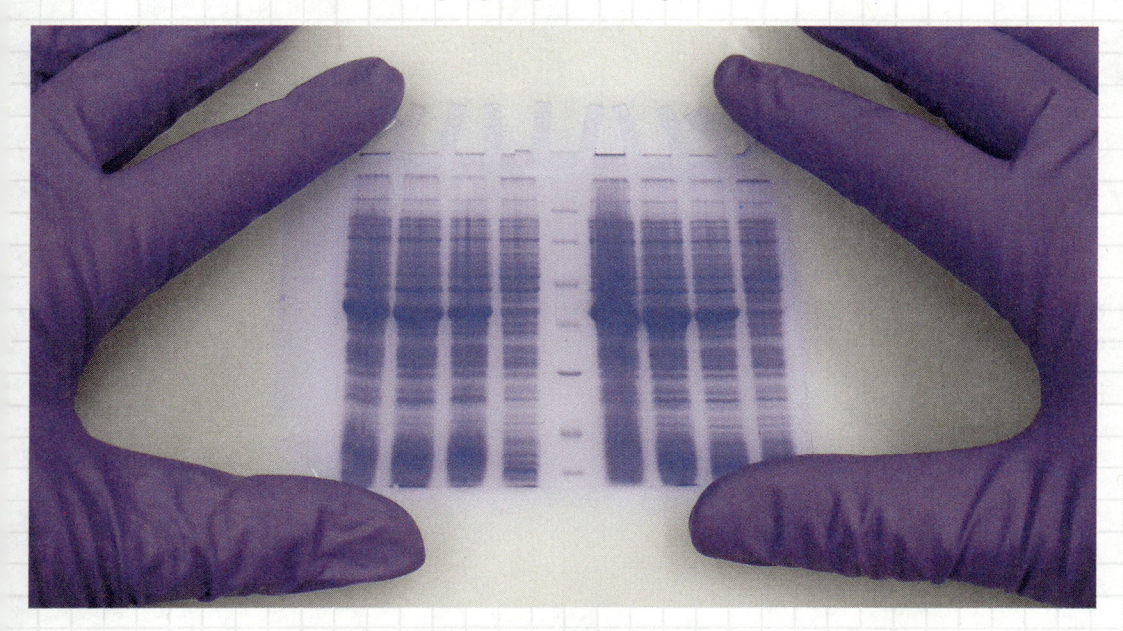

The steps below will help guide you to develop and carry out your plan.

1. **Conduct Research** Research examples of situations in which gel electrophoresis is used and the types of molecules that scientists separate using this technique.

UNIT 2 PERFORMANCE TASK

2. **Ask a Question** How do scientists take advantage of differences between the properties of substances to make this technique work?

3. **Construct an Explanation** Based on your research, write a report that explains how gel electrophoresis works and how a scientist can interpret the results in an electrophoresis gel.

4. **Develop a Model** Create your own physical model representing how electrophoresis is used to separate substances.

5. **Communicate** Present your findings to the class, and share your model of gel electrophoresis.

✓ Self-Check

	I conducted research on how gel electrophoresis is used and examples of its application.
	I explained how gel electrophoresis separates molecules based on differences in their properties and how scientists can interpret the results.
	I developed a model to show how electrophoresis works.
	I communicated my results by presenting my findings to the class and sharing my model.

UNIT 3

Chemical Processes

How do matter and energy change in chemical processes?

Unit Project	134
Lesson 1 Matter Changes Identity in Chemical Reactions	136
Lesson 2 Chemical Equations Model Chemical Reactions	154
Lesson 3 Engineer It: Using Thermal Energy in a Device	174
Lesson 4 Synthetic Materials Are Made from Natural Resources	194
Unit Review	219
Unit Performance Task	223

This is a crystal of progesterone, an important hormone in the human body. It can be synthetically produced from plant materials using a series of chemical reactions known as the Marker degradation.

You Solve It **How Can You Design a Heat Pack?** Design the chemical system for a heat pack by testing different amounts of chemical components to see which combination best meets the design criteria.

Go online and complete the You Solve It to explore ways to solve a real-world problem

UNIT 3 PROJECT

Design a Chemical Cold Pack

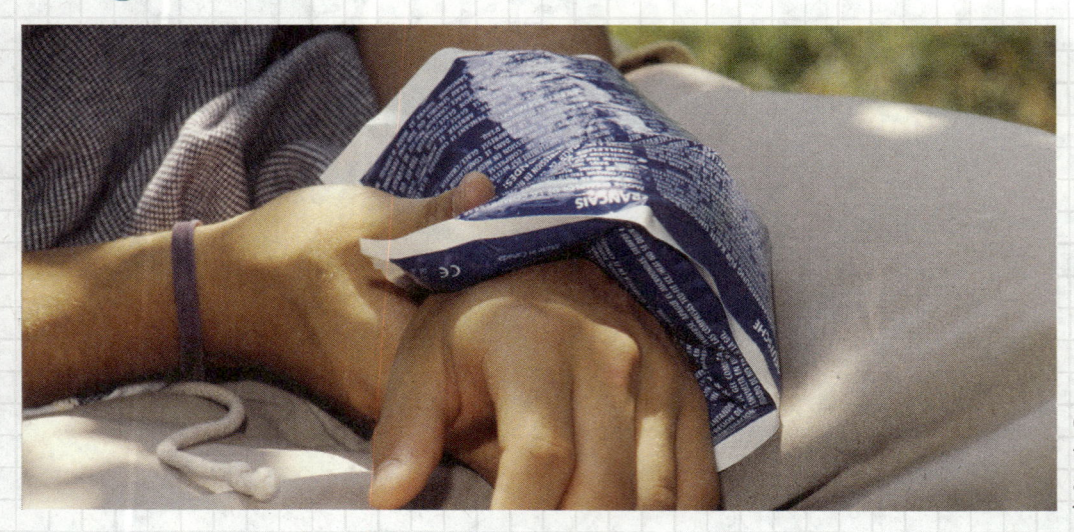

Cold packs are used to reduce swelling after an injury.

A. Look at the photo. On a separate sheet of paper, write down as many different questions as you can about the photo.

B. Discuss With your class or a partner, share your questions. Record any additional questions generated in your discussion. Then choose the most important questions from the list that are related to designing a chemical cold pack. Write them below.

C. Based on your experience using cold packs in the past, what are some ways that you think you could improve cold packs?

D. Use the information above to help design a cold pack.

Discuss the next steps for your Unit Project with your teacher and go online to download the Unit Project Worksheet.

UNIT 3

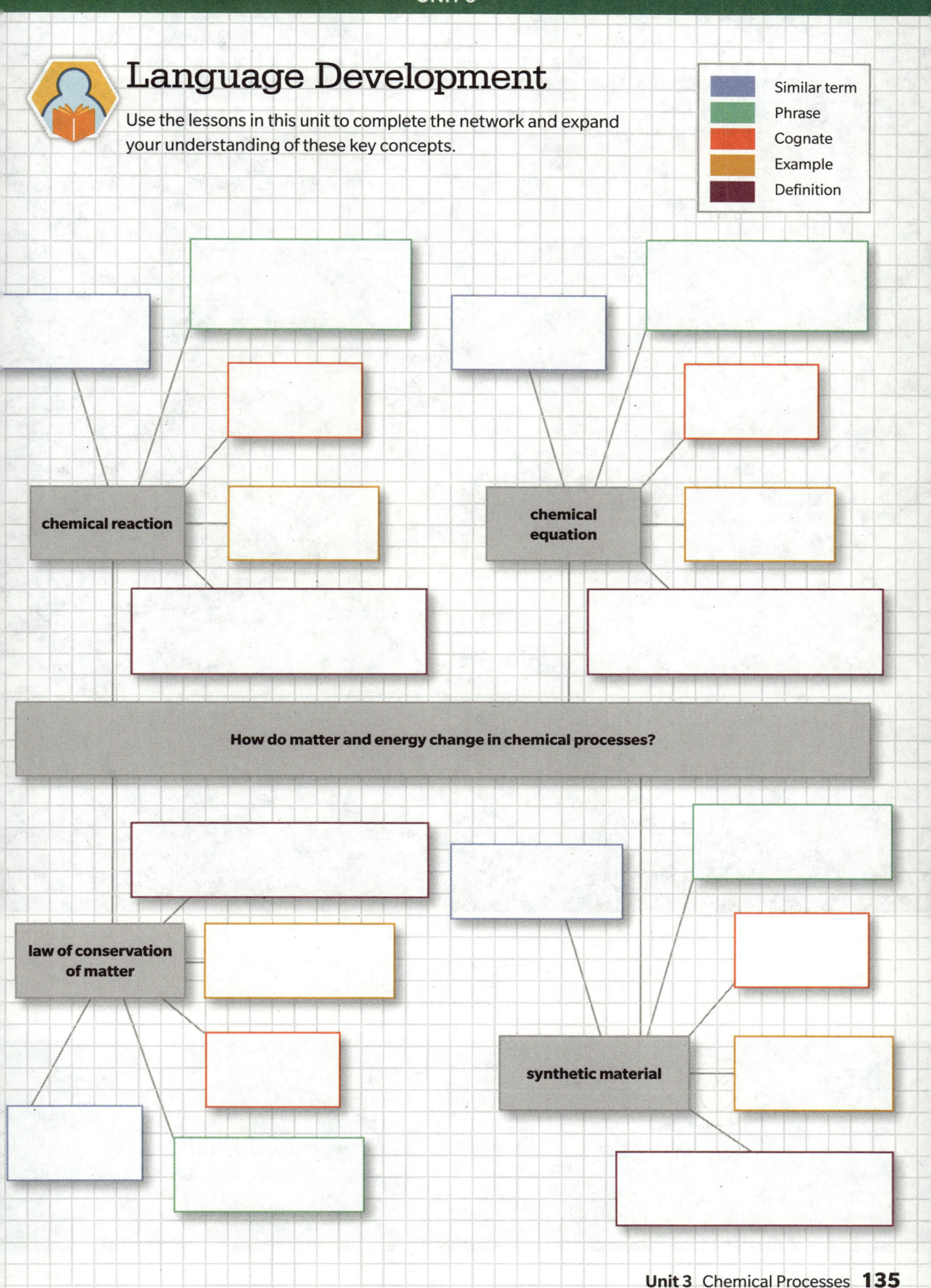

Language Development

Use the lessons in this unit to complete the network and expand your understanding of these key concepts.

- Similar term
- Phrase
- Cognate
- Example
- Definition

chemical reaction

chemical equation

How do matter and energy change in chemical processes?

law of conservation of matter

synthetic material

Unit 3 Chemical Processes **135**

LESSON 1

Matter Changes Identity in Chemical Reactions

Fireflies, also called lightning bugs, are small insects that generate their own light using chemical reactions.

Explore First

Reorganizing Materials Build a structure out of building blocks. Make a sketch of your structure and then trade structures with a partner. Disassemble your partner's structure and build one or two new structures using the same blocks. Make a sketch of your new structures. How are the original structure and the new structures different?

CAN YOU EXPLAIN IT?

What happens to the matter when sulfuric acid is added to powdered sugar?

These photos shows concentrated sulfuric acid mixing with powdered sugar.

Explore Online

1. What do you observe when sulfuric acid is added to the powdered sugar?

2. Is the black substance that grows out of the beaker the same as the white sugar? Explain your answer.

EVIDENCE NOTEBOOK As you explore the lesson, gather evidence to help explain what happens to matter when the sulfuric acid is added to the sugar.

Lesson 1 Matter Changes Identity in Chemical Reactions 137

EXPLORATION 1

Analyzing Natural Systems

You can look at the universe as a collection of systems. A system can be tiny, such as a cell, or it can be huge, such as a solar system. A system can also be an event or phenomenon. When you look at a system, you can identify the different pieces and how they interact with one another. You can also identify the inputs, which are things entering the system, and the outputs, which are things leaving the system. By identifying the inputs and outputs, you can track how different parts of the system behave. For example, you can track matter and energy by modeling their movements in a system. You can identify how matter and energy change or how the parts of the system interact.

A volcanic eruption can be treated as a system. Some of the inputs include thermal energy and magma from below Earth's surface. The outputs include ash and lava.

3. **Discuss** What are five possible inputs and outputs of Earth as a system?

Matter and Energy

While Earth as a system has inputs and outputs, matter and energy cycle through many smaller systems on Earth. For instance, water evaporates out of lakes and rivers. In the atmosphere, the water then condenses and forms clouds. Eventually, that same water can become rain and return to Earth's surface. Energy also moves through systems. Grass takes in energy from the sun to grow. Cows eat grass in order to get that energy. Millions of processes occur every second, and these processes cycle atoms and molecules through Earth's systems.

4. Describe two examples of how matter moves through a cycle on Earth.

5. Classify the following items as either inputs or outputs of a forest.

Inputs	Outputs

word bank
- sunlight
- nutrients
- wood
- oxygen

Changes in Matter and Energy

When matter and energy cycle through Earth's systems, they are often transformed. When you burn a piece of wood, you are not destroying matter or making energy. You are transforming both. The matter that makes up the wood becomes ash, smoke, and gases. The chemical energy that was stored in the wood is transformed into thermal energy and light. Matter and energy are conserved. When an object changes, the matter and energy that were associated with it are redistributed.

Trees use nutrients from the ground and air as well as energy from the sun to grow. They produce oxygen and wood.

While different molecules are formed when something undergoes a chemical change, atoms are not created or destroyed. For instance, oxygen atoms are used by organisms and are bonded to carbon atoms to make carbon dioxide. Plants then use carbon dioxide during photosynthesis and separate the molecule back into carbon and oxygen. Oxygen atoms can be involved in many chemical changes, but they never disappear.

Model a System

6. **Draw** Treat your classroom as a system. Draw a diagram showing the inputs, outputs, and internal components of the system.

139

EXPLORATION 2

Using Properties to Identify Substances

Properties of Matter

If someone offers you a choice of two fruits—a banana or an orange—you can make your choice based on which kind of fruit you like better. But how do you know which fruit is which? You know that a banana is long and yellow, and an orange is round and orange. You may know how each tastes. In a similar way, you can identify most substances by identifying their properties.

7. **Discuss** Iron pyrite is commonly called "fool's gold" because it looks like real gold, but it is not valuable. Both fool's gold and real gold may be found in the same area, but they have different properties. Why would it be important for a miner to know about the properties of real gold and fool's gold?

Which substance is real gold?

These two substances look similar. The one on the left is gold, but the other is a mineral called iron pyrite. One property that miners use to identify gold is density. Gold has a much higher density than iron pyrite.

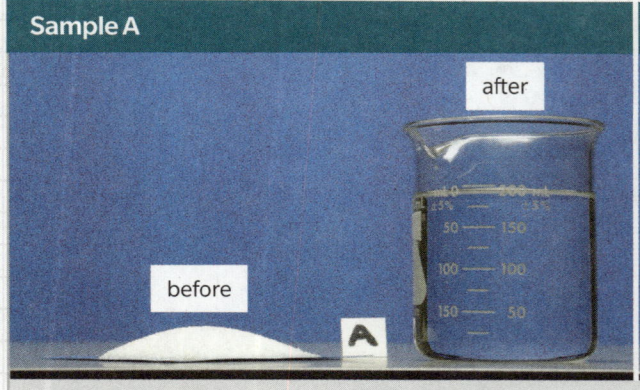

Sample A — before / after

Sample B — before / after

Two unknown samples, Sample A and Sample B, are shown before and after they are stirred into a beaker of water.

8. Are Sample A and Sample B in the photos the same substance? Explain.

140 Unit 3 Chemical Processes

Physical Properties

All substances have properties that can be used to identify the substance. Each substance has a unique combination of properties. The more properties of a substance you can determine, the more likely you are to correctly identify that substance.

The physical properties of a substance are those that can be observed or measured without changing the substance's identity. Physical properties include density, melting point, boiling point, color, texture, odor, solubility, malleability, and conductivity. There are many more physical properties that can be measured.

Every substance has a set of physical properties that are used to describe the substance. Scientists use physical properties to describe and to help identify substances. The two unknown samples in the previous photos are different substances; one substance dissolved in water and the other substance did not dissolve in water.

Chemical Properties

Another type of property, a chemical property, can be determined by observing whether or not a substance can change into another substance under a given set of conditions.

9. The two nails in the photos are shown before and after being left outside in the rain. Are the two nails made of the same substance? Explain.

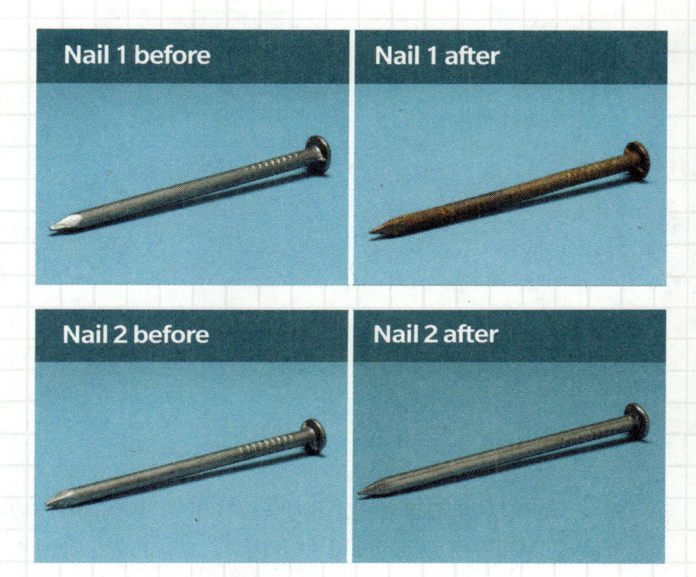

All substances have chemical properties. Chemical properties describe ways a substance can change to form different substances. Some examples of chemical properties are flammability and reactivity. When a substance changes to form a new substance, the atoms in the original substance are arranged in different ways. In the new substance, the original atoms form new molecules or arrangements of atoms. As a result, the new substance has its own unique set of properties that differ from the original substance.

When the two nails that looked alike were left outside, only one changed in a way that indicated that a new substance had formed. Nail 1 rusted, while nail 2 did not. The rust is made of particles that are different from the particles in nail 1. The particles that make up nail 2 did not change into a new substance. Therefore, the two nails left outside are not made of the same substance.

> **EVIDENCE NOTEBOOK**
> 10. How might the properties of a substance help you explain what happened when sulfuric acid was mixed with powdered sugar? Record your evidence.

Do the Math
Compare Properties of Matter

Different substances may have some similar properties, but not all of their properties will be the same. You may need evidence about several different properties to determine whether two substances are identical.

11. Use the information in the table to calculate the density of each sample, and enter it in the table. Then compare the properties of these two samples.

	Sample A	Sample B
Color	colorless	colorless
Odor	odorless	odorless
Boiling Point	100 °C	100 °C
Freezing Point	0 °C	75 °C
Mass	5.5 g	10.4 g
Volume	5.5 mL	7.0 mL
Density = $\frac{mass}{volume}$	_____ $\frac{g}{mL}$	_____ $\frac{g}{mL}$

12. Using the data in the table for color, odor, and boiling point, circle the correct words to complete each statement.

    The colors of Sample A and Sample B are **the same** / different.

    The odors of Sample A and Sample B are **the same** / different.

    The boiling points of Sample A and Sample B are **the same** / different.

13. Now use the data in the table for freezing point and density. Circle the correct words to complete each statement.

    The freezing points of Sample A and Sample B are the same / **different**.

    The densities of Sample A and Sample B are the same / **different**.

14. Based on all the data from the table, are these two samples the same substance? Explain why it is important to look at several properties before drawing a conclusion. Cite evidence to verify your claim.

Unit 3 Chemical Processes

EXPLORATION 3

Comparing Physical Changes and Chemical Reactions

Changes to substances take place all around you every day. Changes such as water freezing or metal being hammered into a thin sheet do not alter the identity of the substance. Changes such as milk spoiling or silver tarnishing do change the identity of the substance.

15. Discuss Explain in your own words what changes you see taking place in the photo.

Physical Changes

When a physical change takes place, the identity of a substance remains the same after the physical change. The particles that make up the substance are the same before and after the physical change. When you bend a paper clip, it is still a paper clip made of all the same particles. Physical changes only change the appearance of the substance.

Ice is solid water. When ice melts, it becomes liquid water. If liquid water boils, it becomes water vapor, a gas. Whether the water is a solid, liquid, or gas, it is the same substance. There is no change to the identity of the water molecules. Physical changes do not change water into a new substance.

This wood is being cut with a saw.

16. The photo shows wood undergoing a physical change. Compare the cut wood to the original piece of wood. Write *the same* or *different* to complete each sentence.

After cutting, the size and shape of the wood are _____. The smaller pieces of wood are _____ substance as the original, larger piece of wood. The smaller pieces of wood are made of _____ particles as the original, larger piece of wood. The identities of wood and sawdust are _____.

17. Why doesn't a change in a physical property change the identity of the substance? Explain in terms of the particles of a substance and give a new example.

Lesson 1 Matter Changes Identity in Chemical Reactions **143**

Chemical Changes

When substances are mixed together, a chemical change may or may not take place. When a chemical change does take place, the original substance changes into a different substance with different properties.

Mixing Baking Soda and Vinegar

A student measures baking soda into a balloon, attaches the balloon to the top of a flask containing vinegar, and empties the baking soda into the flask.

Explore Online

18. Observe what happens in the flask as the baking soda is added to the vinegar. Why do you think the balloon inflates?

19. What happens when the baking soda and vinegar are mixed? Circle the correct words to complete the explanation.

When these two substances are mixed, a *gas / liquid* forms.

The baking soda and vinegar react with each other and *change state / form a new substance*.

A chemical reaction changes the identity of a substance. A **chemical reaction** is the process in which atoms are rearranged to produce different substances. The original substance or substances in a chemical reaction are called **reactants**. The substance or substances that form in a chemical reaction are called **products**. During a chemical reaction, the atoms that make up the reactants regroup into different particles to form the products. The particles that make up the products can be atoms, molecules, or subunits of extended structures.

In a chemical reaction, all the atoms present in the reactants will also be present in the product. Chemical reactions generally follow defined patterns each and every time they occur. Under the same conditions, the same reactants will always form the same products in a chemical reaction.

20. Write *chemical reaction* or *physical change* to label each photo.

[photo] _____

[photo] chemical reaction

[photo] _____

[photo] _____

Analyze a Change in Matter

21. Look at the photo. Which changes have happened to the bucket? Circle all that apply.

   A. A chemical reaction has formed a new substance.

   B. The metal has reacted with air to form rust.

   C. The metal has changed to a different state.

   D. The color has changed to dark, reddish color.

22. How do you think the chemical reaction has affected how the bucket can be used?

_____
_____
_____

23. Engineer It | Collaborate You have been asked to design a pipe system to deliver water. What criteria might you need to consider when choosing materials to use? Work together with a partner to develop a list. Choose one or two items from your list to incorporate into a short presentation for the class.

_____
_____

Lesson 1 Matter Changes Identity in Chemical Reactions **145**

EXPLORATION 4

Analyzing Substances Before and After a Change

In a chemical reaction, the atoms of the reactants are rearranged to form new products. The products are different from the reactants, and they have different properties. A change in properties is evidence of a chemical reaction.

Signs of a Possible Chemical Reaction

You cannot always see new substances form in a chemical reaction. But there are some signs that you can observe to indicate that a chemical reaction may have taken place.

24. Each photo shows an indication that a chemical reaction may have taken place. Write the letter to label each photo.

A. Energy is released.
B. A solid forms.
C. The color changes.
D. A gas appears.
E. The odor changes.

[C] [ ] [ ] [ ] [ ]

Some observations that are signs of a chemical reaction include a change in color, a change in odor, the appearance of a gas, the release of energy as light or heat, and the formation of a precipitate. A precipitate is a solid that is produced as a result of a chemical reaction in a liquid.

Most of these changes could also happen in ways that are not the result of a chemical reaction. The appearance of bubbles can indicate formation of a new gas, but bubbles also form when water boils. The only way to know for sure whether a chemical reaction has taken place is to perform more testing.

Evidence of a Chemical Reaction

To determine whether a chemical reaction has taken place, you can test the properties of the substances both before the change and after the change. The products of a chemical reaction are different substances from the reactants and will have different properties. These different properties can help identify the products.

> **EVIDENCE NOTEBOOK**
> 25. How might knowing the signs of a chemical reaction help you explain what happened when sulfuric acid was mixed with powdered sugar? How does this relate to the rearrangement of atoms that occurs in a chemical reaction? Record your evidence.

Hands-On Lab
Observe Substances Before and After a Change

Mix substances together, and then determine whether a chemical reaction has taken place.

Procedure and Analysis

STEP 1 In bag 1, add 1 level spoonful of baking soda and 1 level spoonful of powdered sugar. Record observations in the table.

STEP 2 In bag 2, add 1 level spoonful of baking soda and 1 level spoonful of road salt. Record observations in the table.

STEP 3 Add 10 mL of water to each of the small containers.

STEP 4 Carefully place a container of water into each bag. Do not spill the water. Zip each bag closed with little air in it.

STEP 5 Tip the container over in bag 1. Observe what happens and record observations in the table. Repeat for bag 2.

MATERIALS
- bags, sealable plastic, gallon size (2), labeled *bag 1* and *bag 2*
- baking soda (sodium bicarbonate)
- calcium chloride
- film canisters or small containers (2)
- graduated cylinder
- spoons, plastic (3)
- sugar, powdered

	Observations
Bag 1: baking soda + powdered sugar	
Bag 2: baking soda + road salt	
Bag 1: baking soda + powdered sugar + water	
Bag 2: baking soda + road salt + water	

STEP 6 Do you think a chemical reaction occurred in the bag with baking soda, powdered sugar, and water? What about the bag with baking soda, road salt, and water? Give evidence to support your answers.

26. Which observations could be evidence of a chemical reaction? Circle all that apply.

   A. A substance dissolved.

   B. A precipitate formed.

   C. A substance changed state.

   D. A gas was produced.

27. Draw lines to match each list of observations with the conclusion that it indicates.

• a gas was produced • the color changed	does not indicate a chemical reaction
• the sample melted • the sample dissolved in water	may indicate a chemical reaction
• bubbles formed • the temperature climbed	definite evidence of a chemical reaction

Observations such as the formation of a precipitate, the production of light or heat, or a change in color suggest that a chemical reaction has taken place. However, these signs do not always mean a chemical reaction took place. Definite evidence for a chemical reaction requires proof that at least one new substance is present after the change. The presence of a new substance is determined by comparing the physical properties and chemical properties of the substances before and after the change.

Analyze Physical Changes and Chemical Reactions

28. Circle the correct terms to complete each sentence.

   A. The burning of the candle wick shows a
   chemical reaction / physical change.

   B. The melting of the wax shows a
   chemical reaction / *physical change*.

   C. The ~~change of state~~ / *generation of light and heat* indicates a chemical reaction may be occurring.

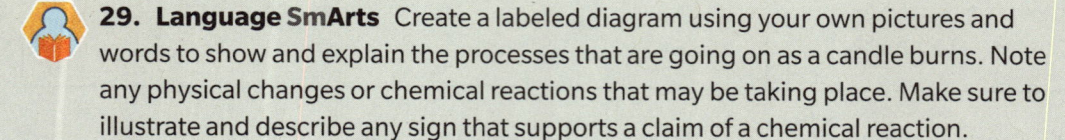

29. Language SmArts Create a labeled diagram using your own pictures and words to show and explain the processes that are going on as a candle burns. Note any physical changes or chemical reactions that may be taking place. Make sure to illustrate and describe any sign that supports a claim of a chemical reaction.

TAKE IT FURTHER

Continue Your Exploration

Name: _____ Date: _____

Check out the path below or go online to choose one of the other paths shown.

Chemistry and Engineering: Airbags

- Chemical Reactions Are Essential for Life
- Hands-On Labs
- Propose Your Own Path

Go online to choose one of these other paths.

Using Chemical Reactions in a Product

Chemical reactions take place all around us. One chemical reaction you hope you never need is the one that takes place in the airbags of cars. During certain accidents, airbags inflate very quickly and cushion the people in a car to protect them from serious injury. An airbag inflates because a chemical reaction happens quickly after a crash sensor is activated. The chemical reaction produces a large volume of gas that fills the airbag. Airbags are not meant to replace safety belts. They are additional safety features.

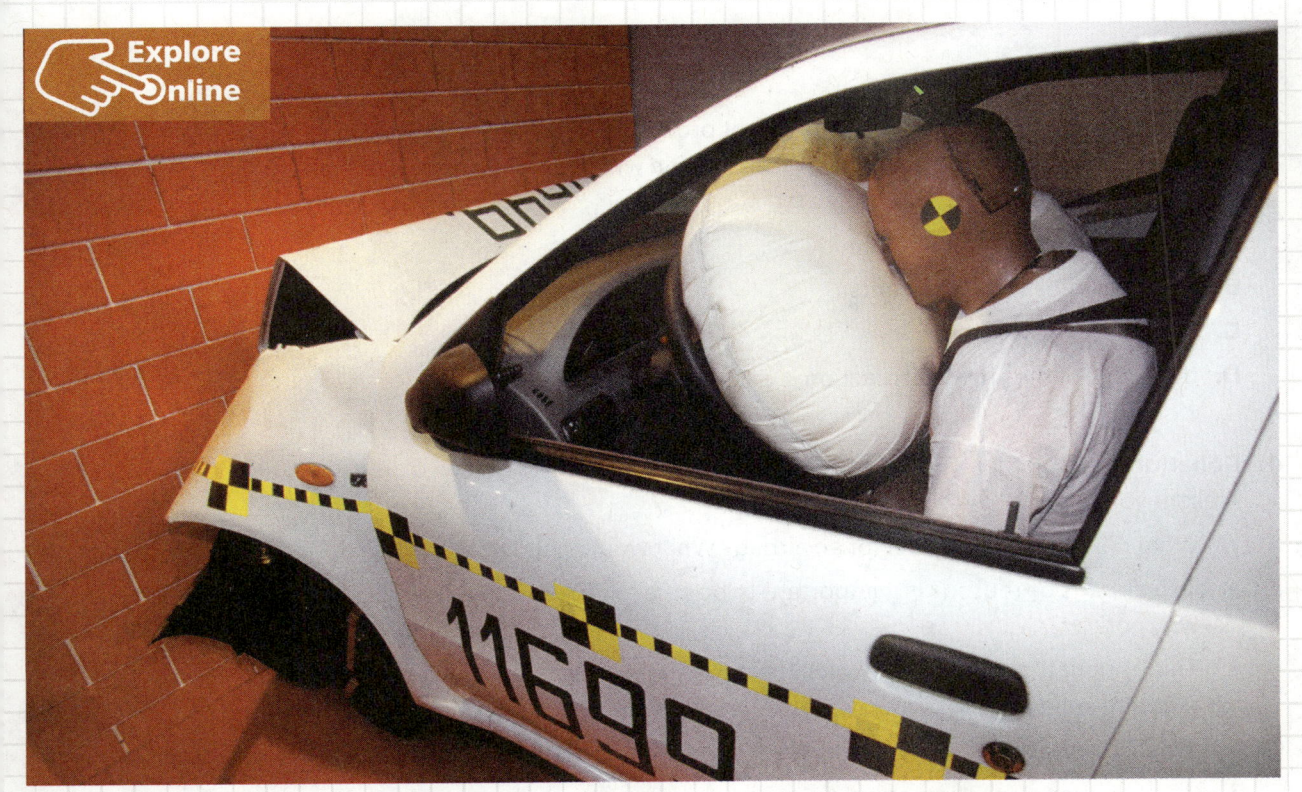

Explore Online

The chemical reaction that inflates an airbag happens very quickly. The time it takes for the airbag to fully inflate is less than a second!

Lesson 1 Matter Changes Identity in Chemical Reactions   149

TAKE IT FURTHER

Continue Your Exploration

Inside an airbag is a chemical called sodium azide, which is made up of sodium and nitrogen atoms. When the crash sensor is triggered, thermal energy is sent to the sodium azide. This energy causes the sodium azide to undergo an explosive chemical reaction. The sodium azide molecules break apart and produce a large volume of nitrogen gas. This causes the airbag to inflate rapidly.

1. Which best describes how the chemical reaction that produces nitrogen gas inflates the airbag?
    A. The sodium azide quickly breaks apart.
    B. The sodium azide suddenly melts.
    C. The sodium azide rapidly forms a precipitate.

2. What indicates that a chemical reaction has taken place? Explain why the indicator would be a sign of a chemical reaction and not a sign of a physical change.

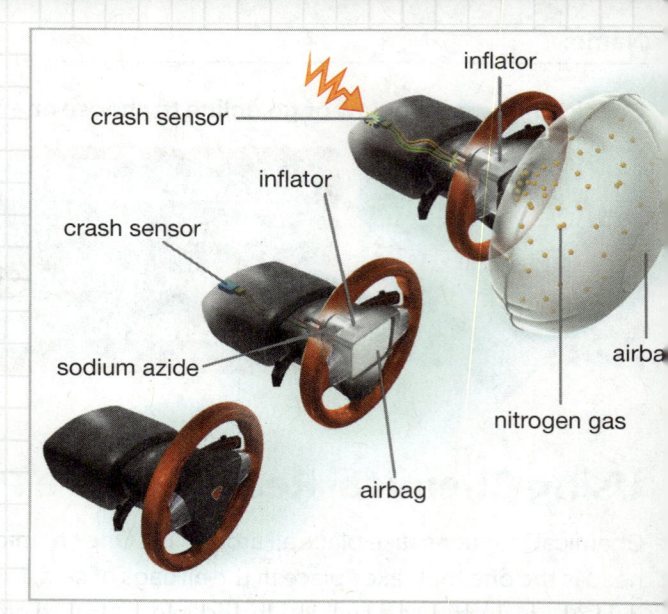

3. Chemical reactions are part of many different products. Which are important considerations about a particular chemical reaction when it is used as part of the product design? Circle all that apply.
    A. the properties of product formed
    B. the properties of the reactants
    C. the cost of the reactants
    D. the safety of the chemical reaction

4. **Collaborate** Together with a partner, choose one of the topics below to discuss. Present your ideas to the class.
    - What criteria are important for an airbag? What would need to be tested?
    - Can airbags be reused? Is it important to be able to reuse airbags? Why or why not?
    - Think about the problem for which the airbag was designed. Can you think of a different solution? Make a drawing or diagram to illustrate your idea.
    - What safety issues would need to be considered when designing airbags?
    - What environmental issues would need to be considered when designing airbags?

LESSON 1 SELF-CHECK

Can You Explain It?

Name: _____   Date: _____

What happens to the matter when sulfuric acid is added to powdered sugar?

EVIDENCE NOTEBOOK
Refer to the notes in your Evidence Notebook to help you construct an explanation for what you observed when sulfuric acid was added to powdered sugar.

1. State your claim. Make sure your claim fully explains what happens when these two substances are mixed.

2. Summarize the evidence you have gathered to support your claim and explain your reasoning.

Lesson 1 Matter Changes Identity in Chemical Reactions   151

LESSON 1 SELF-CHECK

Checkpoints

Answer the following questions to check your understanding of the lesson.

3. Students were given a solid Sample A and made these observations. Write *physical property* or *chemical property* to indicate what kind of property is being tested.

   Sample A melted when heated to 52 °C. _____

   Sample A floated when dropped into water. _____

   Sample A burned when held in a flame. _____

4. A science class did an experiment in which two substances were mixed. After 15 minutes, everything looked the same, but the students noticed an odor coming from the experiment. What does this likely indicate?

   A. A liquid was formed.

   B. A temperature change occurred.

   C. A chemical reaction occurred.

   D. A physical change occurred.

Use the photo to answer Question 5.

5. Which of the following is the best evidence that a chemical change has taken place?

   A. The apple is smaller in size after cutting.

   B. The apple is turning brown.

   C. The apple has changed shape.

Use the photo to answer Questions 6 and 7.

6. Two metal samples are each placed in a beaker containing the same solution. What evidence indicates that a chemical reaction is taking place in one of the beakers? Circle all that apply.

   A. A gas is being given off.

   B. There is a change in color.

   C. The solution is clear and colorless.

   D. Bubbles are forming.

7. Based on what you observe in the beakers, which of the following statements is true?

   A. Chemical reactions can always be seen.

   B. The two samples of metal are different substances.

   C. Chemical reactions are unpredictable.

   D. New substances are formed in each beaker.

LESSON 1 SELF-CHECK

Interactive Review

Complete this section to review the main concepts of the lesson.

Using a systems approach to examining phenomena allows matter and energy to be tracked through chemical changes and through Earth's systems.

A. Describe how analyzing the inputs and outputs of a system can help you to determine what occurred in the system.

Physical properties and chemical properties are used to identify a substance.

B. Explain the difference between a physical property and a chemical property and give at least one example of each.

Physical changes do not form new substances but chemical reactions do.

C. Explain the changes that happen in a chemical reaction in terms of atoms.

The products of a chemical reaction have different properties than the reactants.

D. How can you gather evidence to determine whether a chemical reaction has taken place?

Lesson 1 Matter Changes Identity in Chemical Reactions   153

LESSON 2

Chemical Equations Model Chemical Reactions

When copper sulfate reacts with ammonia, a solid precipitate forms and the solution color changes to deep blue.

Explore First

Writing Formulas Gather ten small items. Divide them into at least two groups. Describe the items in each group using symbols or numbers, but not words. Trade items and written descriptions of the groups with a partner to see if you can replicate one another's groups. How well were you able to communicate your groups to one another?

CAN YOU EXPLAIN IT?

How does this chemical equation explain what happens when copper reacts with silver nitrate?

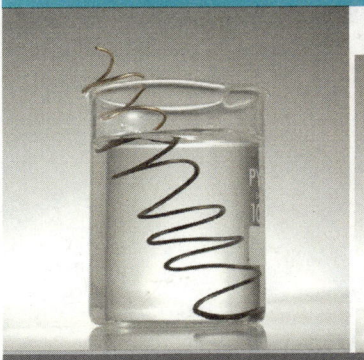

$$Cu + 2AgNO_3 \rightarrow Cu(NO_3)_2 + 2Ag$$

When a copper wire is placed in a solution of silver nitrate, copper nitrate and silver metal form.

Explore Online

1. Based on the photos, what do you think happens when copper reacts with silver nitrate?

2. What do you think the letters, numbers, and arrow represent in the chemical equation?

EVIDENCE NOTEBOOK As you explore the lesson, gather evidence to help you account for the matter that is rearranged in a chemical reaction.

Lesson 2 Chemical Equations Model Chemical Reactions

EXPLORATION 1

Using Chemical Formulas

Students connected blocks together in three different combinations. They labeled each group with a code to describe how it was built.

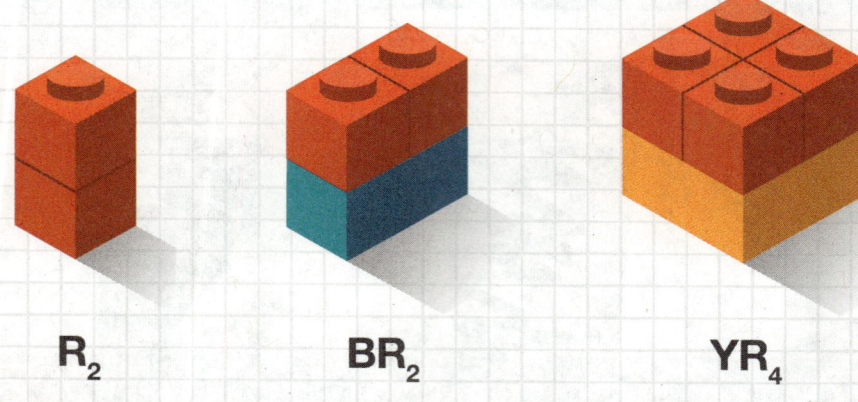

Each code represents the group of blocks above it.

R$_2$ BR$_2$ YR$_4$

3. Explain how the code describes each group of blocks in the images above.

Chemical Formulas

You and everything around you, including air, water, your desk, and your clothes, are made of chemical substances. These substances are made of the atoms of chemical elements combined with one another in different ways.

Think about the code used to show the combinations of blocks. How could a similar code be used to represent a chemical substance? Each element has a one-, two-, or three-letter chemical symbol associated with it. A combination of chemical symbols and numbers that is used to represent a single unit of a substance is known as a **chemical formula**. For many substances, this single unit is a molecule. A molecule is a specific group of atoms held together by chemical bonds. In other substances, the single unit is part of a larger, repeating pattern of atoms. The chemical formula shows the exact atoms in each molecule or unit.

In any pure substance containing atoms of different elements, the atoms are always present in the same ratio. In other words, a chemical formula shows the relative numbers of atoms of each kind in a chemical compound.

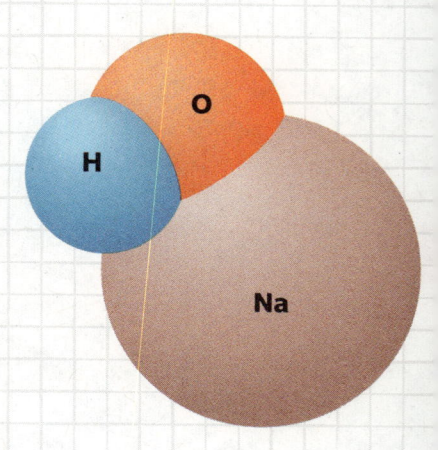

Sodium hydroxide (NaOH) is made up of a sodium atom (Na), an oxygen atom (O), and a hydrogen atom (H).

156 Unit 3 Chemical Processes

Water Molecule

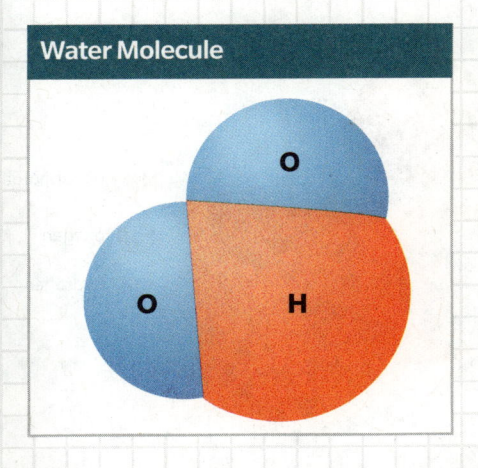

4. The chemical formula for water is H_2O. Explain how this chemical formula describes the model of a water molecule shown in this diagram.

A chemical formula uses chemical symbols of the elements that make up the substance. A *subscript*, a number below and to the right of the symbol, shows how many atoms of that element there are. If there is no subscript, then one atom of that element is present.

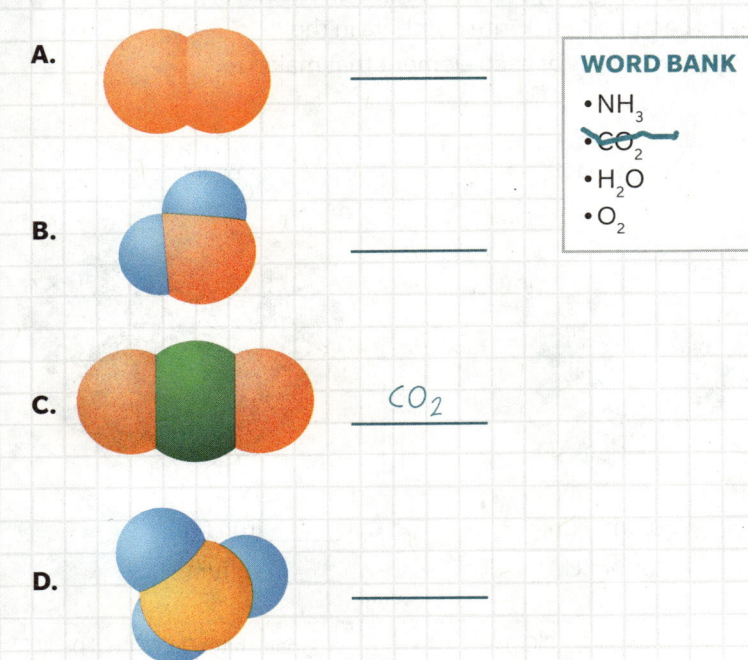

Chemical Formula of Sulfuric Acid

A molecule of sulfuric acid is made up of 2 hydrogen atoms, 1 sulfur atom, and 4 oxygen atoms.

symbol — H_2SO_4 — subscript

5. Write the chemical formula to identify each model shown.

A. _____

B. _____

C. CO_2

D. _____

WORD BANK
- NH_3
- ~~CO_2~~
- H_2O
- O_2

Sometimes a formula includes a group of symbols in parentheses. Symbols in parentheses represent atoms that are held together as a group within the compound. Subscripts outside the parentheses show the number of groups there are in the compound. For example, the chemical formula $Al_2(SO_4)_3$ describes a compound that contains 2 aluminum atoms, 3 sulfur atoms, and 12 oxygen atoms.

6. How many atoms of each element are in the compound described by this chemical formula?

$(CH_3)_2N$

Each molecule of the compound has __2__ atom(s) of carbon (C), _____ atom(s) of hydrogen (H), and _____ atom(s) of nitrogen (N).

Lesson 2 Chemical Equations Model Chemical Reactions 157

7. The chemical formula below describes the model shown in the diagram, but a subscript is missing. Write the subscript. Then write numbers to show how many atoms of each element are in the formula.

H₃PO[ ]

The chemical formula shows there is (are):

_____ atom(s) of hydrogen
_____ atom(s) of phosphorus
_____ atom(s) of oxygen

- phosphorus
- oxygen
- hydrogen

Analyze the Chemical Formulas of Minerals

8. Minerals are natural substances that form as a result of processes in the rock cycle. Most minerals consist of repeating units of atoms or groups of atoms. The chemical formula given for each mineral describes its composition. Write numbers in the blanks below each photo to show the number of atoms of each element that make up a unit of the mineral.

hematite: Fe₂O₃

A. __2__ iron (Fe),
   __3__ oxygen (O)

halite: NaCl

B. _____ sodium (Na),
   _____ chlorine (Cl)

pyrite: FeS₂

C. _____ iron (Fe),
   _____ sulfur (S)

diamond: C

D. _____ carbon (C)

grossular: Ca₃Al₂(SiO₄)₃

E. _____ calcium (Ca),
   _____ aluminum (Al),
   _____ silicon (Si),
   _____ oxygen (O)

malachite: Cu₂CO₃(OH)₂

F. _____ copper (Cu),
   _____ carbon (C),
   _____ oxygen (O),
   _____ hydrogen (H)

EXPLORATION 2

Analyzing Chemical Equations

During a chemical reaction, new substances form. Atoms grouped together in molecules or chemical units in the reactants rearrange and form different molecules or units in the products. The products of the chemical reaction have properties that are different from the reactants, because the molecules that make up the products are different from those in the reactants.

The changes in these robots model the kinds of changes that happen in a chemical reaction.

9. Explain what is happening in the image. How are the changes in the robots like a chemical reaction?

10. **Draw** Make your own drawing to model reactants rearranging and forming new products.

Lesson 2 Chemical Equations Model Chemical Reactions 159

Chemical Equations

Chemical formulas model chemical substances. A **chemical equation** uses chemical formulas to model what happens in a chemical reaction. It shows how the reactants change and form the products of the reaction. The way a chemical equation is written is similar to that of a mathematical equation.

On the left side of a chemical equation, one or more chemical formulas are shown, separated by addition signs. Those formulas are followed by an arrow pointing to the right. This arrow indicates the direction of the reaction. Then one or more different chemical formulas are shown on the right side of the equation. The formulas for the reactants are to the left of the arrow, and the formulas for the products are to the right.

11. Look at the chemical equation below. There is a number in the chemical equation that is not a subscript. What do you think the number 2 on the right side of the chemical equation represents?

$$H_2 + Cl_2 \rightarrow 2HCl$$

In a chemical equation, a *coefficient* is a number placed in front of a chemical formula to show how many molecules of the substance are represented in the chemical equation. In the reaction shown above, the coefficient of HCl is 2, because two molecules of hydrogen chloride are formed in the reaction for every one molecule of H_2 and Cl_2.

The Electrolysis of Water

When an electric current passes through water, the water breaks down into hydrogen and oxygen. The stable products of this reaction are molecules of hydrogen gas and oxygen gas, which are both composed of two of each atom. To model this reaction correctly, the chemical equation shows hydrogen and oxygen as the gas molecules H_2 and O_2. The coefficients of the water and of the hydrogen gas are 2. Only one molecule of oxygen is produced, so no coefficient appears in front of the chemical formula for the oxygen gas.

$$2H_2O \rightarrow 2H_2 + O_2$$

A Chemical Equation

$$\underbrace{CH_4 + 2O_2}_{\text{reactants}} \rightarrow \underbrace{CO_2 + 2H_2O}_{\text{products}}$$

coefficient — 2, subscript — 2

12. Circle the correct word to make each sentence true.

   A. A chemical **equation** / formula shows both the reactants and the products of a chemical reaction.

   B. The same number of **atoms** / substances are present on both sides of a chemical equation.

   C. The arrow in a chemical equation points to the **products** / reactants.

Use a Model to Write a Chemical Equation

13. Write formulas in the boxes to show the chemical equation for this model of a chemical reaction.

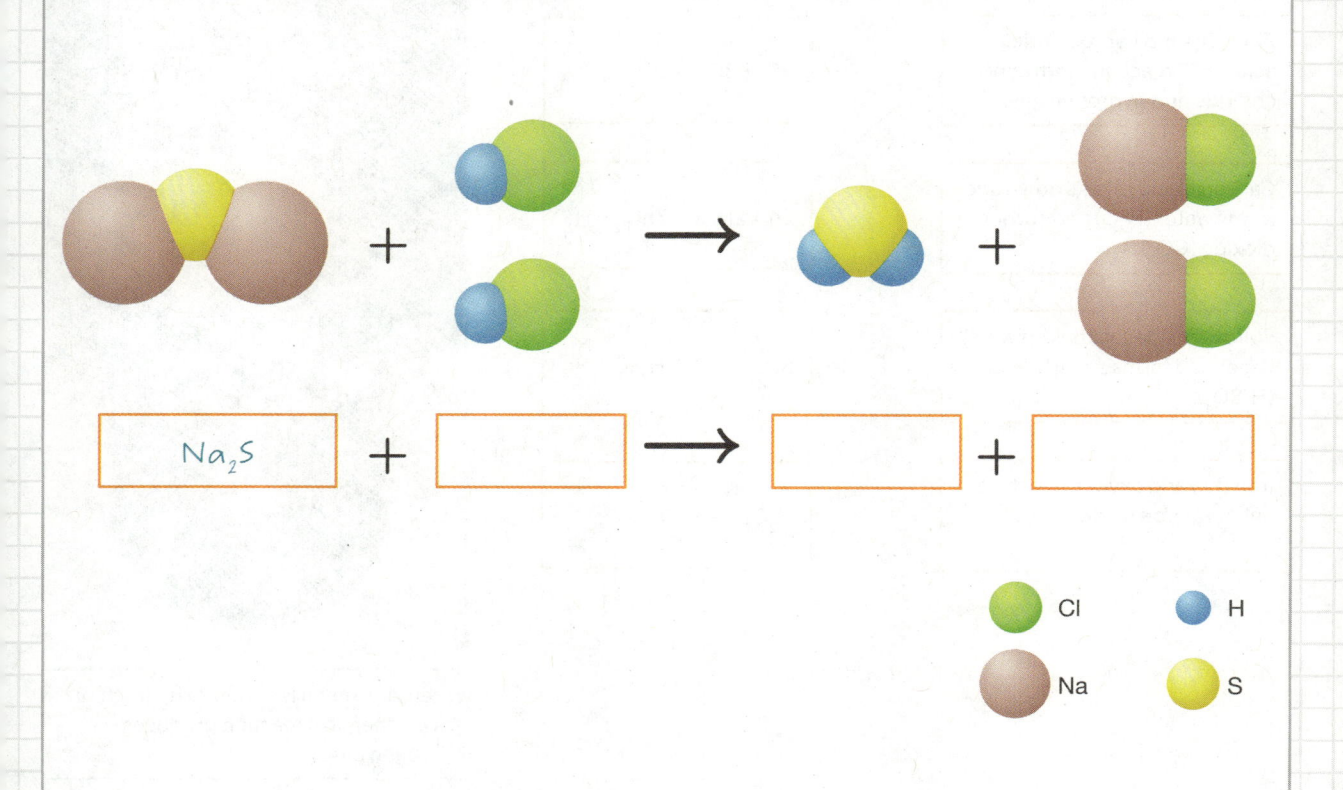

   ~~Na_2S~~ | H_2S
   2NaCl | 2HCl

   Na_2S + ☐ → ☐ + ☐

   Cl — green, H — blue, Na — brown, S — yellow

Lesson 2 Chemical Equations Model Chemical Reactions 161

Chemical Equations and Chemical Reactions

During a chemical reaction, the reactants change into different substances, which are called the products. A chemical equation is a model that represents that change. Models help people learn about things that cannot be observed directly. The rearrangement of atoms that is happening in the chemical reaction cannot be directly observed, but the chemical equation helps to keep track of the rearrangement that is taking place.

A chemical equation shows that the same atoms are present before and after a reaction. Each side of the equation contains the same number and types of atoms. For example, think about the chemical equation that describes how glucose, a type of sugar, is broken down by cells to release energy:

$$C_6H_{12}O_6 + 6O_2 \rightarrow 6CO_2 + 6H_2O$$

This chemical equation models a chemical reaction. The chemical bonds between carbon, hydrogen, and oxygen and between oxygen atoms are broken. New chemical bonds form between carbon and oxygen and between hydrogen and oxygen.

The substances on one side of the arrow are different from the substances on the other side of the arrow. Atoms have recombined into new molecules, which are modeled by the chemical formulas.

The equation shows what happens to the reactants under a certain set of conditions. If an experiment is carried out under the same conditions that were used to determine the equation, the same reactants will always form the same products.

14. Language SmArts Draw a line to match each description of a chemical reaction with the equation that models it.

Zinc (Zn) and hydrochloric acid (HCl) react and form zinc chloride and hydrogen gas.	$4Fe + 3O_2 \rightarrow 2Fe_2O_3$
Carbonic acid breaks down and forms water (H_2O) and carbon dioxide (CO_2).	$Zn + 2HCl \rightarrow ZnCl_2 + H_2$
Sulfur trioxide reacts with water vapor and forms sulfuric acid (H_2SO_4).	$SO_3 + H_2O \rightarrow H_2SO_4$
Iron (Fe) and oxygen gas react and form iron oxide (rust).	$H_2CO_3 \rightarrow H_2O + CO_2$

When zinc metal is added to hydrochloric acid, a chemical reaction produces hydrogen gas.

Hands-On Lab
Observe a Chemical Reaction

Plan and carry out an investigation to observe what happens when acetic acid and baking soda are mixed. Acetic acid is a liquid ingredient in vinegar, that gives vinegar its distinctive odor and taste.

MATERIALS
- bag, sealable plastic, sandwich-size
- baking soda
- cup, 3-ounce, paper or plastic
- graduated cylinder, 50 mL
- pan or tray
- scale
- spoon, plastic
- vinegar

Procedure and Analysis

STEP 1 Measure an amount of baking soda between 5–10 grams into the bag. Record the amount in the table.

STEP 2 Measure 30 mL of vinegar using the graduated cylinder. Pour the vinegar into the cup.

STEP 3 Place the bag into the pan. Place the cup of vinegar upright into the bag. Be careful not to spill the vinegar. Get as much air out of the bag as possible, and zip the bag closed.

STEP 4 Tip the cup over in the bag. Observe what happens, and record your observations in the table.

Vinegar/Baking Soda Experiment		
Baking soda (g)	Vinegar (mL)	Observations
	30	

STEP 5 The chemical equation for the reaction that you observed is:

sodium bicarbonate + acetic acid → sodium acetate + water + carbon dioxide
(solid) (liquid) (solution) (liquid) (gas)

$$NaHCO_3 + C_2H_4O_2 \rightarrow NaC_2H_3O_2 + H_2O + CO_2$$

How can you use the chemical equation to explain what you observed when you added vinegar (acetic acid) to baking soda (sodium bicarbonate)? Explain what happens to the atoms of the different elements involved in the reaction.

EVIDENCE NOTEBOOK

15. How does a chemical equation help to keep track of what happens in a chemical reaction? Record your evidence.

Identify a Chemical Equation

A solution of hydrogen peroxide can be used to kill germs on a small cut. Over time, the peroxide becomes less effective.

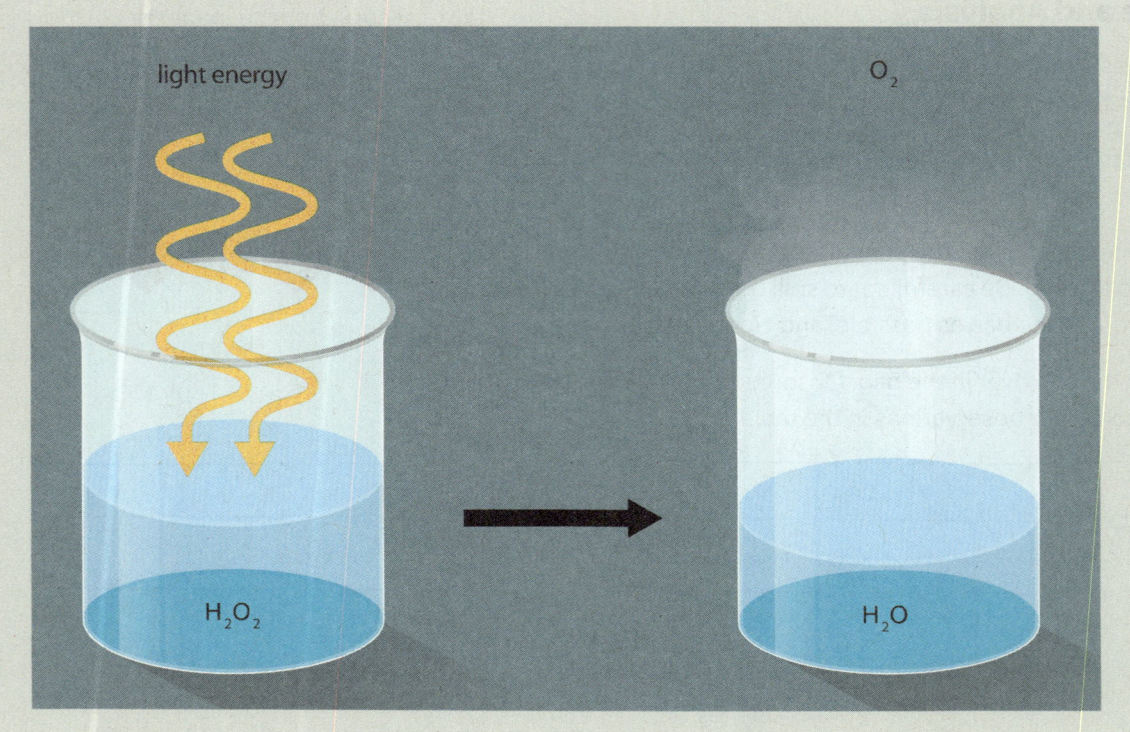

light energy

O_2

H_2O_2 → H_2O

16. The image shows that hydrogen peroxide (H_2O_2) changes to oxygen gas and water. What chemical equation models this reaction?

   A. $H_2O_2 \rightarrow H_2O$
   B. $2H_2O_2 \rightarrow O_2 + 2H_2O$
   C. $O_2 + 2H_2O \rightarrow 2H_2O_2$

17. **Engineer It** A packaging engineer is designing a container to hold hydrogen peroxide. The engineer knows that light speeds up the chemical reaction that changes hydrogen peroxide into oxygen and water. How might the engineer use that information when designing the container?

_____
_____
_____
_____
_____
_____

164 Unit 3 Chemical Processes

EXPLORATION 3

Modeling Chemical Reactions

Any change that produces a new substance, or substances, is a chemical reaction. Chemical reactions occur around you all of the time. Some reactions, such as a log burning in a campfire, occur quickly and are easy to observe. Some reactions, such as the reactions that cause a green banana to ripen over several days, are much slower. Other reactions are harder to observe, such as the formation of ozone in the atmosphere.

18. In some chemical reactions, such as photosynthesis, several different compounds take part in the reaction. How do you think that the atoms present at the end of this kind of reaction compare to the atoms present at the beginning of the reaction? Explain.

In the green parts of trees, the chemical reaction photosynthesis uses energy from the sun to convert carbon dioxide and water into sugar and oxygen.

The Law of Conservation of Matter

Chemical reactions do not always produce a visible product. For example, one product of photosynthesis, oxygen, cannot be observed by looking at a leaf. Scientists have measured the amount of carbon dioxide and water that react during photosynthesis. When they compared the mass of reactants and the mass of oxygen and plant material produced, they confirmed that the reactants and the products have the same mass.

The **law of conservation of matter** states that matter cannot be created or destroyed in ordinary chemical or physical changes. During any ordinary chemical or physical change, the total mass of the substances involved in the change is the same before and after the change. Matter is conserved during chemical reactions because atoms are conserved. The new substances formed during a chemical reaction are made up of exactly the same atoms as the atoms of substances that reacted. Because the same atoms are present before and after the reaction, the mass of the reactants is the same as the mass of the products.

19. How do you think a chemical equation shows that matter is being conserved?

Lesson 2 Chemical Equations Model Chemical Reactions **165**

Balanced Chemical Equations Model the Conservation of Matter

Because a chemical equation is a model of a chemical reaction, the equation must show that the number of atoms does not change during the reaction. A chemical equation is *balanced* when it has the same number of each type of atom on both sides of the equation.

The fact that chemical equations have the same number and types of atoms on both sides of the equation demonstrates the law of conservation of matter.

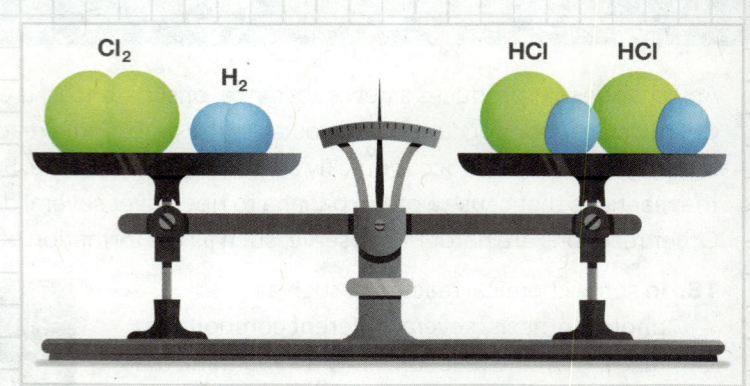

When H_2 and Cl_2 react and form 2HCl, the same number and types of atoms are in the reactants and in the products. The two sides balance.

Balanced Chemical Equations

Hydrogen and chlorine can combine and form hydrogen chloride, as shown in the diagram and modeled by this chemical equation:

$$H_2 + Cl_2 \rightarrow 2HCl$$

20. If the reactants contain one chlorine molecule, do you know how many chlorine atoms will be in the product? Include conservation of matter in your explanation.

21. How do you think subscripts and coefficients help to tell whether a chemical equation is balanced?

You can determine whether a chemical equation is balanced by comparing the number of atoms of each element on both sides of the arrow. Every element must have the same number of atoms in the reactants and in the products for the equation to be balanced. As you count atoms in a chemical formula, remember that the subscript following a symbol tells you the number of atoms of that element present in one molecule or unit of a substance. If a coefficient is in front of a chemical formula, multiply the number of atoms of each element in that formula by the coefficient. For example, if an equation includes the term $2H_2O$, then 4 hydrogen atoms and 2 oxygen atoms are present.

The Conservation of Matter

A chemical equation is a model of what happens during a chemical reaction. It shows what reactants are changed and what products form. Because every chemical reaction follows the law of conservation of matter, the chemical equation must also demonstrate that law.

When a chemical equation is balanced, all matter on one side of the equation is also shown on the other side of the equation. The equation correctly models the chemical reaction by showing that matter is conserved.

Model a Balanced Chemical Equation

22. As methane burns, it reacts with oxygen and forms carbon dioxide and water. The balanced chemical equation below models this chemical reaction. Examine each molecule represented in the chemical equation. Write the numbers of each type of atom in the reactants and products. Compare the numbers when you are finished.

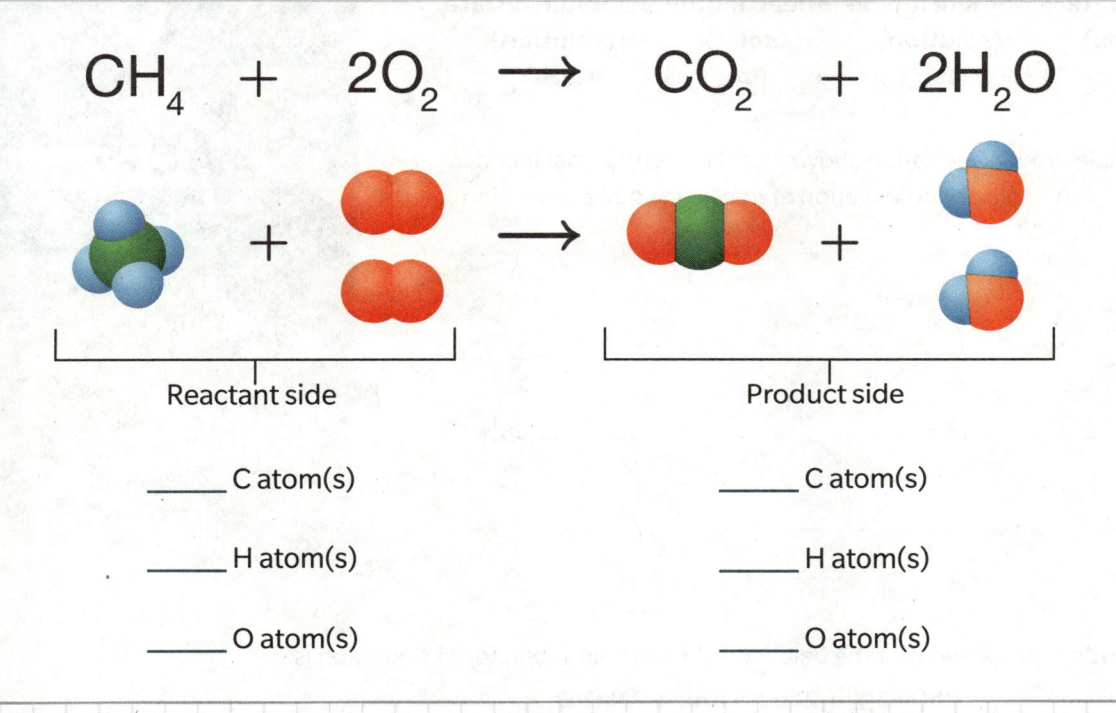

$$CH_4 + 2O_2 \rightarrow CO_2 + 2H_2O$$

Reactant side

Product side

_____ C atom(s)   _____ C atom(s)

_____ H atom(s)   _____ H atom(s)

_____ O atom(s)   _____ O atom(s)

23. Act Work with a group to demonstrate the law of conservation of matter by acting out this chemical equation:

$$CH_4 + 2O_2 \rightarrow CO_2 + 2H_2O$$

EVIDENCE NOTEBOOK

24. How do balanced chemical equations help to account for everything that happens in a chemical reaction? Record your evidence.

25. **Do the Math** Compare the number of atoms of each element on both sides of each chemical equation. Write *balanced* or *not balanced* to describe each equation.

   A. $C_2H_6 + 5O_2 \rightarrow 2CO_2 + 3H_2O$ _____

   B. $3CO + Fe_2O_3 \rightarrow 2Fe + 3CO_2$ _____

   C. $H_2SO_4 + 2NaOH \rightarrow Na_2SO_4 + 2H_2O$ _____

   D. $2AgNO_3 + CaCl_2 \rightarrow 2AgCl + Ca(NO_3)_2$ _____

Evaluate a Chemical Equation

The photo shows that when a clear, colorless solution of lead nitrate is added to a clear, colorless solution of sodium iodide, a yellow solid, lead iodide, forms.

lead nitrate + sodium iodide → lead iodide + sodium nitrate
(solution)   (solution)   (solid)   (solution)
$Pb(NO_3)_2$ + NaI → PbI_2 + $NaNO_3$

26. Explain how the equation shown is not currently a balanced equation. Include conservation of matter in your explanation.

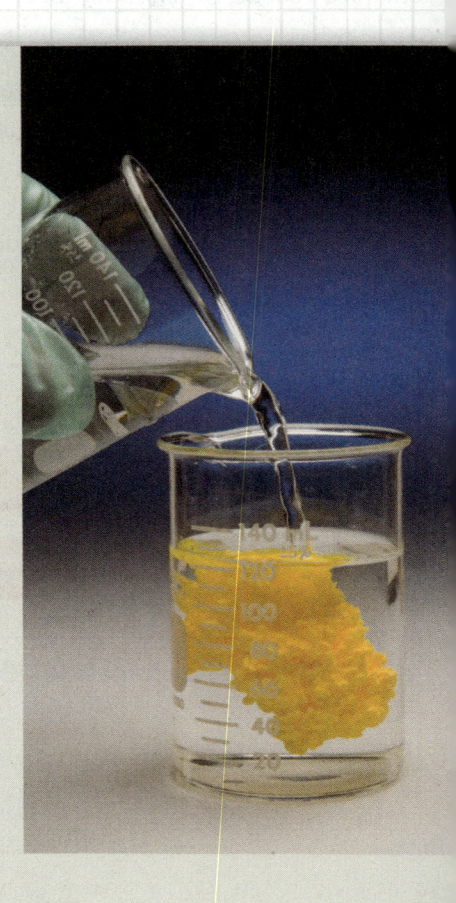

   _____
   _____
   _____
   _____
   _____
   _____
   _____

27. A student proposed that the balanced chemical equation for this reaction is:

   $$Pb(NO_3)_2 + 2NaI \rightarrow PbI_2 + 2NaNO_3$$

   Determine whether this is a correctly balanced equation and give evidence for your conclusion.

   _____
   _____
   _____
   _____
   _____
   _____
   _____
   _____

168 Unit 3 Chemical Processes

TAKE IT FURTHER

Continue Your Exploration

Name: _____   Date: _____

Check out the path below or go online to choose one of the other paths shown.

| Balancing a Chemical Equation | • People in Science
• Chemistry in the Kitchen
• Hands-On Labs
• Propose Your Own Path | Go online to choose one of these other paths. |

If you know the reactants and the products of a chemical reaction, you can write a balanced chemical equation. You can model balancing a chemical reaction by using parts of an object that combine to form a complete object.

As in a balanced chemical equation, all of the parts on the left are shown in the bike on the right.

1. To build a bicycle, you need to start with the number of each part needed for the finished bicycle. A word description for constructing a bicycle could be written as:

   frame + wheels + seat + pedals → bicycle

   With a partner, write a "balanced equation" for a bicycle. Use F, W, S, and P as symbols for the "reactants." Use subscripts and coefficients to balance the bicycle equation. Include the formula for the finished bicycle.

Lesson 2 Chemical Equations Model Chemical Reactions

TAKE IT FURTHER

Continue Your Exploration

To balance a chemical equation, change the coefficients to balance each type of atom. Subscripts are part of the chemical formula and cannot be changed.

$$C + O_2 \rightarrow CO$$

C = 1   O = 2   C = 1   O = 1

$$2C + O_2 \rightarrow 2CO$$

C = 2   O = 2   C = 2   O = 2

Count the atoms in the reactants and in the product. There are more oxygen atoms in the reactants than in the product. There are two oxygen atoms in the reactants, so you need two oxygen atoms in the product.

In order to have two oxygen atoms in the product, place a coefficient 2 in front of CO. Now the oxygen atoms balance, but the carbon atoms do not. Placing the coefficient 2 in front of the C reactant balances the equation.

2. Count the atoms of each element in the reactants and product in the unbalanced chemical equation. Write the numbers in the blanks below the model.

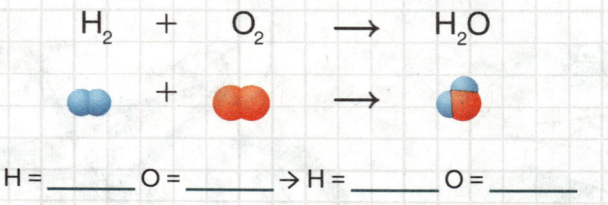

$$H_2 + O_2 \rightarrow H_2O$$

H = _____ O = _____ → H = _____ O = _____

3. To balance the number of each type of atom, place coefficients in front of the appropriate chemical formulas. Then sketch the products and reactants, showing the correct number of molecules of each. Write the number of hydrogen and oxygen atoms in the reactants and products for the balanced reaction.

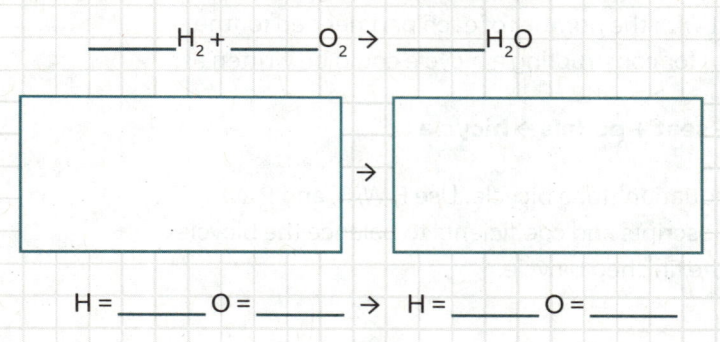

_____ H_2 + _____ O_2 → _____ H_2O

H = _____ O = _____ → H = _____ O = _____

4. **Collaborate** Work with a partner. Choose one of the unbalanced chemical equations shown. Find the coefficients needed to balance the equation and model the balanced equation by sketching the products and reactants. Present your sketch to the class and explain how it shows the balanced chemical equation.

$$Al + O_2 \rightarrow Al_2O_3$$

$$Na + H_2O \rightarrow NaOH + H_2$$

170 Unit 3 Chemical Processes

LESSON 2 SELF-CHECK

Can You Explain It?

Name: _____ Date: _____

How does this chemical equation explain what happens when copper reacts with silver nitrate?

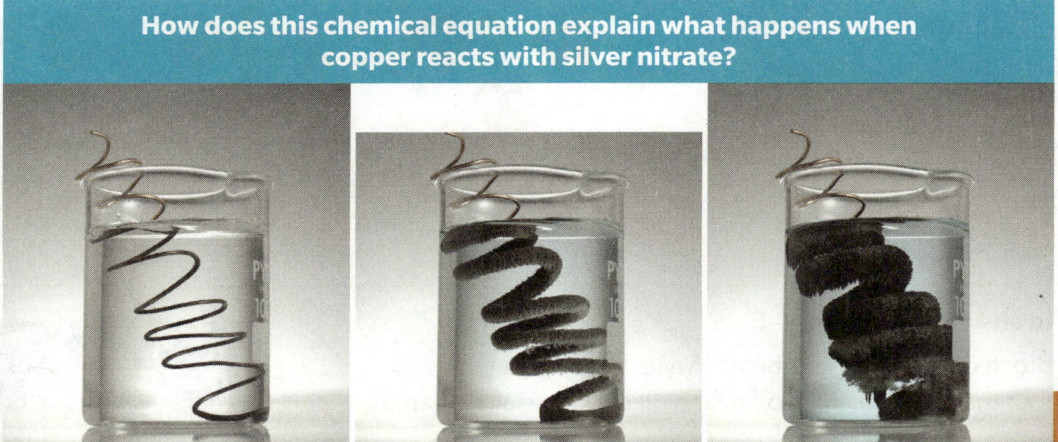

EVIDENCE NOTEBOOK
Refer to the notes in your Evidence Notebook to help you construct an explanation for the solid that forms when a copper wire is placed in a silver nitrate solution.

1. State your claim. Make sure your claim fully describes how the chemical equation explains what happens when copper reacts with silver nitrate.

2. Summarize the evidence you have gathered to support your claim and explain your reasoning.

Lesson 2 Chemical Equations Model Chemical Reactions 171

LESSON 2 SELF-CHECK

Checkpoints

Answer the following questions to check your understanding of the lesson.

Use the model to answer Question 3.

3. This model shows a single unit of a compound containing several elements. What is the chemical formula for the substance?

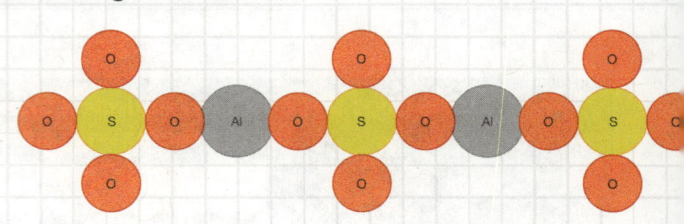

   A. Al_2SO_4
   B. $Al_2(SO_3)_4$
   C. $Al_2(SO_4)_3$
   D. $(AlO)_2(SO_4)_3$

Use the photo to answer Questions 4–5.

4. Zinc and hydrochloric acid are combined in a test tube. What can you conclude about the chemical reaction taking place? Circle all that apply.

   A. The mass of the products is exactly the same as the mass of the reactants.
   B. At least one new product formed is a gas.
   C. Molecules are changing into different molecules.
   D. Atoms are changing into different atoms.

5. The photo shows the reaction between zinc and hydrochloric acid that forms zinc chloride and hydrogen gas. Which of these is a correctly balanced equation that models the reaction?

   A. $Zn + HCl \rightarrow ZnCl_2 + H_2$
   B. $Zn + 2HCl \rightarrow ZnCl_2 + 2H_2$
   C. $Zn + 2HCl \rightarrow ZnCl_2 + H_2$
   D. $Zn + 4HCl \rightarrow ZnCl_2 + 2H_2$

6. What is shown by this balanced chemical equation? Select all that apply.

   $$H_2 + Cl_2 \rightarrow 2HCl$$

   A. The atoms in the original substances regroup and form a different substance.
   B. The product is a new substance made up of different atoms than the reactants.
   C. The total number of atoms changes in the reaction.
   D. The same atoms are present before and after the reaction.
   E. Matter is conserved.

7. How many oxygen (O) atoms are involved in this chemical reaction?

   $$2Fe(OH)_3 \rightarrow Fe_2O_3 + 3H_2O$$

   A. 2
   B. 3
   C. 6
   D. 12

LESSON 2 SELF-CHECK

Interactive Review

Complete this section to review the main concepts of the lesson.

A chemical formula is a model of a molecule or unit of a substance.

A. What information about a molecule can you determine from its chemical formula?

A chemical equation models what happens in a chemical reaction. It shows how the substances that are reacting change and form the products of the reaction.

B. Explain how a chemical equation shows that the reactants change and form the products.

The law of conservation of matter states that matter is not created or destroyed in ordinary chemical or physical changes.

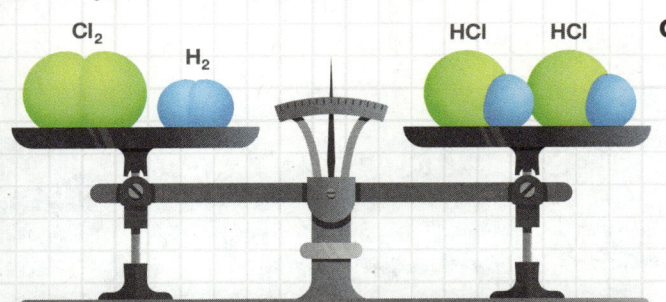

C. How does a balanced chemical equation show that a chemical reaction obeys the law of conservation of matter?

Lesson 2 Chemical Equations Model Chemical Reactions 173

LESSON 3 | ENGINEER IT

Using Thermal Energy in a Device

As the chemical reactions of the bonfire proceed, the air around the fire becomes hot.

Explore First

Measuring Changes in Energy Measure the temperature of a small glass of water. Place several ice cubes into the glass of water and measure the temperature again after several minutes. Is the ice absorbing or releasing energy? Mix some of the powdered laundry detergent into a small amount of water and measure the temperature. Is this chemical process absorbing or releasing energy?

CAN YOU EXPLAIN IT?

How can a device warm food without using fire or electricity?

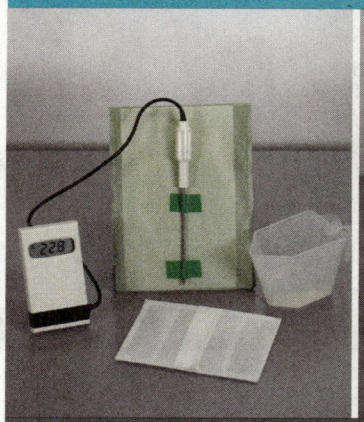

These photos show a digital thermometer measuring the temperature of a flameless heater. Flameless heaters produce energy for cooking without flames or electricity. This heater contains a mixture of iron and magnesium. Once water is added to the heater, the heater begins to warm quickly. A bag of food can be warmed by putting it inside the heater.

1. Observe the photos. What could be occurring inside the device to release thermal energy for cooking?

EVIDENCE NOTEBOOK As you explore the lesson, gather evidence to help explain how a device could warm food without using fire or electricity.

Lesson 3 Engineer It: Using Thermal Energy in a Device

EXPLORATION 1

Exploring Systems and Energy Flow

When you shoot a basketball, kinetic energy from your hand is transferred to the ball. Thermal energy can also be transferred between objects. Think about what happens when you touch a warm pan. How do you know that the pan is warm? Thermal energy from the pan is transferred to your hand. You experience this energy transfer as a feeling of warmth.

2. The hot metal in the photo cools quickly and soon stop glowing. What happens to the energy as the metal parts cool?

During the production of steel goods, the metal becomes so hot that it glows. After each piece of metal is removed from the furnace, it begins to cool and to glow less brightly.

Energy Flow in Systems

A system is a set of interacting parts. Systems can include matter, energy, and information. By grouping a set of related parts or events into a system, scientists and engineers can study how matter and energy behave.

A system can have inputs (things that enter the system) and outputs (things that leave the system). Inputs and outputs can be matter, energy, or information. New matter or energy cannot be created or destroyed. Instead, matter and energy can only be transformed into new forms or move in or out of the system. To accurately model a system, you must understand the inputs and outputs of that system. You also have to understand the flow of matter, energy, and information through the system.

For example, an automobile engine uses energy to make a car move. The inputs of the system are gasoline and air. When gasoline and air enter the engine system, they react with one another. The chemical energy released by the gasoline-air reaction is converted into thermal energy and then kinetic energy by the engine. The kinetic energy is an output of the engine system and is used to move the car. By tracing the flow of energy, you can understand how the system functions.

3. Use the temperatures of the water, the metal object, and the air to explain the flow of thermal energy in this system. What do the arrows show?

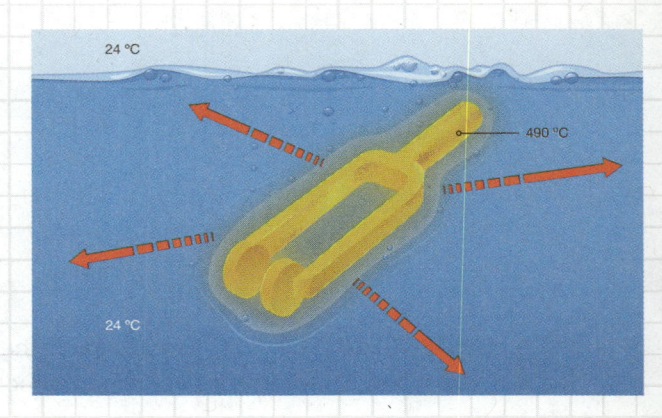

Unit 3 Chemical Processes

4. Why do the contents of the ice chest in the photo stay cold even though the air around the chest is warm?

   A. Thermal energy flows from the ice to the drink containers.

   B. Thermal energy flows from the drink containers to the ice chest.

   C. The ice chest accelerates the flow of thermal energy to the environment.

   D. The ice chest slows the flow of thermal energy from the environment to the ice and drinks.

The ice chest and its contents can be studied as a system.

Types of Energy Transfer

All matter is made up of tiny particles that are in constant motion. The particles of matter that make up an object move faster when the object is warm than when the object is cold. When thermal energy flows from one object to another, it always flows from the warmer object to the cooler object. As a result, the motion of the particles in the two objects changes. The thermal energy being transferred is known as **heat**. While heat will always move from a warmer object to a colder object, the way this energy is transfered is not always the same. Thermal energy can be transferred between objects through conduction, convection, or radiation.

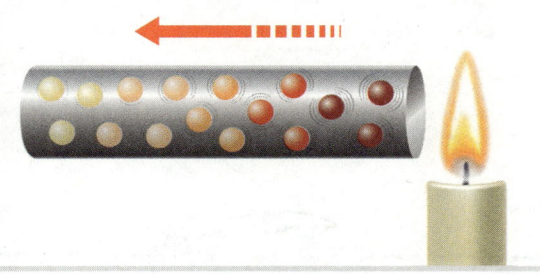

Conduction, Convection, and Radiation

Conduction Thermal energy is transferred between particles through conduction. In this example, the candle is warming one end of the metal bar. The particles in the metal bar start to move faster as they gain more thermal energy. As the particles move faster, they bump into each other and transfer thermal energy through the metal rod.

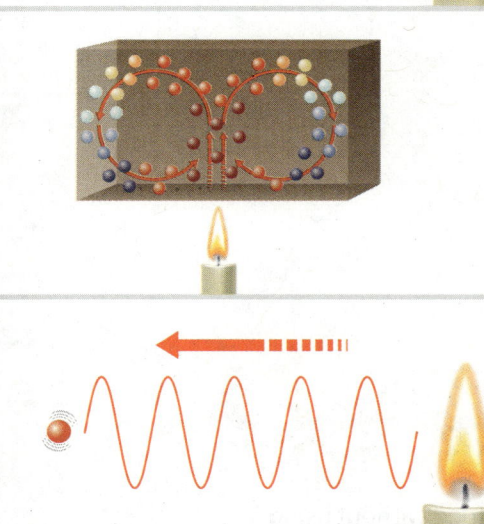

Convection Thermal energy is transferred throughout liquids and gases through convection. In this example, the candle is heating the box. As air in the box warms, the air particles begin to move faster, and the air becomes less dense. The colder, denser air sinks and pushes up the warmer air. This movement transfers thermal energy through liquids and gases.

Radiation Radiation is the transfer of energy through electromagnetic waves. In this example, the candle produces infrared radiation. This radiation travels through air. As the radiation is absorbed by particles, it is converted into thermal energy. Radiation can also travel through empty space, which is how thermal energy is transferred from the sun to Earth.

Lesson 3 Engineer it: Using Thermal Energy in a Device   177

5. The airless vacuum of space is extremely cold, but objects in space do not cool nearly as fast as you might expect. Which statement most likely explains this?

   A. Objects in space are already cold, so they do not transfer thermal energy.
   B. There is no matter in space to transfer thermal energy to by conduction or convection.
   C. Convection carries thermal energy from the sun to objects in space and keeps them warm.
   D. Radiation does not occur in space because of the lack of air.

Specially designed suits protect astronauts from the cold and airless space around them.

Model Energy Movement

If you want to understand a device that uses energy, it is important to know how energy will move through the device and any system that the device could be part of. You can map energy flows with arrows to visualize how energy flows through any system.

6. Show how thermal energy would flow through this system. Draw arrows to show the direction of thermal energy flow.

EVIDENCE NOTEBOOK
7. How would the energy flow in a device that warms food without using a flame or electricity? Record your evidence.

178 Unit 3 Chemical Processes

EXPLORATION 2

Analyzing Energy in Chemical Processes

Thermal energy is not the only form of energy. Many systems produce thermal energy when a different form of energy is transformed into thermal energy. For example, pavement can feel hot in the summer, because it absorbs energy from the sun's radiation. Other forms of energy that can be changed into thermal energy include chemical, kinetic, and electrical energy.

Energy Changes in a Hand Warmer

When a small tab in this hand warmer is bent, the sodium acetate inside the hand warmer starts to form crystals. As the crystals form, the sodium acetate releases thermal energy.

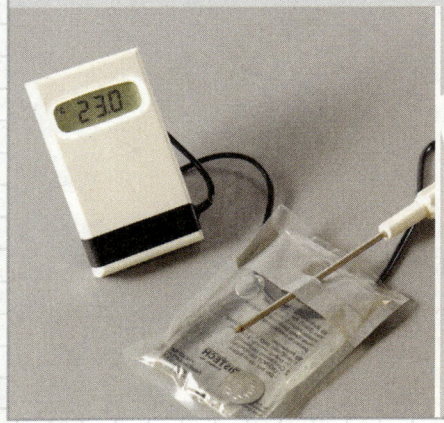

8. Which type of energy is likely changed into thermal energy in this hand warmer?
   A. electromagnetic energy
   B. electrical energy
   C. chemical energy
   D. gravitational potential energy

Energy and Chemical Processes

One way that energy can be transformed is through chemical processes. Chemical processes include chemical reactions in which the identity of matter changes, and physical changes such as a change of state or the dissolution of a solid in a liquid. Chemical processes can transform the energy stored in chemical bonds or in the arrangement of molecules into thermal energy.

Most chemical processes involve a change in energy. Some processes, such as melting ice cubes, absorb thermal energy. Other processes, like the burning of paper, release thermal energy. The change in thermal energy will depend on the change in the energy stored in the chemical bonds or molecular structures. If a large amount of a solid melts, the amount of thermal energy absorbed will be larger than if a small amount of the solid melts.

Chemical Processes and Thermal Energy

The temperature of the steel wool increased from 20.6 °C to 26.5 °C when the iron in the steel wool rusted. Vinegar was used to accelerate this normally slow reaction.

The temperature of this solution dropped from −0.8 °C to −8.0 °C when the rock salt was dissolved in the water.

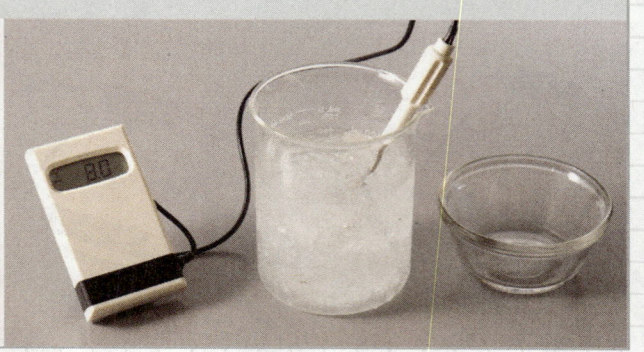

9. Draw a line connecting the chemical processes shown in the photos to the change in thermal energy that occurs during the process.

| iron rusting | absorbs thermal energy |
| salt dissolving in water | releases thermal energy |

Rates of Energy Transformation

Chemical processes do not all transform energy at the same rate. The rate of energy transformation depends on the type of chemical process. A fire releases thermal energy very quickly. Inside a muscle, a similar chemical reaction releases the energy that the muscle needs to move. This process transforms chemical energy into thermal energy at a slower rate than a fire does. The rate of energy transformation also depends on how quickly a chemical process occurs. A candle burning quickly will release energy faster than a candle that is barely burning. The muscles of a hamster running on a wheel will release energy faster than those of a sleeping hamster. Both the chemical process and the rate of the chemical process affect how quickly energy is transformed in a given situation.

EVIDENCE NOTEBOOK

10. How might the rates of energy transformation affect how the flameless heater is able to warm objects? Record your evidence.

Unit 3 Chemical Processes

Do the Math
Analyze Thermal Energy

Two things must be considered when you use a chemical process to release thermal energy. One factor is the amount of chemical energy that a process can transform into thermal energy. This can be measured as the number of joules of energy produced by one unit of reactant. The second factor to consider is how quickly the process releases energy. This rate is the number of units of reactants that react per second.

This table shows the amount of energy released when one unit of each substance combines with oxygen in a combustion reaction. Combustion reactions usually involve a fire or explosion.

Reactant	kJ/unit Released in combustion
hydrogen	286
ethanol	1,371
propane	2,219

11. Which reactant releases the most energy when a single unit is combusted?

12. In each sentence, choose the number that represents the correct answer.
   A. Under certain conditions, 6 units of hydrogen will burn in 1 second. This process releases energy at a rate of 286 / 572 / *1,716* kJ per second.
   B. Under the same conditions, 1 unit of ethanol will burn in 1 second. This process releases energy at a rate of 686 / *1,371* / 8,226 kJ per second.
   C. Under these conditions, *hydrogen* / ethanol will release more energy in 1 second.

13. Which of the following factors affect how quickly burning hydrogen, ethanol, and propane will release energy? Choose all that apply.
   A. whether the reactant burned
   B. the number of reactants in the chemical process
   C. the time when the chemical process takes place
   D. the amount of reactant burned per second

Lesson 3 Engineer It: Using Thermal Energy in a Device **181**

Factors That Affect Reaction Rates

In order to use a chemical process to control the flow of thermal energy, you must understand how the process works. Knowing the type of process and how to control the rate at which it takes place allows you to adjust the rate of the process. There are many factors that control the rates of chemical processes. The diagrams show some important factors that can be used to control the rates of chemical reactions.

Chemical Reaction Rate Variables

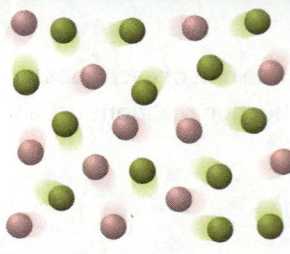

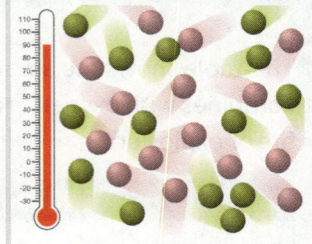

Concentration Increasing the concentration of reactants can cause a reaction to occur faster. This happens because increasing the concentration means that the reactants come into contact more often.

Temperature Increasing temperature can cause the reaction to occur faster. When particles have more energy, they move faster. The faster particles are moving, the more often they will come into contact with each other.

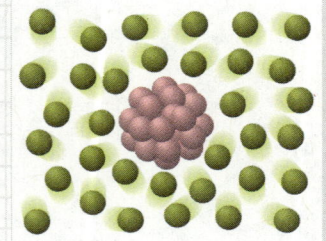

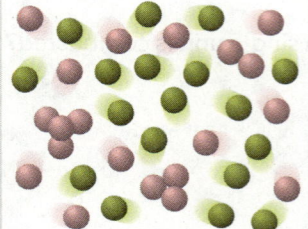

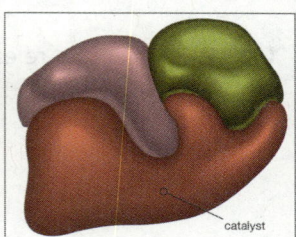

Surface Area Increasing the surface area of a solid reactant increases the reaction rate because the increased surface area allows more particles of the other reactants to collide with the particles of the solid.

Catalysts Catalysts are materials that increase the rate of a chemical reaction by bringing together reactants. The catalyst itself is not used up or changed very much.

Chemical reactions are only one type of chemical process. The rates of other chemical processes, such as dissolution or state changes, can be affected by some of these same factors. For instance, temperature can affect how quickly a solid dissolves in a liquid. The surface area of a solid can affect how quickly the solid changes state to a liquid. Not all chemical processes will be affected in the same way by these factors and some chemical processes may be affected by other factors as well. For instance, a catalyst may not have much effect on how quickly a liquid boils, but elevation of the liquid above sea level will.

14. Which statement correctly explains how increasing the reaction rate affects the thermal energy of a chemical reaction?

    A. It increases the total amount of energy absorbed or released.

    B. It decreases the total amount of energy absorbed or released.

    C. It increases the rate at which energy is transformed, but not the amount of energy of the reaction.

    D. It increases the total amount of energy transformed, but not the rate at which energy is transformed.

Language SmArts
Analyze a Chemical Process

Ammonium chloride is a white crystalline compound. When crystals of ammonium chloride are mixed with water, they dissolve to form a solution. As the crystals dissolve, the solution absorbs thermal energy. The temperature of the solution will decrease. The temperature of the solution can decrease enough to cause water on the outside of the container to freeze.

15. **Draw** Make a sketch that shows how thermal and chemical energy interact in the system made up of water and ammonium chloride.

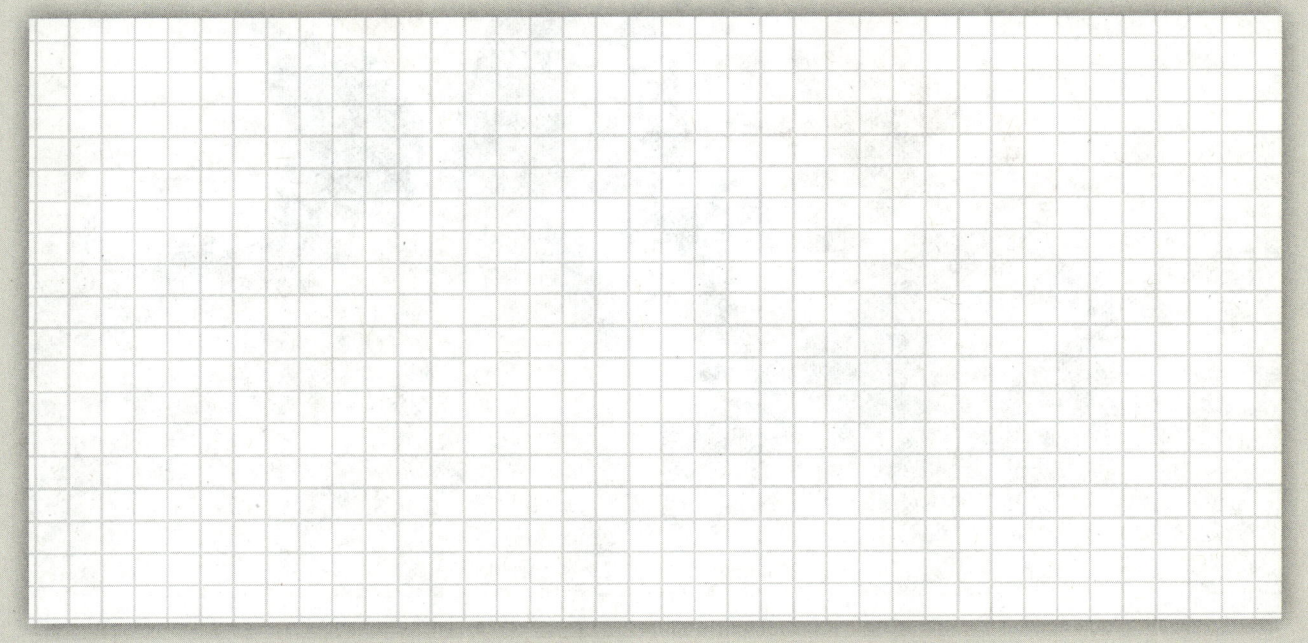

16. Describe the flow of energy shown in your sketch of the water and ammonium chloride system.

Lesson 3 Engineer It: Using Thermal Energy in a Device **183**

EXPLORATION 3

Designing a Cold Pack

When you twist an ankle or sprain your wrist, an ice pack can help reduce the swelling and pain from the injury. If you are hiking in the wilderness or playing on a ball field, ice might not be easy to find. In that case, how could you treat your hurt ankle? A chemical cold pack might be just what you need. You can carry the cold pack with you. You do not need a cooler or ice to store it. When you do need a cold pack, you just start the chemical process inside the sealed package. Within a few seconds, the pack will begin to cool.

To keep swelling down, treat a sprained ankle as soon as possible.

17. Which of the following would be included in the criteria for a chemical cold pack that you could take along on a hike? Choose all that apply.

    A. small and easy to carry
    B. becomes cold quickly when activated
    C. flexible enough to form around injured area
    D. packaging that transfers thermal energy well

Hands-On Lab
Choose a Chemical Process

Test different chemical processes that might be used in a chemical cold pack. Then calculate the temperature changes that occur. Make observations about how each chemical process might behave in a cold pack.

To design a chemical cold pack, determine what characteristics a process should have in order to be a solution to your engineering problem. Think about the criteria and constraints of the problem as you test each process. The cold pack must get cold as a result of a chemical process. The process must occur rapidly so that the cold pack is available when needed.

MATERIALS
- ammonium chloride
- baking soda
- balance
- beakers, 500 mL, (4)
- calcium chloride
- graduated cylinders, 100 mL (2)
- paper towels
- steel wool, fine
- stirrers
- thermometer
- vinegar
- water

Procedure

STEP 1 Choose a pair of liquid and solid components from Table 1 at the bottom of the page. Measure 100 mL of the liquid component into a beaker. Measure the temperature of the liquid. Record your measurement in Table 2 on the next page.

STEP 2 Add 10 grams of the solid component to the beaker. Stir the mixture. Record any changes that you observe in Table 1.

STEP 3 After 2 minutes, measure the temperature of the liquid. Record your measurement in Table 2.

STEP 4 Repeat Steps 1–3 with each of the other combinations of materials. Note any observations that might affect the usefulness of each combination.

Table 1

Liquid component	Solid component	Observations
vinegar	steel wool	
vinegar	baking soda	
water	calcium chloride	
water	ammonium chloride	

Lesson 3 Engineer It: Using Thermal Energy in a Device **185**

Analysis

STEP 5 Calculate the temperature change that takes place during each chemical process by subtracting the initial temperature from the final temperature. Record your answers in Table 2.

Table 2

Liquid component	Solid component	Starting temperature (°C)	Ending temperature (°C)	Temperature change (°C)
vinegar	steel wool			
vinegar	baking soda			
water	calcium chloride			
water	ammonium chloride			

STEP 6 Which chemical processes absorbed thermal energy? Select all that apply.
  A. vinegar/steel wool
  B. vinegar/baking soda
  C. water/calcium chloride
  D. water/ammonium chloride

STEP 7 Which process would you choose to use for your instant cold pack? What adjustments to the chemical process, if any, would you make? Include an explanation of the flow of energy in your answer and cite evidence from your observations to justify your reasoning.

How to Design a Container

After you determine the best chemical process to use for the cold pack, you will design the cold pack itself. For the cold pack to be useful, it must be ready to become cold when you need it. However, the components of the chemical process cannot mix too soon because the process cannot be repeated. You must design a way to keep the two components apart until it is time to use the cold pack. Your design should be one package that is able to keep the two components separate, so that they do not accidentally mix. Your design should also have a way to mix the two components easily, so that you can use the cold pack when you need it.

18. What criteria would apply to the packaging or container in order to make the product useful? Select all that apply.
    A. flexible
    B. brightly colored
    C. keeps components separate during storage
    D. allows easy mixing when needed

19. **Draw** Make a sketch of a possible design for the device.

20. Explain your sketch and how the components would be separated in your device. How could they be combined easily when needed?

21. **Draw** Make a sketch of the outside of your device. You may design a name and logo for your device if you like.

Choose a Material

When you choose materials for your device, you must consider how those materials could affect the function of the entire system. The device must be durable and able to form to an injured body part. It should also transfer thermal energy well. The table lists several different materials that you can consider. It shows the thermal conductivity value, which is the rate at which thermal energy passes through a material. Thermal conductivity is higher for materials that transfer thermal energy faster. Other factors may be as important, or even more important, than thermal conductivity.

Material	Thermal conductivity	Characteristics
Aluminum foil	205.00	Flexible, tears easily, hard
Glass	1.05	Rigid, strong, hard, breakable
Polythene	0.33	Flexible, strong, soft
Polystyrene	0.03	Rigid, easily punctured
Rubber	0.13	Flexible, very strong, soft

22. Which material would best meet the criteria and constraints of the cold pack? Would using multiple materials improve your design? Explain your reasoning.

TAKE IT FURTHER

Continue Your Exploration

Name: _____ Date: _____

Check out the path below or go online to choose one of the other paths shown.

People in Science
- Researching Chemical Processes
- Hands-On Labs
- Propose Your Own Path

Go online to choose one of these other paths.

Fritz Haber and Carl Bosch, Chemists

Ammonia is an important chemical in many industries and in fertilizer. The Haber-Bosch process was developed to address the need for a renewable source of ammonia. Fritz Haber, a German research chemist, developed the initial process. Haber's process reliably produced ammonia from nitrogen and hydrogen. Carl Bosch, a German industrial chemist, later engineered high-pressure equipment that could mass produce ammonia using Haber's initial process. Both men received Nobel Prizes for their work.

This process was the first industrial chemical process to use high pressure in chemical production. It combines nitrogen with hydrogen under very high pressures and temperatures. An iron catalyst allows the reaction to be carried out at a lower temperature, a still very high 400 °C to 650 °C, than would otherwise be possible.

Fritz Haber was a chemical researcher and professor who developed the chemical reaction still used to make ammonia.

Carl Bosch used the engineering design process to develop equipment to produce ammonia on a large scale.

1. How does the Haber-Bosch process demonstrate the connection between science and engineering?

TAKE IT FURTHER

Continue Your Exploration

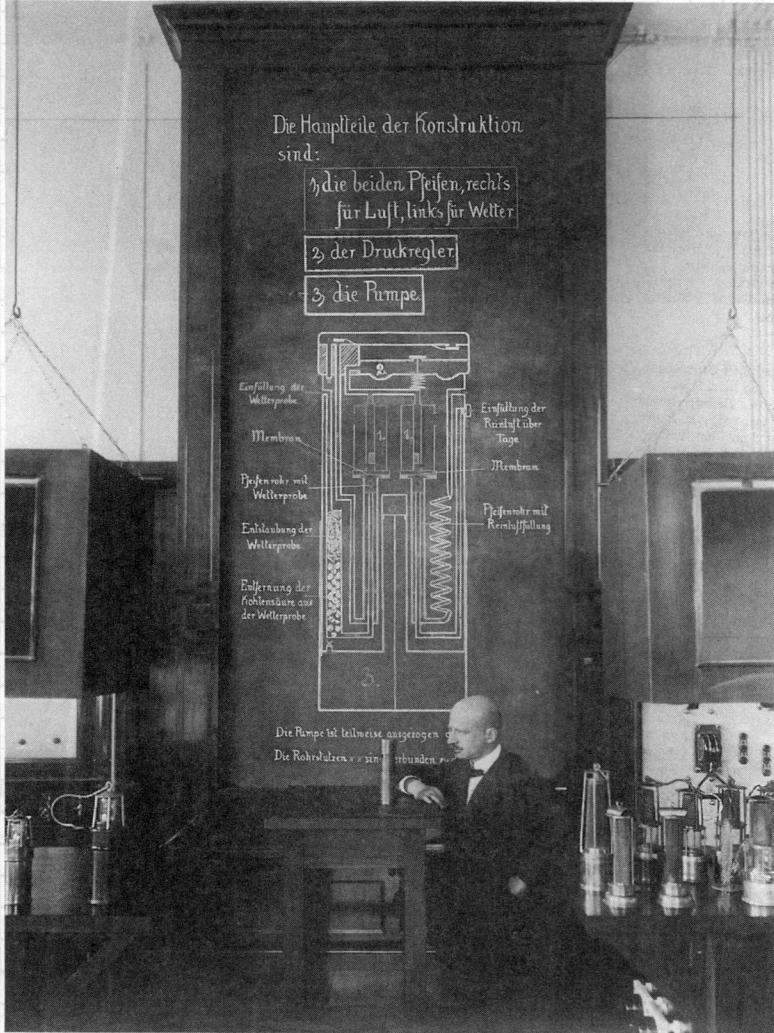

A Haber-Bosch reactor uses catalysts and a series of pipes to combine nitrogen and hydrogen under high pressure.

2. Haber's original lab reaction worked on a very small scale. Once Bosch began to scale it up, it was apparent that the reaction produced large amounts of thermal energy. Which statement best explains why this might be a problem?
   A. Higher temperature increases the reaction rate.
   B. Too much thermal energy could damage equipment.
   C. Chemical processes work better when there is less thermal energy.
   D. Catalysts are never useful when the temperature is high.

3. High temperatures can damage equipment. Which of the following are ways to keep a Haber-Bosch reactor from getting too hot? Choose all that apply.
   A. Insulate the outside of the reaction vessel.
   B. Perform the reaction in a system that transfers thermal energy well.
   C. Surround the reaction vessel with flowing water that absorbs thermal energy.
   D. Remove some catalysts from the reaction.

4. **Collaborate** As a team, research ways that chemical industries control thermal energy involved in manufacturing processes. Prepare a report or presentation to describe one method. Use a poster, models, or diagrams to assist your report or presentation.

LESSON 3 SELF-CHECK

Can You Explain It?

Name: _____ Date: _____

How can a device warm food without using fire or electricity?

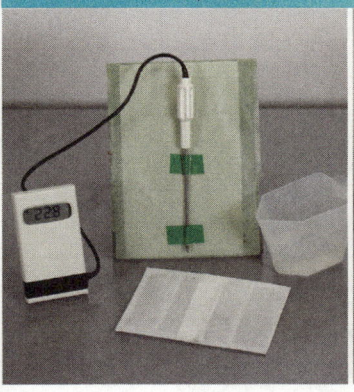

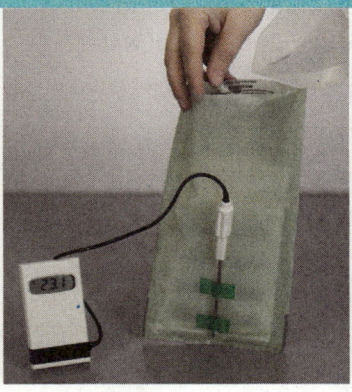

EVIDENCE NOTEBOOK
Refer to the notes in your Evidence Notebook to help you construct an explanation for how thermal energy could be released and transferred in order to warm food in a flameless cooking device.

1. State your claim. Make sure your claim fully explains how a device can warm food without using fire or electricity.

2. Summarize the evidence you have gathered to support your claim and explain your reasoning.

LESSON 3 SELF-CHECK

Checkpoints

Answer the following questions to check your understanding of the lesson.
Use the table to answer Question 3.

3. When ammonium chloride is mixed into water to form a solution, the solution absorbs thermal energy. Which process might represent 3 g of ammonium chloride mixed into a certain amount of water, and which process might represent 6 g mixed into the same amount of water?

   A. Process E represents 3 g and Process F represents 6 g.
   B. Process F represents 3 g and Process E represents 6 g.
   C. Process G represents 3 g and Process H represents 6 g.
   D. Process H represents 3 g and Process G represents 6 g.

Process	Temperature change (°C)
E	3.0
F	5.0
G	−4.0
H	−7.0

4. A high-quality sleeping bag will keep you warm even during a winter camping trip high in the mountains. How do you stay warm when the air around you is very cold?

   A. The sleeping bag produces thermal energy that keeps you warm.
   B. The sleeping bag transfers thermal energy from the air to your body.
   C. The sleeping bag slows the transfer of thermal energy produced by your body into the air.
   D. The sleeping bag increases the production of thermal energy by your body.

5. Samples of baking soda and vinegar at room temperature are mixed together. The resulting solution has a lower temperature than the original temperature of the vinegar. Which statement correctly describes how the system could be modified so that thermal energy is absorbed faster?

   A. Decrease the amount of baking soda used.
   B. Increase the concentrations of the chemicals used.
   C. Increase the size of the container used.
   D. Decrease the temperature of the environment so more energy flows away from the solution.

Use the photos to answer Question 6.

6. Which statement correctly describes what is occurring in the photos? Choose all that apply.

   A. The hand warmer is absorbing thermal energy.
   B. The hand warmer is releasing thermal energy.
   C. The hand warmer's temperature increased.
   D. The liquid in the hand warmer underwent a chemical process.

192 Unit 3 Chemical Processes

LESSON 3 SELF-CHECK

Interactive Review

Complete this page to review the main concepts of the lesson.

Systems can be used to model the flow of energy between objects.

A. Why is it useful to model systems that use energy?

Chemical processes can release or absorb thermal energy.

B. Explain how different factors affect how thermal energy is absorbed or released by a chemical process.

A chemical process can be used in a device designed to release or absorb thermal energy.

C. Describe the process that you would go through when deciding on a chemical reaction to use in a device.

Lesson 3 Engineer It: Using Thermal Energy in a Device **193**

LESSON 4

Synthetic Materials Are Made from Natural Resources

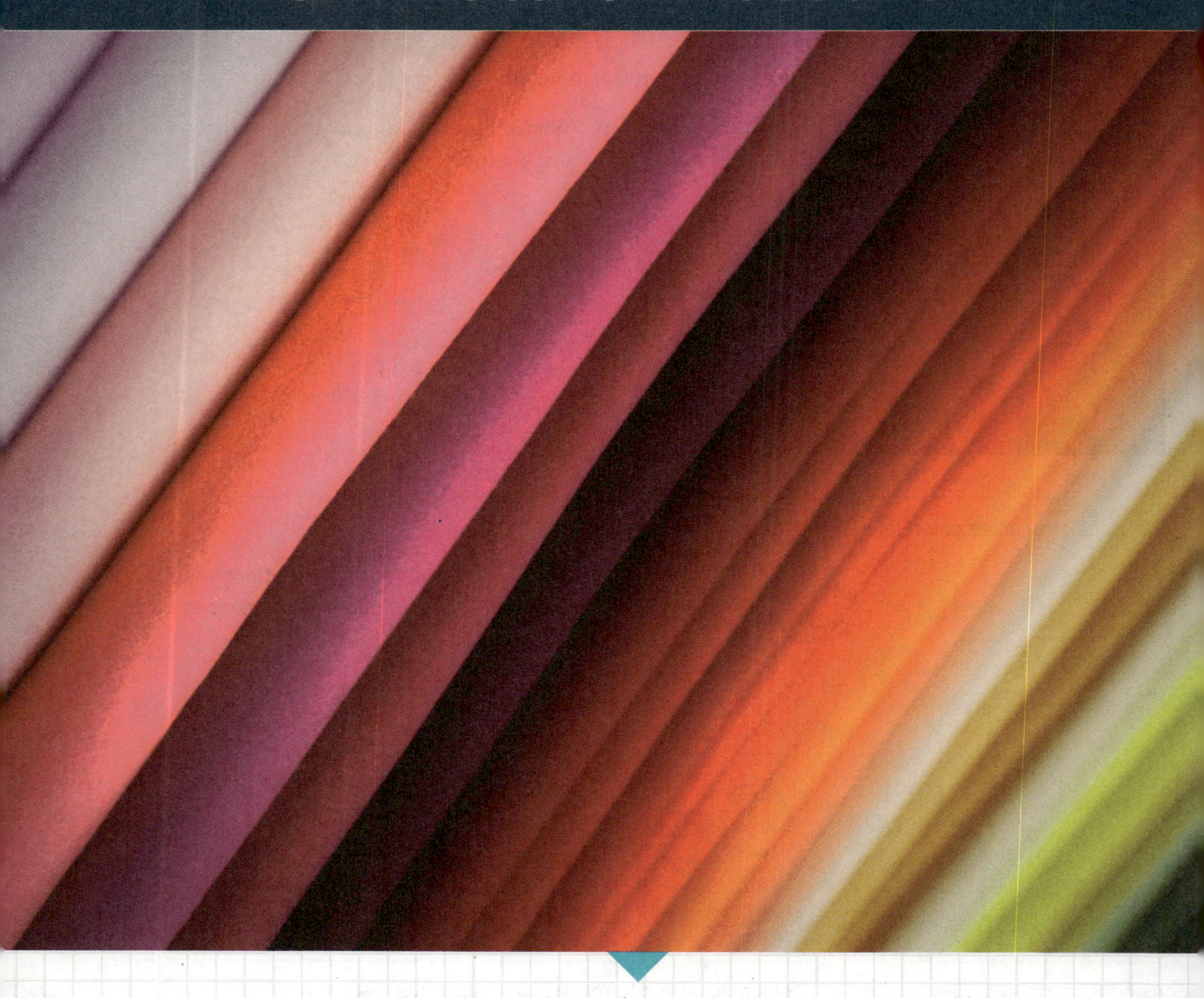

The material that makes up these fabrics is ideal for clothing. Fabric can be made with natural or synthetic materials.

Explore First

Categorizing Substances Find at least five different objects in the room and identify what substances they are made of. Categorize each of these objects as being made of either a natural or synthetic substance. Identify where the natural substances came from. How might the synthetic materials have been made?

Go online to view the digital version of the Hands-On Lab for this lesson and to download additional lab resources.

CAN YOU EXPLAIN IT?

How can a plastic kayak be made from oil?

crude oil

The synthetic material that makes up this kayak cannot be harvested or mined. It is made from crude oil, which is found naturally on Earth. Scientists and engineers have developed different types of plastics with different properties. Some synthetic materials make great kayaks, and others make beautiful fabrics.

1. How do the properties of the oil and of the plastic of the kayak differ? What makes the plastic a good choice for kayak material?

2. How do you think oil could be made into a plastic kayak?

EVIDENCE NOTEBOOK As you explore this lesson, gather evidence to help explain how oil can be made into a plastic kayak.

Lesson 4 Synthetic Materials Are Made from Natural Resources **195**

EXPLORATION 1

Analyzing Natural Resources

If you go on a picnic in the park, you are surrounded by nature. Trees, grass, birds, rocks, and water are all parts of nature. The fruit in your picnic basket comes from nature. In fact, many of the materials around you every day come from nature, including materials found inside your classroom. A desk is made by people, but the wood of the desk comes from trees. The metal comes from rocks. The fabric of your cotton clothing is made from cotton plants. Even chalk originally came from nature.

The materials and objects at this picnic are obtained from different sources.

3. What materials do you see in the photo? Which of those materials come from nature?

Natural Resources

Trees are a natural resource. A **natural resource** is a substance, material, object, or source of energy that is found in nature and that is useful or valuable to humans. Humans use natural resources as sources of food and fuel. They may also use them to make other substances or materials. Some resources are used in many ways. Trees are used to produce lumber and paper, and wood from trees is sometimes used as fuel for heating people's homes.

Natural resources may be living things or nonliving things. Plants and animals provide food and materials, such as cotton, wool, and leather. Rocks and ores provide building materials, such as granite and iron. Sources of energy, such as coal, petroleum, natural gas, and sunlight, are also natural resources.

4. Choose an object near you. Explain whether the materials that make up the object are natural resources.

Material and Energy Resources

Animals and plants provide food, materials, and fuel. Cows give us meat, milk, and materials for leather. Corn gives us food and materials to make fuel and starch.

Metals come from ores that are mined. Copper is separated from other materials in this ore by chemical reactions and physical processes.

5. Describe how you use two living and two nonliving natural resources every day.

Properties of Natural Resources

Natural resources have physical and chemical properties that make them useful. Some natural resources are used primarily for their physical properties. Copper is a good conductor of electricity and is used to make wire. Granite, a type of rock, is hard and dense. It is used in buildings. Natural resources are even used for their color. Many dyes are made from plants. For example, indigo, a blue dye that gives jeans their color, is made from the indigo plant.

Some natural resources are mainly used for their chemical properties. Fuels such as petroleum, coal, and natural gas are highly flammable. They are used as fuels. Other resources, such as metals, are not flammable. They can be used to build stoves and cookware.

Plant materials, such as grass and the grains stored in these silos, are made of many substances, including cellulose. Cellulose makes plants useful in the manufacturing of paper, fabric, and building materials.

Chemical Makeup of Natural Resources

Natural resources have many different chemical makeups. Most elements occur naturally—from aluminum to gold to uranium. However, very few elements are found in their pure form. Instead, they are combined in different ways in the compounds found in nature. Graphite is a form of pure carbon found in nature. Carbon also combines with other elements, such as oxygen and hydrogen, to make up the huge variety of substances in living things.

Most natural resources are mixtures of substances. Rocks are mixtures of different compounds. Petroleum is a mixture of carbon-based compounds. Plants and animals are made up of many substances. Cellulose is one of the many substances found in plants. It is the main substance in cotton fabric, and it makes wood strong.

Graphite is found naturally. It is soft and feels greasy. It is used to make pencil lead and lubricants.

Lesson 4 Synthetic Materials Are Made from Natural Resources 197

Natural Resources for Different Uses

The way people use natural resources has changed as technologies and needs have changed. Ancient civilizations made tools from copper, because pure copper was found in nature. They eventually learned to mix copper with other metals to make the harder material, bronze. Today, copper is used to make electrical wire and computer parts.

The resources used to meet needs have also changed. People have used trees for energy and building materials for a long time. Once engines were invented, the use of fossil fuels for energy increased. Wood is still used in building materials, but steel has made taller buildings possible.

A hickory tree is made up of many substances that give it certain physical and chemical properties.

energy

Hickory wood is flammable. When it burns, energy is released.

materials

Hickory wood is strong and hard. It is used for floors because it does not dent or scratch easily.

6. Write some of the chemical and physical properties and uses of each natural resource shown in the photos below.

Natural resource	Properties	Uses
granite		
natural gas		
wool		

198 Unit 3 Chemical Processes

Do the Math
Analyze Natural Resource Use

A single natural resource may be used in different ways. Trees are used as building materials, to make paper, for fuel, and for other applications. The way wood is used depends on the type of wood, the size of the tree, and the quality of the wood. Saw mills inspect the properties of the logs before deciding how to process them. On average, saw mills use about 25% of the wood for lumber and other building materials, 25% for paper, 35% for fuel, and 15% for other uses. The percentages may vary from mill to mill depending on the logs that they accept and the way they process the wood.

After being cut down, trees are sent to mills where they are cut and processed into lumber products.

7. A saw mill produces about 28 m³ of dried lumber each day. About 70% of the lumber is cut into boards for use in construction, 25% is used to make thin sheets of wood used in plywood, and 5% is ground into pulp and used for paper products. Fill in the table below with the cubic meters of wood that are turned into each type of material each day.

Lumber produced	70% boards	25% plywood	5% paper
28 m³			

8. It takes about 38 m³ of boards and plywood to build an average-size, single-family home. About how many days will it take for the saw mill to produce enough lumber to build a neighborhood of 100 average-size homes? Show how you found your answer.

EXPLORATION 2

Evaluating the Effects of Using Resources

Imagine that you and a friend take a long bike ride. You fill your water bottles and start out on your ride. The day is hot, and you both drink all of your water quickly. You can drink as much water as you want when you get home. But right now your water supply is gone.

9. **Discuss** Think about everything you use in a day, such as water. What are some things that affect how quickly you are able to replace the materials you used?

This bike rider has used up his supply of water to drink.

The Availability of Natural Resources

The more a resource is used, the sooner it will be used up, unless it can be replaced. As people use a resource, its supply decreases. The ability to replace a resource depends on how much of it can be found, grown, mined, or processed. When some resources are used up, no more is available. Other resources are easily replaced. Resources can be categorized by how quickly they can be replaced.

10. Look at the list below. Think about how each resource grows or forms. Determine whether it could be replaced within a human lifetime (quickly) or whether it would take many human lifetimes (slowly).
    Write _quickly_ or _slowly_ to describe how fast each resource can be replaced.
    - A. trees _____
    - B. cotton _quickly_
    - C. petroleum _____
    - D. fish _____
    - E. soil _____
    - F. coal _____

Crop resources, such as the cotton shown here, can be replaced quickly. Quickly may mean a time period as short as a growing season or as long as a human lifetime.

Unit 3 Chemical Processes

11. The following conditions occurred in a town one summer. Which could negatively affect the replacement rate of the town's water resources? Circle all that apply.

   A. The town put a limit on how often people could water their lawns.

   B. More rain fell than normal.

   C. Temperatures were higher than normal.

   D. Twice as many tourists visited the town than normal.

Nonrenewable Resources

A **nonrenewable resource** is a natural resource that cannot be replaced as quickly as it is used. Rocks and minerals form beneath Earth's surface over millions of years. Coal, petroleum, natural gas, and uranium do not form as quickly as they are used. People cannot control or speed up the geologic processes that form rocks, minerals, or fossil fuels. Therefore, these resources are almost always nonrenewable.

Cassiterite, the main ore of tin, forms in veins of rock.

Renewable Resources

A **renewable resource** is a natural resource that can be replaced at the same rate it is used, or faster. Hydroelectric energy, wind energy, solar energy, and biomass are renewable energy resources. One type of renewable resource is an *inexhaustible* resource. These resources cannot be used up by human activity. Wind and solar energy are inexhaustible renewable resources because the supply of these resources is not affected by human use.

   Another type of renewable resource is a *potentially renewable resource*. Air, water, fish, animals, and plants can be renewable material resources, but they must be managed so they do not run out. If they are used too quickly, they may not be able to be replaced. For example, passenger pigeons, such as the one in the photo, were hunted to extinction. Today in some places, there are conservation limits on hunting and fishing. These limits are designed to allow the populations of those species of animals to be maintained. Water can also be a renewable resource, but it must be managed so that it is not polluted or used more quickly than it can be replaced. Water, biomass, and animals are examples of renewable resources that could be used up if not managed.

The passenger pigeon was once the most common bird in North America, numbering 3–5 billion pigeons. Mass hunting led to extinction within 300 years. In 1914, the last passenger pigeon died in the Cincinnati Zoo.

12. Resources that come from living things can be considered either nonrenewable or renewable. Crude oil and corn both were originally living things, but oil is considered nonrenewable while corn is considered renewable. Why is there a difference in how we treat these resources?

Lesson 4 Synthetic Materials Are Made from Natural Resources   **201**

The Cycling of Matter and Energy

Matter and energy naturally cycle through Earth's systems. Living organisms will consume other organisms and move matter and energy through an ecosystem. Nonliving resources move through their own cycles, such as water's evaporating, condensing into clouds, and then raining back to the ground. The time that each of these cycles and processes take affects the availability of different natural resources. For instance, some types of bamboo can grow a foot or more a day. The giant panda, which eats bamboo, can live for over twenty years in the wild. Earth has some cycles that can last seconds and others that last thousands or millions of years.

Natural resources cycle through Earth's systems at varying rates.

Humans can dramatically affect different cycles on Earth. Due to our technology and the number of people on Earth, humans can have wide-ranging impacts on the planet. A farm can disturb how nutrients cycle through an ecosystem. A city dramatically affects the ecosystems and water cycles around it. Humans are able to affect Earth's systems in ways no other organisms are can through activities like shipping, mining, and driving cars.

Do the Math
Compare Rates of Renewal

Pine trees are harvested as building material after growing for about 40 years. About 14 acres of pine are needed to build a 1,000 ft² house. About 2 acres of bamboo are needed for the same size house. A bamboo stand regrows and is ready for harvesting in about 5 years.

Complete the equation. Then solve it.

13. About how many times as many acres of pine are needed to produce the same amount of building material as using bamboo?

    $x =$ _____ $\div$ _____

    $x =$ _____

    About _____ times as many acres of pine are needed to produce the same amount of building material as using bamboo.

14. About how many harvests of bamboo can be collected during the time it takes to fully grow one pine tree?

    $y =$ _____ $\div$ _____

    $y =$ _____

    About _____ harvests of bamboo can be collected in the same time it takes to fully grow one pine tree.

Bamboo is a fast-growing alternative to wood. It can be used as a building and flooring material.

Consequences of Using Natural Resources

A *consequence* is a result that follows naturally from the actions of a person or group. Consequences may be good or bad. They can occur immediately or over a long time. For example: You choose to ignore the alarm clock one morning. You get more sleep, but you arrive late to school and get detention. These are immediate consequences of your decision to sleep later than usual.

15. Discuss Imagine that you earn ten dollars for babysitting. You decide to go to the movies with your friends, and spend all of your money on the ticket. What is a positive consequence of this decision? What is a negative consequence of this decision?

The extraction of resources can negatively affect other resources. Offshore drilling for oil can pollute marine environments, which are resources for food and medicine.

Human use of resources results in consequences for people and the environment. Imagine a paper factory near a forest and a river. The paper is made using trees from the forest and water from the river. Paper is an important resource, but the processes used to make it pollute the river, forest, and the air. Also, using river water and trees can degrade and destroy habitats. These negative effects can be reduced by using less paper, recycling paper, using less-polluting processes in the factory, and by replanting trees.

Positive and Negative Consequences

Human use of resources has positive and negative effects on people and on the environment. For example, nuclear power plants provide energy and do not pollute the air. But they produce radioactive wastes that must be handled and stored safely for thousands of years or more.

Management of resources can help reduce negative consequences. For example, clear-cutting is a way of harvesting trees in which every tree in an area is cut down and removed. It destroys forests and increases soil erosion. But selective cutting and replanting allows trees to be used while still conserving forest resources. New energy technologies, such as those that use solar or wind power, reduce human use of nonrenewable fossil fuels.

Resources can be protected. For example, The Pacific Remote Islands Marine National Monument is an area that is protected from practices such as offshore drilling.

Lesson 4 Synthetic Materials Are Made from Natural Resources

Consequences of Resource Use

Wind is an energy resource that does not pollute the environment. It also reduces dependence on fossil fuels.

Road construction cuts through a natural ecosystem. This can interrupt migration patterns and cause animals to cross dangerous roads.

Because resource use can have both positive and negative consequences, choices have to be made about how to use them. A *tradeoff* is a situation that involves giving something up in return for gaining something else. For example, crude oil can be processed into gasoline. The tradeoff is that we gain gasoline so that people can travel, but we lose air quality because the processing and the burning of the gasoline sends pollutants into the air.

16. Give an example of how using soil, trees, or air might result in a tradeoff.

Short-Term and Long-Term Consequences

Human use of resources has both short- and long-term effects on people and on the environment. A short-term effect would last a human lifetime or less. A long-term effect would last longer than a human lifetime. Burning fossil fuels introduces pollutants to the air, including greenhouse gases and chemicals that cause acid rain and affect human health. In the short-term, these pollutants affect air quality and may affect people with asthma and other respiratory conditions. In the long-term, acid rain may cause damage to structures and environments. Greenhouse gases cause a warming of Earth's atmosphere that can last for centuries.

Wetlands are areas with standing water that covers the soil. Wetlands filter pollutants from water before they reach rivers and streams. Many wetlands have been drained or filled in so that crops can be grown or structures can be built. Short-term consequences of wetland loss include increased erosion and chemical pollution of rivers. Fish populations also decrease because wetlands are fish nurseries. Long-term consequences of wetland loss include habitat loss, extinction of organisms, and increased vulnerability of the area to severe weather and climate events.

Examples of Short-Term and Long-Term Consequences

Oil spills from deep-sea drilling can have short-term, negative consequences for wildlife. For example, oil from an oil spill coated this bird's feathers, preventing it from flying. Rescuers washed the bird with dish soap to remove the oil.

Mountaintop removal mining has long-term, negative consequences for the environment. For example, explosives are used to remove rock and soil above this coal deposit. This practice destroys habitats and leaves behind pollutants.

17. Write S to label the event as a *short-term* effect or write L to label the event as a *long-term* effect.

_____ A large, fast-flowing river is cloudy and muddy for a few days after 1000 kilograms of soil is spilled by a barge.

_____ People who live near an oil refinery are advised to avoid outdoor activity for a week after a smokestack filter malfunctions and releases toxic chemicals.

_____ A nuclear energy accident results in a permanent evacuation of a 40-kilometer radius because of radioactive contamination.

_____ An oil spill in the ocean coats penguins' feathers with oil until volunteers can clean them up.

Engineer It
Identify the Effects of an Engineering Solution

An engineering team has developed an idea for a drinking straw that filters out parasites from polluted water.

18. Identify at least one way this engineered solution might affect the health of people in a positive way or a negative way. Explain.

_____
_____
_____
_____

19. Identify at least one way this engineered solution might affect the health of the environment in a positive way or a negative way. Explain.

_____
_____
_____
_____

Lesson 4 Synthetic Materials Are Made from Natural Resources

EXPLORATION 3

Investigating Synthetic Materials

Some of the materials that make up many objects around you are not natural materials. If you look around the room, you will see a lot of plastic—in chairs, the parts of pens, eyeglasses, shoes, and even some fabrics. You will not find plastic occurring naturally in the environment. Instead, plastic must be made using chemical reactions.

Many materials that are not plastic are also not natural materials. The bicycle frame in the photo might look like painted metal, but it is much stronger and lighter than metal. Plastic and carbon fibers are mixed together to make a new material. In this case, the new material is made by a physical process and has properties of both plastic and carbon fibers.

A bicycle is made of many kinds of materials. Some are natural materials, and others are made by chemical or physical processes that form a new material.

20. **Discuss** On a separate sheet of paper, make a list of the parts of the bicycle in the photo and the materials that they might be made of. Sort your list into materials that might be natural resources and those that might not be natural resources. With a partner, compare and discuss your lists. Revise your list as you come to an agreement about the types of materials used in the bike. Share your final list with the class.

Synthetic Materials

Many parts of a bicycle are synthetic materials rather than natural materials. **Synthetic materials** are human-made materials that are produced using natural or synthetic materials. Plastics are one type of synthetic material. There are many types of plastic, from the soft plastic that makes up a water bottle to the harder plastic that is used to make eyeglass lenses. Glass and ceramics are also synthetic materials. You will not find clear window glass in nature. Many foods, medicines, and personal care products are synthetic materials or contain synthetic materials. Some fuels, such as biodiesel and ethanol, are synthetic materials as well.

21. Which of the following items are most likely made from synthetic materials: a drinking glass, orange juice, a dinner plate, a paper bag, an insulated lunch bag? Explain your reasoning.

Synthetic materials, such as this nylon, can be made in a lab.

206 Unit 3 Chemical Processes

Formation of Synthetic Materials

Most synthetic materials are formed through chemical reactions. The reactants may be natural or synthetic substances. The diagram shows the reaction that forms polyethylene, a solid used to make plastic bottles. The reactant is ethylene, a gas made from crude oil. The ethylene molecules join together to form polyethylene, the product. Polyethylene is one of the most common plastics used to make bags. Reactants change into new products in all chemical reactions. Bonds between the atoms break and new bonds form. As a result, the atoms are rearranged to make one or more new products.

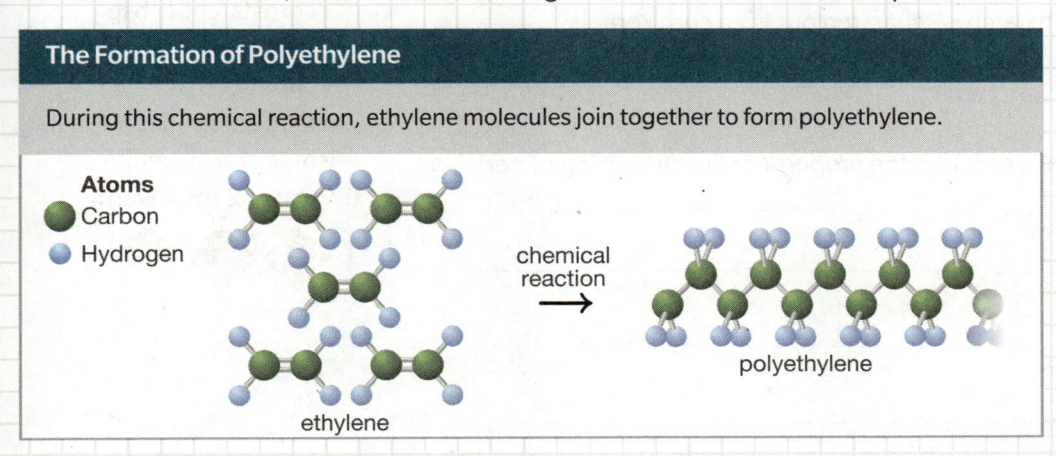

The Formation of Polyethylene

During this chemical reaction, ethylene molecules join together to form polyethylene.

Atoms
- Carbon
- Hydrogen

ethylene → chemical reaction → polyethylene

22. Act With a group, model how ethylene molecules react to form polyethylene.

Properties of Synthetic Materials

The properties of a pure substance depend on the identity and the arrangement of the atoms that make up the substance. Therefore, the products of a reaction have different chemical and physical properties than the reactants have. Ethylene and polyethylene have different properties because their atoms are arranged differently.

Some synthetic materials, such as composites, are made by mixing together materials to form a new material. Mixing is a physical change. The materials that make up the composite keep their original properties, but the composite material also has new properties. Concrete, plywood, and fiberglass are composites.

23. How do the properties of polyethylene compare to the properties of ethylene?

24. Why do synthetic materials have different properties than the materials used to make them?

EVIDENCE NOTEBOOK
25. How might the substances in oil change into the substances that make up the plastic of a kayak? Record your evidence.

Hands-On Lab
Make a Synthetic Material

Use a chemical reaction to make a ball out of a synthetic material.

Your reactants are glue, water, borax, and cornstarch. Glue is a synthetic material. Water, borax, and cornstarch are natural materials. Borax is mined from rocks, and cornstarch is separated out from corn kernels.

MATERIALS
- borax, $1\frac{1}{2}$ tsp
- cornstarch, 1 tbsp
- craft stick
- cups (2)
- food coloring (optional)
- glue, 1 tbsp, white
- water, 2 tbsp, warm

Procedure

STEP 1 In the table, describe the properties of each starting material.

Materials	Properties
borax	
cornstarch	
water	
white glue	

STEP 2 Make a borax solution by adding $1\frac{1}{2}$ tsp borax to 2 tbsp warm water in a cup. Stir until the borax disappears.

STEP 3 Add 1 tbsp glue to the second cup. If you are using food coloring, add about 3 drops.

STEP 4 To the glue, add $\frac{1}{2}$ tsp of the borax solution and 1 tbsp of cornstarch.

STEP 5 Wait 10 seconds, and then stir the contents of the cup until you cannot stir anymore.

STEP 6 Roll the mixture in your hands until it forms a smooth ball. Explore the properties of the new material.

Analysis

STEP 7 How do the properties of the synthetic material you made compare to the properties of the starting materials?

STEP 8 What caused the properties to change?

How Synthetic Materials Are Used

Synthetic materials have a wide variety of chemical and physical properties. Some are very strong and hard, while others are soft and flexible. Some have low reactivity and others undergo very specific chemical reactions. The synthetic material used to make a bouncy ball is soft and it bounces. The carbon fiber reinforced bike frame is strong and light. A medicine reacts in the body in a certain way. The properties of each of these synthetic materials make them well-suited for the ways that they are used.

Polyester is a synthetic material that is used to make clothes. It is lightweight and does not shrink when washed and dried.

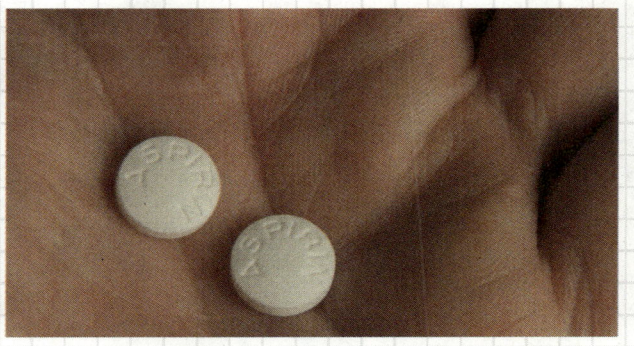

Aspirin is a synthetic material that is used as medicine. It reacts in the body to relieve pain.

26. Nylon is a synthetic material that can be made into string. Mountain climbers use ropes that are made of nylon string that is woven together and braided. What properties of the nylon rope are important for the mountain climbers who use it?

Relate the Properties and Uses of a Synthetic Material

Fiberglass is a composite material made of glass fibers mixed in plastic. The mixture of the glass fibers and plastic makes a strong, lightweight material that can be molded into many shapes. Fiberglass does not conduct electricity well.

27. List two ways that fiberglass could be used. Explain how the properties of fiberglass would be important for each use.

Fiberglass is a composite synthetic material.

EXPLORATION 4

Analyzing the Design of Synthetic Materials

Take a glance around the room and you will see many types of synthetic materials. Why are there so many kinds of synthetic materials? Scientists and engineers design them to meet specific needs. The polyester used in clothes needs to be able to be drawn into soft threads. The glass in a window needs to let in light. Engineers have even designed glass, such as the glass in the photo, that does not break as easily as other glass.

28. What are two uses of glass? How do the requirements of these two uses differ?

This glass might shatter when an object hits it, but it does not break apart. This glass can help reduce damage when it is used for windows in places where there are hurricanes.

Types of Synthetic Materials

All synthetic materials are made by chemical and physical processes, instead of being extracted from a natural resource. Plastic is one type of synthetic material. The starting materials for most plastics come from oil, which is a natural resource.

Plastics are polymers. **Polymers** are long molecules that are made up of five or more repeating units. Recall the reaction of ethylene to form polyethylene. Polyethylene is a polymer that is made of repeating ethylene units.

29. Nonstick cooking pans are easy to clean, because they are coated with a polymer. What properties of the polymer meet the specific needs of this application?

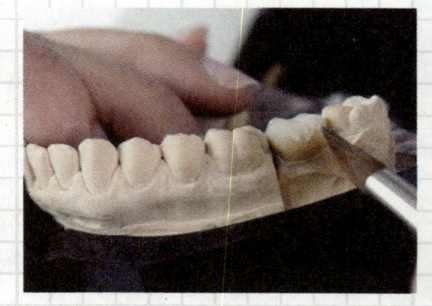

A strong composite made of a polymer and glass is used in tooth-colored fillings and crowns.

Composites are synthetic materials that are made from a mixture of two or more materials. Polymers are used to make some composites, such as fiberglass. Dental fillings and tooth-shaped caps that cover teeth, called crowns, can be made using composite material made from a polymer and glass. This material is strong and the same color as teeth.

EVIDENCE NOTEBOOK
30. How could a chemical reaction change oil into a new material with different properties? What properties of the plastic are important for a kayak? Record your evidence.

Medicine

Most medicines are synthetic materials that are designed to have specific chemical properties. Medicines are used to treat specific conditions, such as diabetes, pain, and allergies. Many people with diabetes take insulin. While some substances, such as insulin, are found naturally in the body or environment, it is often easier and more economical to synthesize the substance. Genetically modified bacteria produce most of the insulin that is used as medicine today.

Materials for Products

Synthetic materials are used in many products, including paints, building materials, clothing, and electronics. Different materials are made by using different combinations of starting substances, which may be natural or synthetic materials. Plastics can have a variety of properties for different uses—from thin plastic films used for sandwich bags to hard plastic used for car bumpers. Materials such as concrete and plywood are used in construction. Some synthetic materials even glow to light up computer screens.

Synthetic materials are designed for use in some electronic screens to provide properties such as resolution and brightness.

31. Engineer It Synthetic materials such as organic light-emitting diodes, called *OLEDs*, are used to make some computer and television screens. These materials glow when an electric current is applied to them. OLEDs that glow different colors are combined to make screens. What are some of the criteria to consider when designing a computer or phone screen? What properties of OLED materials would engineers try to produce when they make the materials?

Foods

Synthetic materials are added to many foods today to help them last longer or add color and flavor. Preservatives, such as citric acid, make food last longer by slowing chemical reactions or the growth of mold and bacteria. Some synthetic materials in food are found in nature. Citric acid and banana flavoring are found in fruits or seeds. However, citric acid and banana flavoring are also made from other materials.

Fuels

Some fuels are synthetic materials that are made from natural materials. Ethanol is added to gasoline. Ethanol is made from materials in plants, such as corn and wood. Algae can also be used to make fuel. Algae produce oils that can be turned into biodiesel. The algae may also be genetically modified to produce more oil than they normally would.

32. The plant and algae resources used to make biofuels can be regrown after they are used. How does this make biofuels different from fossil fuels?

Algae make oils that can be turned into biodiesel, which is a fuel that is used in some vehicles.

Lesson 4 Synthetic Materials Are Made from Natural Resources

Language SmArts
Determine Sources and Uses of Synthetic Materials

Vanilla is a common flavor in many foods, including ice cream, cookies, and cereal. It is also used as a scent in candles. It is found naturally in vanilla beans, but most vanilla flavoring that is added to food is the synthetic substance vanillin. Synthetic vanillin is chemically the same as the main substance that gives vanilla beans their vanilla flavor and scent. How and why is synthetic vanillin made?

You can find information about how synthetic vanillin, or almost any synthetic material, is made and how it is used. However, some of that information may not be reliable. When you are looking for information about chemical reactions, primary sources such as scientific journals with research articles are reliable sources of information. But, they may not be easy to understand. Secondary sources like university websites, chemical societies, and science magazines are good places to look. They try to present accurate information, even if they did not gather it. Company websites may be reliable sources for certain types of information. The companies are experts on how they make materials and the properties of those materials. However, the companies have biases because they make money from the material. Websites for organizations that promote certain points of view are also likely to present biased information.

Possible sources of information
a nationally accredited college research department
an independently funded science organization
a government website
a national research lab
a company that makes the material
an organization that supports a natural diet
a society of professional materials scientists or chemists
an organization that promotes the use of food additives
a popular science magazine

33. Which of the sources listed above would be the most reliable sources of information about synthetic vanillin? Would some sources be reliable for certain types of information, but not others?

_____
_____
_____
_____
_____

34. Research how synthetic vanillin is made. What are the sources of the starting materials? Are there advantages or disadvantages to using synthetic vanillin? Should people choose foods with natural vanilla over synthetic vanillin? On a sheet of paper, write a marketing pitch for synthetic vanillin for a consumer audience.

TAKE IT FURTHER

Continue Your Exploration

Name: _____ Date: _____

Check out the path below or go online to choose one of the other paths shown.

Careers in Engineering
- Desalination
- Hands-On Labs
- Propose Your Own Path

Go online to choose one of these other paths.

Biomass Engineer

Biomass is organic matter that can be processed to make fuel. Biomass engineers apply engineering practices to process biomass into biofuel. Some biomass engineers focus on ensuring that the source of the biomass remains a renewable resource.

Biomass engineers and biologists work together in teams. These teams develop and test cost-efficient ways to make biofuels. They conduct research and use technology to find ways to turn plant waste into biofuel sources. They come up with environmentally safe ways to get rid of or use biomass waste. Biomass engineers also help design machines that use biofuel. Biomass engineers need at least a bachelor's degree in engineering or a related science field.

This biomass engineer investigates the quality of biofuel made from algae, a type of organism that grows in many parts of the world.

Making Biofuel

Using biomass for fuel began when humans first built fires with wood. Wood is still the largest biomass energy resource worldwide.

Many types of biomass can be used to produce biofuel. For example, used vegetable oils and animal fats can be turned into biodiesel fuel to run a school bus. Any plant matter—such as wood shavings, grass, leaves, algae, wheat straw, and corncobs—can be turned into biofuel. Some common biofuel sources include soybeans, corn, and waste products from wood production. In the future, biomass engineers hope to find new ways to make fuel, plastics, chemicals, and other products from plant matter.

Farmers used to harvest soybeans only for food. Now they harvest the soybeans and the rest of the plant matter too. Stalks, stems, and leaves are used to produce biofuel.

TAKE IT FURTHER

Continue Your Exploration

Use the circle graph to answer Questions 1–2.

1. What can you conclude from the information shown in the graph?
   A. Used cooking oil is used more than canola oil to produce biofuels in the United States.
   B. People in the United States use twice as much animal fat for biofuel as they do soybean oil.
   C. More corn oil is used for biofuel in the United States than was used in the past.
   D. More people in the United States would use corn oil if there were no canola oil.

Sources of Biofuels in the United States

- Soybean oil: 52%
- Animal fats: 14%
- Used cooking oil: 14%
- Corn oil: 11%
- Canola oil: 8%
- Other: 1%

Source: U.S. Energy Information Administration, Monthly Biodiesel Production Report with data for December 2015, February 2016

2. A biomass engineering team is developing a new way to power lawnmowers by using biofuel. What might influence their decision about which oil to use? Circle all that apply.
   A. Soybean oil is the most common source of biofuels in United States.
   B. A new opportunity for using used cooking oil might encourage people to recycle.
   C. Canola oil is one of the least common sources of biofuels in the United States.
   D. Engineers would not want to use a type of biofuel that is already in use.

3. Which of these is a positive consequence of using biomass as an energy resource?
   A. No burning is required.
   B. More new machines are designed.
   C. It is potentially renewable.
   D. No waste is produced.

4. **Collaborate** Biofuel can be made from wood, grass clippings, leaves, crops, or crop waste. Methane can be collected from rotting garbage and community landfills to produce biofuel. Ethanol can be made from fruit or other crops, such as corn. These energy resources can be used to do the same work as fossil fuels.

   Together with a partner, come up with an idea to power a household item with a biofuel. Draw and label a diagram to show your idea. Present your diagram to the class, along with any new or different ideas you and your partner had about promoting biomass energy.

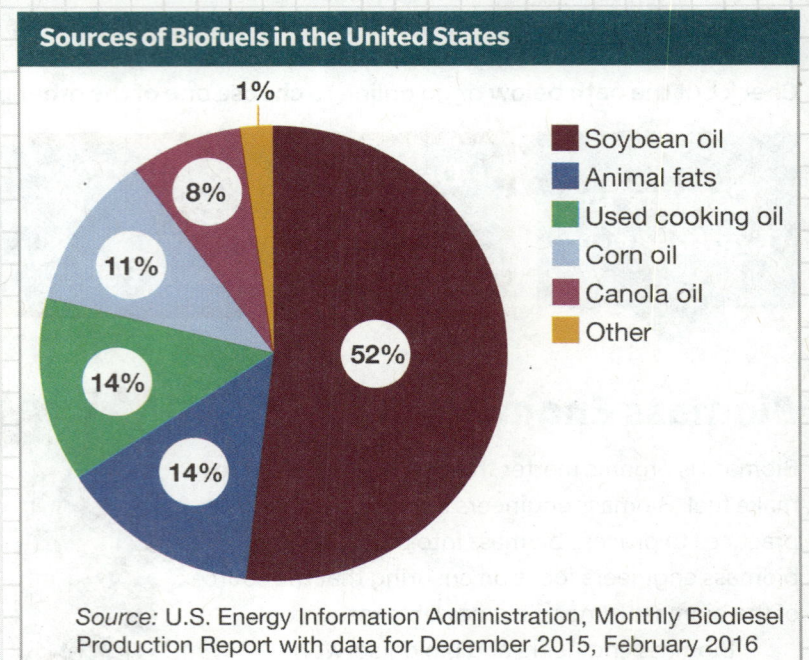

LESSON 4 SELF-CHECK

Can You Explain It?

Name: _____   Date: _____

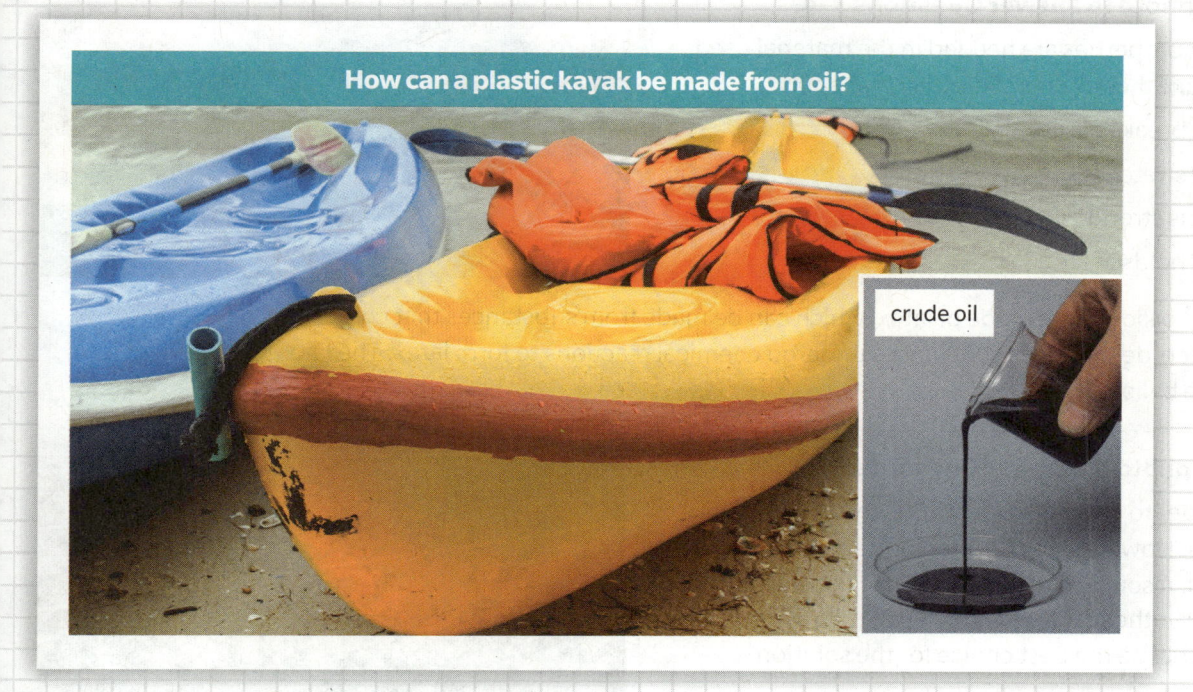

How can a plastic kayak be made from oil?

crude oil

📋 **EVIDENCE NOTEBOOK**
Refer to the notes in your Evidence Notebook to help you construct an explanation for how a plastic kayak can be made from crude oil.

1. State your claim. Make sure your claim fully explains how a plastic kayak can be made from oil.

2. Summarize the evidence you have gathered to support your claim and explain your reasoning.

Lesson 4 Synthetic Materials Are Made from Natural Resources **215**

LESSON 4 SELF-CHECK

Checkpoints

Answer the following questions to check your understanding of the lesson.

Use the photo to answer Questions 3–4.

3. What properties are needed in the material used to make these items? Select all that apply.
   A. It breaks easily.
   B. It stretches.
   C. It is strong.
   D. It holds in air.

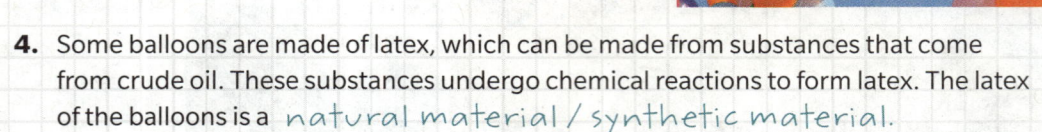

4. Some balloons are made of latex, which can be made from substances that come from crude oil. These substances undergo chemical reactions to form latex. The latex of the balloons is a *natural material / synthetic material.*

Use the photo to answer Questions 5–6.

5. In order to use a field for sports, the field needs grass. However, sports often quickly destroy grass. A solution to this problem can be achieved with synthetic materials. Why might a synthetic material be the best choice for the solution?
   A. Synthetic materials can be designed to fit a certain need.
   B. Synthetic materials are easier to make than obtaining natural materials.
   C. The use of natural materials has a negative impact on the environment.

6. What properties of plastic make it useful for fake grass? Select all that apply.
   A. It can be colored green.
   B. It is durable.
   C. It can be made into thin strips.
   D. It breaks down in the sun.

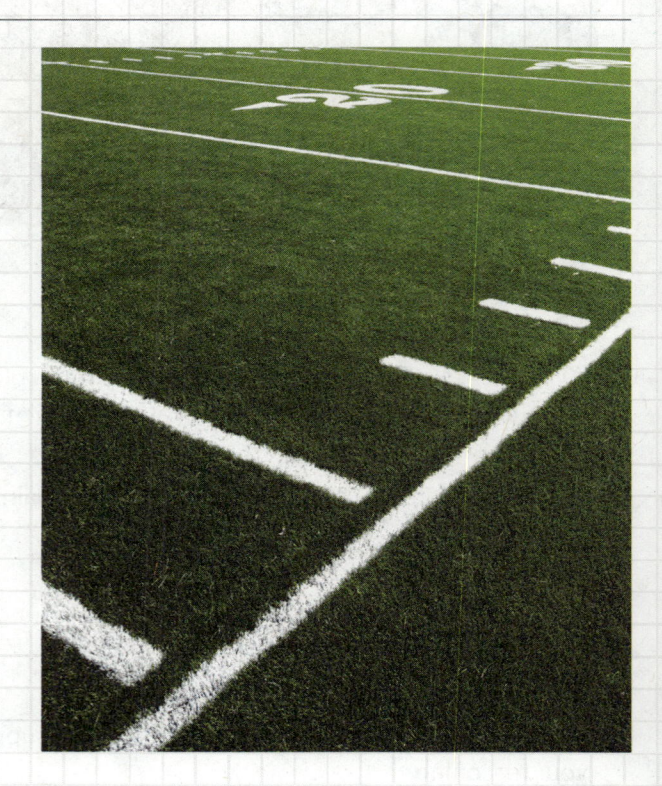

7. Are plants and animals potentially renewable natural resources?
   A. Yes, because some plants and animals are resources that can be replaced at the same rate they are used, if managed well.
   B. No, because it is not possible for humans to use plant and animal resources at a faster rate than they can be replaced.
   C. No, because plants and animals are inexhaustible resources.
   D. Yes, because we use plant resources at the same rate as we use animal resources.

LESSON 4 SELF-CHECK

Interactive Review

Complete this section to review the main concepts of the lesson.

Natural resources are found in nature and are used by humans.

A. What properties of a natural resource make it useful to humans as a material or energy source?

Natural resources can be classified as renewable or nonrenewable.

B. What is the difference between a renewable resource and a nonrenewable resource?

Synthetic materials are made by people using chemical reactions or by mixing together materials.

C. Explain why chemical reactions are used to form synthetic materials.

Engineers design synthetic materials to meet specific needs.

D. Why are synthetic materials sometimes used when designing a way to improve existing materials?

Lesson 4 Synthetic Materials Are Made from Natural Resources

UNIT 3 CONNECTIONS

Choose one of the activities to explore how this unit connects to other topics.

☐ People in Engineering Connection

Mahmooda Sultana, Engineer Dr. Mahmooda Sultana has a PhD in chemical engineering and is a researcher at NASA. She develops sensors using nanocrystal semiconductors and graphene, a one atom thick material made of carbon. The sensors made from nanocrystal semiconductors are designed to detect the chemical make-up of substances and the graphene-based sensors are designed to detect oxygen concentrations.

Research ways that the chemical make-up of a substance can be measured. Develop a presentation that discusses one way that chemicals can be measured and the importance of these measurements.

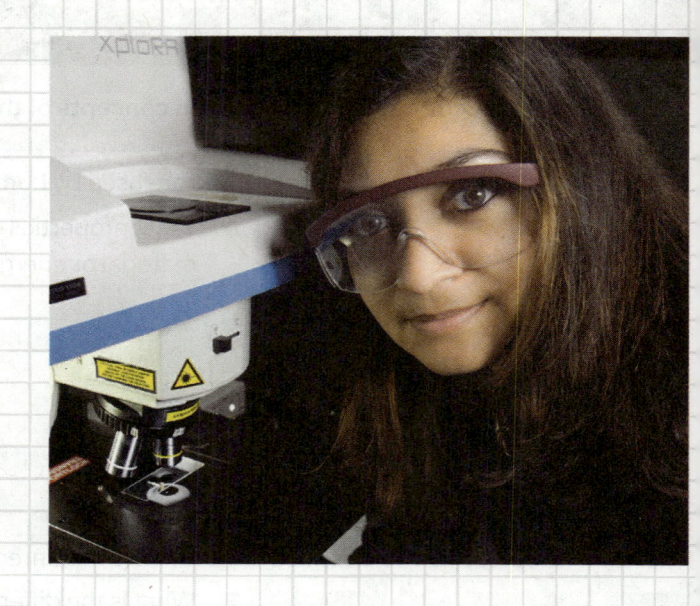

☐ Health Connection

The Chemistry of Digestion When you eat food, it is physically changed into small pieces through chewing. Carbohydrates, proteins, and fats are then chemically changed by reactions with enzymes and are absorbed into the bloodstream. Carbohydrates are converted to glucose, proteins become amino acids, and fats become glycerol and fatty acids.

Research the main category of your favorite food: carbohydrates, proteins, or fats. Then investigate how long it takes for that food to be chemically converted in your body and how your body uses the digested products. Create a short presentation on your findings.

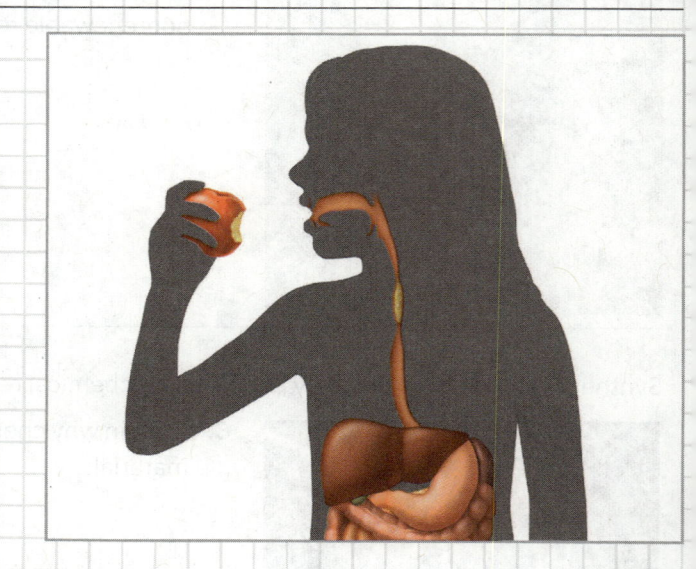

☐ Environmental Science Connection

Acid Rain Burning fossil fuels produces sulfur dioxide and nitrogen oxides. These oxides react with water and oxygen in the atmosphere, producing sulfuric acid and nitric acid. Acid rain results when these products are carried to the ground with precipitation. Acid rain is harmful when it gets into soil and waterways because it can damage structures and organisms.

Research a specific animal or plant, and describe how it is affected by chemical reactions from acid rain. Create a pamphlet, including visuals, to showcase your findings.

This statue has been damaged by acid rain.

UNIT 3 REVIEW

Name: _____ Date: _____

Complete this review to check your understanding of the unit.

Use the photos to answer Questions 1–2.

1. The image of the fried eggs is / *is not* an example of a chemical reaction. The image of the whisked eggs is / *is not* an example of a chemical reaction.

2. Which of the following statements are true about the reaction rates of cooked eggs? Circle all that apply.
   A. Increasing the temperature causes the reaction to occur more slowly.
   B. Increasing the temperature causes the reaction to occur more quickly.
   C. Increasing the temperature causes the eggs' particles to have more energy and move faster.
   D. Increasing the temperature causes the eggs' particles to lose energy and move more slowly.

3. What are some possible benefits of using a synthetic material? Select all that apply.
   A. Synthetic materials can replace all natural materials.
   B. Synthetic materials can help preserve food and are used in medicine.
   C. Synthetic materials can be less expensive alternatives to natural materials.
   D. All synthetic materials can be recycled.

Use the graph to answer Question 4.

4. Why does increasing the temperature of the water increase the rate of the chemical reaction shown in the graph?
   A. Faster moving particles will come into contact with each other less frequently.
   B. Faster moving particles will come into contact with each other more frequently.
   C. Changing the temperature does not change the motion of the particles.
   D. Warmer water contains more water particles.

Effect of Temperature on Effervescent Tablets

This graph shows the time it takes for an effervescent tablet to finish reacting in water at different temperatures.

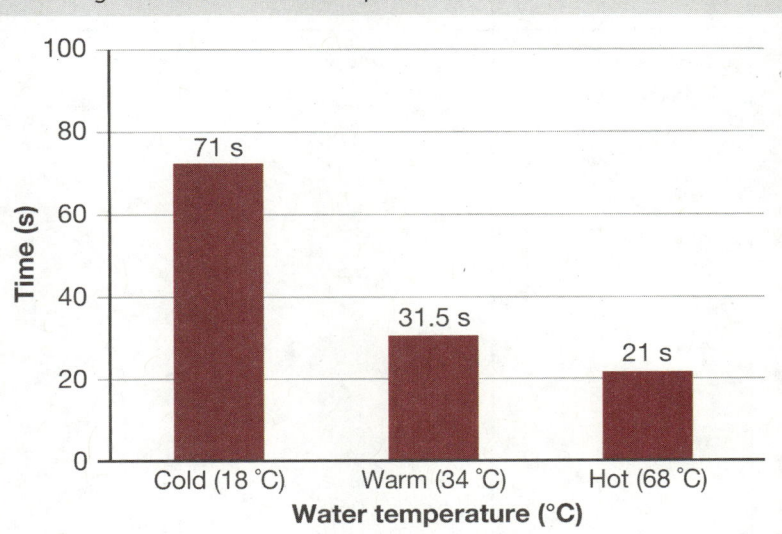

Water temperature	Time (s)
Cold (18 °C)	71 s
Warm (34 °C)	31.5 s
Hot (68 °C)	21 s

Unit 3 Chemical Processes

UNIT 3 REVIEW

5. Complete the table by providing descriptions of how each of type of change relates to the properties of matter.

Properties of Matter	Physical Changes	Chemical Reactions	Changes in Energy
Arrangement of Atoms	During physical changes, the arrangement of atoms (molecular structure) of a substance remains the same.		
Physical Properties of Matter			
Chemical Properties of Matter			

220 Unit 3 Review

UNIT 3 REVIEW

Name: _____   Date: _____

Use the image and the molecular model to answer Questions 6–9.

The rust forming on this bike is the product of a chemical reaction between iron and oxygen, as shown in the molecular model.

iron + oxygen → iron oxide

6. Describe how particles of iron (Fe) and oxygen (O_2) react to produce iron oxide (Fe_2O_3), also known as rust.

7. Write a balanced chemical equation based on the molecular model shown in the image. Describe the equation in a sentence.

8. The formation of iron oxide is a slow reaction that releases thermal energy. Describe what that means and explain the transfer of energy that is occurring.

9. Salt can act as a catalyst to the formation of iron oxide. What would happen if the bike were exposed to saltwater?

Unit 3 Chemical Processes   221

UNIT 3 REVIEW

Use the image to answer Questions 10–12.

10. Rubber, which is made from latex, is very water resistant, slip proof, and durable. Describe some useful everyday applications for rubber.

11. A special tapping knife is used to shear off a thin layer of the bark so that latex can flow into a bucket. After the latex is collected, formic acid is added to coagulate the liquid latex into solid rubber. What problems would arise if synthetically-produced formic acid were not added to the natural latex?

Latex is collected from a rubber tree in Phuket Province, Thailand.

12. Rubber production influences the local people harvesting latex, the trees and environment from which it is harvested, and the land where rubber products are discarded. What are possible negative and positive effects of rubber production and disposal?

UNIT 3 PERFORMANCE TASK

Name: _____   Date: _____

Save the Sea Turtle Eggs!

As a marine biologist, you are responsible for transporting sea turtle eggs that may be in danger after a storm. It is important to keep the eggs at a safe temperature (approximately 27 °C to 33 °C) for the 30 minutes it takes to drive to the animal hospital. You have three possible combinations of materials available to create an egg warmer to maintain the proper temperature:

- ammonium nitrate crystals and a pouch of water
- fine iron powder, salt, and water
- sodium acetate solution and a small metal disc

The steps below will help guide your research to develop an egg warmer.

Engineer It

1. **Define the Problem** Clearly define the criteria and constraints associated with the design of the egg warmer.

UNIT 3 PERFORMANCE TASK

Engineer It

2. **Conduct Research** Research each of the three possible material combinations you could use to make an egg warmer. Are you looking for a chemical process that releases or absorbs thermal energy?

3. **Analyze Data** Create a decision matrix to analyze each material option. Describe the strengths and weaknesses of each choice.

4. **Identify and Recommend a Solution** Based on your research, construct a written explanation describing which combination of materials would make the best egg warmer. How would you design the warmer to safely carry eggs?

5. **Communicate** Prepare a presentation of your recommendation explaining the best materials and design to make a portable egg warmer.

✓ **Self-Check**

	I identified the problem.
	I researched the three combinations of materials to determine how well they meet the criteria and constraints of the problem.
	I analyzed my research and data to create a decision matrix.
	My solution is based on evidence from research, data, and an analysis of my decision matrix.
	My recommended design was clearly communicated to others.

UNIT 4

Matter and Energy in Organisms and Rock

How does the flow of energy drive the cycling of matter in natural systems at different scales?

Unit Project	226
Lesson 1 The Flow of Energy Drives the Cycling of Matter in Organisms	228
Lesson 2 Chemical Reactions Provide Energy for Cells	248
Lesson 3 The Flow of Energy Drives Weathering, Erosion, and Deposition	266
Lesson 4 The Flow of Energy Drives the Rock Cycle	284
Unit Review	309
Unit Performance Task	313

Mountain goats are adapted to life on the rocky peaks formed by Earth's processes.

You Solve It How Does a Tabletop Biosphere Work?

Choose the organisms to place in your tabletop biosphere. Estimate the biomass of each organism required and run a simulation to see if your biosphere is sustainable.

Go online and complete the You Solve It to explore ways to solve a real-world problem.

UNIT 4 PROJECT

Investigate Fossil Fuels

This refinery is producing gasoline from crude oil.

A. Look at the photo. On a separate sheet of paper, write down as many different questions as you can about the photo.

B. Discuss With your class or a partner, share your questions. Record any additional questions generated in your discussion. Then select the most important questions from the list that are related to how the use of fossil fuels cycles matter among Earth's subsystems. Write them below.

C. Select a fossil fuel, such as coal, natural gas, or oil, to research. List some resources you might use to find out how fossil fuels are formed, extracted, and used by humans.

D. Use the information above, along with your research, to develop a model that shows how the use of fossil fuels cycles matter in the Earth system.

Discuss the next steps for your Unit Project with your teacher and go online to download the Unit Project Worksheet.

UNIT 4

Language Development

Use the lessons in this unit to complete the network and expand your understanding of these key concepts.

- Similar term
- Phrase
- Cognate
- Example
- Definition

molecule

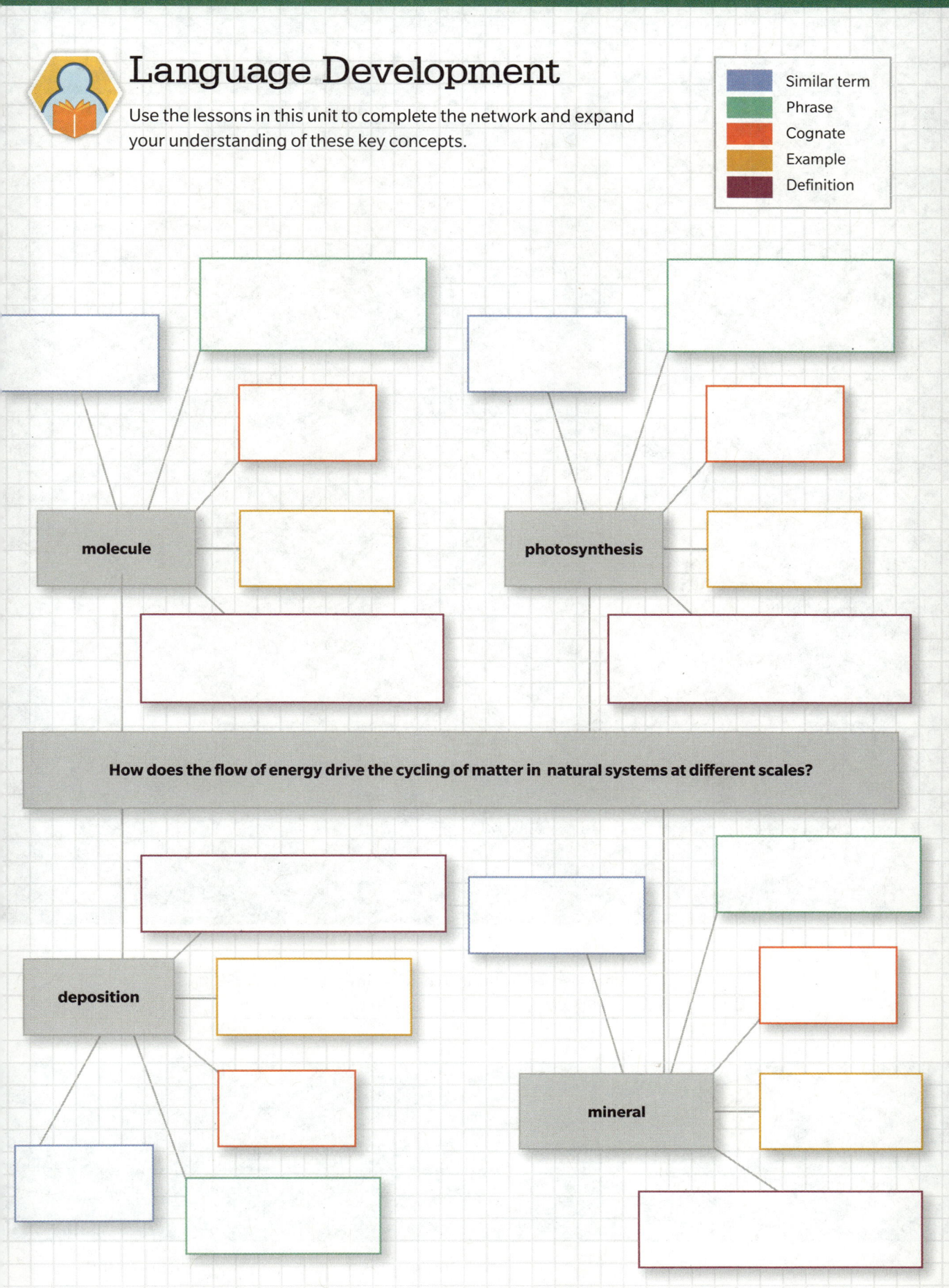

photosynthesis

How does the flow of energy drive the cycling of matter in natural systems at different scales?

deposition

mineral

Unit 4 Matter and Energy in Organisms and Rock **227**

LESSON 1

The Flow of Energy Drives the Cycling of Matter in Organisms

This kingfisher gets matter and energy from eating fish and other animals.

Explore First

Analyzing Food Labels Collect nutrition information labels from a variety of foods. Construct a table to compare the amounts of fat, protein, sugar, and vitamins in the different foods. Which foods do you think are the most nutritious? Which are the least nutritious?

CAN YOU EXPLAIN IT?

What happened to the matter and energy that were in these fruits when they were first picked?

These fruits were once part of living plants. After they were picked they began to *decompose*, or break down. Eventually, a person looking at the space where these fruits lay will see no trace of them.

1. **Discuss** What is another example in which matter changes over time? How does your example compare or contrast with the example shown here?

EVIDENCE NOTEBOOK As you explore this lesson, gather evidence to explain what happened to the matter and energy in the decomposed fruits.

Lesson 1 The Flow of Energy Drives the Cycling of Matter in Organisms 229

EXPLORATION 1

Describing Matter and Energy in Organisms

Over 250 million years ago, many species of plants and animals, including pine trees, dinosaurs, giant sea reptiles, and tiny mammals, lived on Earth. A mass extinction event 66 million years ago resulted in the loss of many species, including all dinosaurs and plesiosaurs. What happened to their bodies? Did they just disappear?

Plesiosaurs were giant sea reptiles that lived at the same time as dinosaurs.

2. **Discuss** What do you think happened to the materials that made up the bodies of plesiosaurs? Do you think these materials are still on Earth today?

Matter in Organisms

The bodies of all living things are made of matter. **Matter** is anything that has mass and takes up space. A tree's leaves, trunk, and roots are made of matter. All the parts of your body are also made of matter. Even the tiniest organism, such as a single-celled bacterium, is made of matter. Nonliving things, such as rock, water, and air are all made of matter.

Living things need matter to survive because it provides them with the materials needed to grow and carry out life processes. For example, the food you eat and the air you breathe are made of matter.

230 Unit 4 Matter and Energy in Organisms and Rock

Atoms Are the Building Blocks of Matter

Most of the matter in organisms is contained in cells, the smallest unit of living things. Cells are made of even smaller units called atoms. An *atom* is the smallest unit of a substance that maintains the properties of that substance. Substances that contain only one type of atom are called *elements*. Nearly 100 elements occur naturally on Earth. Elements are the most basic substances on Earth. Oxygen and hydrogen are examples of elements. A substance made of atoms of two or more different elements is a *compound*. For example, oxygen and hydrogen combine to form water.

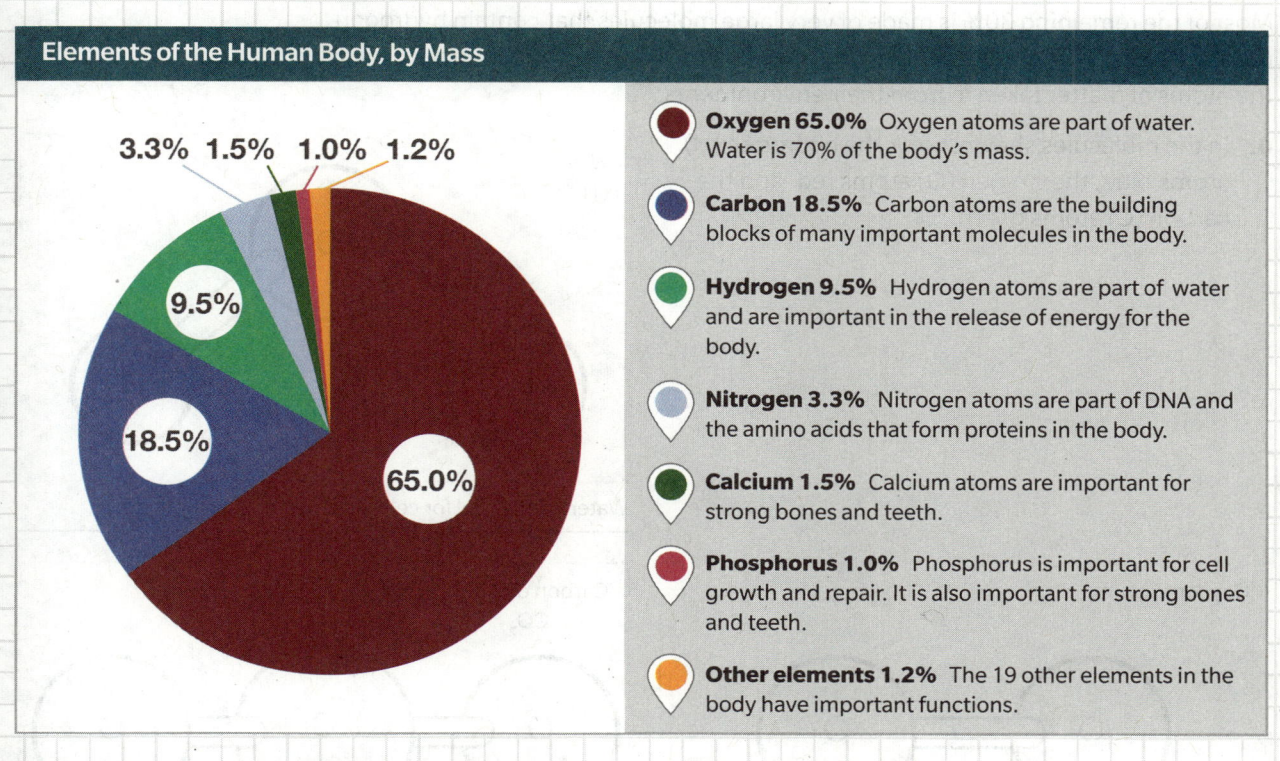

Elements of the Human Body, by Mass

Element	Percentage	Description
Oxygen	65.0%	Oxygen atoms are part of water. Water is 70% of the body's mass.
Carbon	18.5%	Carbon atoms are the building blocks of many important molecules in the body.
Hydrogen	9.5%	Hydrogen atoms are part of water and are important in the release of energy for the body.
Nitrogen	3.3%	Nitrogen atoms are part of DNA and the amino acids that form proteins in the body.
Calcium	1.5%	Calcium atoms are important for strong bones and teeth.
Phosphorus	1.0%	Phosphorus is important for cell growth and repair. It is also important for strong bones and teeth.
Other elements	1.2%	The 19 other elements in the body have important functions.

3. Which element makes up most of the mass of the human body? Why do you think the body is made of a large percentage of this element? Use evidence from the text and the diagram to support your answer.

Lesson 1 The Flow of Energy Drives the Cycling of Matter in Organisms **231**

Atoms Bond to Form Molecules

Organisms need many different kinds of molecules, such as water, protein, and carbohydrates, for life processes. A **molecule** is made up of two or more atoms held together by chemical bonds. Molecules provide the matter and energy needed for cell structure and function. For example, cells use the atoms and the energy stored in the bonds of food molecules for growth, reproduction, and the processes needed for life.

Some molecules are very simple. For example, two hydrogen atoms and one oxygen atom form a water molecule. Water makes up about 70% of the human body. Most of the remaining 30% is made of very large molecules that contain hydrogen, carbon, and other elements. Organisms make some of these large molecules by using the atoms of matter taken in from their environments.

4. In the molecules shown, color the hydrogen (H) atoms blue, the oxygen (O) atoms red, and the carbon (C) atoms green.

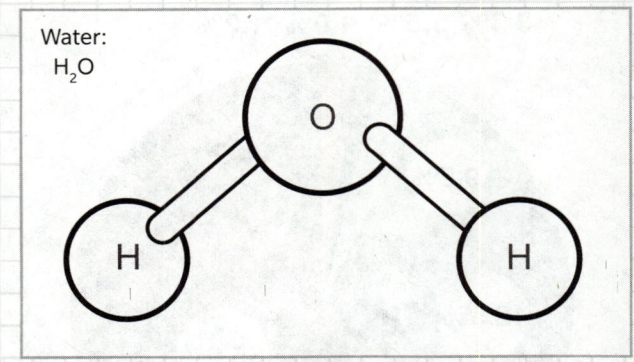

Water: H_2O

Water is essential for cell and body system functions.

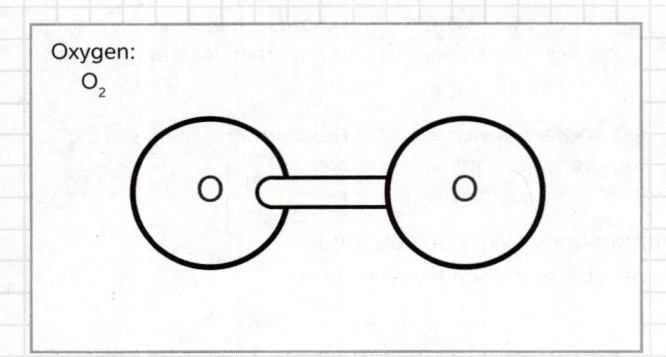

Oxygen: O_2

Oxygen is used by cells to extract energy from food.

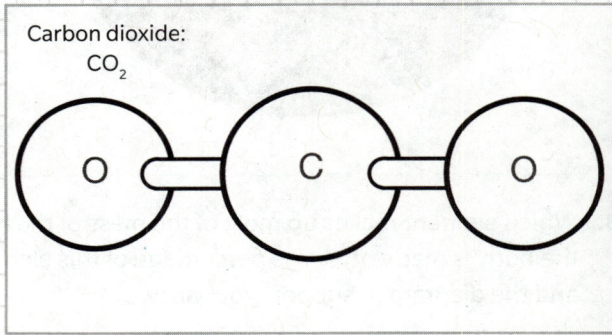

Carbon dioxide: CO_2

Plants use carbon dioxide, water, and sunlight to make food.

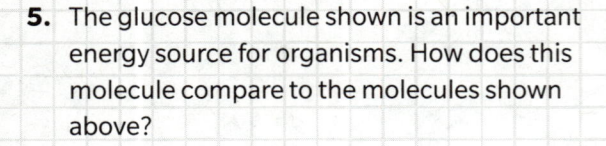

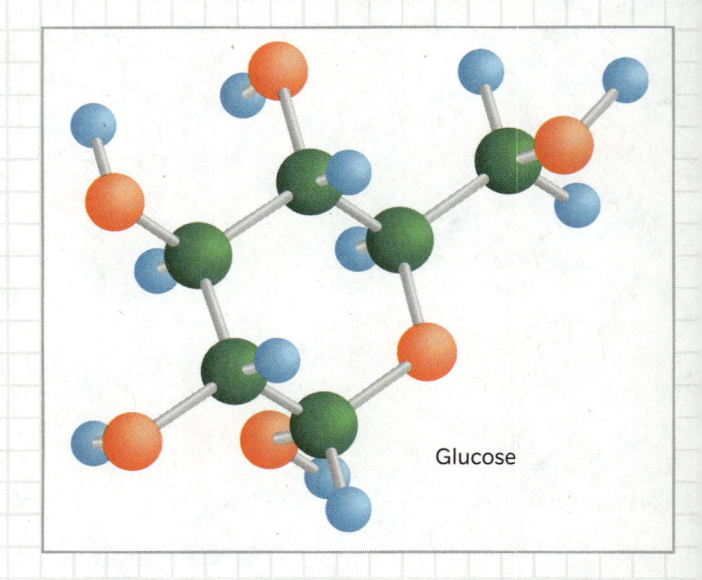

5. The glucose molecule shown is an important energy source for organisms. How does this molecule compare to the molecules shown above?

Glucose

232 Unit 4 Matter and Energy in Organisms and Rock

Do the Math
Analyze Size and Scale of Matter

Measuring between 4 and 6 meters tall, giraffes are the tallest mammals on Earth. They prefer to eat leaves and buds from trees, but will also eat grasses, flowers, and fruits.

Giraffes get much of their water from eating acacia leaves. They can eat as much as 65 kilograms (about 140 pounds) of leaves each day!

6. Which choice below shows the matter that makes up the giraffe in order from smallest to largest?

   A. atoms → molecules → cells → giraffe
   B. atoms → cells → molecules → giraffe
   C. cells → atoms → molecules → giraffe

7. Giraffes can weigh 1,300 kilograms (kg) or more. If they eat 65 kg of food each day, what percentage of their body weight do they consume in food each day?

Energy in Organisms

Organisms need a constant source of energy to live, grow, and reproduce. **Energy** is the ability to cause change. Energy comes in many forms, including light energy from the sun and the energy stored in the bonds of food molecules. When an organism eats food, the energy in the bonds of the food molecules becomes available to the organism for use in life processes. Some energy is stored for later use or converted to heat.

Different organisms get food in different ways. For example, plants depend on the sun's energy to make food molecules. Animals cannot make their own food, so they must get energy by eating plants or other animals.

Energy Sources of Plants and Animals

energy from the sun

energy in plants

energy in animals

- Earth receives only a small fraction of the sun's energy. Of the sunlight that does reach Earth, some is absorbed by matter, including air, water, rocks, and living things, and some is reflected back into space.

- Plants use energy from the sun to make food molecules. Plants use most of the energy stored in food molecules for life processes, but some of the energy is stored or transferred to the environment as heat.

- Animals must eat plants or other animals to get energy. When an animal eats, most of the energy from food molecules is used for life processes, but some of the energy is stored or transferred to the environment as heat.

Make an Analogy

Organisms need both matter and energy to perform functions. For example, organisms need matter and energy to move, keep their bodies warm, and control heart rhythms.

Other types of systems also need matter and energy to perform functions. For example, a car engine uses gasoline to produce the motion that makes the car move. Stoves and furnaces use natural gas to produce heat that cooks food and warms homes. Batteries use elements and compounds to produce electrical energy that powers cell phones, computers, and flashlights.

8. Organisms get energy from the bonds that hold together food molecules. How do you think a car engine gets energy from gasoline?

___

9. Describe the similarity between the way an organism uses the energy from food and the way a car uses the energy from gasoline.

___

234 Unit 4 Matter and Energy in Organisms and Rock

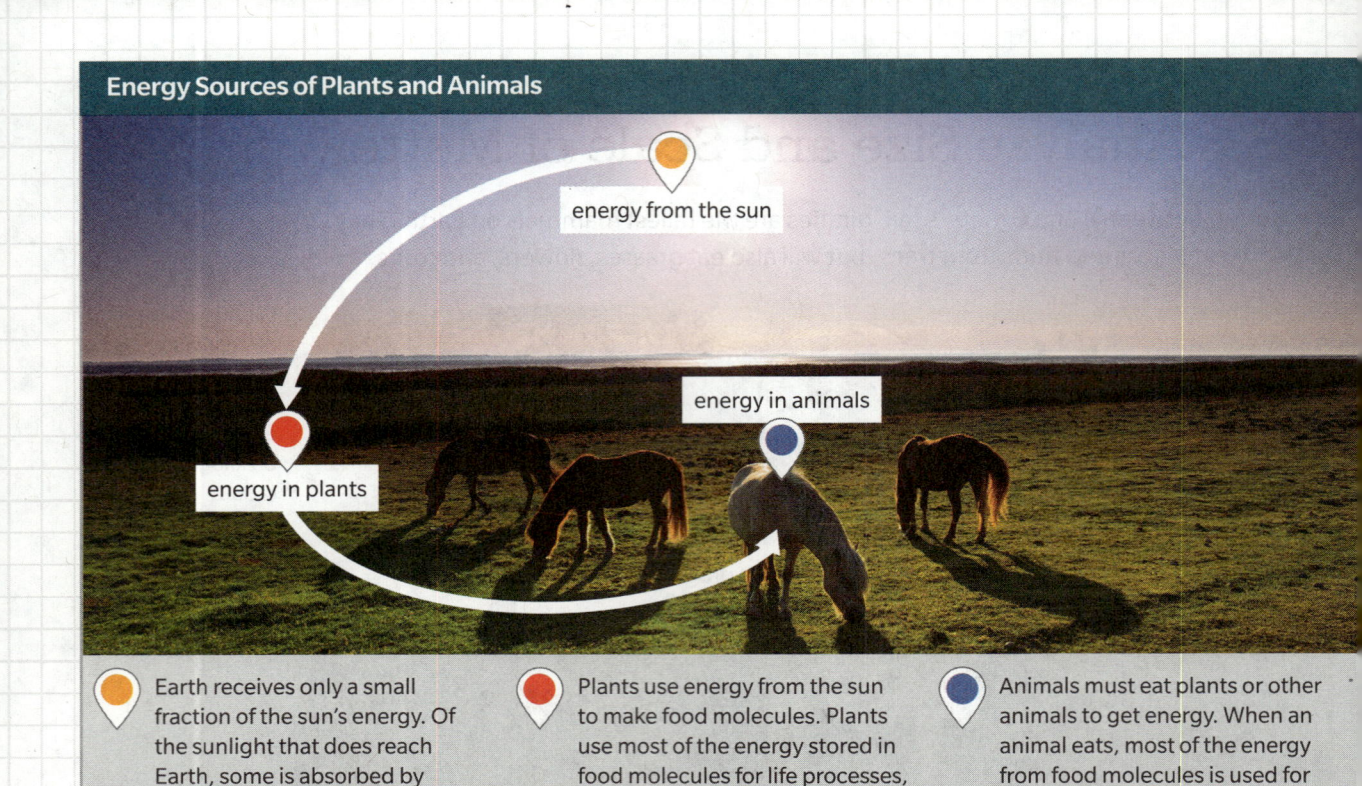

EXPLORATION 2

Explaining How Organisms Obtain Matter and Energy

Organisms Need Sources of Matter and Energy

A hungry rabbit is nibbling on the lettuce that is growing in your garden. The lettuce provides some of the matter and energy the rabbit needs to find your garden, escape from predators, grow a thick fur coat for winter, and many other functions necessary for reproduction and survival. Like the rabbit, all living organisms need a source of matter and energy.

10. **Discuss** Brainstorm some common foods that people eat. Think about whether each food comes from a plant or an animal. Record the foods in the table.

This apple is only one source of matter and energy for the girl.

Plant	Animal

Lesson 1 The Flow of Energy Drives the Cycling of Matter in Organisms

11. Read about the organisms in the photos. Do you think they get their matter from the nonliving environment or from other organisms? Do you think they get their energy from the sun or other organisms? Record your answers.

	These rhinos spend most of their time roaming through their environment to find plants to eat.	Matter: Energy:
	When a tree falls in a forest, these fungi soon begin to live on its decaying trunk.	Matter: Energy:
	Lianas are vines that climb tall trees, so their leaves can reach the sunlight at the top of the canopy.	Matter: Energy:

Producers

An organism can be categorized by the way it obtains matter and energy. A **producer** is an organism that uses energy and matter from the environment to make its own food molecules. Producers get energy from the sun and matter, such as carbon dioxide, water, and nutrients, from soil and air.

Many producers, such as plants, algae, and some bacteria, use energy from sunlight to make glucose molecules from carbon dioxide and water. They use the glucose molecules as food. When producers break down the glucose molecules they have made and form new molecules, energy is released. This energy is used for life processes. Producers provide energy and matter for other living organisms that consume them.

The plants in this forest provide food for most of the other organisms that live there.

Consumers

Many organisms cannot make their own food. A **consumer** is an organism that gets energy and matter by eating other organisms. Humans and all other animals are consumers. Some consumers, such as rabbits, eat only plants. These consumers may eat any plant matter they can find. For example, elephants will eat grasses, bark, leaves, and fruit. Other consumers may specialize and eat only one part of a plant. Koalas eat only the leaves of eucalyptus trees, and pandas feed almost entirely on bamboo.

Not all consumers eat plants. Some consumers, such as spiders, frogs, and sharks, eat other animals. Other consumers have more variety in their diets. Animals such as ants, raccoons, and bears eat both plants and animals.

This lesser anteater's diet is mostly ants and termites.

Decomposers

The matter left behind when a plant or animal dies becomes food for a different type of organism. A **decomposer** is an organism that gets energy and matter by breaking down the remains of other organisms that have died. Decomposers also break down the wastes expelled by other organisms. Like consumers, decomposers use the bodies of other organisms as sources of matter and energy because they cannot make their own food. Fungi, such as mushrooms, often grow on dead tree trunks or in soil that is rich in decaying matter. Some bacteria, earthworms, and slugs are also decomposers.

Without decomposers, the matter that makes up organisms would not be recycled back to the nonliving environment. When decomposers break down remains and wastes, nutrients enter the soil and become available for use by other organisms. Often, several different species of decomposers are involved in breaking down the dead organism.

Slugs process dead plant material and deposit the nutrients into the soil.

EVIDENCE NOTEBOOK

12. Which group of organisms is breaking down the matter and using the energy in the decaying fruit from the beginning of the lesson? Record your evidence.

Hands-On Lab
Investigate Decomposition

You will observe the decomposition of plant matter in different soil types and explain how soil type affects the rate of decomposition. You will then develop your own procedure to test other variables that can affect the rate of decomposition.

Decomposers break down the matter in this compost bin.

Procedure

STEP 1 List factors that you think might affect the rate of decomposition.

MATERIALS
- dry sand and potting soil
- graduated cylinder
- sealable plastic bags
- variety of fruits and vegetables, cut into pieces
- water

STEP 2 Label three bags for each condition (9 total): control, dry sand, and potting soil. Do not add sand or soil to the control bags. Add 1 cup dry sand and 1 cup potting soil to the corresponding bags. To each bag, add pieces of fruits and/or vegetables. The contents of each bag should be identical, except for the type of soil.

STEP 3 Use the graduated cylinder to add 100 mL of water to each bag.

STEP 4 Put the bags in a cool, dark place, such as a closet or a drawer.

STEP 5 For five days, at the same time each day, take the bags out and observe them. Write your observations in the table. Note any variation observed between bags within a condition.

238 Unit 4 Matter and Energy in Organisms and Rock

Observations

Day	Control	Dry sand	Potting soil
1			
2			
3			
4			
5			

Analysis

STEP 6 What are the differences between the dry sand and the potting soil? How do you think these differences affect the rate of decomposition you observed?

STEP 7 Explain how this activity is similar to and different from decomposition that takes place outdoors.

STEP 8 What other factors could you test? Choose one of these factors and plan an experiment to test the relationship between that variable and rate of decomposition. Perform your experiment, record your results, and construct a graph using your data to show the relationship between your variable and decomposition. Prepare a slide show presentation to share your results.

Engineer It | Explore Bioremediation Suppose that the next time you spill something, you could call on a team of microorganisms to clean up the mess. Bioremediation does just that. At a site where soil or water is contaminated by pollutants, scientists can use microorganisms, such as bacteria, to help break down the pollutant that is causing the problem. For example, oil spills contaminate soil and damage aquatic ecosystems. Not many organisms can decompose oil molecules because of the molecules' very stable, ringlike structures. But scientists have identified naturally occurring bacteria that can break down the oil molecules and use them as food. Chemical reactions change the oil molecules into water and other nontoxic substances as the bacteria break down the oil molecules.

This bioremediation pit contains soil contaminated with crude oil. Scientists are observing the pit to see if bacteria that are able to break down the oil can help clean this contaminated site.

13. Which of the following are constraints scientists need to consider when designing a bioremediation solution? Select all that apply.
    A. the maximum number of oil-digesting bacteria available
    B. the temperature range in which the oil-digesting bacteria grow best
    C. the cause of the oil contamination
    D. regulations about adding nonnative organisms to ecosystems

14. Explain how using bioremediation to clean contaminated soil is similar to the process of decomposition in a natural environment.

Explain the Need for Plant Food

15. You may have heard someone say they need to feed their plants. Products called *fertilizers* or *plant foods* are available for this purpose. A potted plant often grows better if it is given plant food. Explain why a potted plant might need plant food if it is getting enough sunlight and water.

EXPLORATION 3

Relating Cycling of Matter to Transfer of Energy

How tall was the tallest tree you have ever seen? That tree was made of matter. Some trees can be more than 90 meters tall. That's a lot of matter! The tree also needed energy to grow. It did a lot of growing, so it needed a lot of energy.

Trees and other producers use the sun's energy and matter from the environment to make food molecules. First, energy flows through a tree as sunlight energy is transferred to food molecules. Food molecules store energy that the tree can use later. This stored energy is released through chemical reactions that form new molecules, providing the tree with energy for growth and life processes. Some energy is also released from the tree as heat.

A tree grows from a seed into a young sapling.

Over many years the sapling grows into a fully mature tree.

16. Discuss Think about how this tree got bigger. With a partner, construct an explanation about where the matter came from.

Energy and Matter Are Conserved

Luckily, the sun is a nearly limitless source of energy for plants. Matter, however, is limited. Matter continually moves, or cycles, between the living and nonliving parts of the environment. Energy changes form as it flows through a system, but it is not created or destroyed. For example, energy enters the tree as light. It is transformed to chemical energy, and exits the tree in the form of heat. Energy transfers drive the chemical reactions that rearrange matter taken in by the tree into new molecules needed for growth and life processes. The matter in the tree will eventually return to the environment when the tree decomposes, completing the cycle.

> **EVIDENCE NOTEBOOK**
> **17.** Could any of the matter and energy in the decaying fruits have disappeared? Record your evidence.

Lesson 1 The Flow of Energy Drives the Cycling of Matter in Organisms

18. **Draw** Complete the diagram by drawing illustrations to show how matter cycles and energy flows in the life of a tree.

The sunlight shines on a sapling that has grown from a seed.

The tree uses matter and sunlight to grow taller and thicker.

The tree has died and decomposers in the soil are breaking it down and returning the matter to the soil.

The tree has lived for many years and has a large canopy of leaves.

Language SmArts
Cite Evidence for Conservation of Matter and Energy

19. Use your illustrations of the life of a tree to write a short explanatory text that explains how matter and energy were not created or destroyed over the course of the tree's life. Describe the flow of matter and energy in your explanation.

_____
_____
_____
_____
_____
_____
_____

TAKE IT FURTHER

Continue Your Exploration

Name: _____   Date: _____

Check out the path below or go online to choose one of the other paths shown.

Chemotrophs → • Cosmic Dust
• Hands-On Labs
• Propose Your Own Path

Go online to choose one of these other paths.

The sun is the source of almost all energy on Earth. *Phototrophs* (FOH-tuh-trofs)—most plants, algae, and some bacteria—use energy from the sun to change water and carbon dioxide into glucose and oxygen. However, some organisms live in deep in the ocean where sunlight does not reach. Organisms called *chemotrophs* (KEE-muh-trofs) can use energy stored in chemical bonds to live.

On the ocean floor, extremely hot water gushes from below Earth's surface through hydrothermal vents. In the absence of sunlight, organisms living in and around these vents must find another source of energy to make their food. *Chemosynthesis* is the process by which chemotrophs convert carbon dioxide to glucose molecules by using the energy stored in molecules, such as hydrogen sulfide. When chemotrophs break the bonds between atoms, and new bonds are formed, energy is released that can be used to make food, much like phototrophs that use energy from the sun to make food. The chemotrophs are a source of food for other organisms that live near these deep-sea vents, much like producers are a source of food for consumers on land.

The compounds rising from this vent store energy that some organisms can use.

Lesson 1 The Flow of Energy Drives the Cycling of Matter in Organisms   243

TAKE IT FURTHER

Continue Your Exploration

1. In addition to chemotrophs, a variety of other organisms live near hydrothermal vents, including shrimp, crabs, tubeworms, and octopuses. Which statements describe matter and energy in deep-sea vent ecosystems? Select all that apply.
   A. Crabs are consumers that get matter and energy from eating other organisms that live near deep-sea vents.
   B. Chemotrophs get matter and energy from the compounds coming out of the sea floor.
   C. Chemotrophs get matter, but not energy from the compounds coming out of the sea floor.
   D. Chemotrophs provide most of the matter and energy that is available to the other organisms that live near the deep-sea vent.

2. How are phototrophs and chemotrophs similar and different?

3. What would happen to chemotrophs if the sun suddenly stopped releasing energy? Would the chemotrophs survive? Why or why not?

4. **Collaborate** Conduct research with a classmate to learn more about chemotrophs. Find out about species of chemotrophs that have been discovered as well as the technologies that help scientists explore deep-sea vents. You can also explore topics related to chemotrophs, such as the origin of life on Earth and the possibility of life on other planets. Prepare a multimedia presentation to share with the class.

LESSON 1 SELF-CHECK

Can You Explain It?

Name: _____ Date: _____

What happened to the matter and energy that were in these fruits when they were first picked?

EVIDENCE NOTEBOOK
Refer to the notes in your Evidence Notebook to help you construct an explanation for what happened to the matter and energy in the fruits as they decomposed.

1. State your claim. Make sure your claim fully explains where the matter and energy went as the fruits decomposed.

2. Summarize the evidence you have gathered to support your claim and explain your reasoning.

Lesson 1 The Flow of Energy Drives the Cycling of Matter in Organisms 245

LESSON 1 SELF-CHECK

Checkpoints

Answer the following questions to check your understanding of the lesson.

Use the photo to answer Questions 3 and 4.

3. What happens to the food after the snail eats it? Select all that apply.
   A. The snail breaks apart the food molecules to get energy.
   B. The snail uses the matter in the food to grow.
   C. The snail uses the matter in the food to produce its own food.
   D. The snail uses energy from the sun to make food.

4. The plants in the photo get energy from the ~~air~~ / sun. The plants store the energy in the bonds / ~~matter~~ between ~~atoms~~ / cells that make up the food molecules. When the snail eats a plant, it uses the energy stored in bonds / ~~atoms~~ of the molecules to get energy. Matter ~~is~~ / is not destroyed in the process.

Use the diagram to answer Question 5.

5. Why do you think the starch molecule shown is a good source of energy for an organism?
   A. The many bonds in the starch molecule store energy.
   B. The starch molecule is made of atoms.
   C. Starch is the only type of molecule that provides energy.
   D. A starch molecule is made of more than one kind of atom.

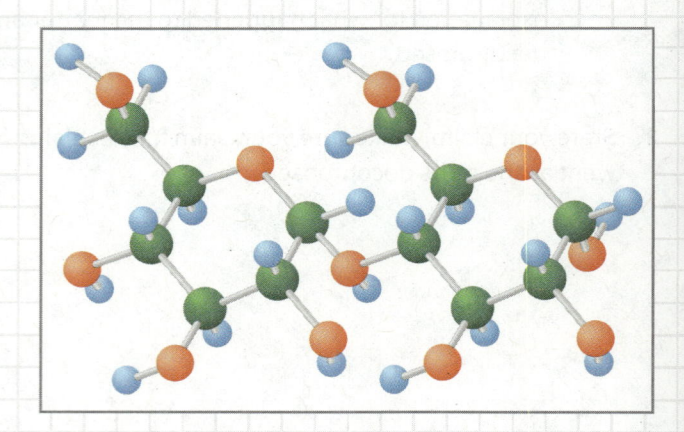

6. Number the sentences to show what will happen to an apple's matter and energy.

   _____ A deer eats the apple to get matter and energy.

   _____ The apple passes through the digestive system of the deer, returning some of the apple's matter and energy to the environment.

   _____ An apple tree uses the matter from the soil and air for life processes.

   _____ An apple falls from a tree and lands on the ground.

   _____ Decomposers break down the deer's waste to get matter and energy and return some matter to the soil and air.

Unit 4 Matter and Energy in Organisms and Rock

LESSON 1 SELF-CHECK

Interactive Review

Complete this section to review the main concepts of the lesson.

All living things need matter and energy to survive. Organisms get matter and energy from food.

A. Describe how food molecules provide matter and energy for organisms.

Different types of organisms get matter and energy in different ways.

B. Construct a concept map to show how producers, consumers, and decomposers get matter and energy.

The transfer of energy drives the cycling of matter in organisms.

C. Construct a diagram that illustrates how energy flows and matter cycles through an organism.

Lesson 1 The Flow of Energy Drives the Cycling of Matter in Organisms

LESSON 2

Chemical Reactions Provide Energy for Cells

Underwater forests of kelp provide food and shelter for many species including fish, sea urchins, and sea lions.

Explore First

Investigating Plants Fill a clear cup with water. Place a fresh, green leaf from a plant in the cup and set in a sunny location. Observe the leaf and the side of the cup after one hour. What do you see? What do you expect to see if you leave the cup in sunlight for several more hours?

> **Go online** to view the digital version of the Hands-On Lab for this lesson and to download additional lab resources.

CAN YOU EXPLAIN IT?

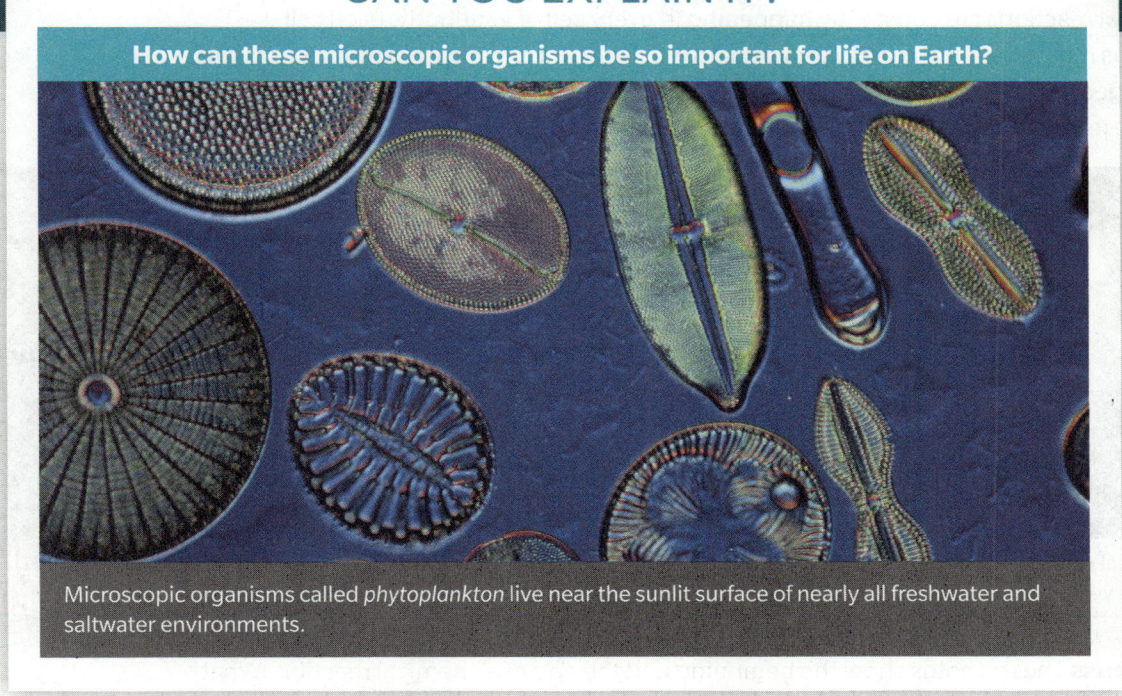

How can these microscopic organisms be so important for life on Earth?

Microscopic organisms called *phytoplankton* live near the sunlit surface of nearly all freshwater and saltwater environments.

1. Phytoplankton are a diverse group of unicellular organisms that are neither plants nor animals. Phytoplankton use sunlight, carbon dioxide, and nutrients to live and grow. Do you think phytoplankton are producers, consumers, or decomposers? Explain your reasoning.

EVIDENCE NOTEBOOK As you explore this lesson, gather evidence to explain why phytoplankton are so important for life on Earth.

Lesson 2 Chemical Reactions Provide Energy for Cells 249

EXPLORATION 1

Analyzing the Chemistry of Cells

Chemical reactions are constantly happening in every cell of your body. Each cell performs many chemical reactions every second. During a chemical reaction, atoms are rearranged into new substances. The new substances formed by chemical reactions in cells are used as matter and energy for life processes.

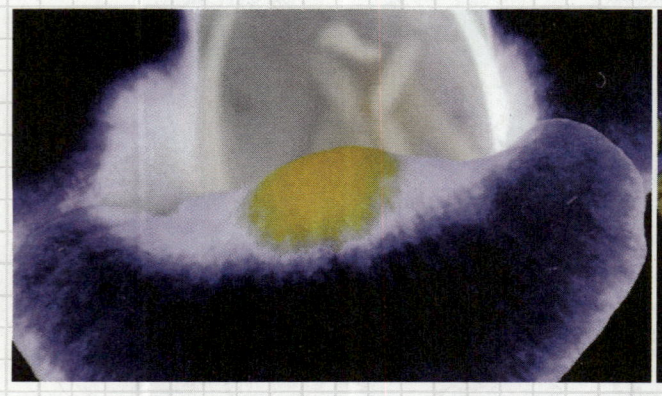

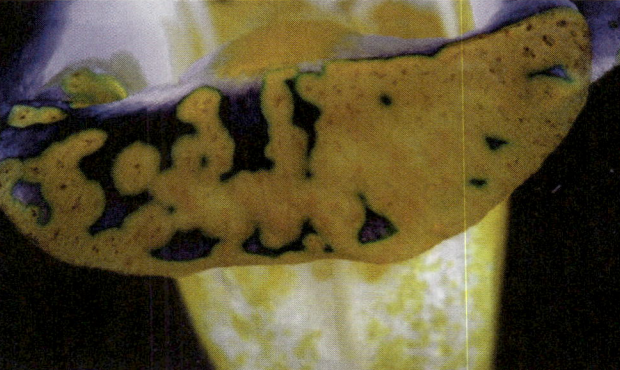

A chemical reaction has occurred that causes the color of the flower's petals to change from purple to yellow.

Explore Online

2. **Discuss** These photos show the beginning and the end of a chemical reaction. What do you think happens to the atoms in the petals during this chemical reaction?

Chemical Reactions

A **chemical reaction** is a process in which atoms are rearranged to produce new substances. The starting substances in a chemical reaction are called *reactants*. The substances formed in a chemical reaction are called *products*. During a chemical reaction, bonds that hold atoms together may be broken or formed. An energy input is needed to break the bonds between atoms, and energy is released when new bonds are formed. Neither matter nor energy is created or destroyed during a chemical reaction.

Many different chemical reactions take place in living systems. For example, the production of food molecules in the cells of producers involves chemical reactions. The cells of all organisms use chemical reactions to release energy from food molecules.

Explore a Chemical Reaction

water + carbon dioxide → carbonic acid

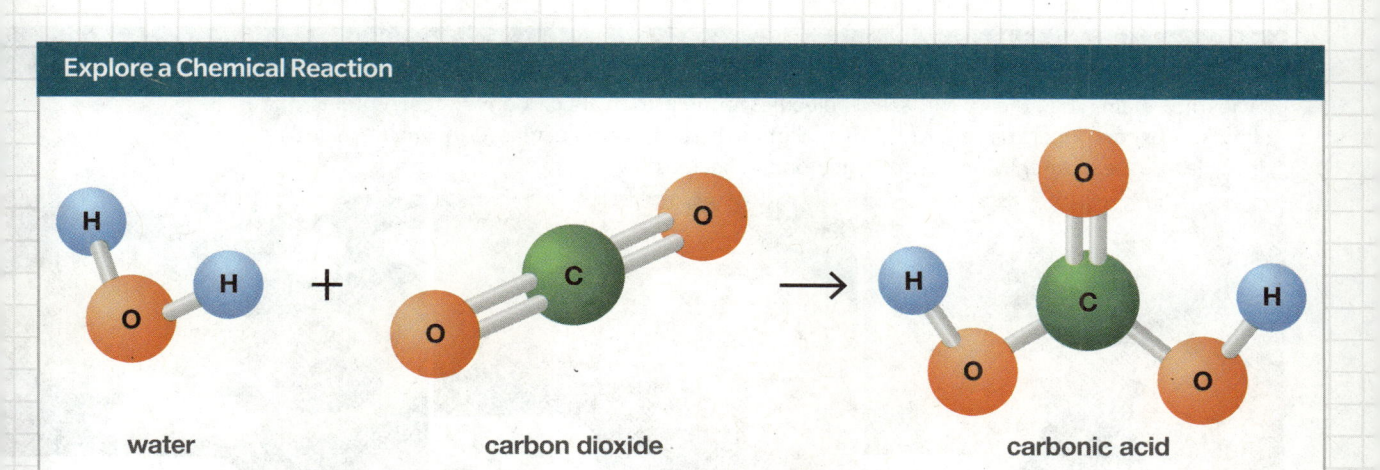

Reactants Water molecules are composed of two hydrogen atoms and one oxygen atom. Carbon dioxide molecules are composed of two oxygen atoms and one carbon atom. An energy input is needed to break the bonds between the atoms.

Changes in Energy Energy is released when new bonds form. Depending on the overall change in energy between the reactants and products, some chemical reactions absorb energy and others release energy.

Products The atoms of the carbon dioxide molecule and the water molecule have been rearranged to form a molecule of carbonic acid. The carbonic acid has the same number and types of atoms as were in the carbon dioxide and water molecules.

Chemical Equations

A chemical reaction can be modeled by writing a chemical equation, which uses symbols to show the relationship between the starting materials and the materials produced in the reaction. Each type of atom is indicated by its symbol.

3. Complete the chemical equation using the molecules in the Word Bank. Refer to the model above to help you.

   ☐ + ☐ → ☐

   WORD BANK
   - CO_2
   - H_2O
   - CH_2O_3

4. The molecular model in the illustration and the chemical equation above both model the same chemical reaction. Compare and contrast these two models.

Carbon-Based Molecules in Cells

Carbon-based molecules are the building blocks of living things. Carbon is unique, because carbon atoms can bond together to form large chains and other large molecules. Each carbon atom can form four bonds. The sugar and fat molecules that provide energy to cells are made up of carbon, hydrogen, and oxygen atoms. Nucleic acids that give the instructions to make proteins, as well as the amino acids that form proteins, are also carbon-based molecules. All animal and plant cells use energy that comes from carbon-based molecules.

Lesson 2 Chemical Reactions Provide Energy for Cells

Molecular Structure of Foods

The three main types of carbon-based molecules found in food are carbohydrates, proteins, and lipids. Most producers use energy from sunlight to make food molecules. Consumers, including people, must eat other living things to get food molecules.

Sweet potato plants store starches, a type of carbohydrate, in specialized roots. Carbohydrates are an important source of energy and matter used to build cell parts.

Salmon flesh is high in protein. Proteins are responsible for most of the work performed in cells, including transport, growth, and repair.

The fruit of an avocado plant is high in fat, which is a type of lipid. Lipids are a rich source of energy in the form of stored reserves.

5. How does chemical energy become available to the cells of consumers? Number the statements to show the sequence of events.

   _____ Consumers eat food to get carbon-based molecules.

   _____ Producers absorb energy from the sun.

   _____ Chemical reactions release the energy stored in sugar molecules.

   _____ Energy from sunlight is used to produce sugar molecules.

Analyze a Chemical Reaction

6. The equation that represents the chemical reaction shown is $CH_4 + 2O_2 \rightarrow CO_2 + 2H_2O$. Which molecules are the reactants? Which molecules are the products?

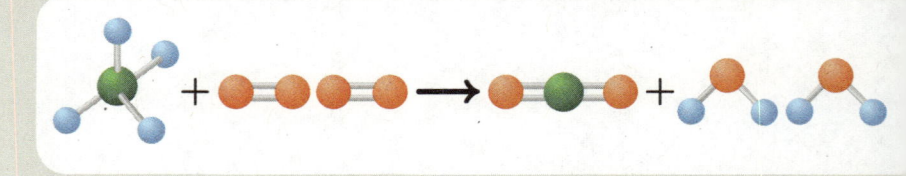

   _____
   _____
   _____

7. What does the equation and the model tell you about the number of atoms of each kind in the reactants and products?

   _____
   _____
   _____
   _____

252 Unit 4 Matter and Energy in Organisms and Rock

EXPLORATION 2

Investigating Photosynthesis

What did you eat for breakfast this morning? Maybe you had scrambled eggs and some toast. These breakfast foods help to provide the cells of your body with the energy they need.

Producers, such as plants and algae, don't "eat" their food. Most producers use energy from sunlight to make food from carbon dioxide and water. The energy from sunlight is needed for chemical reactions that produce carbon-based food molecules.

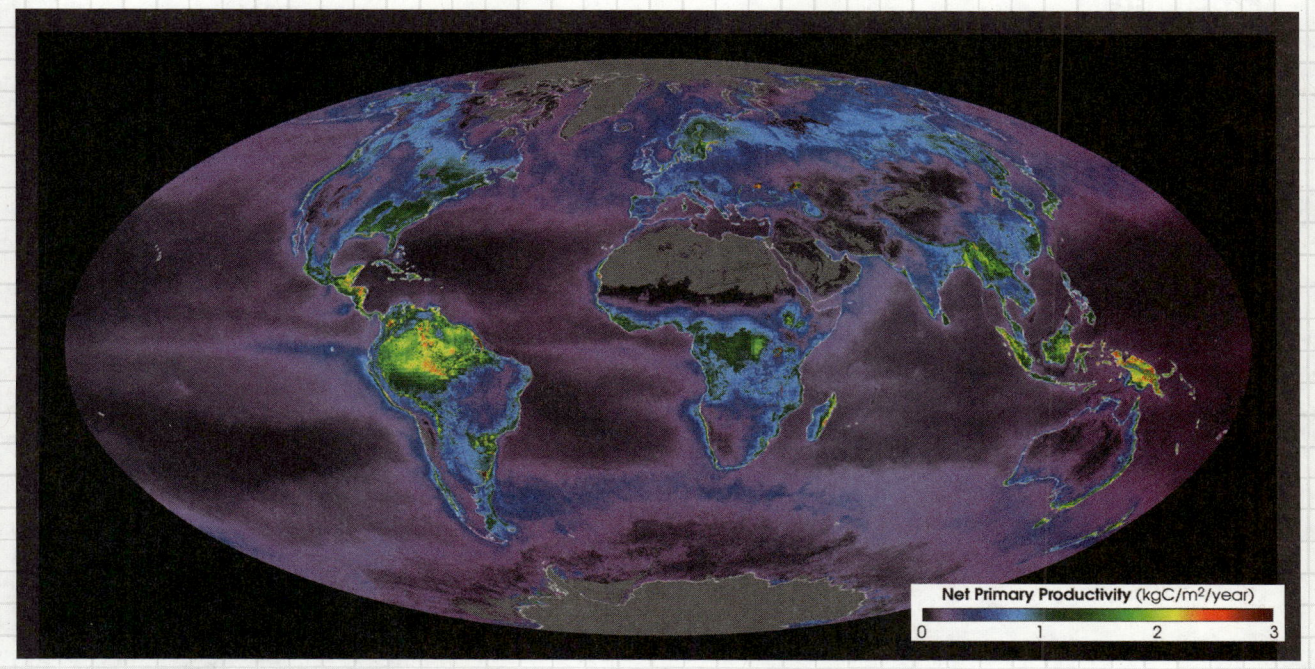

Net Primary Productivity ($kgC/m^2/year$)
0 1 2 3

Primary productivity is a measure of the rate of conversion of the sun's energy into matter by the producers in an ecosystem.

8. **Discuss** Primary productivity is an indicator of how much matter and energy is available in the producers within a given area. With a partner, discuss the patterns you see in the map. Why do you think primary productivity is important for the health of an ecosystem?

EVIDENCE NOTEBOOK

9. Phytoplankton are found in fresh and saltwater environments. How much primary productivity is found in areas where phytoplankton are abundant? Record your evidence.

Lesson 2 Chemical Reactions Provide Energy for Cells 253

Hands-On Lab
Investigate the Effect of Sunlight on *Elodea*

You will observe an aquatic plant, *Elodea*, to determine the relationship between sunlight and the amount of carbon dioxide absorbed by the plant.

MATERIALS
- beaker, 500 mL, or tube rack
- bromothymol blue
- *Elodea* plants
- eyedropper
- flask, 250 mL
- foil
- graduated cylinder, 200 mL
- light source
- straw
- test tubes, large, or bottles with caps (3)
- water

Procedure

STEP 1 Based on your understanding of how producers make food, make a prediction about the relationship between sunlight and carbon dioxide uptake by a plant.

STEP 2 Bromothymol blue is a dye that turns yellow in the presence of an acid. A solution containing bromothymol blue will turn yellow when carbon dioxide and water react to form an acid. Prepare the bromothymol blue solution by measuring 150 mL of water into the graduated cylinder. Pour the water into a flask and add 20–25 drops of bromothymol blue. Swirl gently to mix. Observe and describe the color of the solution.

This *Elodea* plant is in a solution of water and bromothymol blue.

STEP 3 Label three large test tubes for each variable: control, wrapped, and unwrapped. Cover "wrapped" tubes in foil, making sure that light cannot reach inside of the tube.

STEP 4 Use a straw to gently blow carbon dioxide from your lungs into the flask containing the bromothymol blue. Stop immediately when you see the color change to yellow. Use extreme caution to be sure not to inhale the solution through the straw. Notify your teacher immediately if you accidentally do so.

STEP 5 Fill each tube about halfway with the solution. Clean up any spills on the table or floor immediately. Place a piece of *Elodea* into each of the wrapped and unwrapped tubes. Do not place *Elodea* in the control tubes. Top off the tubes with solution to be sure the *Elodea* is completely submerged. Cap all three tubes tightly. Be sure to wash your hands thoroughly.

STEP 6 Describe the importance of having one tube that does not contain *Elodea*.

254 Unit 4 Matter and Energy in Organisms and Rock

STEP 7 Place the tubes in a beaker or tube rack and position them near a window or light source. Allow the tubes to sit in a well-lit location for 24 hours. Record your observations in the data table.

Observations						
Control		Unwrapped		Wrapped	
Start	24 h	Start	24 h	Start	24 h

Analysis

STEP 8 What do you observe about the three tubes? Do they look the same or different? Why or why not?

STEP 9 Explain whether or not your data support your prediction.

STEP 10 What do your observations tell you about the relationship between sunlight, carbon dioxide, and oxygen? Use your observations of the three tubes to provide evidence for your argument.

Photosynthesis

Photosynthesis is a series of chemical reactions in which the cells of producers—including plants, algae, and some bacteria—use energy from the sun to make carbon-based food molecules, known as sugars or *glucose*. In these reactions, carbon dioxide and water combine to form sugar molecules and release oxygen. Chemical energy is released when sugar molecules are broken down and their atoms are used to form new products. The sugar can be used by the plant immediately for life processes, or can be stored for later use. The oxygen is released into the atmosphere.

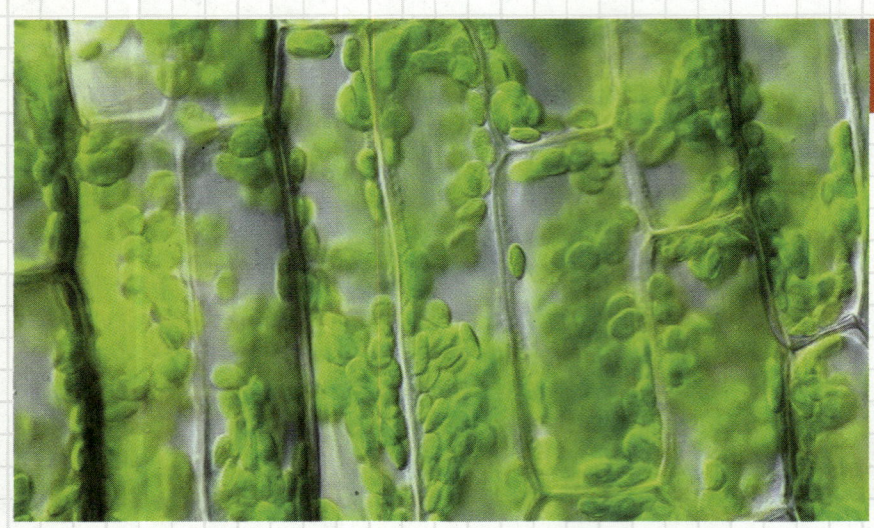

Movement of the cytoplasm in *Elodea* cells allows the chloroplasts to move around the cell in response to light.

Explore Photosynthesis

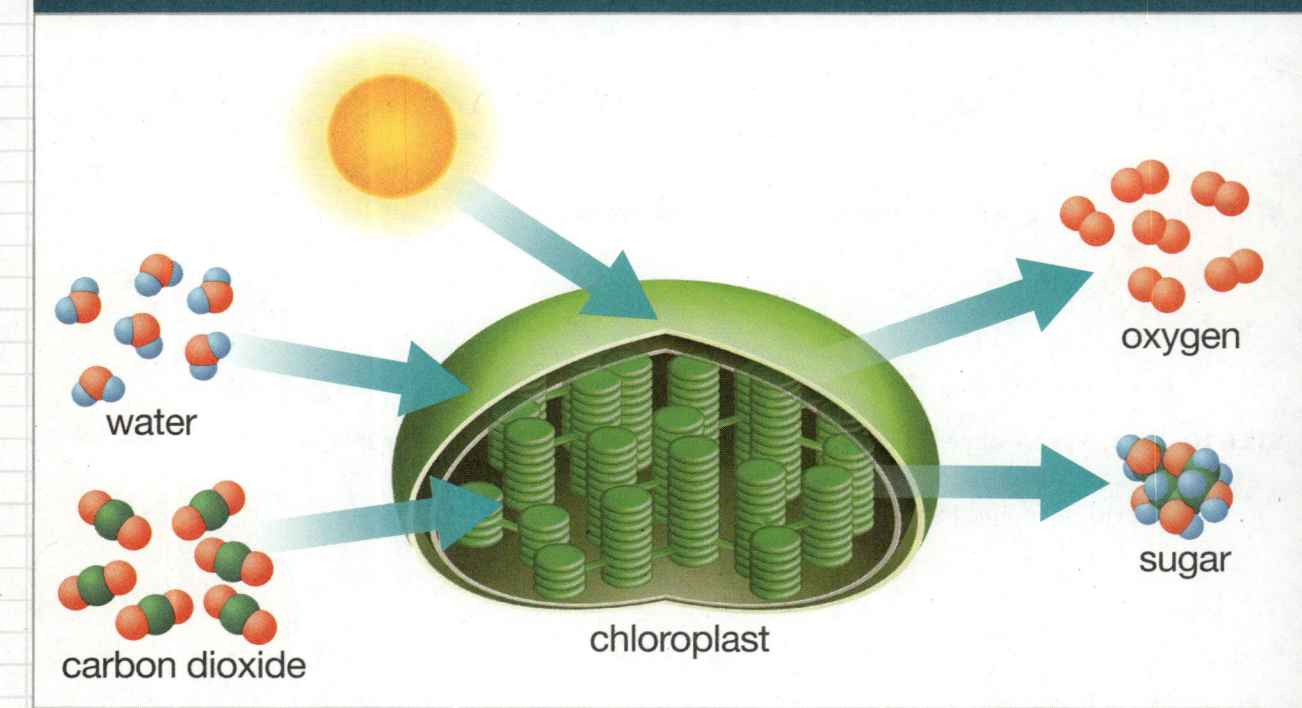

Reactants The starting materials of photosynthesis are carbon dioxide (CO_2), water (H_2O), and light energy from the sun.

Changes in Energy Photosynthesis takes place inside organelles called *chloroplasts*. These reactions absorb and store energy.

Products The products of photosynthesis are oxygen (O_2) and sugar molecules ($C_6H_{12}O_6$). The sugar molecules will be used as an energy source or stored by the cell.

Unit 4 Matter and Energy in Organisms and Rock

Capturing Light Energy

Photosynthesis needs an input of light energy. Cell structures called *chloroplasts* capture light energy from the sun. Chloroplasts are only found in the cells of plants and other producers that use photosynthesis. Photosynthesis takes place in the chloroplasts.

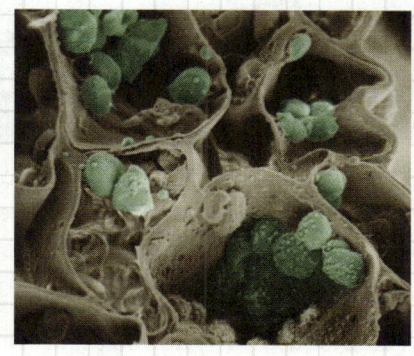

Storing Energy in Chemical Bonds

All chemical bonds are sources of energy. During photosynthesis, light energy is used to make sugar molecules. These molecules can be broken down and the atoms rearranged by cells to provide energy for life processes. In plants, the sugar that is not used is stored in the plant's body. It is often stored as starch in the plant's stem and roots, such as asparagus or a sweet potato.

This scanning electron micrograph (SEM) of the cut edge of a leaf shows the chloroplasts inside each of the cells.

WORD BANK
- $6O_2$
- $6CO_2$
- $6H_2O$
- light energy
- $C_6H_{12}O_6$

10. Use the Word Bank to complete the chemical equation for photosynthesis.

☐ + ☐ + ☐ → ☐ + ☐

Engineer It
Explore Use of Algae as Biofuel

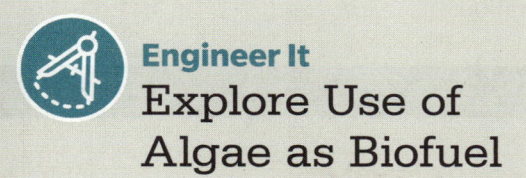

Biofuels are fuels that are produced from plant or animal matter. The gasoline we use to fuel our cars is ancient biofuel, or *fossil fuel*, because it is made from decomposed plants and animals that have been buried in the ground for millions of years. Because fossil fuels are not renewable and extracting them from the ground can harm the environment, engineers are looking for new sources of biofuel. Biofuel made from algae is one possibility.

Algae can be grown in freshwater, saltwater, and even wastewater environments. Algae grow quickly, producing a large amount of energy-rich lipids that can be converted to fuel.

11. Which statements identify possible advantages of algal biofuel? Select all that apply.

A. Algae grow quickly and are a renewable source of energy.

B. Algae can be grown in water sources that cannot be used for drinking or agriculture.

C. Algal biofuel use is not established on a large scale, so farming and fuel production methods cannot meet current global needs for energy.

D. Algae can be supplied with the carbon dioxide they need to grow using emissions from power plants and other sources.

EXPLORATION 3

Describing Cellular Respiration

Think of the last time you tried to hold your breath. It is not easy! That's because you—like nearly all living things—need a constant supply of oxygen to live. Organisms get oxygen from their environment.

12. Discuss Why do you think living things need oxygen?

Oxygen can enter this frog's body through its skin.

Cellular Respiration

The cells of all living things need energy, which they get from food. When cells break down food molecules, the energy stored in chemical bonds is released. **Cellular respiration** is a process that uses oxygen to release the energy stored in food molecules. Producers, consumers, and some other types of organisms use cellular respiration.

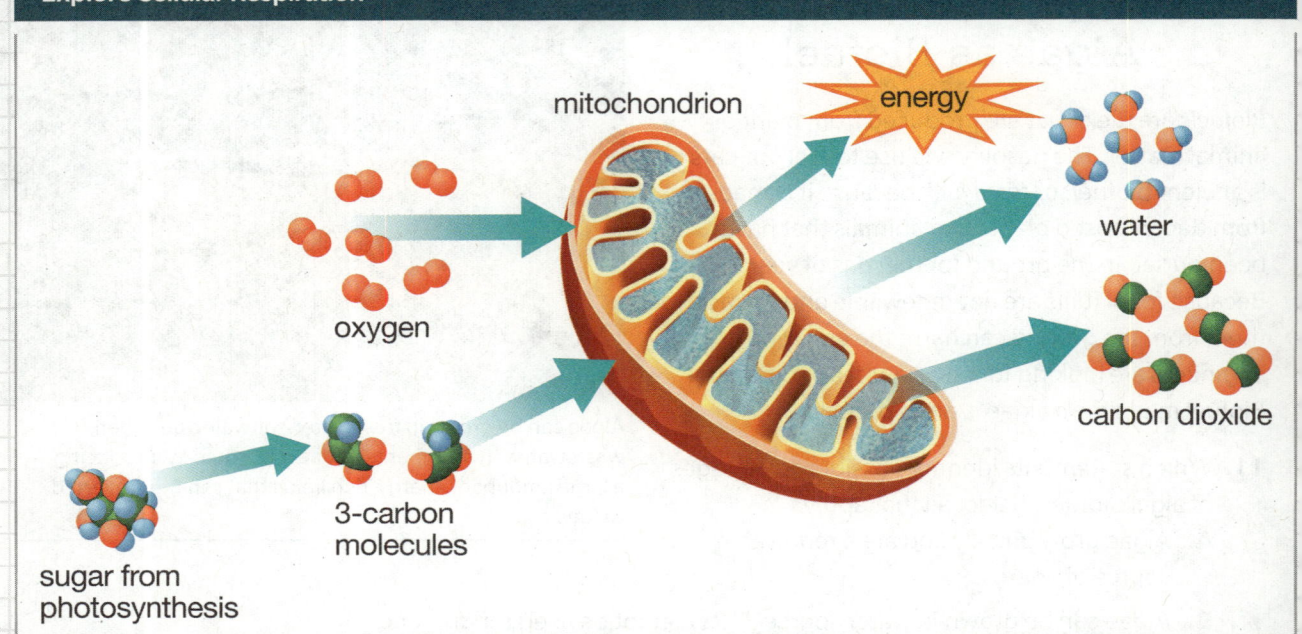

Explore Cellular Respiration

mitochondrion

energy

water

oxygen

carbon dioxide

3-carbon molecules

sugar from photosynthesis

Reactants The starting materials of cellular respiration are sugar molecules ($C_6H_{12}O_6$) and oxygen (O_2).

Changes in Energy In plant and animal cells, cellular respiration takes place in membrane-bound organelles called *mitochondria*. These chemical reactions release energy.

Products The products of cellular respiration are water (H_2O), carbon dioxide (CO_2), and energy.

258 Unit 4 Matter and Energy in Organisms and Rock

Using Oxygen

Cellular respiration occurs in several stages. In plant and animal cells, the first stage takes place in the cytoplasm, where each sugar molecule is broken down into smaller molecules. The next stages take place in the mitochondria. There, the smaller molecules are broken down even more. The chemical reactions that take place in the mitochondria require a lot of oxygen.

Releasing Energy

Energy is released during all stages of cellular respiration. A small amount of energy is released when the sugar molecules are broken down in the cytoplasm. A large amount of energy is released by the chemical reactions in the mitochondria. Cells use this energy for life processes. The other products of cellular respiration—water and carbon dioxide—are released by the cell.

The many folds and compartments of the inner mitochondrial membrane increase the total surface area.

13. Use the Word Bank to write the chemical equation for cellular respiration.

WORD BANK
- $6H_2O$
- $6CO_2$
- $6O_2$
- energy
- $C_6H_{12}O_6$

☐ + ☐ → ☐ + ☐ + ☐

Do the Math
Compare Reactants and Products

In a chemical reaction, bonds are broken and formed as atoms are rearranged to produce new substances. You can analyze the equation for cellular respiration to see how the reactants are rearranged to form the products.

14. Count the number of each type of atom in the reactants and products of cellular respiration. Use the diagram and text about cellular respiration to help you.

Type of atom	Number of atoms in reactants	Number of atoms in products
carbon (C)		
hydrogen (H)		
oxygen (O)		

15. What do your calculations tell you about the conservation of matter?

Lesson 2 Chemical Reactions Provide Energy for Cells

Language SmArts
Relate Photosynthesis and Cellular Respiration

16. Use the terms *energy*, *oxygen*, *sugar*, and *carbon dioxide* to complete the diagram.

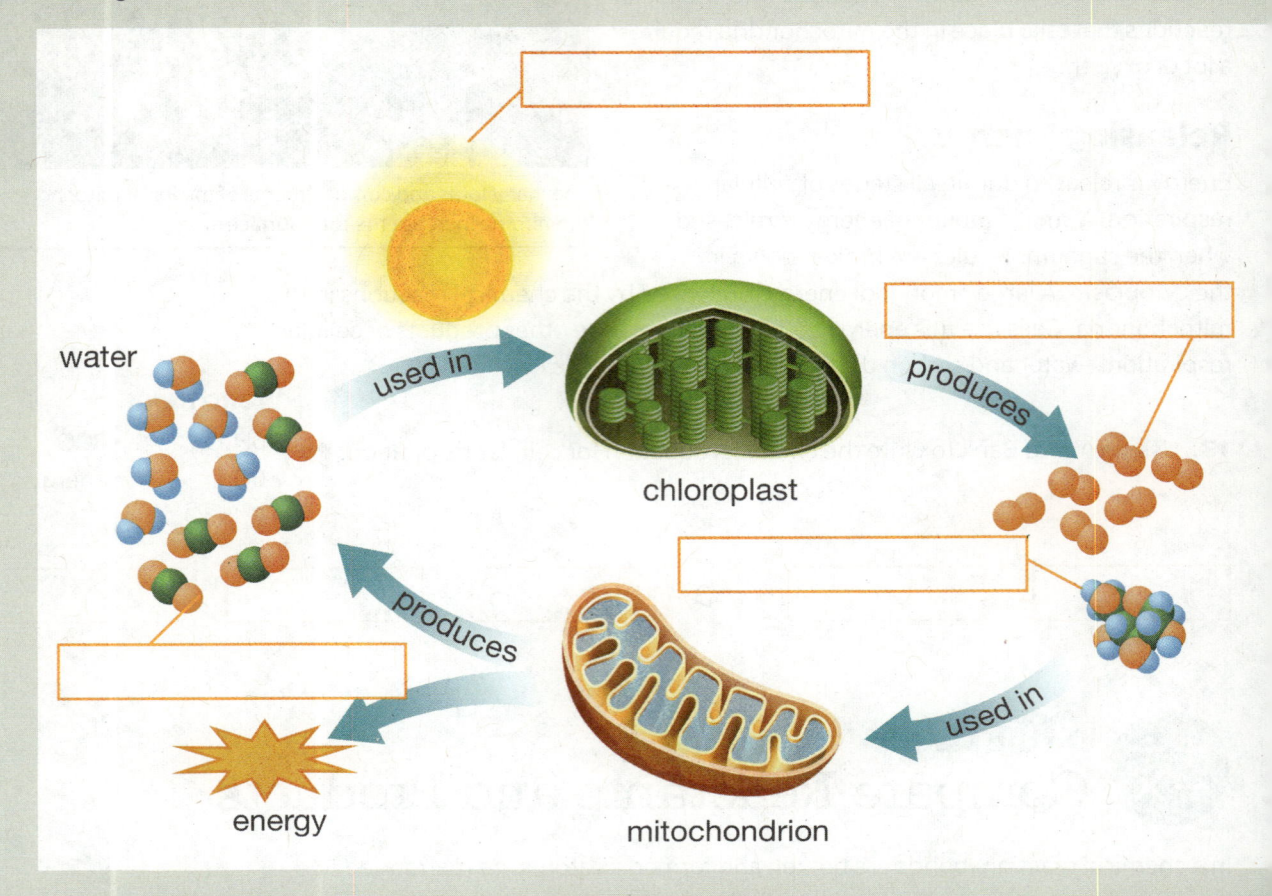

[Diagram: Sun labeled with blank box (energy) → "used in" → chloroplast → "produces" → blank box (oxygen). Water labeled on left. Chloroplast produces oxygen on right, which is "used in" → mitochondrion. Mitochondrion "produces" → blank box (water/energy) on left, returning to water and energy. Middle blank box between chloroplast and mitochondrion (sugar). Bottom left labeled "energy"; bottom right labeled "mitochondrion".]

17. How are the reactants and the products of photosynthesis and cellular respiration related? Use evidence from the diagram to support your explanation.

_____
_____
_____
_____
_____
_____
_____
_____

> **EVIDENCE NOTEBOOK**
>
> **18.** How do other organisms use the products of photosynthesis from phytoplankton? Record your evidence.

260 Unit 4 Matter and Energy in Organisms and Rock

TAKE IT FURTHER

Continue Your Exploration

Name: _____ Date: _____

Check out the path below or go online to choose one of the other paths shown.

Fermentation

- Primary Productivity
- Hands-On Lab 👋
- Propose Your Own Path

Go online to choose one of these other paths

When there isn't enough oxygen available for cellular respiration, organisms can release energy from sugars through a process called *fermentation*. Like cellular respiration, fermentation releases energy that cells can use. However, it does not require oxygen, and it does not release as much energy as cellular respiration. Two main types of fermentation are lactic acid fermentation and alcoholic fermentation.

Think about the last time you exercised so hard that your muscles became sore. That soreness is evidence of *lactic acid fermentation*. When your muscle cells run out of oxygen, they use this type of fermentation to release more energy. Lactic acid fermentation also produces carbon dioxide and lactic acid. The buildup of lactic acid causes muscles to feel weak and sore. Some types of bacteria also use lactic acid fermentation. Yogurt and cheese are made by adding these types of bacteria to milk. The buildup of lactic acid thickens the milk, eventually turning it into yogurt or cheese.

Many yeasts, which are single-celled fungi, use *alcoholic fermentation* to release energy. Carbon dioxide and alcohol are also produced in this process. Alcoholic fermentation is important to bakers because the carbon dioxide produced by yeast creates air pockets in bread dough, causing it to rise.

Cheese is a food that is made by lactic acid fermentation.

When you perform rapid, vigorous exercise, fermentation releases energy in your muscles.

Lesson 2 Chemical Reactions Provide Energy for Cells **261**

TAKE IT FURTHER

Continue Your Exploration

1. Ethanol is a biofuel made from corn. The corn is ground and water is added. The substance goes through several more steps before yeast is added, and the sugars in it are converted to ethanol and carbon dioxide. What process is part of the making of this biofuel?

    A. cellular respiration

    B. alcoholic fermentation

    C. lactic acid fermentation

2. How are cellular respiration and fermentation similar and different?

3. Some bakers of sourdough and a few other types of bread have what they call "starter dough." This dough contains yeast from which they make all their bread. Some starter dough is more than 100 years old. The dough has to be "fed" more flour and water on a regular basis for it to remain usable. Why must the starter dough be "fed"?

4. **Collaborate** Discuss with a classmate that even though fermentation is necessary when our muscles cannot get enough oxygen, it causes a sore feeling in the muscles. Research lactic acid fermentation in the body to find out the physiological reason for muscle soreness. Prepare a multimedia presentation to share your findings.

LESSON 2 SELF-CHECK

Can You Explain It?

Name: _____   Date: _____

How can these microscopic organisms be so important for life on Earth?

> **EVIDENCE NOTEBOOK**
> Refer to the notes in your Evidence Notebook to help you construct an explanation for why phytoplankton are so important for life on Earth.

1. State your claim. Make sure your claim fully explains why phytoplankton are so important for life on Earth.

2. Summarize the evidence you have gathered to support your claim and explain your reasoning.

Lesson 2 Chemical Reactions Provide Energy for Cells **263**

LESSON 2 SELF-CHECK

Checkpoints

Answer the following questions to check your understanding of the lesson.

Use the photo to answer Questions 3–4.

3. Which of the statements below are true? Select all that apply.
    A. The tree uses photosynthesis to get energy from food molecules; the elephant uses cellular respiration to get energy from food molecules.
    B. The tree and the elephant both use cellular respiration to get energy from food molecules.
    C. Sunlight is the ultimate source of energy for both the tree and the elephant.
    D. The tree and the elephant both use photosynthesis to make food molecules.

4. The tree uses energy from the sun to produce _oxygen / carbon dioxide_ as a product of _photosynthesis / cellular respiration_. The elephant and the tree take in the _oxygen / carbon dioxide_ and use it to break down sugars through the process of _photosynthesis / cellular respiration_.

Use the equations to answer Question 5.

5. Which of the statements are true about the two chemical reactions? Select all that apply.
    A. Equation A summarizes photosynthesis, and Equation B summarizes cellular respiration.
    B. Equation A summarizes cellular respiration, and Equation B summarizes photosynthesis.
    C. Both chemical reactions produce oxygen and energy.
    D. The products of Equation A are the starting materials for Equation B.

Equation A:
$6CO_2 + 6H_2O + \text{energy} \rightarrow C_6H_{12}O_6 + 6O_2$

Equation B:
$C_6H_{12}O_6 + 6O_2 \rightarrow 6CO_2 + 6H_2O + \text{energy}$

6. Animals that eat only meat, such as dolphins, do not get much sugar from their diets. Select the statement below that best explains how a dolphin gets the energy it needs from its food.
    A. The dolphin does not use cellular respiration to get energy from food.
    B. The dolphin is not very active so it does not need a lot of energy to function.
    C. The dolphin's body is able to break down other carbon-based molecules, such as proteins and fats, to use as an energy source for cellular respiration.
    D. The dolphin gets the energy it needs directly from sunlight.

LESSON 2 SELF-CHECK

Interactive Review

Complete this section to review the main concepts of the lesson.

Chemical reactions provide the energy that cells need to perform functions.

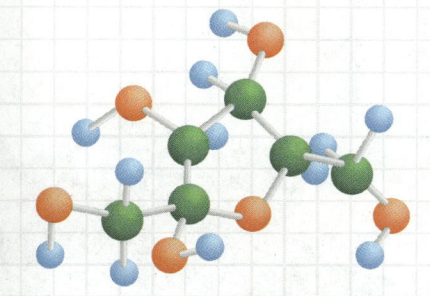

A. Explain how carbon-based molecules provide energy to cells.

Photosynthesis is a series of chemical reactions in which producers convert light energy from the sun to energy that is stored in the bonds of sugar molecules.

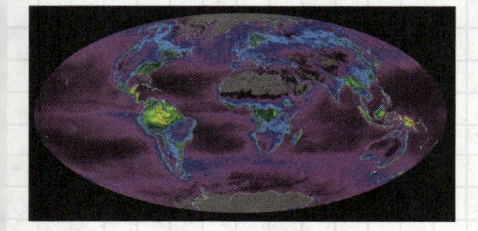

B. Construct a diagram or concept map that models photosynthesis.

Cellular respiration is a process that uses oxygen to release energy stored in food molecules.

C. Construct a diagram or concept map that models cellular respiration.

Lesson 2 Chemical Reactions Provide Energy for Cells

LESSON 3

The Flow of Energy Drives Weathering, Erosion, and Deposition

The rock structures on Praia do Camilo in Lagos, Algarve region, Portugal, have formed as a result of wave action over many years.

Explore First

Investigating Changes to Matter Break an effervescent antacid tablet into pieces with your fingers into a clear, plastic cup. Place another tablet in a cup filled with water. How does the tablet change using each method? Brainstorm ways these changes could occur to rocks in a natural system.

Go online to view the digital version of the Hands-On Lab for this lesson and to download additional lab resources.

CAN YOU EXPLAIN IT?

What caused these changes at Port Campbell National Park?

before 1990

after 1990

The photo on the left shows a rock formation just offshore of Port Campbell National Park in Australia before 1990. The photo on the right shows the same rock formation after 1990.

Earth's surface can change in the blink of an eye, or so it seems. While some events can appear to happen quickly, it may have taken many years to build up to that point. As you look at the photographs of the rock formation in Port Campbell National Park, evidence of change appears obvious, but the story may be more complex.

1. What types of changes do you observe between the rock formations in the two images?

2. Based on the visible changes in the rock formation, do you think the changes occurred quickly or slowly over time? Explain your reasoning.

EVIDENCE NOTEBOOK As you explore the lesson, gather evidence that will explain what happened to the rock formation in Australia over time.

Lesson 3 The Flow of Energy Drives Weathering, Erosion, and Deposition   267

EXPLORATION 1

Identifying Effects of Weathering

Energy Drives the Process of Weathering

Rocks, minerals, and landforms that make up Earth's surface are matter. Matter cannot be created or destroyed, but it can be changed. **Weathering** is the process by which rock materials are broken down by the action of physical and chemical processes. Energy that drives surface processes comes from gravity, and the sun, which provides thermal energy and causes movements of wind and water.

Weathering changes rocks by breaking them into smaller and smaller pieces, or by dissolving and removing some chemicals within the rock. Fragments of weathered rock, called **sediment,** are an important part of soil. Sediment can build up in layers on Earth's surface to form rock formations, sand dunes, and other features.

When it comes to weathering, not all rocks are created equal. Some rocks are more resistant to weathering than other rocks. Resistance to weathering is affected by the composition of, or substances that make up, the rock. Surface area also affects a rock's tendency to weather. A large block of rock will weather more slowly than smaller, broken pieces of the same rock will. This difference is because the smaller pieces have more surface area exposed to agents of physical and chemical weathering. Physical and chemical weathering are the two main types of weathering.

Look closely at the shape of this rock formation in South Coyote Buttes Wilderness in Arizona.

3. **Discuss** Study the photo of the rock formation. Many features found in South Coyote Buttes have this same striking appearance. With a partner, think of what could cause rocks to be shaped this way.

Physical Weathering

Physical weathering is the mechanical breakdown of rocks into smaller pieces. Physical weathering involves only physical changes. Temperature changes caused by the sun's energy or ice can cause cracks that eventually break rocks apart. Energy transfers caused by wind, water, and gravity can smooth rock surfaces, wear down rock, and transfer rock matter to other locations on Earth's surface.

Plants, animals, and humans also contribute to physical weathering of rocks. Plant growth can break rocks apart. Burrowing animals can expose and displace soil and rock. A well-worn walking path in a meadow exposes buried rocks to wind, water, air, and other agents of weathering.

Examples of Physical Weathering

Water can seep into tiny cracks in rocks and then freeze. Water expands when it freezes, causing the cracks in the rocks to widen. Cycles of repeated freezing and thawing eventually fracture the rock.

Plant roots can grow into gaps in rocks. Over time, as the roots grow, they force the gaps wider, causing the rock to break apart.

Abrasion occurs when rock is broken into smaller pieces by the scraping action of other materials. Abrasion is driven by water, wind, ice, or gravity. For example, a strong wind can blow sediments against rock surfaces, wearing down the rock. Abrasion can make angular rocks smooth and rounded.

4. Which statements describe physical weathering? Select all that apply.
   A. Two rocks hit against each other in a fast-flowing stream and break apart.
   B. Oxygen and water change the composition of the minerals in a rock.
   C. Small rocks are pushed together when a mole digs an underground den.
   D. Mosses grow on a rock and produce acids that wear away the rock over time.

Chemical Weathering

Chemical weathering is the breakdown and decomposition of rocks as a result of chemical reactions and processes. Unlike physical weathering, chemical weathering changes the composition of rocks through a chemical process. It weakens or dissolves rock over time. Interactions with components of other Earth systems such as water, oxygen, and plants can result in chemical weathering. For example, groundwater is water that flows through rock below Earth's surface. Groundwater can contain natural acids that dissolve rocks. Underground caves form in this way.

Examples of Chemical Weathering

Acid precipitation is rain or other precipitation that is more acidic than normal. Acid precipitation reacts with certain types of rocks, weakening them and making them more susceptible to physical weathering. The rocks break down over time.

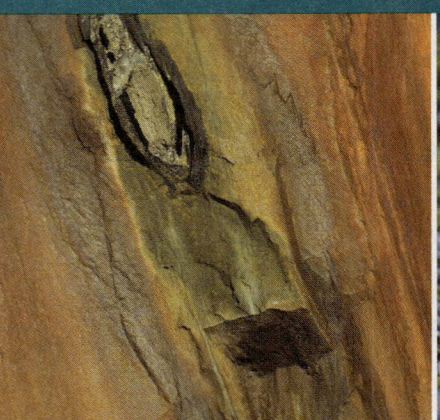

Iron-containing rocks can react with oxygen and water in a process called oxidation. Oxidation can give the rocks a reddish color, similar to rust. In fact, the same process causes rust to form on bicycles left out in the rain.

Plants, such as lichens and mosses, produce weak acids. When the plants grow on rocks, the acids slowly, but steadily, wear down the rocks.

Study the equation that shows the reaction of water with a mineral commonly found in rock.

$$KAlSi_3O_8 + H_2O \rightarrow HAlSi_3O_8 + KOH$$

5. The equation shows that chemical weathering *does / does not* result in the formation of new substances and matter *is / is not* conserved.

Other factors that affect rates of weathering include location and climate. Rocks on steep slopes are more likely to be displaced by gravity and exposed to wind, water, and air. Rocks in cold climates are more likely to experience physical weathering caused by cycles of freezing and thawing. In contrast, chemical weathering occurs more rapidly in warm, wet climates because warm temperatures increase rates of chemical processes. Both types of weathering tend to happen more slowly in dry climates.

> **EVIDENCE NOTEBOOK**
> 6. Does the collapsed rock formation in Australia show signs of weathering? If so, identify the type of weathering that could have occurred. Record your evidence.

7. **Language SmArts | Find Evidence for Weathering** Analyze each photo and identify the correct terms to complete each statement. Then provide evidence to support your answer choices.

Weathering Example	Weathering Type or Agent	Evidence
	This rock shows evidence of chemical / **physical** weathering as a result of acid / wind / **ice**.	
	This rock shows evidence of chemical weathering as a result of **acid** / wind / ice.	
	This rock shows evidence of physical weathering as a result of acid / **wind** / ice.	

Analyze the Effects of Weathering

Weathering is an important process that changes Earth's surface. These changes happen on different scales of time and space. A rock tumbles to the ground and breaks apart—this is a fast change that affects a small area. Water and wind steadily wear down a mountain over millions of years—this is a slow change that affects a large area.

8. **Discuss** With a partner, look at the stone bricks used to build this building and think about how they changed over time. What process may have caused them to change? Do you think these changes occurred quickly or slowly? Explain.

Lesson 3 The Flow of Energy Drives Weathering, Erosion, and Deposition

EXPLORATION 2

Exploring Agents of Erosion and Deposition

Picture a fast-flowing stream. Rocks tumble together, breaking up into sediment that is carried away and dropped in a new place. Some of the rock material dissolves in the water and is carried downstream. **Erosion** is the process by which wind, water, ice, or gravity transport weathered materials from one location to another. **Deposition** occurs when the eroded materials are dropped, or laid down. Like weathering, energy drives the processes that cause erosion and deposition and transfers matter to other locations on Earth's surface.

Wind and Water

Recall that wind and water can cause weathering through abrasion. Wind and water are also agents of erosion and deposition. Water erodes as it flows above ground through streams or underground through spaces in rock. Wind erodes as it blows over surfaces and lifts or pushes sediments. When wind and water lose energy and slow down, they drop their sediments and deposition occurs.

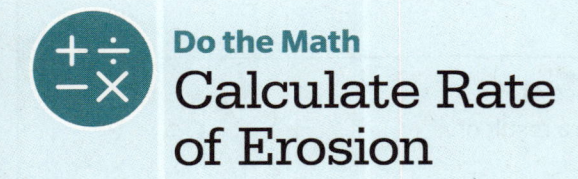

Do the Math
Calculate Rate of Erosion

The environment, very much like an equation, is balanced. Although matter cannot be created or destroyed, it can move and cycle through Earth's subsystems. As erosion occurs, it removes, or subtracts, sediment from one location and deposits, or adds, it to another location.

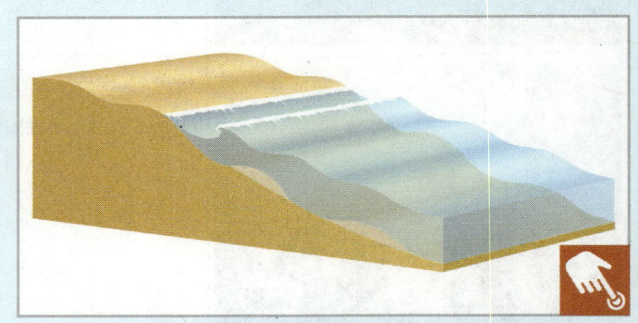

As ocean waves erode and deposit sand, features such as sandbars and beaches form.

9. Identify the correct type of change that occurs.
   A. Erosion represents a(n) ~~increase~~ / decrease in volume.
   B. Deposition represents a(n) increase / ~~decrease~~ in volume.
   C. As sand is eroded by waves and deposited on the sandbar, the sandbar increases / ~~decreases~~ in volume.

10. During a storm, sand is eroded from a beach at a rate of 2 m³ per hour. What equation can be used to represent the volume of sand in cubic meters, c, on the beach? Let b represent the amount of sand in cubic meters at the beginning of the storm and h represent time in hours. Complete the equation using +, −, ×, or ÷.

    $c = b\ \boxed{}\ 2h$

11. Suppose the total volume of sand on the beach is 1,278 m³. What will its volume be after 24 hours of erosion?

272

Erosion and Deposition by Wind and Water

How will water and wind shape the land in each of these areas?

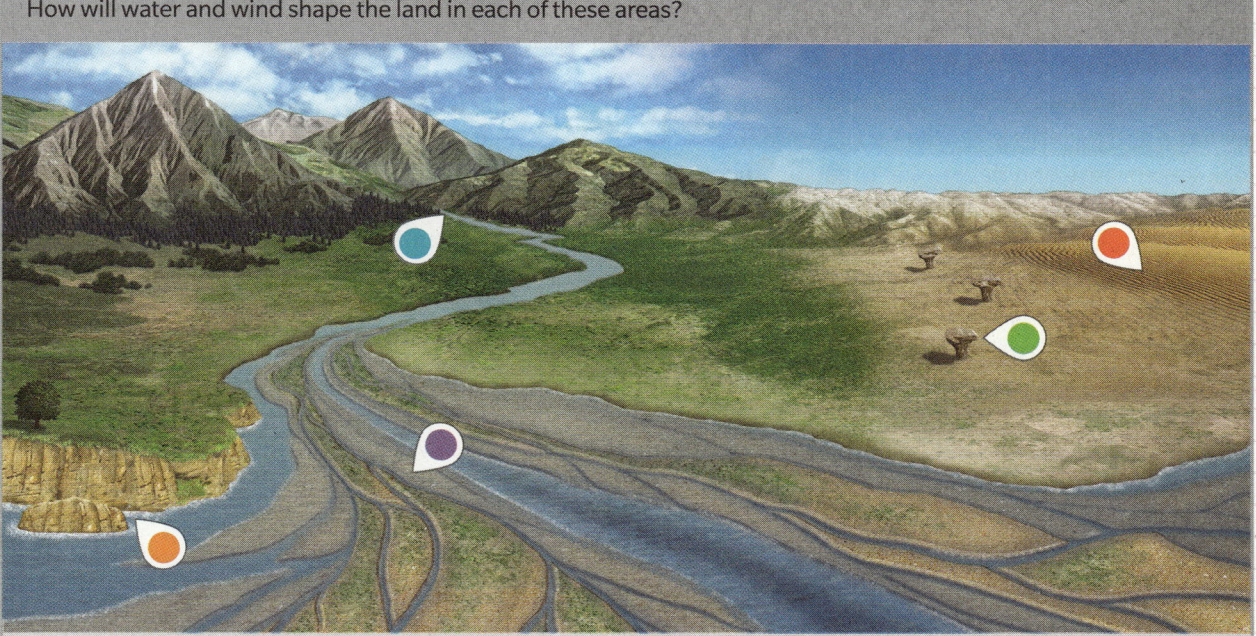

Waves constantly crash against the shoreline, weathering and eroding this rocky coast. Waves also erode sediments from sandy beaches.

Over millions of years, a river can carve a valley by the processes of weathering and erosion.

This rock formation has been shaped by wind abrasion, a type of weathering. Wind erosion then transported the weathered sediments to a new place.

A river slows down when it reaches the ocean. When the water loses energy, the sediments it was carrying are deposited. At the mouth of a stream or river, this action forms a feature called a *delta*. The shape of a delta changes constantly as sediments are deposited and eroded.

Sand dunes form when wind deposits sediments. Sand dune patterns are constantly changing due to erosion and deposition. Patterns can shift in time scales that range from hours to years.

12. **Discuss** A friend looks at these images and says that sand and sediment are being destroyed during the process of erosion. Form into small groups and discuss whether you think the friend is correct. Use evidence to support your response.

Lesson 3 The Flow of Energy Drives Weathering, Erosion, and Deposition

Ice

One of the most powerful agents of erosion and deposition is ice. A glacier is a large mass of ice that exists year-round and flows slowly over land. Gravity moves the glacier over land. As glaciers move, they act like a conveyor belt, eroding soil, sediment, and rock—even large boulders—over great distances, and then depositing the materials elsewhere. Glaciers can form jagged peaks or flatten and scoop out large sections of land, creating valleys. The Great Lakes are huge depressions formed by glaciers and later filled in with water. Glacial deposits can create long winding ridges or rocky mounds of sediment.

This cutaway view of a glacier reveals the sediment and rocks that can be picked up, carried, and deposited by the glacier as it flows across the surface of Earth.

13. How will the glacier affect surrounding land as it moves and melts over time?

Gravity

Energy from the sun powers the movement of wind and water. But the force of gravity, which attracts matter to Earth's center, also plays a role in driving these agents of erosion. When wind slows down, its load of sediment drops to the ground because of gravity. Rocks, boulders, and soil fall down slopes because of gravity. Water flows downhill, through valleys and waterfalls, because of gravity. Gravity is the main force behind sudden rock falls and landslides that can change the shape of a mountain.

landslide

waterfall

14. Explain the role of gravity in the landslide and in the waterfall.

15. Look at the photo of the rock formation. What factors could contribute to a collapse of the horizontal ledge? Select all that apply.
    A. wind
    B. water
    C. ice
    D. gravity

16. Explain how each of the contributing factors would play a role in the collapse of the ledge.

Found near the coast of Palau, Italy, this rock formation shows evidence of erosion.

EVIDENCE NOTEBOOK
17. Will gravity always play a role in erosion of a shoreline feature, such as the collapse of a rock formation in Australia? If so, identify the process, or processes, that would lead up to the collapse. Record your evidence.

Identify Areas of Erosion and Deposition

Weathering, erosion, and deposition are geologic processes that are mostly powered by energy from the sun. These changes happen on different scales of time and space. Yet, each change can be studied to help predict how Earth will change in the future.

18. On the map, label the areas where erosion occurs with an E and then label the areas where deposition occurs with a D. Some areas may have both.

Lesson 3 The Flow of Energy Drives Weathering, Erosion, and Deposition 275

EXPLORATION 3

Modeling Weathering, Erosion, and Deposition

You cannot re-create an actual flood in a lab, but you can use models to investigate the processes of weathering, erosion, and deposition during flood conditions. Computer simulations can also be used as models that can help you learn about past events and predict future ones. Computer models can be used to re-create events that cannot be studied directly, such as a massive flood in prehistoric times.

Case Study: The Missoula Floods

The Missoula Floods took place over 10,000 years ago. These floods stretched across a large portion of the northwestern United States, leaving visible evidence of their path. In the early 1920s, scientists began to study these historic floods and the research continues today.

The map and photos model the area affected by several floods over time. Deposition and erosion caused by repeated cycles of flooding resulted in the landforms visible today.

During the last Ice Age, a huge ice dam held back Glacial Lake Missoula, a large body of water in western Montana. On multiple occasions, the dam burst. Water rushed out, carrying ice, rock, and soil, and reshaping the land.

Erosion caused by the rushing water carved out a landscape of huge waterfalls, deep canyons, and the giant ripple marks shown here.

When the rushing floodwaters reached narrow Wallula Gap, they would back up and halt for several days, forming a temporary lake about 240 m deep.

The Scablands cover at least 5,000 km^2 of land affected by the ancient floodwaters. The ice dam reformed and broke several times. During each flood, the land was scoured and stripped bare.

19. **Discuss** With a partner, use the map and the photos to explain why large quartzite rocks from Idaho were discovered in Washington and Oregon.

Hands-On Lab
Model Erosion and Deposition

You will model Earth's surface with sand and soil and then investigate the effects of erosion and deposition by water and wind.

MATERIALS
- container of water
- colander with small holes
- flat trays (2)
- sand
- soil

Procedure and Analysis

STEP 1 Make a mound of soil on a tray to represent a hill and a mound of sand on the other tray to represent a dune.

STEP 2 Predict what will happen to both features after a heavy storm. Record all your predictions and observations in the spaces provided.

STEP 3 Blow on the sand dune to simulate a coastal storm. Observe what happens.

STEP 4 Pour water through the colander and onto the hill, simulating rain. Observe what happens.

STEP 5 Pour water around the base of the dune. Carefully tilt the tray to model wave action. Observe what happens to the dune.

	Predictions	Observations
water		
wind		
wave		

STEP 6 What agents of erosion and of deposition did you model?

STEP 7 **Engineer It** Models like this one can help scientists and engineers better understand natural hazards related to erosion and deposition, such as landslides. Describe a limitation of this model and propose a design solution to improve your model.

Lesson 3 The Flow of Energy Drives Weathering, Erosion, and Deposition

Scales of Weathering, Erosion, and Deposition

Weathering, erosion, and deposition can happen over a wide range of timescales. Wind can change the shape of a sand dune in minutes. The erosion that forms a canyon can take place over millions of years. The size of the changes caused by weathering, erosion, and deposition can vary too. Some changes, such as acids weathering a rock, affect Earth's surface on a small, localized scale. Changes such as the movement of an ice sheet can affect a whole continent. By studying these processes, you can reconstruct past geologic events, such as the massive flood that occurred in the northwestern United States over 10,000 years ago. You can also make predictions about future events.

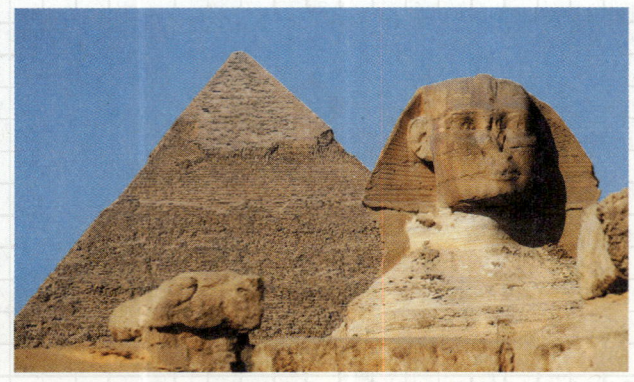

The Great Sphinx of Giza, Egypt.

20. The Sphinx in Egypt was likely built about 4,500 years ago. If weathering and erosion continue to have the same effect on the Sphinx, what do you think it will look like in 4,500 more years?

   A. It will not change.
   B. It will look more defined.
   C. It will look much less defined.
   D. It will disappear completely.

Predict Effects of Erosion

21. **Discuss** Water and wind have shaped Mesa Verde Canyon in Arizona for millions of years. With a partner, look for evidence of weathering and erosion in the canyon.

22. **Draw** If water continues to flow through the canyon, what do you think it will look like 1 million years from now? Use the space below to make a drawing of the canyon.

TAKE IT FURTHER

Continue Your Exploration

Name: _____ Date: _____

Check out the path below or go online to choose one of the other paths shown.

Gold Rush

- People in Science
- Sailing Stones
- Hands-On Lab
- Propose Your Own Path

Go online to choose one of these other paths.

Did you ever wonder why gold prospectors are often shown knee-deep in a shallow stream panning for gold? Why do they look there?

The prospectors know that gold is subject to the natural processes of weathering, erosion, and deposition. Gold can be found in the rocks of mountains, in the sediment at the bottom of streams, and even along the ocean floor. Gold is often found in veins, which are narrow zones within rock that contain minerals different from the rest of the rock. Weathering can expose these veins, wearing away nuggets or flakes of gold. Erosion carries the gold into streambeds. Deposition drops it in places where the stream flow slows down, such as near pools or sandbars.

When looking for gold in a stream, pans are used to sift through sediment and rocks.

TAKE IT FURTHER

Continue Your Exploration

Use your knowledge of erosion and deposition to answer the questions.

1. The rocks that make up this mountain contain gold. What processes can explain the discovery of gold in the stream, far away from the mountain?

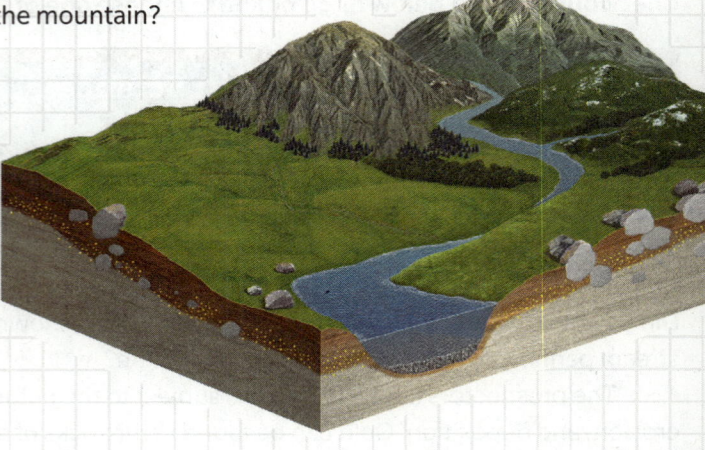

2. How could your understanding of erosion and deposition help identify where to pan for gold?

3. In which area(s) would you search for gold? Explain.

4. **Collaborate** Discuss with a classmate the locations where you would search for gold. Construct your own model and label the areas where you would search. Present an argument based on evidence to support your model.

LESSON 3 SELF-CHECK

Can You Explain It?

Name: _____ Date: _____

What caused these changes at Port Campbell National Park?

EVIDENCE NOTEBOOK
Refer to the notes in your Evidence Notebook to help you construct an explanation of the causes of the changes at Port Campbell National Park.

1. State your claim. Make sure your claim fully explains how the changes at Port Campbell National Park occurred.

2. Summarize the evidence you have gathered to support your claim and explain your reasoning.

Lesson 3 The Flow of Energy Drives Weathering, Erosion, and Deposition   281

LESSON 3 SELF-CHECK

Checkpoints

Use the photo to answer Questions 3–4.

3. For which of the following can you find evidence in this photo? Select all that apply.
   A. erosion
   B. deposition
   C. chemical weathering
   D. physical weathering

4. Which processes could be primarily responsible for the formation of the alluvial fan shown in the photo?
   A. wind storms coming through the base of the mountains into the valley
   B. water flowing down from the mountains and depositing sediment at the base
   C. rocks and boulders falling down the mountains and piling up at the base

Use the photo to answer Questions 5–6.

5. Which of the following is a factor in weathering caused by gravity?
   A. presence of living organisms on the rocks
   B. presence of water at one end of the glacier
   C. slope of the ground that the glacier is on
   D. size of the boulders at the base of the glacier

6. Which evidence in the photo best illustrates the occurrence of deposition?
   A. the glacier ending in the water
   B. the color of the rock formations
   C. areas of water where the glacier may be melting
   D. rocks and sediment at the edges of the glacier

7. What type of physical weathering could cause a rock to break apart?
   A. abrasion of the surface caused by rocks being moved under a sliding glacier
   B. gravity acting upon the loose rocks and dirt in the area
   C. water refreezing in the rock crevasses

282 Unit 4 Matter and Energy in Organisms and Rock

LESSON 3 SELF-CHECK

Interactive Review

Complete this interactive study guide to review the lesson.

Weathering is all of the processes that break down rocks. Physical weathering mechanically breaks down rocks. Chemical weathering breaks down rock by chemical reactions or processes such as dissolving rock in water.

A. List and describe different types of physical and chemical weathering.

Erosion is the process by which wind, water, ice, or gravity transport weathered materials from one location to another. Deposition occurs when materials are transferred by wind, water, ice, or gravity.

B. Explain how wind and water contribute to weathering, erosion, and deposition.

Weathering, erosion, and deposition can occur in minutes or over millions of years. Changes can be very large and noticeable, or small and seemingly insignificant.

C. Describe how weathering, erosion, and deposition operate on both small and large time and spatial scales.

Lesson 3 The Flow of Energy Drives Weathering, Erosion, and Deposition **283**

LESSON 4

The Flow of Energy Drives the Rock Cycle

Arches National Park in Utah is known for its beautiful sandstone arches.

Explore First

Modeling Rock Formation Use a grater to make crayon shavings using crayons of several colors. Wrap the shavings in a piece of foil and press down on the foil as hard as you can. Record your observations. Now float the foil of shavings on a cup of hot water. How has heat changed the appearance of the shavings?

Go *online* to view the digital version of the Hands-On Lab for this lesson and to download additional lab resources.

CAN YOU EXPLAIN IT?

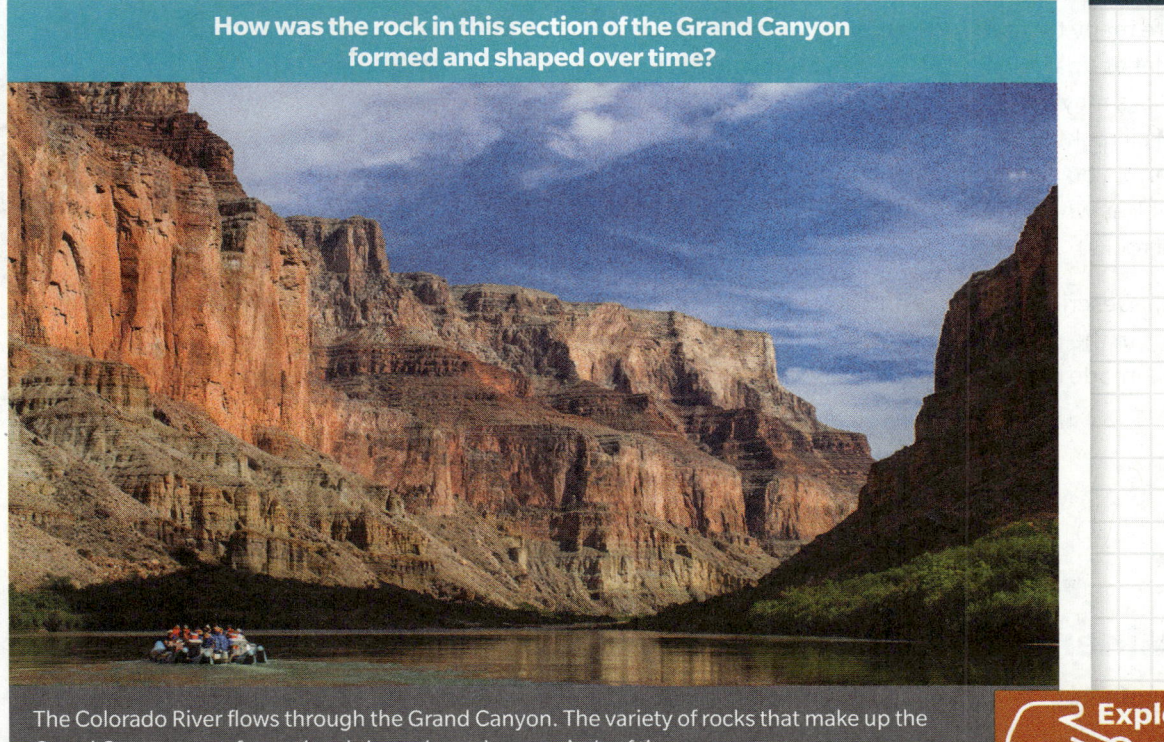

How was the rock in this section of the Grand Canyon formed and shaped over time?

The Colorado River flows through the Grand Canyon. The variety of rocks that make up the Grand Canyon were formed and shaped over long periods of time.

Explore Online

1. Look closely at the rock layers that make up the walls of the Grand Canyon in the photo. How do you think these rock layers form? Do you think these rock layers always looked the way they do now? Explain your answer.

EVIDENCE NOTEBOOK As you explore the lesson, gather evidence to help explain how the Grand Canyon formed and changed over time.

Lesson 4 The Flow of Energy Drives the Rock Cycle 285

EXPLORATION 1

Comparing Minerals and Rocks

Many parts of Earth are made up of solid rock. There are many types of rock beyond the layered rock that makes up the walls of the Grand Canyon. Although rocks may differ in appearance, the key ingredients of all rocks are minerals. To understand how rocks form, you must understand mineral formation as well as which minerals make up different kinds of rocks.

2. Describe the colors and appearance of the rock in the photograph. Do you think the whole rock is made of the same materials? Why or why not?

Different colors and patterns can be seen in this rock found near the edge of a lake in Sweden.

Minerals

A **mineral** is a naturally occurring and usually inorganic solid. It has a definite chemical composition and an orderly internal structure. A mineral's properties depend on the kinds of atoms or molecules that make up the mineral. The conditions under which the mineral forms also affect a mineral's properties. Minerals form by different natural processes. Some minerals form when magma or lava cools. Magma is molten rock inside Earth. Lava is molten rock on Earth's surface. As magma or lava cools, the atoms join together to form different minerals.

Minerals can also form when temperature and pressure within Earth cause the atoms in existing minerals to reorganize, forming a new mineral. When substances that are dissolved in liquid water are left behind as water molecules evaporate, minerals also form.

Minerals are made up of crystals. A crystal is a solid with its atoms or molecules arranged in a repeating pattern. The way the crystal forms determines its size. Some crystals are very large and some can only be seen with a microscope.

3. Which of the following processes can form a mineral? Select all that apply.
   A. cooling of melted rock
   B. changing heat and pressure
   C. erosion of sediments

This cave in Mexico was once full of water. Over millions of years, dissolved minerals in the water slowly formed these gypsum crystals. These are now considered to be the largest mineral crystals in the world!

286 Unit 4 Matter and Energy in Organisms and Rock

Rocks

Where do rocks come from? Rocks come from other rocks or from cooling magma or lava. Over long periods of time, natural processes change one type of rock into another type of rock. For example, weathering can break down rocks into smaller particles called sediment. Over time, the sediment can be deposited in layers in low-lying areas. Sediment can be buried, hardened, and cemented to form new rock.

Rocks can also form when existing rock experiences an increase in temperature or pressure. This change may happen when rock is buried deep below Earth's surface or when rock is stretched or squeezed during the formation of mountains. If the pressure and temperature are high enough, the minerals in a rock can change into new minerals. The changing of the minerals forms a new type of rock. Very deep below Earth's surface, rock may get hot enough to melt and form magma. Magma can eventually cool and solidify to form new rock.

This rock is made up of layers of sand that were pressed together and then cemented over time.

This rock is made up of light and dark bands of minerals that were chemically changed from their original form by intense pressure and temperature.

This rock formed when magma cooled far beneath Earth's surface.

4. What role do you think the minerals that make up a rock and the way a rock forms play in the appearance of rocks?

EVIDENCE NOTEBOOK

5. What characteristics do you see in the rocks that form the layers of the Grand Canyon? Record your evidence.

Identify Types of Rock

6. **Discuss** With a partner, write some observations of the rock formation in the photo. How might this rock have formed?

_____
_____
_____
_____
_____

7. This rock's formation likely resulted from changes in *temperature* / pressure.

Lesson 4 The Flow of Energy Drives the Rock Cycle

EXPLORATION 2

Relating Igneous Rocks to the Earth System

Igneous Rock

Cooling magma below ground and cooling lava above ground both form **igneous rocks.** Magma cools below ground in large chambers, in cracks, or between surrounding rock layers. Intrusive igneous rock forms when magma pushes, or intrudes, into the rock below Earth's surface and cools. Extrusive igneous rock forms when lava erupts, or is extruded, onto Earth's surface. Extrusive igneous rock is common at the sides and base of volcanoes.

Lava flows often cool quickly, hardening into rock.

The mineral composition of igneous rocks depends on the chemical make-up of the magma or lava that formed it and on how quickly that magma or lava cooled. Some igneous rocks are made up of many types of minerals. Other igneous rocks have fewer minerals in their make-up.

8. **Discuss** Do you think that the rock in the photo took more or less time to cool than rocks formed from magma beneath Earth's surface? Together with a partner, discuss why you think your conclusion is correct.

Geological Processes

The processes on Earth that form rock take such a long time that it is hard to imagine that they happen continuously. All rock that is on and inside Earth was magma at some point in the past. Likewise, rock that exists now may eventually end up back below Earth's crust. Then it may melt to form magma. These processes in the rock cycle may take hundreds of millions of years.

The flow of energy and cycling of matter that forms most rock may not be noticeable. However, if you have ever seen video of an erupting volcano, you have seen a few moments of the process of rock formation.

9. What happens to the matter in rock when it melts beneath Earth's surface? How does the melting process eventually lead to igneous rock forming?

Lava from a volcanic eruption flows through a tropical forest in Hawaii.

Explore Online

288 Unit 4 Matter and Energy in Organisms and Rock

Hands-On Lab
Model Crystal Formation

You will use salt to observe crystal formation and draw conclusions about the factors that affect crystal size.

Salt is found in natural bodies of water all over the world, especially in oceans and in some inland lakes. When salt water evaporates or changes temperature, salt crystals may form.

MATERIALS
- beakers, 250 mL (3)
- Epsom salts
- graduated cylinder, 100 mL
- hot plate
- small saucepan
- spoon or stirring rod
- tongs
- test tubes, tempered glass (3)
- terrycloth hot gloves

Procedure

STEP 1 Add the following to each of the three beakers until each is $\frac{2}{3}$ full
- beaker 1—water and ice cubes
- beaker 2—water at room temperature
- beaker 3—hot tap water

STEP 2 Place 120 mL of water in a saucepan. Heat the water on a hot plate over low heat until warm. Add 90–100g of Epsom salts and stir until dissolved. DO NOT let the mixture boil. Keep adding small amounts of salt until the crystals no longer dissolve in water.

STEP 3 Using a graduated cylinder, carefully pour equal amounts of the Epsom salts mixture into three test tubes, making sure not to include any salt from the bottom of the pan. Use tongs to steady the test tubes as you pour. Drop a few crystals of Epsom salt into each test tube. Then gently shake them. Place a test tube into each beaker.

STEP 4 Cool the test tubes for 15 minutes. Observe what happens. You may write or draw what you observe.

Beaker Observations - 15 minutes		
Beaker 1	Beaker 2	Beaker 3

Analysis

STEP 5 In which beaker did the largest crystals form? How did the temperature and the amount of time affect the size of the crystals?

Lesson 4 The Flow of Energy Drives the Rock Cycle

Timescale

The timescale for the formation of igneous rocks varies from minutes to hundreds of thousands of years. When igneous rock forms below Earth's surface, the magma is well insulated by surrounding rock, so it cools very slowly. The longer the cooling takes, the more time crystals have to grow. Rocks formed under these conditions generally have large, visible crystals. These rocks are described as "coarse-grained." Examples of igneous rocks that form below Earth's surface are granite and dolerite.

On the other hand, magma that reaches Earth's surface, called lava, cools very quickly when exposed to air. Because there is little time for crystals to form, these rocks are made up of very small crystals. These rocks are said to be "fine-grained." Basalt and andesite are common igneous rocks that form on Earth's surface.

Rocks that have the same chemical composition can have very different appearances when they cool at different rates. Remember: slow cooling results in larger crystals. Fast cooling results in smaller crystals. Super-fast cooling of magma can result in no crystals at all. Obsidian (ahb•SID•ee•uhn) is an igneous rock that cools so rapidly that no crystals form. Obsidian is glassy in appearance and is called volcanic glass.

dolerite | granite | basalt

These igneous rocks cooled at different rates.

10. Compare the igneous rocks in the photo. Which of the three rocks shows evidence of the longest cooling process? What evidence do you see to support your answer?

Igneous Rock in the Geosphere

Extrusive igneous rock, such as basalt, is easily found on Earth's surface. This is where it formed. Intrusive igneous rock is located beneath Earth's surface, where it formed. However, not all intrusive rock remains underground. For example, large regions of Earth's crust are pushed toward the surface during a process called uplift. Then, the intrusive igneous rock may be exposed at Earth's surface if the layers above are eroded. The Rockies, the largest mountain range of western North America, are made mostly of intrusive igneous rock, especially granite.

Igneous Rock

The igneous rock columns making up Devils Tower, Wyoming, show the result of magma forcing its way up toward Earth's surface. Geologists hypothesize that the columns formed underground. The columns later became exposed after the surrounding rock eroded away.

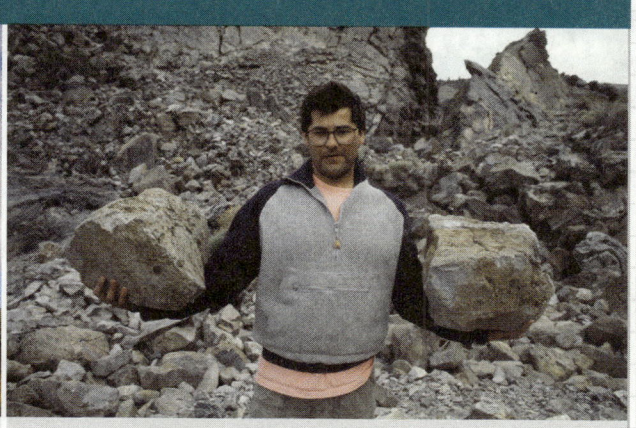

Quick-cooling igneous rocks, such as these pumice boulders, often have a spongy appearance because the lava contained bubbles of gas. The bubbles leave pockets of air in the rock. The pumice is light enough to hold over your head with little effort.

11. Compare and contrast the two rock formations shown above. What do these formations have in common, as related to energy flow in the Earth system?

Describe How Igneous Rock Forms and Changes

As with all rocks, igneous rocks can be weathered by wind, water, and organisms. Climate changes may also be a factor in the weathering of rocks. For example, as glaciers grow and shrink during ice ages, the granite of massive mountains may be weathered and eroded.

12. Order the events that likely led to the formation of Half Dome. Write numbers 1–4 on the lines to order the events.

    ___ The granite was uplifted with the surrounding rock.

    ___ A glacier moved over the exposed granite and eroded the rock.

    ___ A body of magma cooled underground and formed granite rock.

    ___ The surrounding rock was weathered and eroded.

One of the iconic rock formations found in Yosemite National Park, California, is Half Dome. It is made of intrusive igneous granite that has weathered with time.

Lesson 4 The Flow of Energy Drives the Rock Cycle

EXPLORATION 3

Relating Sedimentary Rocks to the Earth System

Sedimentary Rock

When sediments are compacted or are cemented together by new minerals, **sedimentary rock** forms. This process is gradual and may take up to millions of years to occur. Like the name suggests, sedimentary rock is made of sediment. The mineral "glue" that cements sediment into rock may be mixed with the sediment when it is deposited or it may enter the rock later. The minerals quartz and calcite are common sedimentary cements.

Sedimentary rocks are named according to the size and type of fragments they contain. For example, one type of sedimentary rock called mudstone is made up mostly of cemented mud particles.

Some sedimentary rock, like this breccia (BREHCH-ee-uh), is made up of large, compacted rock fragments.

13. What processes form the sediment that makes up sedimentary rock? Explain how sedimentary rock is part of the cycling of Earth materials over time.

Sedimentary rock may form in distinct layers. The layers can be different colors and thicknesses, depending on the type and amount of sediment deposited.

Geological Processes

How does sediment get pressed together, or compacted, and cemented? Often these processes happen when the weight of overlying layers of soil and sediment press down on lower layers of sediment. At the same time, dissolved minerals solidify between sediment pieces and cement them together.

Sedimentary rocks may also form from the remains of once-living plants and animals. For example, when layer upon layer of plant material is buried, compacted, and exposed to the higher temperatures and pressures beneath Earth's surface, its atoms rearrange. Over millions of years, this process may form coal.

Sedimentary rock, however, does not always form from layers of sediment. Sometimes minerals form when the water in which they are dissolved evaporates. The chemicals that remain crystallize to form minerals. Salt and various kinds of limestone form this way.

One Way Sedimentary Rock Forms

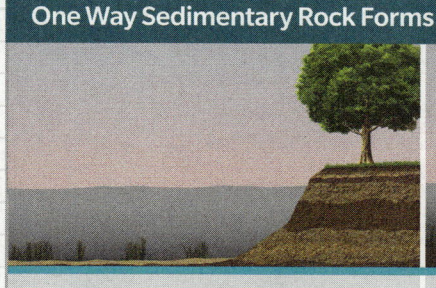

Sediment and organic material are deposited in a lake over time.

As these materials break down and settle, they form layers.

These layers are compacted and cemented to form sedimentary rock.

Explore Online

14. Select the statements that correctly describe a part of the process shown above.
    A. The oldest rocks are found in the top layers.
    B. The sediment is broken down rock from the edge of the lake.
    C. Rock layers formed when magma beneath the lake cooled.
    D. The rocks in this scene contain once-living things.

15. **Engineer It** Sandstone is a type of sedimentary rock that can be formed in a lab environment. How would your knowledge of the formation of sedimentary rock help when designing a machine that could create sandstone in a lab?

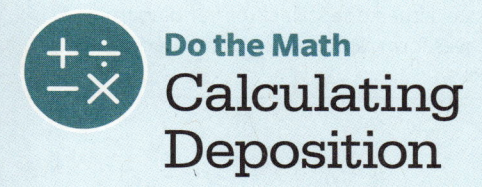

Do the Math
Calculating Deposition

The top of the travertine layer (white material) shown in the photo is 3 m below the top of the sarcophagus. Assuming a rate of deposition of 2 mm/year on average, how many years will it take for the sarcophagus to be completely buried in travertine? Complete the steps below to find out.

In Turkey, calcium-rich hot springs leave behind mineral deposits that cause this rock formation to slowly bury this 2,000-year-old sarcophagus while the rock formation grows.

16. How long will it take for the sarcophagus to be completely buried?

    STEP 1 First, convert meters to millimeters: 3 m = _____ mm

    STEP 2 Then, set up a proportion. Use the variable n to represent the unknown:

    $$\frac{2 \text{ mm}}{1 \text{ yr}} = \frac{\boxed{} \text{ mm}}{\boxed{} \text{ yr}}$$

    STEP 3 Solve the proportion.

Timescale

Sedimentary rock forms slowly over time. A person could observe a travertine deposit growing very slowly over a period of years—about 2 cm in 10 years. But the deposition of calcium carbonate out of solution is actually one of the faster ways that sedimentary rock can form. Sedimentary rock formed from the compaction and cementation of sediments may take many thousands or even millions of years to form. For example, some types of limestone form as the remains of tiny aquatic organisms build up on the floor of the ocean or a lake. These sediments accumulate slowly and are buried and compacted for a long time to form limestone.

Shale may take millions of years to form by slow accumulation, burial, and compaction of very fine clay sediments.

Limestone may form by the deposition of dissolved calcium carbonate. Limestone stalactites hanging from the ceilings of caves form rapidly when compared to other sedimentary rocks.

17. **Discuss** Look at the photos and read about the formation of shale and limestone. Together with a partner, compare and contrast the process of shale and limestone formation.

Sedimentary Rock in the Geosphere

Sedimentary rock is often identified by its visible layers. Even though you can see these sedimentary rocks, that does not mean they were formed on or near the surface. The pressure needed for compaction of some sedimentary rocks happens under many layers of sediment and rock, over thousands or millions of years.

Water plays a key role in forming, as well as exposing, sedimentary rock. Water contains many dissolved minerals and salts. Water can flow through sediments and leave the minerals and salts behind, which can cement the sediments together. After a sedimentary rock forms under the surface, uplift can push the rock up toward the surface. Then, weathering and erosion might expose and shape the rock into the formations seen today. For example, over millions of years the Colorado River has helped to shape the Grand Canyon and expose the many colorful layers that make up the canyon walls.

Examples of Sedimentary Rock

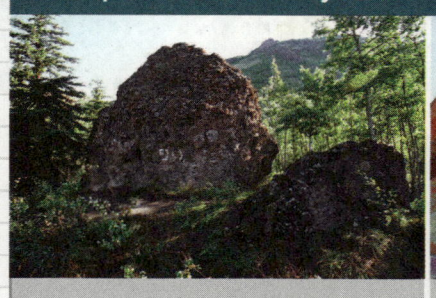

Conglomerate rocks are made of large pieces of sediment later cemented together.

The Rainbow Mountains of Gansu Province, China, are sandstone. The different colors and textures are due to differences in the mineral composition and grain size.

The White Cliffs of Dover, England, are made of chalky limestone. They are composed largely of the calcium carbonate shells of tiny ocean-dwelling organisms.

18. Which of these three words applies to all types of sedimentary rock: *weathering*, *compaction*, or *deposition*? Explain your answer.

EVIDENCE NOTEBOOK

19. Do you see any evidence of sedimentary rock in the Grand Canyon? If so, how long do you think it took to form and how has the rock changed over time? Record your evidence.

Identify How Sedimentary Rock Forms and Changes

Like other types of rock, sedimentary rock can be affected by its surroundings. Wind and water can weather and erode sedimentary rock, sometimes exposing new layers.

20. Use what you know to write a series of three events that could have led to the formation of Monument Valley as it appears today.

The sedimentary rock of Monument Valley, Arizona, formed approximately 300 to 100 million years ago at what was then near sea level. Since then, dramatic uplift has moved the rock to its current position of 2000 m above sea level. Amazingly its horizontal layers are undisturbed! However, rivers that flooded over it at various times over millions of years have carried much of the rock away.

Lesson 4 The Flow of Energy Drives the Rock Cycle

EXPLORATION 4

Relating Metamorphic Rocks to the Earth System

Metamorphic Rock

Imagine a rock that is buried deep in Earth's crust. The temperature and pressure are very high. Over millions of years, the solid rock may change to a different kind of rock.

When large changes of temperature, pressure, or both cause the texture and mineral content of existing rock to change over millions of years, **metamorphic rock** forms. Contact with hot fluids can also cause changes to rock. *Metamorphism* is another word for this change. Rocks undergo metamorphism when their temperatures typically reach ranges of 200 °C to 1200 °C.

Gneiss (NYS) is a metamorphic rock. It forms at high temperatures deep within Earth's crust.

21. Discuss Together with a partner, discuss why the gneiss rock shown in the photo has both light bands and dark bands.

Geological Processes

When rock is exposed to physical or chemical conditions that cause the rock's minerals to change and form new minerals, the rock then becomes a new metamorphic rock. Each type of metamorphic rock forms under a certain range of temperatures and pressures, and each contains particular kinds of minerals.

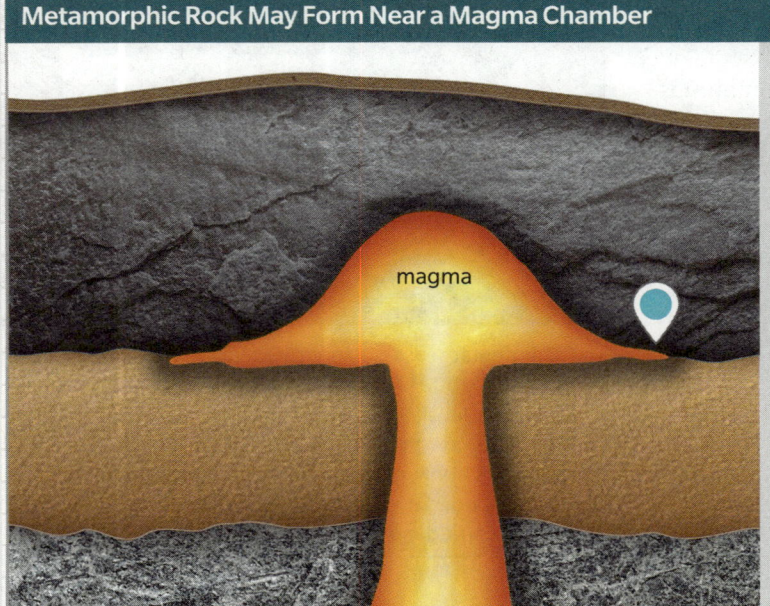

Metamorphic Rock May Form Near a Magma Chamber

magma

Hornfels is a metamorphic rock that forms in the zone of shale closest to magma, where the shale is exposed to very high temperatures.

296 Unit 4 Matter and Energy in Organisms and Rock

Metamorphic Rock Formation

All three kinds of rock—sedimentary, igneous, or metamorphic—can change into new metamorphic rock. Increased temperature and pressure can cause changes to both the physical and chemical make-up of the rock. These changes result in the formation of a new type of rock—a metamorphic rock different from the original rock. The kind of metamorphic rock that forms depends on the parent rock and the conditions of formation.

Metamorphic rock can form in areas that are in contact with or close to a magma chamber. The intense heat of the magma chamber can change the minerals in nearby rock. Rock can also undergo metamorphism when it is buried deep enough in Earth that a large region of rock is subjected to intense heat and pressure. In this situation, large areas of rock can be changed into different types of rock.

An example of metamorphic rock transformation is quartzite. Quartzite forms when sandstone, a sedimentary rock, is exposed to high temperature and pressure. This causes the sand grains to fuse and grow larger and the spaces between the sand grains to disappear.

Before	Metamorphosis	After
 shale	Slate results from exposing shale to moderate pressure and temperature increases over a very long period of time—perhaps millions of years. Slate is a metamorphic rock in which the minerals have become squeezed into flat, sheet-like layers.	 slate
 slate	Metamorphic rocks can change into other types of metamorphic rock. Slate can become phyllite when it is exposed to increased temperature and pressure. Tiny plates of a sparkling mineral called mica form during metamorphism. This gives phyllite a slight sheen.	 phyllite
 basalt	Basalt is an igneous rock that can change into amphibolite when exposed to temperatures between 500 °C and 850 °C. Amphibolite has grains coarse enough for individual minerals to be seen.	 amphibolite

22. Circle the answer that best completes each statement.

   A. A sedimentary rock is most likely to change into metamorphic rock after _heating_ / erosion / deposition.

   B. Metamorphic rocks are _usually_ / sometimes / never produced by changes to other metamorphic rock.

Lesson 4 The Flow of Energy Drives the Rock Cycle

Timescale

The formation of metamorphic rock is generally a very slow process because the changes happen to rock in its solid state. The process to form coarser-grained metamorphic rocks with larger mineral crystals, such as gneiss, may take tens of millions of years.

23. How does the time it takes to form metamorphic rock compare to the time it takes to form extrusive igneous rock?

24. What happens to the minerals in rocks that undergo metamorphism?

Metamorphic Rocks in the Geosphere

If metamorphic rock forms deep inside Earth, how are you able to see it? The ridges making up much of the Appalachian Mountains are metamorphic rock. This rock formed when the edges of North America and Africa crashed together hundreds of millions of years ago. Metamorphic rock may be moved to the surface by uplift or after erosion removes layers of rock.

Some rocks are easy to identify as metamorphic. When a metamorphic rock forms, pressure on the rock may force the mineral crystals into parallel dark and light bands. Other kinds of metamorphic rocks will not show this kind of structure. Instead, these rocks will have large grains that are arranged in an unstructured manner.

Schist is often categorized by color. Greenschists, like this one, form under high pressure and high temperature, far below Earth's surface. Blueschists form under high pressure but relatively low temperature.

Exposing schist to higher temperature and pressure can eventually cause its minerals to separate into alternating bands of light and dark minerals as it transforms into another metamorphic rock called gneiss.

25. **Discuss** Is it possible for metamorphic rock to form on Earth's surface? Together with a partner, discuss your answer and explain your reasoning.

marble

This marble formed beneath the ocean floor millions of years ago. It was uplifted and carved by erosion into vast cliffs. When this marble formed, the calcite crystals in the original limestone grew, filling the spaces in the limestone. This resulted in harder and longer lasting marble. Marble is not as hard as granite. However, marble is chosen as a building material for grand monuments due to its beauty.

Describe How Metamorphic Rock Forms

Metamorphic rock often shows evidence of the strong forces that helped form it. These forces can even change metamorphic rock into different kinds of metamorphic rock. Uneven pressures applied to rock affect the rock's appearance. Many metamorphic rocks have wavy patterns of minerals caused by the reorganization of the solid crystals. Some rocks may be bent or folded by intense pressure.

Metamorphic rocks, just like igneous and sedimentary rock, can also be weathered over time. The weathering may expose mineral patterns.

This metamorphic rock was exposed after glacial movement eroded part of it away. The wavy bands of minerals are a clue to the intense forces experienced during its metamorphism.

26. Use what you know about the formation of metamorphic rock to describe three events that could have led to the formation of the rock as it appears today.

Lesson 4 The Flow of Energy Drives the Rock Cycle

EXPLORATION 5

Modeling the Rock Cycle

Although rocks seem solid and unchanging, they can be affected by temperatures and pressure beneath Earth's surface and weathering on Earth's surface. As a result, rocks undergo changes. These changes sometimes form new kinds of rock. This series of processes, in which rocks change from one type to another, is called the *rock cycle*. The rock cycle is one way that matter is recycled on Earth.

The action of waves has broken up shells at the beach into tiny fragments.

This limestone rock is made up mostly of shells that settle to the ocean floor.

Marble forms when limestone is subjected to heat and pressure.

27. Draw Processes in the rock cycle result in the formation of limestone and change limestone to sediment and other types of rock. Construct a diagram to show the processes that change limestone to sediment and marble.

The Rock Cycle

Think about all the processes that form the three kinds of rock—igneous, sedimentary, and metamorphic—and the factors that influence those processes. How are these processes related to each other? How do they recycle matter on Earth?

The processes that form different kinds of rock and recycle matter on Earth do not have one defined pathway. The pathways are more like a web. You can use a model of the rock cycle to show how the processes that form different kinds of rocks are related.

28. Circle the energy source for these processes in the rock cycle.
  A. Melting and cooling: sun / *Earth's interior*
  B. Erosion and deposition: *sun* / Earth's interior
  C. Changing temperature and pressure: sun / *Earth's interior*

A Model of the Rock Cycle

29. Complete the rock cycle diagram by writing *sedimentary rock* or *igneous rock*. *Metamorphic rock* has been filled in for you.

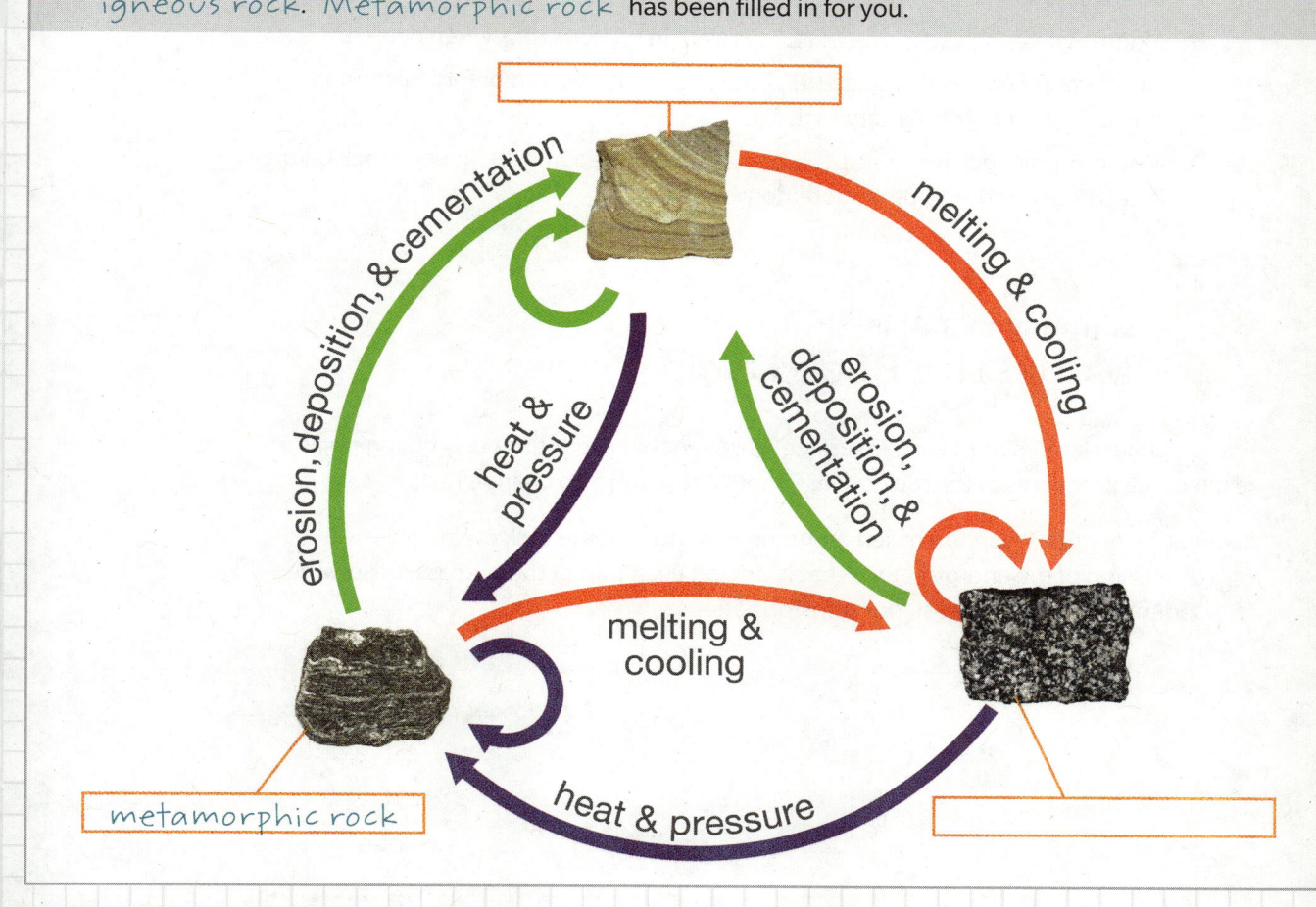

[Rock cycle diagram with three rocks connected by arrows showing processes: erosion, deposition, & cementation (green); melting & cooling (orange/red); heat & pressure (purple). Top box: sedimentary rock. Bottom-left labeled: metamorphic rock. Bottom-right box: igneous rock.]

30. Discuss What information about the rock cycle is shown in this model? What information about the rock cycle is not shown in this model? With a partner, discuss the advantages and disadvantages of this model.

Paths in the Rock Cycle

With pressure and temperature changes, sedimentary rock may become metamorphic rock. Sedimentary rock may melt and cool to form igneous rock. Sedimentary rock at Earth's surface may break down into sediment that will form new sedimentary rock.

Igneous rock can change directly into metamorphic rock while still beneath Earth's surface, or it might melt and then cool again to form a new igneous rock. Igneous rock at Earth's surface can be weathered to form sediments that form sedimentary rock.

Metamorphic rock can melt and form magma. The magma cools to form igneous rock. Metamorphic rock can also be changed by temperature and pressure to form a different type of metamorphic rock. Weathering can change metamorphic rock into sediments that will become sedimentary rock.

> **EVIDENCE NOTEBOOK**
> **31.** How did the processes in the rock cycle play a role in the formation of the Grand Canyon? Record your evidence.

Lesson 4 The Flow of Energy Drives the Rock Cycle **301**

32. Write *always*, *sometimes*, or *never* to complete the statements.

   A. Igneous rock will _____ change as a result of temperature and pressure.

   B. Magma will _____ result in igneous rock when cooled.

   C. Sedimentary rock will _____ be eroded before becoming another type of sedimentary rock.

   D. Metamorphic rock will _____ become an igneous rock before it becomes another type of metamorphic rock.

Language SmArts
Model the Rock Cycle

Rocks define a large part of Earth's surface. Those rocks are continuously changing as a result of the processes of the rock cycle. Other factors can also change rock.

33. Tell a story of a teaspoon of sediment moving through the rock cycle. Include a discussion of the energy source that is driving each part of the process. Follow the sediment through at least four transformations.

34. **Draw** In the space provided, draw a rock cycle diagram to go with your story.

TAKE IT FURTHER

Continue Your Exploration

Name: Date:

Check out the path below or go online to choose one of the other paths shown.

Coal Mining

- Geodes
- Hands-On Labs
- Propose Your Own Path

Go online to choose one of these other paths.

Minerals and rocks are used for many purposes, such as building homes, paving roads, and manufacturing consumer items. Before they can be used, rocks and minerals must be mined, or removed from the ground. Some materials are mined from large open pits, called quarries. Others must be removed from deep, underground tunnels.

Some common mineral resources are granite, limestone, marble, sand, gravel, gypsum, iron, and copper. Some rocks, such as coal, are burned for heat and to generate electrical energy. Coal is burned in power plants to release chemical energy that is converted to electrical energy. In fact, more than 90% of the coal mined in the United States is used to generate electrical energy.

The original source of the energy stored in coal is the sun. Plants absorb sunlight and convert the solar energy into chemical energy that is stored in their stems, roots, and leaves. Hundreds of millions of years ago, remains of plants that died were buried beneath sand, rock, or mud. This created a pocket of carbon-rich materials that were trapped in layers of sediment and rock. Over time, temperature and pressure from these sediments changed the buried plant materials into the coal that we mine today.

coal seam

Coal seams are layers of sedimentary rock that are formed from organic matter over millions of years.

TAKE IT FURTHER

Continue Your Exploration

1. Based on how it is formed, what type of rock is coal?
   A. sedimentary
   B. igneous
   C. metamorphic

2. Explain why you think mining for coal almost always requires miners to dig deep into the ground.

3. Draw a model of how the flow of energy relates to the formation, mining, and burning of coal by humans as an energy source.

4. **Collaborate** Discuss with a classmate how mining for coal may have changed over the years. Research different ways coal is mined. What processes are best used to extract the coal? Present evidence for your argument using an oral presentation.

LESSON 4 SELF-CHECK

Can You Explain It?

Name: Date:

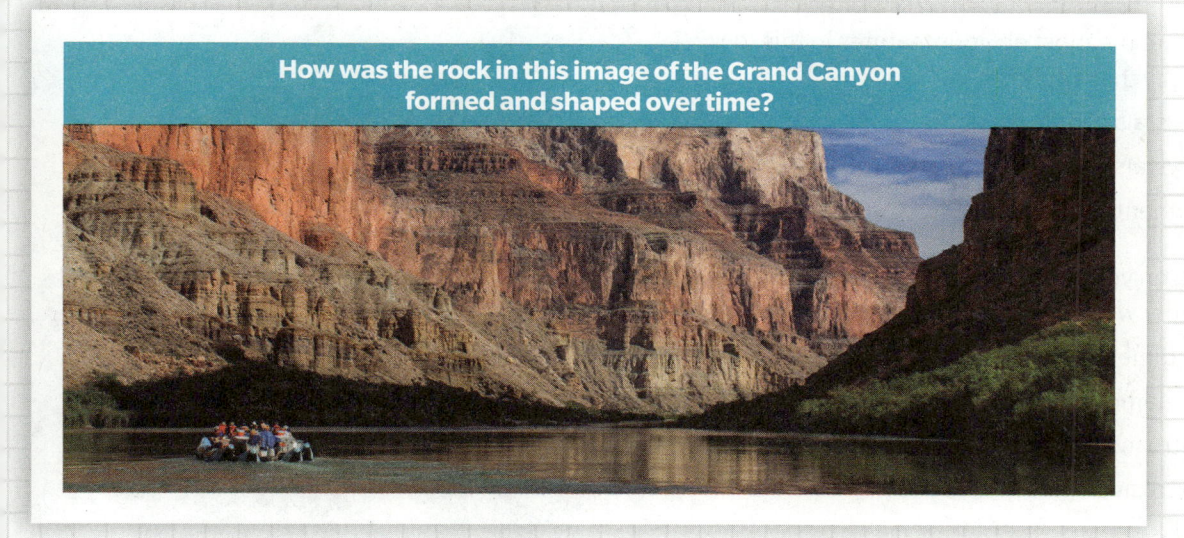

How was the rock in this image of the Grand Canyon formed and shaped over time?

> **EVIDENCE NOTEBOOK**
> Refer to the notes in your Evidence Notebook to help you construct an explanation for how the rock layers formed and were shaped over time.

1. State your claim. Make sure your claim fully explains how the rocks in the Grand Canyon formed and were shaped over time.

2. Summarize the evidence you have gathered to support your claim and explain your reasoning.

Lesson 4 The Flow of Energy Drives the Rock Cycle **305**

LESSON 4 SELF-CHECK

Checkpoints

Answer the following questions to check your understanding of the lesson.

Use the photo to answer Questions 3–5.

3. What are the most obvious features in this rock? Select all that apply.
   A. crystals of different sizes
   B. crystals of different colors
   C. cemented sediments

4. Based on your observations, in which general category would you place this rock?
   A. sedimentary
   B. metamorphic
   C. intrusive igneous
   D. extrusive igneous

5. In which order did these events most likely occur during this rock's formation? Write numbers 1–4 on the lines to order the events.
   ___ Magma began cooling.
   ___ Uplift moved the rock to the surface.
   ___ Heat from Earth's interior formed magma.
   ___ Crystals formed in the rock.

Use the photo to answer Questions 6–7.

6. Based on your observations, in which general category would you place this rock?
   A. sedimentary
   B. metamorphic
   C. intrusive igneous
   D. extrusive igneous

7. What type of rock fragments could be part of this rock? Choose all that apply.
   A. sedimentary
   B. metamorphic
   C. intrusive igneous
   D. extrusive igneous

LESSON 4 SELF-CHECK

Interactive Review

Complete this section to review the main concepts of the lesson.

Rocks are composed of minerals.

A. What characteristics do minerals have in common?

The three rock types are igneous, sedimentary, and metamorphic rock.

B. What do all rocks have in common? How is the formation of the three rock types similar? How is their formation different?

Igneous, sedimentary, and metamorphic rocks are all part of the rock cycle.

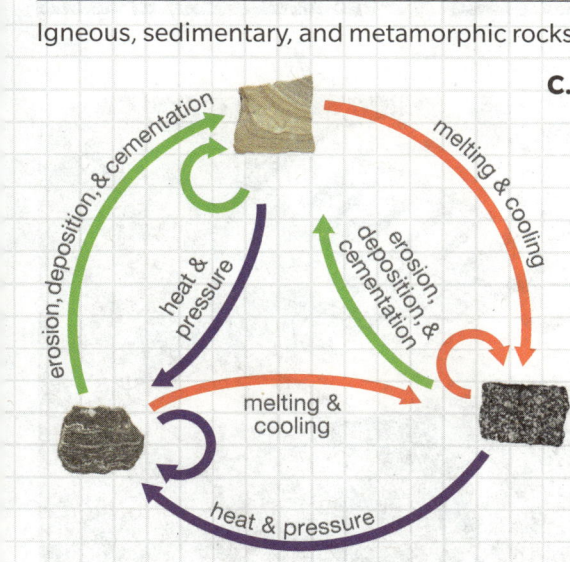

C. Use the rock cycle diagram to explain how a sedimentary rock could become a metamorphic rock.

Lesson 4 The Flow of Energy Drives the Rock Cycle 307

UNIT 4 CONNECTIONS

Choose one of the activities to explore how this unit connects to other topics.

☐ People in Science/Engineering

Dr. Jayne Belnap, Research Ecologist
Biological soil crusts are communities of organisms on the surface of soil that include lichen, mosses, cyanobacteria, and fungi. Soil crusts are commonly found in dry areas of the world. Dr. Belnap has worked for over 30 years researching the role of soil crusts in the stability of dryland ecosystems. Her expertise has contributed to the development of creative and cost-effective ways to restore soil crusts that have been damaged by land use and climate change.

Research the effects of temperature and precipitation changes on the structure and function of biological soil crusts. Present your findings in a poster or infographic.

☐ Physical Science Connection

Energy Transformations An energy transformation takes place when energy changes from one form into another. For example, plants transform light energy from the sun into chemical energy stored in the bonds of sugar molecules. The Hoover Dam transforms the mechanical energy of rushing water into electrical energy that can be used by homes, offices, and buildings within the region.

Using library or Internet sources, research three different examples of energy transformation. Identify the primary forms of energy involved in each transformation. Use visuals to present your findings.

Hoover Dam

☐ Health Connection

The Gluten-Free Craze Looking around a grocery store, many products are labeled "gluten free." A gluten-free diet is recommended to help people with certain immune disorders. The gluten-free trend has also been adopted by other people as a way to lose weight and increase energy levels. However, these claims have not been proven by research.

Using library or Internet sources, find out what gluten is. Research the effects of adopting a gluten-free diet. Create a poster or other visual display that explains how a gluten-free diet could affect a person's energy levels.

UNIT 4 REVIEW

Name: _____   Date: _____

Complete this review to check your understanding of the unit.

Use the graph to answer Questions 1–3.

1. What conclusions can be made about the rate of photosynthesis shown in the graph? Select all that apply.

   A. The rate of photosynthesis changes over a day.
   B. The rate of photosynthesis decreases at night.
   C. The rate of photosynthesis decreases at midday.
   D. The rate of photosynthesis is lowest only at 10 p.m.
   E. The rate of photosynthesis is constant.

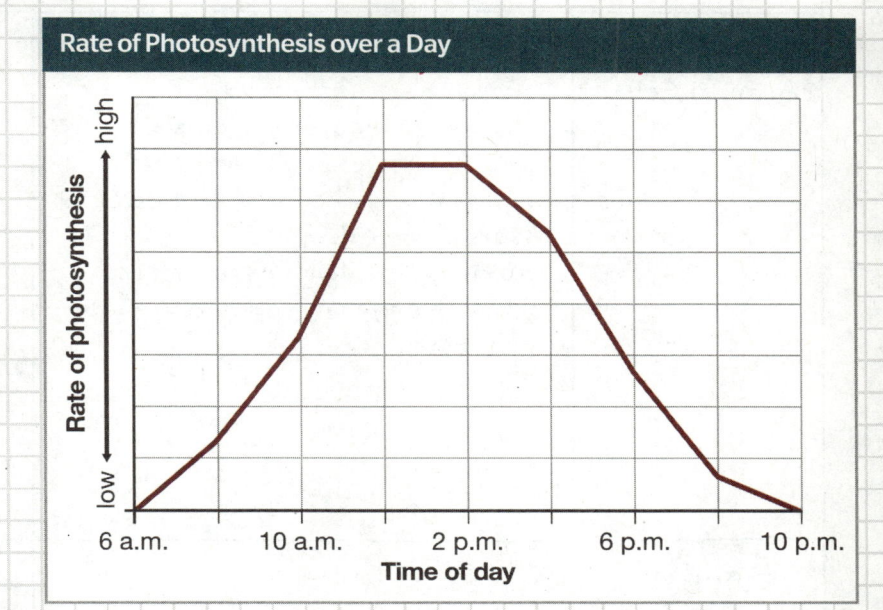

   Rate of Photosynthesis over a Day

2. Based on the graph, when is the rate of photosynthesis expected to be the lowest? Select all that apply.

   A. 6 a.m.
   B. 10 a.m.
   C. 2 p.m.
   D. 6 p.m.
   E. 10 p.m.

3. Sunlight is the ~~matter~~ / *energy* input required for the process of photosynthesis. The rate of photosynthesis increases during parts of the day that have *more* / ~~less~~ sunlight. The rate of photosynthesis decreases during parts of the day that have ~~more~~ / *less* sunlight.

4. Grasses get matter and energy from the environment. Grasses are *producers* / ~~consumers~~. Mice get matter and energy from eating grasses and other plants. Mice are ~~producers~~ / *consumers*.

Use the photo to answer Question 5.

5. The tree's roots *physically* / ~~chemically~~ weather the rock, breaking the rock apart. The type of matter that makes up this rock ~~changes~~ / *does not change* as a result of this process.

Unit 4 Matter and Energy in Organisms and Rock **309**

UNIT 4 REVIEW

6. Complete the table by describing the flow of energy and the cycling of matter at different scales of natural systems.

Scale	Flow of Energy	Cycling of Matter
Plant and Animal Cells	Plant cells use light energy from the sun to produce sugar molecules through photosynthesis. Plant and animal cells release the energy stored in sugar molecules during cellular respiration. This energy is used for life processes.	
Organisms		
Rocks		

UNIT 4 REVIEW

Name: Date:

Use the rock cycle diagram to answer Questions 7–10.

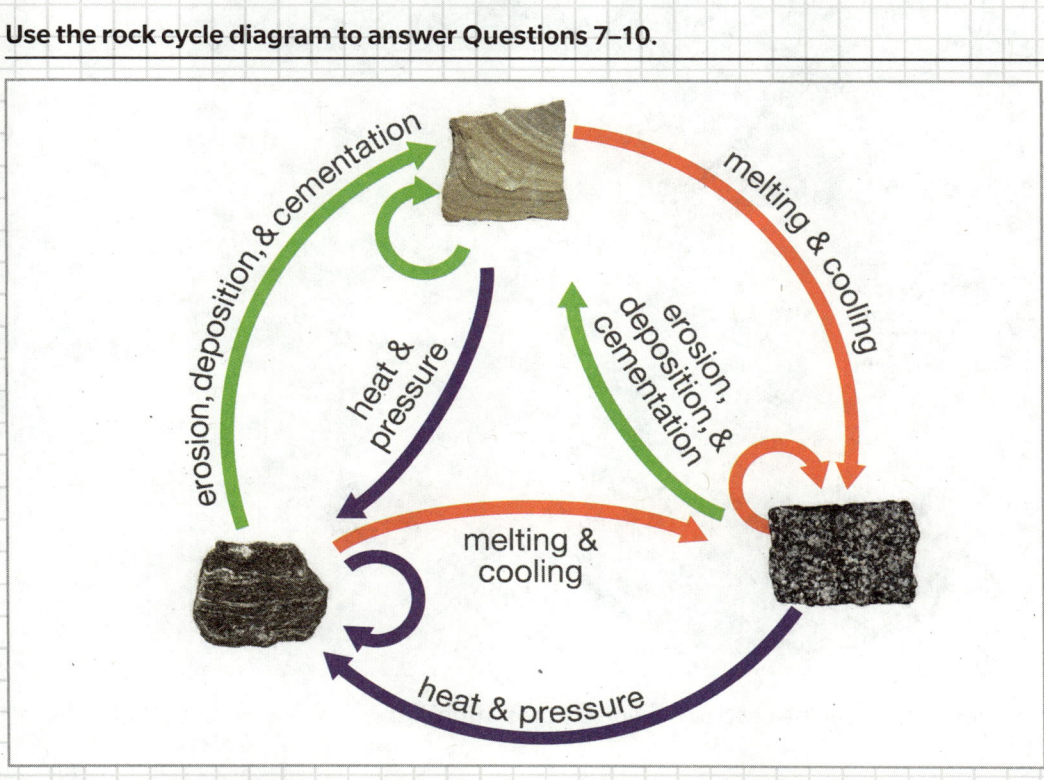

7. Based on the diagram, what changes between types of rock can occur as part of the rock cycle process?

8. Earth began as a molten mass of material that slowly cooled and became mostly solid. What type of rock would have been formed first during Earth's history? Explain your reasoning.

9. Identify parts of the rock cycle that can only occur deep beneath the surface, and provide evidence to support your reasoning.

10. Close examination of a rock sample shows that it has many tiny fossils of seashells. Explain how you could determine whether the rock is igneous, metamorphic, or sedimentary.

Unit 4 Matter and Energy in Organisms and Rock 311

UNIT 4 REVIEW

Use the diagram to answer Questions 11–14.

Photosynthesis Investigation

In this investigation, a plant is contained in water with a light shining down on it. Tubing connects the container to a syringe that measures oxygen production, which can be seen in the container in the form of oxygen bubbles.

11. Explain how this investigation can be used to observe photosynthesis.

12. Which reactants (starting materials) and products of photosynthesis can be observed in this diagram?

13. How would you expect the amount of oxygen to change if the intensity of the light is increased or decreased? Explain your reasoning.

14. Explain why plants such as this one need to perform both photosynthesis and cellular respiration to survive.

312 Unit 4 Review

UNIT 4 PERFORMANCE TASK

Name: _____ Date: _____

Should your school use vermicomposting?

Composting is a natural process that breaks down food and yard waste into a rich, fertile soil additive. Vermicomposting is one method of composting that has become popular recently. Your task is to help determine if vermicomposting is a good option for disposing of food waste from your school's cafeteria.

Research the use of vermicomposting units. Explain how a vermicomposting unit works, describe the flow of energy and cycling of matter within the system, and determine the advantages and disadvantages of using this type of system to dispose of food waste from your school's cafeteria.

Vermicomposter

This vermicomposter shows a three-bin system for using worms to decompose food and yard waste into a nutrient-rich mixture that can be added to soil.

Labels: cover, holes for air, food waste and worms (active area), bedding material, storage bin, compost, compost collection, brick support

The steps below will help guide your research and develop your recommendation.

Engineer It

1. **Define the Problem** Write a statement defining the problem you have been asked to solve. Define the criteria and constraints of the design problems based on what is reasonable for your school and the cafeteria.

UNIT 4 PERFORMANCE TASK

Engineer It

2. **Conduct Research** What is vermicomposting? Explain how worms break down food waste and how the compost that is produced can be used.

3. **Develop a Model** Use a labeled diagram or another model of a vermicomposting unit to describe the function of each layer and explain how energy and matter flow through the system.

4. **Make a Recommendation** List the advantages and disadvantages of using a vermicomposting unit. Write a recommendation that explains whether this would be a good solution for disposing of food waste from your school.

5. **Communicate** Create a multimedia presentation of your findings to present to the principal. Use your labeled diagram or model to summarize how vermicomposting works, and explain whether or not you should use vermicomposting at your school. Provide evidence and reasoning for your recommendation.

✓ **Self-Check**

	I defined the criteria and constraints of the design problem.
	I researched the process of vermicomposting to determine the advantages and disadvantages.
	I used a diagram or model to explain the function of each layer in a vermicomposting unit and how energy and matter flow through the unit.
	My recommendation was clearly communicated during my presentation.

UNIT 5

Earth's Resources and Ecosystems

How do natural processes and human activities shape Earth's resources and ecosystems?

Unit Project		316
Lesson 1	The Movement of Earth's Plates Affects Earth's Surface	318
Lesson 2	Natural Resources Are Distributed Unevenly	340
Lesson 3	Resource Availability Affects Organisms	360
Lesson 4	Patterns Can Be Observed in Interactions between Organisms	382
Lesson 5	The Flow of Energy Drives the Cycling of Matter in Ecosystems	400
Unit Review		417
Unit Performance Task		421

We depend on forests for many resources, including paper, furniture, medicines, and biofuels.

You Solve It What Is Causing Earthquakes In Oklahoma?
Several earthquakes have been recorded in Oklahoma in recent years. What is causing these earthquakes? Is it the same as the cause of earthquakes elsewhere?

Go online and complete the You Solve It to explore ways to solve a real-world problem.

UNIT 5 PROJECT

Analyze the Impacts of Resource Use

This wetland contains resources such as fish and drinking water.

A. Look at the photo. On a separate sheet of paper, write down as many different questions as you can about resource use and human population changes.

B. Discuss With your class or a partner, share your questions. Record any additional questions generated in your discussion. Then choose the most important questions from the list that are related to natural resources humans depend on and how those resources form and are distributed. Write them below.

C. Choose a natural resource from a specific ecosystem that you would like to research.

D. Use the information above, along with your research, to explain how the extraction, processing, and use of that resource affects ecosystems and is related to human population change.

Discuss the next steps for your Unit Project with your teacher and go online to download the Unit Project Worksheet.

316 Unit 5 Earth's Resources and Ecosystems

UNIT 5

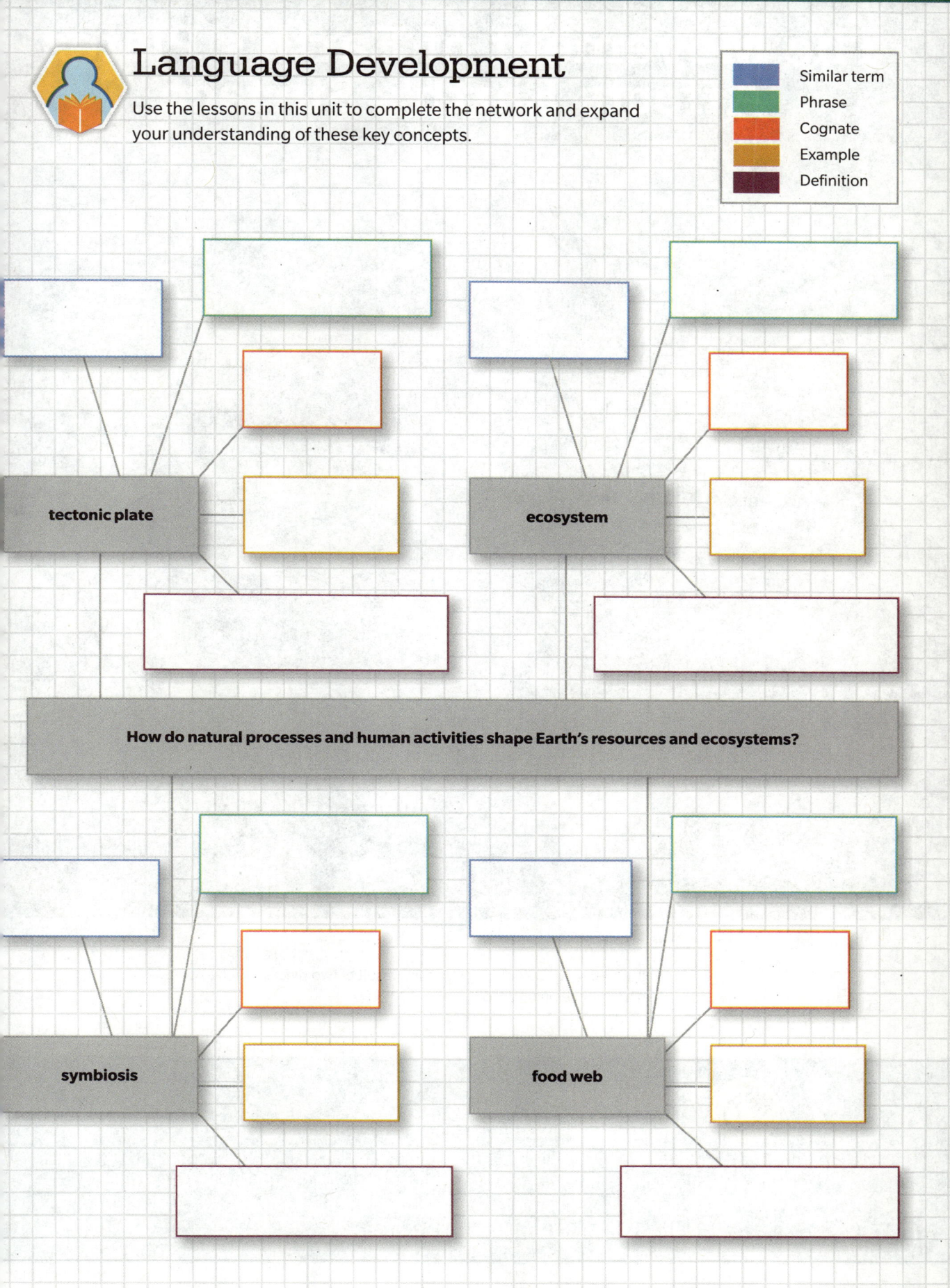

Language Development

Use the lessons in this unit to complete the network and expand your understanding of these key concepts.

- Similar term
- Phrase
- Cognate
- Example
- Definition

tectonic plate

ecosystem

How do natural processes and human activities shape Earth's resources and ecosystems?

symbiosis

food web

Unit 5 Earth's Resources and Ecosystems 317

LESSON 1

The Movement of Earth's Plates Affects Earth's Surface

This underwater canyon in Iceland is a result of two pieces of Earth's surface pulling apart.

Explore First

Constructing Puzzles Make a puzzle with at least five pieces, using any material you would like. Take your puzzle apart and trade puzzles with a partner. Try to put your partner's puzzle back together. Write a brief statement explaining how you know which pieces connect. What clues helped you put the puzzle back together?

Go online to view the digital version of the Hands-On Lab for this lesson and to download additional lab resources.

CAN YOU EXPLAIN IT?

How might this island have appeared overnight?

In November 2013, off the coast of Japan, an island formed virtually overnight. The view quickly changed from calm Pacific waters to boiling water and plumes of smoke. By the next morning, an entirely new island had appeared. The new island continued to grow for about two years.

Explore Online

1. What explanation can you suggest for how an island could suddenly appear? Could this happen anywhere, or might there be something special about the location that made this possible?

2. **Draw** Include a drawing to illustrate your explanation.

EVIDENCE NOTEBOOK As you explore the lesson, gather evidence to help explain how an island could suddenly appear.

Lesson 1 The Movement of Earth's Plates Affects Earth's Surface **319**

EXPLORATION 1

Analyzing Continental Data

Continental Observations

Long ago, people noticed that some continents, such as Africa and South America, looked as if they could fit together. Explorers also discovered rocks and landforms of the same ages and compositions on different continents. They also found fossils of the same plants and animals across continents. What could explain these findings?

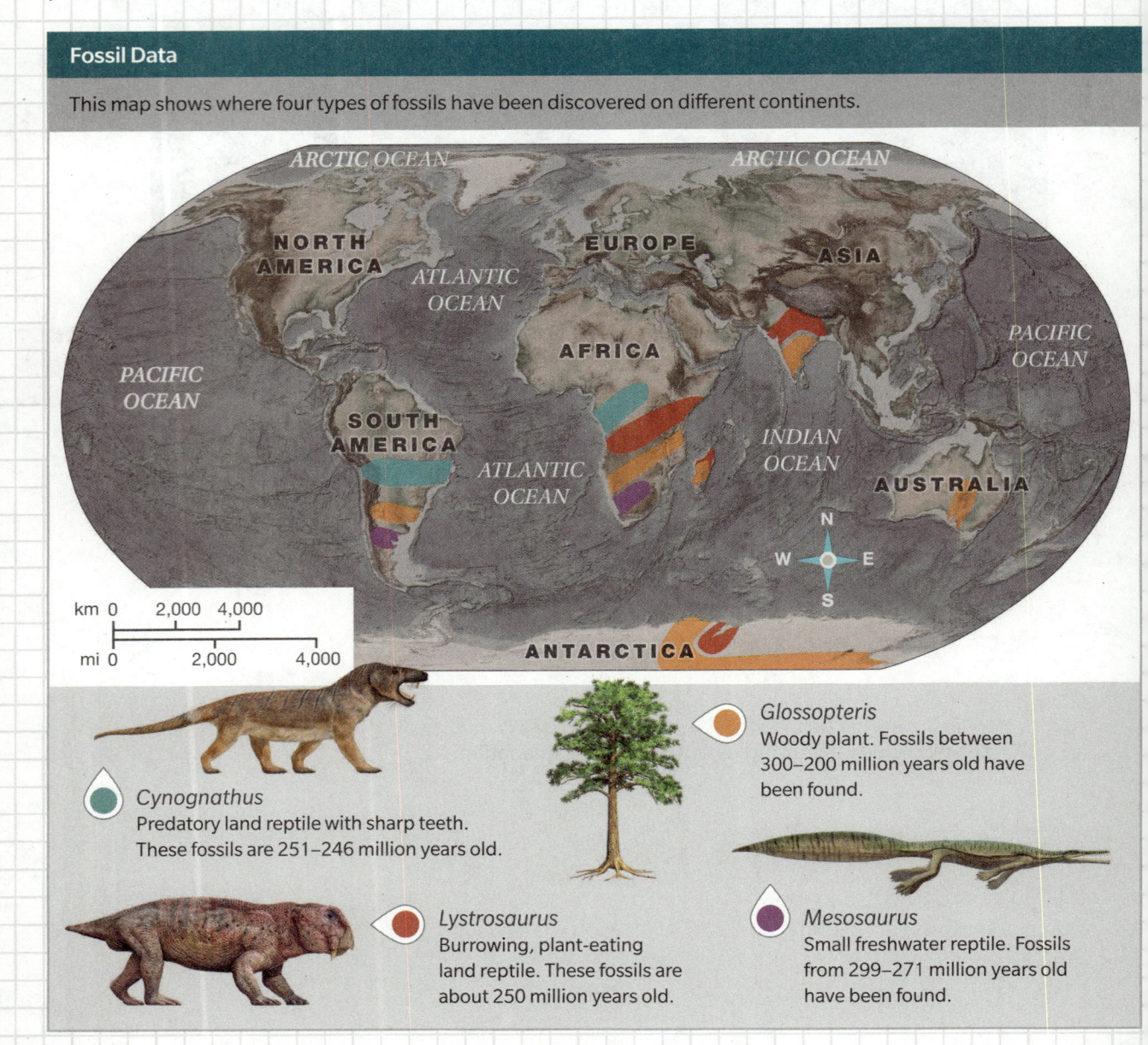

Fossil Data

This map shows where four types of fossils have been discovered on different continents.

Cynognathus
Predatory land reptile with sharp teeth. These fossils are 251–246 million years old.

Glossopteris
Woody plant. Fossils between 300–200 million years old have been found.

Lystrosaurus
Burrowing, plant-eating land reptile. These fossils are about 250 million years old.

Mesosaurus
Small freshwater reptile. Fossils from 299–271 million years old have been found.

3. **Discuss** Observe the shapes and locations of the continents. Do you think they have always been in the same locations, or do they move? State your claim and cite specific evidence to explain your reasoning.

320 Unit 5 Earth's Resources and Ecosystems

4. Fill in the table with your observations as you explore the map. Think about the following points:
- What was the plant or animal like?
- When and where did it live, according to the map?
- Use the scale bar to estimate how far apart fossils of the same type were found.

Fossil Data Observations

Fossil Type	Observations and Notes
Cynognathus	
Glossopteris	
Lystrosaurus	• Land reptile • Lived around 250 million years ago. • Lived in Africa, Asia, and Antarctica. • Fossils in Africa are about 3,000 km from those in Asia and about 7,000 km from those in Antarctica.
Mesosaurus	

Fossil Data

Fossils are the traces or remains of organisms that lived long ago. Fossils are most commonly preserved in rock. Fossils may be skeletons, burrows, footprints, or body parts such as shells that have been replaced by minerals.

Fossils can give us clues about what the environment was like when the organism was alive. For example, fish fossils indicate that an aquatic environment existed. Palm leaf fossils mean a tropical environment existed. Scientists have found fossils of trees and dinosaurs in Antarctica, so the climate there must have been warmer in the past.

Mesosaurus fossils like this one have been found in both South America and Africa.

Lesson 1 The Movement of Earth's Plates Affects Earth's Surface

Landform Data

Look at the dashed lines on the map below that follow along the continental shelves of North America, South America, Europe, and Africa. A *continental shelf* is the edge of a continent that is underwater. Just past the edge of the shelf is a steep drop-off into the deep ocean.

The map below also shows where mountain ranges formed many millions of years ago. The mountains have since been weathered and eroded, so the land is now flatter. The rocks from these weathered mountains have been analyzed by geologists who found that many of the rocks are the same age and made up of the same materials. These pieces of evidence led to the conclusion that parts of these mountain ranges formed at the same time and in the same location.

Continental Shelf

A continental shelf is the edge of a continent that is covered with water.

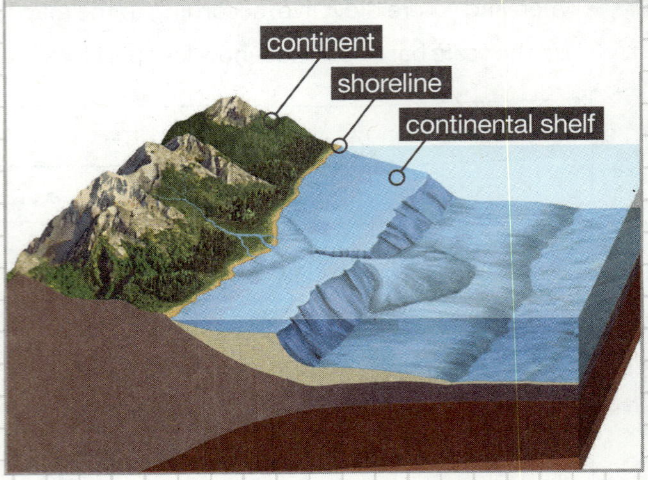

Matching Landforms Across the Atlantic Ocean

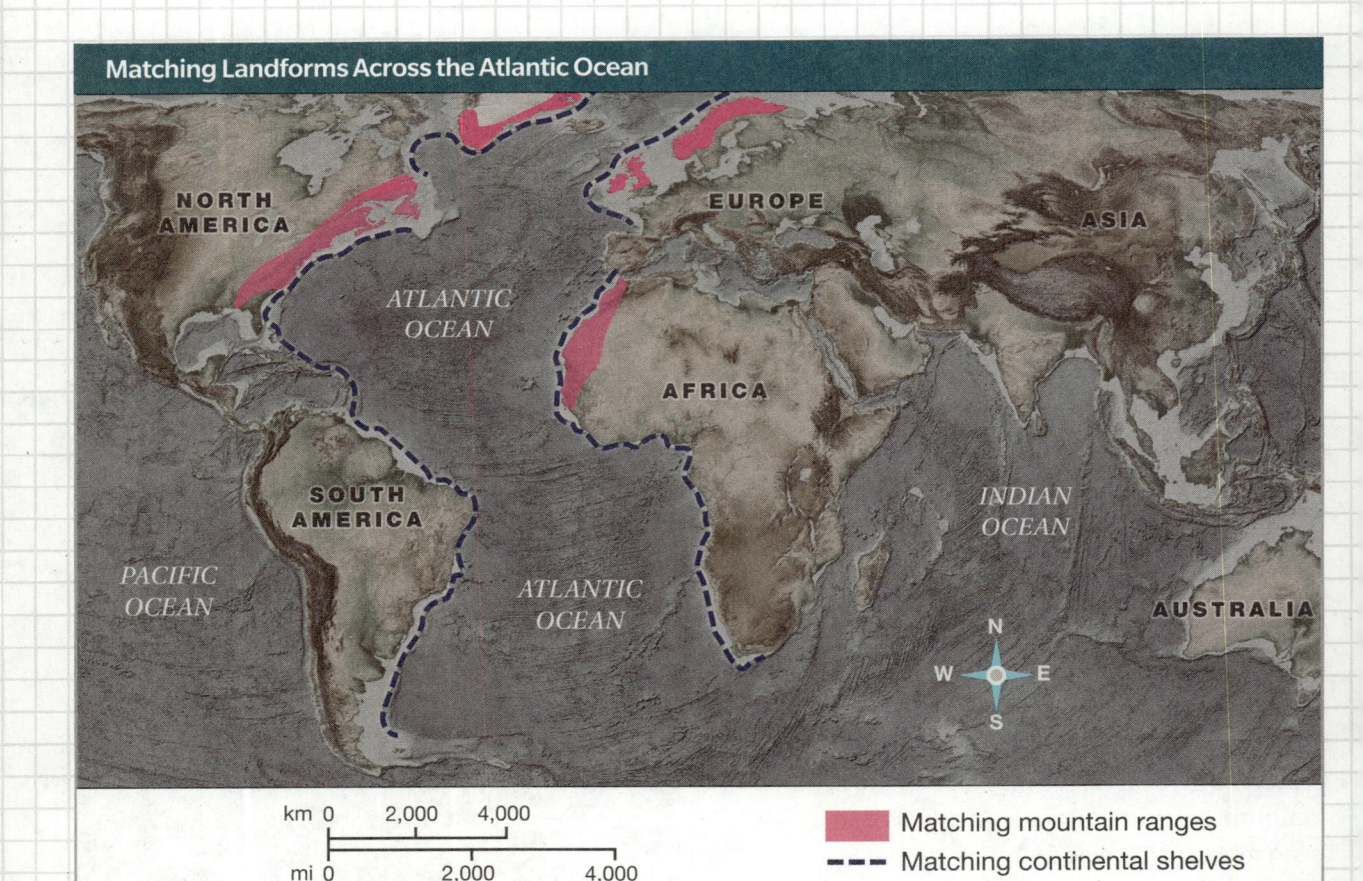

Matching mountain ranges
- - - Matching continental shelves

Matching Mountain Ranges
Look at the mountain ranges within the colored areas on the map. Many parts of these mountains match in age and composition. Scientists have concluded that the mountains formed around the same time.

Matching Continental Shelves
The dashed outlines trace along continental shelves that were measured and mapped in the 1960s. The continental shelves match up even more closely than the shorelines of the continents do.

322 Unit 5 Earth's Resources and Ecosystems

5. Fill in the table with your observations as you explore the map.

Landform Data Observations	
Data	Observations and Notes
Mountain Ranges	
Continental Shelves	

Language SmArts
Explain Your Observations

Since the 1800s, people have attempted to explain the matching fossils and landforms on the continents. Some people thought that land bridges once connected the continents, which allowed plant and animal populations to spread. Some thought that the entire planet expanded and tore the continents apart, then water filled the spaces between them. Others thought the continents were once part of a single landmass surrounded by a large ocean, and when the landmass broke up, the pieces drifted apart.

6. Recall your discussion about whether the continents have moved over time. You may wish to revise your claim based on your observations so far. Write your claim, then compare and contrast your claim to the claims listed above.

_____
_____
_____
_____
_____
_____

7. Explain the reasoning behind your claim. What evidence supports your claim? Think about using words such as *evidence, observations, measurement,* and *data,* and phrases such as *the evidence supports* or *the evidence does not support*.

_____
_____
_____
_____
_____

Lesson 1 The Movement of Earth's Plates Affects Earth's Surface

EXPLORATION 2

Analyzing Ocean-Floor Data

Discoveries in the Ocean

In the mid-1900s, new technology allowed scientists to map the ocean floor. They found a giant continuous mountain range they called the *mid-ocean ridge*. One part, the Mid-Atlantic Ridge, runs along the entire middle of the Atlantic Ocean. Scientists also found *deep-ocean trenches*, which are the deepest valleys on Earth's surface.

Mid-Ocean Ridges and Deep-Ocean Trenches

This map shows the locations of mid-ocean ridges in red and deep-ocean trenches in yellow. The diagram beneath the map shows what these features look like.

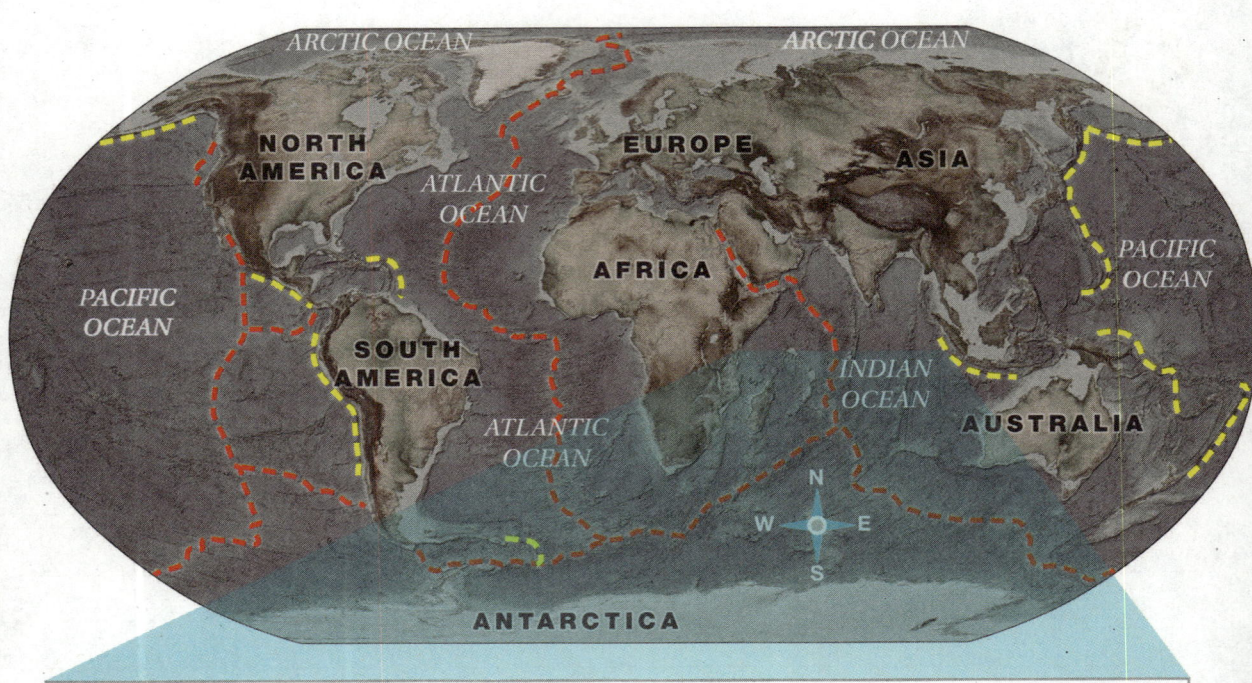

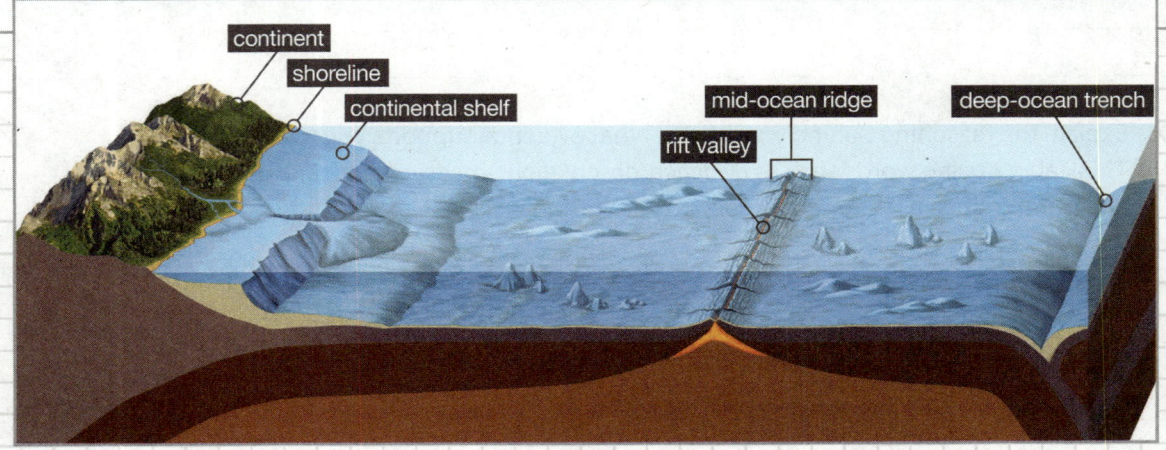

324 Unit 5 Earth's Resources and Ecosystems

8. **Discuss** Compare this map of ridges and trenches to the fossil and matching landforms maps. Discuss patterns you see with a partner.

The Mid-Atlantic Ridge can be seen above water in Iceland.

Sea-Floor Spreading and Mid-Ocean Ridges

Did you know that the oceans can form, change, and disappear over millions of years? Oceans form by the process of *sea-floor spreading*. In this process, the crust stretches and magma rises from Earth's interior. The stretching forms a long narrow valley called a *rift valley*. Along the rift valley, earthquakes and volcanic eruptions occur, and the eruptions release lava that cools to form new rock on the surface. As long as forces continue to stretch the crust, the rift valley widens. The valley may eventually fill with seawater and become a *linear sea*, like the Red Sea between Africa and Asia. Over time, the linear sea eventually widens into an ocean basin.

As eruptions add rock in a rift valley, old rock is pushed outward and slowly moves away from a rift valley on either side, like two conveyor belts. As old rock moves away, it gets cooler and denser and sinks deeper beneath the water. Closer to the rift valley, the ocean floor is elevated because the new rock there is warmer and less dense. This elevated ridge is called a *mid-ocean ridge*.

9. Complete the captions to describe how an ocean basin forms by the process of sea-floor spreading.

WORD BANK
- linear sea
- ocean basin
- ~~rift valley~~

A. Earth's crust is stretched by forces within Earth. A ___rift valley___ forms and volcanic eruptions occur.

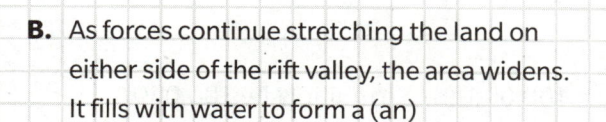

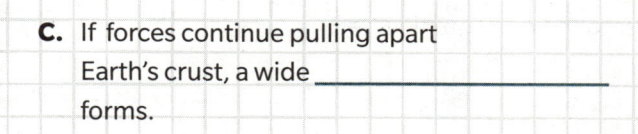

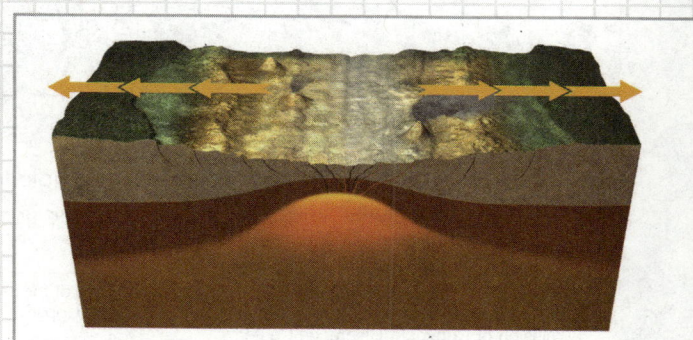

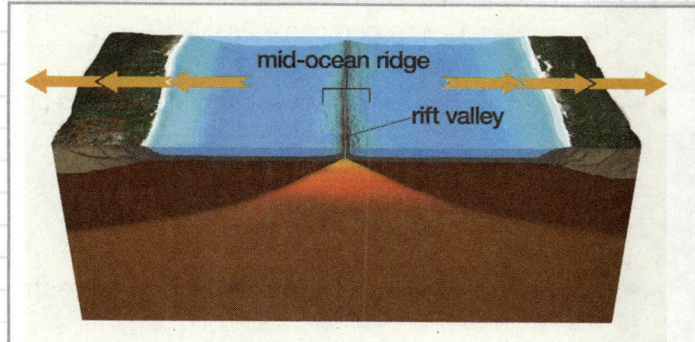

B. As forces continue stretching the land on either side of the rift valley, the area widens. It fills with water to form a (an) _____.

C. If forces continue pulling apart Earth's crust, a wide _____ forms.

Lesson 1 The Movement of Earth's Plates Affects Earth's Surface

Do the Math
Calculate the Rate of Sea-Floor Spreading

How fast does the Atlantic Ocean grow? To find out, we can calculate the rate of sea-floor spreading. The map shows the age of the ocean floor and three rock samples. For example, rock B is 55 million years old. So is any rock on the red line labeled "55." Rock B formed 55 million years ago at the ridge, then traveled to its current location. Rock C is now at the ridge. To find the rate of spreading, first estimate the distance between rocks B and C by using the scale bar. Divide that by the difference in their ages. In other words, rate is distance divided by time (age difference): $r = \frac{d}{t}$. So $r = \frac{200,000,000 \text{ cm}}{55,000,000 \text{ y}}$, or about 3.6 $\frac{cm}{y}$.

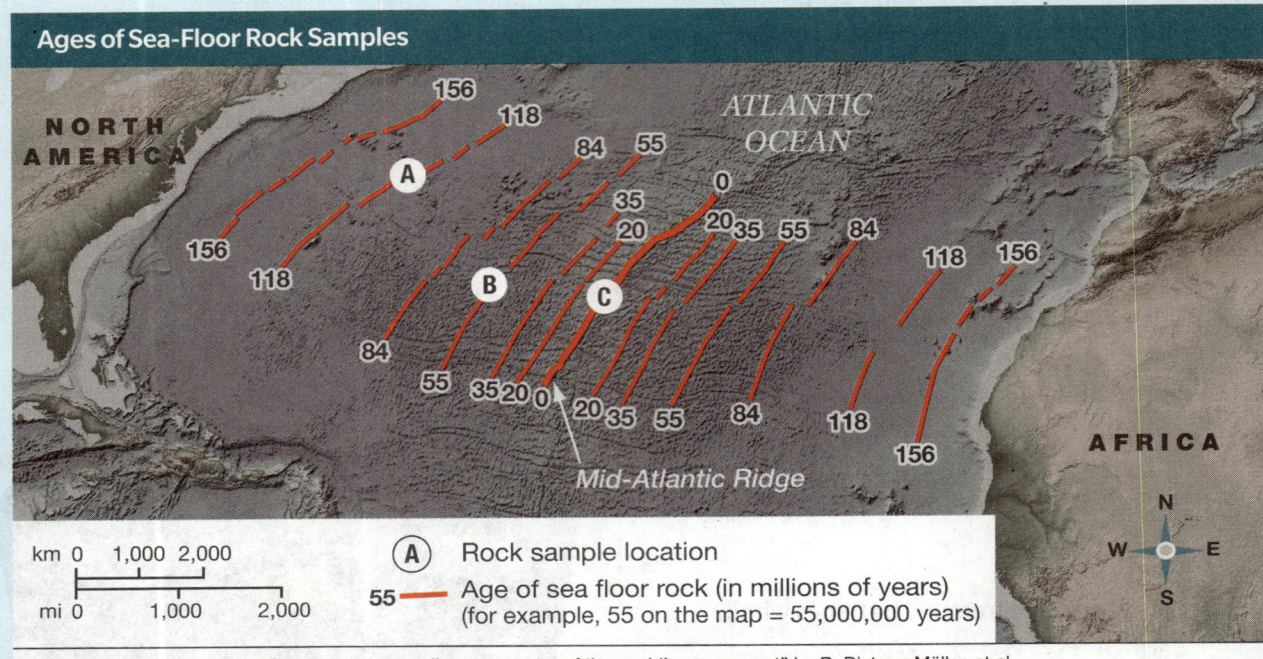

Ages of Sea-Floor Rock Samples

[Map showing the Atlantic Ocean between North America and Africa with Mid-Atlantic Ridge. Rock samples labeled A, B, and C with age contours at 0, 20, 35, 55, 84, 118, and 156 million years.]

Scale: km 0, 1,000, 2,000; mi 0, 1,000, 2,000

- **A** Rock sample location
- **55** — Age of sea floor rock (in millions of years) (for example, 55 on the map = 55,000,000 years)

Credit: From "Age, spreading rates, and spreading asymmetry of the world's ocean crust" by R. Dietmar Müller, et al, from Geochemistry, Geophysics, Geosystems, April 3, 2008. Copyright © 2008 by John Wiley and Sons. Used with permission of Copyright Clearance Center.

10. Find the rate using rocks A and C. Express your answer in centimeters per year $\left(\frac{cm}{y}\right)$.

STEP 1 Use the scale bar to estimate the distance from rock A to rock C.

d = _____ km

STEP 2 Convert the distance from km to cm. 1 km = 100,000 cm. So multiply by 100,000.

d = _____ km × 100,000 $\frac{cm}{km}$ = _____ cm

STEP 3 Find the age difference between rocks A and C.

t = 118,000,000 y − 0 y = _____ y

STEP 4 Plug in the values for distance and time into the rate equation $r = \frac{d}{t}$.

r = $\frac{\boxed{}}{\boxed{}}$ $\frac{cm}{y}$

STEP 5 Divide and round to the nearest tenth.   r = _____ $\frac{cm}{y}$

Deep-Ocean Trenches

At mid-ocean ridges, new oceanic crust forms as eruptions bring magma from the interior to the surface. New ocean floor becomes cooler and denser as it moves away from the mid-ocean ridge, and millions of years later, it can sink at a deep-ocean trench. Deep-ocean trenches exist at plate boundaries where the edge of an oceanic plate is cool and dense enough to sink under another plate. The sinking oceanic crust eventually melts into Earth's interior. One day, that recycled rock may rise again to the surface.

Volcanic mountain chains often run parallel to deep-ocean trenches because sinking slabs of ocean floor cause magma to form. The magma may erupt at volcanoes that become mountains over time. The motion at trenches also causes earthquakes.

> **EVIDENCE NOTEBOOK**
> 11. Think about the island that appeared overnight. What processes and features might relate to the formation of an island like this?

Explain the Age of the Ocean Floor

In the mid-1900s, new technology allowed scientists to determine the age of sea-floor rock. They discovered the interesting patterns you see on this map. They also discovered that ocean-floor rock is generally much younger than continental rock.

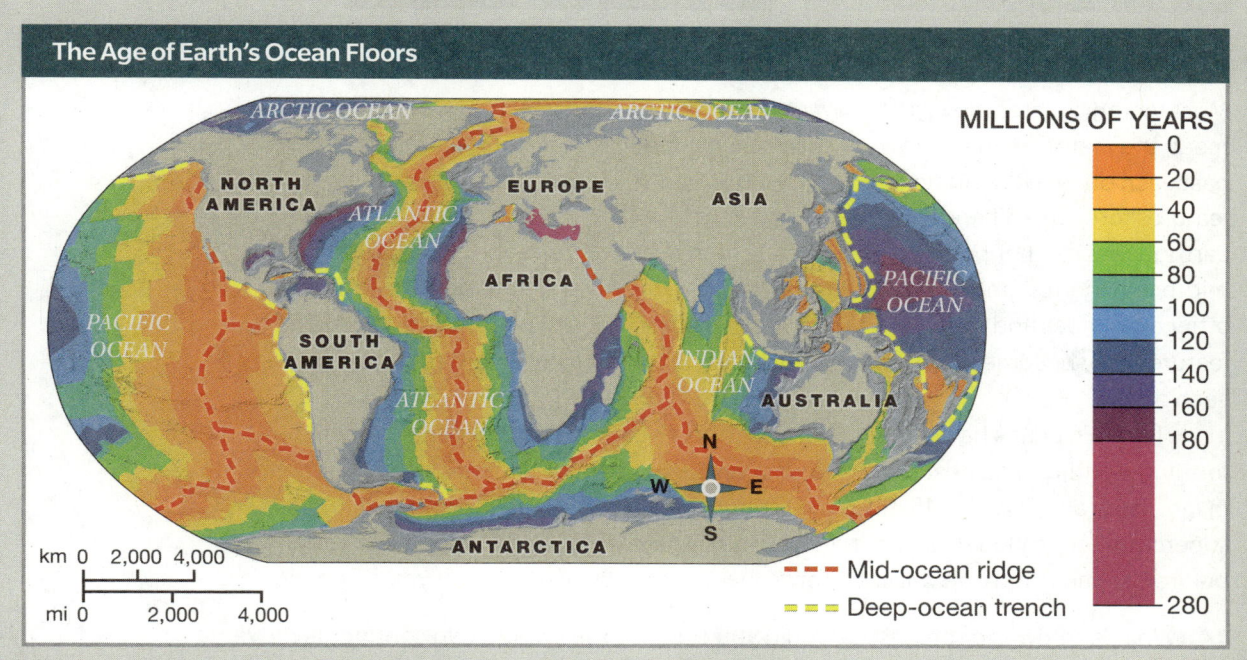

The Age of Earth's Ocean Floors

12. Rock near mid-ocean ridges is the _oldest / youngest_ rock.

13. Compare the age of sea-floor rock near mid-ocean ridges and near trenches. Cite evidence to explain these patterns in ocean-floor age.

EXPLORATION 3

Modeling Earth's Surface

Earth's Broken Surface

Evidence has led scientists to conclude that Earth's entire surface, including the ocean floor and the continents, is broken into large moving pieces. These pieces, called **tectonic plates**, fit together like a jigsaw puzzle to form Earth's outer shell, but the pieces are thousands of kilometers wide and hundreds of kilometers thick!

Earth's thin and rigid outer shell is broken into giant moving pieces called tectonic plates.

Plate Motion

Most tectonic plates move just a few centimeters per year. Where two tectonic plates meet, the plates can move toward each other, away from each other, or horizontally past each other. Depending on the type of motion at a tectonic plate boundary, different features form and different processes occur. At most every type of plate boundary, earthquakes can happen. Where two plates move apart from each other, volcanoes, mid-ocean ridges, and ocean basins may form. Where two plates move toward each other, volcanoes and mountain chains may form. Where two plates slide past each other, features may become offset. However, volcanoes do not form where two plates slide past each other.

Tectonic plates have been moving for hundreds of millions of years, all while forming, shifting, and destroying features on Earth's surface, including the continents. In fact, from about 280–245 million years ago, all the continents were joined into a supercontinent called *Pangaea* (pan•JEE•uh). There were several supercontinents before Pangaea, and one will likely form again hundreds of millions of years from now.

14. What landforms or processes would you expect to see where two continents move toward each other? Explain your reasoning.

EVIDENCE NOTEBOOK

15. What type of plate motion could be related to the formation of the new island off of Japan's coast? Record your evidence.

Plate Boundaries and Surface Features

Each colored line represents a different type of plate boundary. The diagrams show the different features that result from the different types of plate motion at each boundary.

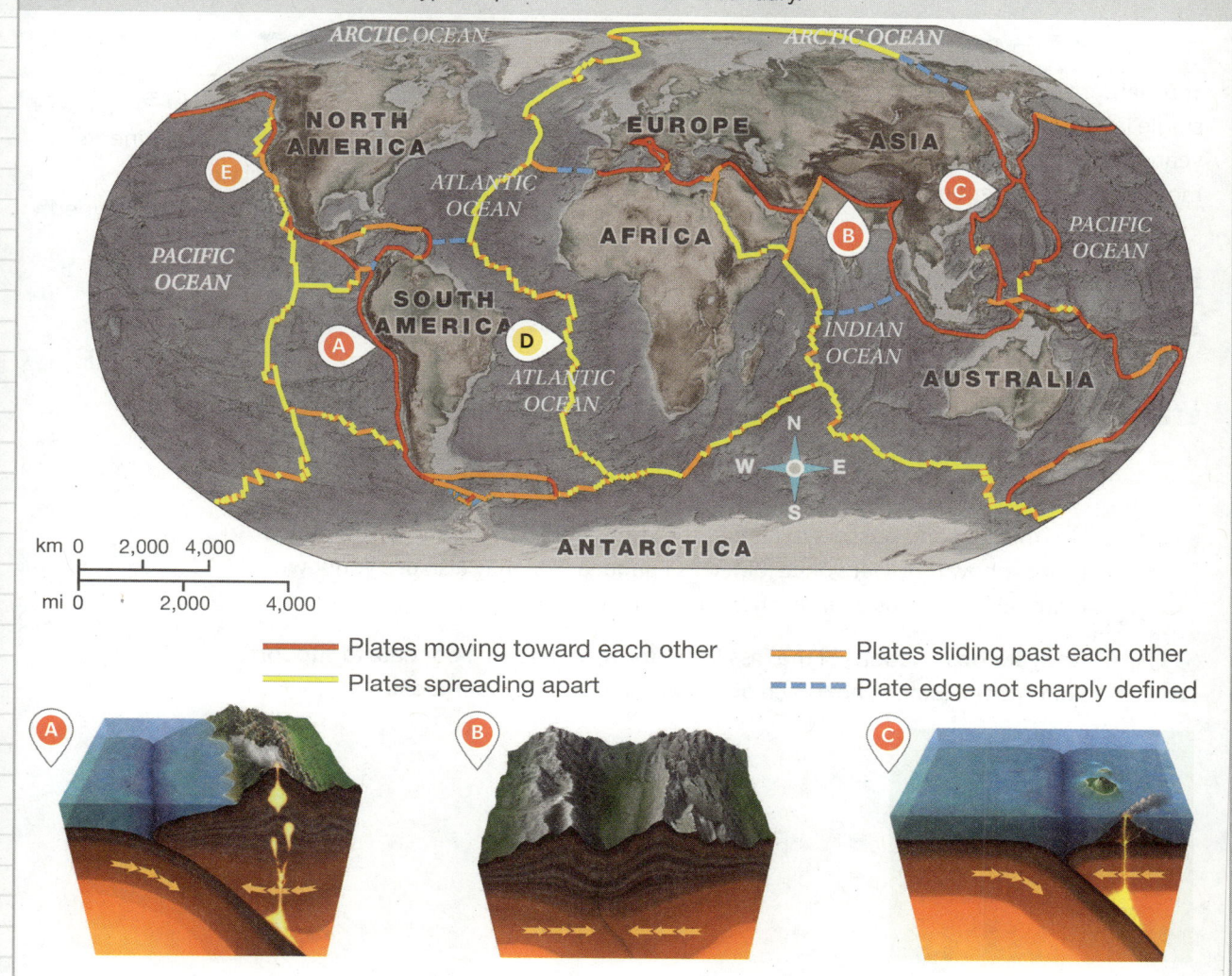

— Plates moving toward each other
— Plates spreading apart
— Plates sliding past each other
-- Plate edge not sharply defined

16. These diagrams show plates moving ~~toward~~ / ~~away from~~ / past each other. Where an oceanic plate sinks, deep-ocean trenches, volcanic mountains, or volcanic islands can form. Where two continental plates collide, mountains form.

17. Here, two plates move ~~toward~~ / away from / ~~past~~ each other. Magma rises in the rift valley that runs along the center of the mid-ocean ridge and causes eruptions. These eruptions form volcanic mountains that may become volcanic islands.

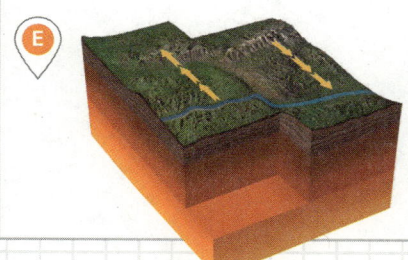

18. Here, two plates move ~~toward~~ / ~~away from~~ / past each other. This offsets features on the surface. Eruptions do not usually occur here. Earthquakes happen at all plate boundaries.

Lesson 1 The Movement of Earth's Plates Affects Earth's Surface

Hands-On Lab
Model the Movement of Continents

You will construct a model to show how the continents once fit together as a single landmass called Pangaea, which existed from about 280–245 million years ago. Brainstorm ways you can use the model to show how the continents moved to their current positions.

MATERIALS
- map of continents
- scissors
- animation (provided by your teacher)

Procedure and Analysis

STEP 1 Review the observations you made about the fossils, landforms, and the ocean floor's features and processes.

STEP 2 Think about how your observations can be used to construct your model. For example, think about when the plants and animals from the fossil map lived and where these fossils are now located.

STEP 3 Use the map and scissors to cut out the continents and construct your model to show how they were once joined as Pangaea. You may also use your own materials as long as your teacher has approved them first.

STEP 4 Use your observations of the fossil, landform, and ocean floor data to support your model. Explain how each observation supports your model.

STEP 5 Look at a map of the plate boundaries with the continents in their current positions. Using your model of Pangaea, explore how the plates may have moved to result in the current positions of the continents.

330 Unit 5 Earth's Resources and Ecosystems

STEP 6 Observe how scientists reconstructed the breakup of Pangaea and compare this to your model. Record similarities and differences.

245 million years ago
About 245 million years ago, the continents we know today were joined into a single landmass.

PANGAEA
PANTHALASSA
PANTHALASSA

135 million years ago
As tectonic plates moved at just a few centimeters a year, this landmass slowly broke apart.

STEP 7 Evaluate your model to describe which aspects of plate motion are represented and which are not.

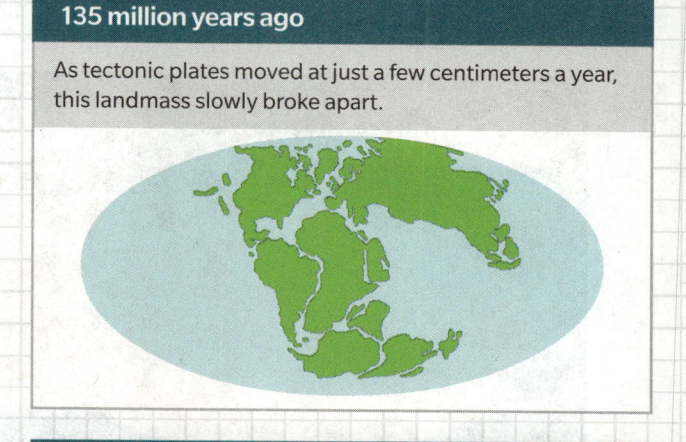

Present Day
Fossils, rocks, and other evidence help us understand how the continents came to be in their current positions.

- Lystrosaurus
- Cynognathus
- Matching mountain ranges
- Mesosaurus
- Glossopteris
- Matching continent shapes

Describe Plate Motion

19. Look back to the map of plate boundaries. If current plate motions continue, what will happen to the shapes, sizes, and relative positions of South America, Africa, and the Atlantic Ocean? Support your claim with evidence and reasoning.

_____
_____
_____
_____

Lesson 1 The Movement of Earth's Plates Affects Earth's Surface

EXPLORATION 4

Explaining Plate Motion

You cannot feel it, but the ground beneath you is in constant motion. In fact, you are on top of a moving tectonic plate as you read this! Even though plates move slowly, they can cause sudden events, such as volcanic eruptions and earthquakes.

20. Explore the photos below. Which type of plate motion is responsible for all three of these features?

    A. plates moving apart
    B. plates sliding past each other horizontally
    C. plates moving toward each other

This is just one of the 80 islands of Vanuatu (vahn•wah•TOO). This long chain of volcanic islands runs parallel to a deep-ocean trench.

The West Mata volcano is nearly 1,200 meters deep and lies on the floor of the Pacific Ocean near a deep-ocean trench.

The Himalayas are mountains that have been growing for millions of years. These mountains are in the middle of a continent.

The Theory of Plate Tectonics

Plate tectonics is the theory that describes how Earth's outer layer is broken up into moving tectonic plates. It also explains how plates shape Earth's surface. Some of the first pieces of evidence supporting this theory were matching fossils and landforms on separate continents. Next came discoveries in the ocean, such as sea-floor spreading. Today, additional evidence comes from Global Positioning System (GPS) instruments that directly measure the speeds and directions of Earth's moving plates.

21. **Engineer It** Models help us understand concepts such as plate tectonics. Think about items you could use to represent tectonic plates or their motion. List or draw two items, explaining how each item represents Earth's plates.

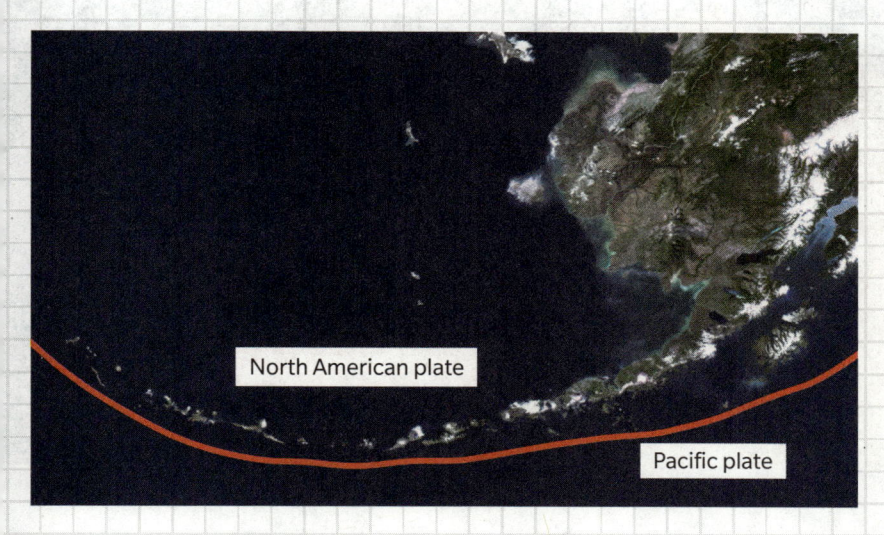

Alaska has a long chain of islands that extends across the ocean. Volcanic eruptions and earthquakes frequently happen in this island chain.

22. Complete the following sentences to describe the photo. You may want to refer to the other maps in this lesson that show plate boundaries.

    The red line below these Alaskan islands shows a plate boundary where the Pacific plate is sinking beneath the North American plate. This motion forms a _deep-ocean trench_ / mid-ocean ridge. The sinking edge of the Pacific plate triggers melting that results in eruptions on the North American plate. Repeated eruptions have built up these basins / _islands_.

> **EVIDENCE NOTEBOOK**
> 23. As you continue exploring this section, identify the energy source that drives plate motion. How does the flow of energy and cycling of matter relate to the formation of the island in Japan?

Lesson 1 The Movement of Earth's Plates Affects Earth's Surface   333

Causes of Plate Motion

Energy from deep within Earth drives temperature and density differences in Earth's interior. Along with gravity, this causes the mostly solid interior to slowly cycle. These cycles are called **convection currents**. Earth's outer shell of moving plates is part of this cycle. Where the edge of a plate sinks into Earth, it pulls the rest of the plate along with it. At mid-ocean ridges, new, warm rock sits higher than surrounding older, denser rock. Gravity causes the weight of the rock at the ridge to "push" the rest of the plate away from the ridge.

How Plates Move

24. Choose from the phrases to label this diagram. You may use a phrase more than once.

| Plates move toward each other | Plates move away from each other |

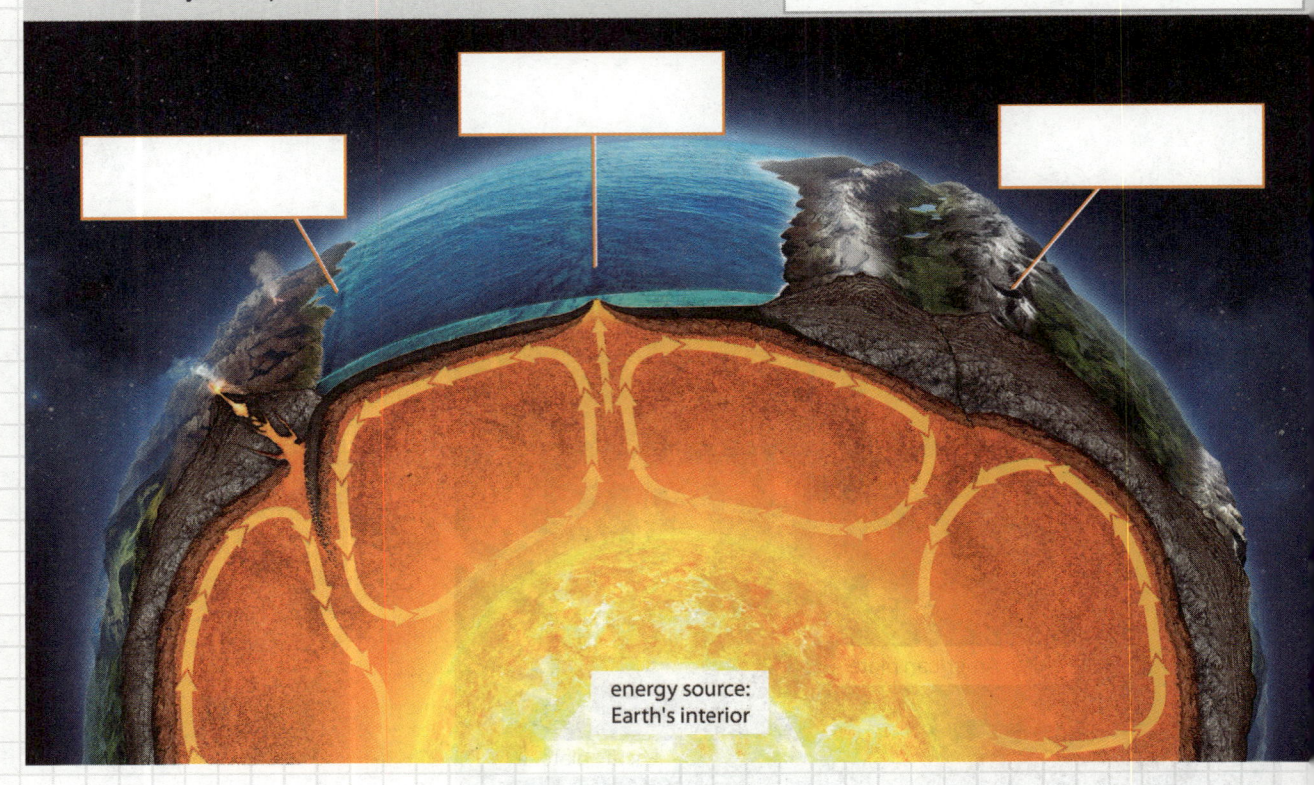

energy source: Earth's interior

Language SmArts
Cite Evidence for Plate Tectonics

25. Use the information you gained from the lesson so far to explain how GPS instruments and studies of Earth's fossils, landforms, and ocean floor provide evidence for plate tectonics.

TAKE IT FURTHER

Continue Your Exploration

Name: _____ Date: _____

Check out the path below or go online to choose one of the other paths shown.

People in Science
- Deep-Sea Resources Debate
- Hands-On Labs
- Propose Your Own Path

Go online to choose one of these other paths.

Doug Gibbons, Research Scientist Engineer

In and around Seattle, Washington, earthquakes are a major hazard. This is where Doug Gibbons lives and works, not too far from a tectonic plate boundary where one plate is sinking beneath another. The motion at this plate boundary can cause major earthquakes that damage buildings and roads and cause injury or death.

Part of Doug's job is installing and maintaining instruments that detect earthquakes for the Pacific Northwest Seismic Network (PNSN). He also speaks with the media and schools to inform people about earthquakes and the importance of monitoring them. Doug's favorite part of the job is traveling. He has spent time at the beach, in remote parts of the forest, and even at the tops of volcanoes. However, he occasionally travels to less exciting places, such as dusty basements, to install and check his earthquake instruments.

An Earthquake Warning System

Doug and others at PNSN are working toward building an earthquake warning system that will alert people before shaking occurs. This is one reason the earthquake detection instruments Doug works on are so important. Earthquakes are unpredictable, so how is it possible to warn people before shaking occurs? When an earthquake happens, it sends out waves of energy in all directions. P-waves travel the fastest, but do not cause much shaking. S-waves are slower and can cause major shaking. Sensors in the earthquake instruments detect the faster P-waves, which arrive before the S-waves. The instruments communicate data almost instantly to an earthquake alert center, where it is determined if shaking will happen and if so, when and where. This triggers a warning message that is sent to people's phones and computers, possibly giving them several seconds to prepare for the shaking that S-waves can bring.

Doug graduated from the University of Washington with degrees in Earth and Space Sciences and History.

Lesson 1 The Movement of Earth's Plates Affects Earth's Surface   335

TAKE IT FURTHER

Continue Your Exploration

An Earthquake Warning System

This diagram shows how the waves sent out from an earthquake are detected by sensors. The sensors communicate with an alert center where an earthquake warning message is generated.

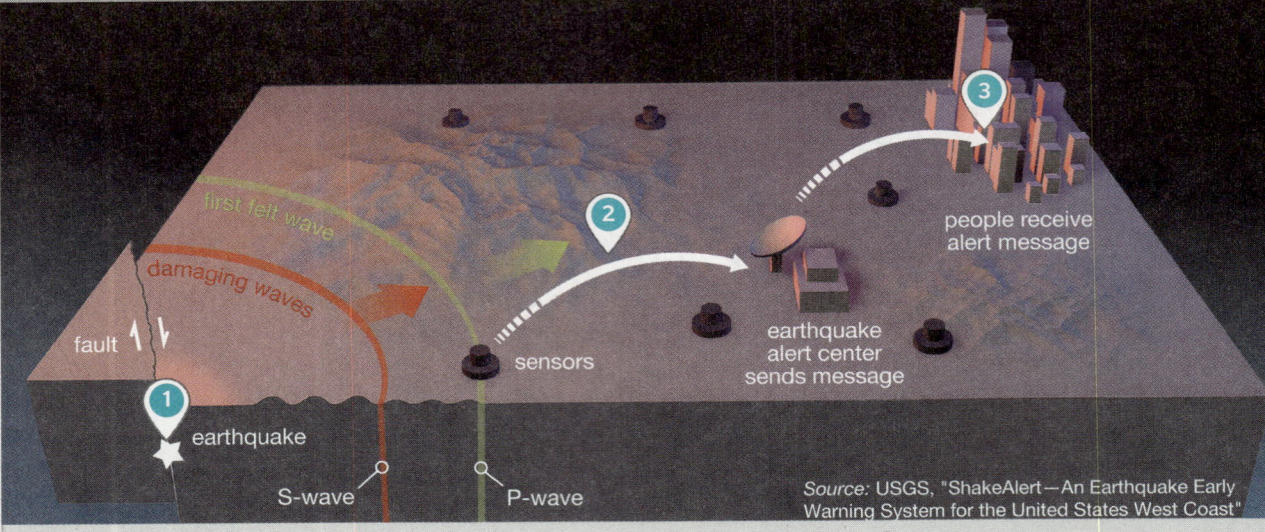

Source: USGS, "ShakeAlert—An Earthquake Early Warning System for the United States West Coast"

1. When an earthquake happens, waves of energy are sent out. Faster P-waves reach locations first. Slower S-waves follow and can cause shaking and damage.

2. P-waves are detected by sensors that immediately communicate with an alert center. Here, alert messages are generated and sent to people in the area.

3. The farther people are from the earthquake source, the more warning time they will have, as the S-waves will take longer to reach them.

1. Explain why an earthquake warning system is useful even though earthquakes cannot be predicted.

2. The team at PNSN is working to make the transfer of data faster from the sensors to the alert center. Explain why this is important.

3. An earthquake warning could give people a few seconds to prepare. Apply what you've learned to provide examples of ways people could prepare for shaking.

4. **Collaborate** With a partner, research the chance of an earthquake happening in your local area. Are you near a plate boundary? Are there any warning systems in place locally? Write an informative brochure to present your findings.

LESSON 1 SELF-CHECK

Can You Explain It?

Name: _____   Date: _____

How might this island have appeared overnight?

> **EVIDENCE NOTEBOOK**
> Refer to the notes in your Evidence Notebook to help you construct an explanation for how this island suddenly appeared.

1. State your claim. Make sure your claim fully explains how the island could have suddenly appeared.

2. Summarize the evidence you have gathered to support your claim and explain your reasoning.

Lesson 1 The Movement of Earth's Plates Affects Earth's Surface   337

LESSON 1 SELF-CHECK

Checkpoints

Answer the following questions to check your understanding of the lesson.

Use the map to answer Questions 3–4.

3. This map shows four kinds of _____. They are now separated by a(n) _____ that they could not have crossed. Their locations could be explained if South America and Africa were _____ at the time the plants and animals lived.

4. In the map key, circle the colored ranges that serve as evidence of the former positions of South America and Africa.

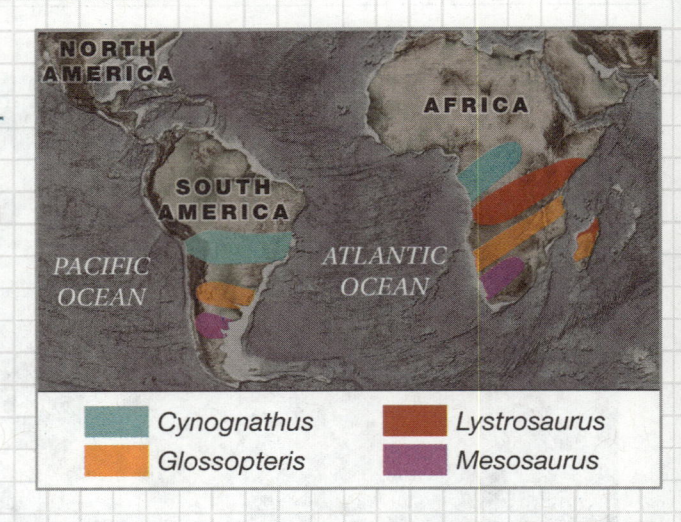

5. Around the world, scientists have found matching fossils, landforms, and continental shelves. Mid-ocean ridges and trenches were discovered on the _____. Together these findings serve as evidence that Earth's surface is made up of moving _____.

Use the map showing plate boundaries to answer Questions 6–7.

6. The Aleutian Trench is a deep-ocean trench that resulted from the sinking of the Pacific plate beneath the North American plate. These plates move *toward / away from / past* each other at a rate of 6–7 cm/y. Also resulting from this motion are *mid-ocean ridges / ocean basins / volcanic islands.*

7. Based on the data in the map, where are eruptions most likely to happen?
   A. along the Aleutian Trench
   B. along the east coast of North America
   C. inland, far from any coastlines shown

8. Which statements correctly describe the nature of plate motion? Circle all that apply.
   A. Energy from the sun drives plate motion.
   B. Energy from Earth's interior drives plate motion.
   C. Plates move in different directions.
   D. Most plates do not move.

338 Unit 5 Earth's Resources and Ecosystems

LESSON 1 SELF-CHECK

Interactive Review

Complete this section to review the main concepts of the lesson.

Fossil and landform data provide evidence that continents have moved and changed.

A. How do patterns in fossil locations provide evidence that Earth's continents have moved?

At mid-ocean ridges, new rock forms. At deep-ocean trenches, rock sinks into Earth's interior. These features provide evidence that the ocean floor moves and changes.

B. Describe the different processes that occur at mid-ocean ridges and deep-ocean trenches.

Earth's surface is made up of tectonic plates that move in different ways. This motion forms and reshapes Earth's surface features over long time periods.

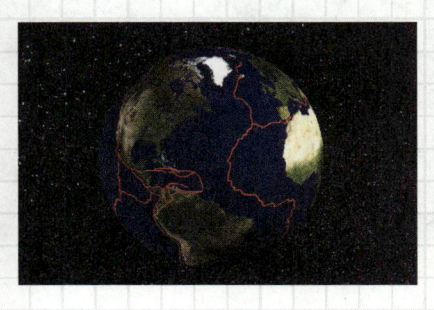

C. Provide an example of a surface feature that forms at each type of plate boundary.

The theory of plate tectonics describes how and why Earth's plates move over time.

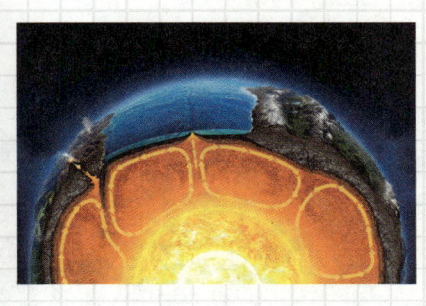

D. What causes convection currents in Earth's interior and how does it relate to plate motion?

Lesson 1 The Movement of Earth's Plates Affects Earth's Surface 339

LESSON 2
Natural Resources Are Distributed Unevenly

The mineral fluorite is used in the production of hydrofluoric acid, in ceramics, and in iron and steel production.

Explore First

Mapping Resources Create a map of "resources" in your school or home. You might include items such as chairs, desks, water fountains, tables, doors, rugs, or sinks. Describe patterns in the distribution of the resources you mapped. What determines each item's placement or distribution?

CAN YOU EXPLAIN IT?

What determines where gold is found in nature?

Gold is an important natural resource. It is used to make reliable computer circuits, repair damaged teeth, and lubricate machinery in space vehicles.

Gold deposits that are worth mining exist only in certain places in the world. In the United States, major gold deposits are found in Alaska, California, Colorado, and Nevada. The United States is among the top gold-producing countries in the world, which also include China, Australia, Russia, and Canada.

1. Why do you think gold deposits are found in the places listed above? Do you think natural processes, human processes, or both have an impact on these places?

EVIDENCE NOTEBOOK As you explore the lesson, gather evidence to help explain where gold is found in nature.

Lesson 2 Natural Resources Are Distributed Unevenly 341

EXPLORATION 1

Explaining Patterns in Natural Resource Distribution

Humans depend on resources from the Earth system, which includes the geosphere, hydrosphere, biosphere, and atmosphere. Minerals, oil, and many other resources are not renewable. That is, they cannot be replaced as quickly as we use them.

Plate Boundaries and Landforms in the United States

Alaska shown at a smaller scale
Source: U.S. Geological Survey

2. **Discuss** Do you think you could use this map to predict where certain natural resources are found? Why or why not?

Natural Resource Distribution

Many resources are unevenly distributed because the processes that formed them long ago only happened in specific places. For example, colliding tectonic plates formed mountains in specific areas in the past. During this time, rock and underground fluids were heated. The hot fluids dissolved minerals, such as gold and copper, and redistributed them in more concentrated forms in the crust. Therefore, copper and gold deposits are often found near plate boundaries that existed in the past. Water, forests, and soil are also resources. Their locations are due to past and present climate conditions and landforms. The landforms you see today were shaped by plate motion, weathering, erosion, and deposition.

Some resources are moved after they form. For example, explore the diagram showing weathering and erosion removing gold from the rock it formed in.

Gold deposits can become exposed at the surface by processes such as uplift and erosion. The exposed gold-bearing rock is broken down, eroded, and deposited into valleys and streams.

342 Unit 5 Earth's Resources and Ecosystems

Mineral Resources

What does a school building have in common with a smart phone? They are both made from minerals. In fact, many synthetic, or human-made, items come from minerals, including computers, paint, bicycles, concrete, and steel. Most mineral deposits take millions of years to form. Therefore, most mineral resources are nonrenewable.

Minerals are usually found alongside several other minerals in a rock. A rock with a high enough concentration of a specific mineral to be worth mining is called an *ore*. Ores are mined and processed to separate the desired mineral from rest of the rock.

Mineral Mines in the United States

Legend:
- Cobalt
- Copper
- Gold
- Iron ore
- Lead
- Molybdenum
- Salt
- Silver

Alaska is shown at a smaller scale

Source: USGS, Mine and Mineral Processing Plant Locations, 1997

Gold is found in and around intrusive igneous rocks below ground, or above ground where it has been uplifted by geologic processes. Some gold is also found in stream bottoms and valleys.

Iron ore is found where iron-rich oceans existed billions of years ago. These deposits formed on the ancient ocean floors as iron reacted with oxygen and other substances in the water.

Table salt is made from a mineral called *halite*. It forms when salt water evaporates. Halite is forming today in the Great Salt Lake in Utah and in other places around the globe.

The locations of mineral deposits depend on the past processes by which the minerals formed. For example, as tectonic plate motion squeezes Earth's crust and forms mountain belts, the crust and its underground fluids become very hot. The heated fluids dissolve minerals and metals in the crust. The hot fluids rise toward the surface through tiny underground passages. The fluids rise because they are less dense than the surrounding rock. Near the surface, the pressure and temperature around the fluids decrease, so the dissolved metals solidify and become concentrated in deposits.

3. Relate the mineral map back to the map of landforms and plate boundaries. Note any patterns you observe.

EVIDENCE NOTEBOOK

4. How can gold deposits form? How could gold be moved from its original location to a new location? Record your evidence.

Soil

Soil provides nutrients for plants and shelter for animals, and humans use soil to grow food. Soil even plays an important role in storing water, which helps prevent flooding. Soil forms on land where rock is broken down by chemical and physical weathering processes. Explore the diagram to learn more.

Steps in Soil Formation

parent rock — Rock is broken down into smaller and smaller pieces by the processes of weathering and erosion. These fragments of rock are called *sediment*.

young soil — Sediment mixes with air, water, and organic matter present in the ground to become soil. The soil can now support some plant life.

mature soil — More organic matter is added as organisms die and decompose. This process makes a nutrient-rich layer of soil at the surface called *topsoil*.

The conditions required for soil to form only exist in certain areas on Earth, so soil distribution is not uniform. For example, soil tends to form in valleys and basins where wind and water deposited sediment in the past. The tops and sides of hills and mountains often have little or no soil. This is because sediment is eroded from the tops of hills and mountains by factors such as wind and rain.

There are different types of soil and some are more fertile than others. Soil fertility depends on how much organic matter and other nutrients the soil has. A fertile soil contains a lot of organic matter and nutrients. Organic matter in the soil comes from dead organisms and animal waste. Bacteria and fungi break down organic matter and release chemical byproducts that mix with the top layer of soil. These materials are the nutrients that make the soil better able to support plant life.

The Sierra Nevada Mountains were uplifted by tectonic forces millions of years ago. Weathering and erosion later brought sediment from the mountains down into the central valley, shown here. Soil formed as the sediment mixed with organic matter, water, and air.

5. Soil can take hundreds of years to form. Soil's formation rate depends on rock type, climate, and the presence of organisms. Is fertile soil a renewable or nonrenewable resource? Use evidence and scientific reasoning to support your claim.

344 Unit 5 Earth's Resources and Ecosystems

Fossil Fuels

Fossil fuels include oil, coal, and natural gas. Fossil fuels have many uses. For example, coal can be burned to generate electrical energy and provide lighting in buildings. Natural gas and oil can be used to heat homes. Oil can also be processed to make plastics and gasoline. Fossil fuels are nonrenewable resources because we are using them faster than the natural processes that form them. Even though the processes that form oil, coal, and gas are happening today, these processes take millions of years.

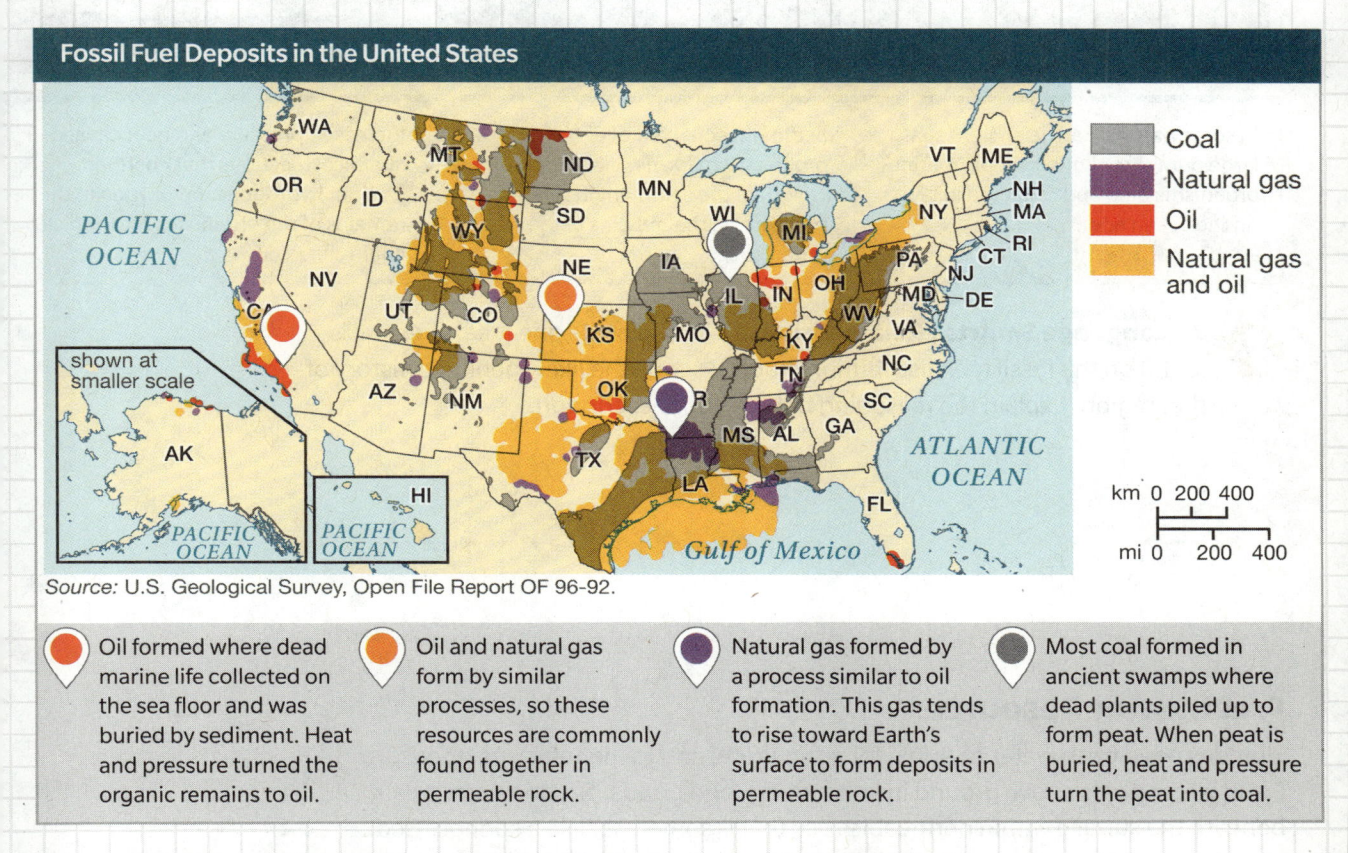

Fossil Fuel Deposits in the United States

Legend:
- Coal
- Natural gas
- Oil
- Natural gas and oil

Source: U.S. Geological Survey, Open File Report OF 96-92.

- **Oil** formed where dead marine life collected on the sea floor and was buried by sediment. Heat and pressure turned the organic remains to oil.
- **Oil and natural gas** form by similar processes, so these resources are commonly found together in permeable rock.
- **Natural gas** formed by a process similar to oil formation. This gas tends to rise toward Earth's surface to form deposits in permeable rock.
- **Most coal** formed in ancient swamps where dead plants piled up to form peat. When peat is buried, heat and pressure turn the peat into coal.

6. Compare this map to the map you explored in the beginning of this lesson. Do you notice any patterns? Write your observations.

Deposits of oil and natural gas found today formed millions of years ago in ancient seas. Sediment and the remains of organisms collected at the bottoms of the seas and formed sedimentary layers rich in organic matter. Over time, heat and pressure converted the organic matter into oil and natural gas.

Coal is a sedimentary rock. Coal is found today where swamp environments once existed. As plants died and collected at the bottoms of these swamps, a material called peat formed. The peat was buried as matter continued collecting in the swamp. This increased heat and pressure and eventually turned the peat into coal.

Steps in Oil Formation

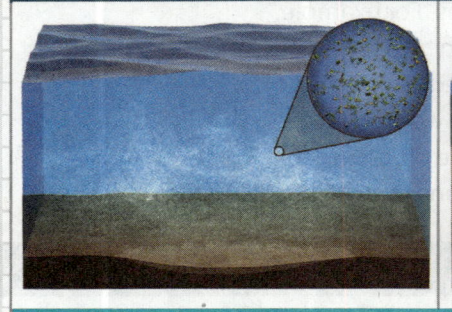

In some parts of Earth's ancient seas, large numbers of microscopic marine organisms died and collected in layers on the ocean floor.

Sediment collected over the organisms to form rock layers. The weight of the sediment increased pressure on the remains of the organisms.

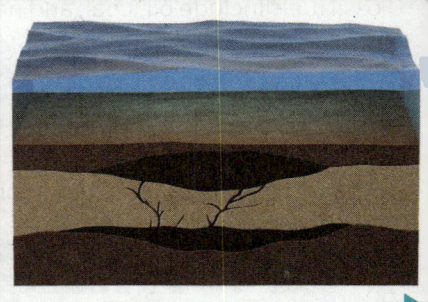

Increased pressure and heat caused chemical reactions that changed carbon, hydrogen, and oxygen in the remains of the organisms into a thick liquid called *oil*.

7. **Language SmArts | Relate Visuals to Text** Locate one area where oil is found on the fossil fuel distribution map. Describe the likely geologic history of that region. Explain the reasoning behind your description.

Freshwater Resources

Humans need fresh water to drink, for agriculture, and to manufacture goods. Fresh water exists above ground in lakes, rivers, and ponds. Groundwater exists beneath the surface within permeable rock that is somewhat like a sponge. Bodies of rock containing water are called *aquifers*. Aquifers exist almost everywhere on Earth. Groundwater flows through aquifers and connects to water on the surface. Groundwater levels can increase as precipitation and surface water seep through soil and rock. Groundwater levels can decrease during droughts, or as water is pumped by humans at a faster rate than the water is replenished.

The Huacachina Oasis near Ica, Peru, formed in the desert where groundwater rises to Earth's surface.

Groundwater and Surface Water Distribution

Aquifers are found in many places on Earth. Aquifers are connected to surface water in springs, lakes, streams, and rivers. Water can flow back and forth between these reservoirs.

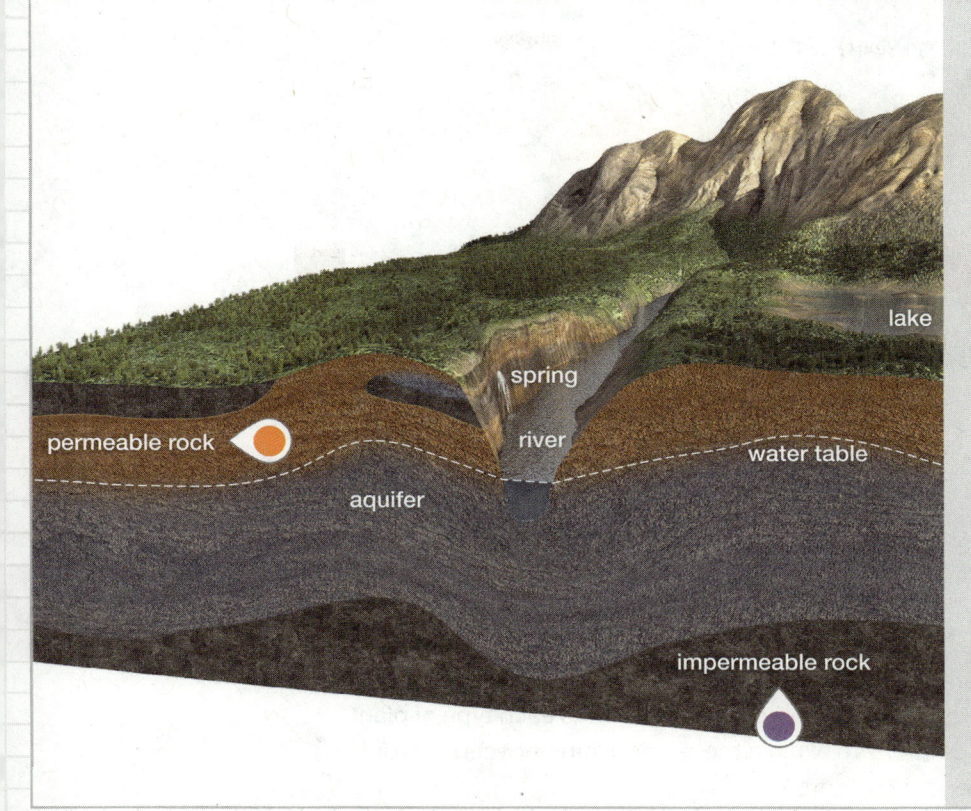

Aquifers consist of permeable rocks that hold groundwater. Like a sponge, permeable rocks allow liquid or gas to pass into and through them.

Water and other fluids cannot flow through impermeable rock. Impermeable layers prevent groundwater from entering or leaving aquifers.

Earth's supply of usable fresh water is limited. Some is polluted and unusable, or it costs a lot to remove the pollution. Some freshwater is not accessible, for example, it can be frozen in glaciers or be stored too deep underground.

Tectonic plate motion along with surface processes like erosion and deposition shaped the mountains and valleys we see today. The locations of freshwater resources depend on these landforms and on climate. Water flows downhill from snowmelt, springs, glaciers, and rainfall to form bodies of water such as streams and lakes. During droughts, water can evaporate from lakes and seas.

Renewable Resources

Like fossil fuels, minerals, and fresh water resources, most renewable resources are unevenly distributed on Earth. Sunlight, wind, water, and biomass are a few examples. Biomass is plant matter that can be burned for heat or used to make other fuels. Crops, plant waste, and trees are all types of biomass. Biomass is considered renewable because it can be replenished faster than humans use it.

Wind and water resources are also unevenly distributed. Wind can be harnessed to generate electrical energy where wind blows consistently and in a predictable direction. Hydroelectric energy is usually generated by harnessing large amounts of moving river water. Dams are built to control the flow of water in some rivers, but not every river has enough water or a strong enough flow for a hydroelectric dam.

Worldwide Distribution of Solar Energy

8. This map shows the relationship between latitude and solar energy. Most areas near the equator receive more / ~~less~~ solar energy than the poles receive.

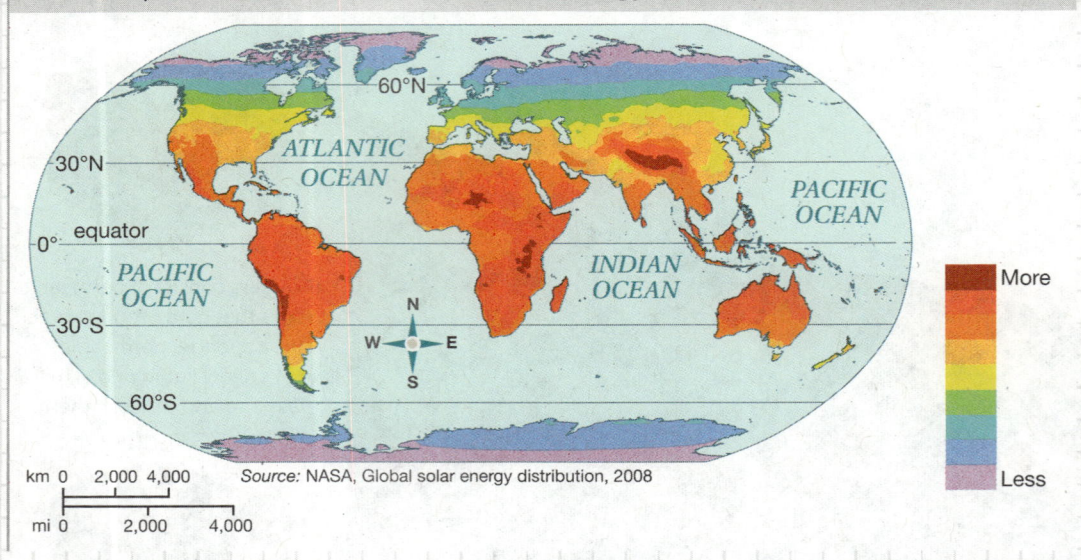

Source: NASA, Global solar energy distribution, 2008

Analyze Energy Resource Locations

Geothermal and nuclear plants are used to generate electrical energy and heat buildings. Explore the map to see the patterns in distribution of each type of plant. Complete the following descriptions to explain the relationship between geologic processes and two types of energy resources.

9. Earthquake risk is high along the west coast of the United States due to an active plate boundary. There are several geothermal / ~~nuclear~~ plants and there are no ~~geothermal~~ / nuclear plants where earthquake risk is highest.

10. Radiation from a nuclear power plant disaster could make people and other living things very sick. ~~Geothermal~~ / Nuclear plants are not built near plate boundaries because earthquake risk is high there and could result in a disaster.

U.S. Plate Boundaries, Earthquake Risk, and Nuclear and Geothermal Plants

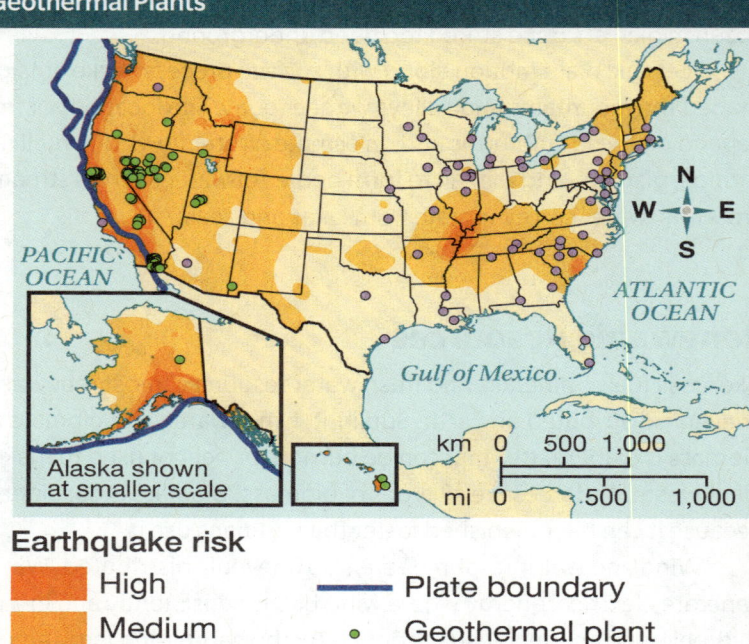

Earthquake risk:
- High
- Medium
- Low
- Plate boundary
- Geothermal plant
- Nuclear plant

Source: U.S. Geological Survey, U.S. Department of Energy, and National Renewable Energy Laboratory

348 Unit 5 Earth's Resources and Ecosystems

EXPLORATION 2

Explaining Human Impact on Natural Resource Distribution

Many resources, such as clean drinking water and soil, are a result of Earth's natural systems and cycles, such as the water cycle. As humans extract and use resources, they can disrupt the natural systems they rely on. As humans use more resources, the availability of these resources may be reduced. Once a nonrenewable resource, such as oil, is used up, it is unlikely more will become available. Other resources, such as water and wind, are renewable resources. People can conserve renewable resources such as trees or biomass by careful management and use.

11. Act Create a skit that explains how the use of natural resources has short-term and long-term effects on both human health and on the environment.

Human Impact on Soil Distribution

Human actions can negatively change soil quality and can promote erosion. Soil polluted with pesticides and fertilizers is not a valuable resource. Repeatedly growing nutrient-depleting crops in the same fields can also lead to unhealthy soil. Unhealthy soil is less able to support plant growth, and its value as a resource is reduced. Strip mining, overgrazing cattle, and clearing forestland for building encourage soil erosion and can cause the loss of healthy soil. These processes may contribute to the expansion of deserts, a process called *desertification*. To protect soil resources, human activities can be designed to prevent soil loss or degradation. Planting diverse crops, rotating crops, planting trees and cover crops, and contour farming help prevent erosion and degradation of soil.

Human Activities and Soil Erosion

For years, Great Plains farmers over-plowed and overgrazed the land. In 1931, drought and poor farming practices caused extensive soil erosion. These practices caused the Dust Bowl.

Loss of tree cover increases soil erosion. Humans did not form the Sahara desert. But human activity, such as removing trees, allows the Sahara to grow. This is an example of desertification.

Crop rotation and contour plowing enrich soil and prevent erosion. Adding mulch retains water. Planting ground cover and trees holds soil in place. These practices protect soil resources.

12. Can human activities change the distribution of nonrenewable resources, such as oil or minerals? Could we change the distribution of renewable resources, such as sunlight and wind? Support your claim with evidence and reasoning.

Engineer It
Reduce Erosion

Soil erosion caused by heavy rains is threatening to reduce the harvests of farms in your hilly community. Work with a small group to develop a solution to reduce erosion.

13. Identify the criteria and constraints for your problem. What needs must your solution address? What resources do you need to implement your solution? Describe any issues that limit your solutions.

14. **Discuss** Brainstorm and list ideas to prevent soil erosion. Be sure to consider the criteria and constraints. Choose the most promising solution based on your criteria and constraints. Describe or draw your solution here.

Human Impact on Fossil Fuel and Mineral Distribution

Before humans can use minerals and fossil fuels, these resources must first be extracted from the ground. Extracting resources changes their distribution because the resources are removed and carried to a new location. For example, when oil is pumped out of the ground for human use, the amount of oil in that reservoir is reduced or completely depleted. Once nonrenewable energy and mineral resources are used, they are not replaced for millions of years. As humans extract and use nonrenewable mineral and energy resources, the total amount of these resources available for future use declines.

Gold Mining and Distribution

In 1848, gold was discovered at Sutter's Mill in California. Thousands of people moved to California to look for gold in the streams and hills of California in the years that followed.

Valuable gold deposits are rare. As gold is taken from a mine, less and less gold remains in that location. As the supply of gold at the mine gets smaller, miners must ask: Is there enough gold to continue mining this location?

Although some deposits have been depleted, the demand for gold continues. Used gold can be reclaimed and recycled. Recycling gold becomes more important as accessible gold deposits become harder to find.

As deposits and reservoirs get smaller and disappear, we must find new deposits of the resources to use. These new deposits may be of lower quality or may be more challenging to acquire than the original deposits. We may also develop new technologies for extracting valuable resources. Some nonrenewable resources can be recycled. For example, gold can be extracted from some existing products, such as jewelry, and used again in other products, such as electronics. Recycling mineral resources reduces the need for mining and processing new ore deposits. Managing and reducing the use of nonrenewable minerals and fossil fuels is important to ensure that resources will remain available for future generations.

EVIDENCE NOTEBOOK

15. How does human activity change the distribution of gold? Record your evidence.

Human Impact on Freshwater Distribution

Humans cannot control Earth's water cycle, but they do change the distribution of fresh water on Earth. Humans cannot live without fresh water. We use water in most activities, including drinking and bathing, raising livestock and crops for food, manufacturing goods, and generating electrical energy.

Human activities can change the distribution of surface water. Dams block off flowing water to form reservoirs. As a result, water that would have flowed farther down the river stays in the area above the dam. Dams make more fresh water available upstream from the dam, but they make fresh water less available downstream. Humans also build canals to force water to flow in different directions. Canals are used to transport fresh water into and through regions where natural streams and rivers do not exist. Canals are also used to transport other materials by boat. Reservoirs and dams in dry areas also increase the rate of evaporation of freshwater supplies.

Humans extract groundwater from aquifers by using wells to pump the water up from below the surface. This process, called withdrawal, reduces the amount of water in the aquifer. In some places, water is used up faster than it is replenished by precipitation. The process by which water seeps through the ground and enters an aquifer is called *recharge*. When the rate of withdrawal exceeds the recharge rate, the water level in the aquifer may drop, and deeper wells have to be drilled. Over time, an aquifer can be completely drained if the rates of use and recharge remain unbalanced. Removal of too much groundwater may also destabilize the ground and cause sinkholes to form.

The Shrinking Aral Sea

Before 1960, the Aral Sea in Central Asia was the world's fourth largest lake. It supported villages and a small fishing industry. Then, people began using the water to irrigate crops. The sea shrank. The water became polluted with fertilizer. In 2000, the Aral Sea was less than half its historic size. By 2016, it had almost dried up.

2000   **2008**   **2016**

16. The cause of the shrinking Aral Sea is the overuse of its water by humans. What do you think the Aral Sea will look like in 2024? Support your claim with evidence and reasoning.

352 Unit 5 Earth's Resources and Ecosystems

Hands-On Lab
Model Recharge and Withdrawal in an Aquifer

You will model an aquifer to explore how groundwater levels change.

Procedure

STEP 1 Build a landscape made up of permeable rock. In your landscape, make a depression to represent a low-lying area of land. What material models the permeable rock?

STEP 2 Add a few drops of blue food coloring to the pitcher of water to make the water a medium blue color. Carefully pour the blue water over your landscape until it partially fills the depression you made. What do the blue water and the depression represent?

MATERIALS
- fish tank hand siphon, pump, or syringe
- food coloring, blue
- graduated cylinders, 50 mL (2)
- gravel or aquarium pebbles, light colored (3 cups)
- pitcher, with water
- plastic container, clear, large, rectangular
- ruler

STEP 3 Use a ruler to measure the height of the groundwater starting from the bottom of the container. Measure the height of the water in the depression starting from the bottom of the depression. Record your observations in the table.

STEP 4 Using a pump, model how a well can be used to withdraw groundwater from an aquifer. Pump out 50 mL of groundwater. Measure and record the depth of the groundwater and the surface water in the depression. Record your observations in the table.

STEP 5 An aquifer is refilled when precipitation occurs. Add 50 mL of water to the aquifer. Measure and record the depth of the groundwater and the surface water in the depression. Record your observations in the table.

	Groundwater depth (mm)	Surface water depth (mm)	Observations
STEP 3			
STEP 4			
STEP 5			

Lesson 2 Natural Resources Are Distributed Unevenly

STEP 6 How do precipitation and pumping each affect the water in an aquifer? How do changes in the groundwater level affect the level of surface water?

STEP 7 How could you model the effects of humans using water from the aquifer more quickly than precipitation could recharge the aquifer?

STEP 8 In your model, you withdrew and added water in seconds. Explain how this differs from the rate at which groundwater levels change in the real world.

STEP 9 **Engineer It** Think about your aquifer model. What does it tell you about the properties of rock in aquifers? How could you use your model to inform the design of a driveway that allows water to enter the ground below it?

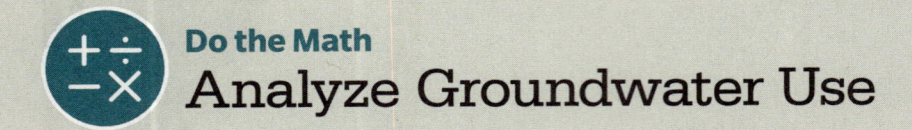

Do the Math
Analyze Groundwater Use

v = overall change in volume in one month
s = starting volume
w = withdrawal rate
r = recharge rate

Caleb's farm uses groundwater from an aquifer that holds 100,000 gallons of water. The farm withdraws about 5,000 gallons per month. Precipitation adds about 2,000 gallons of water per month back into the aquifer.

17. With a partner, use the variables to write an equation to represent the overall change in volume per month, taking into account both withdrawal and recharge. Next, use your equation to find the overall change in volume each month. Hint: For the rate of withdrawal, use a negative value.

18. What will the total volume of water in the aquifer be after 6 months? Recall the initial volume is 100,000 gallons.

19. The well only reaches a certain depth into the aquifer. Once the aquifer's volume is less than 50,000 gallons, the well will no longer be able to pump water. At the current rate of usage, how long will this take?

TAKE IT FURTHER

Continue Your Exploration

Name: _____   Date: _____

Check out the path below or go online to choose one of the other paths shown.

Rare Earth Elements and Technology
- Resources in Space
- Hands-On Labs
- Propose Your Own Path

Go online to choose one of these other paths.

Suppose you send a text message. For you, it means tapping a screen. For Earth, it means more rare earth elements (REEs) in shorter supply. Seventeen elements are considered REEs, and most are elements few people recognize.

Over time, scientific discoveries and advances in engineering have led to several uses for REEs. They are used in cell phones, tablets, and televisions. REEs are also used to make rechargeable batteries and the world's strongest magnets. You can even find REEs in wind turbine generators and hybrid cars.

Extracting and Processing REEs

REEs are nonrenewable resources, and currently, less than 1% are recycled. The demand for REEs increases as the demand increases for technology. Scientists and engineers are trying to answer several questions about REEs. How many more REE deposits exist on Earth? Can other elements be substituted for REEs? Because REEs are nonrenewable, what will happen to technologies that depend on REEs if they are used up?

REEs accumulated on Earth as the planet was forming, so they are found deep below the surface. As a result, mining REE deposits with currently available tools and technology is difficult and costly.

When people get new cell phones, they can give their old phones to someone who can recycle the REEs in them.

TAKE IT FURTHER

Continue Your Exploration

In the geosphere, REEs combine with other elements to form chemical compounds. Most REE compounds form as crystals. Processing REEs means separating the elements from these crystals, which can be expensive. The waste from these processes includes radioactive material and toxic chemicals. Disposal of the waste can endanger the environment, so safe disposal also adds to the cost of using REEs.

Because REEs have so many uses today, humans will eventually use up all of the REEs in the geosphere. Recycling REEs is critical to maintaining supplies. Most products contain very small amounts of REEs. The average television has trace amounts of yttrium (IT•ree•uhm), europium (yoo•ROH•pee•uhm), and terbium (TER•bee•uhm) while cell phones may have lanthanum (LAN•thuh•nuhm) and neodymium (nee•oh•DIM•ee•uhm). Even at trace amounts, recycling is worthwhile. However, recycling means extracting each REE individually from millions of used cell phones, laptops, and televisions.

1. What are some ways we could ensure that rare earth elements are used wisely? Circle all that apply.

    A. require recycling of used electronics

    B. eliminate their use in electronics

    C. develop ways to use less REEs per device

    D. replace REEs with common elements

    E. make electronics that last longer

2. As REEs are used up and the available supply goes down, do you think the cost of electronics, such as cell phones, will go up or down? Support your claim with evidence and reasoning.

3. What is a possible way to increase the supply of REEs other than recycling?

4. **Collaborate** With a partner, discuss ways to increase the number of people who recycle electronic products. Choose the idea that you think would work best and present it to the class.

LESSON 2 SELF-CHECK

Can You Explain It?

Name: _____   Date: _____

What determines where gold is found in nature?

EVIDENCE NOTEBOOK
Refer to the notes in your Evidence Notebook to help you construct an explanation about where gold is found in nature.

1. State your claim. Make sure your claim fully explains what determines where gold is located in nature.

2. Summarize the evidence you have gathered to support your claim and explain your reasoning.

Lesson 2 Natural Resources Are Distributed Unevenly

LESSON 2 SELF-CHECK

Checkpoints

Answer the following questions to check your understanding of the lesson.
Use the photo to answer Questions 3–4.

3. These mountains in Peru contain gold deposits that formed as
   ~~precipitation / plate motion / erosion~~ deformed the rock
   millions of years ago.

4. Which of these processes could change the gold's distribution? Choose all that apply.
   A. evaporation of water
   B. weathering and erosion
   C. burial of plant matter
   D. mining by humans

5. Which of these activities or processes might affect the supply of groundwater in an aquifer? Select all that apply.
   A. raising livestock on a farm
   B. processing materials in a factory
   C. drought
   D. excessive rainfall

Use the table to answer Question 6.

6. Which of the following resources are most commonly used by this city?
   A. Oil, coal, and natural gas resources
   B. Solar, wind, and biomass resources
   C. Nuclear resources

| Energy Resource Use by a City ||
Resource	Consumption Percentage
Fossil fuels	71%
Nuclear	9%
Renewables	20%

358 Unit 5 Earth's Resources and Ecosystems

LESSON 2 SELF-CHECK

Interactive Review

Complete this section to review the main concepts of the lesson.

The distribution of resources, such as minerals, soil, fossil fuels, and water, depends on both past and current geologic processes.

A. Explain why the distribution of mineral and freshwater resources is uneven in the Earth system.

As humans use nonrenewable resources, the distribution of those resources changes, and their availability becomes limited. Human activities can also affect the quality of some resources, such as water and soil.

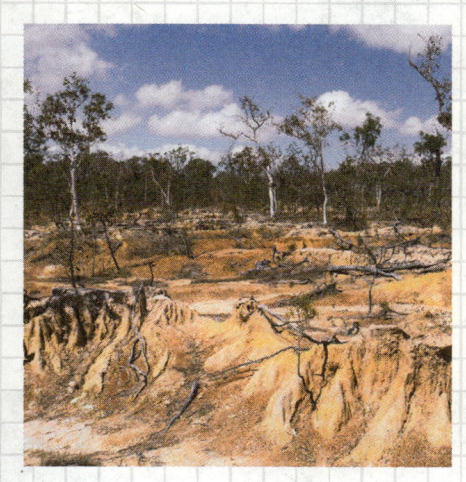

B. Describe the cause-and-effect relationship between human use of a nonrenewable resource and the distribution of that resource on Earth.

Lesson 2 Natural Resources Are Distributed Unevenly

LESSON 3
Resource Availability Affects Organisms

This coniferous forest provides resources, such as food and shelter, for a wide variety of organisms.

Explore First

Planning a Terrarium Write a plan to build a terrarium with at least two plants. What resources will the plants need to survive within the terrarium? What resources outside the terrarium will they need? If time allows you to construct your terrarium, be sure to check with an adult to ensure your materials and plants are safe to use.

CAN YOU EXPLAIN IT?

How does a wildfire affect resources and populations in a forest?

Some wildfires are caused by humans, but fires can also start because of a natural factor such as a lightning strike.

1. Imagine that you saw a huge green forest one day, and the next day you saw the scene in the photo above. Describe what you observe in this photo.

2. Think about all the organisms that live in a forest. How do you think living things were affected by this fire?

EVIDENCE NOTEBOOK As you explore this lesson, gather evidence to help explain how a wildfire affects resources and populations in a forest ecosystem.

Lesson 3 Resource Availability Affects Organisms **361**

EXPLORATION 1

Analyzing Parts of an Ecosystem

An **ecosystem** is all the organisms living together in a particular place along with their nonliving environment. Ecosystems contain everything that organisms need to survive. Think about an earthworm living in the soil. The earthworm interacts with other living things when it eats fallen leaves for food or when a predator captures it. The earthworm also needs air and water, which are nonliving parts of the ecosystem.

These robins depend on other parts of the ecosystem, including trees and earthworms.

3. **Discuss** Together with a partner, discuss how these baby birds are interacting with the living and nonliving parts of their environment.

The Living Environment

The parts of an ecosystem that are living, or that result from the activities of living things, are called **biotic factors**. For example, think about a dragonfly that lives in a meadow near a pond. Biotic factors in the dragonfly's ecosystem include the tadpoles, green algae, and insects that the dragonfly eats. Green plants are also biotic factors—dragonflies lay their eggs on the leaves of plants. Other biotic factors that interact with the dragonfly are the animals that eat dragonflies, such as fish, salamanders, and frogs, and other insects that compete with dragonflies for food. A decaying log that dragonflies perch on would also be considered a biotic factor because it is the remains of a living thing.

The Nonliving Environment

An **abiotic factor** is a nonliving part of an ecosystem. Some abiotic factors are air, nutrients, sunlight, water, wind, and temperature. A dragonfly spends the first part of its life cycle in the water. The water must be a certain temperature for the young dragonfly to survive. The adult dragonfly also needs a certain air temperature to be able to fly. Both young and adult dragonflies need oxygen to breathe.

362 Unit 5 Earth's Resources and Ecosystems

Forest Ecosystem

Explore how different organisms in this forest ecosystem depend on the abiotic and biotic factors of their environment.

🔴 This flying squirrel glides through the air from tree to tree and eats the seeds and nuts produced by plants.

🔵 Many different organisms, such as this salmon, depend on streams for oxygen, nutrients, shelter, and water.

🟠 Shelf fungi absorb nutrients and minerals from decaying plants and animals. This fungus is absorbing nutrients from tree bark.

🟢 Soil contains nutrients and water that organisms, such as earthworms and plants, need. Soil also provides shelter for burrowing animals, such as this mole.

Lesson 3 Resource Availability Affects Organisms

The Distribution of Ecosystems

Not all ecosystems are the same. One reason ecosystems differ is that Earth has different landforms, which are shaped by geologic processes over long periods of time. For example, tectonic plate motion crumples Earth's crust into tall mountain ranges. Streams erode valleys and canyons. As you might imagine, a stream ecosystem in a valley differs from a forest ecosystem in the mountains.

Climate types vary with elevation, landforms, and latitude, and specific ecosystems are found in each. For example, warm and rainy climates along the equator promote the growth of dense trees and other vegetation in rain forest ecosystems. Tree-dwelling animals are therefore common in these ecosystems. Hot, dry climates are common along latitudes thirty degrees north and south of the equator. Desert ecosystems often develop here. Plants that can hold water for long periods thrive and many animals avoid the heat by interacting at night. Climates, and therefore ecosystems, are also influenced by oceans, global wind patterns, and even by human activities.

4. The warm air and rainfall in a tropical rain forest ecosystem are *abiotic / biotic* factors that influence the growth of plants. The plants provide food and shelter for many animals. The plants and animals are *abiotic / biotic* factors.

Levels of Organization in Ecosystems

An ecosystem can be organized into different levels. The smallest level is a single organism. The largest level is the entire ecosystem. Each level of organization gets more complex as more of the environment is considered.

Florida Everglades Ecosystem

The Florida Everglades is a wetland ecosystem that includes communities of living organisms and nonliving factors such as water, rocks, and air.

osprey

great blue herons

alligators

Individual

An individual is a single organism, such as one alligator. Each type of organism belongs to a different species. A **species** includes organisms that are of the same kind and can successfully reproduce, resulting in fertile offspring.

Population

A **population** is a group of individuals of the same species that live in an ecosystem. Individuals within a population can compete with each other for resources. For example, alligators in the Everglades ecosystem compete for food, space, and mates.

Community

A **community** is made up of all the populations of different species that interact in an area. The species within a community depend on each other for things such as shelter and food. For example, animals get energy and nutrients by eating other organisms.

Populations in a community compete with other populations for resources. One example is two bird populations with similar nesting habits that may compete for nesting space. Two populations with similar diets may compete for food resources.

Ecosystem

An ecosystem is a community of organisms and their nonliving environment, such as the Everglades ecosystem. Energy flows through an ecosystem, starting with sunlight that powers plant and algal growth. Energy continues to flow through the ecosystem as one organism eats another. Ecosystems occur at all scales, from a tiny puddle to a vast forest.

Describe Human Impact on an Ecosystem

The rivers, swamps, and thick soils of the Florida Everglades provide food, water, shelter, and other resources to organisms, including humans. Humans pump water from the Everglades to grow crops nearby. As the human population in the area grows, the amount of water pumped out of the ecosystem often exceeds the amount of rainfall and water that flows into the ecosystem.

5. If the human population near the Everglades continues to grow, the water levels in the ecosystem will likely increase / *decrease* / stay the same. This will likely have *a positive* / a negative / no impact on the plants and animals that depend on the swamps, lakes, and rivers.

6. Healthy, functioning ecosystems provide *ecosystem services* to humans. For example, the Everglades provide flood control because wetland soils and plants can soak up a lot of rain. The development of buildings, parking lots, and roads would increase / *decrease* / not change the ability of the ecosystem to provide flood control.

EXPLORATION 2

Relating Resource Availability to Growth

You may think you are very different from a robin or an earthworm, but humans, hummingbirds, and earthworms all have the same basic needs. In fact, *all* organisms require the same basic resources to survive, grow, develop, respond to the environment, and reproduce. Can you think of what some of these key resources are?

7. All organisms need energy to survive. A plant that stops receiving energy from the sun ~~will~~ / will not be able to perform life functions. As a result, the plant will continue / ~~stop~~ growing and will eventually ~~reproduce~~ / die.

8. Rank each organism according to the amount of energy you think it needs to sustain its life processes, with 1 being the least and 4 being the most.

This single-celled amoeba is microscopic.

The common octopus's arms can grow up to one meter long.

Adult African elephants can reach four meters in height.

The tiny leaves of this moss plant are only millimeters in length.

Growth Requires Resources

All living things must get resources from their environment because their cells need a source of materials and energy. The resources that organisms need to live and grow include food, water, and shelter. Some of these resources are living. Food and some types of shelter, such as a tree, are living resources. Water and some types of shelter, such as a burrow in the ground, are nonliving resources. Minerals found in soil and energy from the sun are also nonliving resources. Organisms get all of the resources they need from the ecosystem in which they live. The growth of both individuals and populations depends on resource availability within an ecosystem.

Individual Growth

A hatchling from a tiny egg can become a large sea turtle, and an acorn can grow into a towering oak tree. These individual organisms—like all individual organisms—require resources to grow. Only with sufficient resources can an individual survive, grow, and eventually reproduce.

Population Growth

The growth of a population depends on the availability of resources, including food, water, and shelter. Suppose that the organisms in an ecosystem have an abundance of the resources that they need to grow and reproduce. Under these conditions, the number of organisms in a population will likely increase and the population will grow. Now think about conditions in which some resources are scarce. Under conditions of scarce resources, not all organisms can get the resources they need. Fewer organisms are able to reproduce and the population does not grow. If resources are very scarce, some individuals may not survive. Other organisms may reproduce at such a low rate that the population gets smaller. If the amount of resources changes, a population may become larger or smaller.

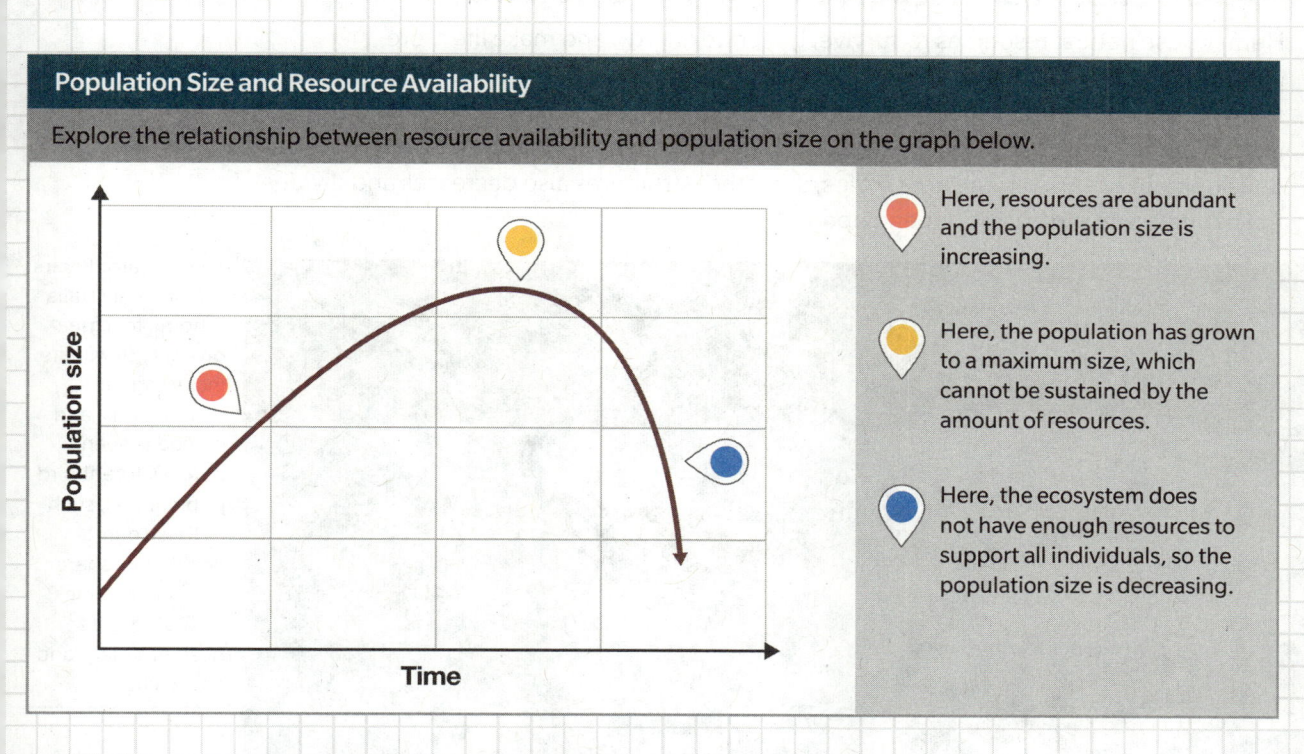

Population Size and Resource Availability

Explore the relationship between resource availability and population size on the graph below.

🔴 Here, resources are abundant and the population size is increasing.

🟡 Here, the population has grown to a maximum size, which cannot be sustained by the amount of resources.

🔵 Here, the ecosystem does not have enough resources to support all individuals, so the population size is decreasing.

9. A decrease in a population's rate of reproduction can cause a decrease in population size, such as the one shown on this graph. Which factors might cause a decrease in the rate of reproduction? Select all that apply.

   A. a decrease in the availability of food resources
   B. an increase in resources such as water
   C. conditions that limit the availability of shelter resources
   D. conditions that allow access to new resources that were not previously available

Lesson 3 Resource Availability Affects Organisms

Factors That Influence Resource Availability

Resource availability influences the growth and survival of individual organisms as well as the sizes of populations. In fact, the types of resources that individuals need are also critical for the population as a whole. Resource availability depends on a variety of factors.

Individuals within a population share the same resources. These individuals may compete with each other for access to these resources. An increase in population size may mean that fewer resources are available for each individual of the population. Different populations of organisms may also share resources, such as water or food. Competition between different populations may result in fewer resources for some populations or individuals.

Environmental factors can also affect resource availability. For example, after a rainy season, plants may produce many leaves and seeds. This large amount of food may allow a deer population to grow. However, when the rain stops and plants produce less, the deer population may decrease. Natural events, such as wildfires and droughts, can limit resource availability temporarily, leading to population decreases.

Human Impact on Resource Quality and Quantity

Humans use natural resources to survive, generate energy, and make life more convenient. This can decrease the availability of natural resources used by other plants and animals. For example, growing crops requires water. When farms and ranches use water from a nearby stream or lake over time, that water supply may be decreased. The development of agricultural fields, cities, and other structures also decreases and divides the habitats that organisms depend upon.

The Alligator Rivers region in Australia is home to a great diversity of wildlife, including the plants, birds, and crocodile seen here. Different bird populations, such as these egrets and storks, share certain resources, including water, nest materials, and fish to eat.

10. What factors might affect the availability of fish to eat for the egret and stork populations?

11. A red-tailed hawk is a bird that eats other birds and small animals including mammals. Label each scenario to tell whether it would likely *increase* or *decrease* the availability of food resources for a red-tailed hawk population.

Scenario	Effect on red-tailed hawk food resources
A drought causes plants to produce fewer seeds than usual, limiting food resources for small mammals.	
A disease causes decreases in the populations of mice, voles, ground squirrels, and other small mammals.	
Corn crops left in the field provide abundant food for mice and other small mammals.	

EVIDENCE NOTEBOOK
12. Think about the organisms that live in a forest. What resources do they need for survival? Record your evidence.

Engineer It
Control Population Growth

Mosquitoes can feed off of the blood of almost any animal, including humans. Their bites can be very unpleasant. They can also transmit a variety of serious diseases. Because of these problems, global efforts exist to design solutions to help limit the sizes of mosquito populations. Mosquitoes require standing water, such as ponds or puddles, to reproduce because their larvae live in these types of water environments.

13. Suppose you are tasked with decreasing the mosquito population in a large city with many people. A decrease in which resource would be most effective in decreasing the mosquito population?
    A. food resources
    B. water resources
    C. plant resources
    D. sunlight resources

14. **Discuss** Brainstorm actions that might limit the availability of this resource for mosquitoes in the area. How might other species be impacted by this change?

EXPLORATION 3

Predicting Effects of Limited Resources

Resources in an ecosystem are often limited, so individuals must compete for the existing resources to meet their needs. *Competition* occurs when two or more individuals or populations try to use the same limited resource.

Competition can happen among individuals within a population. For example, deer in a forest compete with each other for the same plants to eat. This competition increases in winter when many plants die. If an organism does not get the resources it needs, it may not survive to reproduce. Competition also happens among populations. For example, different species of trees in a forest compete with each other for sunlight, water, and space.

Turtles sun themselves to warm their bodies. These turtles are competing for a sunny spot on this rock.

Some bird species only nest in forested areas that are large and continuous.

Human activities can divide large forests into smaller parts. This means some birds may not find nesting sites.

15. Which of the following is most likely to happen when birds cannot find nesting sites?

   A. The birds wait until a tree becomes available for nesting.
   B. The birds move to another area with more shelter resources.
   C. The birds build a different kind of shelter instead of a nest.

16. **Write** Think about the birds that are left without nesting sites. Write a short story from the point of view of one of those birds. In your story, describe the types of resources you depend on for survival, a situation that led to the lack of resources, and how you responded to the lack of resources.

Hands-On Lab
Investigate Effects of Limited Resources

Plan and conduct an investigation of how a specific resource can limit the growth of bean plants. Resources and other factors that affect the growth and health of living things are called *limiting factors*.

MATERIALS
- cups with sprouted bean plants, 8 oz (4)
- marker
- ruler
- water

Procedure

STEP 1 Choose to investigate water or sunlight as a limiting factor. Write a hypothesis related to the limiting factor and the bean plants.

STEP 2 Plan a two-week investigation to test your hypothesis. On a separate sheet of paper:

- Describe the steps of your procedure
- Identify the variables and controls of the investigation
- Identify the types of data that you will collect
- Describe how you will measure the limiting factor and the plant growth, including the tools and units of measurement will you use.
- Explain what format you will use to record your data and observations, and note how often you will record them.

STEP 3 Have your teacher approve your procedure. Revise it as necessary and then begin your investigation. Record your data and observations on a separate sheet of paper.

Analysis

STEP 4 Do your data support your hypothesis?

STEP 5 Make a claim about how the limiting factor you chose affects bean plants. Use your data as evidence to support your claim. Explain your reasoning.

STEP 6 How could you improve your procedure to obtain clearer results?

Lesson 3 Resource Availability Affects Organisms

Limited Abiotic Resources

Abiotic factors are the nonliving parts of an ecosystem, such as air, water, nutrients, soil, sunlight, and rainfall. Individuals of a population depend on an ecosystem's abiotic resources for survival. For example, the amount of oxygen dissolved in lake water is an important abiotic resource for fish that live in the lake. If there is plenty of oxygen and other resources that fish need, fish will be healthy and fish populations may increase in size. But if oxygen becomes limited, the health of individual fish may suffer, and fish populations may decline.

Rain Forest Ecosystem

17. **Draw** The availability of light varies in different layers in a rain forest. Use a pencil to shade the band to the right of the diagram—darkest where the forest receives the least amount of light and lightest where it receives the most light.

18. The layers of a rain forest are, from bottom to top, the forest floor, the understory, the canopy, and the emergent layer. Explain where light is likely a limiting factor in this rain forest. What factors do you think are limited at other levels in the forest?

Limited Biotic Resources

Biotic factors are the parts of an ecosystem that are living or are related to the activity of living things. Bacteria, algae, fungi, plants, and animals are all biotic factors. Decaying organisms are also considered biotic factors. Biotic resources can also become limited. For example, suppose that a fungus destroys the fruits of a tree on which a certain kind of insect feeds. The insect population will decrease because less food is available to individuals. In turn, other animals that feed on the insect will also have less food. The decrease in food would continue to the top of the food chain. An ecosystem's biotic factors are interconnected, so limits to any single factor can affect all other factors.

19. Draw a line to connect each change in resource availability with its effect.

Change in Resources

- A region experiences drought conditions for several years.
- A disease greatly decreases the size of a population of woodpeckers.
- A population of fish greatly increases in size after a short-term increase in food availability.

Effects

- Population size decreases as individuals compete for access to food resources.
- Mates become harder to find.
- Plant growth is greatly limited.

> **EVIDENCE NOTEBOOK**
> **20.** Wildfires not only burn down trees and other plants, they also burn much of the materials and nutrients in the top layer of soil. Think about the abiotic and biotic resources that may become limited after a wildfire. How would individual organisms and populations be affected? Record your evidence.

Predict Effects on a Population

Lions and hyenas—like the ones in the photo—live in similar habitats in a number of African ecosystems. Lions and hyenas rely on the same food resources.

Populations of lions and hyenas compete for the same food resources.

21. Predict how an increase in the hyena population would affect the population of lions. Then think of a similar interaction in a different ecosystem. Predict how an increase in one population from your example would affect the other population.

Lesson 3 Resource Availability Affects Organisms

EXPLORATION 4

Predicting Effects of Abundant Resources

Some resources are abundant in certain ecosystems. An example is sunlight, which is usually an abundant resource on the prairie. In other cases, resources may become abundant for a short time. For example, a species of insect known as periodical cicadas (sih•KAY•duhz) have 13- or 17-year life cycles. Every 13 or 17 years, large numbers of these cicadas emerge after developing underground and provide an abundance of food for their predators. Birds and other animal predators eat the cicadas.

These photos show an example of resource abundance caused by humans. Rainwater runoff carries garden and agricultural fertilizers into aquatic ecosystems. The abundant nutrients cause extreme growth of algal populations, called an *algal bloom*.

Algal Bloom Caused by Nutrient Abundance

The aerial photographs show a body of water with a typical amount of nutrients and a body of water during an algal bloom. During an algal bloom, nutrient resources that were once limited became abundant, allowing the algal populations to grow.

typical state

algal bloom

22. Discuss If the algae in an algal bloom never run out of nutrients, what other factor do you think might limit their population growth?

Abundant Abiotic and Biotic Resources

An abundance of abiotic or biotic resources can result in the growth of individuals and populations. An abundance of food, which is a biotic factor, can specifically lead to population growth. However, an excess of certain resources can sometimes limit growth. For example, a plant that thrives in shaded areas may not survive in direct sunlight.

23. Weeks of rainfall have provided an abundance of water resources in a region that is usually dry. Which of the following are likely effects of the sudden abundance of water? Select all that apply.
   A. Some plants may thrive.
   B. Some plants may be washed away.
   C. Some plants may have limited growth.

Do the Math
Analyze Population Growth Data

If resources are abundant, a population may grow at an increasing rate. When the population size increases by a factor repeatedly, the growth is called *exponential growth*.

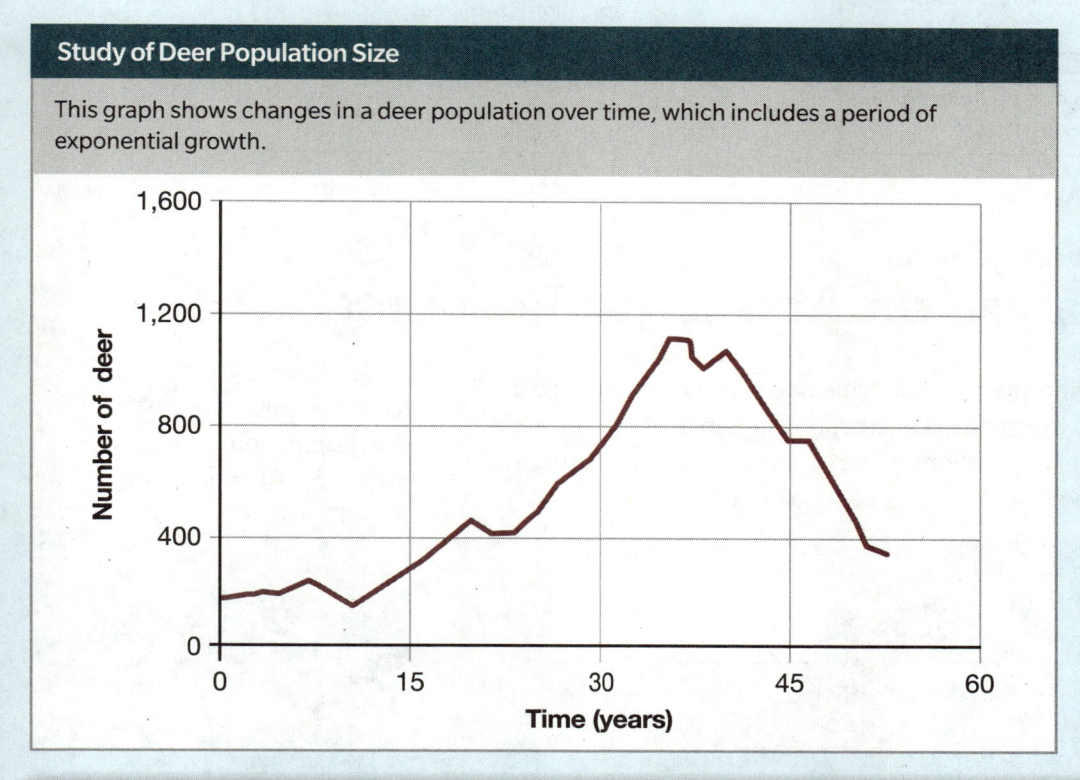

Study of Deer Population Size

This graph shows changes in a deer population over time, which includes a period of exponential growth.

24. The largest deer population during the study was about ~~1,100~~ / 1,300 / ~~1,500~~ and occurred about ~~20~~ / ~~30~~ / 40 years into the study.

25. The deer population experienced exponential growth from about 14 years to about 40 years into the study. Which of the following are possible reasons for this growth? Select all that apply.

    A. an abundance of plants that deer eat
    B. a scarcity of plants that deer eat
    C. an increase in a population of predators to deer
    D. a decrease in a population of predators to deer

26. Form an argument for why a large decrease in the deer population occurred following the period of exponential population growth. Cite evidence from the text and the graph to support your argument.

27. Draw a line to connect each change in resource availability with its effect.

Change in Resources	Effects
Resource availability remains steady.	Population size decreases.
Availability of resources becomes more limited.	Population size increases.
Resources become abundant for a period of time.	Population size remains the same.

Language SmArts
Analyze an Abundant Resource

28. The diagram shows the relationship between a type of fish and crabs that the fish eat. How might an abundance of one resource affect the other populations in the ecosystem? Use the terms in the box to label the cause-and-effect diagram.

- crab population decreases
- fish population increases
- fish population decreases

crab population increases

29. Describe the limitations of your diagram. For example, what other abiotic or biotic factors could influence the populations of these organisms?

_____
_____
_____
_____

376 Unit 5 Earth's Resources and Ecosystems

TAKE IT FURTHER

Continue Your Exploration

Name: _____ Date: _____

Check out the path below or go online to choose one of the other paths shown.

Analyzing Types of Population Growth

- Monarch Butterfly Survival
- Hands-On Labs
- Propose Your Own Path

Go online to choose one of these other paths.

Population growth is often represented by two different models: an exponential growth model and a logistic growth model. *Exponential growth* occurs when resource abundance allows for a continued increase in the growth rate of a population. In *logistic growth*, the rate of population growth slows as the population approaches a maximum size. Logistic growth occurs because one or more resources limit the growth of the population. When a population has reached the maximum size that can be sustained by available resources, the population size levels off.

The population growth of these harbor seals exhibits a logistic growth pattern because their population size is limited by competition for resources and predation.

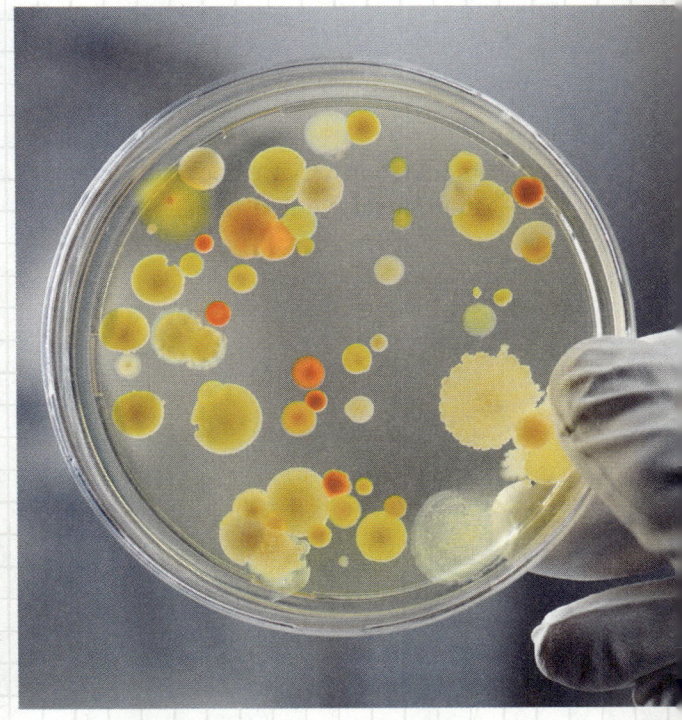

In a Petri dish with plenty of nutrients and space, these bacteria exhibit an exponential growth pattern until resources become limited.

Lesson 3 Resource Availability Affects Organisms

TAKE IT FURTHER

Continue Your Exploration

1. In both growth models, population growth occurs when resources are ~~abundant~~ / limited. ~~Exponential~~ / Logistic growth continues to increase while resources are abundant, while exponential / ~~logistic~~ growth slows down due to limits in resource availability.

2. What is the greatest difference between the two growth models? Explain your answer.

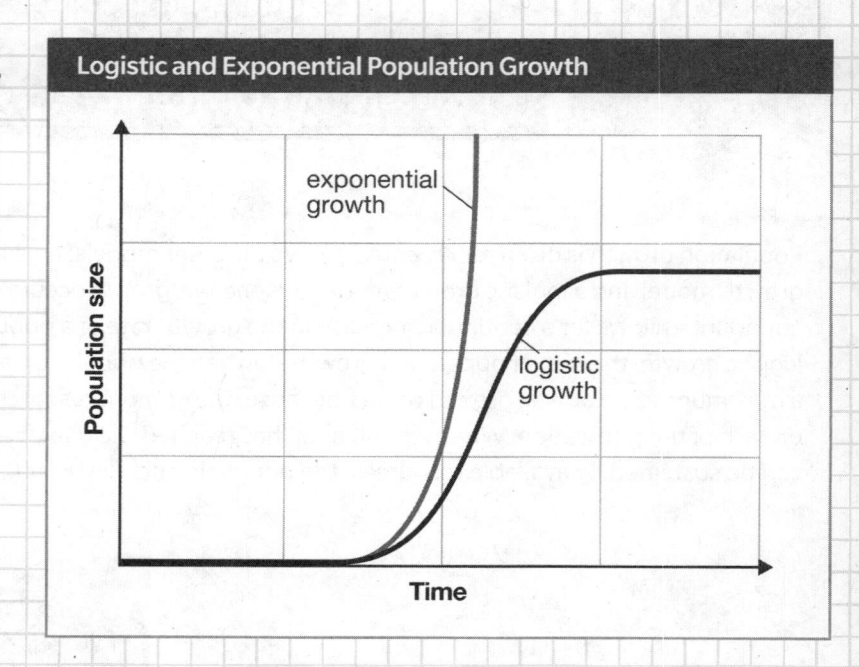

Logistic and Exponential Population Growth

(Graph showing Population size vs. Time, with exponential growth curve rising steeply and logistic growth curve leveling off at a carrying capacity.)

3. Which population growth model do you think best describes most populations in an ecosystem? Justify your response.

4. **Collaborate** Research another species that experiences logistic growth and another species that experiences exponential growth. For each example, describe a key resource that affects population size, and describe the availability of that resource. Plan and deliver an oral presentation that explains each example.

LESSON 3 SELF-CHECK

Can You Explain It?

Name: _____   Date: _____

How does a wildfire affect resources and populations in a forest?

> **EVIDENCE NOTEBOOK**
> Refer to the notes in your Evidence Notebook to help you construct an explanation for how a wildfire affects resources and populations in a forest ecosystem.

1. State your claim. Make sure your claim fully explains how a wildfire affects resources and populations in a forest ecosystem.

2. Summarize the evidence you have gathered to support your claim and explain your reasoning.

LESSON 3 SELF-CHECK

Checkpoints

Answer the following questions to check your understanding of the lesson.

Use the information in the table to answer Questions 3–4.

| Resource Availability in Three Marine Habitats ||||
Resource	Habitat 1: Coral reef	Habitat 2: Open water zone	Habitat 3: Deep water zone
sunlight	high	low	none
temperature	warm	moderate	cold
shelter	medium	none	none
nutrients	high	medium	low

3. Which of the resources listed would organisms most likely compete over in the deep water zone?
   A. shelter
   B. sunlight
   C. nutrients
   D. temperature

4. The most diverse community would typically be found in the *coral reef / open water zone / deep water zone* because it has the *least / greatest / same* amount of basic resources.

Use the caribou photo to answer Questions 5–7.

5. How might an abundance of food resources affect the caribou population? Select all that apply.
   A. The population would increase in size.
   B. The population would decrease in size.
   C. The caribou would start to eat other types of food.
   D. There would be less competition between the caribou for food.

6. How would a shortage of water likely affect the caribou? Select all that apply.
   A. The population would increase in size.
   B. The population would decrease in size.
   C. The growth of individual caribou would increase.
   D. The growth of individual caribou would decrease.

7. Developing roads here could affect the caribou by disrupting their migration patterns. This is an example of a *negative / positive / neutral* human impact.

LESSON 3 SELF-CHECK

Interactive Review

Complete this section to review the main concepts of the lesson.

Ecosystems are made up of organisms that live together and interact in an environment.

A. Provide at least two examples of abiotic and biotic factors.

The growth of individuals and populations depends on resource availability.

B. What basic resources do organisms and populations need to grow?

Biotic and abiotic factors can limit population growth.

C Describe one biotic factor and one abiotic factor that can limit population growth.

Resource abundance can promote population growth.

D. Explain the relationship between resource availability and population growth.

Lesson 3 Resource Availability Affects Organisms **381**

LESSON 4
Patterns Can Be Observed in Interactions between Organisms

These fish enjoy a feast of algae on the sea turtle's shell. It is an easy meal compared to foraging among ocean plants or reefs.

Explore First

Observing Resource Use Fill a basket with two or three kinds of small items, such as pens. Set the basket somewhere in your school with a sign that says your fellow classmates can take some. Make observations as people take items. Which items were the most popular? Were any items left in the bowl, or did it run out?

CAN YOU EXPLAIN IT?

How could a devastating drought lead to a population increase of coyotes?

Surface waters in California gradually shrink during a long drought. All ecosystem populations are deprived of a needed resource. Resourceful coyotes found ways to adjust to the new environmental conditions.

1. Think about what happens to an ecosystem's plant and animal life during a drought. Suggest possible impacts to a plant, a freshwater fish, and a rabbit.

2. What ecosystem changes might lead to an increase in the population of a predator, such as a coyote? Consider the changes to both living and nonliving resources in the ecosystem.

EVIDENCE NOTEBOOK As you explore the lesson, gather evidence to explain how a severe drought could cause an increase in a coyote population.

Lesson 4 Patterns Can Be Observed in Interactions between Organisms

EXPLORATION 1

Analyzing Feeding Relationships

Think about all the ways you are connected to other organisms. Both plants and animals provide resources that humans need. You may eat meat from a variety of animals. You get food and fiber from plants. Humans also provide resources to some animals, such as the blood a mosquito gets when it bites a person. Another way humans are connected with other animals is through social interactions. For example, you laugh with your friends or play fetch with your dog.

3. **Discuss** Together with a partner, compare the feeding habits of the animals in the photos. Which animal has the most diverse diet? Which animal has the least diverse diet? Discuss two advantages of each feeding strategy.

A koala's diet consists almost solely of eucalyptus leaves. Koalas are one of three organisms in the world that can feed on eucalyptus leaves, which are low in nutrients and contain many toxins.

Feeding Interactions between Organisms

Feeding interactions and relationships are important connections between organisms. Organisms need the energy and nutrients provided by food to survive. Plants make their own food in a process driven by energy from the sun. Animals must eat other organisms to get energy and nutrients. Some animals eat plants, some eat other animals, and some eat both.

4. The photos show different ecosystems, but a similar pattern in the interactions between animals and their food. The animals must eat other organisms to obtain energy. Compare this to the way plants obtain food and energy.

Lions feed only on meaty animals of the savanna, such as zebra or gazelle. They may catch prey from the large herds that graze near watering holes.

The pink color of flamingos' feathers comes from red pigments in their food, which includes red algae and shrimp. They also eat aquatic plants, insects, and small fish.

Predators Eat Prey

With its toothless duck-like bill, webbed feet, and cat-sized furry body, you might be surprised to learn that the platypus is a feisty predator. A **predator** is an animal that captures and eats other animals. The platypus is a *carnivore*, an organism that feeds exclusively on animal flesh. Its **prey,** or hunted food source, includes shellfish, worms, insects, and fish larvae. Most carnivores have sharp teeth to hold or rip their prey. But platypuses use gravel scooped up with their water-dwelling prey to grind food into small pieces. As with other carnivores, the number of platypuses in an area depends on the availability of prey. Factors that limit the number of prey therefore limit the number of platypuses.

5. The photos show an example of how similar predatory interactions occur in different ecosystems. The spider and platypus are both <u>predators</u> / prey. The worms and insects are both predators / <u>prey</u>.

The platypus is sticking its bill in the bottom of the stream in search of animals, such as worms, to eat.

A spider wraps an insect tightly with the silk threads of its web. The spider will then eat the insect.

Herbivores Eat Plants or Algae

Unlike carnivores, some organisms get energy and nutrients from plants or algae. These organisms are called **herbivores.** Some herbivores feed only on the leaves of particular plants. Others take advantage of a range of plant parts. The mountain gorilla, for example, feeds on the leaves and shoots of trees. The monarch butterfly feeds on milkweed leaves as a caterpillar and on nectar from flowers as a winged adult.

Algae are unicellular or multicellular organisms that can make their own food through photosynthesis. Algae live in water ecosystems, where they collect light energy from sunlight. They provide food for large numbers of herbivores. Kelp is a type of algae that can grow to be more than 50 m in length. Crabs and many other shellfish eat kelp. These animals are food for carnivores, such as the red octopus.

Manatees are herbivores. These manatees are feeding on lettuce and other plants in a natural spring in Homosassa, Florida.

Hands-On Lab
Simulate Feeding Relationships

Use a model to simulate the interactions among plants, herbivores, and omnivores over several seasons. Then, use evidence to analyze patterns of change in clover, rabbit, and coyote populations as they experience typical seasonal weather interrupted by unexpected events.

Carnivores consume animals and herbivores only eat plants or algae. *Omnivores* are organisms that consume both plants and animals. In this simulation, coyotes eat rabbits. However, in a real ecosystem, they are omnivores and eat a variety of plants and animals.

MATERIALS
- beans, red kidney (coyotes)
- beans, white navy (rabbits)
- graph paper
- peas, split green (clover)
- pencils, colored
- penny
- ruler

Cottontail
Sylvilagus floridanus

Attributes
Shy, Evasive, Adaptable, and Quick

Type: Mammal
Diet: Herbivore
Habitat: Fields and Meadows
Average Life Span: Less than 3 years
Size: 39.5 to 47.7 cm
Weight: 800 to 1533 g

Red Clover
Trifolium pratense

Attributes
Drought Resistant, Edible, Nonnative

Type: Perennial
Growth: Short-lived, highly productive
Habitat: Fields and Meadows
Stem: hollow stems, 60 to 80 cm
Leaf: Palmately trifoliate, variegated
Flower: rose, purple, or magenta

Coyote
Canis latrans

Attributes
Clever, Sneaky, Adaptable, and Swims

Type: Mammal
Diet: Omnivore
Habitat: Prefers Fields and Prairies
Average Life Span: Up to 14 years
Size: Head and body, 81 to 94 cm; Tail, 41 cm
Weight: 9 to 23 kg

Procedure

STEP 1 Place beans that represent 20 clover plants, 12 rabbits, and 6 coyotes on your table. This models a stable community during the winter.

STEP 2 Using the sample below, create a line graph on graph paper to track population sizes over four seasons. Choose a different colored pencil for each type of organism. Then plot each starting population number for the winter on your graph. Continue to plot the size of each population as you complete Step 3.

Population size

Winter   Spring   Summer   Fall

STEP 3 Use the instructions in the table to model seasonal population changes. Follow these guidelines:

- For each season, add or remove beans according to the information in the *Seasonal Changes* column. Then flip a coin to complete either the heads (H) or tails (T) directions for that season.
- Remove beans for organisms that die. Add beans for births, new growth, or organisms that migrate into the area.
- Recount each type of bean. As you finish each season, plot the end-of-season population on your graph.
- If a population reaches zero organisms, it exits the simulation.

Seasonal Changes	Coin Flip
Spring The clover population doubles. Each rabbit eats 2 clover plants. Each coyote eats 1 rabbit.	**H:** Heavy rains cause 15 more clover plants to grow. For every 2 rabbits, 5 more are born, but 2 coyotes die from disease. **T:** For every 2 rabbits, 6 more are born. Construction forces 3 more coyotes to join the population.
Summer The clover population triples. Each rabbit eats 2 clover plants. Each coyote eats 1 rabbit.	**H:** Drought wipes out half the clover population. For every 2 rabbits only 2 rabbits are born. One coyote dies from dehydration. **T:** Late rains allow 10 new clover plants to grow. For every 2 rabbits, 6 new rabbits are born.
Fall The clover population doubles. Each rabbit eats 2 clover plants. Each coyote eats 1 rabbit.	**H:** Over-grazing kills half the clover population. Five rabbits die for lack of food. Two coyotes also die of starvation. **T:** A warm fall spurs growth of 9 new clover plants and a longer breeding season for rabbits. For every 2 rabbits, 4 more rabbits are born.

STEP 4 Connect the population plots on your graph to show the changes in population size for each organism. Remember to use a different color for each type of organism.

Analysis

STEP 5 Which populations were the most strongly affected by seasonal changes? Use evidence from your data to support your argument.

STEP 6 Look at your graph to analyze how changes to one population affect changes to other populations. Using your data, predict how the following winter might affect the three populations in this activity. Cite evidence to explain your reasoning.

STEP 7 Model the population changes for the following winter season to evaluate your prediction.

Lesson 4 Patterns Can Be Observed in Interactions between Organisms **387**

Relationships Between Population Sizes

When mice begin to invade grain storehouses, farmers may bring a few cats to their farm. Elsewhere, conservationists work to increase impala populations so that endangered cheetahs have plenty of food to raise healthy cubs. These farmers and conservationists understand that populations of carnivores and herbivores are related. If one population in a feeding relationship increases or decreases, the other population is affected. For example, the cheetah population can only grow when there is an abundance of energy from food resources. An increase in the impala population results in an increase of available food energy. If food resources for the cheetah became scarce enough, the cheetah population could be eliminated.

> **EVIDENCE NOTEBOOK**
> 6. What does a population of coyotes need in order to increase in size? How might a drought help to fulfill the need? Record your evidence.

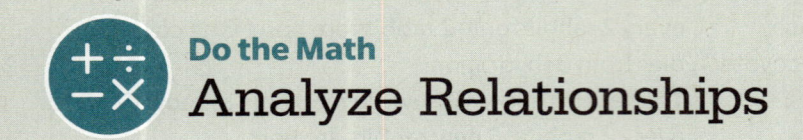

Do the Math
Analyze Relationships

Graphs of population size are one tool used to identify patterns in ecosystem interactions. Analyzing moose and wolf population data helps scientists understand their relationship. As predators and prey, these animals are closely linked.

7. Analyze the graph to determine what is happening near points A, B, and C. Write the letter next to each description of population change.

    _____ Both populations are increasing.

    _____ Wolf populations are decreasing.

    _____ More wolves are eating moose.

8. ~~Time~~ / population size is the dependent variable. The independent variable is time / ~~population size~~.

Predator and Prey Populations Over Time

(Graph showing Moose and Wolf populations over Time, with points A, B, and C labeled, and dashed lines indicating average moose population and average wolf population)

9. Describe how the dependent and independent variables help explain the feeding relationship between moose and wolves.

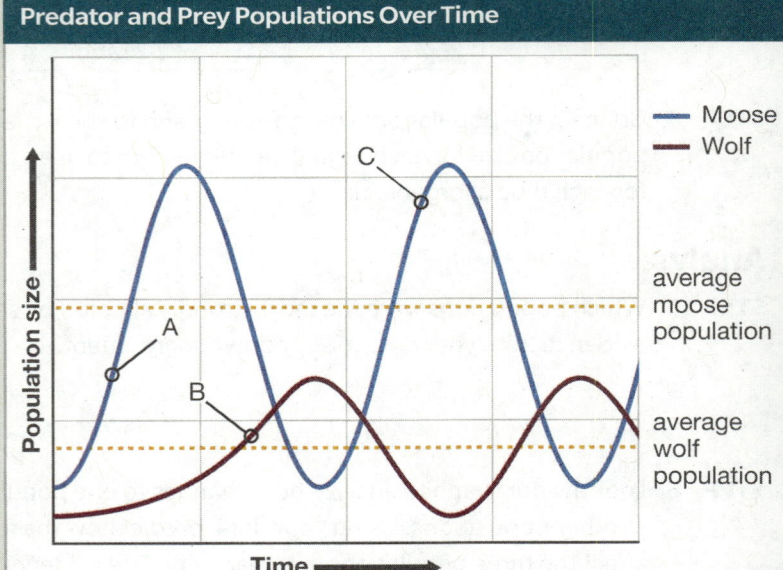

_____
_____
_____
_____

EXPLORATION 2

Explaining Symbiotic Relationships

Some species within an ecosystem interact very closely. For example, clownfish live in anemones, birds nest in trees, and humans and dogs have loyal relationships. One species may depend completely on another for survival. Without the hardworking actions of the fig wasp, for example, fig trees could not reproduce. Fig trees produce flowers. But these flowers are all grouped together inside a structure that has a tough skin. This structure is often referred to as the fig's "fruit." Only tiny fig wasps will bore into the fruit, pollinating the figs as they feed.

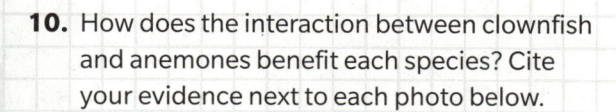

Clownfish make their home within the stinging tentacles of sea anemones. The clownfish is not harmed by the anemone, but potential predators can be. The darting clownfish bring a rush of fresh ocean water to the anemone. This water clears away the nutrient-depleted water trapped between its tentacles.

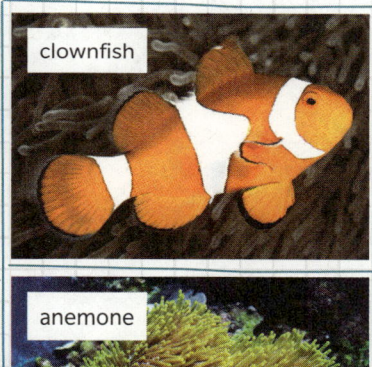

10. How does the interaction between clownfish and anemones benefit each species? Cite your evidence next to each photo below.

clownfish

anemone

Symbiotic Relationships

As scientists study ecosystems, they observe patterns in the strategies organisms use to survive and reproduce within a community. Many of these patterns include symbiotic relationships. **Symbiosis** refers to the close, long-term relationship between two species within an ecosystem. Many symbiotic relationships help organisms get important nonliving resources from the environment. For example, animals gain nitrogen for making proteins from their food. But plants also need a source of nitrogen. Bacteria living in the roots of many plants provide nitrogen. In turn, the plant roots provide energy-rich sugars to the bacteria.

There are three types of symbiotic relationships. They are categorized based on whether each organism benefits, is harmed, or is unaffected by the relationship.

11. After reading about the interactions in the photos below, write whether each organism *benefits, is not affected,* or *is harmed* in the space provided.

The tick lives in the dog's fur and feeds off the dog's blood. As it feeds, the tick exposes the dog to microorganisms through the transfer of blood.

Remora fish follow or attach themselves through suction to the whale shark. Remoras feed on leftovers from the shark's meals.

Pollen from the flower sticks to the bee as it drinks nectar. While visiting the flower, the bee may transfer pollen from another flower. As a result of pollination, the plant can reproduce.

A. The dog _____ by the interaction, while the tick _____.

B. The remora _____ by the interaction, while the whale shark _____.

C. The bee _____ by the interaction, while the flower _____.

Mutualism

Mutualism occurs when both organisms benefit from an interaction. These relationships usually occur between species that do not compete with each other, but there are exceptions. For example, zebra and wildebeest each feed on the wild grasses of the savanna. Yet, they migrate together in large numbers across the Serengeti plains in Kenya each year. By doing so, they deter predators such as lions or cheetahs. Some mutualistic interactions are so close that they involve one organism hosting another within its body. *Trichonympha* (trik•uh•NIM•fuh) are unicellular organisms that live within the intestines of termites. They gain energy and a safe home while helping termites break down hard-to-digest wood.

Commensalism

In commensalism, one organism benefits from an interaction, and the other is unaffected. For example, antbirds in tropical forests follow behind army ants. They eat small insects driven from plant leaves by the stampeding ants. High above the ground, certain bromeliad plants wrap tough roots around the upper branches of rain forest trees to get enough sunlight. The ants, trees, and snails are unaffected by these interactions. Organisms that benefit from commensalism are able to take better advantage of environmental resources.

Parasitism

Predators kill and eat their prey, but parasites may feed on host organisms without killing them. Parasites get energy and nutrients as they feed on their host. While the parasite benefits from this interaction, the host is harmed. Fleas, ticks, and leeches are examples of parasites that feed on the blood of their animal hosts. These parasites attach to the hosts. Some parasites enter the host's body to obtain what they need. Tapeworms live within the intestines of some animals. They eat from their host's undigested food. As a result, fewer nutrients are left for the host.

12. What type of symbiotic relationship does the dodder plant have with the host plant? Which plant benefits from this interaction?

    A. mutualism; the dodder plant benefits
    B. predation; the host plant benefits
    C. commensalism; the dodder plant benefits
    D. parasitism; the dodder plant benefits

13. **Act** Pair with another student to act out a symbiotic relationship while your classmates guess the type of interaction.

    a. As you act, briefly describe your interactions.
    b. Discuss another way you could model this interaction.

This dodder plant has no chlorophyll. It winds its stems around another plant, called a host plant. Then the dodder sends rootlike organs into the host plant's tissues to steal food.

Predict Population Changes

14. In the dark depths of the ocean, a female anglerfish extends a glowing ball from a modified spine to lure prey. The glow comes from symbiotic bacteria that give off light from certain chemical reactions. The anglerfish "lure" provides the bacteria with nutrients and a place to live. What type of interaction is this? Explain how each of these populations might be affected by a decline in the other population.

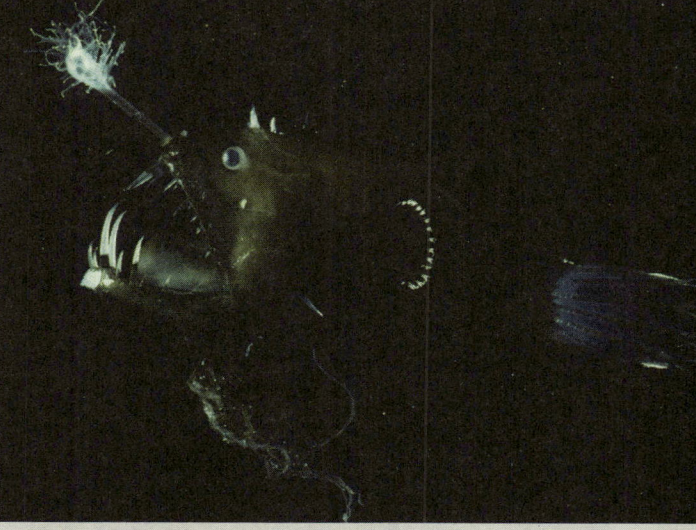

_____
_____
_____
_____
_____
_____
_____
_____

The anglerfish attracts prey by "fishing" with a lure protruding from a spine near the top of its mouth. Only female anglerfish have lures to attract prey.

Lesson 4 Patterns Can Be Observed in Interactions between Organisms

EXPLORATION 3

Predicting Effects of Competitive Interactions

Athletes train for years to compete in the Olympic games. Each athlete uses a large amount of resources to compete, including time, water, and food for energy. Competition encourages all athletes to build on their strengths and reduce their weaknesses over time. Competition for limited resources among populations also involves costs and benefits.

15. Discuss Working with a partner, brainstorm a list of abiotic and biotic resources that populations might compete for in an ecosystem. Choose one resource from your list. What evidence might you gather to determine whether two populations compete for this resource?

Competition for Resources

Organisms with similar needs tend to compete for resources. All plants, for example, require sunlight. The tallest trees in a rain forest create a canopy that blocks sun. Therefore, plants below must compete for the limited light passing through the leaves of taller trees. Some plants have adaptations that help them gather light. They compete effectively and build a stable population size. Liana vines, for example, may grow as long as 915 m to reach sunlight available at the rain forest canopy.

The interactions that occur between organisms when they both seek the same resource in an ecosystem are called **competition**. Each organism or population gets less of the resource than it would if there were no competitors. For example, in dry environments, many types of organisms compete for limited water resources.

Water is a limited resource in the Namib Desert in Africa. These zebras and hartebeest compete for access to the same watering hole.

392 Unit 5 Earth's Resources and Ecosystems

16. Complete the cause-and-effect table about interactions in the Namib Desert.

Cause	Effect
A population of lions grows too large to share their current territory.	
	Several male hyenas compete to mate with the females present in their area.
	Lions, leopards, and cheetahs compete for zebras to eat.
Zebras and wildebeests both feed on savanna grasses. Recent heavy rains have caused the grass population to flourish.	

Language SmArts
Explain Evidence of Competition

The green anole lizard is native to southern Florida. The anoles climb trees to hunt insects and return to the ground to lay eggs. Sightings of green anoles have been declining over the last two decades. A species of brown anole from Cuba seems to be taking over the area. They are effective hunters. Researchers observe that as brown anoles continue to move in, green anoles shift their activities higher in trees.

green anole

brown anole

Habitat: They are native to the southeastern United States, prefer bushes and trees, and may climb up to canopy level.
Diet: They eat insects, spiders, and flies.
Predators: They are eaten by skinks, snakes, birds, and other lizards.

Habitat: They are native to Cuba and the Bahamas, are mainly ground dwelling, and may climb up to 1.5 m.
Diet: They eat insects, spiders, worms, snails, slugs, and other small reptiles (including hatchling green anoles).
Predators: They are eaten by skinks, snakes, and birds.

17. Use evidence from the text to explain why brown and green anoles are competitors. What might happen if the population of green anoles decreased?

393

18. Look again at the pattern of population growth for wolves and moose presented in the graph. If grizzly bears, which also feed on moose, are introduced to the same ecosystem, how might the graph change?

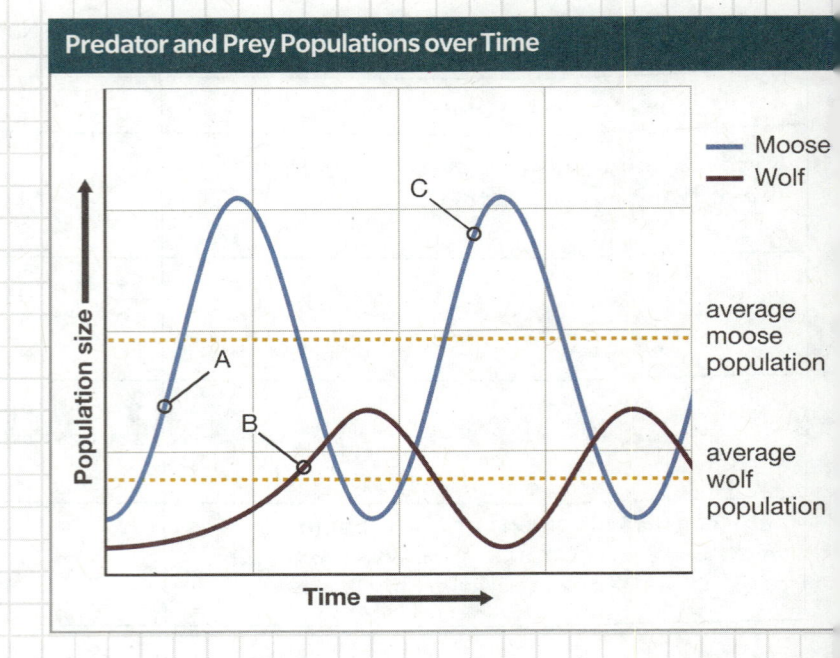

EVIDENCE NOTEBOOK

19. Explain how a drought might change a coyote's normal feeding habits. What effect could the change have on competition? Record your evidence.

Engineer It
Use Competition to Control Population Size

A nonnative fish is causing trouble in the Mississippi River. Asian carp came to the United States from China in the ballast (BAL•uhst) water of ships. The carp reproduce quickly and eat large amounts of plankton. They increase water cloudiness by eating shoreline plants and jump easily over barriers made to control their migration. Populations of native mussels and small fish that also feed on plankton are declining. Larger fish species also suffer because their prey populations have decreased and their shoreline nurseries have been destroyed. As carp numbers rise, ecologists seek solutions.

20. Which of the following methods would cause competition for resources among carp and therefore help control the carp population?

    A. Ecologists sprout plants distasteful to carp along unvegetated river shoreline.
    B. Thousands of mussels are relocated from the Great Lakes to the Mississippi River.
    C. State officials offer free licenses to fishermen that catch more than 100 Asian carp each year.
    D. Conservationists build protective barriers around grasses where native plankton-eating fish lay their eggs.

TAKE IT FURTHER

Continue Your Exploration

Name: Date:

Check out the path below or go online to choose one of the other paths shown.

Environmental Changes and Interactions

- People in Science
- Cleaning Symbiosis
- Hands-On Labs
- Propose Your Own Path

Go online to choose one of these other paths.

Large-scale changes in environmental conditions can change patterns of interaction in ecosystems. During El Niño (el•NEEN•yoh) weather cycles, for example, global winds and ocean currents shift. These shifts cause changes to ecosystems around the world. In 2016, an intense El Niño cycle caused severe droughts in Zimbabwe (zim•BAHB•way). Crops and livestock populations there decreased rapidly. As a result, competition for food increased among human groups. Half a world away, the same El Niño cycle caused flooding in Paraguay (PAR•uh•gwy). Mosquito populations flourished. Viral diseases in humans that are transmitted by mosquitoes, such as dengue (DENG•gay), spread.

El Niño cycles have natural causes and are temporary. However, human influences on the environment can last a very long time. For example, the use of fossil fuels can lead to ocean warming, a difficult trend to reverse. Warmer waters draw tiger sharks from their normal feeding grounds along tropical coasts into northern waters and the open ocean. As they move to new territories, sharks affect the interactions among organisms.

Difference from Average Precipitation Amount, December 2015 to February 2016

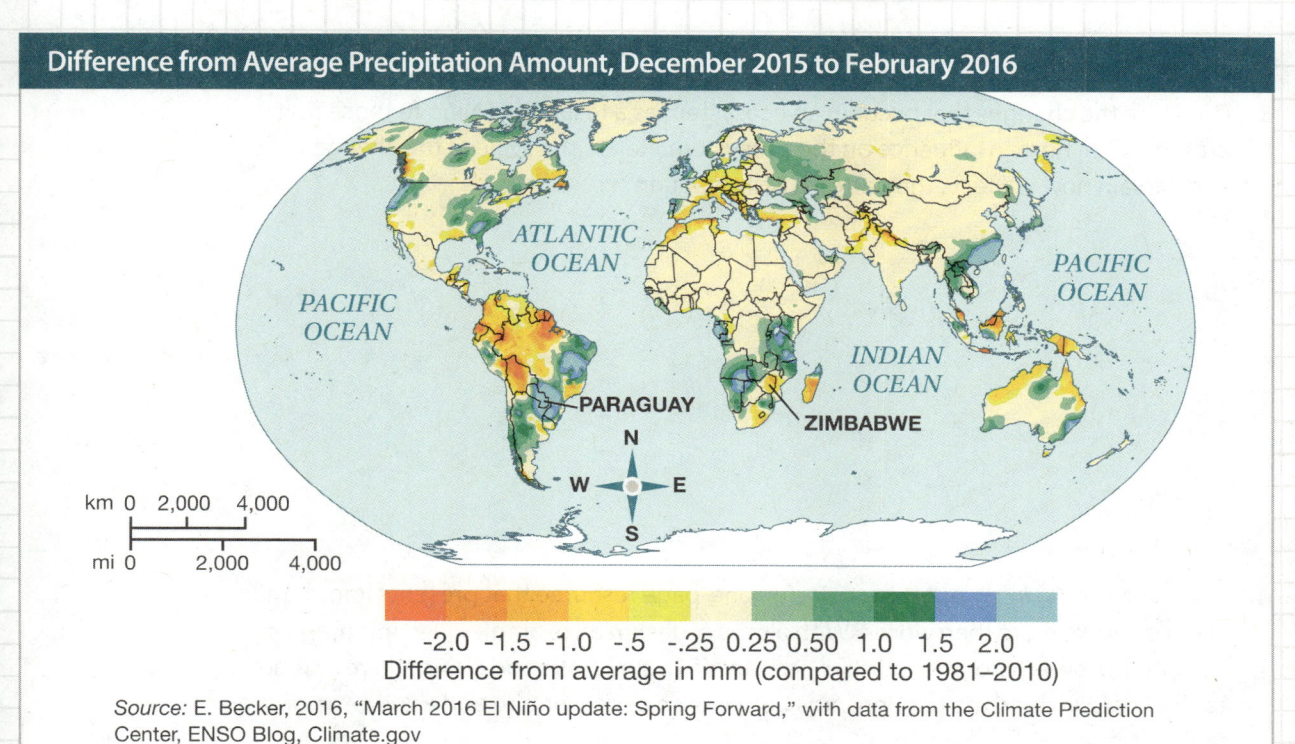

Difference from average in mm (compared to 1981–2010): -2.0, -1.5, -1.0, -.5, -.25, 0.25, 0.50, 1.0, 1.5, 2.0

Source: E. Becker, 2016, "March 2016 El Niño update: Spring Forward," with data from the Climate Prediction Center, ENSO Blog, Climate.gov

TAKE IT FURTHER

Continue Your Exploration

1. How will warmer ocean temperatures likely affect the competitive interactions of tiger sharks? Explain what might happen to the size of shark and competitor populations.

As apex predators, tiger sharks consume many types of ocean prey.

2. As humans use natural gas, coal, and oil for energy, the amount of carbon dioxide in the air and oceans increases. The increasing concentration of oceanic carbon dioxide depletes resources used by coral in coral reefs to build skeletons. Nutrient pollution and increasing ocean temperatures are also linked to reef decline. Predict what might happen to populations that have mutualistic, commensal, and parasitic interactions with the coral.

3. Compare the changes that occur in an ecosystem as a result of El Niño to those that are a result of human influence on the ecosystem. Relate the scale of the changes, and explain how it affects the patterns of interaction.

4. **Collaborate** An *infographic* is a colorful, one-page resource that presents information using symbols more than words. With a group, design an example-filled infographic explaining how environmental changes can affect symbiotic and competitive interactions. Topics could include the relationships between an oxpecker bird and a zebra, an orca and a seal, or a mosquito and a deer.

LESSON 4 SELF-CHECK

Can You Explain It?

Name: _____   Date: _____

How could a devastating drought lead to a population increase of coyotes?

EVIDENCE NOTEBOOK
Refer to the notes in your Evidence Notebook to help you construct an explanation for how a coyote population might increase during a drought.

1. State your claim. Make sure your claim fully explains the role of feeding relationships and community interactions in the increase of the coyote population during a drought.

2. Summarize the evidence you have gathered to support your claim and explain your reasoning.

Lesson 4 Patterns Can Be Observed in Interactions between Organisms

LESSON 4 SELF-CHECK

Checkpoints

Answer the following questions to check your understanding of the lesson.

Use the photo to answer Questions 3–4.

3. Which statements describe the feeding interaction between frogs and insects? Circle all that apply.
   A. The frog is a predator.
   B. The interaction is mutualistic.
   C. The frog is a parasite.
   D. The number of insects can influence the number of frogs in the ecosystem.

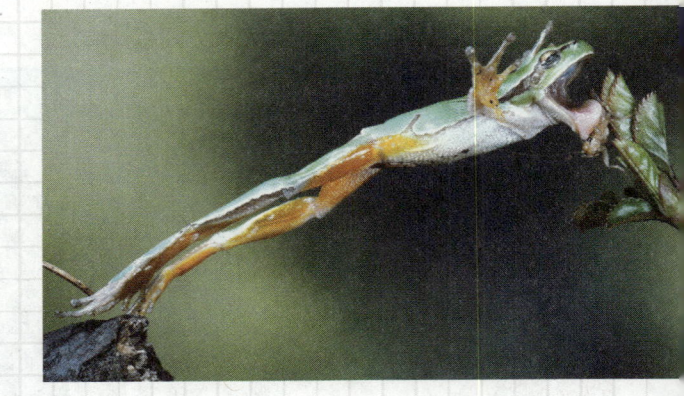

4. If a drought causes insect populations to decrease, the frog population will likely *increase / decrease / remain stable*. If populations of birds that eat insects increase, the frog population will likely *increase / decrease / remain stable*.

Use the photo to answer Questions 5–6.

5. Hundreds of pounds of barnacles may be attached to the surface of a whale at a given time. Unnoticed by the whale, barnacles avoid predators and filter plankton from ocean water while the whales feed. In this interaction, the barnacles *benefit / are unaffected / are harmed* while the whale is unaffected.

6. Whale lice live on the surface of whales. They are very small, and they feed on whale skin. Which statement best describes the relationship between lice and barnacles?
   A. They have a predator-prey relationship.
   B. They are both whale parasites.
   C. They compete for food resources.
   D. They do not compete for food resources, but may compete for space on a whale.

7. Atlantic salmon migrate to rivers in New England to reproduce and migrate to the coast of Greenland to feed. Which of these scenarios could cause a decrease in salmon populations due to competition? Circle all that apply.
   A. abundant food resources in Greenland
   B. limited food resources in Greenland
   C. increased predation by birds
   D. limited space for reproduction in New England rivers

LESSON 4 SELF-CHECK

Interactive Review

Complete this page to review the main concepts of the lesson.

While plants can make their own food, animals must eat other organisms for survival. Carnivores eat animal prey, while herbivores eat plants or algae.

A. Explain how the population sizes of two species in a feeding relationship are linked.

Symbiotic interactions are close, long-term relationships between species. At least one species benefits from the relationship, while the other species may benefit, be harmed, or be unaffected.

B. Compare the interactions of predators with prey to the interactions of parasites with host organisms.

Organisms that seek the same limited resources will compete with each other.

C. What happens to competition when resources are abundant in an ecosystem? Use an example to explain your answer.

Lesson 4 Patterns Can Be Observed in Interactions between Organisms **399**

LESSON 5

The Flow of Energy Drives the Cycling of Matter in Ecosystems

This wetland ecosystem supports a large community of plants, birds, fish, and other animals.

Explore First

Modeling the Flow of Energy Construct a model to show how a person gets energy and how they use energy. Use arrows to show the transfers of energy that take place.

CAN YOU EXPLAIN IT?

How could the reintroduction of wolves to Yellowstone have led to an increase in the beaver population?

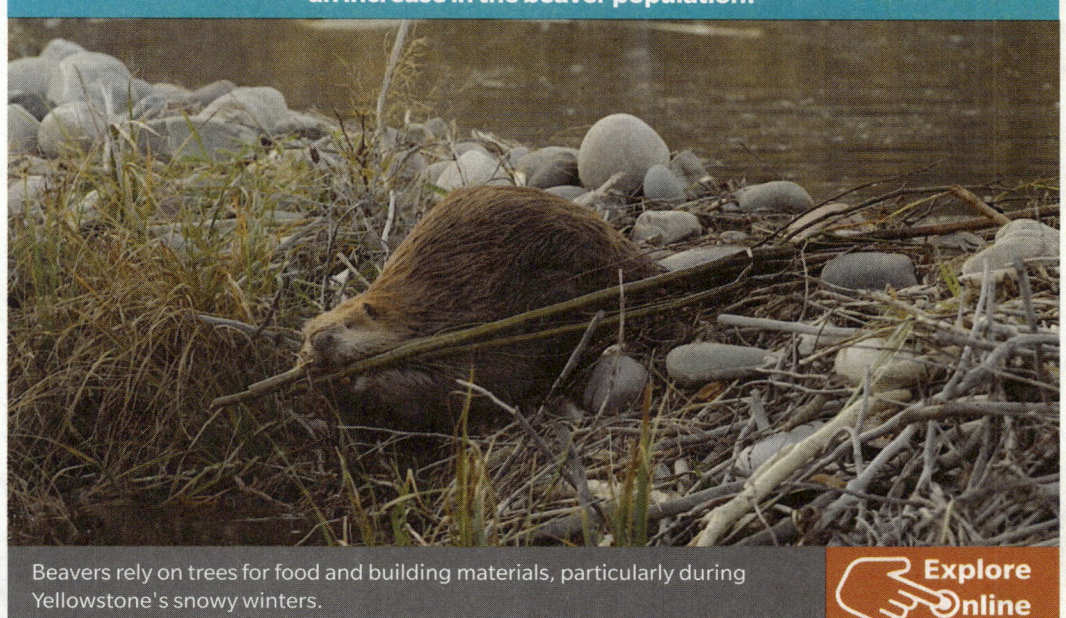

Beavers rely on trees for food and building materials, particularly during Yellowstone's snowy winters.

Explore Online

By 1926, after decades of targeted hunting, the last wolves were removed from Yellowstone National Park. The wolves were reintroduced to Yellowstone in 1995, causing a ripple of change through the park. Elk, coyotes, beavers, birds, and plant life were all affected by the reintroduction of Yellowstone's top predator.

1. Think about the resources that wolves and beavers in Yellowstone might share. Record at least three possible connections between wolves and beavers.

EVIDENCE NOTEBOOK As you explore the lesson, gather evidence to explain how the return of wolves caused Yellowstone's beaver population to increase.

Lesson 5 The Flow of Energy Drives the Cycling of Matter in Earth's Ecosystems

EXPLORATION 1

Analyzing Energy Flow in Ecosystems

Energy Transfer in Ecosystems

A pond may seem quiet, but interactions are taking place at all times. A pond ecosystem, like all ecosystems, involves the flow of energy and cycling of matter through a web of producers, consumers, and decomposers. Plants are *producers* that capture energy from the sun to make food. *Consumers,* such as birds, eat other organisms to gain energy. *Decomposers,* such as earthworms, gain energy by breaking down the waste and remains of living and nonliving matter. The broken down matter is returned to the environment and made available for use by other organisms. As these interactions and processes take place, energy flows into, within, and out of ecosystems. Energy changes form, but it is never created or destroyed. Matter changes and cycles as ecosystem processes take place, but every single atom of matter is conserved.

2. Label each organism in this pond ecosystem as a *producer, consumer,* or *decomposer*.

- grasses: _____
- raccoon: _____
- turtle: _____
- water lily: _____
- heron: _____
- earthworm: _____
- fish: _____
- algae: _____

Human Activities

Energy and matter are continuously exchanged between humans and ecosystems because humans rely on ecosystems for natural resources, such as plants and soil. Healthy, functioning ecosystems also provide *ecosystem services,* such as clean air and water. Human activities can negatively affect ecosystems by disrupting important cycles. A healthy, diverse ecosystem can recover from, or adjust to, human activities if the activities are short-term or small in scale. Humans can try to ensure their activities have minimal, or even beneficial, impacts on ecosystems.

3. Provide at least two examples of human activities that depend on or benefit from ecosystem services.

Food Chains

A *food chain* is a pathway that energy and nutrients can follow through an ecosystem. Producers make up the first level of a food chain. For example, the producers in a tropical rain forest include many species of grass, flowering ground plants, and fruit trees. Insects and other plant eaters get energy by eating these producers. Other consumers, such as lizards and birds, eat the insects. Large snakes and jaguars are at the top of the food chain. They hunt and eat lizards, birds, and smaller mammals that live in the rain forest. Decomposers complete the food chain. They break down nonliving plant and animal matter and return nutrients to the soil, where they can be used by producers.

Construct a Food Chain

4. Draw Construct a diagram that shows these organisms arranged into a food chain. You can use organism names or drawings. Use arrows to show the flow of energy.

Food Webs

Different types of animals may share food sources. In the tropical rain forest, grasshoppers, fruit bats, and relatives of rhinos called *tapirs* feed on plants. Monkeys, iguanas, and birds eat plants, grasshoppers, and butterflies. Jaguars eat iguanas, tapirs, and monkeys. These interconnected food chains are an example of a **food web,** a model that shows how energy flows between organisms in an ecosystem. The size of a food web depends on the nonliving resources available to producers in the ecosystem. Food web diversity depends on various factors. One factor is how predators control the population size of lower-level consumers.

Arrows in a food web diagram show the direction of energy flow. The arrows come from where energy is stored in an organism, then point to where energy travels when that organism is consumed. All energy paths begin at the producer level.

Feeding Relationships in a Tropical Rain Forest

Explore this tropical rain forest food web. Identify one of the food chains that is shown with arrows. Trace this chain with your finger, starting with the producer. As you trace the chain, think about how matter and energy are flowing between living things at each step.

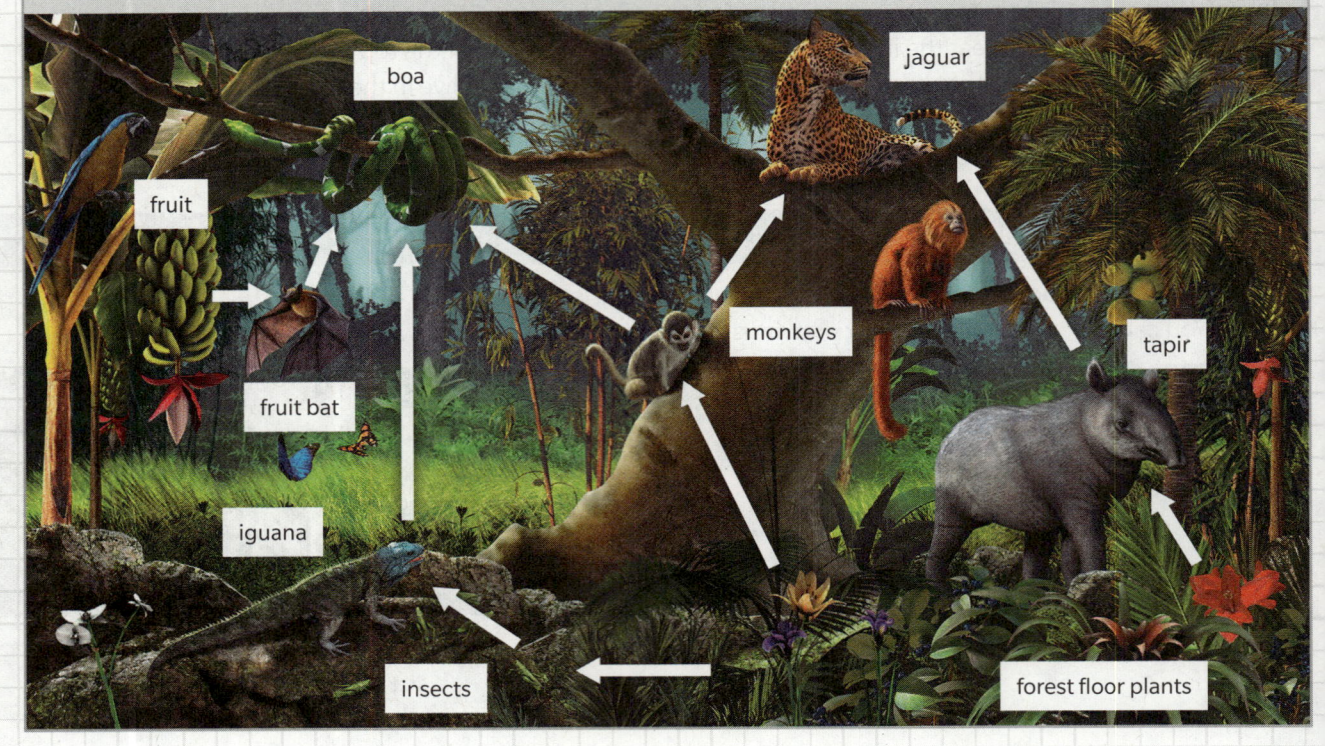

5. Identify two food chains that share at least one organism. Write each food chain below, showing the flow of energy with arrows.

6. If iguanas were removed from the ecosystem, the population of grasshoppers would most likely increase / decrease. The population of boas would most likely increase / decrease.

EVIDENCE NOTEBOOK

7. Beavers use plant material for food and building their homes. Elk and deer are also plant consumers in Yellowstone. How are the beavers, elk, deer, and wolves related in a food web? Record your evidence.

404 Unit 5 Earth's Resources and Ecosystems

Hands-On Lab
Model Energy Flow in an Ecosystem

Model energy transfer in a meadow ecosystem. Use evidence from your model to explain why the ecosystem supports different numbers of organisms at different feeding levels.

> **MATERIALS**
> - index cards (18), labeled: sun (1), grass plants (10), rabbits (5), fox (1), weasel (1)
> - resealable bags (10), each holding 100 dried beans
>
> **MODEL PARAMETERS**
> - Energy is represented in the model by the packets of beans. One packet of 100 beans is required to support one grass plant.
> - 20 beans are required to support one rabbit.
> - 30 beans are required to support one fox.
> - 10 beans are required to support one weasel.

Procedure and Analysis

STEP 1 On a table, lay out the sun card, all plant and rabbit cards, and the fox card. Place all bean packets around the sun.

STEP 2 Model photosynthesis by moving one packet of beans to each grass card. Place 10 beans from each packet on each grass card to represent the energy stored in the grass. Set the rest of the beans aside to represent energy used by the grasses and transferred to the environment as heat.

STEP 3 Model the rabbits eating grasses. Have each rabbit try to obtain 20 beans from the grass plants. Do all the rabbits survive? Is there extra energy?

STEP 4 Leave 2 beans on each rabbit card to represent the energy stored in each rabbit's body. Set the rest of the beans aside to represent energy used by the rabbits and transferred to the environment as heat.

STEP 5 Model the fox eating rabbits. Have the fox try to obtain 30 beans from the rabbits. Were there enough rabbits to support the fox? How many more rabbits will the food chain need to support two foxes?

STEP 6 **Do the Math** What percentage of the sun's energy provided to the grasses was available to the rabbits? What percentage of all energy provided by the grasses to the rabbits was available to the fox?

STEP 7 Return to Step 1 to run the model again using the weasel instead of the fox. Does the weasel survive? Given the energy available from the sun, which animal can be successful in this ecosystem—the fox or the weasel?

STEP 8 Why are some organisms more numerous in the ecosystem than others? Use numbers from the modeling activity to support your answer.

STEP 9 How does your model show how energy and matter are conserved?

Energy Pyramids

When an organism obtains energy, most of the energy is used for life processes. Some of the energy is given off to the environment as heat. A small amount of energy is stored in an organism's body. Only this stored energy can be used by a consumer that eats the organism.

An **energy pyramid** is a representation of the energy available at each level of a food web. The shape of the energy pyramid shows that there is less energy available as you go toward the top. The number of organisms that can be supported at each level is limited by the amount of energy available. The bottom level—the producers—has the most energy. The other levels are consumers. Consumers at the highest level have the least amount of available energy.

The shape of this energy pyramid shows that the energy availab[le] decreases as you move up this arctic tundra food chain.

8. Explain how energy is conserved even though the amount of energy available decreases as you move up the pyramid.

EVIDENCE NOTEBOOK

9. What happens to producer populations in Yellowstone when elk and deer populations become smaller? How might these changes explain the increase in the beaver population? Record your evidence.

Describe Energy Transfer between Ecosystems

10. Ecosystems do not have clear boundaries—matter and energy can move from one ecosystem to another. The energy available in ecosystems is constant / *constantly changing*. As grass-seeking wildebeest migrate from the Serengeti of Tanzania to Kenya each year, the energy available in the Serengeti ecosystem *increases* / decreases.

11. **Collaborate** With a partner, brainstorm other ways in which matter and energy move between ecosystems.

These wildebeest move matter and energy from one ecosystem to another as they cross the Mara River in Tanzania.

406 Unit 5 Earth's Resources and Ecosystems

EXPLORATION 2

Describing the Cycling of Matter in Ecosystems

Energy Drives the Cycling of Matter

Driven by energy from the sun or from Earth's hot interior, matter cycles through the living and nonliving parts of ecosystems. As one organism eats another organism, energy and matter are transferred to the consumer. Eventually, the matter that makes up the bodies of living things is returned to the environment by decomposers. Matter is conserved as it is transformed and transferred in the Earth system.

12. **Discuss** In any system, energy is required to move matter. For example, windmills require wind energy, and spinning wheels require engines. With a partner, discuss other ways that energy drives circular motion.

The Water Cycle

Water moves continuously through Earth's systems. The force of gravity drags massive glaciers, pulls raindrops from clouds, and draws streams into lakes and oceans. The sun's energy causes water to evaporate into the air, where wind then transports it. Water also moves through living things, where it flows into and out of cells. Organisms use energy when they take in and release water. Wherever water moves, energy is at work.

13. Uphill from here is an old landfill. Heavy rains sometimes carry pollutants from the landfill through this area and into the *clouds / mountains / lake*. However, many of the pollutants are removed from the water as it seeps into the soil and is taken up by plants. Imagine if a city with streets, parking lots, and other hard surfaces replaced much of the land. Water that ran through the area would likely contain *more / less / no* pollutants.

> **EVIDENCE NOTEBOOK**
>
> **14.** Decreased plant growth near a river can result in excess soil entering and clogging the water. How might the wolves help increase the plant growth that stabilizes the riverbanks? Record your evidence.

The Carbon Cycle

Carbon is essential to life because all cells are made of carbon-based molecules. Organisms obtain more than energy from food. They also gain carbon and other elements needed for growth and life. The carbon cycle makes this possible when physical and chemical changes transfer carbon between the environment and living cells.

Photosynthesis, cellular respiration, and the digestion of food are processes that cycle carbon between the environment, food molecules, and cells. Decomposition is also part of the carbon cycle. Decomposition returns carbon stored in the remains of organisms to the environment. These transfers of carbon are driven by the energy flowing through ecosystem food webs.

Energy also drives carbon transfers between land, water, and air, without using living organisms. Human activities affect some of these transfers. Burning fossil fuels speeds up the transfer of carbon from the geosphere to the atmosphere. Cutting down forests slows down the transfer of carbon from the atmosphere to the biosphere. These changes affect the stability of ecosystems over time.

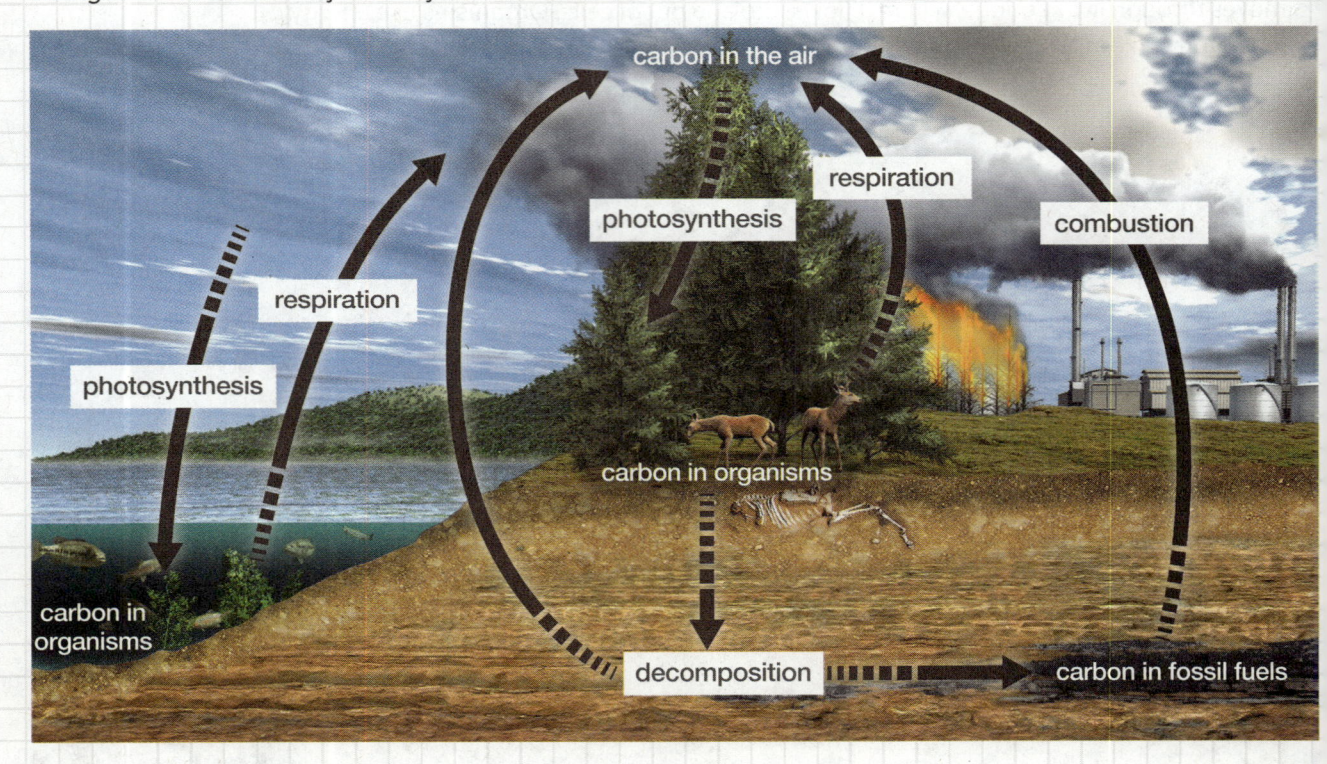

15. Describe how carbon enters and exits a consumer, such as the deer shown in the diagram.

408 Unit 5 Earth's Resources and Ecosystems

Engineer It
Analyze a Solution

Artificial trees are human-made systems engineered to collect carbon pollutants from the air. These systems can be used in locations where it may be difficult to grow real trees, such as dense, urban areas. Artificial trees can be powered by wind and solar energy. They can also be powered with energy generated by swings or seesaws that are attached to the system. The energy generated by the motion of people swinging can be transferred to the artificial tree and used to power the carbon collection process.

This tower removes carbon from the air and compresses it into cubes that are used to make jewelry. The profits from the sale of the jewelry are used to make more towers.

16. Trees use the carbon dioxide they get from the environment to make water / ~~sugar~~ / oxygen that stores energy. Like trees, engineers could find a way to use captured carbon dioxide to make fuel / ~~sugar~~ / water that stores energy.

The Nitrogen Cycle

Cells use nitrogen to build many life molecules, including DNA. Bacteria in soil and water change nitrogen into chemical forms that plants and algae can use. Nitrogen enters most food webs when plants or algae take up these forms of nitrogen. Decomposers return nitrogen to the soil and water, where bacteria can change it back to a gas form, returning it to air.

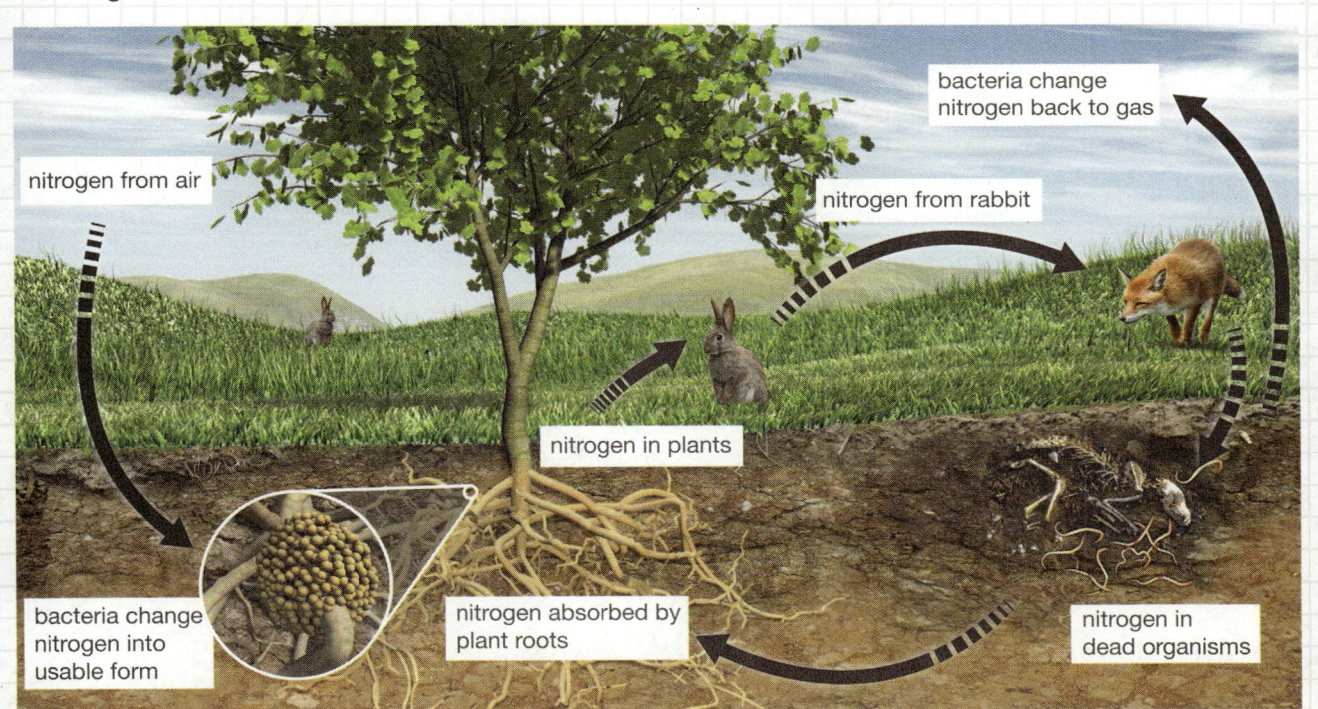

- nitrogen from air
- bacteria change nitrogen back to gas
- nitrogen from rabbit
- nitrogen in plants
- bacteria change nitrogen into usable form
- nitrogen absorbed by plant roots
- nitrogen in dead organisms

17. All organisms need a source of nitrogen and other matter. Explain how the nitrogen and other matter in your body came from other living things and the environment.

Lesson 5 The Flow of Energy Drives the Cycling of Matter in Ecosystems

Language SmArts
Model the Cycling of Matter

Eagles prefer to eat fish. Therefore, they tend to live in forested borders of inland lakes and rocky shorelines of North America. They also feed on turtles and other reptiles, rodents, and dead animals. As lakes freeze over in winter, the eagles migrate to warmer areas. Their diet switches to include more birds, which are easier to find during cold months.

Explore Online

18. **Draw** Model the flow of carbon in the eagle's winter or summer food chain. Include producers and other consumers. Use arrows to indicate the cycling of carbon through the living and nonliving parts of the ecosystem.

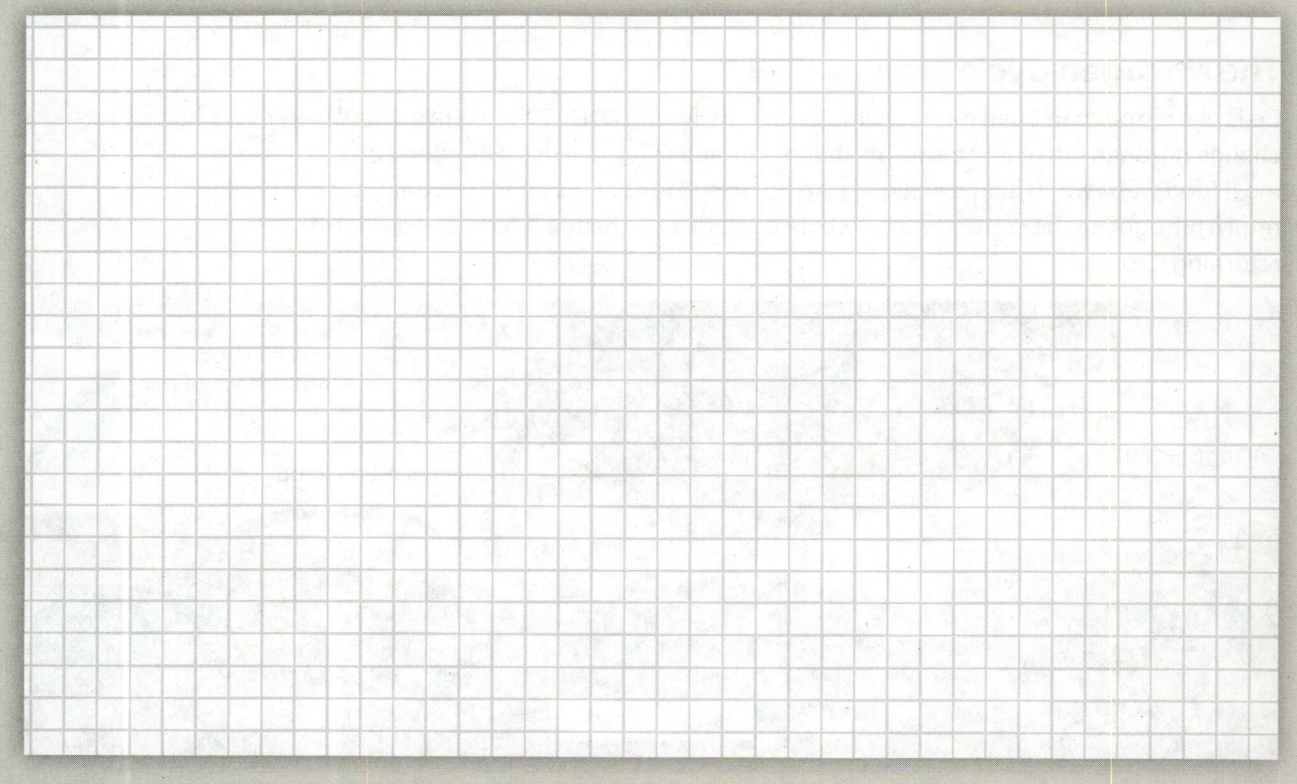

19. Use your model to describe how matter and energy cycle between the eagle and the other living and nonliving components of its ecosystem.

_____
_____
_____
_____
_____
_____
_____

Continue Your Exploration

Name: _____ Date: _____

Check out the path below or go online to choose one of the other paths shown.

- **People in Science**
- Biomagnification
- Hands-On Labs
- Propose Your Own Path
- Go online to choose one of these other paths.

Charles Elton, Ecologist

Charles Elton was an English biologist who lived during the early 1900s. He is credited with establishing ecology as a scientific field. He gathered a large amount of data to draw conclusions about ecosystem populations. Before Elton's work, most people studied the natural world by observing and describing, rather than experimenting and collecting data. Elton discovered that food chains display a "pyramid of numbers." That is, producers have the largest population sizes and top consumers have the smallest population sizes. Later scientists built upon Elton's work to develop the energy pyramid model used today to represent the amount of energy available at each feeding level.

One of Elton's later books described the ecology of voles. Voles are a favorite meal for birds of prey. Their populations rise and fall wildly in different ecosystems. This made the voles an intriguing subject for Elton. He spent his life to trying to explain ecosystem dynamics using reliable numbers.

1. Charles Elton needed to gather data from several different ecosystems to be certain that the pyramid of numbers explains a real pattern in food chains. What does this tell you about the connection between the nature of science and the use of evidence?

A hungry owl catches a vole. An owl might eat up to three voles each day.

TAKE IT FURTHER

Continue Your Exploration

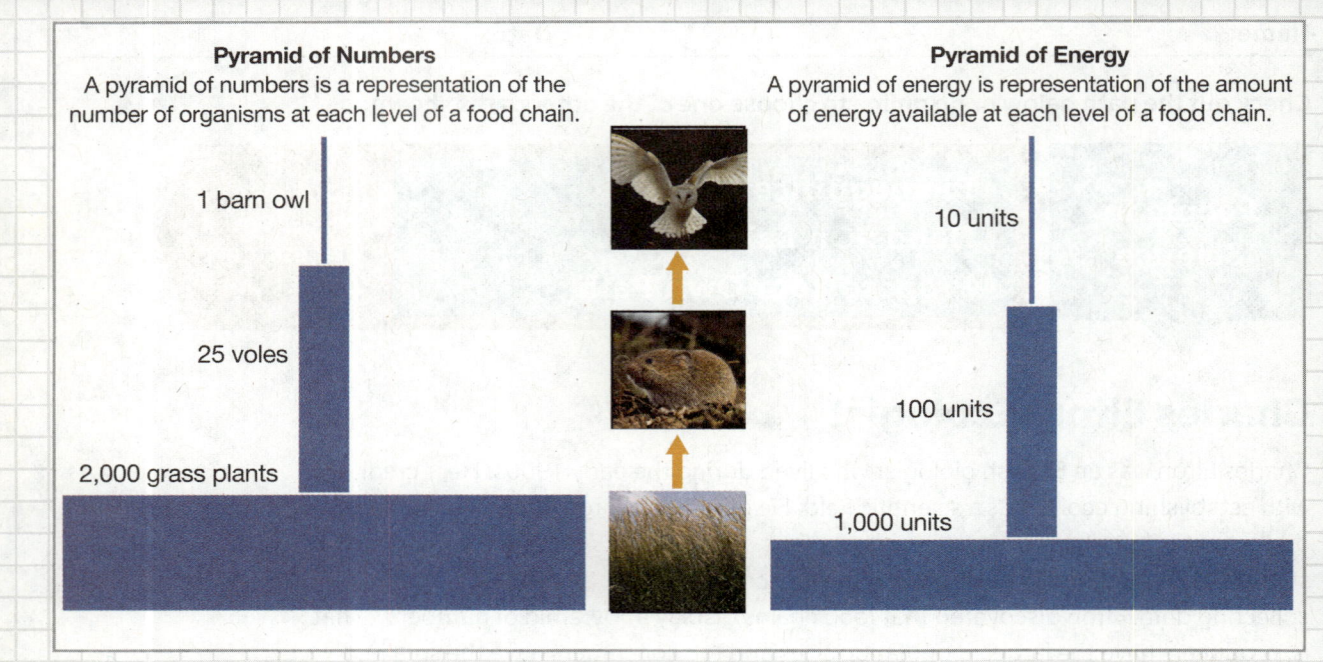

Pyramid of Numbers
A pyramid of numbers is a representation of the number of organisms at each level of a food chain.

- 1 barn owl
- 25 voles
- 2,000 grass plants

Pyramid of Energy
A pyramid of energy is representation of the amount of energy available at each level of a food chain.

- 10 units
- 100 units
- 1,000 units

2. Construct a pyramid of numbers for the food chain below.
   1 oak tree ⟶ 200 caterpillars ⟶ 4 robins ⟶ 1 hawk

3. Do you expect the energy pyramid for this food chain to have the same shape as the pyramid of numbers? Why or why not?

4. **Collaborate** In addition to being credited with the concepts of the pyramid of numbers and food webs, Charles Elton contributed to studies related to conservation, invasive species, and wildlife disease ecology. Work with a group to research the career of Charles Elton. Present your biography as a multimedia presentation. Lead a post-presentation discussion about how Charles Elton's methods may have influenced new generations of ecologists.

412 Unit 5 Earth's Resources and Ecosystems

LESSON 5 SELF-CHECK

Can You Explain It?

Name: _____   Date: _____

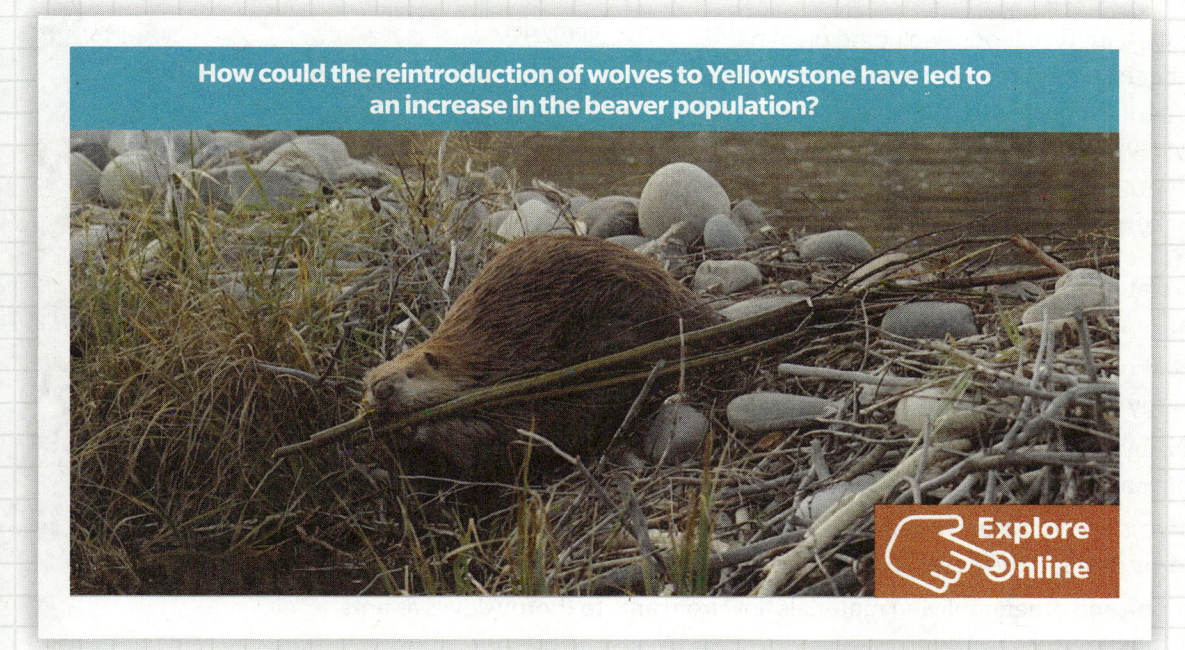

> **How could the reintroduction of wolves to Yellowstone have led to an increase in the beaver population?**
>
> Explore Online

EVIDENCE NOTEBOOK
Refer to the notes in your Evidence Notebook to help you construct an explanation for how the reintroduction of wolves to Yellowstone influenced the park's beaver population.

1. State your claim. Make sure your claim fully explains why the beaver population increased after wolves were reintroduced to Yellowstone National Park.

2. Summarize the evidence you have gathered to support your claim and explain your reasoning.

Lesson 5 The Flow of Energy Drives the Cycling of Matter in Ecosystems   **413**

LESSON 5 SELF-CHECK

Checkpoints

Answer the following questions to check your understanding of the lesson.

Use the photo to answer Questions 3–4.

3. Ants eat a variety of foods, including plants and other insects. A reptile called a *thorny devil* eats ants. If a food chain that includes the thorny devil and ants is represented by an energy pyramid, the ants would occupy the ~~bottom / middle / top~~ pyramid level.

   thorny devil

4. Which statement about thorny devils and ants is true?
   A. The thorny devil stores almost all of the energy it receives from eating ants.
   B. Thorny devils get all the matter they need from eating ants.
   C. There is likely an equal number of ants and thorny devils in the desert ecosystem.
   D. Carbon and other nonliving materials flow from ants to thorny devils as ants are eaten.

Use the photo to answer Question 5.

5. Which statement(s) describe how the river moves matter between land and water ecosystems? Select all that apply.
   A. The river provides water to many land animals.
   B. The river draws soil nutrients into water for use by aquatic plants.
   C. The pull of gravity allows water to move from where it falls as rain, returning it to the ocean.
   D. Rivers carry rocks downstream.

6. What processes drive the flow of carbon between living and nonliving components of ecosystems? Select all that apply.
   A. photosynthesis
   B. evaporation
   C. decomposition
   D. cellular respiration

414 Unit 5 Earth's Resources and Ecosystems

LESSON 5 SELF-CHECK

Interactive Review

Complete this section to review the main concepts of the lesson.

Energy is transferred in ecosystems through a network of producers, consumers, and decomposers that are connected.

A. Use a concept map to illustrate the role of producers, consumers, and decomposers in the transfer of energy through ecosystems.

Matter continuously cycles between the living and nonliving parts of an ecosystem. The flow of energy drives the cycling of matter through ecosystems.

B. The water, carbon, and nitrogen cycles share patterns in the flow of matter and energy through ecosystems. Describe two different patterns that can be observed in all three cycles.

Lesson 5 The Flow of Energy Drives the Cycling of Matter in Ecosystems

UNIT 5 CONNECTIONS

Choose one of the activities to explore how this unit connects to other topics.

☐ People in Science

Alfred Wegener, Geophysicist Alfred Wegener was educated in astronomy, meteorology, and physics. He worked as a professor and meteorologist and even built Greenland's first meteorological station. On the side, Wegener did research that led him to propose that Earth's continents were joined together millions of years ago.

Do research and plan an oral presentation to describe the claim and supporting evidence Wegener presented in his book, *The Origin of Continents and Oceans*. Note why he revised his book several times. Did counterarguments exist at the time? Provide a conclusion regarding his impact on today's understanding of continental movements.

☐ Earth Science Connection

Cycling of Resources Many types of resources are involved in cycles. For example, carbon, water, and nitrogen all cycle through Earth's systems, including the atmosphere, hydrosphere, geosphere, and biosphere. Each of these resources is essential for living things.

Using library and Internet sources, research the parts of one of these cycles. Draw a labeled illustration of how the resource cycles through an ecosystem of your choosing. Include a prediction as to how a change in that cycle would impact the different populations living in the ecosystem.

☐ Environmental Science Connection

Drilling in the Arctic Under the snow and ice of the Arctic are millions of gallons of oil. This oil would be very useful to people. However, drilling in the ice can threaten Arctic ecosystems.

Investigate the oil drilling that takes place in the Arctic and research the pipeline that moves the oil from the far north. What might happen to Arctic ecosystems if this pipeline were to leak or break? Research the solutions that have been developed to make these pipelines safe. Make a recommendation for at least one of these solutions to be implemented in the Arctic pipeline, and explain your reasoning.

UNIT 5 REVIEW

Name: Date:

Complete this review to check your understanding of the unit.

Use the food web diagram to answer Questions 1–2.

1. This food web shows how energy is transferred within a forest ecosystem. The squirrel ~~gains~~ / loses / creates energy by eating nuts and berries from plants. Plants grow by using energy from ~~the sun~~ / deer / wind.

2. Mining activities in this ecosystem resulted in the loss of many plants that produced nuts and berries. A decrease in nuts and berries would result in a(n) increase / ~~decrease~~ in the fox population because the squirrel and bird populations would increase / ~~decrease~~ / stay the same.

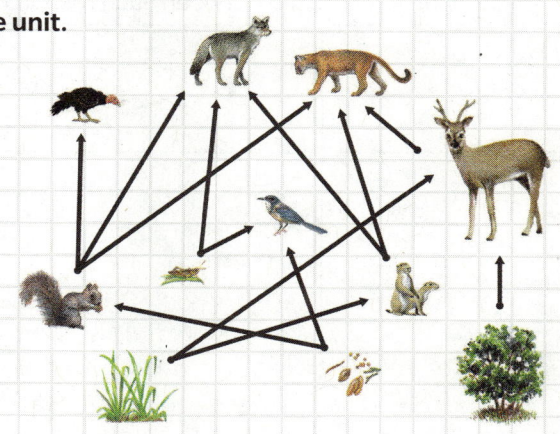

Use the graph to answer Questions 3–4.

3. Sea ice is an example of a living / ~~nonliving~~ factor in the Arctic ecosystem. The overall trend in the extent of Arctic sea ice, shown by the blue line, is that it has increased / ~~decreased~~ / remained the same. Since 1979, the greatest extent of ice was in ~~1983~~ / 1999 / 2009 and the least amount was in 1980 / 1995 / ~~2012~~.

4. Walruses use sea ice as a diving platform to swim to the sea floor and feed on clams. What prediction can be made about sea ice and walruses in 2024?

   A. The ice cover will continue to increase and walrus populations will grow.

   B. The ice cover will continue to decrease and walrus populations will decline.

   C. The ice cover will continue to decrease but walruses will move to new areas and populations will grow.

   D. The ice cover will continue to increase but there will not be enough space for walruses to live.

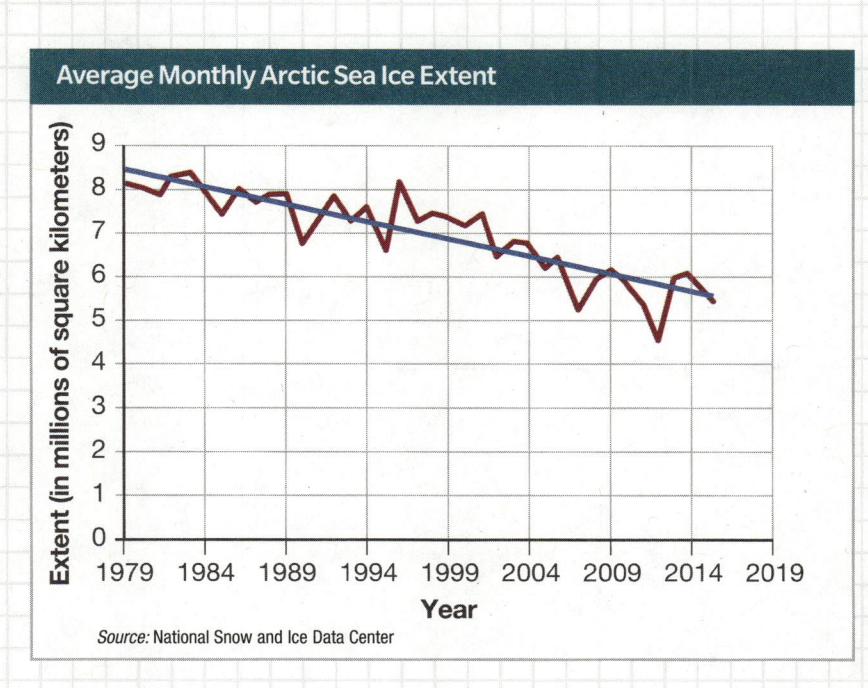

Average Monthly Arctic Sea Ice Extent

Extent (in millions of square kilometers) vs. Year (1979–2019)

Source: National Snow and Ice Data Center

Unit 5 Earth's Resources and Ecosystems   417

UNIT 5 REVIEW

5. Complete the table by describing patterns in the distribution of each resource, as well as the relationship between each resource with ecosystems and humans.

Natural resources	Patterns in distribution	Matter and energy in ecosystems	Relationship to humans
Plants	Different plants are found in different climates and ecosystems. For example, in the desert, only plants that can go without water for a long time will grow.		
Healthy soil			
Clean freshwater			
Clean air			

UNIT 5 REVIEW

Name: _____   Date: _____

Use the graph to answer Questions 6–9.

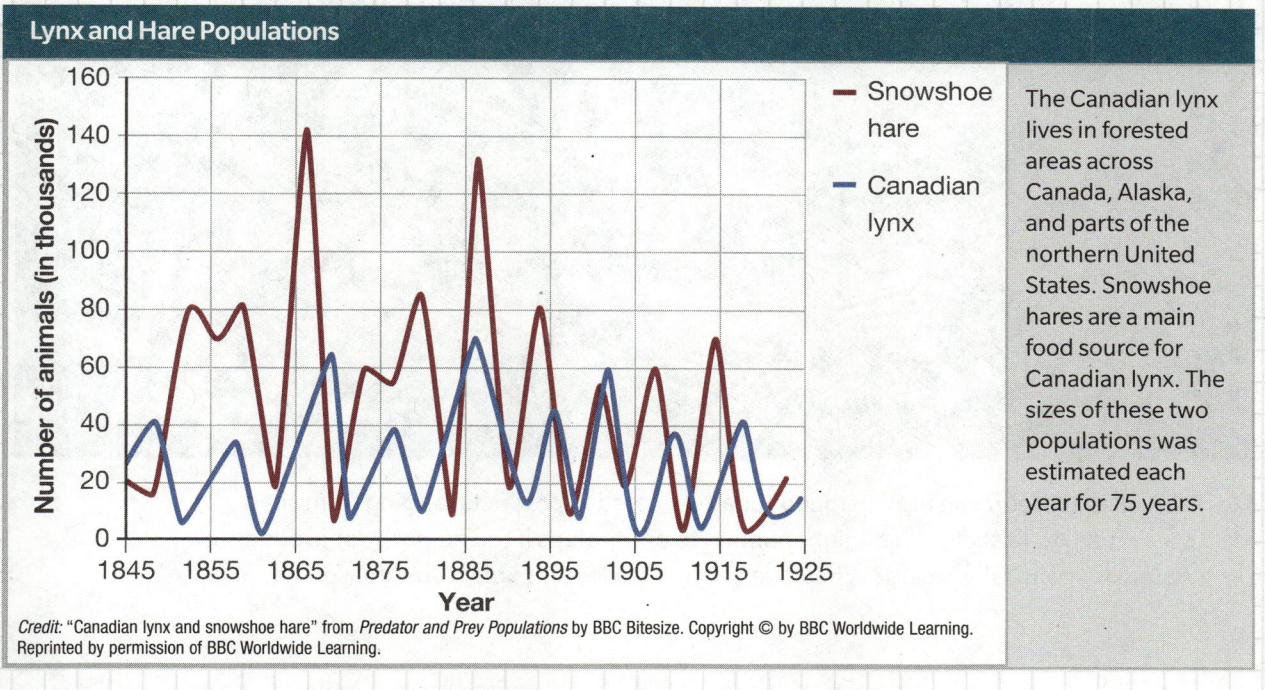

Lynx and Hare Populations

— Snowshoe hare
— Canadian lynx

The Canadian lynx lives in forested areas across Canada, Alaska, and parts of the northern United States. Snowshoe hares are a main food source for Canadian lynx. The sizes of these two populations was estimated each year for 75 years.

Credit: "Canadian lynx and snowshoe hare" from *Predator and Prey Populations* by BBC Bitesize. Copyright © by BBC Worldwide Learning. Reprinted by permission of BBC Worldwide Learning.

6. Explain the pattern displayed in this graph in terms of the relationship between predator and prey population sizes.

7. Snowshoe hares eat grasses, small leafy plants, and flowers. When hare populations peak, these plant food sources can become scarce. What can you conclude about the size of these plant populations from 1910–1915?

8. How would decreased availability of plant food sources affect the populations of snowshoe hares? Would competition for food likely increase or decrease?

9. Provide different examples of how changes in biotic and abiotic resources could affect the stability of this ecosystem.

Unit 5 Earth's Resources and Ecosystems

UNIT 5 REVIEW

Use the photos and text to answer Questions 10–13.

Palm Oil Plantations are Replacing Tropical Rain Forests

Endangered orangutans in the native rain forests of Indonesia and Malaysia depend on resources such as bark, leaves, insects, and fruits. These rain forests are being replaced by palm oil plantations.

10. Palm oil is a resource in high demand today. It is used in products ranging from soap to ice cream to lipstick. What might happen to orangutans if the demand for products containing palm oil goes up? What if demand goes down? Explain your reasoning.

11. Imagine that an area was set aside to relocate orangutans displaced from their rain forest habitats. A solution like this would involve many groups of people and careful considerations. Review the questions below, then develop at least two additional questions that could be considered.
    - What do orangutans use for shelter in their native ecosystem?
    - How much area does a specific number of orangutans need?

12. Healthy rain forest ecosystems provide ecosystem services, such as clean air, shade, food, and water. How might an increase in palm oil plantations affect humans who live nearby?

UNIT 5 PERFORMANCE TASK

Name: _____   Date: _____

How do lionfish affect relationships in local ecosystems?

The red lionfish (*Pterois volitans*) is native to the South Pacific. However, this species is now found in the Atlantic Ocean, ranging from the North Atlantic Ocean near Rhode Island down to the Caribbean Sea and the Gulf of Mexico. These fish were introduced to the Atlantic by human activities. Lionfish are damaging native ecosystems in the Atlantic and are therefore an *invasive species*. Lionfish have no natural predators here and can live to be 30 years old. A single female lionfish lays about 2 million eggs each year.

You will research how the introduction of lionfish has caused changes to the existing interactions among native species in the Gulf of Mexico. You will then provide possible solutions for the problem.

The red lionfish is an invasive species that is causing much damage to the ecosystem in the Gulf of Mexico.

Lionfish Sightings in Three Areas in the Florida Garden Banks National Marine Sanctuary

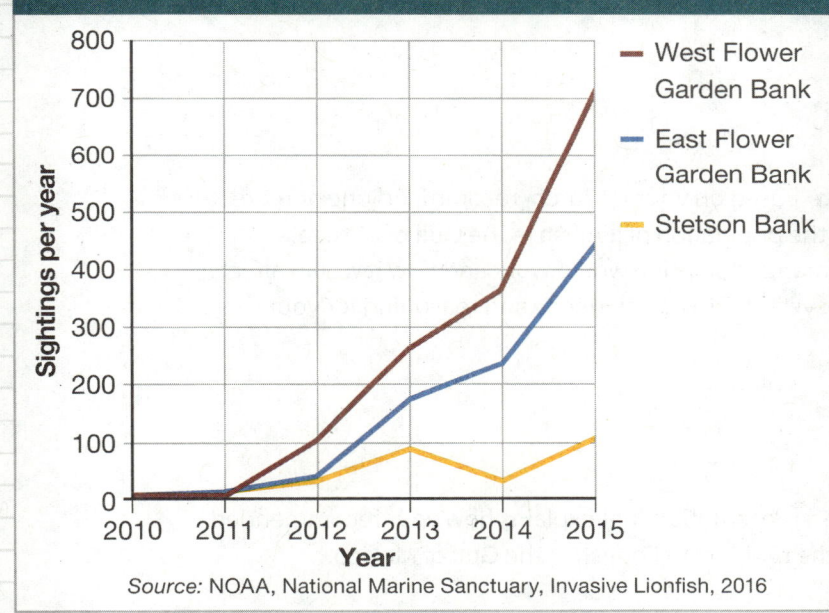

[Graph showing Sightings per year (0–800) vs Year (2010–2015) for three locations: West Flower Garden Bank, East Flower Garden Bank, and Stetson Bank]

Source: NOAA, National Marine Sanctuary, Invasive Lionfish, 2016

The number of lionfish sightings has greatly increased in recent years. This graph shows population sizes in three different areas in the Florida Garden Banks National Marine Sanctuary. In each area, the sightings of lionfish have been increasing.

The steps below will help guide your research and help you develop your recommendation.

Engineer It

1. **Define the Problem** Write a statement defining the problem you will be researching and recommending solutions for. With a classmate, discuss how this problem began and what impact it has on local ecosystems. What questions do you have about this problem?

Unit 5 Earth's Resources and Ecosystems   421

UNIT 5 PERFORMANCE TASK

Engineer It

2. **Conduct Research** Investigate lionfish and their impacts on other species living in the Gulf of Mexico. How do lionfish interact with native species? How do they affect the availability of resources for native species? What is being done to try to control their population size?

3. **Conduct Research** How do increasing lionfish populations affect humans that depend on the Gulf of Mexico's marine ecosystems for resources?

4. **Construct an Explanation** Use evidence from your research to explain why lionfish have been able to thrive as an invasive species in the Gulf of Mexico. Cite your sources and be sure to quote and paraphrase the data and conclusions from your research while avoiding plagiarism.

5. **Recommend a Solution** Based on your research, recommend one or more solutions for controlling the population of lionfish in the Gulf of Mexico. Explain how your recommended solution would work and how it would affect native species in the ecosystem. Provide evidence and reasoning for your recommendation.

6. **Communicate** Prepare a presentation that explains how your recommended solution would address the problem of lionfish in the Gulf of Mexico.

Self-Check

	I identified and defined the problem.
	I researched the interactions that lionfish have with native species in the Gulf of Mexico and efforts to control lionfish populations.
	I analyzed my research and constructed an explanation for why lionfish have been able to thrive in the Gulf of Mexico.
	I recommended a solution based on evidence from research, data, and an analysis of how lionfish populations can be managed.
	My recommendation was clearly communicated to others.

UNIT 6

Earth's Surface and Society

How do natural processes and human activities affect Earth's surface and society?

Unit Project	424
Lesson 1 Geologic Processes Change Earth's Surface	426
Lesson 2 Natural Hazards Disrupt Earth's Surface	444
Lesson 3 Some Natural Hazards Can Be Predicted and Mitigated	466
Lesson 4 Human Use of Synthetic Materials Affects Earth's Surface	492
Unit Review	517
Unit Performance Task	521

Wildfires, such as this one in the Rocky Mountains, can destroy thousands of acres of forest and can threaten human cities and homes.

You Solve It Where and When Do Most Human-Caused Fires Occur? Analyze data about wildfires to decide when and where to run a public awareness campaign about preventing fires.

Go online and complete the You Solve It to explore ways to solve a real-world problem.

UNIT 6 PROJECT

Develop a Natural Hazard Mitigation Plan

Students practice taking cover during an earthquake drill.

A. Look at the photo. On a separate sheet of paper, write down as many different questions as you can about the photo.

B. Discuss With your class or a partner, share your questions. Record any additional questions generated in your discussion. Then choose the most important questions from the list that are related to preparing for a natural hazard. Write them below.

C. Choose a natural hazard to research, and create a plan to minimize the effects of that hazard. Here's a list of natural hazards you can consider:

avalanche	flood	sinkhole
blizzard or ice storm	hailstorm	tornado or waterspout
cold wave	hurricane or tropical cyclone	tsunami
drought	landslide	volcanic eruption
earthquake	lightning or electrical storm	wildfire

D. Use the information on this page, along with your research, to explore how people prepare and respond to a natural hazard.

Discuss the next steps for your Unit Project with your teacher and go online to download the Unit Project Worksheet.

424 Unit 6 Earth's Surface and Society

UNIT 6

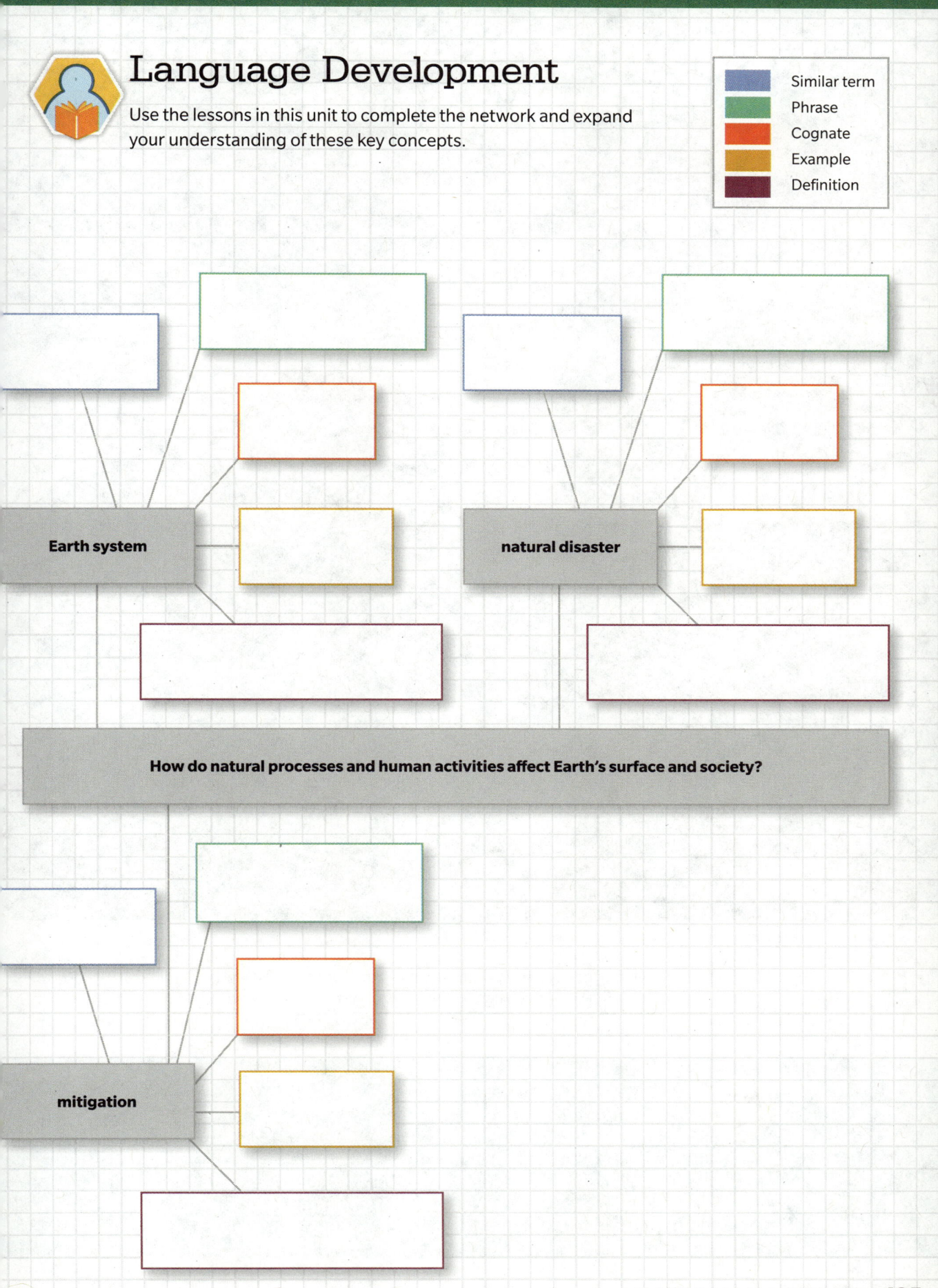

Language Development

Use the lessons in this unit to complete the network and expand your understanding of these key concepts.

- Similar term
- Phrase
- Cognate
- Example
- Definition

Earth system

natural disaster

How do natural processes and human activities affect Earth's surface and society?

mitigation

Unit 6 Earth's Natural Hazards 425

LESSON 1

Geologic Processes Change Earth's Surface

This mountain range in Banff National Park, Alberta, Canada, was formed by interactions among Earth's systems.

Explore First

Classifying Events Make a timeline of the events in your life. Use a key with symbols to indicate which of these events were large scale and which ones were small scale. Show which ones were short term, and which ones took longer. Compare your timeline with others'. Do any of your events overlap? Are they categorized in the same way?

CAN YOU EXPLAIN IT?

How has this area of the Arizona desert changed in the last 50,000 years?

The Barringer Meteorite Crater is 1.3 km wide and extends 174 m into Earth. The crater formed about 50,000 years ago, when a meteorite with a mass of 300,000 metric tons hurtled through Earth's atmosphere nearly 50 times faster than a commercial jet. It struck Earth in what is now the Arizona Desert.

1. What immediate effects might the meteorite impact have had on Earth's surface?

2. Which changes might have happened after a longer time had passed?

EVIDENCE NOTEBOOK As you explore the lesson, gather evidence to help explain the changes to Earth's surface in this area over the last 50,000 years.

Lesson 1 Geologic Processes Change Earth's Surface **427**

EXPLORATION 1

Analyzing Interactions Within the Earth System

The Earth System

A system is a group of related parts that work together as a whole. Earth itself is one large system, from its core to the outer edge of its atmosphere. The **Earth system** is all the matter, energy, and processes within this boundary. The Earth system is different from the systems of other planets and moons. Human survival depends on natural systems and cycles, as well as human-made systems. For example, food can only be grown in certain places at certain times. When humans disrupt natural systems and cycles, they also affect the ability of those systems to provide necessary resources, including food. As the human population increases, it has a growing influence on many of Earth's systems. Humans are using many resources at a faster rate than the resources can be replaced. As a result, many species are going extinct. The biodiversity that helps sustain stable Earth systems has been affected by human-made systems.

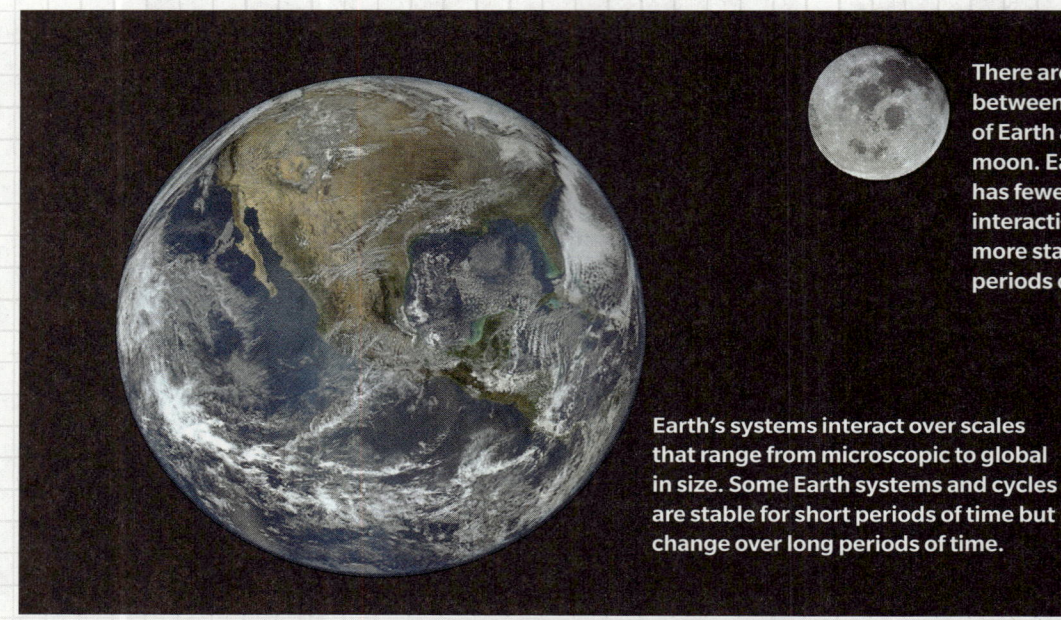

There are differences between the systems of Earth and its moon. Earth's moon has fewer systems interacting and is more stable over long periods of time.

Earth's systems interact over scales that range from microscopic to global in size. Some Earth systems and cycles are stable for short periods of time but change over long periods of time.

3. What difference or differences do you see between Earth and its moon? Put a check mark to show which statements are true for Earth and for the moon.

Earth	Moon	Statements
✓		Water covers much of the surface.
		The surface receives energy from the sun.
		It has a thick atmosphere and weather.
		The surface includes solid materials.
		Living organisms are visible on the surface.

Earth's Subsystems

The Earth system has many different parts that make up Earth's four major subsystems: the geosphere, hydrosphere, atmosphere, and biosphere. Many of Earth's materials are part of more than one subsystem. For example, fog is part of the atmosphere and the hydrosphere. These subsystems change over time, but also have periods of stability.

The interactions between Earth's subsystems happen over time spans that range from fractions of a second to billions of years. These interactions have shaped Earth's history. Earth's future will continue to be determined by these interactions as well as the decisions humans make about natural systems and resource use.

Earth's Subsystems

Atmosphere
The atmosphere is the part of the Earth system that includes all of the gases in a layer that surrounds Earth. Earth's weather and climate result from interactions between the parts of this subsystem. Human influences are affecting the long term stability of Earth's weather and climate systems.

Geosphere
The geosphere is the part of the Earth system that includes all of the rocks, minerals, and landforms on Earth's surface and all the matter in Earth's interior. The geosphere usually changes slowly and so it appears stable.

Biosphere
The biosphere is the part of the Earth system that includes all living organisms, from the smallest bacterium to the largest tree. The biosphere is constantly changing as organisms migrate, evolve, or become extinct.

Hydrosphere
The hydrosphere is the part of the Earth system that includes all Earth's water that is cycling between the surface, underground, or the atmosphere. The hydrosphere includes liquid water, water vapor, and the solid water in ice and snow.

EVIDENCE NOTEBOOK

4. Which of Earth's subsystems was most obviously affected by the meteorite impact? What changes occurred in that subsystem? Record your evidence.

Lesson 1 Geologic Processes Change Earth's Surface **429**

Identify the Subsystems

5. Label each image with the appropriate subsystem. Some images may be labeled with more than one subsystem.

- geosphere
- biosphere
- atmosphere
- hydrosphere

_____   _____   _____

6. **Discuss** How do you use resources from each of Earth's four subsystems on any given day?

The Cycling of Matter and Energy

Earth's subsystems constantly interact, and as they do, energy and matter cycle through the Earth system. Energy and matter also cycle between natural systems and human-made systems. Natural and human-made systems are dependent on each other and can affect each other over both short and long periods of time.

Energy from the sun and from Earth's interior is transferred by several processes, including wind, water waves, and movements of rock. In fact, energy from the sun is one of the main drivers of erosion and deposition. Interactions between the hydrosphere and the atmosphere also drive weather and climate systems. While the climate of a region may stay stable for decades, seasonal differences in solar radiation result in changes in weather throughout the year.

Explore Online

Energy from the sun drives interactions between subsystems on Earth's surface.

7. _____ causes rain to fall to Earth's surface. Energy from _____ causes water to evaporate.

430 Unit 6 Earth's Surface and Society

Energy from Earth's Interior

Energy from Earth's interior is transferred upward through Earth's layers. Several processes transfer energy and matter through the geosphere. For example, hot magma in Earth's upper mantle and lower crust can rise to the surface in a volcanic eruption. The eruption can cause heat and small particles of rock and minerals from deep within Earth's crust to enter the atmosphere. The energy and matter from the eruption can kill organisms and destroy habitats, causing stable ecosystems to change very quickly. Hot ash and lava can heat the water in streams or lakes, sometimes changing liquid water into steam. The eruption also brings minerals from within Earth to its surface, where they can be used by organisms. Other energy transfers from Earth's interior cause the melting of rock, earthquakes, and the movement of Earth's plates.

8. The rocks that make up Earth's interior and surface melt and form _____, which pushes up through rock to form volcanoes. Volcanoes underwater release energy from Earth's interior into the _____.

Energy from Earth's interior causes the movement of tectonic plates and the formation of volcanoes. These movements affect all four of Earth's subsystems.

Explain Earth Systems Interactions

The interactions among Earth's subsystems are often quite complex. A single event, such as a forest fire, results in the cycling of energy and matter among the systems in many different ways. Effects on the subsystems can be positive, negative, or both.

9. **Discuss** Together with a partner, study the scene shown in the photograph. Describe subsystem interactions you can infer from the scene and explain the cycling of matter and energy that could be occurring with each interaction.

A forest fire can affect more than just the biosphere.

EXPLORATION 2

Explaining the Changes on Earth's Surface

Some changes to Earth's surface are easy to see—they are big changes that happen quickly, such as a landslide. Other changes can start out small and occur slowly but become big changes over many years. An example is the erosion of Earth's mountains. The changes to Earth's surface—big or small, fast or slow—are the result of Earth's subsystems interacting.

10. **Discuss** Together with a partner, examine the photo of the cone-shaped deposit. Did this deposit form recently, or did it form many years ago? What evidence do you observe to support your answer?

This cone-shaped deposit of sediment is caused by the deposition of sediment and rock where a stream leaves a narrow channel such as a canyon and spreads out in a wider area such as a plain.

Large-Scale and Small-Scale Changes

Most changes on Earth's surface are the result of interactions of Earth's subsystems. Changes on Earth's surface range from microscopic to global in scale. A smaller-scale change may be crystal formation, while ocean shore erosion is a larger-scale change. Global-sized changes, such as movements of Earth's tectonic plates, affect all of Earth.

Changes at Different Scales

Larger-scale changes happen when the plates in Earth's crust move slowly as the mantle beneath them moves. Plate motion squeezes, stretches, and breaks Earth's crust. These motions slowly shape global-scale features, such as wide ocean basins, deep ocean trenches, and long mountain chains, like the Himalayas pictured here.

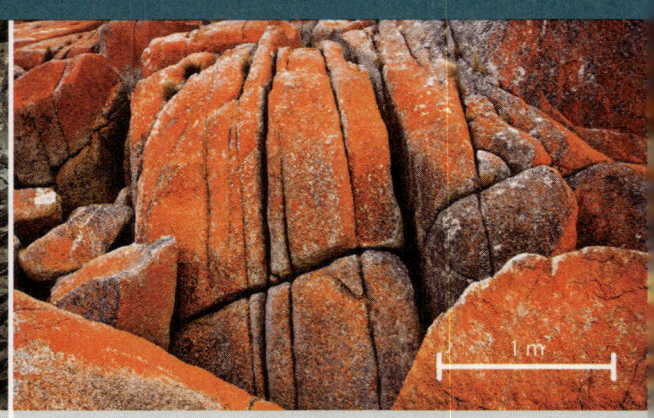

Smaller-scale changes happen when oxygen and water chemically react with minerals in rocks. These reactions cause the rocks to change and break down. Similarly, organisms that live on rocks, such as lichen, produce chemicals that cause rocks to break down. These changes affect much smaller areas on Earth's surface.

432 Unit 6 Earth's Surface and Society

11. The events listed below describe changes to Earth's surface. Classify the changes as smaller-scale, medium-scale, or larger-scale by writing the correct label on the line next to each event. Assign each scale to only two events.

WORD BANK
- smaller-scale change
- medium-scale change
- larger-scale change

A. Water and ice weather and erode a rock.   *smaller-scale change*

B. Two plates collide, causing a mountain range to form.   _____

C. Heavy rainfall causes a landslide.   _____

D. An oil spill damages a coastal ecosystem.   _____

E. Gravity causes a rock structure on a beach to collapse into the ocean.   _____

F. A plant dies and decays, and its nutrients become part of the soil.   _____

EVIDENCE NOTEBOOK
12. How would you classify the scale of the change to Earth's surface due to the impact of the meteorite? Provide evidence to support your answer.

Time Scales of Changes

Geologic processes happen on varying time scales. Some events that change Earth's surface happen very quickly, such as erosion and deposition caused by floods. Other processes happen slowly, such as the growth of cave formations caused by groundwater. The processes may take so long, in fact, that we may think nothing is happening. When wind, water, and ice cause erosion and deposition over a long time scale, mountains and valleys form. However, because these changes sometimes occur over millions and billions of years, humans usually can observe only a small part of most processes that change Earth's surface. The geosphere usually appears very stable.

The same processes that shaped Earth's surface in the past continue to shape Earth's surface today. Some of these processes may have occurred more often or less often in the past than they do today. An example is the large meteorites that impacted Earth early in its history. Meteorite impacts occur much less frequently today.

Do the Math
Compare Rates of Change

Changes on Earth's surface happen at many different rates. Both rapid and slow processes can cause changes to landforms on Earth's surface. For example, when plate movement happens suddenly, it can trigger earthquakes. When plate movement happens slowly, continents can break apart and mountain ranges can form. Three changes that usually happen at different rates are:

- flow of a fast glacier (17 km/year)
- spreading at the Mid-Atlantic Ridge (2 cm/year)
- formation of a stalactite in a cave (1 mm/year)

The dark gray area is the Mid-Atlantic Ridge in the Atlantic Ocean.

13. In the table below, use what you know about the original rate data to complete the order column by ranking the processes as fastest or slowest.

Process	Original Data	Order	Converted Data
glacier flow	17 km/year		
sea-floor spreading	2 cm/year	middle	2 cm/year
stalactite formation	3 mm/year		

14. Complete the converted data column by converting all the rates to cm/year. Remember: 1 km = 100,000 cm and 1 cm = 10 mm

15. What is the difference between comparing the rates using the original rate data and the data converted to cm/year? Which data set is easier to use to compare the rates of change? Explain your reasoning.

16. **Engineer It** How could you measure the speed of a glacier if it takes a year to move several kilometers? What is one additional challenge scientists face in measuring the spreading rate at a mid-ocean ridge compared to measuring the speed of a glacier?

Fast and Slow Changes

Earth's surface has been changing over billions of years. Many of the changes happen in a matter of minutes, while others may take millions of years to occur. As you look at events that change Earth's surface, comparisons can be made to give you a sense of these time scales. For example, you can compare two events—the formation of a river delta and a river flooding—that can occur in your lifetime. A river delta forms when sediments carried by a river are deposited where it empties into the ocean. A river delta might grow slowly each day, with changes visible in a couple of months or a year's time. In comparison, floods may occur when there is heavy rainfall in a short period of time. This can cause lakes and rivers to overflow and flood the surrounding area. Humans can influence the rate at which many changes occur. For example, building a dam along a river changes cycles of flooding. This may benefit farmers by controlling the flow of water, but may harm ecosystems downstream. Humans can build a dam quickly, but both Earth and human systems will be changed for a long time.

This river delta formed from sediments deposited by the river that flows into the sea here.

The level of this river is higher than normal. It can erode sediment and other materials, depositing them in new locations in a matter of hours, days, or weeks.

17. Relative to a human lifetime, delta formation is a large, *slow* / fast process that involves small / medium / *large* amounts of energy and matter over a longer time. A flash flood is a slow / *fast* process that involves small / *large* amounts of energy and matter over a shorter time.

> **EVIDENCE NOTEBOOK**
> 18. When the meteorite hit Earth in Arizona, did its impact cause fast or slow changes to Earth's surface? Support your claim with evidence.

Lesson 1 Geologic Processes Change Earth's Surface **435**

Hands-On Lab
Analyze Visual Evidence

What changes can a volcanic eruption cause? You will use maps to analyze the visible changes to the Mount St. Helens area that were caused by a powerful eruption.

The eruption of Mount St. Helens, a volcanic mountain in the Cascade Range in the state of Washington, is an example of a rapid change that caused medium-scale changes to Earth's surface.

The volcano had been dormant since 1857, but on the morning of May 18, 1980, a massive earthquake (magnitude 5.1 on the Richter scale) caused the volcano's north side to collapse. An avalanche of rock fell onto the land below. Then gases that had been under pressure inside the mountain shot out sideways, destroying 500 km² of surrounding forest. Ash rose thousands of feet into the air, and pyroclastic flows streamed down the mountain's sides. After nine hours, the eruption was over, but Earth's surface in the area was dramatically changed.

MATERIALS
- colored pencils

This satellite image of Mount St. Helens was taken after the eruption in 1980.

Procedure and Analysis

STEP 1 In this activity, you are provided with information about Mount St. Helens and two maps of the area. One map is from the time between 1970 and 1980, before the eruption. The other map is from 1980, after the eruption.

STEP 2 Compare the two maps. Look for differences between them. What changed in the area around Mount St. Helens after the eruption?

Before 1980

436 Unit 6 Earth's Surface and Society

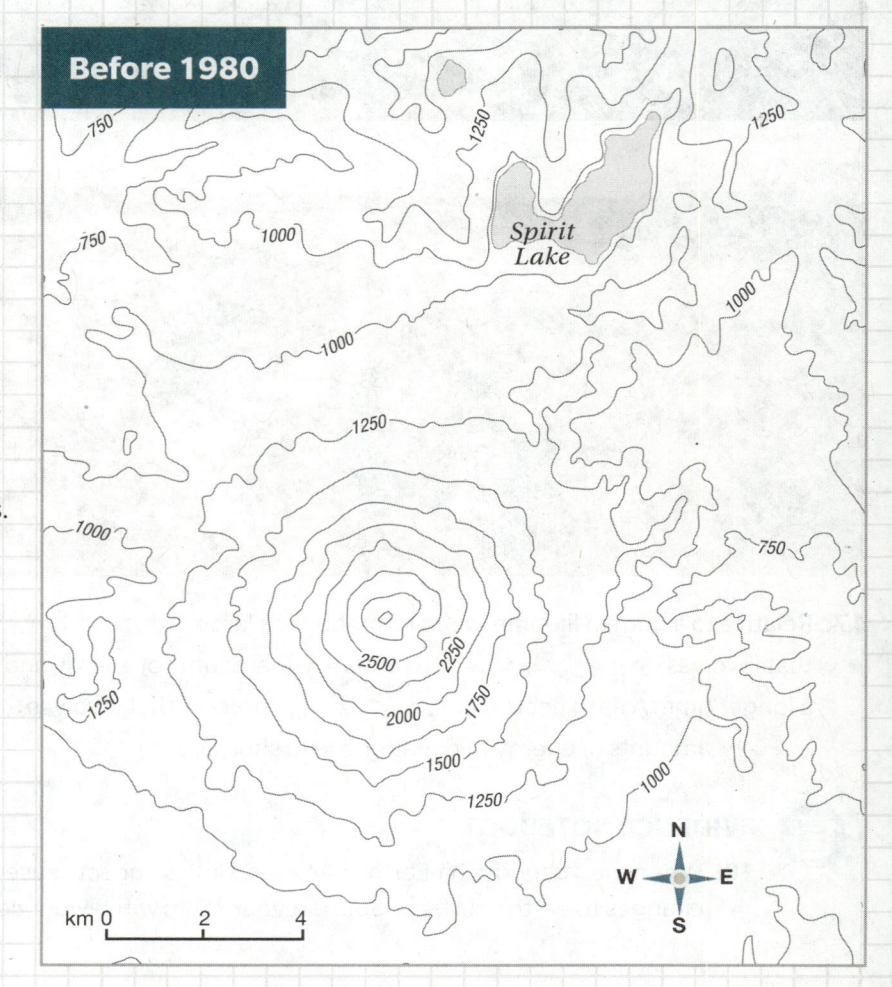

STEP 3 From among your observations, choose something that changed after the eruption. Use the colored pencils to indicate the feature on the "before" map and where it has changed on the "after" map. Outline or color the feature in a way that makes it clear to a viewer what feature you are highlighting.

STEP 4 Choose at least two other changes and mark your maps to show them.

STEP 5 Create a map legend that explains the colors and their meanings.

STEP 6 Based on evidence from the maps, which statement describes Mount St. Helens after the changes occurred as a result of the eruption? Circle all that apply.

    A. The shape of Spirit Lake was not affected by the eruption.

    B. The land south of Mount St. Helens was changed more than the land to the north.

    C. The eruption caused the erosion and deposition of rocks and sediment.

    D. The eruption left a large crater on Mount St. Helens that reduced the overall height of the mountain.

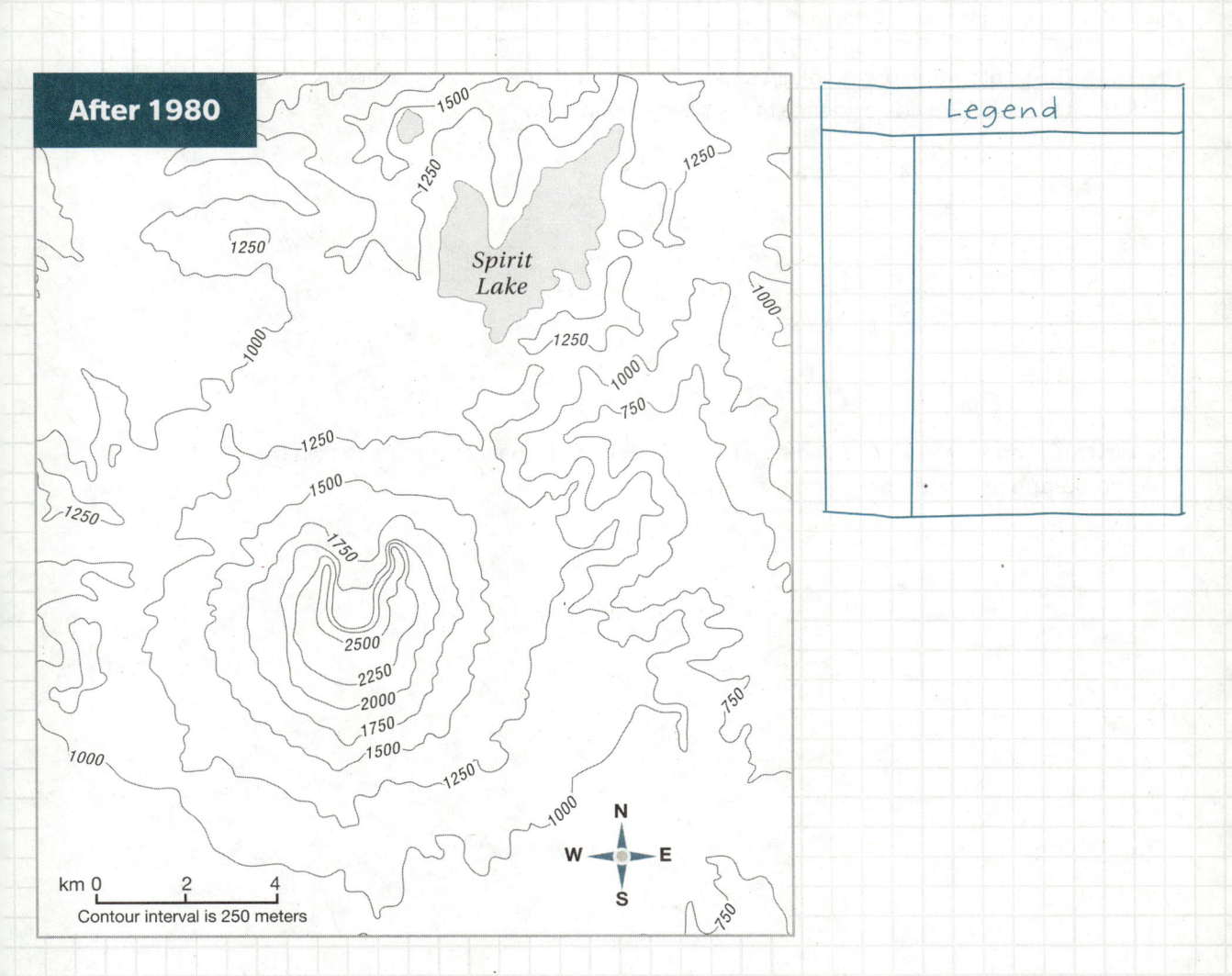

After 1980

Contour interval is 250 meters

Legend

Lesson 1 Geologic Processes Change Earth's Surface 437

Language SmArts
Examine Changes over Time

This volcanic rock has been sitting on the coastline of Maui, Hawaii, for many years. The rock, a result of cooled lava, has changed over time.

19. Study the photograph of the volcanic rock. Do you think the rocks have always looked like this? Provide evidence to support your answer.

_____
_____
_____
_____
_____
_____

20. Write Compose a story about the fast and slow changes that caused the rock in the photograph to look the way it does today.

_____
_____
_____
_____
_____
_____
_____
_____
_____
_____

TAKE IT FURTHER

Continue Your Exploration

Name: _____ Date: _____

Check out the path below or go online to choose one of the other paths shown.

- **Geologically Active Yellowstone**
- Destination Mars
- Hands-On Labs
- Propose Your Own Path

Go online to choose one of these other paths.

Yellowstone National Park covers parts of Wyoming, Montana, and Idaho. About 640,000 years ago, magma in a chamber below the surface pushed Earth's crust up, creating a dome. A huge volcanic explosion emptied the magma chamber. The dome cracked and collapsed, forming the Yellowstone Caldera. A caldera is a depression formed when a magma chamber below a volcano empties.

Today, there is still a magma chamber below the Yellowstone Caldera. In some places it is less than 10 km below the surface. About 9% of the chamber is molten rock, or magma, found in small pockets within very hot solid rock. There are also many fractures and faults, or breaks in rock, in and around the caldera. When rocks move along a fault and release energy, earthquakes occur. Many earthquakes happen near the Yellowstone Caldera.

Yellowstone National Park also contains about 10,000 hydrothermal features, such as geysers and hot springs. The energy source for all these features is the magma chamber below the Yellowstone Caldera. If water flows through or over hot rock, it can become very hot or even turn into steam. Hot springs are places where hot groundwater rises to Earth's surface. Geysers are hot springs where water and steam erupt periodically from surface pools or small vents. The geyser eruption empties an underground chamber where the water had collected. The chamber then refills with groundwater and erupts again after the water is hot enough to boil.

1. Describe an interaction between Earth's subsystems that is happening in Yellowstone National Park today. Describe the cycling of matter and flow of energy involved in this interaction.

A geyser erupts at Yellowstone National Park.

Lesson 1 Geologic Processes Change Earth's Surface **439**

TAKE IT FURTHER

Continue Your Exploration

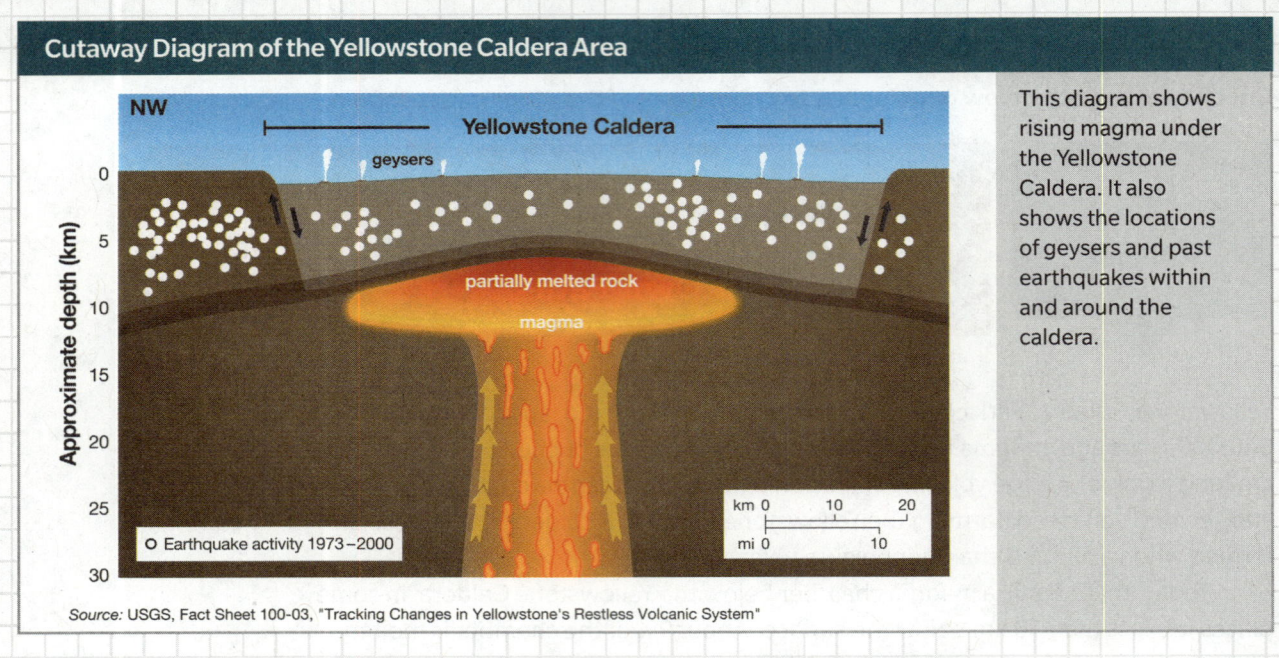

Cutaway Diagram of the Yellowstone Caldera Area

This diagram shows rising magma under the Yellowstone Caldera. It also shows the locations of geysers and past earthquakes within and around the caldera.

Source: USGS, Fact Sheet 100-03, "Tracking Changes in Yellowstone's Restless Volcanic System"

2. There are large faults at the edges of the Yellowstone Caldera. The caldera formed when the magma chamber emptied. How do the movement arrows on the faults in the diagram explain what happened when the caldera formed?

3. Describe the locations of the geysers in this diagram. Develop an explanation for why the geysers are found inside of and not outside of the caldera.

4. **Collaborate** Discuss with a classmate how Earth's surface may change in Yellowstone over the next 100 years. What features may be affected? Provide evidence from the image to support your argument.

LESSON 1 SELF-CHECK

Can You Explain It?

Name: _____ Date: _____

How has this area of the Arizona desert changed in the last 50,000 years?

EVIDENCE NOTEBOOK
Refer to the notes in your Evidence Notebook to help you identify the immediate effects of the meteorite on Earth's systems, as well as the changes that were observed over time.

1. State your claim. Make sure your claim fully explains how this area of the Arizona desert has changed over the last 50,000 years.

2. Summarize the evidence you have gathered to support your claim and explain your reasoning.

Lesson 1 Geologic Processes Change Earth's Surface **441**

LESSON 1 SELF-CHECK

Checkpoints

Answer the following questions to check your understanding of the lesson.

Use the photo to answer Questions 3–4.

3. Which phrases apply to the formation of the Grand Canyon? Select all that apply.
   - A. medium scale
   - B. long-term
   - C. small scale
   - D. short-term
   - E. large scale

4. What is the primary source of energy that drove the cycling of matter that formed the Grand Canyon?
   - A. the sun
   - B. weathering
   - C. erosion

Use the photo to answer Questions 5–6.

5. This photo shows evidence of the interaction of Earth's subsystems. Which of Earth's subsystems are interacting during a landslide? Select all that apply.
   - A. geosphere
   - B. biosphere
   - C. atmosphere
   - D. hydrosphere

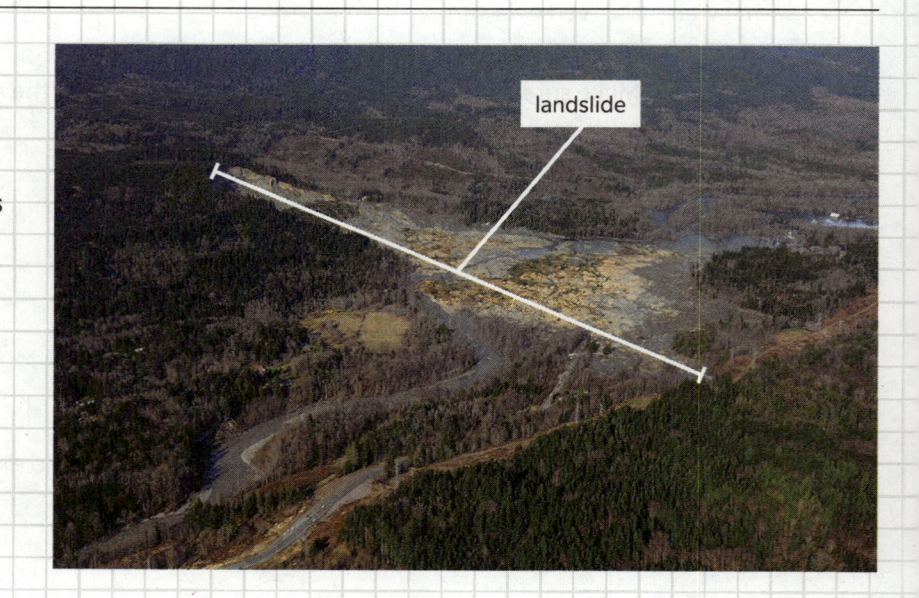

6. The devastation from the landslide shown—the disturbed soil, the knocked-over trees, the blocked waterway and road—are evidence that the change happened _rapidly / slowly_ over time.

442 Unit 6 Earth's Surface and Society

LESSON 1 SELF-CHECK

Interactive Review

Complete this section to review the main concepts of the lesson.

Earth's subsystems are the geosphere, atmosphere, hydrosphere, and biosphere. Energy and matter are transferred when Earth's subsystems interact with each other and with human-made systems.

A. Describe which of Earth's subsystems are involved when an oil spill occurs in a coastal ecosystem. Explain how these different subsystems may be affected over a long period of time.

Geologic processes change Earth's surface on varying scales of space and time. They range from rapid to very slow; from global to microscopic. Humans can also change Earth's surface and speed up or slow down some geologic processes.

B. How can humans change the time scale at which some geologic processes take place when a dam is built along a river?

Lesson 1 Geologic Processes Change Earth's Surface

LESSON 2
Natural Hazards Disrupt Earth's Surface

In 2015, this wildfire near Clear Lake, California, destroyed property and devastated the environment.

Explore First

Modeling a Sandstorm Spread a cup of sand evenly in the bottom of an open top shoe box. From a distance of about one meter, blow air from a hairdryer towards the sand in the box. What happens to the sand in the box? How might this process affect Earth's surface?

CAN YOU EXPLAIN IT?

How was this city suddenly buried without warning?

In the 1700s, scientists in Italy discovered a city that had been buried for over 1,900 years. As they dug down to see more and more of the city, it appeared that the city had been buried very suddenly. They discovered that the buildings and other structures were still standing, and there were cavities in the ground in the shapes of people and animals all over the city. The city's inhabitants had been buried suddenly, and over hundreds of years the bodies had decayed. Scientists began filling the cavities with plaster or cement and letting it dry. Then they carefully removed the material around the cement so they could see the shape of the cavity. One of these cement casts is shown in the photo.

1. What could have buried this city and its inhabitants so suddenly?

EVIDENCE NOTEBOOK As you explore this lesson, gather evidence to help explain what could have suddenly buried this ancient city.

Lesson 2 Natural Hazards Disrupt Earth's Surface 445

EXPLORATION 1

Describing Natural Hazards and Natural Disasters

A naturally occurring event that can have a negative effect on humans or the environment is called a **natural hazard**. Natural hazards include floods, storms, droughts, avalanches, wildfires, earthquakes, tsunamis, hurricanes, tornadoes, and volcanic eruptions. Natural hazards also include the spread of disease and space-related hazards, such as meteorite impacts. Humans cannot control the causes of natural hazards, but some human activities may influence the intensity and frequency of some natural hazards. Understanding these events can help humans find ways to make these events less destructive. Humans can identify areas where natural hazards are likely to occur and find ways to prepare for these events.

Natural Hazard Risk in the United States

This map shows where the risk is greatest for tornadoes, hurricanes, and earthquakes.

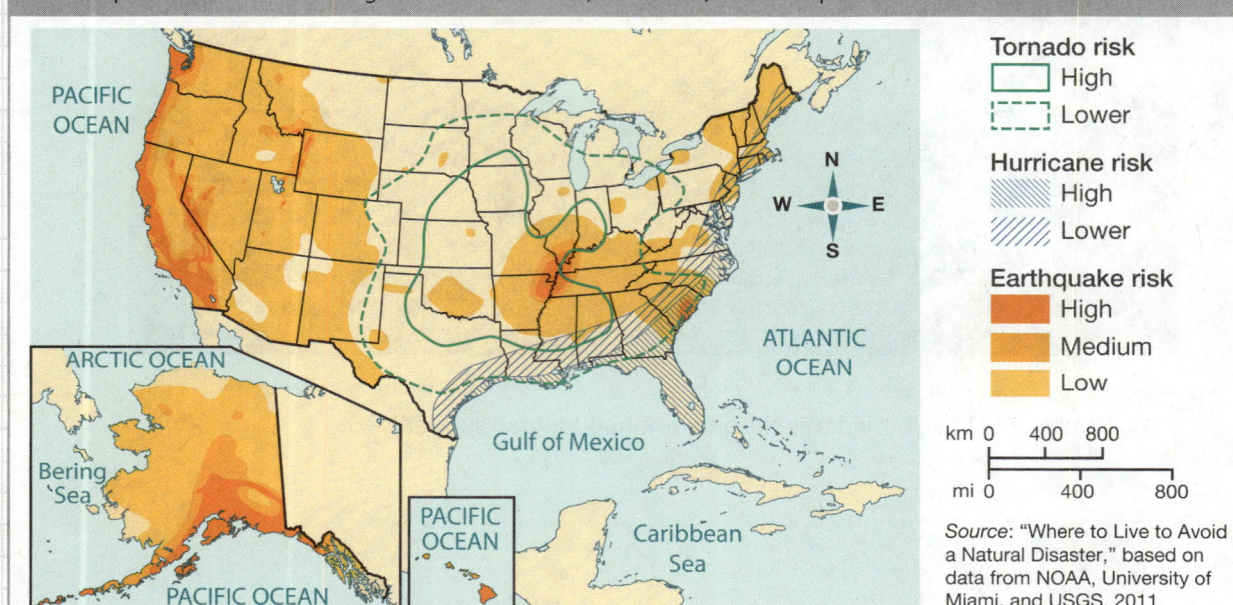

Source: "Where to Live to Avoid a Natural Disaster," based on data from NOAA, University of Miami, and USGS, 2011

Earthquakes are sudden, short-term, geologic events in which the ground shakes violently.

Hurricanes are massive storms that are characterized by high winds, heavy rain, and coastal flooding.

Tornadoes are weather events that involve strong, rotating winds and may involve hail and rain.

2. **Discuss** Do any of the natural hazards shown on the map occur where you live? Do you know why or why not? Discuss your ideas with a partner.

446 Unit 6 Earth's Surface and Society

Natural Hazards and Natural Disasters

Any natural hazard can become a **natural disaster** if it causes widespread injury, death, property damage, or damage to an ecosystem. A natural disaster may occur in only one small area, or it may cover large areas—even several countries. As the human population increases, the number of natural disasters increases as well. Whenever a natural hazard affects a heavily populated area, the chance of it becoming a natural disaster increases. For example, a heavy rain that would soak into the ground may cause a flood in an area that has been covered in roads and buildings.

3. Label each photo to show whether it is a *natural hazard* or a *natural disaster*.

[natural hazard]

Sometimes, hurricanes occur over the ocean and never reach land. This satellite image shows several large hurricanes. Hawaii is in the middle of the image.

[natural disaster]

Hurricanes with strong winds and heavy rain can cause flooding and structural damage if they reach land. This photo shows Hurricane Isaac when it struck Gulfport, Mississippi, in 2012.

Lesson 2 Natural Hazards Disrupt Earth's Surface **447**

Types of Natural Hazards

There are many types of natural hazards. Weather hazards include thunderstorms, tropical storms, lightning, and tornadoes. Too much rain can cause floods, erosion, and landslides. Too little rain can cause droughts, which are climate hazards that can disrupt ecosystems. Geologic hazards include earthquakes and volcanic eruptions. Earthquakes can cause ground shaking, landslides, and tsunamis. Volcanic eruptions can bring molten rock, hot gases, and volcanic ash to Earth's surface. Other types of natural hazards include wildfires, space-related hazards such as asteroid impacts, and widespread diseases. Sometimes natural hazards are related to each other. For example, an area is more likely to have wildfires during a drought. Earthquakes can cause tsunamis that rapidly flood coastal areas.

Worldwide Natural Disasters, 1995–2015		
Natural hazard type	Number of occurrences	Percentage of total (%)
Flood	3,062	43
Storm	2,018	28
Earthquake	562	8
Extreme temperature	405	6
Landslide	387	5
Drought	334	5
Wildfire	251	3
Volcanic eruption	111	2

Source: The Centre for Research on the Epidemiology of Disasters, United Nations Office for Disaster Risk Reduction, *The Human Cost of Weather Related Disasters, 1995–2015*

4. **Draw** Create a circle graph or another type of graphic to show what percentage of all worldwide natural disasters each hazard type represents.

448 Unit 6 Earth's Surface and Society

Geologic Hazards

Geologic hazards are caused by geologic processes such as tectonic plate motion or erosion. Some geologic hazards, such as landslides, earthquakes, tsunamis, and volcanic eruptions, can happen quickly or without warning.

When groundwater dissolves rock below the surface, the ground can suddenly collapse to form a *sinkhole*.

Earthquakes occur when slabs of Earth's crust move and release energy, causing violent shaking.

A *tsunami* is a powerful wave caused by movement of ocean water after an earthquake, a landslide, or an eruption.

Weather and Climate Hazards

Weather describes the conditions in the atmosphere at any given time. *Climate* describes long-term weather patterns. Weather and climate hazards include droughts, hurricanes, tornadoes, blizzards, severe thunderstorms, and floods. Severe storms can have heavy rain, lightning, high winds, and hail, and they can lead to tornadoes and floods.

When heavy rain cannot soak into the ground it runs over Earth's surface and causes a *flood*.

During a *drought*, too little rain causes the land to dry out, and plants are unable to get the water they need.

Very cold temperatures and strong winds combined with extreme amounts of snowfall cause a *blizzard*.

EVIDENCE NOTEBOOK

5. What kinds of natural hazards could suddenly bury a city and the people who live there? Record your evidence.

Natural Hazard Data

Historical data from past natural hazards help us understand the causes and effects of natural hazards and allow us to see patterns in hazard occurrences. Depending on the natural hazard, data could include location, time, and duration. It may also include *frequency*, or how often events occur, and *magnitude*, or how large events are. These data help researchers identify how human activity may affect the magnitude and frequency of some natural hazards. Current conditions are also monitored to learn about natural hazards. For example, weather instruments collect data on current atmospheric conditions. Meteorologists analyze these data to determine when and where a storm might occur.

6. **Discuss** Look at the data in the two maps. Is there a correlation between historic earthquake locations and earthquake hazard level?

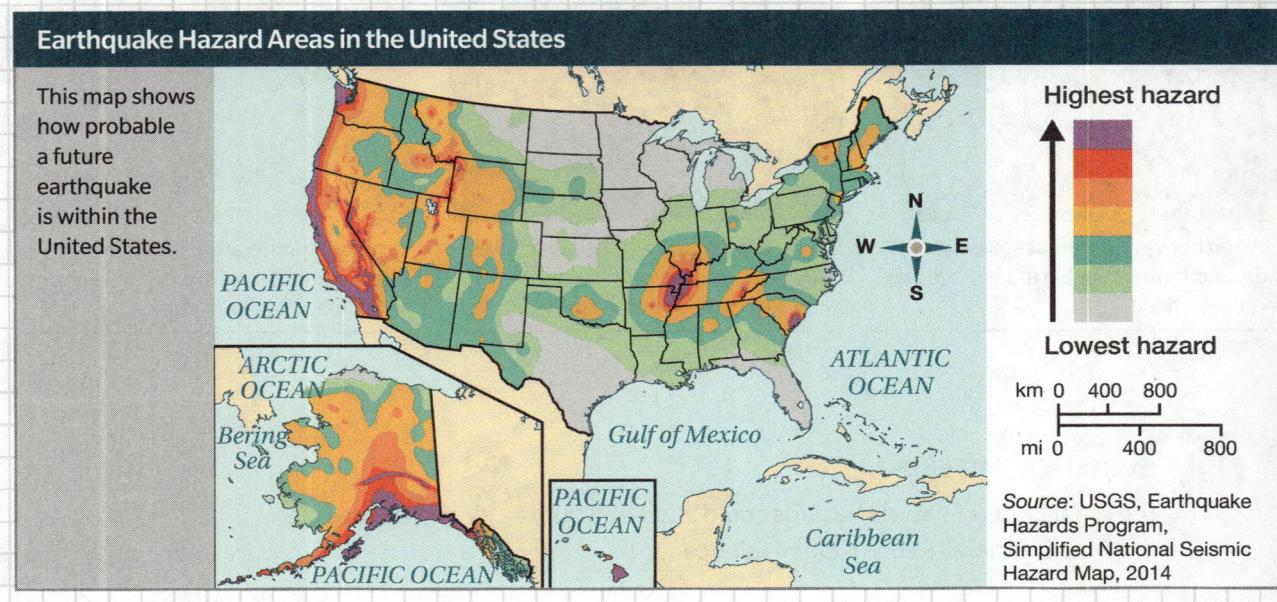

Historic Earthquakes in the United States

This map shows the locations of some significant earthquakes that have happened in the United States since the 1800s. It also shows the locations of tectonic plate boundaries.

Source: U.S. Geological Survey

Earthquake Hazard Areas in the United States

This map shows how probable a future earthquake is within the United States.

Source: USGS, Earthquake Hazards Program, Simplified National Seismic Hazard Map, 2014

450 Unit 6 Earth's Surface and Society

Do the Math
Interpret Natural Disaster Data

The table shows the number of people affected by weather and climate disasters.

Effects of Weather and Climate Disasters Worldwide, 1995–2015	
Natural hazard type	Number of people affected (excluding deaths)
Flood	2,300,000,000
Drought	1,100,000,000
Storm	660,000,000
Extreme temperatures	94,000,000
Landslide and wildfire	8,000,000

Source: The Centre for Research on the Epidemiology of Disasters, United Nations Office for Disaster Risk Reduction, *The Human Cost of Weather Related Disasters, 1995–2015*

7. One researcher claimed, "Between 1995 and 2015, more than twice as many people were affected by floods as were affected by all of the other natural hazard types combined."

   STEP 1 Use the variables to write an expression to represent the researcher's claim. You can divide the number of people affected by floods by the total number of people affected by other natural hazard types.

   $$\frac{\text{number affected by floods}}{(\text{number affected by other natural hazard types})} = \underline{}$$

   f = number affected by floods
   a = number affected by all other natural hazard types combined

   STEP 2 Simplify the expression by dividing. Round to the nearest hundredth.

   STEP 3 Do the data support the researcher's claim? Explain.

8. Based on your results, do you think the researcher should reword the claim? Explain.

Lesson 2 Natural Hazards Disrupt Earth's Surface

EXPLORATION 2

Interpreting Patterns in Volcanic Data

A *volcano* is a place where molten rock and gases can rise from Earth's interior to the surface. Volcanoes are located on continents and at the bottom of the ocean. Some volcanoes are tall mountains, while others are just cracks in Earth's surface. A *volcanic eruption* is a geologic hazard in which molten rock—called *magma* or *lava*—gases, ash, and other materials are released onto Earth's surface and into the atmosphere.

9. Match these terms to the photos: explosive, quiet.

A. During _____ eruptions, lava oozes downhill.

B. During _____ eruptions, lava, ash, and gases shoot into the air.

Volcanic Eruptions

When a volcano erupts, molten rock reaches Earth's surface. Once at the surface, the molten rock is called *lava*. Not all volcanic eruptions are the same. Some are explosive, forcefully throwing hot lava, ash, and gases into the air. Volcanic eruptions may also be quiet or slow, with lava oozing out and flowing downhill.

Volcanoes erupt on Earth every day, but most eruptions are small or far from human populations. Only some of Earth's volcanoes have erupted in the past 10,000 years. These are considered *active volcanoes*. Those that have not erupted in the past 10,000 years are considered *dormant volcanoes*. If geologists agree that a volcano is not likely to erupt ever again, it is considered an *extinct volcano*.

Volcano Classification and Volcanic Hazards

Volcanic eruptions are natural disasters when they cause property damage, injury, or death. Lava flows can burn down structures and start wildfires. Gases can cause breathing issues. A dense cloud of hot ash over 1,000 °C can flow along the ground. This is called a *pyroclastic flow*. Heat from volcanoes can melt ice and snow and form a mudflow called a *lahar*. Both pyroclastic flows and lahars move rapidly downhill and disrupt ecosystems. Ash from explosive eruptions can be spread by wind in the atmosphere and partially block sunlight, lowering Earth's temperature over a period of months to years. Volcanic ash can also contaminate water supplies. Large eruptions may cause earthquakes and tsunamis. Shaking from earthquakes can damage buildings and roads. *Tsunamis* are powerful ocean waves that can flood coastal areas.

Volcanic Explosivity Index (VEI)			
VEI number	Type of eruption	Minimum volume of material erupted (cubic kilometers, km³)	Eruption cloud height (km)
0	nonexplosive	0.000001	<0.1
1	gentle	0.00001	0.1–1
2	explosive	0.001	1–5
3	severe	0.01	3–15
4	cataclysmic	0.1	10–25
5	paroxysmal	1	>25
6	colossal	10	>25
7	super-colossal	100	>25
8	mega-colossal	1,000	>25

Scientists compare the magnitudes of volcanic eruptions by using the Volcanic Explosivity Index (VEI). The scale starts at 0 and has no upper limit. The largest known eruption had a magnitude of 8.

Source: USGS, "How Big Are Eruptions?" 2017

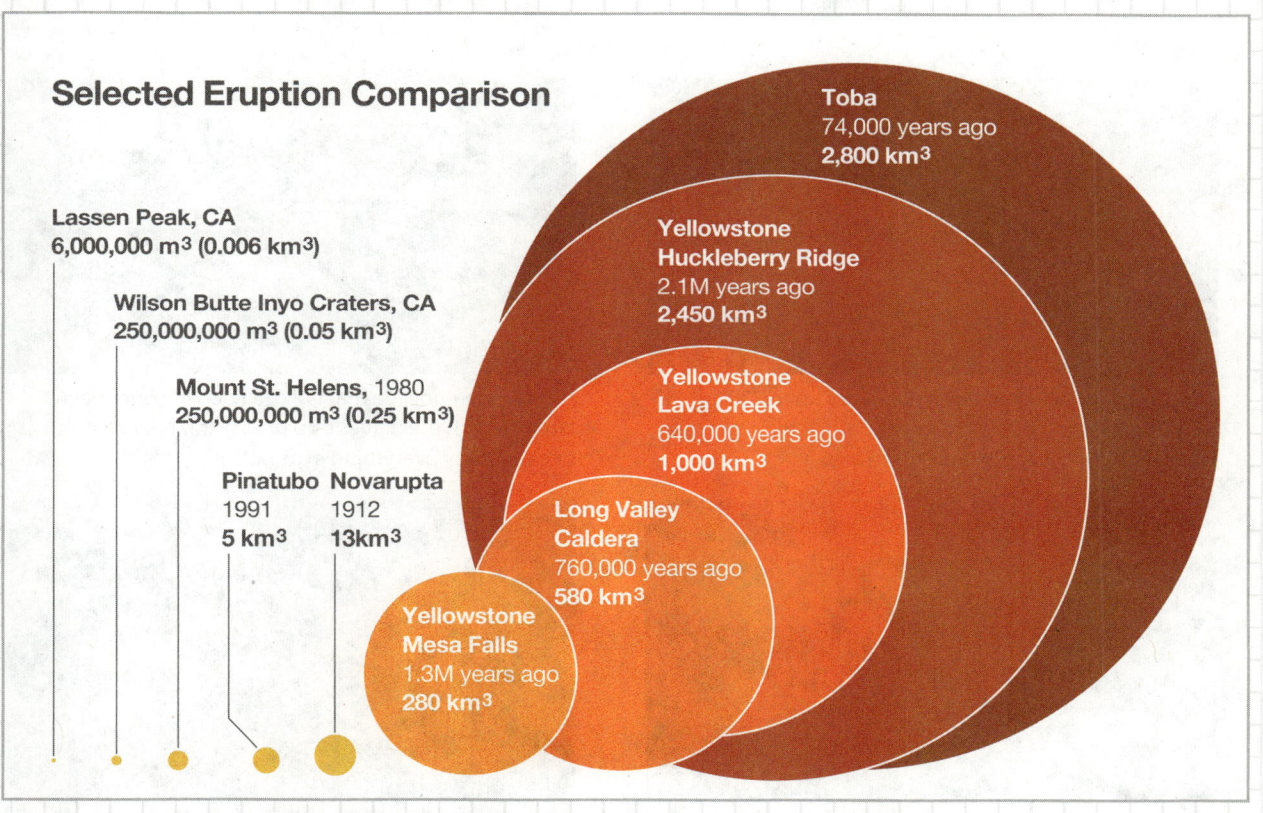

Selected Eruption Comparison

Lassen Peak, CA
6,000,000 m³ (0.006 km³)

Wilson Butte Inyo Craters, CA
250,000,000 m³ (0.05 km³)

Mount St. Helens, 1980
250,000,000 m³ (0.25 km³)

Pinatubo 1991
5 km³

Novarupta 1912
13 km³

Yellowstone Mesa Falls
1.3M years ago
280 km³

Long Valley Caldera
760,000 years ago
580 km³

Yellowstone Lava Creek
640,000 years ago
1,000 km³

Yellowstone Huckleberry Ridge
2.1M years ago
2,450 km³

Toba
74,000 years ago
2,800 km³

Source: USGS, Yellowstone Volcano Observatory, "How Much Magma Erupts?" 2015

10. Use the table and the chart to complete the sentence. Mount Pinatubo erupted in 1991, as a(n) _____ on the VEI and is therefore categorized as a(n) _____ eruption.

Lesson 2 Natural Hazards Disrupt Earth's Surface 453

Volcanic Hazards

The diagram and photos illustrate some of the hazards associated with a volcanic eruption.

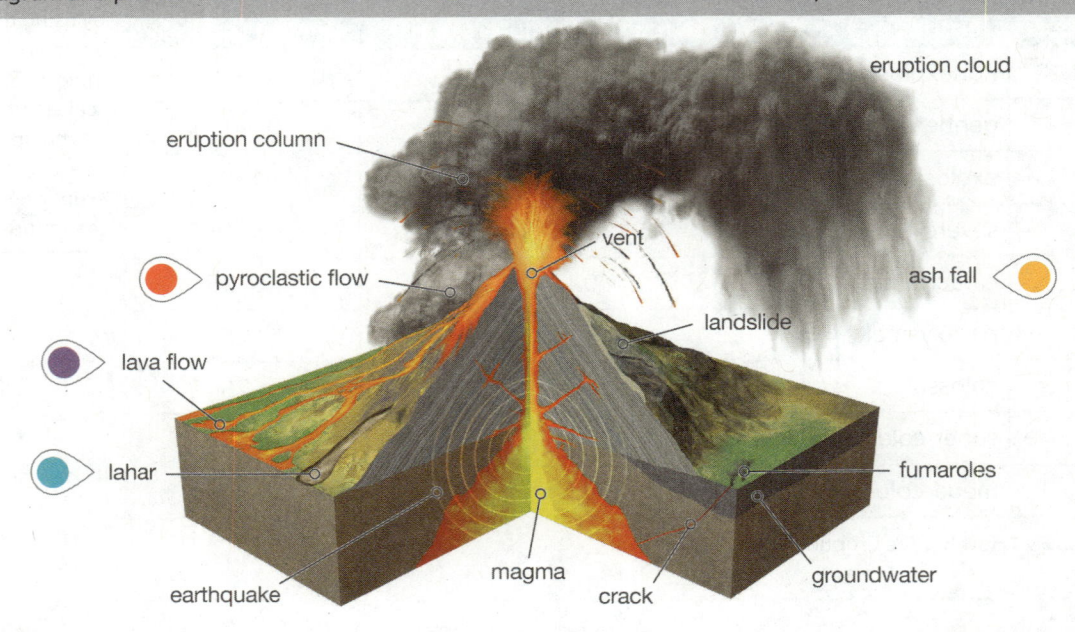

Diagram labels: eruption cloud, eruption column, vent, pyroclastic flow, ash fall, lava flow, landslide, lahar, fumaroles, earthquake, magma, crack, groundwater

A *pyroclastic flow* can travel at speeds of up to 700 km/h and kill or destroy everything in its path. It may take many years for the local ecosystem to recover.

A *lahar* is a mudslide that is like a flood of concrete. A lahar can travel at speeds up to 200 km/h and can crush or carry away everything in its path.

Lava can surround and cover objects in its path. When lava cools, the objects are buried under hardened rock. Lava can flow at speeds up to 60 km/h and can also trigger wildfires.

As volcanic ash falls from the sky for hours to weeks after an eruption, it can bury everything, including buildings, homes, forests, and crops.

EVIDENCE NOTEBOOK

11. Could a volcanic eruption suddenly bury a city and its inhabitants? Record your evidence.

Hands-On Lab
Assess Building Sites Near a Volcano

You will assess potential building sites near an active volcano.

Kilauea (kee•low•AY•uh) volcano, located on the Big Island of Hawaii, has been erupting constantly since 1983. Lava has been continually flowing out of vents, or cracks, on the side of the volcano. Depending on where the lava is flowing from and the shape of the land it flows over, the direction of the lava flow changes. The volume of lava can also change.

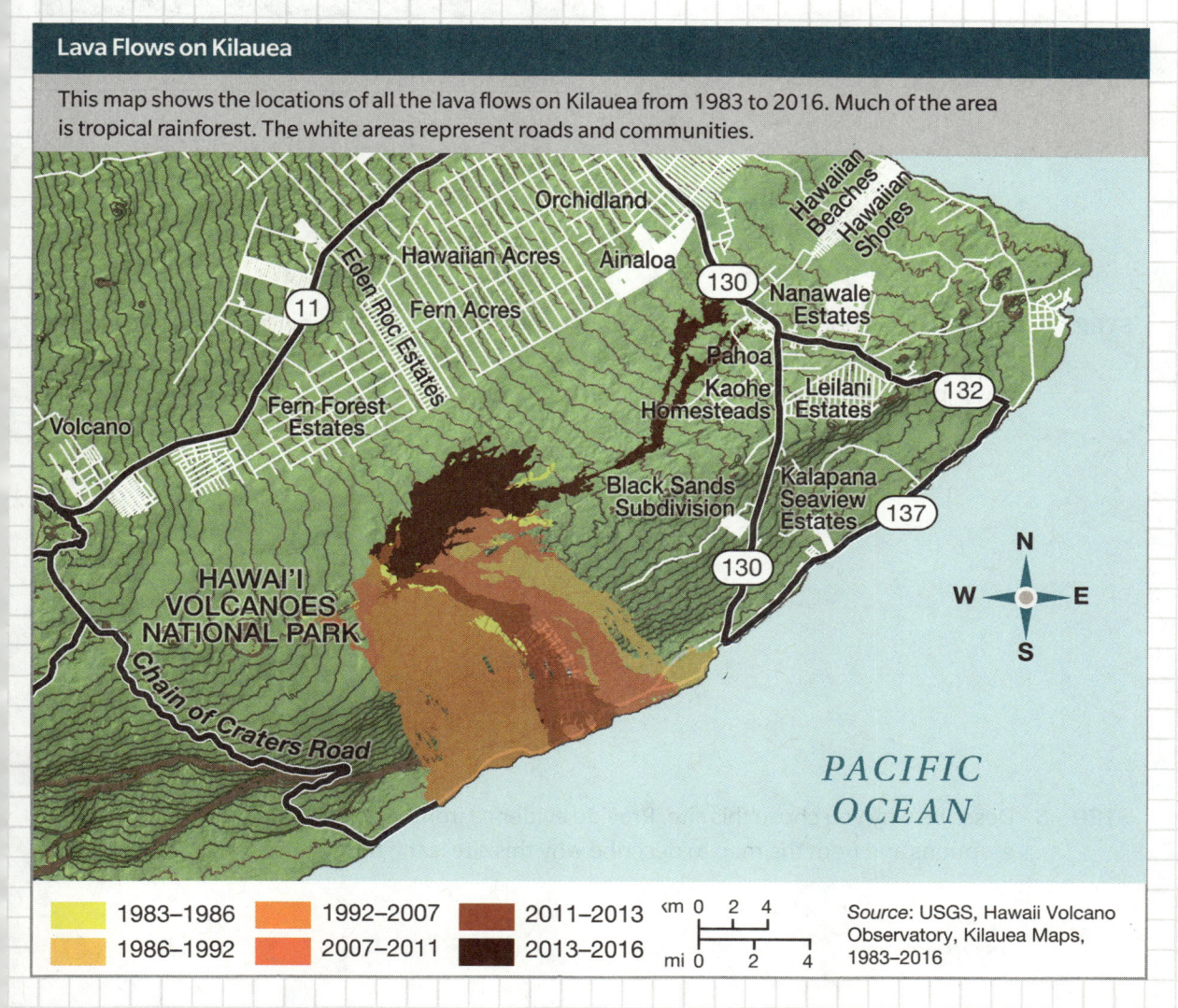

Lava Flows on Kilauea

This map shows the locations of all the lava flows on Kilauea from 1983 to 2016. Much of the area is tropical rainforest. The white areas represent roads and communities.

Legend:
- 1983–1986
- 1986–1992
- 1992–2007
- 2007–2011
- 2011–2013
- 2013–2016

Source: USGS, Hawaii Volcano Observatory, Kilauea Maps, 1983–2016

Procedure and Analysis

STEP 1 Use the map to identify where and when past lava flows occurred.

STEP 2 In the past, Kilauea has had many devastating and deadly eruptions. Today, the eruption of Kilauea is quiet rather than explosive. Hazards associated with the current type of eruption of Kilauea include poisonous _____ around the crater, _____ that burn vegetation and structures, and _____ that flows downhill.

WORD BANK
- wildfires
- lava
- gases

Lesson 2 Natural Hazards Disrupt Earth's Surface **455**

Engineer It

STEP 3 Imagine that a developer wants to build a hotel near the national park. What factors should the developer consider when deciding where to build? How would these factors affect where the hotel is built?

These homes near the town of Pahoa were destroyed by lava flowing from Kilauea in 2014.

STEP 4 Use the map to identify the best places to build the hotel. Select a building site that would be at a relatively low risk from the hazards of the volcano. Describe its location on the map.

STEP 5 Describe why you chose this site. Provide evidence from your knowledge of eruptions and from the map to describe why this site is the best choice.

Do the Math
Analyze Eruption Data

Although every volcanic eruption is different, scientists can compare the explosiveness, frequency, and size of volcanic eruptions. The table compares eruption size to eruption frequency and provides examples of volcanoes that fall into each category.

Mount Vesuvius, on the coast of Italy, has produced eight major eruptions within the last 17,000 years. These eruptions have included lava, pyroclastic flows, and ash clouds.

Volcanic Eruption Frequency and Size		
Eruption size (km^3)	Eruption frequency (approximate)	Volcano example(s)
< 0.001	Daily	Kilauea, Stromboli
0.001–0.01	Weekly to monthly	Etna
0.01–0.1	Annually	St. Helens (1980)
1–10	Once every 10 to 100 years	Pinatubo (1991), Vesuvius (79)
10–100	Once every 100 to 1,000 years	Krakatau (1883), Katmai (1912)
100–1,000	Once every 1,000 to 10,000 years	Tambora (1815)
> 1,000	Once or twice every 100,000 years	Yellowstone, Toba

Source: USGS, "How Big Are Eruptions?" 2017

12. Look at the table. Eruption size is the volume of material erupted. Eruption frequency is approximately how often an eruption of that size occurs. How would you describe the relationship between eruption size and eruption frequency?

Lesson 2 Natural Hazards Disrupt Earth's Surface

EXPLORATION 3

Interpreting Patterns in Tornado Data

A *tornado* is a rapidly spinning column of air extending from a storm cloud to the ground. Tornadoes are weather hazards that are most common in spring and summer. This time of year is sometimes referred to as "tornado season."

This mobile Doppler radar truck was used to collect data from a storm in Nebraska that caused several tornadoes like the one shown in the inset. These data help scientists better understand how, when, and where tornadoes form and end.

Tornadoes

Severe thunderstorms can bring heavy rain, hail, high winds—and tornadoes. Tornadoes can develop when rotating thunderstorms, called *supercells*, occur. However, not all supercells form tornadoes. A combination of factors must be present for a tornado to form. A body of warm, moist air must collide with a body of cooler, drier air. As a result, winds at different altitudes blow at different speeds and cause a column of air in the thunderstorm to spin. Because the air pressure is low in the middle of the spinning column, air in the middle of the column rises. The result is that the spinning column of air rotates in a vertical direction and drops below the thunderstorm to form a funnel cloud. When the funnel cloud touches the ground, it becomes a tornado.

A tornado can last anywhere from a few seconds to more than an hour. Most tornadoes last less than ten minutes. More than 1,000 tornadoes occur in the United States each year, but they are not evenly distributed across the country. Most tornadoes occur in the middle of continents. In the United States, the area where most tornadoes happen is called "Tornado Alley." You can find out about the average number of tornadoes per year in each state by studying the map.

> **EVIDENCE NOTEBOOK**
> **13.** As you explore this section, think about whether a tornado could suddenly bury a city and its inhabitants. Record your evidence.

Average Annual Number of Tornadoes in the United States, 1991–2010

14. This map shows the average number of tornadoes per year in each state. Color in the ten states that have the highest average number of tornadoes.

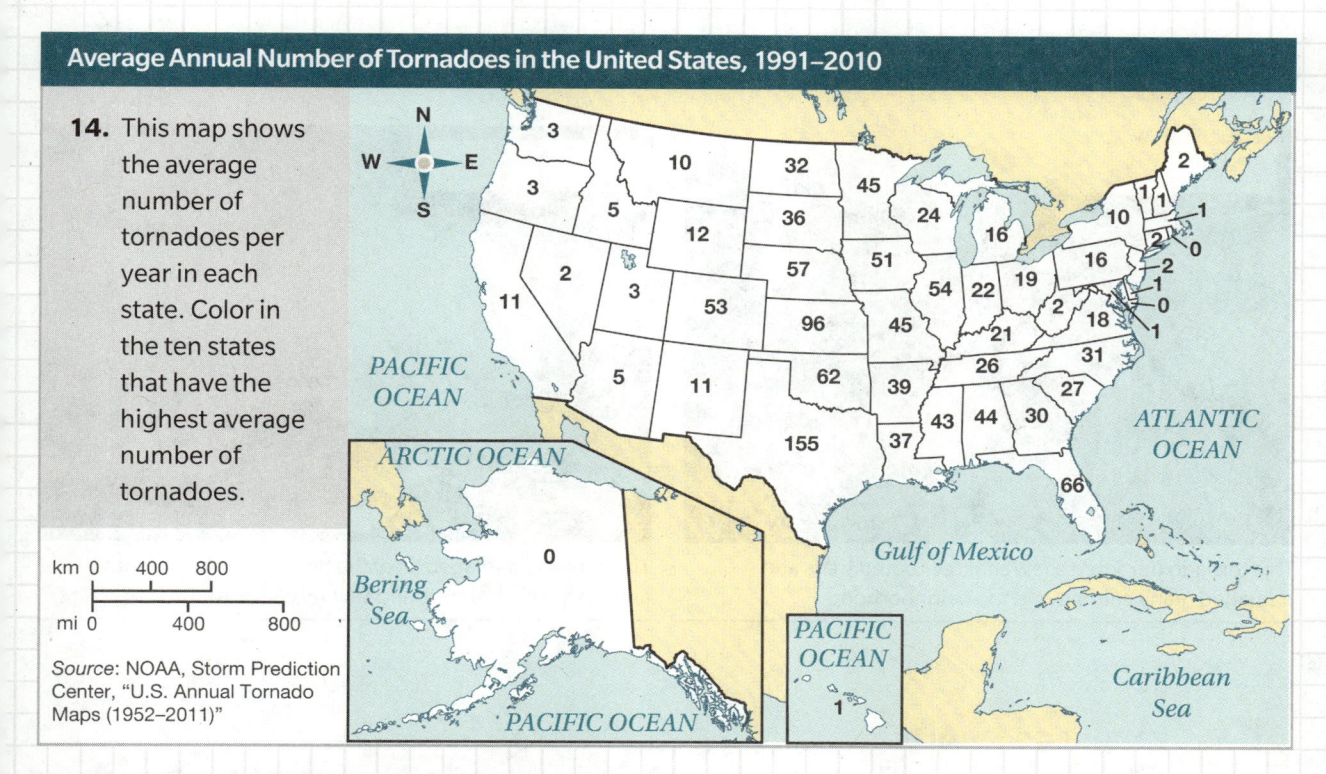

Source: NOAA, Storm Prediction Center, "U.S. Annual Tornado Maps (1952–2011)"

Tornado Classification and Hazards

When a tornado strikes a populated area and is strong enough, it can cause damage, injury, or death. Its strong winds destroy many objects in its path, including buildings, roads, trees, crops, and sometimes people and other animals. A tornado that causes these types of damage is considered a natural disaster.

Meteorologists collect tornado data, such as a tornado's path, wind speeds, duration, and temperatures. These data are organized into tables, graphs, and maps and then analyzed to help us understand the causes of tornadoes and their effects on people and the environment. Tornado data are also analyzed to identify areas at risk for tornado hazards and to make predictions about when and where tornadoes might occur. The Enhanced Fujita (foo•JEE•tuh) Scale, also known as the EF Scale, describes tornado damage.

The Enhanced Fujita Scale		
EF rating	Wind speeds (km/h)	Expected damage
EF-0	105–137	Chimneys damaged; tree branches broken; shallow-rooted trees toppled.
EF-1	142–177	Roof surfaces peeled off; windows broken; some tree trunks snapped; garages may be destroyed.
EF-2	179–217	Roofs damaged; manufactured homes destroyed; trees snapped or uprooted; debris entered air.
EF-3	219–265	Roofs and walls torn from buildings; some small buildings destroyed; most forest trees uprooted.
EF-4	267–322	Well-built homes destroyed; cars lifted and blown some distance; large debris flew through the air.
EF-5	Over 322	Strong houses lifted, concrete structures damaged; very large debris flew through the air; trees debarked.

Source: NOAA

Lesson 2 Natural Hazards Disrupt Earth's Surface

15. These photos show different places where a tornado occurred. How would you rate the damage caused by each tornado based on the Enhanced Fujita (EF) Scale?

This tornado uprooted a few shallow-rooted trees and damaged many chimneys in the neighborhood.

This tornado damaged all of the homes in this community and tossed large debris and several cars through the air.

Language SmArts
Compare Tornado Data

16. A researcher wants to collect tornado data from the three states where tornado risk is highest. Where and when should the researcher collect data? Support your claim by citing evidence from this graph and from the map of tornadoes in the United States.

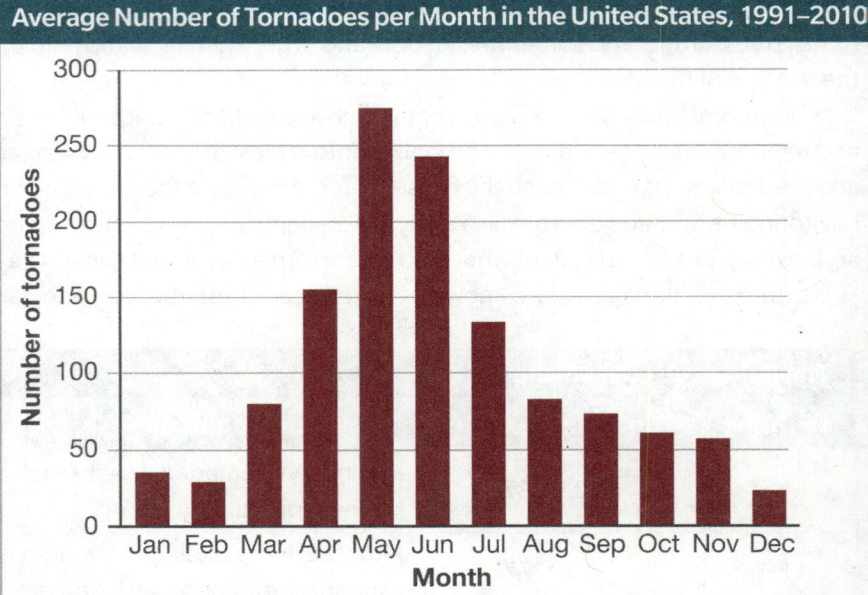

Average Number of Tornadoes per Month in the United States, 1991–2010

Source: NOAA, National Climatic Data Center, "U.S. Tornado Climatology, Historical Records and Trends," 2011

460 Unit 6 Earth's Surface and Society

TAKE IT FURTHER

Continue Your Exploration

Name: _____ Date: _____

Check out the path below or go online to choose one of the other paths shown.

The Cost of Natural Disasters
- People in Science
- Forest Fires
- Hands-On Labs
- Propose Your Own Path

Go online to choose one of these other paths.

Natural disasters can destroy homes, buildings, crops, and sources of clean water. They can also cause injury and death. It can be very costly to repair the damage caused by a natural disaster. The cost can be determined by considering many factors, such as

- What was damaged or destroyed?
- Do the inhabitants of the area need to have those objects or systems repaired or replaced?
- What can be repaired and what must be replaced?
- What materials and labor are needed to repair or replace objects or systems?

Once the necessary work is identified, someone will have to pay for it. The costs are paid by insurance companies; local, state, and federal agencies; government disaster relief programs; nonprofit organizations, and the individuals who live in the area.

Natural Disasters in the United States

In 2015, one of the most expensive types of natural disaster in the United States was the tropical cyclone. *Tropical cyclone* is a term used by scientists to refer to any rotating, organized storm that starts over tropical waters. Environmental changes resulting from rising temperatures have increased the frequency and intensity of tropical cyclones.

These storms cause massive and widespread destruction by bringing high winds, heavy rains, and possible tornadoes and flooding to large areas. The wind and flooding from *tropical cyclones* can affect people in populated areas by damaging buildings, roads, dams, sea walls, and other structures along coastlines and waterways.

These men are pushing a vehicle off a flooded road in Houston, Texas, after heavy rains fell during Hurricane Harvey.

Lesson 2 Natural Hazards Disrupt Earth's Surface **461**

TAKE IT FURTHER

Continue Your Exploration

Billion-Dollar Weather and Climate Disasters in the United States, 1980–2016

Disaster type	Number of events	Cost of damage (in billions of dollars)
Tropical cyclone	35	560.1
Drought/heat wave	24	223.8
Severe local storm	83	180.1
Nontropical flood	26	110.7
Winter storm	14	41.3
Wildfire	14	33.0
Freeze	7	25.3

Source: NOAA National Centers for Environmental Information (NCEI), U.S. Billion-Dollar Weather and Climate Disasters, January 2017

1. **Do the Math** Compare the cost of damage caused by tropical cyclones and by severe local storms, and compare the number of each of those events. Was the average cost of damage per event higher for tropical cyclones or for severe local storms?

2. How could you explain this difference?

3. Which costs would be associated with a severe freeze in an apple orchard? Select all that apply.
   A. recovering from the cost of a loss of apples
   B. replacing damaged or destroyed trees
   C. repairing irrigation lines that burst when they froze
   D. buying new harvesting equipment

4. **Collaborate** With a partner, discuss ways that encouraging volunteers to participate in recovery efforts could reduce the time for recovering from a natural hazard.

LESSON 2 SELF-CHECK

Can You Explain It?

Name: _____   Date: _____

How was this city suddenly buried without warning?

EVIDENCE NOTEBOOK
Refer to the notes in your Evidence Notebook to help you construct an explanation for what could have suddenly buried this city.

1. State your claim. Make sure your claim fully explains what could have suddenly buried this city and its people, and why the people were unable to escape.

2. Summarize the evidence you have gathered to support your claim and explain your reasoning.

Lesson 2 Natural Hazards Disrupt Earth's Surface **463**

LESSON 2 SELF-CHECK

Checkpoints

Answer the following questions to check your understanding of the lesson.

3. A volcanic eruption produces a pyroclastic flow, a dense cloud of hot ash. How might the pyroclastic flow disrupt the local ecosystem? Select all that apply.
   - **A.** by partially blocking the sunlight to the area
   - **B.** by contaminating water supplies in the area
   - **C.** by killing all of the vegetation in its path
   - **D.** by damaging roads and buildings in its path

Use the photo to answer Question 4.

4. Which of the following natural hazards could have caused the ash damage in this photo? Select all that apply.
   - **A.** flood
   - **B.** hurricane
   - **C.** volcanic eruption
   - **D.** earthquake
   - **E.** wildfire

Use the graph to answer Questions 5–6.

5. Which of the following statements is true?
   - **A.** The number of tornadoes per year remains about the same.
   - **B.** The number of tornadoes per year varies from year to year.
   - **C.** The number of tornadoes per year is increasing each year.
   - **D.** The number of tornadoes per year is decreasing each year.

6. Which of the following periods had the fewest tornadoes?
   - **A.** 1960–1964
   - **B.** 1970–1974
   - **C.** 1985–1989
   - **D.** 2005–2009

Number of EF-1 and Larger Tornadoes in the United States, 1954–2014

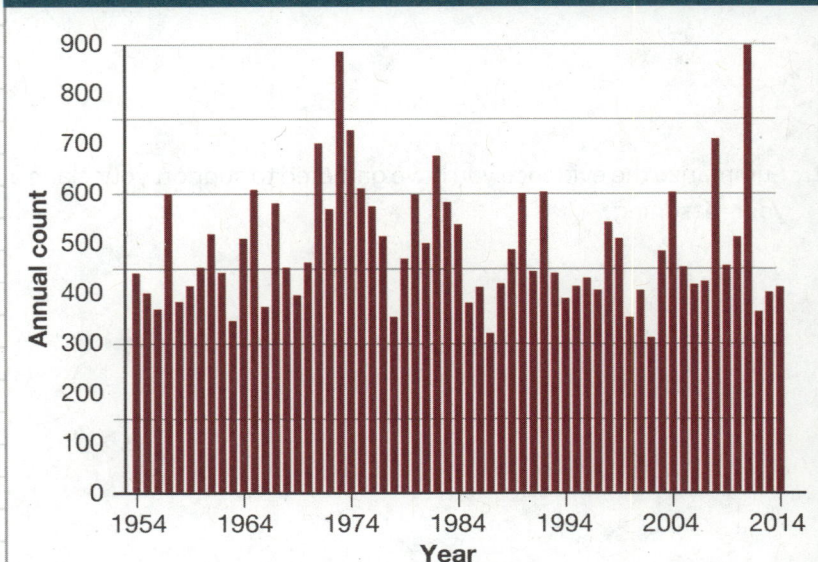

Source: NOAA, National Weather Service Storm Prediction Center, "U.S. Annual Count of EF-1+ Tornadoes, 1954 through 2014"

LESSON 2 SELF-CHECK

Interactive Review

Complete this section to review the main concepts of the lesson.

Natural hazards are naturally occurring events such as wildfires, earthquakes, and hurricanes. Natural disasters are natural hazards that negatively affect humans.

A. Provide two examples of natural hazards that are not natural disasters.

A volcanic eruption is a geologic hazard. Any type of volcanic eruption can become a natural disaster.

B. Describe a volcanic hazard and explain how it could become a natural disaster.

A tornado is a weather hazard that forms quickly and with little warning. A tornado can become a natural disaster.

C. Describe how the terms "Tornado Alley" and "tornado season" are related to the analysis of data about tornadoes.

Lesson 2 Natural Hazards Disrupt Earth's Surface

LESSON 3

Some Natural Hazards Can Be Predicted and Mitigated

This flood in New Jersey was caused by the melting of snow and ice after a major snowstorm. Understanding weather patterns can help people forecast natural hazards like floods.

Explore First

Modeling a Flood What patterns can help us predict when and where a flood might occur? Design a landscape using modeling clay inside a small waterproof container. Use a spray bottle filled with water to model rainfall or pour water slowly from a cup to model a river overflowing its banks. What do you observe as more water is added?

Go online to view the digital version of the Hands-On Lab for this lesson and to download additional lab resources.

CAN YOU EXPLAIN IT?

Why is there a tsunami hazard warning sign on this calm beach?

This beach on the east coast of New Zealand is a popular recreation spot.

1. Some coastal areas are at a higher risk for tsunamis than others are. How do we know which coastal areas are more likely to be affected by tsunamis?

EVIDENCE NOTEBOOK As you explore this lesson, gather evidence to help explain how we know which coastal areas are at risk for tsunamis.

Lesson 3 Some Natural Hazards Can Be Predicted and Mitigated 467

EXPLORATION 1

Predicting Natural Hazards

If the sky is full of dark clouds, you might predict that rain is about to fall. Making predictions is an important part of science. Natural hazard predictions can prevent natural disasters because warnings can be issued to help people prepare.

2. People living near this stream think that if heavy rains continue, the stream will overflow and flood their homes. What information might these people be using to make this prediction?

When it rains, water runs downhill and collects along the lowest elevations in an area, such as this stream.

Natural Hazard Predictions

Natural hazard predictions are efforts to forecast the occurrence, intensity, and effects of natural hazards. Some natural hazards are not predictable. Other hazards follow known patterns, or are preceded by precursor events. If precursor events, or patterns, can be detected far enough in advance, a prediction may be made. For example, a precursor event to a flood may be heavy rainfall over a short period of time. Natural hazard predictions can help people reduce the effects of a natural hazard or even prevent some natural disasters.

Natural hazard predictions involve some uncertainty. Uncertainties can include a hazard's exact location, timing, magnitude, and whether it will actually happen. Certainty generally increases as the time of the predicted event gets closer. Natural hazard predictions are improved by gaining a scientific understanding of hazards, collecting and analyzing data, and using monitoring technology. Advances in science and technology can help improve natural hazard predictions. These advances can help us prepare for the effects of natural hazards. Societal needs, such as keeping people safe, drive development of these advances.

Scientific Understanding

A natural hazard prediction can be improved by gaining scientific understanding of a natural hazard. To gain scientific understanding, you can start by asking questions that can be answered by using scientific methods. For example, if you wanted to understand more about avalanches, you might ask: On which slopes are avalanches most common? What weather conditions are related to avalanches? What types of snow are related to avalanches? To answer these kinds of questions, you can collect and analyze data, use models, or conduct experiments. These practices help scientists better understand natural hazards.

Scientists analyze the snow conditions on slopes to determine how likely an avalanche is to occur.

Historical Data

Historical data are used to evaluate the likelihood that a natural hazard will happen in a given place. Historical data can include the locations of past events, as well as their frequency, magnitude, and effects on the environment and/or people. Some hazards, such as volcanic eruptions, landslides, and earthquakes, tend to occur in specific areas. However, these hazards can happen at any time of the year. Hazards, such as hurricanes and tornadoes, tend to happen in specific places and during specific times of the year.

Historical Hurricane and Tropical Cyclone Paths

The lines on this map show the paths of past hurricanes and tropical cyclones. These data help us identify where hurricanes are likely to occur in the future.

Hurricane Paths
— Hurricane
— Tropical cyclone (intensity below major hurricane)

Atlantic Ocean data: 1851–2013
Pacific Ocean data: 1949–2013

Source: NOAA, Major Hurricane History of the U.S., 2013

Data from Monitoring

Scientists use technology to monitor conditions that relate to the occurrence of natural hazards. For example, satellites orbit Earth and collect weather data. These data go into computer models that help scientists predict weather-related hazards. For hazards that are likely to occur in specific locations, monitoring technology may be designed for and placed in those areas. For example, underwater earthquakes, landslides, and volcanic eruptions can be precursor events to tsunamis. So, scientists monitor ocean water movement after those events in order to predict tsunamis. Tsunami sensors might be put on buoys or on the sea floor to detect water movement in areas at high risk of tsunamis.

This tsunami in Miyako City, Japan, was caused by an earthquake on the ocean floor. The waves arrived less than one hour after the earthquake. Luckily, many people received warnings before the waves struck thanks to monitoring data.

EVIDENCE NOTEBOOK
3. How might scientific understanding, historical data, and monitoring help to determine where tsunami hazard signs should be placed? Record your evidence.

Lesson 3 Some Natural Hazards Can Be Predicted and Mitigated

Hands-On Lab
Predict a Landslide

You will model the relationship between rainfall, hill slope, and landslides.

Heavy rain is forecast for Pineville. Historical data for this area show that heavy rains increase the chance of landslides. Landslides occur when soil and rock slide down a slope and can travel fast and threaten lives and property.

MATERIALS
- duct tape
- gutter, vinyl, U-shaped, 60 cm section (chute)
- plastic scoop
- plastic tub, shallow
- potting soil, saturated
- protractor
- spray bottle

Procedure

STEP 1 Look at the slopes on the map and the slope angles in the table. On which slopes do you predict landslides are likely to occur?

STEP 2 One at a time, model Slopes 1, 2, 3, and 4. Place the chute so one end is at the edge of the plastic tub and tape it to the inside wall of the tub. The other end of the chute should be inside the tub.

STEP 3 To model Slope 1, rest the chute on the edge of the tub. Use the scoop to fill the top $\frac{1}{3}$ of the chute with damp soil.

STEP 4 Outside of the tub and under the chute, set up the protractor to measure the angle between the table and the bottom edge of the chute. Have a partner slowly tilt the chute until the angle is about 10 degrees.

STEP 5 Spray the slope to simulate rainfall until the soil is saturated. Record your observations in the table.

STEP 6 Model Slopes 2, 3, and 4 by repeating STEPS 3–5. Why should you use the same amount of soil and spray the water in a consistent way for all of the trials?

Landslide Model Data

Slope angle (degrees)	Results
Slope 1: 10°	
Slope 2: 15°	
Slope 3: 35°	
Slope 4: 55°	

Landslide Study Area for Pineville

This map shows how the Pineville area is surrounded by hillsides. The hillsides are generally made up of the same type of soil and have little vegetation. Rainfall amounts are even across the area.

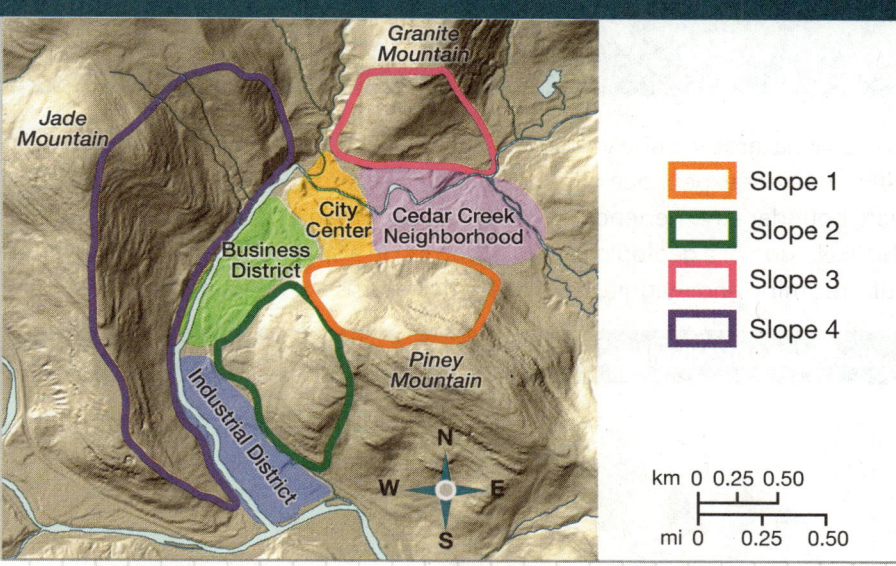

Analysis

STEP 7 Soil on steeper slopes requires less / more rain to result in a landslide than the soil on flatter slopes does.

STEP 8 Compare your prediction to your results. Was your prediction correct?

STEP 9 Based on your model, are any areas in Pineville at risk of damage from a landslide? Explain why or why not.

STEP 10 Evaluate your model. What did your model represent well? What could be changed or added to improve your model?

Engineer It
Designing a Landslide Warning System

4. What information is needed in order to design a landslide warning system that can save lives in Pineville? How would you warn the residents of Pineville that a landslide is likely to occur?

EXPLORATION 2

Predicting Geologic Hazards

Geologic hazards include volcanoes, earthquakes, tsunamis, sinkholes, and landslides. Different areas experience different geologic hazards. For example, areas near tectonic plate boundaries experience more earthquakes than areas far from plate boundaries do. The likelihood of a geologic hazard occurring in a specific location can be determined. But the timing and magnitude of geologic hazards are difficult to predict.

Worldwide Distribution of Earthquakes and Volcanoes

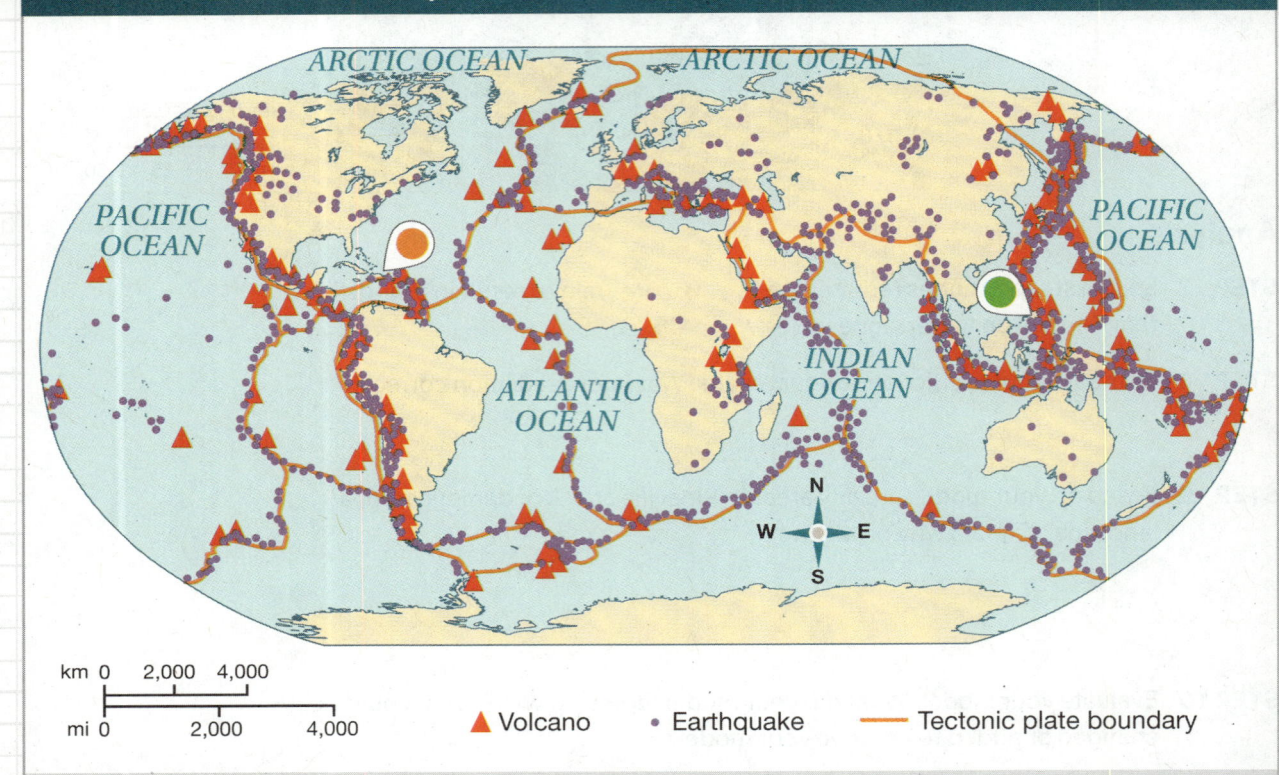

▲ Volcano   • Earthquake   — Tectonic plate boundary

In 2010, a major earthquake shook the ground and toppled buildings in Haiti. Earthquakes happen suddenly and currently cannot be predicted.

Scientists predicted the eruption of Mount Pinatubo in 1991. The predictions helped thousands of people evacuate before falling ash and lahars destroyed villages.

472 Unit 6 Earth's Surface and Society

5. **Discuss** Look at the photo of the effects of the Mount Pinatubo eruption. Predicting volcanic eruptions, such as this one, can save lives and prevent injuries. How do you think scientists predicted this eruption?

Predictions of Volcanic Eruptions

Predictions of volcanic eruptions usually include the likelihood of an eruption within a given time frame. They might also identify possible hazardous effects or related hazards, such as lava flows or wildfires. To determine the likelihood of a volcanic eruption, scientists analyze data, such as the locations of active volcanoes or a certain volcano's past eruptions. Eruption predictions are not always certain because most volcanoes do not erupt on regular schedules. Before some eruptions, specific conditions or precursor events can be identified. Therefore, scientists monitor some volcanoes to watch for changes in conditions and precursor events. Data from monitoring help scientists predict the likelihood of an eruption. However, precursor events and changes in a volcano's conditions may occur without ending in an eruption.

Scientific Understanding

Scientists study the causes and effects of volcanic eruptions. Scientists know that before an eruption, molten rock in Earth's interior, called *magma*, moves closer to the surface. The movement of the magma cracks the surrounding rock and causes swarms of small earthquakes. The moving magma also releases gases into the air and causes the ground surface to change shape.

Scientists study volcanoes to determine whether a volcano is active. They also see whether an eruption could result in a natural disaster. Because scientists have identified where active volcanoes exist around the world, they can identify areas that are at risk for eruption-related natural disasters. For example, the map shows that there are many active volcanoes along the west coasts of North and South America.

This lava flowed over 20 km downhill from the Kilauea volcano. It stopped just outside the town of Pahoa, Hawaii.

Lesson 3 Some Natural Hazards Can Be Predicted and Mitigated 473

Data from Past Eruptions

Past eruption data for a volcano can include eruption timing, precursor events, and eruption types. For example, volcanic rocks and ash layers from past eruptions can tell how often and how explosively a volcano has erupted in the past. This helps scientists determine whether a volcano is active and what type of eruption, if any, is likely to happen in the future. For example, a volcano that explosively erupted and made large amounts of ash in the past most likely will have a similar eruption in the future.

Mauna Loa is an active volcano located on the Big Island of Hawaii. It is a *shield volcano*. This means that it is a broad dome with gently sloping sides. Shield volcanoes often have steady lava flows rather than explosive eruptions. Many eruptions of Mauna Loa have been witnessed by people living in Hawaii. For safety, scientists monitor many active volcanoes near populated areas.

Mauna Loa Eruption Data, 1832–2004

General Information	Eruption History
Location: Mauna Loa, Hawaii	1832, 1843, 1849, 1851, 1852, 1855–1856, 1859, 1865–1866, 1870 (?)*, 1871, 1872, 1873, 1873–1874, 1875, 1876, 1877, 1879, 1880, 1880–1881, 1887, 1892, 1896, 1899, 1903, 1907, 1914–1915, 1916, 1919, 1926, 1933, 1935–1936, 1940, 1950, 1975, 1984
Type and Elevation: Shield volcano, 4,170 m (13,681 ft)	
Eruption Style: Nonexplosive, with steady lava flows	

*The question mark indicates that the exact year of the eruption is not known.
Source: USGS, Hawaii Volcano Observatory, "Summary of Historical Eruptions, 1843–Present", 2004

6. Mauna Loa erupted on average once every four years between 1832 and 1984. From 1870 to 1880, the number of eruptions was **greater / fewer** than average. Beginning in 1940, eruptions were **more / less** frequent than average.

Monitoring Volcanoes

Scientists monitor volcanoes by using technology that detects slight changes in the ground and air around a volcano. They use GPS instruments and thermal imaging sensors set on planes and satellites. These instruments show if magma is moving or if the ground is changing shape. They use *seismometers*, which detect vibrations in the ground, to monitor earthquake activity. Increases in local earthquakes can show movements of magma before a volcanic eruption. Scientists also use *tiltmeters* to monitor changes in the volcano's shape that are related to pressure changes inside the volcano. They also measure the concentration of gases around volcanic vents because the volcano may release more of these gases just before an eruption.

Scientists use tiltmeters to see if a volcano is expanding or shrinking. They use GPS stations to see how much the surface of a volcano is moving.

474 Unit 6 Earth's Surface and Society

Change in Distance Across Mauna Loa's Summit Crater, 2010–2015

GPS units measure the change in distance between Stations 1 and 2.

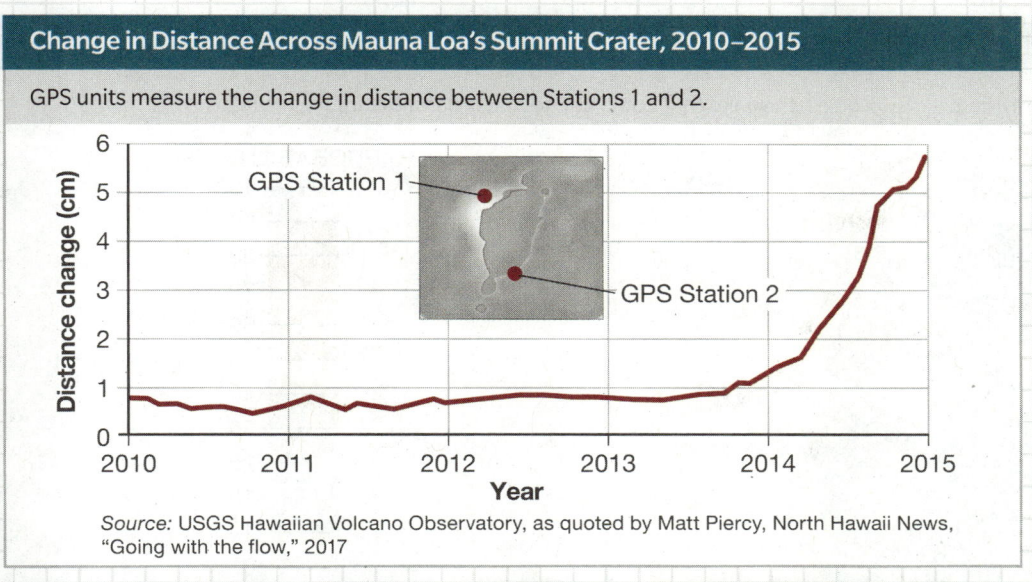

Source: USGS Hawaiian Volcano Observatory, as quoted by Matt Piercy, North Hawaii News, "Going with the flow," 2017

Mauna Loa's Earthquake Activity, 2010–2015

This graph shows the frequency of earthquakes on Mauna Loa.

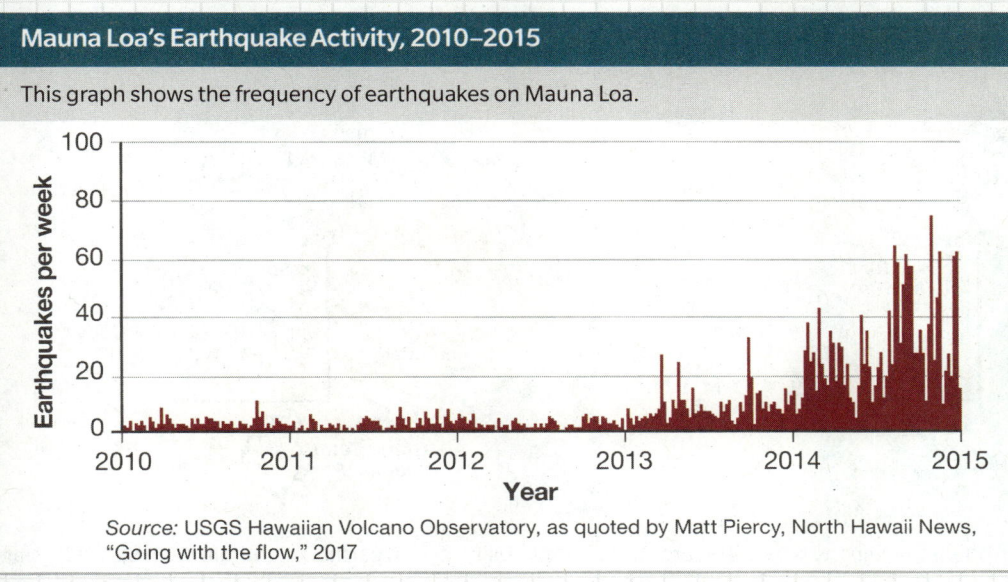

Source: USGS Hawaiian Volcano Observatory, as quoted by Matt Piercy, North Hawaii News, "Going with the flow," 2017

7. The graphs show that Mauna Loa's crater *expanded* / shrank and the number of earthquakes *increased* / decreased.

Earthquake Prediction

Earthquakes can become natural disasters because the shaking can damage structures. Earthquakes can also cause tsunamis, fires, and landslides. Scientists are able to identify areas where earthquakes are likely to happen and cause damage. Scientists use historical data, seismograph data, and GPS data to make earthquake risk maps. These maps show the relative likelihood of an earthquake of a specific size happening in a given area within a given time frame.

EVIDENCE NOTEBOOK

8. What kinds of data might scientists collect in order to identify where tsunamis are likely to occur? How can scientists predict when tsunamis are likely to occur? Record your evidence.

Lesson 3 Some Natural Hazards Can Be Predicted and Mitigated 475

Probability of a Magnitude 7.0 Earthquake near Yellowstone National Park

A magnitude 7.0 earthquake is a large earthquake that could cause major damage, injury, or death.

Probability of a 7.0 earthquake within the next 100 years.

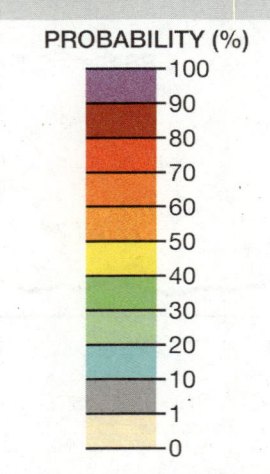

Probability of a 7.0 earthquake within the next 500 years.

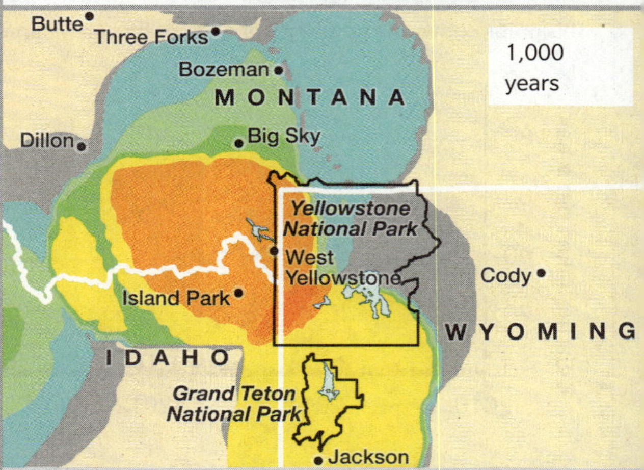

Probability of a 7.0 earthquake within the next 1,000 years.

Source: USGS, Geologic Hazards Science Center, National Seismic Hazard Mapping Project, 2009

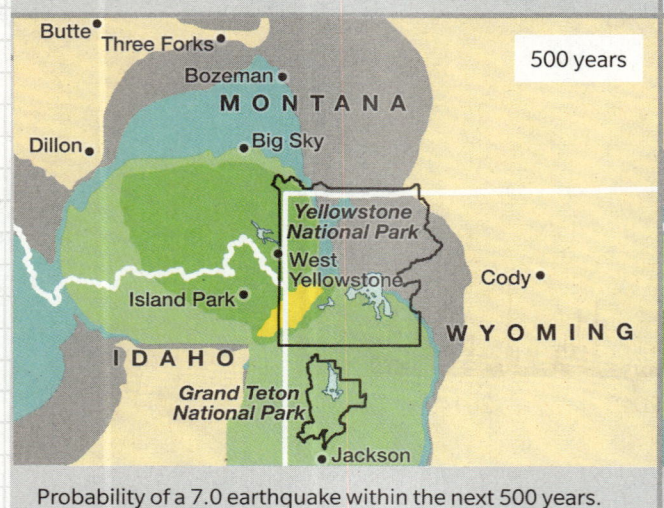

9. The probability of a magnitude 7.0 earthquake happening in Bozeman, Montana, in the next 100 years is 0–1% / 1–10% / 10–20%.

Do the Math
Explain Earthquake Probability

10. Choose Big Sky, Island Park, or Jackson. Use the key to explain how the chance of a magnitude 7.0 earthquake relates to the length of time for which the projection is made for the town you have chosen.

___

476 Unit 6 Earth's Surface and Society

EXPLORATION 3

Predicting Weather and Climate Hazards

Weather hazards include thunderstorms, snowstorms, tornadoes, and floods. These hazards occur in locations where the atmosphere, ocean, and land interact to create specific conditions. Weather predictions describe what the weather is likely to be on a particular day. A weather-hazard prediction indicates when and where dangerous weather conditions are likely to develop. Warnings about weather hazards are issued only minutes to days before a potential event.

Climate hazards are large-scale phenomena that are related to long-term weather patterns. Climate hazards include droughts, sea-level changes, and wildfires.

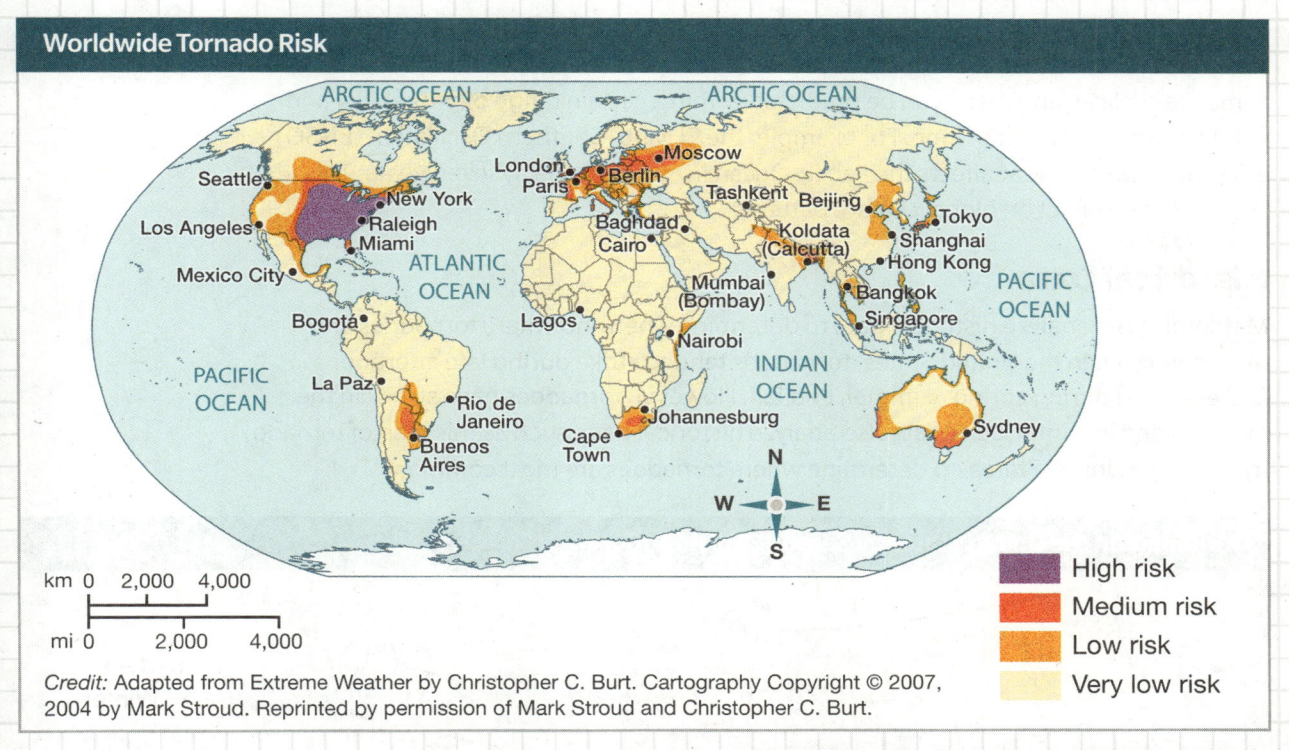

Worldwide Tornado Risk

- High risk
- Medium risk
- Low risk
- Very low risk

Credit: Adapted from Extreme Weather by Christopher C. Burt. Cartography Copyright © 2007, 2004 by Mark Stroud. Reprinted by permission of Mark Stroud and Christopher C. Burt.

11. Look at the map and the photo. We know where tornado risk is high, but do you think we can prevent tornadoes from causing damage and injury? Explain.

12. Look at the map. What is California's tornado risk?

In 2011, a tornado destroyed this house in North Carolina. A tornado warning was issued about 24 minutes before the tornado struck the area.

Lesson 3 Some Natural Hazards Can Be Predicted and Mitigated **477**

Predicting Weather Hazards

Predicting weather and climate hazards relies on understanding the complex ways that the atmosphere, oceans, and topography interact to create weather systems. Some types of weather hazards are related to each other, so scientists use an understanding of those patterns to forecast and predict weather and climate events with varying certainty. Agencies such as the National Oceanic and Atmospheric Administration (NOAA) and the National Weather Service (NWS) continually gather and monitor weather data using technology. For example, although scientists have a pretty good understanding of the conditions that lead to tornadoes, they are difficult to predict with any certainty.

Scientific Understanding

Meteorologists know a lot about conditions that are likely to cause thunderstorms, hurricanes, and even tornadoes. They understand the movement of air masses of different temperatures and moisture content, and that knowledge helps them predict when different weather conditions may occur. Some weather conditions are seasonal, some are cyclical, and many can be predicted within a certain range of probability and within a certain amount of time. For example, the El Niño–Southern Oscillation (ENSO) is a climate pattern that affects the Pacific Ocean in cycles of one to seven years. This system has an effect on global climate patterns.

Historical Data

Meteorologists analyze historical data to determine when and where tornadoes are most common. In the United States, tornadoes tend to strike during late afternoons and evenings during spring, summer, and fall. However, tornadoes have struck in the morning and in winter. Scientists also analyze historical data, such as this map of tornado tracks in the United States, to determine where tornadoes are most common.

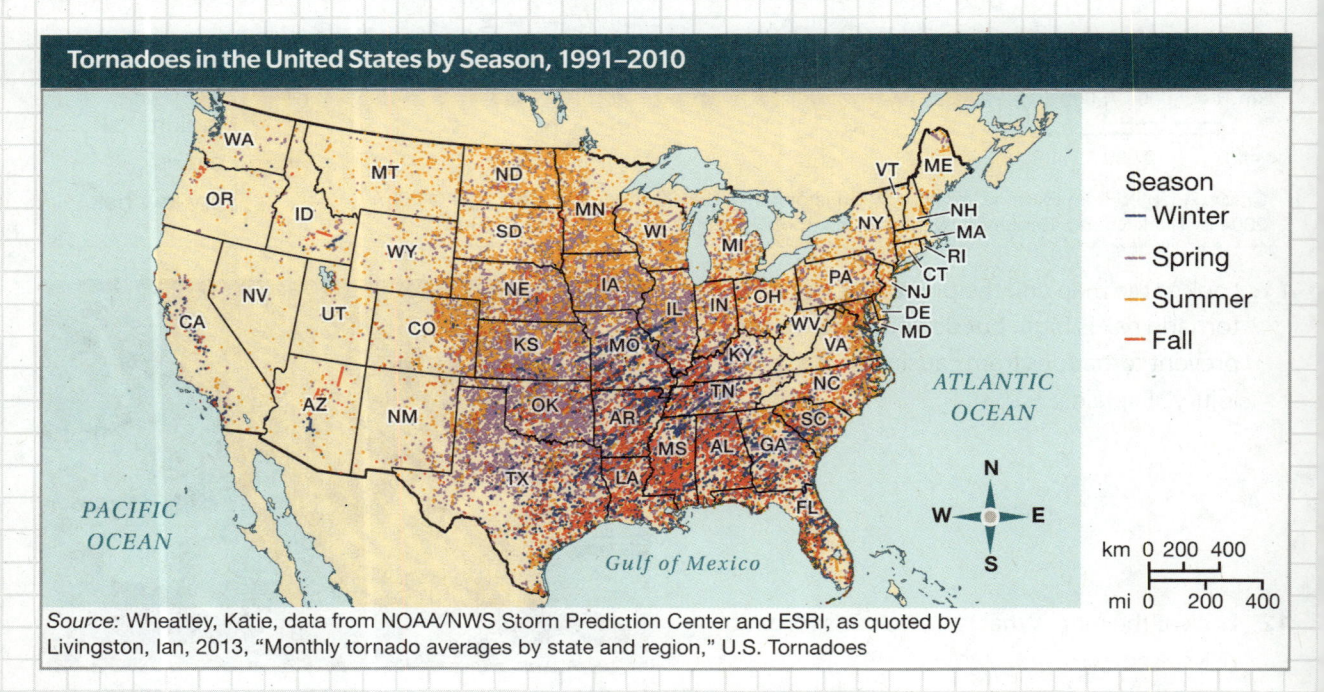

Tornadoes in the United States by Season, 1991–2010

Season
— Winter
— Spring
— Summer
— Fall

Source: Wheatley, Katie, data from NOAA/NWS Storm Prediction Center and ESRI, as quoted by Livingston, Ian, 2013, "Monthly tornado averages by state and region," U.S. Tornadoes

13. The tornado data on this map show a pattern. In the northernmost states where tornadoes occur, most tornadoes occur in the winter / spring / *summer* / fall. In the southeastern United States, most tornadoes occur in the winter / *spring* / summer / fall.

478   Unit 6 Earth's Surface and Society

Forecasting Tornadoes

Meteorologists look at wind patterns in supercell thunderstorms that show rotation. Tornadoes can form where the rotation is strong enough. This table and map were made from weather monitoring data. The data were gathered before and during a tornado outbreak in Raleigh, North Carolina, and the surrounding region in 2011.

Weather Forecasts for Raleigh, NC, from April 12 to April 16, 2011	
April 12, 2011	Forecast mentions a likely threat of upcoming severe weather on the evening of April 15th.
April 13, 2011	Forecast of severe weather is shifted to the daytime of April 16th.
April 14, 2011	NWS issues a prediction of a 30% chance of a major severe weather event on the 16th.
April 15, 2011	The likelihood of a severe weather event is increased to 45% and tornadoes are deemed "likely" to occur.
April 16, 2011	In the morning, NWS issues a warning for afternoon severe thunderstorms and tornadoes. In the afternoon, more than 30 tornadoes strike. Tornado warnings are issued for specific areas an average of 20–30 minutes before the tornadoes strike.

Source: National Weather Service, Raleigh, NC, "April 16, 2011, North Carolina Tornado Outbreak Event Summary," 2012

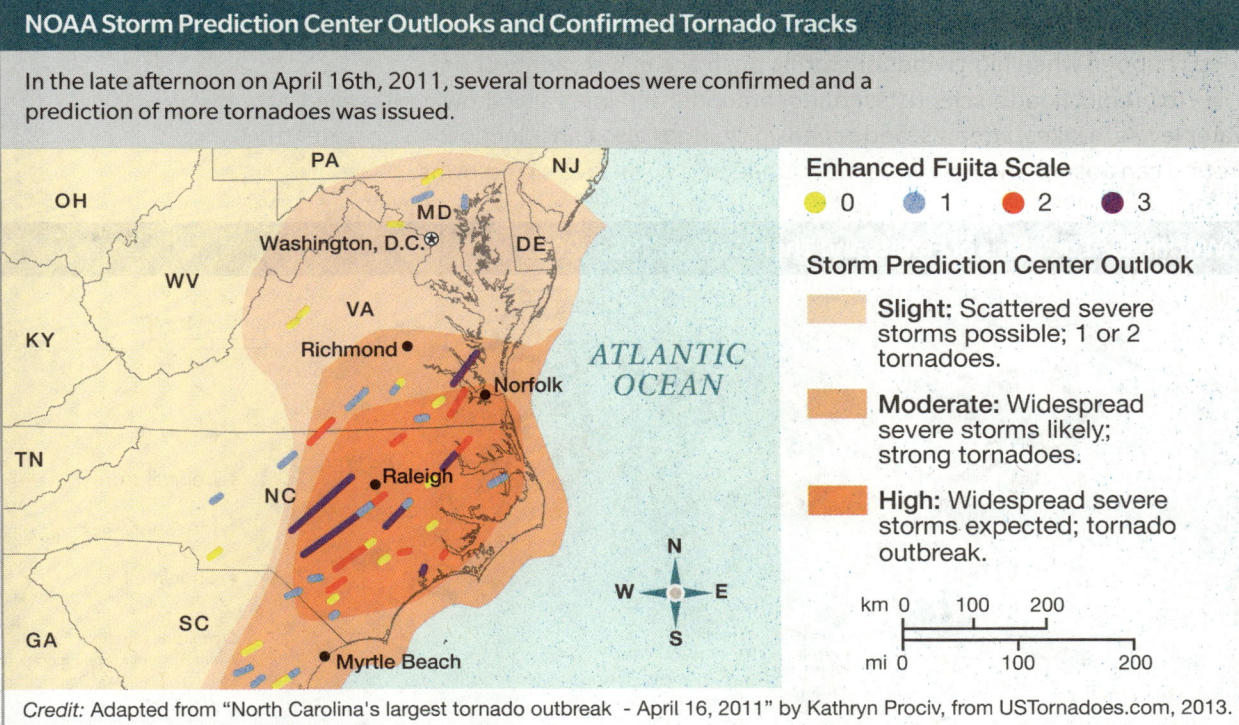

NOAA Storm Prediction Center Outlooks and Confirmed Tornado Tracks

In the late afternoon on April 16th, 2011, several tornadoes were confirmed and a prediction of more tornadoes was issued.

Credit: Adapted from "North Carolina's largest tornado outbreak - April 16, 2011" by Kathryn Prociv, from USTornadoes.com, 2013. Reprinted by permission of Kathryn Prociv.

14. How did the information available in the weather forecasts change in the days leading up to April 16th? Do you think these forecasts gave people enough time to prepare for the tornadoes? Explain.

Lesson 3 Some Natural Hazards Can Be Predicted and Mitigated 479

Monitoring

Several types of technologies are used to monitor weather conditions. For example, Doppler radar uses radio waves to identify direction and intensity of precipitation, wind direction and speed, and the locations of boundaries between large air masses. Weather satellites collect data on cloud systems, snow fields, and ocean currents. Weather stations record temperatures, precipitation, humidity, and wind speed. Historical records are kept and used to determine climate characteristics for a region and to recognize longer-term cycles or patterns.

Weather satellites are sometimes launched from Vandenberg Air Force base in California.

Predicting Floods

Flooding happens when land that is normally dry is covered by water. There are three main types of floods: flash floods, overbank floods, and coastal floods. Flash floods occur suddenly as very fast moving water from excessive rainfall runs over land. Overbank floods happen slowly when rain or melting snow makes river or lake levels rise. Coastal floods happen when high winds or storms push ocean water onto shore.

To predict floods, scientists monitor amounts of rainfall and snow melt, as well as water levels in lakes, streams, and oceans. Scientists also consider how much water the ground can absorb and how water flow is affected by an area's landforms.

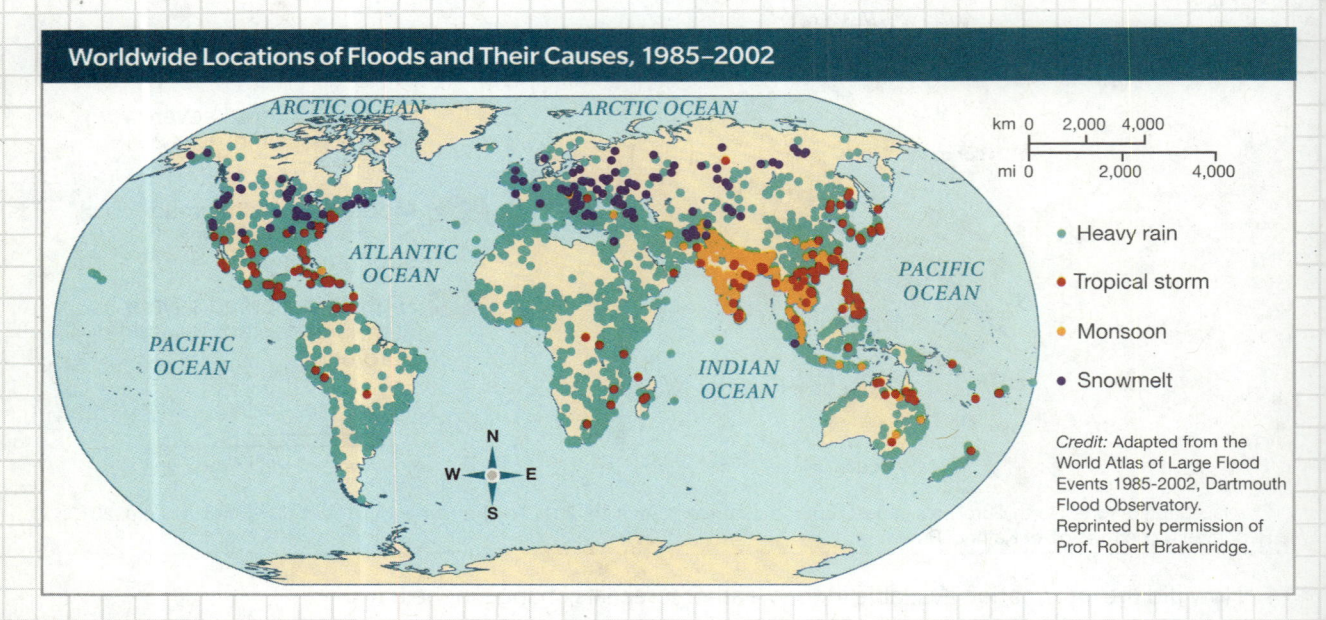

Worldwide Locations of Floods and Their Causes, 1985–2002

- Heavy rain
- Tropical storm
- Monsoon
- Snowmelt

Credit: Adapted from the World Atlas of Large Flood Events 1985-2002, Dartmouth Flood Observatory. Reprinted by permission of Prof. Robert Brakenridge.

15. The most widespread cause of flooding in the world is
    heavy rain / tropical storms / monsoons / snowmelt.
    Flooding caused by snowmelt mainly affected the
    Northern / Southern hemisphere.
    The region most affected by monsoonal rains is
    North America / South America / Europe / Africa / *Asia*.

480 Unit 6 Earth's Surface and Society

Language SmArts
Use Flood Maps

Historical data are used to create flood-risk maps to show how likely areas are to flood under certain conditions. When locations that can flood are identified, the effect of the floods on people can be predicted. It is important that people know safe routes to get out of flood-prone areas. Evacuation routes connect evacuation zones, or areas to be evacuated, to evacuation centers, where people can go to be safe during a flood event.

Flood Risk in New York City

This flood-risk map of New York City shows the evacuation zones for the areas that flood.

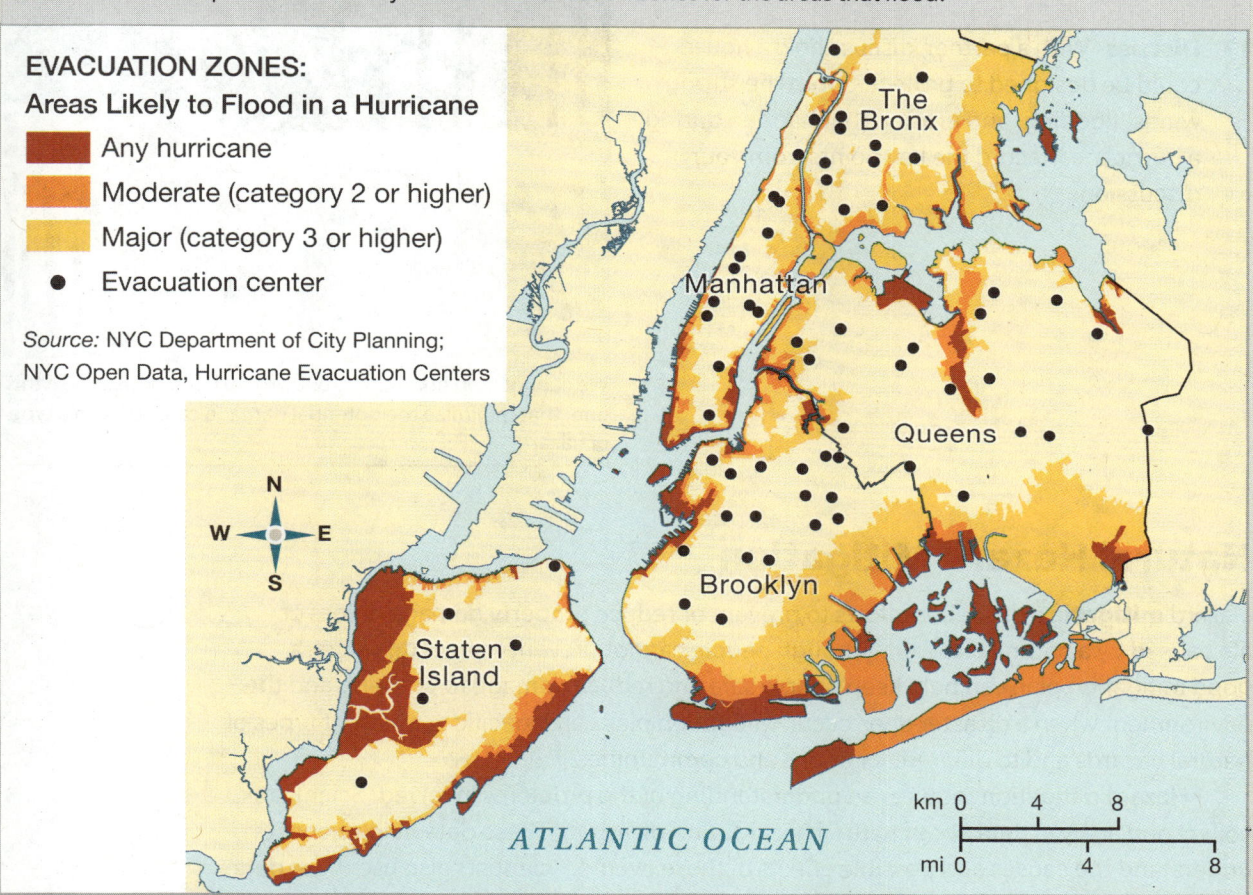

EVACUATION ZONES:
Areas Likely to Flood in a Hurricane
- Any hurricane
- Moderate (category 2 or higher)
- Major (category 3 or higher)
- • Evacuation center

Source: NYC Department of City Planning; NYC Open Data, Hurricane Evacuation Centers

16. A moderate hurricane in the Atlantic Ocean is heading toward New York City. Based on the map, identify the areas that have a high chance of flooding during and after this storm. Suggest which areas people should evacuate based on the coming storm, and support your claim with evidence and reasoning.

_____
_____
_____
_____
_____
_____
_____

Lesson 3 Some Natural Hazards Can Be Predicted and Mitigated   **481**

EXPLORATION 4

Describing Natural Hazard Mitigation

Natural hazards such as floods, earthquakes, and severe storms are dangerous events. These events may cause harm to people and property and, sometimes, they happen without warning. Scientists, engineers, and community officials work together to prepare for and minimize the damage caused by natural hazards.

17. **Discuss** With a partner, discuss how a house could be designed to protect it from the strong winds, flooding, and erosion that happen during a hurricane. Record the key points from your discussion.

We cannot stop hurricanes, but we can build houses, like this one, that minimize the potential damage caused by this type of hazard.

Natural Hazard Mitigation

Hazard **mitigation** describes efforts to prevent or reduce property damage or loss of life caused by a natural disaster. Although people cannot prevent natural disasters, a good mitigation plan can help keep people safe and reduce damage to property and the environment when a disaster does occur. Mitigation plans are specific to different types of natural hazards and to different locations and communities.

Hazard mitigation requires an understanding of the problems involved. Scientists collect and analyze data about natural hazards and disasters. These data help scientists understand the causes and possible effects of these events. Scientists also use these data to determine if an area is at risk for a natural hazard. Scientists work with engineers to apply what they have learned from the data. They design solutions and develop ways to predict and, if possible, to control the hazard or its effects. Engineers and planners use data to develop mitigation strategies. Different strategies are used before, during, and after a natural hazard. Before the event, engineers focus on preparation. After a disaster, their focus shifts to a response to the disaster and recovery from its effects.

18. What types of data might be useful in mitigation efforts for an area that experiences frequent floods? Choose all that apply.
    A. historical information on rainfall patterns
    B. elevation mapping of the area
    C. average income of residents of the area
    D. location of population centers in the region

482 Unit 6 Earth's Surface and Society

Preparation

Preparation is an important mitigation strategy. People prepare for disasters at many different levels. For example, mitigation planning is performed by individuals, families, communities, and local or federal governments.

Governments and other agencies develop and test plans in advance for how to respond to and recover from disastrous events. They work with scientists and engineers to develop technologies to monitor conditions, to make predictions, and to communicate with the public. They monitor conditions and share information before, during, and after natural hazards. Emergency management agencies find good locations for shelters and collect supplies to help people affected by a disaster.

Governments and communities can prepare by setting standards, also called *building codes*. These codes require structures to be likely to survive hazardous events and to protect people during these events. Architects and engineers design and build structures to meet these standards using different materials based on their properties.

Preparation includes education, so that people know what to expect, what to do, and where to go. If you know what hazards exist in your area and pay attention to predictions, you can prepare for the effects of natural hazards. Then, when you need to act, you will know what to do and you will have the things that you need in order to face the emergency.

If you are prepared, you are less likely to be severely affected by an event. If you learn what to expect during and after a natural hazard, you can identify what supplies you will need in case a disaster occurs. You can build an emergency kit as part of your preparations. Many kits include flashlights and batteries, blankets, first-aid supplies, fresh water, and other necessary items.

Being prepared helps people avoid some of the harmful effects of natural hazards. It also helps them recover after an event.

Scientists monitor conditions that lead to volcanic mudflows, called *lahars*, at Mount St. Helens. They use the data to predict lahars and warn people before a disaster occurs.

Television, radio, and emergency websites communicate information about weather hazards before, during, and after an event, such as a hurricane.

Preparation includes actions to prevent disasters. Restored wetlands help control water flow and reduce flooding.

19. A mitigation plan may define how people can be notified about the time and location of potential hazards. Weather forecasts provide information that communities need to <u>prepare for</u> / respond to natural hazards such as severe storms. During the emergency, governments and residents must be ready to prepare for / <u>respond to</u> changing local conditions.

Lesson 3 Some Natural Hazards Can Be Predicted and Mitigated

Response

Natural hazard mitigation continues after the event begins. Appropriate and timely response helps reduce the negative effects of the hazard. Governments, relief agencies, and individuals can all respond to natural hazards. Responding to a natural hazard event means providing people with information and services as an event occurs and later. For example, during a flood, some responders rescue people whose homes or cars are surrounded by water. Others provide first aid and transportation to people who are injured or stranded.

Technology plays an important role in disaster response. Some technologies are used to monitor changing conditions. Other technologies, such as radios and phones, are essential for communication. Modern mapping technology helps responders reach affected locations as quickly as possible. Portable medical equipment and temporary shelters are used by doctors and nurses to provide care wherever or whenever it is needed.

Firefighters respond to a wildfire by using water and other chemicals to keep the fire from spreading.

Recovery

Emergency preparation and response efforts reduce damage and injury but they cannot prevent all damage or loss. Recovery is the final part of a mitigation plan. Recovery generally occurs after a disaster, but planning for recovery takes place long before it is needed. In some cases, recovery efforts may start before the event is over.

Recovering from a natural disaster may involve providing temporary shelter and services until permanent repairs can be made. Recovery involves providing supplies such as food, water, and medical supplies wherever they are needed as quickly as possible. Recovery also involves rebuilding and repairing damaged structures. The final step of recovery involves reviewing and revising mitigation plans for greater success in the future. Recovery is performed by government agencies, volunteer organizations, and members of a community.

Professionals and volunteers work together to help a community recover from a natural disaster.

EVIDENCE NOTEBOOK

20. Which phase of mitigation does a tsunami warning sign on a calm beach mainly support? Record your evidence.

21. These photos show three different parts of earthquake mitigation. Examine each photo and its caption. Then use the words from the word bank to label each photo with the stage of mitigation that is illustrated.

WORD BANK
- preparation
- recovery
- response

preparation	response	recovery
Students practice ways to protect themselves from falling objects during an earthquake.	Teams of volunteers and professionals search through rubble to rescue survivors of an earthquake.	Volunteers travel to areas affected by earthquakes to help residents rebuild homes and infrastructure.

22. Choose one of the examples from the photos. Suggest another mitigation activity that could be performed during that phase of hazard mitigation.

The Role of Technology in Mitigation Planning

Technology is important at all stages of natural hazard mitigation. It is useful in identifying hazard probability, in developing mitigation plans, in testing solutions, in response and recovery, and in evaluating the success of mitigation activities after a hazard. Sometimes, solutions involve developing new technologies, such as equipment or processes, or redesigning existing technologies. The uses of technologies are driven by the needs of the people in an area and the hazards they face. However, the availability of technology may be limited by location or by the economic conditions of a community or region.

One important technology used by scientists and engineers is computer modeling. Data gathered from monitoring stations, drones, and satellites are entered into programs that model and predict hazardous situations. A Graphic Information System (GIS) can then display maps and other visuals. Seeing trends in data over time is important when making decisions such as where to place levees along rivers to prevent flooding. Knowing when and where different kinds of natural hazard are most likely to occur helps reduce response and recovery times. Emergency shelters and medical relief can be sent to where they will be needed more quickly.

Lesson 3 Some Natural Hazards Can Be Predicted and Mitigated

Scientific Knowledge and Engineering Design Principles

Natural hazard mitigation relies on science and engineering for success. Scientists study the causes and effects of natural hazards. They apply what they learn to explain how, where, and why hazardous events may occur. This information is then used to mitigate the events' effects. For example, scientists study the conditions in the atmosphere that may lead to the formation of tornadoes. They use this information to decide which conditions to monitor in order to predict tornadoes. Scientists and engineers can then develop instruments such as satellites and radar systems to monitor the atmosphere. They design computer models to analyze the collected data. When the conditions are right for tornadoes to form, scientists issue warnings that tornadoes may happen.

Mitigation plans are developed by using the engineering design process. Scientists and engineers identify a problem that needs to be solved. Problems may include how to evacuate areas at risk of a disaster or how to get emergency supplies to people affected by a disaster. Once engineers identify a problem or need, they conduct research and more clearly define the problem. They then propose, evaluate, and test solutions to the problem. Solutions related to mitigating natural hazards could involve new tools or equipment. Other solutions could include new systems or processes.

Evaluate Mitigation Technologies

Tsunamis are giant waves that can be caused by an earthquake at the bottom of the ocean. Tsunami waves travel outward in all directions from the source. When the waves reach a shore, they can cause massive damage and loss of life. Scientists and engineers work to mitigate the hazards of tsunamis by developing ways to predict when one will occur and to issue timely warnings.

word bank
- saving lives
- preventing damage
- communication
- data collection
- environmental cleanup

23. Use the word bank to fill in the table to show which needs are met by the technologies that are shown. Some needs may be used more than once. Others may not be used at all.

Technology	Meets Needs
Scientists use seismographs to detect and record earthquakes. When an undersea earthquake occurs, scientists model the earthquake's effects to predict whether tsunamis may occur.	
Evacuation plans are in place long before a tsunami occurs. Evacuation signs direct people to safe areas.	
When data indicate that an earthquake has generated a tsunami, scientists use computers to determine where it is likely to strike. Then, scientists issue warnings to affected areas.	

TAKE IT FURTHER

Continue Your Exploration

Name: _____ Date: _____

Check out the path below or go online to choose one of the other paths shown.

Predicting Asteroid Impacts

- Technology for Hurricane Forecasts
- Hands-On Labs ✋
- Propose Your Own Path

Go online to choose one of these other paths.

An *asteroid* is a large, rocky body that orbits the sun. Tens of thousands of asteroids orbit the sun between Mars and Jupiter. However, some asteroids pass close to Earth, and some even cross Earth's orbit. At times, small fragments of asteroids approach Earth, but most burn up as they travel through the atmosphere. People call these bright streaks of light "shooting stars." Scientists call them *meteors*. Some small fragments do not burn up entirely and they strike Earth, causing little to no damage. A larger asteroid impact could be a worldwide catastrophe, but this type of event is extremely rare. A large asteroid strikes Earth about once every 10,000 years.

Potentially Hazardous Asteroids

Scientists use monitoring technology, such as telescopes, to locate asteroids that orbit close to Earth. Automated systems are used to determine whether these asteroids could pose a threat to Earth. As monitoring technology continues to improve, new asteroids are continually identified. Some of these asteroids pass very close to Earth.

A *potentially hazardous asteroid* (PHA) is one that orbits close enough to Earth to pose a threat. A PHA must be large enough to survive the trip through the atmosphere and hit Earth's surface. Identified PHAs will not necessarily strike Earth's surface, but because an impact is possible, PHAs are continuously monitored. This ongoing monitoring helps scientists better predict whether a PHA poses a threat. The National Aeronautics and Space Administration (NASA) currently monitors more than 1,700 PHAs. As of 2018, no asteroids were categorized as an immediate threat to Earth in the near future.

The Barringer Crater in Arizona is the result of an asteroid impact about 50,000 years ago. The asteroid was about 50 meters wide.

TAKE IT FURTHER

Continue Your Exploration

1. Based on the table, how likely is a large asteroid impact in your lifetime? Explain.

Timeline of the Ten Biggest Known Asteroid Impacts on Earth	
Name of Crater	Time (millions of years ago)
Chesapeake Bay Crater, USA	35
Popigai Crater, Russia	36
Chicxulub Crater, Mexico	66
Kara Crater, Russia	70
Morokweng Crater, South Africa	145
Manicouagan Crater, Canada	214
Woodleigh Crater, Australia	364
Acraman Crater, Australia	580
Sudbury Crater, Canada	1,849
Vredefort Crater, South Africa	2,023

Source: National Geographic. "Asteroid Impacts: 10 Biggest Known Hits," 2013

2. Why are new PHAs continually discovered?

3. An asteroid over 100 meters in diameter could affect an entire country. Scientists predict that there is a 1% chance that an asteroid of this size could strike Earth in the next 100 years. What factors could cause the calculation of this probability to increase or decrease?

4. **Collaborate** Conduct research to evaluate the following statement: "The chances of a small asteroid affecting humans are greater than the chances of a large asteroid affecting humans." Cite evidence to support your evaluation.

488 Unit 6 Earth's Natural Hazards

LESSON 3 SELF-CHECK

Can You Explain It?

Name: _____   Date: _____

Why is there a tsunami hazard warning sign on this calm beach?

📓 **EVIDENCE NOTEBOOK**
Refer to the notes in your Evidence Notebook to help you construct an explanation for how we know which coastal areas are at risk for tsunamis.

1. State your claim. Make sure your claim fully explains why there is a tsunami hazard warning sign on a calm beach.

2. Summarize the evidence you have gathered to support your claim and explain your reasoning.

Lesson 3 Some Natural Hazards Can Be Predicted and Mitigated **489**

LESSON 3 SELF-CHECK

Checkpoints

Answer the following questions to check your understanding of the lesson.

Use the photograph to answer Questions 3–5.

3. What information about the blizzard shown in the photo can be gathered that will help meteorologists make predictions about future blizzards? Select all that apply.
   A. the amount of snow that fell
   B. the location of the blizzard
   C. the amount of moisture in the air
   D. the temperature and wind direction
   E. the types of clouds present

4. A blizzard is a _geologic / weather_ hazard that can be predicted using _satellite images / GPS data_. A hazard mitigation plan to reduce the _negative / positive_ impacts of a blizzard might include sending text messages to warn people before the storm arrives.

5. Many cities do not allow parking on the street when a blizzard has been predicted. How might parked cars interfere with hazard mitigation?
   A. People cannot get the cars out of the parking spaces to drive to work.
   B. Parked cars force traffic to move slower.
   C. Snow-covered cars on the street slow down emergency responders.
   D. The cars make the snow appear worse than it actually is.

Use the table to answer Question 6.

Eruption History of Mt. Etna, Italy, 2002–2015
2002	2003	2005	2006	2008	2009	2010	2011	2013	2014	2015

Source: Smithsonian Institution, Global Volcanism Program, Etna

6. Mt. Etna is an _active / extinct_ volcano. Scientists should _occasionally / continuously_ monitor changes in the shape of the volcano that may signal a volcanic eruption by using _seismometers / tiltmeters_.

7. How does a better scientific understanding of Earth's atmosphere and oceans help scientists predict natural hazards? Choose all that apply.
   A. Changes in the atmosphere and oceans trigger geologic hazards, such as earthquakes and volcanic eruptions.
   B. The atmosphere and oceans are primarily responsible for weather and climate patterns that could lead to hazards such as hurricanes or tornadoes.
   C. Understanding the atmosphere and oceans can help scientists develop new technologies to monitor conditions that could lead to hazardous events.

LESSON 3 SELF-CHECK

Interactive Review

Complete this page to review the main concepts of the lesson.

Scientists gather natural hazard data to improve scientific understanding, analyze historical occurrences, and monitor conditions to better predict natural hazards.

A. How can analyzing historical data and monitoring hazardous events help scientists improve their predictions of natural hazards?

Predicting geologic hazards requires understanding geologic processes, identifying precursor events, and monitoring sites where geologic hazards may occur.

B. Identify two geologic hazards that are related and explain their relationship.

Predicting geologic hazards requires understanding geologic processes, identifying precursor events, and monitoring sites where geologic hazards may occur.

C. How do scientific understanding, historical data, and monitoring help scientists predict weather and climate hazards?

There are three parts to natural hazard mitigation: preparation, response, and recovery.

D. How does a hazard mitigation plan help a community deal with a disaster?

Lesson 3 Some Natural Hazards Can Be Predicted and Mitigated 491

LESSON 4

Human Use of Synthetic Materials Affects Earth's Surface

This sea turtle is eating a plastic bottle. Plastic bags and other synthetic materials are often ingested by marine animals confusing these materials with real food.

Explore First

Exploring Synthetics Plastic objects often have a recycling symbol on them with a number from 1 to 7. These numbers are a code and can tell you if the object can be recycled. How many different recycling numbers can you find on plastic objects in your classroom?

CAN YOU EXPLAIN IT?

How can engineers change the effects of the synthetic materials in the bottles on the environment by reusing the materials to make the jacket?

Plastic bottles and this polyester jacket are made of the same synthetic material.

1. Where have you seen plastic beverage bottles and polyester jackets?

2. What natural resource are the plastic bottles and polyester jacket made from?

EVIDENCE NOTEBOOK As you explore this lesson, gather evidence to explain how using the material from plastic bottles to make a jacket can reduce the environmental effects of the synthetic material on the environment.

Lesson 4 Human Use of Synthetic Materials Affects Earth's Surface

EXPLORATION 1

Analyzing the Life Cycle of Synthetic Materials

You can find synthetic materials in your backpack, your closet, the refrigerator, and the medicine cabinet. Synthetic materials are materials that are made by humans using chemical processes. Synthetic materials are usually designed to have specific properties needed for a particular purpose. However, sometimes new materials are discovered by accident. For example, in the 1960s, Stephanie Kwolek was developing new polymers that could be used to make tires more durable. She discovered a new type of fiber that was extremely strong and lightweight. That fiber is Kevlar®. Its properties make it ideal for use in bulletproof vests and helmets. Engineers have designed different types of Kevlar® that have many uses. Some of the things Kevlar® is used in include vehicle armor, motorcycle racing gear, and tires.

3. How do the properties of Kevlar® determine how it is used?

Between the layers of black fabric in this bulletproof vest is a layer of protective synthetic material called *Kevlar®*.

Synthetic Materials and Society

Engineers look for ways to improve existing materials or design new materials as the needs of society change. New materials have made cars more lightweight, which means they burn less gasoline. New medicines are developed as scientists learn more about the causes of diseases. New materials help computers work faster.

4. Which of the following might drive the development of new materials? Select all that apply.
    A. a desire for affordable, fashionable clothing
    B. an idea that air pollution should be reduced
    C. a need for safe apartment buildings
    D. a change in the availability of natural resources

Needs

Synthetic materials are developed to meet the needs of people. Some needs are basic, such as food and water, energy, housing, and transportation. But even these needs have changed. Foods are now shipped all over the world and may be stored for long periods of time before they reach consumers. Synthetic materials that preserve food help it last longer. The population has increased and cities have grown. Synthetic building materials have made it possible to build larger buildings to house more people and businesses.

Desires

What things would you like to buy—trendy clothes, shoes of a famous basketball player, video games, or a bike like your friends have? People's desires also affect the types of materials that are developed and the way they are used. Materials may be developed to make products people want, such as running shoes or bicycle frames. Synthetic materials may also make products more affordable.

Values

Values affect the development and use of materials. Your values include what you think is good and important. For example, some people think that all-natural food is good for your health. They are likely to choose food without synthetic dyes and preservatives. These choices affect the food that companies make. Food scientists are likely to find natural materials to replace synthetic materials to meet consumer demand.

Materials Meet Needs, Desires, and Values

- The stretchy material of this hair band meets the need to pull back the hair. Its color and style were chosen based on desire.

- This polyester shirt meets the need for clothing. Its style reflects the desire to wear clothes that express personal tastes.

- The game controller meets the desire to play video games and the value that technology should be easy to use.

5. In what ways are needs today different than they were 50 years ago?

6. **Discuss** Think about the plastic casing on a cell phone. Why do you think it is made of plastic? What needs, desires, or values were likely involved in its development?

Phases of the Life Cycle of Synthetic Materials

The polyester in a shirt and the plastic in a cell phone case go through many steps before they reach you. The steps that a material or product goes through are called the *life cycle* of the material. One model of a life cycle includes five steps: obtaining natural resources, production, distribution, consumer use, and disposal. The life cycle describes where a product comes from, how it is used, and where it goes after it is used.

Obtaining Resources
The first step in a life cycle is to obtain the resources needed to make the materials. These resources may be natural resources or recycled materials. A cell phone contains many materials, including metals, plastics, and glass. The metals are produced from ores that are mined. The starting material for plastic comes from crude oil, which is extracted from the ground. Glass is made from resources such as sand and limestone.

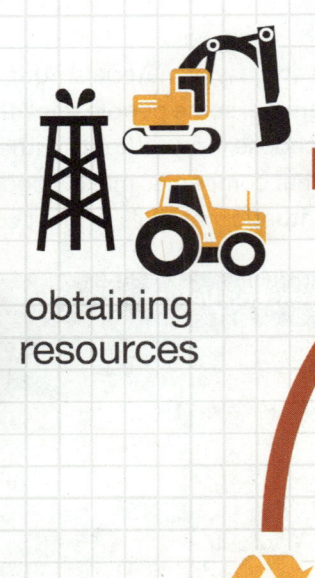

Disposal
Consumers dispose of products when they are done using them. At this point in the life cycle, products and the materials that they contain are discarded, recycled, or reused. Products may be discarded and end up in a landfill where they remain. Some products may be flushed down the drain, where they enter the wastewater system. Many products, including plastic containers and cell phones, may be recycled to produce new materials. Other products, such as electronic devices, may be refurbished and used again.

496 Unit 6 Earth's Surface and Society

Production

During the production stage of a synthetic material, chemical reactions or mixing processes produce the materials in the product. The materials are then shaped into the various parts of the product. Then the parts are put together to make the finished product. Cell phones may be thin, but they have many tiny parts inside the plastic covering.

Distribution

Products must reach consumers, but they are rarely shipped directly from the factory to the consumer. They are likely to be shipped from where they are produced to a warehouse where they are stored. From there, products may be shipped to a store or directly to the consumer.

Consumer Use

Consumers use products in different ways. Some products, such as food and medicine, are consumed. Other products, such as a paper plate, may only be used once. Products such as cell phones may be used frequently for a long time. Products may also be shared and reused by multiple consumers.

Lesson 4 Human Use of Synthetic Materials Affects Earth's Surface

7. Follow the arrows and label the photos to show the life cycle of a nylon rope.

WORD BANK
- consumer use
- disposal
- distribution
- ~~obtaining resources~~
- production

obtaining resources

_____   _____

_____   _____   _____

8. How else could the nylon rope be disposed of?

Natural Resource Use and Synthetic Materials

Natural resources are obtained during the first stage in the life cycle of a material or a product. However, all stages of the life cycle affect the use of natural resources. Some resources are used to make products. Other resources are used as energy resources. Consumers can reuse or recycle products to reduce the need to obtain more natural resources.

The availability of materials also affects how they are used. Some natural resources are scarce and only found in certain locations as a result of geologic processes that occurred in the past. Alternative materials that do not use those resources may be developed.

Excavators are used to harvest trees on a peatland forest on Indonesia's Borneo Island. Synthetic materials that come from trees include rayon fabric, plywood, and some rosin-based adhesives.

9. How can recycling rubber tires into materials that make playground and track surfaces affect the use of natural resources?

498 Unit 6 *Earth's Surface and Society*

EVIDENCE NOTEBOOK

10. How can the end of the life cycle of a plastic bottle be the beginning of the life cycle of a polyester jacket? Record your evidence.

Language SmArts
Model the Life Cycle

11. Write a story about the life cycle of a plastic or paper shopping bag. Remember that plastic is made from petroleum and paper is made from trees.

_____
_____
_____
_____
_____
_____
_____
_____

12. **Draw** In the space below, draw a diagram to model the life cycle of the plastic or paper bag.

499

EXPLORATION 2

Analyzing the Impact of Synthetic Materials

Diamonds can be a symbol of marriage or wealth for many people in the United States. In addition to being desired for their beauty, the hardness of diamonds makes them useful for industrial tasks such as cutting, grinding, drilling, and polishing. Diamonds form naturally deep within Earth, so they must be mined. An increase in the demand for diamonds means that more land must be mined.

Engineers can also make synthetic diamonds to help meet the need for diamonds. Synthetic diamonds usually cost less than natural diamonds. Also, they do not need to be mined.

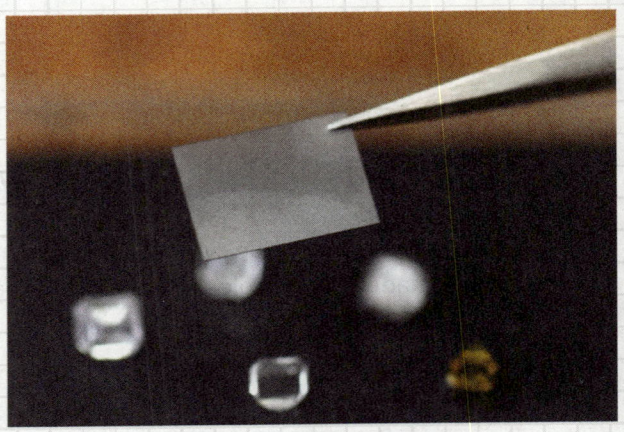

This thin sheet of Chemical Vapor Deposition (CVD) diamond is being held above other synthetic diamond stones. CVD diamonds can take six months to grow using methane gas and are one of the best conductors of heat in the world.

13. How might the life cycle of synthetic diamonds differ from that of natural diamonds?

Impacts Throughout the Life Cycle

The impacts of a product containing synthetic materials can be determined by analyzing the product's life cycle. Each stage of the life cycle may have positive or negative effects on society and the environment. Producing cell phones provides people with jobs but may expose people to some materials that can cause health problems. The need to mine rare-earth minerals used in phones can harm ecosystems and cause pollution. Decisions at each stage of the life cycle can help decrease potential negative effects.

Stages of the Cell Phone's Life Cycle

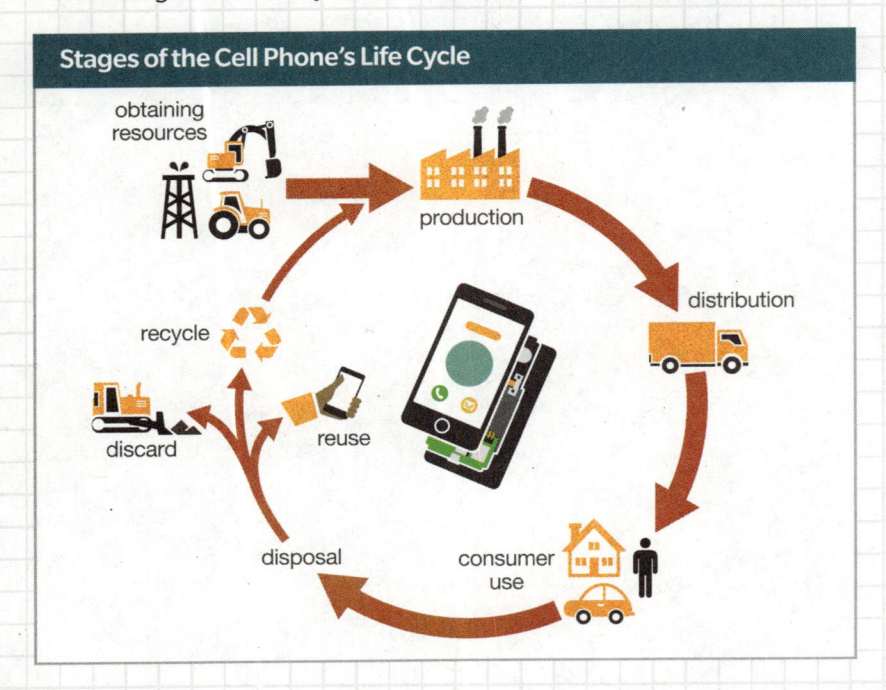

obtaining resources → production → distribution → consumer use → disposal → discard → recycle → reuse

14. How might drilling for oil to make plastic used in a cell phone case impact society? Select all that apply.

   A. Jobs are created for people who work for oil companies.
   B. Oil spills at drilling sites can harm the environment.
   C. Jobs are lost for people who produce alternative fuels.
   D. Pollution from oil is reduced.

Obtaining Resources

Mines and oil rigs are located where resources formed during past geologic processes. As these resources are harvested, the tools used and the waste created can impact the environment. For example, mining and oil drilling can pollute Earth systems. And habitats are destroyed to make way for mines or oil rigs.

On July 18, 2010, an explosion occurred at the *Deepwater Horizon* oil drilling platform. Because of the damage, an estimated 130 million gallons of oil was released into the Gulf of Mexico. The oil spill resulting from the *Deepwater Horizon* explosion affected coastal ecosystems—as shown in the photos—and deep-sea ecosystems. Many organisms died from coming in contact with the oil, and food chains were disrupted.

Obtaining oil resources alters natural cycles and does long-term damage to ecosystems in other ways too. For example, oil companies dredge canals in order to move drilling equipment. These canals destroy habitats and alter the ecosystem by changing the natural interactions of fresh and salt water. The loss of wetlands is important because wetlands protect cities like New Orleans from hurricanes. People are also affected by changes to local ecosystems. Shrimp fishing is an important job along the Gulf Coast. Shrimp depend on the wetlands ecosystem for part of their life cycle. As the wetlands are being destroyed, fewer shrimp are available as a source of food for other organisms as well as for humans.

Relying on natural resources can also affect the availability of a resource in the future. If we use a resource at a rate that is faster than it can be replenished, that resource will be nonrenewable. For example, the rate at which we have been using oil has depleted the supply faster than it can be replenished.

Society is affected in other ways as we obtain natural resources. For example, mining and oil drilling create jobs and provide needed resources, but these jobs can be dangerous for workers. Some people are developing renewable, and less polluting, energy resources that will also provide jobs and needed resources.

Canals are built by oil companies to move equipment.

The *Deepwater Horizon* oil drilling platform was located in the Gulf of Mexico.

This pelican is covered in oil from the *Deepwater Horizon* oil spill.

Shrimping was compromised because of the spill and the fleet stayed in harbor.

15. How have decisions about resource use along the Gulf Coast affected local ecosystems?

Lesson 4 Human Use of Synthetic Materials Affects Earth's Surface **501**

Production

People are employed to produce synthetic materials and then make products out of them. These jobs are often located far away from where the materials are used. For example, most cell phones are manufactured outside of the United States. Factory jobs may provide workers with new opportunities. However, factory workers in other countries may not always have the same protections as workers in the United States have. They may work very long hours for low pay or work in unsafe conditions.

Production can also cause pollution and use energy. The chemical reactions that produce synthetic materials may also produce substances that are toxic. These toxins can pollute the air, water, and ground if they are not disposed of properly. Another source of air pollution during production can be the source of energy for the factories, such as coal power plants. Burning coal releases gases and particles that contribute to air pollution.

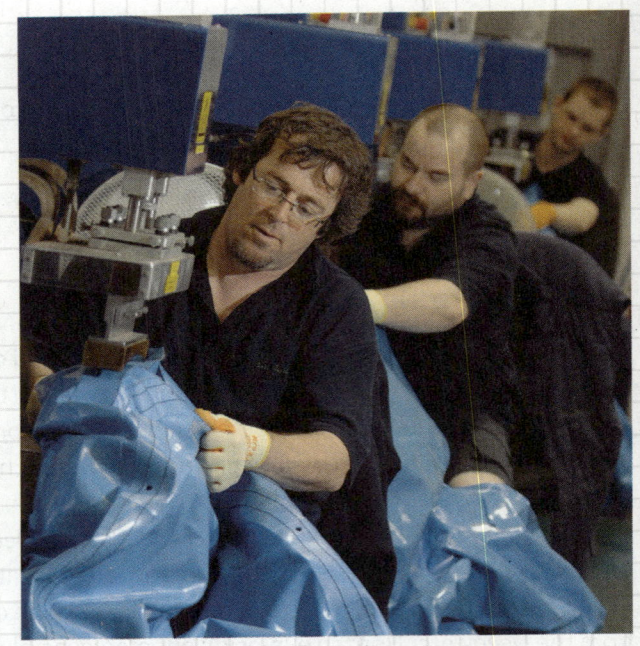

Workers in a plastics factory are making industrial strength plastic bags for use in construction.

16. What questions might an engineer ask when determining whether to produce a product from synthetic materials? Select all that apply.

   A. How are the raw materials acquired?
   B. Is there a more natural alternative that could be used?
   C. How many people will need to be employed to manufacture the material?
   D. What toxins will result if this product is manufactured?

People depend on having a safe and reliable source of fresh water for drinking as well as for manufacturing products. In some places people depend on water collected in human made reservoirs on the surface. In other places people use groundwater that has been pumped to the surface. Both sources of fresh water depend on natural patterns of rainfall to recharge.

Reservoirs and groundwater can both be contaminated when toxic materials are released during the production of synthetic materials. Some of these toxins may break down quickly, but others will continue to pollute the water supply for many years.

When people decide to produce synthetic materials they are making decisions that affect jobs as well as safety and the health of the environment. These decisions are made at the local level as well as nationally and even internationally.

Industrial waste can leak out and enter streams and infiltrate the ground.

Distribution

Today, synthetic materials and the products made from them are shipped around the world. Distribution systems are efficient and can move products to consumers quickly. Products are shipped on trucks, ships, and trains from factories to warehouses. They can also be transported to stores or directly to customers. As a result of these factors, materials and products are less expensive for consumers. However, the distribution stage also has a negative impact. It produces greenhouse gases and other pollutants as products are transported.

Many goods are transported around the world by container ship. These ships may pollute and add greenhouse gases to the atmosphere. Ship collisions are also a threat to endangered whale species.

Consumer Use

Using synthetic materials has both positive and negative effects. Many synthetic materials improve people's quality of life. For example, synthetic medicines can make people feel better and cure diseases. Cell phones help people stay connected over great distances.

Consumer use of synthetic materials can also have negative effects, which are sometimes caused by the choices consumers make. For example, people may use too much fertilizer. Excess fertilizer makes its way to streams, rivers, and oceans where it causes harmful blooms of algae.

Many products use energy and cause pollution when they are used. For example, cell phones need to be plugged in to be recharged and refrigerators constantly use energy.

Digital tablets can have a positive impact because they allow people who are far apart to communicate easily.

EVIDENCE NOTEBOOK

17. How many times does a consumer use plastic water bottles compared to how many times a person uses a new jacket? What effect does this have on all of the steps of the life cycle? Record your evidence.

Lesson 4 Human Use of Synthetic Materials Affects Earth's Surface

Disposal

When people increase their use of materials, the amount of material that is discarded also increases. A huge amount of waste goes to landfills every day. Landfills can be smelly, which is unpleasant for people who live nearby. Improper disposal of some materials can pollute the land and water in areas near and far away from landfills. As the waste breaks down, it produces gases such as methane and carbon dioxide. The methane may be collected and burned. Some landfills are even using methane as an energy resource.

Some waste does not reach landfills, such as when people throw trash along roads or natural areas. This pollution may harm animals. Sometimes they mistake it for food. When animals eat plastic, they can die because it stays in their stomachs. Plastic can also become attached around parts of animals and cause harm to their bodies.

Reusing and recycling can reduce the materials sent to landfills. Materials are reused when they are used more than once. Consumers can also donate or share items so that someone else can use them. Recycling turns used materials into new materials that may be used again. Recycling saves energy and natural resources. It creates jobs for people who work in recycling businesses. For example, cell phone parts, such as metal and some plastics, can be recycled to make new materials. Plastic bottles can be recycled and spun into threads to make fabric.

A cell phone recycling technician works on old cell phones to recover metals and other materials that can be used again.

An employee at a cell phone company refurbishes a used cell phone that still works. The cell phone can then be resold and someone else can use it.

18. It is important for engineers to consider how a _natural / **synthetic**_ material will be disposed of when they are developing the new material. If the material can be _**recycled** / discarded_, energy and natural resources could be saved. The engineer could design the material to _**minimize** / maximize_ harmful environmental pollutants.

504 Unit 6 Earth's Surface and Society

Economic Impact of the Life Cycle

A material's life cycle impacts the economy in numerous ways. All stages of a life cycle provide people with jobs. People may also work in industries that support the life cycle, such as making equipment used for mining or repairing delivery trucks. The life cycle of materials can have a big impact on the economy of countries. Some countries depend on their natural resources, such as oil. Other countries depend on the production of materials and products. Changes to the costs of natural resources or the demand for materials affects the economy. For example, low oil prices can negatively affect the economy of a country that depends on oil extraction.

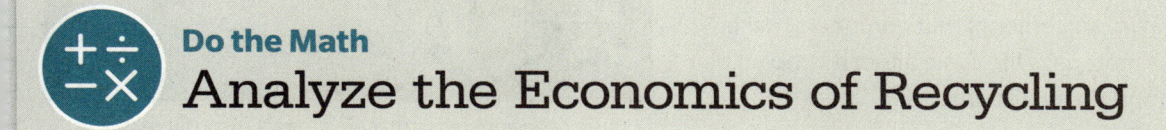

Do the Math
Analyze the Economics of Recycling

Recycling helps the environment by saving energy and reducing the use of natural resources. Because materials do not need to be extracted and made from scratch, recycled materials are often less expensive to produce. The cost of natural resources, the availability of recycled materials, and the processes used to make new materials all determine whether recycling materials is economically useful. The amount of energy used in recycling compared to the amount of energy required to produce new materials is also a consideration.

Plastic water bottles can be recycled to make plastic for new products.

19. A company needs to make at least 75,000 bottles. Twenty-one 20-oz. bottles can be made from one pound of plastic. New plastic costs 83 cents/pound. Recycled plastic costs 55 cents/pound. Determine the economic impact of using new materials and recycled materials.

    The company needs _____ pounds of plastic. This much plastic will cost the company _____ if it uses new plastic and _____ if it uses recycled plastic.

20. Compare the price of the materials needed to make 75,000 bottles. Which type of plastic is the less expensive choice? How much can the company save by using the less expensive plastic?

    _____
    _____
    _____
    _____
    _____
    _____
    _____
    _____
    _____

Lesson 4 Human Use of Synthetic Materials Affects Earth's Surface

EXPLORATION 3

Relating Engineering and the Life Cycle of Synthetic Materials

Engineers have shaped the life cycle of synthetic materials and the products made from them. You might realize that engineers are involved in producing cell phones. They are also involved in making simple products, such as disposable gloves and plastic bottles.

21. How can improvements that engineers make during a material's life cycle affect its impact on society and the environment?

Engineers designed this machine to test disposable gloves made from a polymer to make sure they do not leak.

Engineers Design Materials and Products

Cell phones have changed drastically since they were first invented. The first cell phones were large and could be used only to talk. Cell phones today are thin, sleek, and can be used to talk and text. They can also do almost anything a computer can do. These changes are the result of improvements that engineers made at some stages of a cell phone's life cycle. To improve cell phones, engineers define the criteria and constraints of a problem. These include the costs, safety, energy usage, potential pollution, and how the material needs to work. They find solutions by analyzing and testing possible solutions.

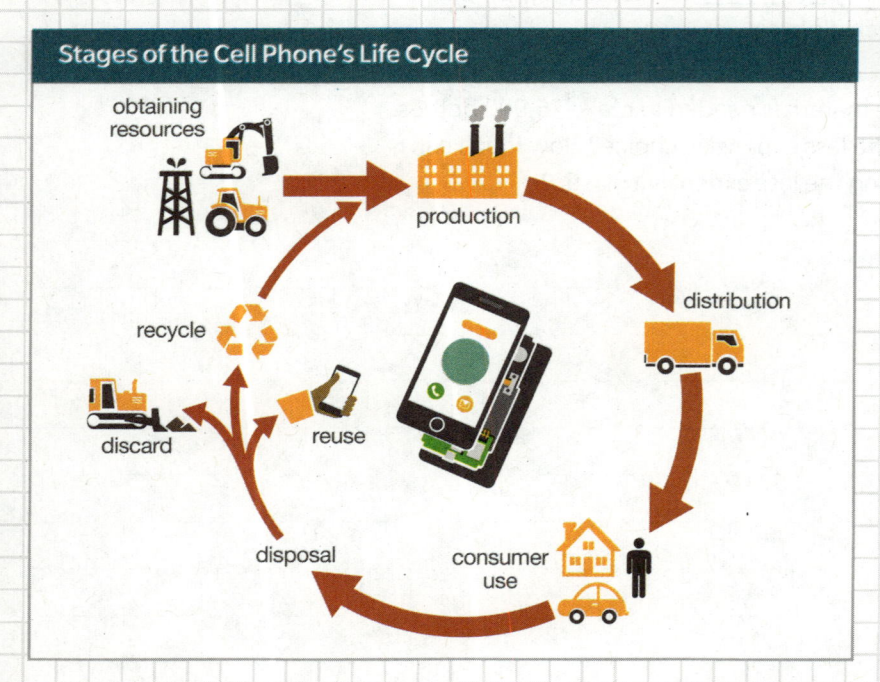

Stages of the Cell Phone's Life Cycle

obtaining resources → production → distribution → consumer use → disposal → discard → reuse → recycle → production

22. **Discuss** What roles might engineers play in the life cycle of a material? Discuss how they might be involved in extracting materials, making and improving materials and products, improving distribution, and sorting recyclables.

506 Unit 6 Earth's Surface and Society

Obtaining Resources

Engineers develop and improve ways of finding and extracting natural resources. They design tools that are used to drill for oil. They have developed new ways of extracting natural gas. These processes provide access to resources that could not be extracted in the past.

One way to extract oil is by hydraulic fracturing, commonly called "fracking." This process involves drilling down to a rock layer that contains oil and injecting a mixture of chemicals at high pressure. The rock fractures, and the oil can then be pumped to the surface. The long-term effects on the groundwater and on the stability of the rock in the area need to be considered along with the benefits that can come from new sources of oil.

23. It is important to know what _natural gases / chemicals_ are being used in hydraulic fracturing operations that are near sources of groundwater. If the chemicals are toxic, they may contaminate the groundwater and may _harm / benefit_ people who consume the groundwater.

This drilling rig is used as part of a hydraulic fracturing operation.

Production

Engineers play many roles in the production of synthetic materials. They oversee the production process. Engineers look for ways to make processes more efficient and cheaper. They figure out ways to minimize waste materials. Engineers also design and improve machines, like the one in the photo. Engineers are also helping to develop and improve renewable resources, including solar and wind energy.

Distribution

Traditional distribution processes include shipping by sea, air, and road. Engineers have been inventing new, "eco-friendly" packaging materials and new ways to use traditional materials. Synthetic materials are involved in the distribution of products in the form of protective packaging, such as packing "peanuts." Engineers are working to help make the processes involved with distribution more efficient. Some companies are considering using drones to deliver their products directly to their customers. The air space above us is a natural resource, and decisions will have to be made about how this resource can be shared. Engineers will have many problems to solve in order to make sure that commercial drones can operate safely.

This machine turns melted plastic into many plastic pieces that are all the same shape.

24. What are some of the problems engineers will have to solve so that commercial drones can deliver products to your home?

Drones can be used to deliver products.

Lesson 4 Human Use of Synthetic Materials Affects Earth's Surface **507**

Consumer Use

Engineers design products to meet the needs and values of consumers. For example, consumers expressed concern about carbon dioxide emissions from gas-powered cars. Engineers worked with scientists to design cars that use less fuel and produce fewer pollutants. As a result, new hybrid cars run on batteries part of the time, and electric cars only use batteries. While battery powered and electric cars reduce or eliminate the need for gas, they still rely on a source of energy to charge their batteries. This energy may come from the sun through solar panels, or from the wind through wind turbines. Both of these technologies use materials that can have long-term effects on the environment.

Solar panels require a lot of space to generate enough energy to meet the needs they were designed to fill.

25. How might using a large area of land for solar panels have a negative affect on a local ecosystem? Select all that apply.

    A. Solar panels can provide energy without creating pollution.

    B. Using land for solar panels disrupts the habitats in the ecosystem.

    C. Solar panels can prevent plants from growing by blocking sunlight from reaching the ground.

    D. Installing solar panels provides jobs for people.

Disposal

While many synthetic materials end up in landfills, or in the oceans, the disposal of natural and synthetic materials can be engineered. For example, engineers have helped improve product packaging so that it has less impact on the environment. Polystyrene foam packing peanuts were once widely used to cushion objects during shipping. The peanuts can be reused, but they cannot be easily recycled. Engineers have developed air-filled plastic pouches and packaging peanuts made out of cornstarch to replace the plastic foam peanuts. These *biodegradable* materials break down without leaving hazardous waste.

Engineers play an important role in the recycling of materials. Materials that can be recycled include metals, glass, paper, and many types of plastic. Not only do the different types of materials need to be separated, the different types of plastics also need to be separated from each other. Engineers have developed methods to separate and clean recycled materials. The materials can then be shredded or melted to make new products.

Food packaging can be made from corn, soy, or sugar cane, which are biodegradable.

26. **Discuss** Why is it important for engineers to consider the entire life cycle of the materials they use when they design new products?

Hands-On Lab
Sort Synthetic Materials Using Properties

You will design a process to separate materials.
You can use only the physical properties of the materials, such as density and attraction to a magnet. Imagine your materials will be going directly from one step to another step. You cannot sort them by picking out the parts by hand. You may make screens with holes in them using scissors and cardboard.

MATERIALS
- bowl of water
- cardboard
- fan
- fine mesh sieve
- magnet
- materials to sort: marbles, metal paper clips, small balls of aluminum foil, plastic straws, pieces of paper
- scissors

Sorting Machine at Recycling Plant

People do sort some materials in recycling centers, but machines do a large part of the sorting based on the properties of the materials.

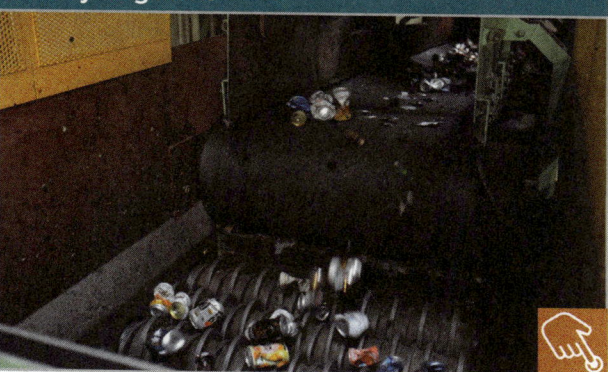

Procedure

STEP 1 Identify the criteria and constraints of the sorting process. Record your notes.

STEP 2 Discuss the properties of the materials and how you might use them to sort the materials. Record your conclusions.

STEP 3 Design a process to sort the materials. Describe your process.

STEP 4 Make a model to test your sorting process. Record your results.

STEP 5 Record any limitations you discovered in your solution. Revise your sorting process as needed to solve any problems you encountered during your tests. Record the changes you make to your process. Record the results of tests using your modified sorting process.

Analysis

STEP 6 Which methods were successful for separating materials by their physical properties, and which methods did not work as expected?

STEP 7 Prepare a presentation for the class to demonstrate how you sorted the materials.

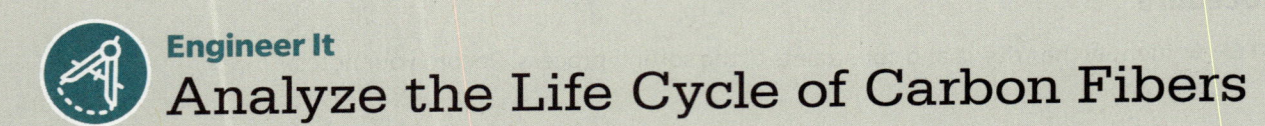

Engineer It
Analyze the Life Cycle of Carbon Fibers

Carbon fiber is a strong synthetic material that has low weight, can resist chemicals, and can withstand high temperatures. It is used in products, such as windmill blades, airplane brakes, and racecar bodies. The process by which carbon fibers are made is relatively expensive because it requires a large amount of energy. The materials must go through several steps of manufacturing, including heating and stretching.

27. Explain how engineers might work to improve the production or consumer use of carbon fiber.

_____
_____
_____
_____
_____
_____
_____

> **EVIDENCE NOTEBOOK**
> 28. At what stage(s) in the life cycle of a plastic bottle could engineers prepare the bottles to become a jacket? Record your evidence.

510 Unit 6 Earth's Surface and Society

TAKE IT FURTHER

Continue Your Exploration

Name: _____ Date: _____

Check out the path below or go online to choose one of the other paths shown.

Careers in Engineering
- Researching Life Cycles
- Hands-On Labs
- Propose Your Own Path

Go online to choose one of these other paths.

Materials Engineer

Materials engineers study how a material's properties are related to its structure. They learn how processing affects the material's properties. Materials engineers develop new materials with specific properties that are suited to their applications. They also develop processes to make these materials, and they test the materials' properties.

Materials engineers work on many kinds of materials in many different products, such as new materials that allow cell phones to work faster or store more information. They make materials that help to restore and protect art. They develop materials that are used inside the body to treat medical conditions. Materials engineers even help protect the environment. They can develop materials that can detect and remove toxic chemicals from water. They are also finding ways to make biodegradable plastics.

This engineer is preparing liquid glass for use in bone implant research. When hardened into foam, the bioactive glass is used as a scaffold for growing human bone.

Lesson 4 Human Use of Synthetic Materials Affects Earth's Surface

TAKE IT FURTHER

Continue Your Exploration

1. A materials engineer is developing new materials that can withstand high-heat environments, such as rocket engines. How might understanding the chemical makeup and properties of materials help the engineer design these materials?

2. People with severe burns need their skin to heal. They often require skin grafts to cover burned areas until they heal. However, the burns can sometimes be too extensive to use the patient's own tissue for the graft. How might this need of burn patients drive materials engineers to design new materials?

3. When boats transporting oil crash or run aground, the water can become polluted with large amounts of crude oil. Because the density of oil is less than that of water, the oil will remain on the water's surface. The oil can then spread and be moved around by water movement and wind. If you were a materials engineer, how might you design a material that could contain the spill and remove as much of the oil from the water as possible?

4. **Collaborate** With a partner, discuss how materials engineers might be involved in the development of synthetic diamonds. What might drive them to want to make diamonds? How might they develop a process to make them? Create a flow chart that shows the life cycle of a synthetic diamond, from inspiration to final product.

LESSON 4 SELF-CHECK

Can You Explain It?

Name: _____ Date: _____

How can engineers change the effects of the synthetic materials in the bottles on the environment by reusing the materials to make the jacket?

EVIDENCE NOTEBOOK
Refer to the notes in your Evidence Notebook to help you construct an explanation for how engineers can change the effects of the synthetic material in the bottles on the environment by reusing the material to make the jacket.

1. State your claim. Make sure your claim fully explains how engineers can change the effects of the synthetic materials in the plastic bottles on the environment by reusing the materials to make the jacket.

2. Summarize the evidence you have gathered to support your claim and explain your reasoning.

Lesson 4 Human Use of Synthetic Materials Affects Earth's Surface 513

LESSON 4 SELF-CHECK

Checkpoints

Answer the following questions to check your understanding of the lesson.

Use the photo to answer Questions 3–4.

3. Which stages of the life cycle of the bowl happen directly before and directly after the stage shown in the photo? Select all that apply.
   A. The production stage happens immediately before.
   B. The distribution stage happens immediately before.
   C. The disposal stage happens immediately after.
   D. The obtaining resources stage happens immediately after.

4. The production of the plastic bowl is driven by the _desire / need_ to have products to prepare food. The color of the bowl reflects the _desire / value_ to have decorative, functional items. The use of the bowl could reflect the _need / value_ that home cooked meals are better than fast food.

Use the photo to answer Questions 5–6.

5. What is a positive impact on society of the synthetic material being consumed in the photo?
   A. Pollution is likely reduced.
   B. Human health is likely improved.
   C. Natural resources are likely conserved.
   D. Carbon dioxide emissions are likely reduced.

6. How are engineers likely to affect the life cycle of a synthetic medicine? Select all that apply.
   A. by optimizing reaction conditions to reduce the cost of making the medicine
   B. by developing ways to package the medicine so that it cannot be opened by children
   C. by determining the price of the medicine to maximize the profit for the company
   D. by regulating the medicine so that it must be prescribed by doctors

7. What negative impact might a factory that produces plastic products have on a local ecosystem? Select all that apply.
   A. Waste from the factory may alter the life cycles of some of the organisms in the ecosystem.
   B. More people from the local area will be employed at the factory.
   C. More roads will be built in the area helping to fragment habitats.
   D. Waste from the factory may be recycled to produce fertilizers for plants in the ecosystem.

LESSON 4 SELF-CHECK

Interactive Review

Complete this section to review the main concepts of the lesson.

Synthetic materials are developed based on consumers' needs, wants, and desires. A five-stage life cycle is one way to model all the ways in which synthetic materials and products can affect society.

A. Make a sketch to show the life cycle of a synthetic material.

Each stage of the life cycle of a material can have positive and negative effects on the environment and society.

B. Explain two positive and two negative effects that synthetic materials could have on society.

Engineers are involved in all stages of the life cycle of synthetic materials.

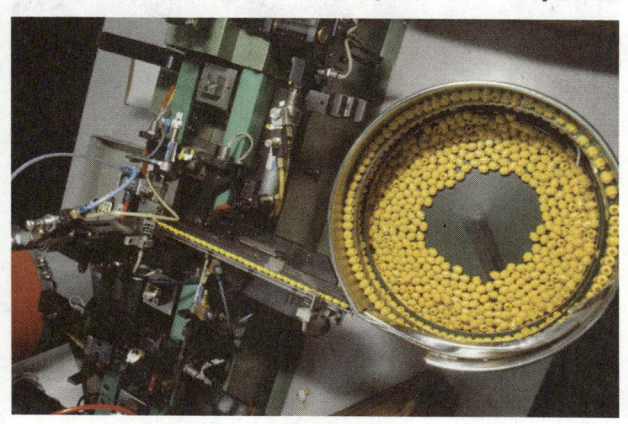

C. Give an example of the type of improvement an engineer could design for two stages of the life cycle of a synthetic product.

Lesson 4 Human Use of Synthetic Materials Affects Earth's Surface

UNIT 6 CONNECTIONS

Choose one of the activities to explore how this unit connects to other topics.

☐ People in Engineering

Dr. Elizabeth Cochran, Geophysicist
Dr. Cochran studies fault zones and ways to monitor earthquakes to better understand the timing and location of earthquakes and how to minimize risks to human populations. Cochran was awarded the Presidential Early Career Awards for Scientists and Engineers for her work on the Quake-Catcher Network, a citizen-science initiative that monitors seismic activity using volunteers' computers.

Research a natural hazard citizen science project, such as the Quake-Catcher Network, that you can participate in individually or as a class. Create a short presentation that describes the objective and methods of the project and your experiences participating in the project.

☐ Life Science Connection

Effects of Plastics on Animals Many animals will be exposed to one or more human-made chemicals in their lifetimes. Many of these chemicals are found in plastic products or are byproducts of plastic manufacturing.

Choose an animal species that has been especially affected by the manufacture and use of plastics. Create an oral presentation of your findings to deliver to your class. Describe how society could help your chosen animal by reducing the effects of harmful chemicals found in plastics.

☐ Health Connection

Natural Disasters and Disease When natural disasters happen, many people lose access to resources such as fresh water and to services such as water and proper sanitation. Without the ability to stay clean and get rid of wastes, people are increasingly likely to become sick.

Research how natural disasters can affect a community's quality of life. Using Hurricane Maria as a case study, analyze how natural disasters can lead to disease outbreaks. Identify ways that this effect of natural hazards could be mitigated. Prepare a multimedia presentation to summarize your findings.

UNIT 6 REVIEW

Name: _____ Date: _____

Use the photograph of the river delta to answer Questions 1–2.

1. At the mouth of a slow-flowing river, a broad, flat delta can form, often extending many kilometers into the sea. Which geologic processes are responsible for the formation of a river delta? Select all that apply.

    A. weathering
    B. erosion
    C. deposition
    D. plate movement

2. What information would you need to determine what natural hazards might affect this region? Select all that apply.

    A. the amount of rainfall it receives
    B. the size of the human population
    C. the distance to the nearest plate boundary
    D. the type of rock that makes up the surface

Use the information provided in the graph to answer Questions 3–4.

3. Between 1900 and 2004, the amount of property damage caused by hurricanes has *increased / decreased* and the number of deaths caused by hurricanes has *increased / decreased*.

4. Which of these factors most likely account for the trends in hurricane damage and deaths over time? Circle all that apply.

    A. decrease in human population in hurricane-prone areas
    B. increase in number of structures in hurricane paths
    C. change in the locations where hurricanes happen
    D. change in the conditions that cause hurricanes
    E. changes in monitoring and forecasting technology

Damages and Deaths from Hurricanes in the United States, 1900–2004

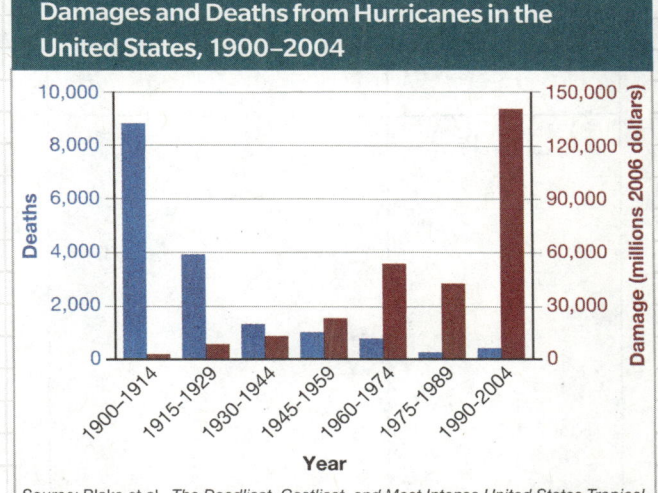

Source: Blake et al., *The Deadliest, Costliest, and Most Intense United States Tropical Cyclones from 1851 to 2006 (and Other Frequently Requested Hurricane Facts)*, NOAA Technical Memorandum NWS TPC-5, updated April 2007

5. As part of the *response to / recovery from* a wildfire, synthetic material combined with water can be dropped on the fire from an airplane.

Unit 6 Earth's Surface and Society **517**

UNIT 6 REVIEW

6. Complete the table by providing at least one example of how these events or processes relate to each big concept.

Hazard or Process	Time and Spatial Scales	Stability and Change	Patterns
Flood			
Earthquake			
Landslide			
Disposal of plastic shopping bag			

UNIT 6 REVIEW

Name: _____ Date: _____

Use the map to answer Questions 7–11.

7. Which regions of Florida have the most sinkholes?

Sinkholes in Florida since 1954

- Bare or thinly covered limestone, with shallow sinkholes
- Sediment cover is 20 to 200 feet thick, mostly sand, with small sinkholes
- Sediment cover is 30 to 200 feet thick, mostly clay, with sinkholes that collapse quickly
- Sediment cover is over 200 feet thick, mostly cohesive sediment, sinkholes are uncommon

Source: USGS, Florida Department of Natural Resources, Florida's Sinkholes, Florida Geological Survey Poster No. 11, 2004

8. What types of sinkholes form most often in each type of rock or soil?

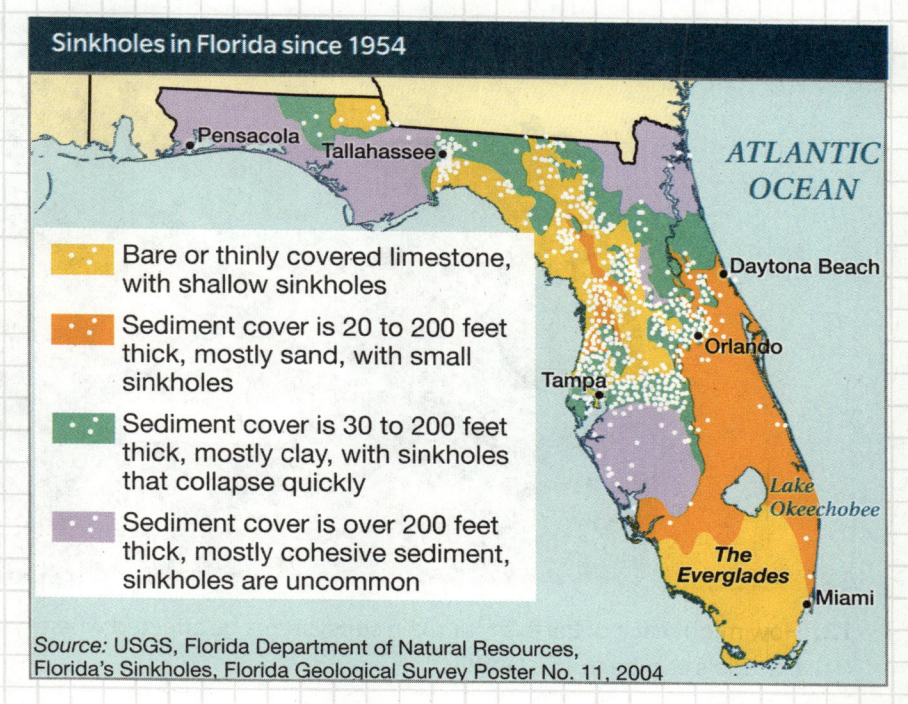

9. What types of monitoring technology and/or precursor events (if any) could be used to forecast sinkhole formation?

10. What would people in Florida need to know in order to develop mitigation protocols for the type of sinkholes that form in a given area? How might mitigation plans differ for people in Pensacola and Orlando?

11. How might synthetic materials be used as part of a sinkhole mitigation plan?

Unit 6 Earth's Surface and Society **519**

UNIT 6 REVIEW

Use the diagram to answer Questions 12–15.

Landfill Exposure Pathways

(diagram showing gas production, surface runoff, and landfill)

12. How might each of Earth's four main subsystems be affected when synthetic materials escape from a landfill?

13. What are some decisions that could be made to reduce the environmental impacts of materials in landfills?

14. What kinds of natural disaster could change the rate at which the waste materials in the landfill enter the surrounding ecosystem?

15. How might the material leaking out of the landfill affect humans living downstream many years after the landfill is closed?

UNIT 6 PERFORMANCE TASK

Name: _____ Date: _____

What is the best plan to improve a park?

Imagine you are on a task force making plans to improve a park near Halls Bayou in Houston, Texas. A bayou is a sluggish stream or river. You want to add features to an existing park for people to enjoy, such as picnic pavilions, playgrounds, soccer fields, a stage, and walking and jogging trails. However, the area is at risk of seasonal flooding. Analyze information about the risk of flooding and use that information to develop a map of your proposed park improvements and a plan for minimizing any flood damage.

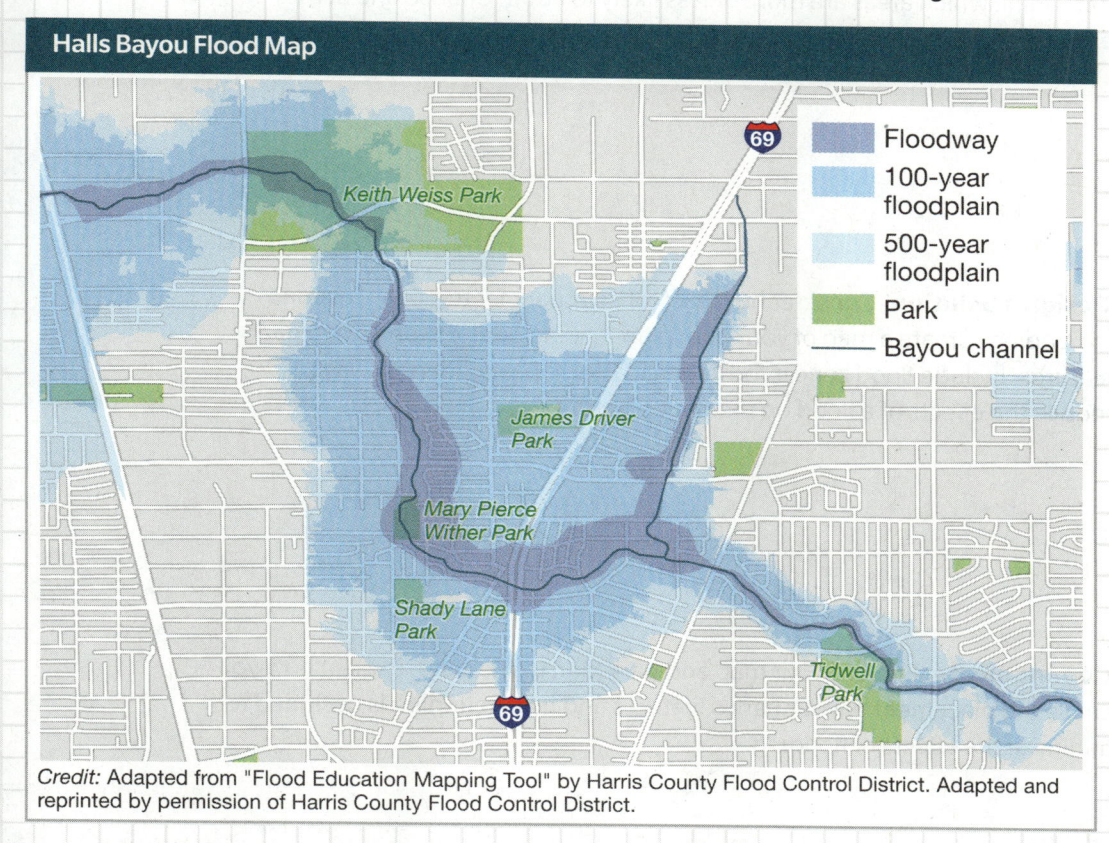

Halls Bayou Flood Map

Legend:
- Floodway
- 100-year floodplain
- 500-year floodplain
- Park
- Bayou channel

Credit: Adapted from "Flood Education Mapping Tool" by Harris County Flood Control District. Adapted and reprinted by permission of Harris County Flood Control District.

The steps below will help guide your research and will help you propose a map of the new park features and a plan to mitigate the effects of flooding.

Engineer It

1. **Ask a Question** What information do you need to know in order to develop your plan?

UNIT 6 PERFORMANCE TASK

Engineer It

2. **Conduct Research** Research the meaning of the different zones on the map: *channel, floodway, 100-year floodplain,* and *500-year floodplain.*

3. **Analyze and Interpret Data** Using past data on floods in this area, determine which areas are more or less likely to flood. Choose one of the existing parks in the area to develop by adding your proposed features.

4. **Design a Solution** Consider how each of your park features will respond to flooding. Create a map of your park plan that includes the proposed park features. Include flood zone information in the map, and identify ways to reduce the effects of a flood on the park's features.

5. **Communicate** Present your map and park plan to the class. Explain how you chose the placement of your park's features and how your park is designed to minimize the effects of flooding.

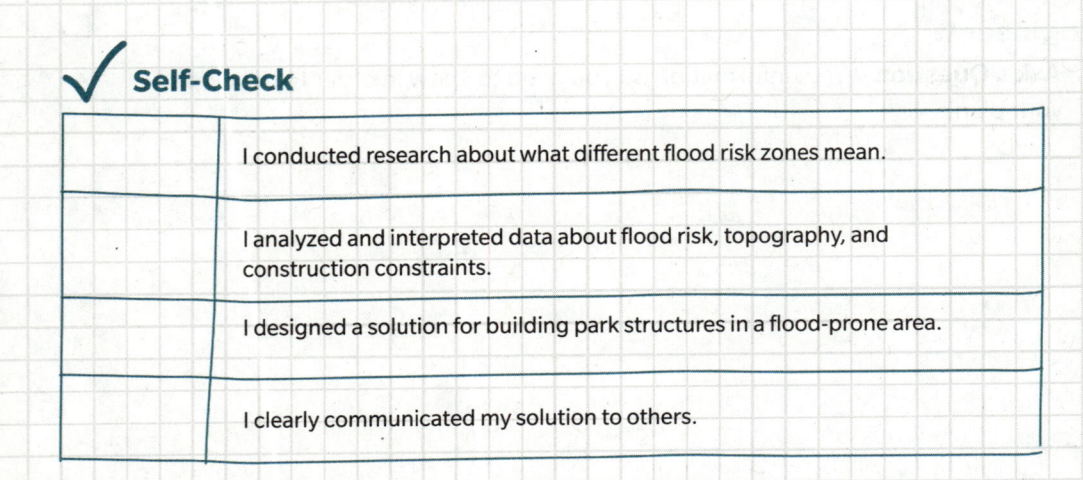

✓ Self-Check

	I conducted research about what different flood risk zones mean.
	I analyzed and interpreted data about flood risk, topography, and construction constraints.
	I designed a solution for building park structures in a flood-prone area.
	I clearly communicated my solution to others.

UNIT 7

Biodiversity and Ecosystem Dynamics

How can humans sustain biodiversity and ecosystem services?

Unit Project	524
Lesson 1 — Biodiversity Indicates Ecosystem Health	526
Lesson 2 — Ecosystems Can Stabilize in Response to Change	544
Lesson 3 — Engineer It: Maintaining Biodiversity and Ecosystem Services	562
Unit Review	589
Unit Performance Task	593

The size and salt level of the Great Salt Lake in Utah change over time. As water evaporates, salt deposits are left behind.

You Solve It Why are Adélie penguin population sizes changing?

Investigate changing penguin populations in Antarctica by analyzing maps and data about climate, food, feeding behaviors, and penguins.

Go online and complete the You Solve It to explore ways to solve a real-world problem.

UNIT 7 PROJECT

Evaluate Biodiversity Design Solutions

This cougar, known as P-22, lives in Griffith Park in Los Angeles. U.S. Route 101 divides cougar habitat in southern California, reducing the animals' natural hunting and breeding range.

A. Look at the photo. On a separate sheet of paper, write down as many different questions as you can about the photo.

B. Discuss With your class or a partner, share your questions. Record any additional questions generated in your discussion. Then choose the most important questions from the list that are related to maintaining biodiversity. Write them below.

C. Choose a problem related to biodiversity loss in your area or in another location to research. Here's a list of problems you can consider:
- extinction of wild native crows on Mauna Loa in Hawaii
- deforestation of Europe
- coral reef bleaching
- local extinction of wild lynx in Colorado
- introduction of mongoose populations in Hawaii
- feral cat populations

What problem related to biodiversity loss will you research?

D. Use the information above, along with your research, to evaluate design solutions for the biodiversity problem you choose.

Discuss the next steps for your Unit Project with your teacher and go online to download the Unit Project Worksheet.

UNIT 7

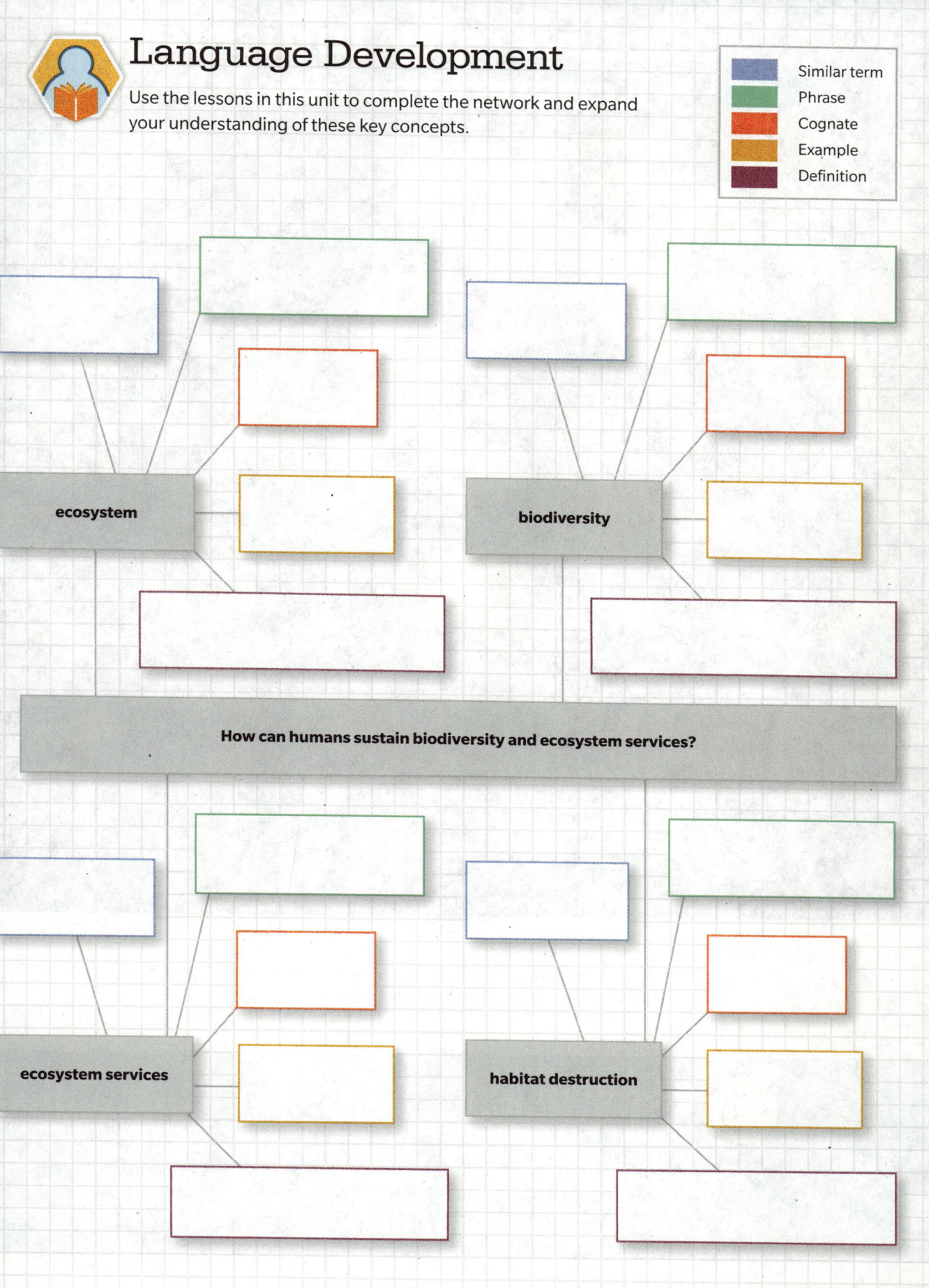

Language Development

Use the lessons in this unit to complete the network and expand your understanding of these key concepts.

- Similar term
- Phrase
- Cognate
- Example
- Definition

ecosystem

biodiversity

How can humans sustain biodiversity and ecosystem services?

ecosystem services

habitat destruction

Unit 7 Biodiversity and Ecosystem Dynamics

LESSON 1

Biodiversity Indicates Ecosystem Health

This coral reef ecosystem in Thailand is home to a large number and variety of animals and other organisms.

Explore First

Modeling Ecosystem Change What contributes to an ecosystem's ability to recover from change? Model an ecosystem by using colored blocks to build a structure. Each color represents a different part of the ecosystem. What happens when you remove all the blocks of one color? How could you change this outcome?

Go online to view the digital version of the Hands-On Lab for this lesson and to download additional lab resources.

CAN YOU EXPLAIN IT?

What factors might influence how this ecosystem would recover from such a large and sudden flood?

before flood

during flood

Several days of heavy rains caused the Vltava River in the Czech Republic to flood extensively in 2002. Towns and cities as well as the natural environment were all affected by this sudden disturbance. Some areas recovered more quickly than others.

1. Study the two photos. Construct a cause-and-effect statement about how the flooding likely affected this ecosystem.

2. What types of living things do you think were the first to return or regrow after the floodwaters receded?

EVIDENCE NOTEBOOK As you explore this lesson, gather evidence to help explain what factors might influence this ecosystem's recovery after a flood.

Lesson 1 Biodiversity Indicates Ecosystem Health **527**

EXPLORATION 1

Describing Biodiversity

Forests, salt marshes, deserts, and lakes are all examples of ecosystems. An ecosystem can be a small pond or extend across a vast grassland. Although there are many different types of ecosystems, they all have some common features. An **ecosystem** is a system made up of all the living and nonliving things in a given area. The living parts of an ecosystem interact with each other and with nonliving parts. Because of these interactions, ecosystems are dynamic—they are always changing. For example, the living components shown in the photos constantly interact with the nonliving and other living components. The macaques, a type of monkey, take in oxygen by breathing air and eat mostly plants and insects. The sea stars take in oxygen from the water through their feet and eat mostly mollusks.

This land ecosystem in Morocco contains several populations of organisms, including the endangered Barbary macaque. Macaques live alongside humans in certain parts of Morocco.

This marine ecosystem also contains several populations of organisms, including sea stars and mollusks. They live alongside many types of fish and coral in this ecosystem.

3. Fill in the table by listing the components in the word bank as living or nonliving parts of the ecosystems in the photos.

Living	Nonliving
	water

WORD BANK
- ~~water~~
- plants
- sand
- air
- fish
- rocks
- macaques
- algae

528 Unit 7 Biodiversity and Ecosystem Dynamics

Biodiversity

One way to evaluate the health of an ecosystem is to consider its biodiversity. **Biodiversity** refers to the variety of life in Earth's land, freshwater, and marine ecosystems. Biodiversity can be studied at different scales. Scales can range from a small area, such as a drop of water, to a large area, such as a forest. An area's biodiversity may be made up of a few species or thousands of species. High biodiversity exists when there are many species and individuals of those species living in an ecosystem. Low biodiversity exists when there is a low number of species in an ecosystem. The biodiversity of an area can be described as the combination of genetic diversity, species diversity, and ecosystem diversity.

Levels of Biodiversity

Genetic diversity refers to the variation of genes within a species or population in a given area. For example, the coyotes living in this prairie may vary in body size, leg length, fur color, or other characteristics. These characteristics are encoded by genes, which are passed from generation to generation. All the possible genetic variations of the coyotes in this prairie make up the population's genetic diversity.

Species diversity refers to both the number of different species that are in a given area and the number of individuals of each species that are there. In this prairie, you can see a variety of plants and animals. If you could see more of this ecosystem, you would most likely see more species. These species interact with each other and with the nonliving parts of the prairie ecosystem.

Ecosystem diversity refers to the variety of ecosystems in a given area. Ecosystem diversity refers to both land and aquatic ecosystems. For example, the area shown here contains several types of ecosystems, including a stream, a prairie, and a riverbank. Ecosystems may be large or very small.

4. Which statement best describes an example of low species diversity?
   A. A population of chorus frogs has a wide variety of skin colors.
   B. A marsh ecosystem is covered by a single species of cattail bulrushes.
   C. A state park includes multiple forest, wetland, and freshwater ecosystems.

Hands-On Lab
Measure Biodiversity

Conduct a simulated measurement of two types of biodiversity: species richness and species abundance.

Bumblebees are important pollinators of plants and crops. Humans rely on them to pollinate food crops. Suppose you are surveying bumblebees within a tall-grass prairie ecosystem. Your job is to provide an estimate of their biodiversity.

Tricolor bumblebees nest underground in colonies.

Procedure and Analysis

STEP 1 Observe the jar of beans. It is a model of the bumblebee population found in a tall-grass prairie ecosystem. The different bean types represent the different bumblebee species. Decide which bean type will represent each species and record this information in the table.

STEP 2 Take a full scoop of beans from the jar. These beans represent individual bumblebees from your sample area.

STEP 3 *Species richness* refers to the number of different species found in a given area. What is the species richness of your sample area?

STEP 4 *Species abundance* refers to the number of individuals of each species found in a given area. Record in the table the species abundance for each species found in your sample area.

STEP 5 **Do the Math** Determine the relative species abundance for each species in the sample area. Relative species abundance will be reported as a percentage. Record your data in the table.

$$\text{Relative abundance} = \frac{\text{species abundance}}{\text{total number of bumblebees in sample}} \times 100$$

MATERIALS
- large jar of dried beans (6 different types)
- scoop or cup

Data for Sample Area

Bumblebee species	Bean type	Species abundance	Relative abundance
Common eastern			
Rusty patched			
American			
Two-spotted			
Tricolored			
Brown-belted			

530 Unit 7 Biodiversity and Ecosystem Dynamics

STEP 6 Draw a second table on a sheet of paper and combine your data with the data from the rest of the class. What is the species richness, according to class data?

STEP 7 Record species abundance in the class data table. Calculate and record relative species abundance using the overall class data.

STEP 8 How did your data differ from the overall class data? What might account for any differences? Discuss these questions in small groups. Then share ideas and listen to others in a whole-class discussion.

STEP 9 Develop hypotheses about the size of the scoop of beans you would need to be able to accurately measure different types of biodiversity and to sample rare bumblebee species in the ecosystem.

Identify Patterns in Biodiversity

A variety of factors, including location, climate, and resource availability, can affect an ecosystem's biodiversity. Certain regions of Earth have very high biodiversity compared to other regions. Some of these regions have been identified as biodiversity hotspots. A *biodiversity hotspot* is a region that has high biodiversity and is threatened with possible destruction. Some land and marine hotspots are identified on the map.

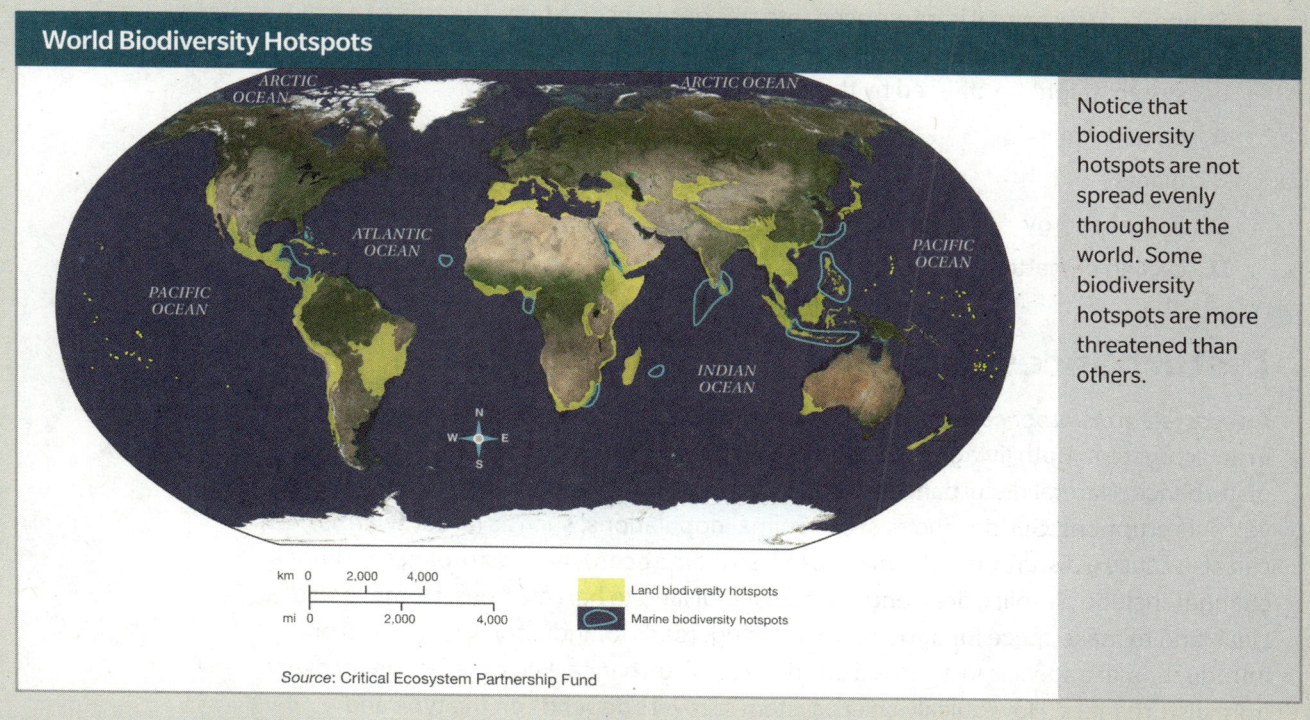

World Biodiversity Hotspots

Notice that biodiversity hotspots are not spread evenly throughout the world. Some biodiversity hotspots are more threatened than others.

Source: Critical Ecosystem Partnership Fund

5. Biodiversity hotspots are common near the equator / poles.
   Hotspots include ecosystems on land only / land and in water .

Lesson 1 Biodiversity Indicates Ecosystem Health **531**

EXPLORATION 2

Evaluating Ecosystem Health

Changes to an ecosystem can affect how the parts of an ecosystem interact. Within a healthy ecosystem, however, factors stay more or less within a certain range and in a mostly stable condition, even as individual parts change. Ecologists call this phenomenon *ecosystem stability*. Recall that matter and energy flow among the living and nonliving parts of an ecosystem. A change to any part of an ecosystem may disrupt the flow of energy and matter.

Ecosystem Interactions Include the Flow of Energy and Matter

- Sunlight is the original source of energy in this desert ecosystem.
- Plants use energy from sunlight to transform water and carbon dioxide into sugars and oxygen during photosynthesis. The plants take in water from the soil and carbon dioxide from the air. They use the sugars they make as food.
- These burros eat plants in the Sonoran desert. Energy and matter move from the plants into the burros.

6. Suppose a new animal is introduced into this desert ecosystem. The animal has no natural predators. It eats the same plants the wild burros do. Which parts of the ecosystem might be affected by this change? Choose all that apply.

   A. other animals
   B. plants
   C. flow of energy
   D. cycling of matter

Disturbances in Ecosystems

An *ecosystem disturbance* is a change in environmental conditions that causes a change in an ecosystem. Both living and nonliving parts of an ecosystem can be affected by a disturbance. Natural disturbances include wildfires, storms, flooding, tsunamis, and volcanic eruptions. Sudden increases in animal populations, such as insect swarms, can also cause a disturbance. Humans can also create ecosystem disturbances. These changes include oil spills, fires, and the clearing of land to harvest trees. Humans also clear land to make space for agriculture, housing, roads, or industry. The removal or introduction of a species in an area also creates a disturbance. Ecosystems can recover from disturbances. How quickly an ecosystem recovers depends on the type and severity of the disturbance.

An Ecosystem Disturbance

A landslide greatly affected this ecosystem in the Philippines. The land was covered by mud and rocks that removed plants and displaced people and other animals.

This photo shows the same ecosystem just one year after the landslide. Plants are growing on the landslide mud. Animals and people have returned to live in the area.

The biodiversity of an ecosystem that experiences a disturbance can influence how well the ecosystem recovers. Ecosystems with high biodiversity have many species fulfilling certain roles, such as pollinator, decomposer, and predator. The graphic below shows how ecosystems with high and low biodiversity can be affected by disturbances.

Biodiversity Impacts Ecosystem Stability

This graphic models the stability of four different ecosystems during years with different amounts of rainfall. The different-colored dots represent different species of insect pollinators. Some of these insects do better in high-rainfall years. Others do better in low-rainfall years.

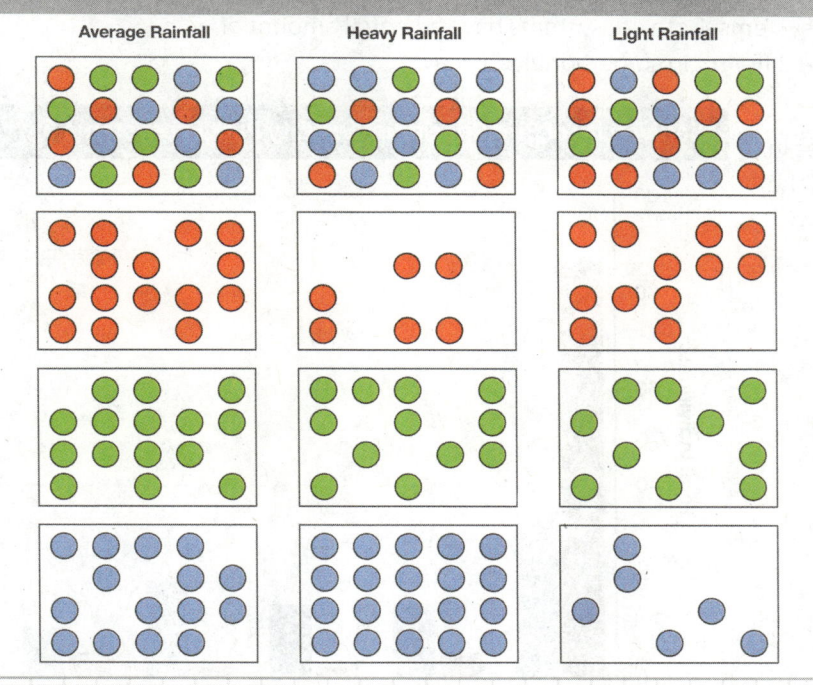

Average Rainfall | **Heavy Rainfall** | **Light Rainfall**

Diverse community Some species do better in wetter years. Others do better in drier years. The total number of pollinators remains stable.

Community made up mostly of red species This pollinator species is negatively affected by high rainfall.

Community made up of mostly green species This pollinator species does poorly in wetter and drier years.

Community made up of mostly blue species This pollinator species is negatively affected by low rainfall.

7. In your own words, explain how rainfall could influence the species abundance over time in the different communities. In which ecosystem is the least amount of change observed in the abundance of pollinators?

Biodiversity and Ecosystem Health

The health of an ecosystem includes its ability to recover from a disturbance. Ecological diversity, species diversity, and genetic diversity all contribute to ecosystem stability. A diverse ecosystem has more ways to recover from a disturbance. If one species dies or leaves a diverse ecosystem, another species can take its place. As a result, the ecosystem can stabilize more quickly.

An ecosystem with lowered biodiversity is less able to recover from a disturbance. Some ecosystems, such as those in polar regions, can maintain stability while naturally having lower biodiversity than warmer regions. Ecosystems generally become less stable when their biodiversity levels are lowered from their baseline levels.

> **EVIDENCE NOTEBOOK**
> 8. How would biodiversity levels affect the recovery of ecosystems along the Vltava River after the floodwaters recede? Record your evidence.

Do the Math
Assess Ecosystem Health

Having many different species in an ecosystem is a sign of high-species diversity. But the size of each population of species is also important. A population can be too small. Fewer individuals means there is less genetic diversity in a population. The graph shows the biodiversity of birds in two ecosystems. Both ecosystems have an equal amount of species diversity. However, they are different in some significant ways.

9. What are the main differences in species abundance between the populations of birds in the two ecosystems?

10. Given the data in the graph, what can you predict about how each ecosystem might recover from a disturbance?

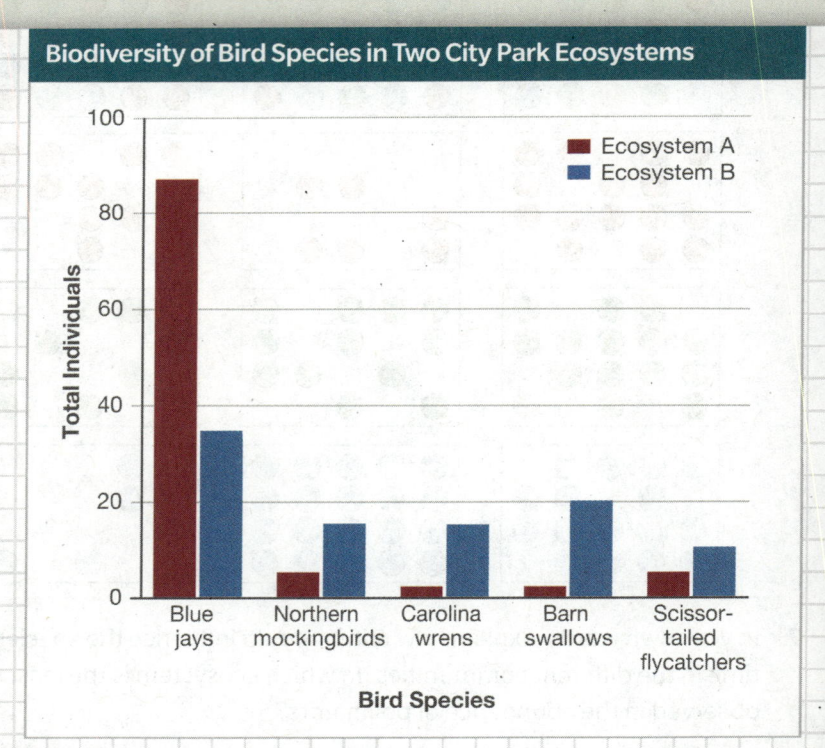

Biodiversity of Bird Species in Two City Park Ecosystems

534 Unit 7 Biodiversity and Ecosystem Dynamics

EXPLORATION 3

Analyzing Human Influences on Biodiversity

Humans have designed structures and developed processes that help them survive in their environments. Ecosystems provide the energy and raw materials that humans need to live and survive. For example, we use wood from trees to build homes. We burn wood and fossil fuels to provide energy. Humans rely on ecosystems to grow crops and raise livestock. Humans also depend on the nonliving parts of ecosystems for clean air, fresh water, and living space. In this way, humans can also affect the health and biodiversity of different ecosystems.

Humans introduced the European honeybee (*Apis mellifera*) to North America. These bees make honey and beeswax.

11. Humans rely on certain services that ecosystems provide. Which ecosystem processes below do humans benefit from? Circle all that apply.

    A. decomposition of wastes
    B. pollination of crops
    C. filtering of fresh water
    D. growth of trees and plants

Humans Are Part of Earth's Ecosystems

Humans rely on and can influence ecosystems. We depend on healthy ecosystems for survival and for a good quality of life. For example, every time you breathe or drink a glass of water, you depend on ecosystem processes to provide oxygen and fresh, clean water. Healthy ecosystems buffer the impact of storms, limit the spread of disease, and recycle nutrients. Humans rely on ecosystems to reduce the effects of droughts and floods, provide fertile soils, pollinate crops and plants, disperse seeds, and control pests by natural predators. These beneficial functions depend on ecosystem health, which is often measured by the integrity of an ecosystem's biodiversity. For these reasons and more, high biodiversity in ecosystems is important to all humans.

Negative Impacts on Biodiversity

Human activities affect the biodiversity of ecosystems. Although we rely on healthy ecosystems, many human activities negatively affect biodiversity. Some activities cause direct negative effects, such as overharvesting of plants or animals. Other activities cause indirect negative effects. For example, constructing new buildings can destroy habitats and reduce biodiversity. Releasing garbage and pollution into the environment can harm or poison organisms and reduce biodiversity.

Habitat Destruction

Activities such as the construction of roads, buildings, towns, and cities cause habitat destruction. Mining and harvesting resources also remove habitats. Less habitat means less biodiversity at all levels—ecosystem, species, and genetic. Human activity can also break large habitats into smaller pieces. When a habitat is broken into smaller pieces, animals that need a large area of habitat can no longer live there.

Habitat destruction occurs when land is cleared for development.

Introduced Species

Tulips, orange trees, and many other highly valued plants are now grown in the United States. However, they are not native to the country. People introduced them to a new environment when they brought them from other countries. These nonnative species are called *introduced species*. Introduced species can have negative impacts on ecosystems. For example, buckthorn, lionfish, emerald ash borers, and Burmese pythons are invasive organisms that threaten native species in several North American ecosystems. These species do not have predators or other natural factors in their new environments that limit their populations' growth.

Pet Burmese pythons that were released into the wild threaten biodiversity in areas of South Florida.

Overharvested Species

Many fish species are harvested for food. The overharvesting of certain fish species threatens marine biodiversity. For example, decades of overfishing led to an extreme drop in populations of Atlantic cod in the early 1990s. This almost caused the collapse of the cod fishing industry. The fishing of Atlantic cod in the north Atlantic was banned in 1992. Overharvesting of plants such as coneflower and American ginseng has greatly reduced their wild population sizes. Land animal species, such as bison, have also been hunted to near extinction. When a population is reduced to a very small size due to overharvesting, genetic diversity is lost.

Atlantic cod populations are closely monitored and are slowly recovering from near extinction in the early 1990s.

Lack of Biodiversity in Food Crops

Many of today's food crops have very little genetic diversity. Some crops, such as bananas, are all genetically identical. Recall that genetic diversity in a population increases the likelihood that some members of a population will survive a disturbance such as a disease. Genetically identical food crops are more likely to be destroyed by a disturbance because every plant reacts in the same way. In the case of bananas, a fungal disease, called *Panama disease,* is destroying banana plants. This disease is threatening banana crops and the livelihood of the people who grow and sell them.

Scientists are working on reintroducing into crops some of the wild-type genes that were lost during domestication. The intention of this bioengineering is to make hardier crops. The wild cousins of crop plants tend to be better able to survive disturbances. Scientists hope that reintroducing wild genes into crop plants will create crops that are more pest and drought resistant and better able to take in nutrients from the soil.

> **EVIDENCE NOTEBOOK**
> 12. Look at the image of the ecosystem before the flood. What evidence of human influence do you see, and how might this affect the ecosystem's recovery after the flood? Record your evidence.

Efforts to Protect Biodiversity

Not all human activities negatively affect biodiversity. Around the globe, people are working to limit the negative impact of human activity and preserve biodiversity. In many locations, nature preserves have been created to protect habitats. Wildlife corridors have been created to connect areas of natural habitat divided by roads or development. Awareness of overharvesting has also become more common. This awareness promotes policies to prevent additional overharvesting and guide the recovery of populations. One way plant biodiversity has been supported is by creating seed banks around the world. These banks help preserve biodiversity by storing different types of plant seeds. Seed banks are a resource for plant breeders.

This forest is managed in a way that provides a sustainable source of wood for industry.

13. **Language SmArts** Construct an argument about why people should work toward having positive influences on biodiversity. Support your claims with clear reasons and relevant evidence. Present your argument to the class.

Engineer It
Monitor and Preserve Biodiversity

Disrupting any part of an ecosystem can change its biodiversity. Suppose a builder clears a field to build houses. In the field, several wildflower species grow. Different animal species living in and around the field depended on the wildflowers for food. Without the food source, those species would die or move away.

Measuring biodiversity before and after a disturbance is one way to monitor changes in an ecosystem. For example, biodiversity counts can be taken before the field is cleared and again after the houses are built. Comparing these counts helps determine the effects the disturbance had on the health of the area. Solutions can be incorporated into building designs to help preserve and protect biodiversity that may be affected by a development.

14. How might biodiversity data be used to design a solution for maintaining biodiversity at a new housing development?

_____

A grid is a tool used to mark sample areas and survey biodiversity. The species within the grid are counted.

15. Describe a design problem that is addressed by the rooftop garden on the building shown in the photo.

_____

The plants on this rooftop are part of a solution to minimize the impact that concrete, asphalt, roof tiles, and other non-absorbent surfaces have on the surrounding environment.

16. Write either a + or a − sign to identify positive or negative impacts on biodiversity.

_____ planting native plants that support native pollinators

_____ collecting rainwater to reuse for irrigation

_____ building a "rain garden" to promote filtering of runoff after rainfall

_____ constructing a road that divides habitat that was once connected

_____ clearing of land to build new buildings

TAKE IT FURTHER

Continue Your Exploration

Name: _____ Date: _____

Check out the path below or go online to choose one of the other paths shown.

Careers in Science
- You Are an Ecosystem
- Hands-On Labs 👋
- Propose Your Own Path

Go online to choose one of these other paths.

Restoration Ecologist

Restoration ecology is a field that focuses on restoring freshwater, marine, and land ecosystems that have been damaged by human activity. Restoration ecologists help design solutions to problems facing ecosystems. These solutions help preserve biodiversity. Restoration ecologists may provide assistance to government agencies and to businesses. Some jobs restoration ecologists might do include:

- controlling and removing invasive species
- helping farmers to use sustainable farming practices
- working to improve habitats for specific species
- planning and developing practices for soil or land conservation
- planning and implementing the restoration of ocean, lake, or stream shorelines

Restoration ecologists may work alone or with others, in the field or in an office. They often collect data in the field and return to an office or laboratory to analyze the data. Then they develop a solution to the biodiversity problem. They may use mapping and computer modeling to help in developing these solutions. Other science disciplines use similar methods and equipment to obtain and evaluate evidence. Accurately collecting and analyzing evidence and applying conclusions in a valid manner is the nature of science.

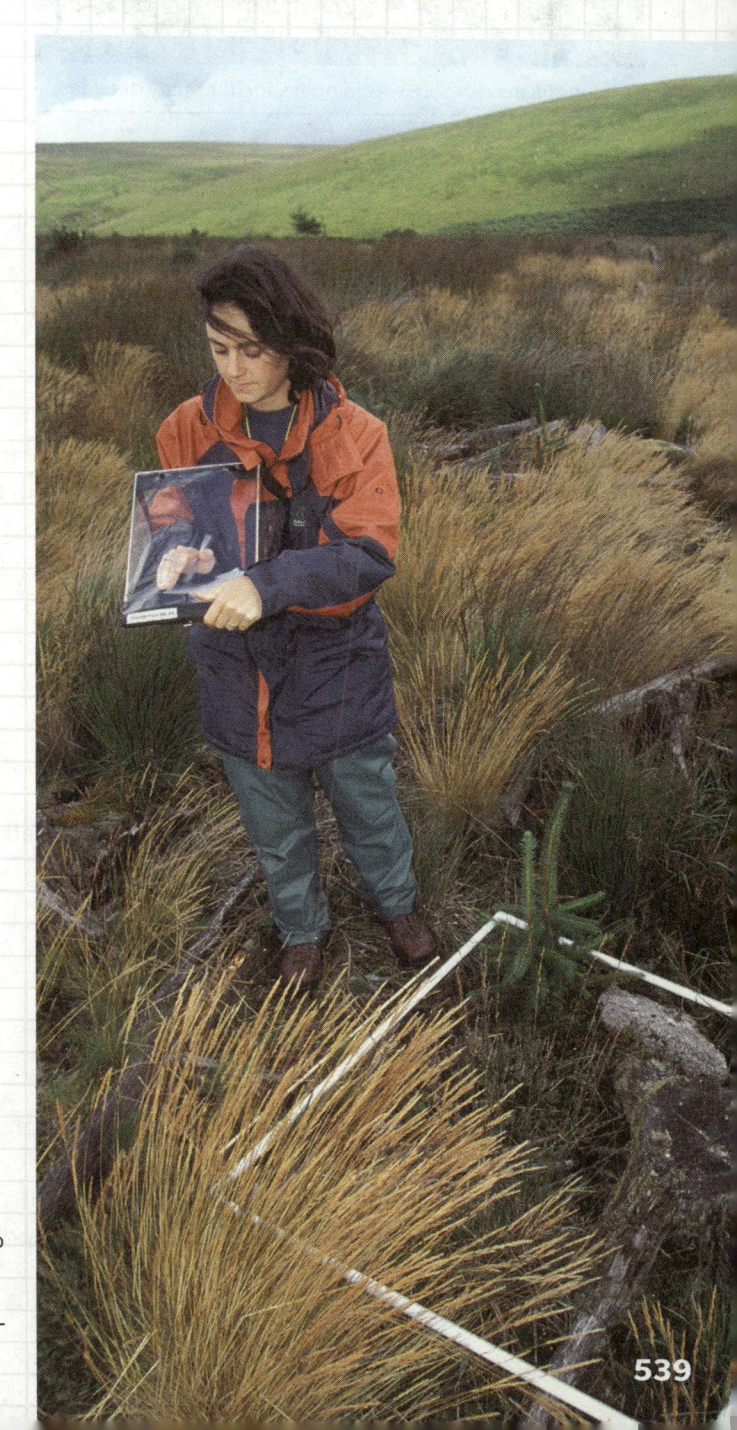

This restoration ecologist is collecting data to study the change in plant communities at a nature reserve in southern England.

539

TAKE IT FURTHER

Continue Your Exploration

This landfill in New York was in operation for many decades.

Through restoration and engineering efforts, the landfill is being transformed into a park that includes wildlife habitats.

1. An organization wants to restore an area's ecosystem to attract bird species that used to live there. How might a restoration ecologist help them?

2. Look at the photos of the landfill area and its restoration. Describe at least two ways that changes to living and nonliving components of the ecosystem have positively affected the biodiversity of the area.

3. What types of evidence might help determine whether the restored ecosystem has high biodiversity?

4. **Collaborate** With a group, outline a restoration project in an area in your community. Suppose that you and your classmates are the restoration ecologists planning and carrying out the work. Develop a short presentation of your proposal. Include an explanation for how the project would positively affect biodiversity in the area.

LESSON 1 SELF-CHECK

Can You Explain It?

Name: _____ Date: _____

What factors might influence how this ecosystem would recover from such a large and sudden flood?

before flood | during flood

EVIDENCE NOTEBOOK
Refer to the notes in your Evidence Notebook to help you construct an explanation for how this ecosystem might have recovered from such a huge and sudden disturbance.

1. State your claim. Make sure your claim fully explains what might influence how this ecosystem would recover from the flood.

2. Summarize the evidence you have gathered to support your claim and explain your reasoning.

Lesson 1 Biodiversity Indicates Ecosystem Health

LESSON 1 SELF-CHECK

Checkpoints

Answer the following questions to check your understanding of the lesson.

Use the photo to answer Question 3.

3. What can you tell about this population of king penguins and their icy Sandwich Island ecosystem from the photo? Choose all that apply.
   A. There is low genetic diversity in this population of king penguins.
   B. It is likely to be one of the largest bird populations in the ecosystem.
   C. Not a lot of species diversity can be seen in this photo.
   D. A lot of species diversity is shown in this photo.

4. An ecosystem with _high / low_ biodiversity is better able to recover from a disturbance because the more biodiverse an ecosystem is, the _more / less_ likely it is that some organisms will survive and continue to grow.

Use the photo to answer Question 5.

5. This photo shows restoration efforts at a former open-pit mine. How will the restoration of this land most likely affect populations of organisms in the surrounding area?
   A. Biodiversity will likely increase.
   B. Population sizes will likely decrease.
   C. Stability will likely decrease.
   D. Disturbances will likely increase.

6. In order to make crop growing more economical, crops such as wheat, corn, and potatoes are often grown on large areas of land where all other plants have been removed. Why can this type of planting style make crops more prone to outbreaks of disease?
   A. The high species diversity associated with croplands leads to poor crop health.
   B. Biodiversity of the cultivated land where the crops grow is very low.
   C. Genetic diversity in crops is typically high, leading to more disease outbreaks.
   D. All ecosystems managed by humans have low biodiversity and poor health.

LESSON 1 SELF-CHECK

Interactive Review

Complete this section to review the main concepts of the lesson.

Biodiversity refers to the variety of life that is a part of Earth's ecosystems. Biodiversity can be studied at the ecosystem, species, and genetic level.

A. Explain why it is important to consider all three levels of biodiversity rather than just one.

An *ecosystem disturbance* is a temporary change in environmental conditions that causes a change in an ecosystem. The health of an ecosystem can be defined by its ability to recover or remain stable when a disturbance occurs.

B. What evidence is used as an indicator of ecosystem health? Explain your answer.

Humans, just like other organisms, need healthy ecosystems in which to survive, but many human activities have negative effects on ecosystems and their biodiversity.

C. Describe how humans can influence biodiversity by using specific examples.

Lesson 1 Biodiversity Indicates Ecosystem Health **543**

LESSON 2

Ecosystems Can Stabilize in Response to Change

Bare rock is exposed for the first time in thousands of years after a glacier retreats from Aialik Bay in Kenai Fjords National Park, Alaska.

Explore First

Thinking About Changes Think of your school as an ecosystem. In groups, brainstorm ways the school could change suddenly and ways it could change gradually. Discuss how each type of change would affect the students, teachers, and staff at the school.

Go online to view the digital version of the Hands-On Lab for this lesson and to download additional lab resources.

CAN YOU EXPLAIN IT?

How would the arrival of a swarm of millions of desert locusts affect an ecosystem?

Desert locusts look and act a lot like grasshoppers, although they are larger. They normally eat plants and live alone. However, certain changes in environmental conditions, such as a drought, can cause them to come together in swarms to travel long distances to find food.

1. Why might a drought cause normally solitary desert locusts to change their behavior and swarm?

2. How might swarming locusts affect planted crops? How might the swarms affect local populations of humans and insect-eating birds?

EVIDENCE NOTEBOOK As you explore the lesson, gather evidence to help explain how an insect swarm would affect an ecosystem.

Lesson 2 Ecosystems Can Stabilize in Response to Change **545**

EXPLORATION 1

Describing Changes in Ecosystems

Yikes! You lift up a rotting log from a forest floor and several insects dash away from it. You disturbed their ecosystem! An *ecosystem* is a natural system in which organisms interact with the living and nonliving parts of their environment.

Insects are not the only living things in a forest floor ecosystem. You might also observe spiders, fungi, snails, mosses, worms, or a toad. Vines, ferns, and other plants might also grow on the forest floor. All of these living organisms depend on each other and the nonliving parts of the ecosystem. The nonliving parts include rocks, nutrients, air, and water. The log on the forest floor is not alive, but it supports lots of life. Some living things break down the log's cells for food. This decomposition releases nutrients from the log back into the soil. In this way, energy and matter cycle between the living and nonliving parts of an ecosystem.

Explore Online

Forest Floor Ecosystem

Ecosystems, even tiny ones, contain living and nonliving parts that interact. Plants take in minerals from the soil and carbon dioxide from the air. Snails eat plants. They also eat soil to get calcium for their shells.

3. A system input is any energy, matter, or information that enters a system. Which factors would be inputs of a forest floor ecosystem? Select the correct answers.

    A. soil
    B. sunlight
    C. rain
    D. trees

4. **Discuss** How do you think a decrease in one of these inputs would affect the forest floor ecosystem?

Ecosystems Change Over Time

Ecosystems are dynamic, which means their characteristics can change over time. Even healthy ecosystems with high biodiversity change a bit every day. In every ecosystem, organisms are born, some die, and all living things respond to changes. Ecosystems with high biodiversity can recover from changes more easily than those with less diversity. Some changes, such as the seasons, are gradual. Other changes, such as a storm or a flood, are sudden.

Seasonal Changes

spring | summer | Changes in temperature, precipitation and sunlight occur during the seasons. They cause changes in ecosystems. This tree goes from budding new leaves in spring to full bloom in summer. Then it loses its leaves in the fall and is inactive through the winter.

fall | winter

5. Classify each statement as a change to a living factor or a change to a nonliving factor.

Change	Change to Living Factor	Change to Nonliving Factor
Birds migrate in fall.		
Ice that covers lakes melts in spring.		
Temperature increases in summer.		
Leaves fall from trees in fall.		
Seeds sprout in spring.		
Water in soil freezes in winter.		

6. Some bird populations that live in the northern hemisphere migrate to warmer climates for the winter. Identify reasons birds might respond this way to a seasonal change in their habitat.

Lesson 2 Ecosystems Can Stabilize in Response to Change 547

Gradual Changes

Gradual changes are going on all the time in every ecosystem. For example, ponds and lakes undergo an aging process that involves gradual changes over hundreds of years. Sediment builds up in a body of water, eventually changing it into land. Sediment buildup also leads to natural *eutrophication*. During this process, nutrients from plants and rock minerals dissolve in the water. The nutrients boost growth of plants and algae. When the plants and algae die, they decompose. Decomposition requires oxygen, so over time, the water becomes depleted of oxygen.

As these changes occur, the pond ecosystem also changes. Fish, amphibian, and insect populations will die out or move to a different pond. Eventually, all populations living in the pond ecosystem will be affected by the change. Gradual changes also take place as glaciers melt, logs rot, and climates change. Even a relatively small increase in temperatures can have a widespread effect on ecosystems.

Over a long period of time, this pond filled up with sediment and changed into a meadow.

sediment builds up

7. The effects of the change to the pond will most likely be ~~short term~~ / **long term** as the pond ecosystem changes to a meadow. The living and nonliving parts of the ecosystems will **change** / ~~stay the same~~.

Sudden Changes

Forest fires, tornadoes, volcanic eruptions, and floods can all cause sudden changes to an ecosystem. For example, if a river floods, its banks may burst. The river banks may erode and cause the river water to become too muddy or too fast flowing for fish and other river organisms to survive. Living things that depend on fish for food may be negatively affected because their food source is gone.

Sudden changes happen quickly and can kill or remove several populations of organisms from an ecosystem at once. Similarly to a slow change, sudden changes can be local or widespread. An event that causes changes to the living or nonliving parts of an ecosystem is called a **disturbance**. Some disturbances are natural processes. Other disturbances are caused by humans when they damage or remove parts of an ecosystem.

In just minutes, a tornado causes a sudden ecosystem change. Powerful winds rip trees and other plants from the soil and may kill or displace many animals.

548 Unit 7 Biodiversity and Ecosystem Dynamics

8. The photos show two different ecosystems after sudden changes. Compare and contrast these two changes. Write your observations in the space provided.

This forest fire caused several changes in the forest habitat. A wildfire can travel about three meters per second.

Ash, gases, and lava flow from a volcanic eruption affect the area around the volcano. Lava can flow about eight meters per second.

9. What organisms or populations do you think might be directly or indirectly affected by each of these sudden changes?

Effects of Changes in Ecosystems

Since each part of an ecosystem is interconnected, a change to any part can affect populations in the larger ecosystem. Consider a population that is removed from an ecosystem for some reason. Another species or population in the same ecosystem may fill the "gap" left by the missing species. Or the species might not be replaced at all.

Small changes in one part of an ecosystem can lead to large changes in other parts of the ecosystem. For example, suppose a disease killed one species of bee in an ecosystem. Bees are important pollinators. In ecosystems with more than one bee species, the remaining species might expand when one dies off. But if there is only one bee species in the area and it dies off, there would be fewer pollinators in the ecosystem. Insect-pollinated plants might not continue to grow, which would mean there would be less food for animals that eat seeds, fruit, or vegetables from these plants. Over time, the change in the bee species would affect many populations.

EVIDENCE NOTEBOOK

10. Think about the swarm of locusts you saw at the beginning of the lesson. Is the swarm a change to a living or a nonliving ecosystem component? Is the change gradual or sudden? Record your evidence.

Lesson 2 Ecosystems Can Stabilize in Response to Change **549**

Ecosystems Recover from Change

After a disturbance, an ecosystem begins to recover. **Succession** is the process of recovery and change that happens after a disturbance. Sometimes the original community may grow back. Other times the changes to an ecosystem are so severe that populations that once lived there die out or do not return. Then, succession begins when certain organisms, called *pioneer species*, begin to grow. For example, after a glacier retreats, only bare rock remains. Pioneer species such as lichens can grow on rock and help to form soil. Over time, other plants and animals return. The ecosystem becomes more complex when it is able to support more types of organisms. Biodiversity gradually increases, and the ecosystem eventually stabilizes. The variety of species and number of individuals in a population tend to increase with time after a disturbance.

Language SmArts
Analyze Rate of Environmental Change

Artificial eutrophication results from pollution and occurs much faster than natural eutrophication. In artificial eutrophication, runoff from farms, mines, or household waste, adds large amounts of nutrients such as phosphorus and nitrogen to a body of water. The nutrients support large algal blooms—population explosions of algae—in the water. As the algae die and decompose, oxygen is depleted from the water. The algae may also produce toxins that kill other living things, such as fish and amphibians. More oxygen is used as their bodies decay. As a result, organisms may not be able to live in the water.

Excess nutrients from fertilizer runoff caused a toxic bloom of cyanobacteria in the Copco Reservoir in California.

11. Compared to natural eutrophication, nutrient pollution is a relatively *sudden* / gradual change to the lake ecosystem. Populations of birds in the area that feed on fish from the lake would likely stay / *move away*. As a result of eutrophication, the biodiversity of the lake ecosystem would likely increase / *decrease*.

12. If artificial eutrophication continues, what changes do you think will occur in the ecosystem and in this area? Use evidence to explain your reasoning.

_____
_____
_____
_____
_____

EXPLORATION 2

Predicting Changes to Populations

An ecosystem disturbance can be caused by the introduction of a nonnative species, such as the introduction of eastern gray squirrels to Europe. Gray squirrels are native to the eastern United States. They were introduced to several locations in the United Kingdom and Ireland between 1876 and 1929. The species quickly adapted to their new forest ecosystems. The total population of gray squirrels in Europe has increased greatly since their introduction.

Red squirrels are native to Europe and northern Asia. Gray squirrels are larger and more aggressive than red squirrels. They eat a larger variety of foods. They also have fewer predators than red squirrels do. As a result, gray squirrels took over much of the red squirrels' resources and the red squirrel population decreased across Europe.

The eastern gray squirrel has quite a varied diet. It eats nuts, flowers, fruits, seeds, tree bark, fungi, frogs, eggs, and bird hatchlings.

Eurasian red squirrels prefer to eat the seeds of trees, but will also eat berries, young plant shoots, and bird eggs.

13. Compare and contrast potential effects of two disturbances on a native population of red squirrels—a storm and the introduction of nonnative gray squirrels. Fill in the Venn diagram using the statements.

WORD BANK
- competes for resources
- decreases available food
- reduces available living space
- causes sudden change
- introduces disease

Gray squirrels | Both | Storm

Lesson 2 Ecosystems Can Stabilize in Response to Change

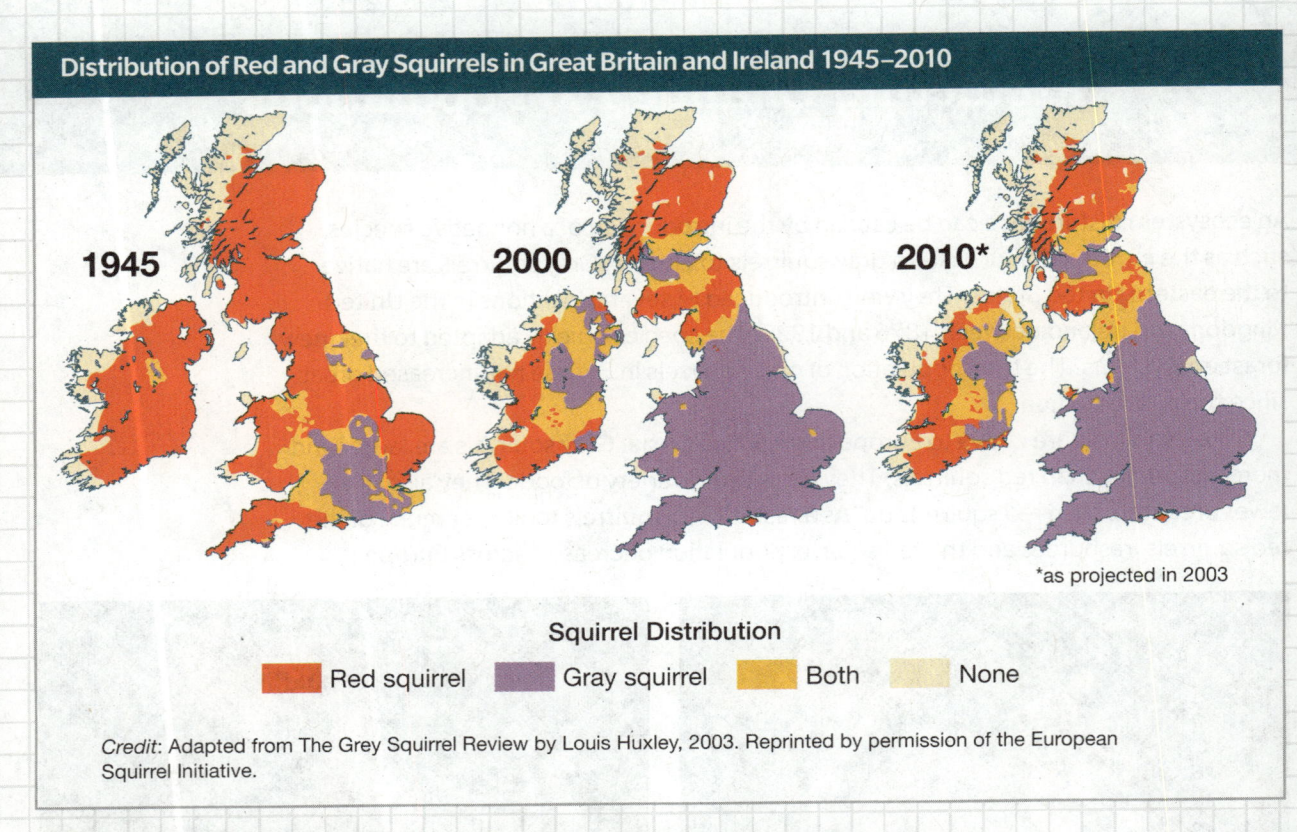

Distribution of Red and Gray Squirrels in Great Britain and Ireland 1945–2010

1945 | 2000 | 2010*

*as projected in 2003

Squirrel Distribution
- Red squirrel
- Gray squirrel
- Both
- None

Credit: Adapted from The Grey Squirrel Review by Louis Huxley, 2003. Reprinted by permission of the European Squirrel Initiative.

14. Language SmArts In your own words, describe the changes in the distribution of red and gray squirrels from 1945 to 2010.

The introduction of gray squirrels into Europe had a negative impact on populations of red squirrels. Scientists also identified that gray squirrels negatively affected populations of songbirds, and likely spread the disease squirrel pox to red squirrels. Gray squirrels also eat the bark from trees in winter, causing the trees to be more prone to disease. However, the presence of gray squirrels helped another species—pine martens—to rebound from the point of extinction.

Scientists determined that gray squirrels likely had a positive effect on the populations of pine martens. Pine martens are weasel-like predators of squirrels. Pine martens were hunted to near extinction in the United Kingdom and Ireland in the early 20th century. Farmers and landowners considered them pests because they ate chickens and young lambs. Since pine martens became a protected species in the 1980s, their numbers have grown. Researchers noted that pine martens prefer eating gray squirrels to red squirrels. Gray squirrels are larger, slower, and spend more time on the ground, which means that pine martens can catch gray squirrels more easily. With more food, pine marten populations in Ireland and Scotland have increased, and the rate of gray squirrel population growth has decreased.

Effects of Ecosystem Changes on Populations

Ecosystem components are connected, so changes to living and nonliving parts can affect populations. The removal of a species, the decrease of a food source, or a change in temperature can cause large changes in the other parts of the ecosystems. For example, several years of increased average winter temperatures can cause seeds to germinate earlier and change the behavior of migrating animals.

A change may displace or kill individuals and populations. A large portion of a population may move because of a disturbance, such as a flood, and not return. If this happens, there may not be enough individuals to sustain the population in that area over time, and the local population could die out.

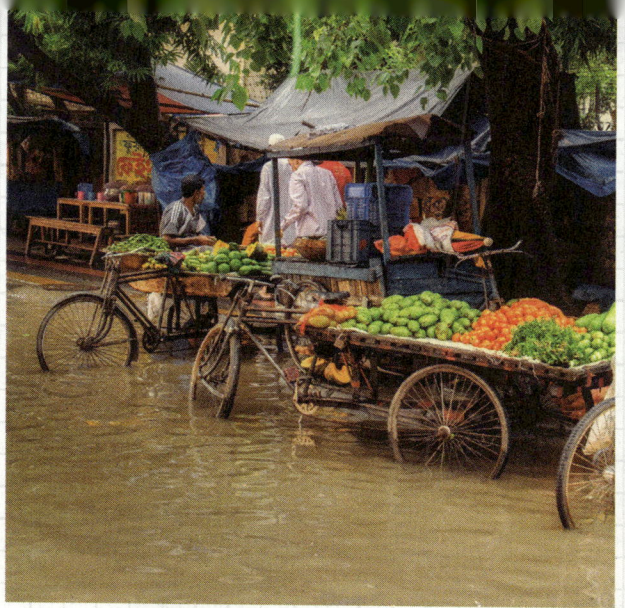

Bangladesh, a country in South Asia, is prone to flooding because it is low-lying and has a long coastline. The frequent flooding affects human, animal, and plant populations.

Do the Math
Identify Factors That Change Populations

Before the arrival of European settlers in North America, about 46% of the land was forested. Early settlers spoke of towering white pine trees. White pines were one of the many native species that were heavily harvested for building ship masts, wagons, fences, and furniture. Clearing of old-growth forests for agriculture and commercial purposes hit its highest rate in the mid-1800s and continued until the mid-1920s.

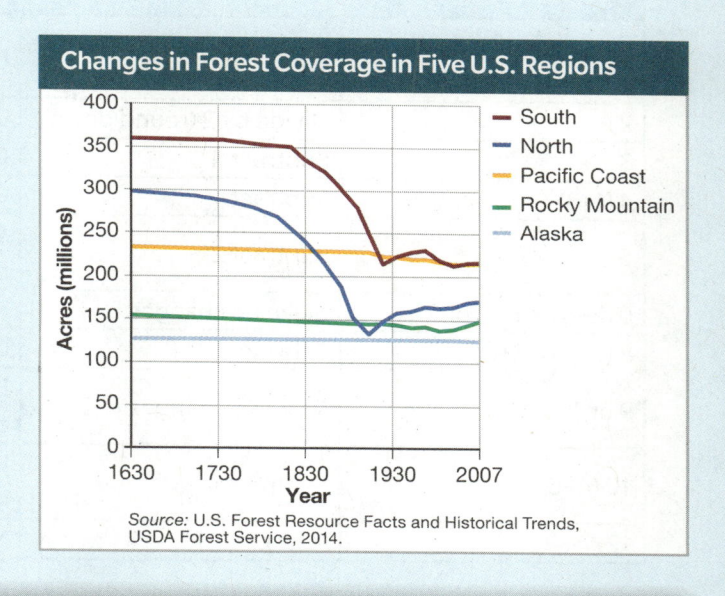

Changes in Forest Coverage in Five U.S. Regions

Source: U.S. Forest Resource Facts and Historical Trends, USDA Forest Service, 2014.

15. What information about forest coverage does the graph tell you?

16. The Carolina parakeet once lived in large flocks in old-growth forests in the eastern and southeastern United States. Their extinction has been linked to the removal of old-growth forests. Based on the graph, when do you think Carolina parakeet populations decreased the most? Give a reason for your answer.

Lesson 2 Ecosystems Can Stabilize in Response to Change

Hands-On Lab
Identify Factors That Influence a Population Change

Simulate population changes in a pack of wolves and identify specific changes that affect this population.

MATERIALS
- cup
- dice (2)
- pencil
- popcorn kernels (generous handful)

Procedure

STEP 1 Place eight popcorn kernels on the table. Two kernels represent adult wolves, the other six represent a litter of pups.

STEP 2 Follow the game play key that is shown below. The game play key will allow you to model ecosystem changes that affect a wolf population by throwing the dice. Some of the changes to the ecosystem are natural events and some are caused by humans.

If you roll...	You...	Reason
Double 2s, 3s, 4s, 5s, or 6s	Subtract 3	Nursing female ingests rat poison; pups die
2	Divide by 2 (round down)	Disease introduced by stray dogs; half the pack dies
3	Subtract 4	Drought occurs, causing food shortage for prey
4 (1+3)	Subtract 1	One wolf dies of natural causes
5	Subtract 2	A harmful pollutant builds up in the tissues of rabbits; wolves eat the rabbits and get poisoned
6 (2+4 or 1+5) or 7	Make no changes	Rains arrive; pack lives well for six months
8 (2+6 or 3+5)	Subtract 1	One pup dies of natural causes
9 or 11	Make no changes	Elk population remains high due to plentiful plant growth; wolves live well for six months
10 (4+6)	Subtract 1	Habitat size decreases due to development; male killed in territorial dispute with another wolf pack
12	Add 1	New, mature wolf joins pack

STEP 3 On a separate sheet of paper, make a table similar to the one below. The table should record the results of 15 years of data.

Year	Last year's total	Add a litter (+6)	First 6 months Reason	Effect on pack	Second 6 months Reason	Effect on pack	Pack subtotal	Subtract matured pups?	Total pack for year
1	2	+6						no	
2								no	
3									

Unit 7 Biodiversity and Ecosystem Dynamics

STEP 4 Roll the dice to represent the passage of six months. Use the total number on the dice to determine what happens to your pack, according to the game play key. Then fill in the information in your data table. As you record data, also record the reason for the population change in the *Reason* column. Adjust the number of kernels that represent your wolf pack.

STEP 5 Repeat Step 4 for the second six months of the year. Count the number of wolves in your pack and fill in the rest of Year 1 in the data table.

STEP 6 Reproduction: After Year 1, adjust the number of kernels to add six pups at the beginning of each year unless a food shortage occurred the previous year.

STEP 7 Maturation: When the pack gets too large, the mature pups leave. Subtract six wolves if your pack has more than nine wolves. Adjust the number of kernels you have accordingly. Record the pack total in the last column of the table.

STEP 8 Repeat Steps 4–7 until you complete 15 years of play or until your pack dies out, whichever comes first.

Analysis

STEP 9 What patterns did you notice in the types of ecosystem changes that affected your wolf pack? Did a relatively small change have a larger impact on the wolf population? Explain your answer.

STEP 10 How might a change to a wolf pack affect other populations, such as the elk or bison that the wolves feed on?

STEP 11 Does evidence from your model suggest that many different types of changes correlate with changes in the wolf population? Explain your answer.

EVIDENCE NOTEBOOK

17. Desert locusts are plant eaters and are eaten by animals such as snakes, birds, and small mammals. What effects might the swarm of locusts have on other populations in an ecosystem? Record your evidence.

Lesson 2 Ecosystems Can Stabilize in Response to Change **555**

Populations That Depend on Disturbance

In the early 1900s, a major goal of the United States Forestry Service was to stop forest fires. One reason for this effort was to prevent the destruction of timber resources. However, around the 1960s, scientists began to recognize that the fires were important to the stability of forest ecosystems. They realized that a forest ecosystem becomes unhealthy if fires do not occur periodically. Scientists observed that if every fire is prevented, trees become overcrowded and dead plant material builds up on the forest floor. Today, scientists know that fires add nutrients to soil. Fires clear the forest floor, providing space for seedlings. They can also thin out the tree canopy, which allows more sunlight to reach the forest floor. Saplings and other plants can then grow.

Sequoias are adapted to survive forest fires. The trees depend on fires to reduce competition from other trees that may crowd out their germinating seedlings.

Some populations depend on fires. For example, populations of sequoias, a type of redwood tree, depend on forest fires to reproduce. They need low-intensity fires to release seeds from their cones. Forest fires also reduce competition from other species.

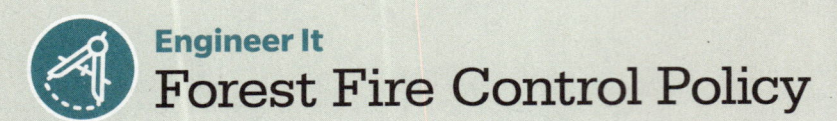

Engineer It
Forest Fire Control Policy

Fire suppression is the process of preventing or putting out forest fires. It was a tool commonly used in the past to prevent forest fires. In the late 1890s, conservationists identified forest fires as a major threat to the U.S. economy because they destroyed the supply of timber. In 1910, the U.S. government began a policy of total fire suppression. The policy involved preventing fires and also putting out a fire as quickly as possible once one started. Later, researchers observed that the fire suppression policy had unintended effects on forest ecosystems. Populations of plants that depended on fires to complete their life cycles were negatively affected and forest ecosystems were changing. Such observations led to a policy change in the 1970s. Today, the U.S. National Park Service manages and controls, rather than totally extinguishes, forest fires.

18. Imagine you are a forest ranger. Define the engineering design problem you face in developing a solution to allow the fire-dependent plants in the forest you manage to carry out their life cycle. You want to minimize fire hazards for people who visit and live near the forest. You also need to be mindful of air pollution laws. List at least three criteria and constraints that would influence your solution.

TAKE IT FURTHER

Continue Your Exploration

Name: _____ Date: _____

Check out the path below or go online to choose one of the other paths shown.

People in Science
- Ecological Succession
- Cockroaches vs. Pandas
- Hands-On Labs
- Propose Your Own Path

Go online to choose one of these other paths.

Rodolfo Dirzo, Terrestrial Ecologist

Rodolfo Dirzo grew up in Morelos in southern Mexico. As a boy, he loved to explore the area's remaining patches of dry tropical forests. Dirzo would capture glowing insects and place them in a plastic bag to make a lantern so that he continue his explorations after dark. This early interest in the natural world led Dirzo to pursue a degree at the local university, where he studied how deforestation impacts the quality and availability of water in southern Mexico. He later earned a doctorate from the University of Wales, where he studied plant and animal interactions. Dirzo's current research examines what happens to ecosystems when animal populations decrease or disappear because of human activity. His research takes him to savannas in east Africa, tropical forests in Mexico, and the oak woodlands of northern California, to name a few.

Rodolfo Dirzo with an elephant in Kenya, where he has studied what happens when large plant-eating animals are removed from ecosystems.

Oak Woodland Regeneration

Oak woodlands are ecosystems dominated by oak trees. Dirzo and his team have found that the number of young oaks in northern California oak woodlands is very limited. Young oaks replace mature oaks in a cycle of regeneration for the woodlands, so the low number of young oak trees may mean that the oak woodlands are unable to regenerate in the future.

Bears and cougars were once top predators in the oak woodland ecosystem. Their numbers have decreased due to hunting and habitat destruction. As these predators decline, the populations of their prey may increase, including deer. Deer graze on oak seedlings, so an increase in the deer population can lead to overgrazing of oak seedlings, reducing the numbers of young oaks. Dirzo hypothesizes that the loss of top predators may also lead to a reshaping of plant communities due to an increase in populations of plant-eating animals and smaller prey animals.

TAKE IT FURTHER

Continue Your Exploration

Oak woodlands like this one provide important ecosystem services, such as water filtration and helping to prevent erosion and mudslides. They are also rich in biodiversity.

1. Develop a diagram that models how a change in the population of a top predator in the oak woodlands could affect regeneration of the oaks.

2. Imagine you have collected data showing that the number of young oaks in the woodlands has decreased as the deer population has increased. Does this finding provide evidence of a causal relationship or of a correlation? Explain your answer.

3. How might cattle grazing of the woodlands impact oak tree regeneration? Explain your reasoning.

4. **Collaborate** Dirzo uses the term defaunation to describe the impact humans have on animal populations. *Deforestation* refers to destruction of trees and plant life due to human activity. *Fauna* refers to animal life. Using these clues, work with a partner to develop a definition for *defaunation*. How might defaunation affect society? Share an example of defaunation and its effects with the class.

LESSON 2 SELF-CHECK

Can You Explain It?

Name: _____   Date: _____

> **How would the arrival of a swarm of millions of desert locusts affect an ecosystem?**

EVIDENCE NOTEBOOK
Refer to the notes in your Evidence Notebook to help you construct an explanation for how a swarm of locusts can affect an ecosystem.

1. State your claim. Make sure your claim fully explains how this disturbance could affect the ecosystem.

2. Summarize the evidence you have gathered to support your claim and explain your reasoning.

Lesson 2 Ecosystems Can Stabilize in Response to Change

LESSON 2 SELF-CHECK

Checkpoints

Answer the following questions to check your understanding of the lesson.

Use the photo to answer Questions 3 and 4.

3. A lahar is a mudflow made up of lava, water, and rocks. How might a lahar affect an ecosystem?

    A. It is a sudden disturbance that affects few populations in the area.

    B. It is a sudden disruption that affects all local populations in the area.

    C. It is a gradual disruption that affects only animal populations in the area.

    D. It is a sudden disruption that has little effect on plant populations in the area.

a lahar

4. In 1980, Mt. St. Helens erupted. The resulting lahar flowed over a wide area of the Cascade Mountains. Which of these statements best describes the effect of the volcanic eruption? Select all that apply.

    A. It affected the living and nonliving components of the ecosystem.

    B. It removed populations of mammals from the mountainside.

    C. It led to succession on the mountainside.

    D. It affected only nonliving components of the ecosystem.

Use the map to answer Questions 5 and 6.

5. Near the coasts there has been *loss only / loss and gain / gain only* of forests. In north-central Washington and British Columbia, there are large patches of *forest loss / forest gain*.

6. Historically, the Pacific Northwest region experienced much less deforestation than other regions of the United States. Therefore, populations of organisms living in Pacific Northwest forest ecosystems are likely to have experienced *relatively few / many* changes to their environment. Changes in the populations of tree species would likely *affect / not affect* other populations living in the forest.

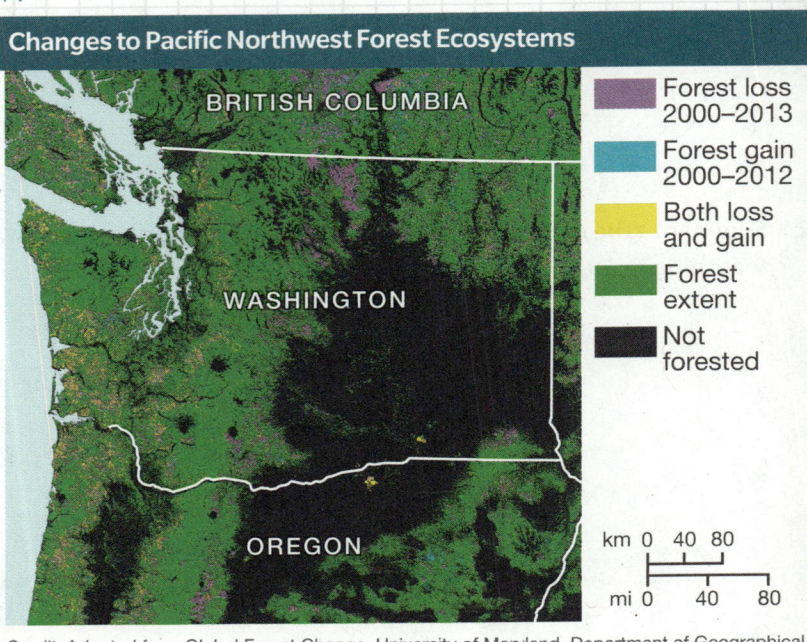

Changes to Pacific Northwest Forest Ecosystems

- Forest loss 2000–2013
- Forest gain 2000–2012
- Both loss and gain
- Forest extent
- Not forested

Credit: Adapted from Global Forest Change, University of Maryland, Department of Geographical Sciences. Reprinted by permission of M.C. Hansen.

LESSON 2 SELF-CHECK

Interactive Review

Complete this section to review the main concepts of the lesson.

Ecosystems contain populations of living organisms as well as nonliving things. Ecosystem disturbances change habitats in different ways.

A. How do sudden and gradual disturbances each affect ecosystems?

Different types of disturbances have different effects on populations. A change in one part of an ecosystem can affect many populations.

B. Use examples to explain how changes to both living and nonliving parts of an ecosystem can affect individuals and populations.

Lesson 2 Ecosystems Can Stabilize in Response to Change

LESSON 3 | ENGINEER IT

Maintaining Biodiversity and Ecosystem Services

These solar-powered Supertrees and elevated walkways are in Singapore's Gardens by the Bay. They are inspiring examples of how human creativity can preserve biodiversity.

Explore First

Choosing Building Materials Imagine you are tasked with building a foot bridge across a stream for hikers in a forest. The stream sometimes floods, so the bridge must be made of a material that is not harmed by water and will not become slippery. What material would you build the bridge out of, and why?

CAN YOU EXPLAIN IT?

How can we develop a solution to biodiversity loss in the Everglades without shutting humans out of this endangered ecosystem?

The manatee is just one of the endangered species living in Florida's Everglades, a large wetland ecosystem. Habitat loss and collisions with watercraft are two major threats to manatees.

1. Which design solutions protect biodiversity and consider human needs? Select all that apply.
   A. installing walkways that leave wildlife undisturbed
   B. building houses on a filled-in wetland
   C. using water from lakes to supply farmland
   D. creating no-fishing zones

2. What ideas do you have for how boaters might enjoy the wetlands of Florida's Everglades without harming manatee habitats?

EVIDENCE NOTEBOOK As you explore this lesson, gather evidence to help you explain how to develop a solution to biodiversity loss in the Everglades.

EXPLORATION 1

Evaluating Biodiversity Loss

As the sun rises on a coastal mangrove forest, all seems quiet and still. But upon closer observation, the forest is full of activity. The forest's network of branches and roots provides enough food for a diverse community of organisms. The underwater roots are a perfect nursery for many fish. The forest is also home to native and migratory birds.

3. A fishing boat by a mangrove forest spills a chemical that is deadly to aquatic plants. What changes might happen as a result? Select all that apply.

    A. Many trees become poisoned and die.
    B. Fish eggs fail due to loss of nursery habitat.
    C. Mangrove shrimp become unsafe for humans to eat.
    D. Erosion from the loss of trees causes decreased water quality.

Mangrove forests are full of life. The dense tangle of roots props the trees above high tides.

Humans Rely on Healthy Ecosystems

Humans depend on resources provided by healthy ecosystems. For example, fish breed in mangrove forests. Therefore, the forests provide food and jobs for people who live nearby. The mangroves' dense roots trap sediments and filter out impurities. So, the forests also provide clean water. Mangrove forests even help protect houses near the shore. They block damaging storm winds, reduce soil erosion, and prevent flooding.

The health of an ecosystem, such as a mangrove forest, can be defined by how well it can recover from disturbances. The higher the biodiversity level within an ecosystem, the healthier it is. However, different ecosystems can differ in their biodiversity and still be thought of as "healthy." For example, an arctic ecosystem naturally has far less biodiversity than a coral reef ecosystem does. It is when the biodiversity of an ecosystem decreases from its "healthiest" level that problems can happen. As an ecosystem loses its biodiversity, natural resources become less available. Services provided by ecosystems with lowered biodiversity may also become less reliable.

4. Scientists and engineers study ways to help coral reefs recover from damage by boats or pollution. How does this show that science and technology can have positive and negative effects on biodiversity?

Coral reefs have stunning biodiversity. However, they recover very slowly from disturbances because corals grow slowly.

Ecosystems Provide Natural Resources

Living and nonliving parts of an ecosystem provide humans with natural resources. A *natural resource* is any natural material that is used by humans. Humans rely on ecosystems for natural resources such as fresh water, food, medicines, energy, clothing, and building materials.

For example, few areas on Earth have more natural resources than the Amazon rain forest. The Amazon River flows more than 6,920 kilometers (4,300 miles) across Peru and Brazil to the Atlantic Ocean. It provides water for drinking, transportation, and agriculture. It supports more than 2,500 species of fish and hundreds of species on land. Chemical compounds in rainforest plants are used as medicines. Plants growing in the forests also provide 20% of Earth's atmospheric oxygen. However, there are many threats to the health of the Amazon rain forest. Trees are cleared and rivers are dammed to generate power. The health of any ecosystem affects the health of communities and the supply of resources to them.

Natural Resources Provided by Ecosystems

Humans use or change Earth's many resources to live comfortably.

5. Match each product with the natural resource used to make it.

concrete	fossil fuels
timber for housing	plants
gasoline	minerals

6. How does the availability of natural resources depend on ecosystem health? Use an example to explain.

Lesson 3 Engineer It: Maintaining Biodiversity and Ecosystem Services

Ecosystems Provide Services

Matter cycles and energy flows through the living and nonliving parts of ecosystems by natural processes. Humans benefit from many of these natural processes. An **ecosystem service** is any ecosystem function that provides benefits to humans. The benefits can be direct or indirect, small or large. Water purification, nutrient recycling, and climate regulation are ecosystem services. Pollination and pest and disease control are also important services.

Analyze Threats to Five Ecosystem Services

7. What environmental changes might threaten each of these ecosystem services? Include those caused by human activities.

Ecosystem Service	Potential Threats
Water filtration: Filtration by soil, rock, and plants provides clean water. Humans use this water for drinking, industry, and recreation. Filtration helps prevent microbe-related illness and the nutrient poisoning of lakes from farmland runoff.	
Decomposition: Soil microbes break down dead matter and nutrients are released into the ecosystem. This improves soil quality and decreases the need for artificial fertilizers.	
Pollination: Many plants must be pollinated by animals to produce fruit and seeds. Such plants include over 150 food crops in the United States. Insects and birds are pollinators. They need enough undisturbed nesting sites to live and reproduce.	
Erosion control: The extensive root systems of native plants and trees anchor soils. Thus, they prevent erosion and reduce the effects of floods. Root systems of crops are not as extensive. Therefore, they do not provide the same benefit.	
Climate regulation: Tiny marine phytoplankton are producers in marine ecosystems. They carry out more than half of all photosynthesis on Earth. They help maintain levels of oxygen and carbon dioxide in the air and in the oceans.	

8. Discuss What ecosystem services do you depend on every day? Brainstorm ways your life would be different if you did not have these services where you live.

Loss of Biodiversity Affects Ecosystem Health

When biodiversity declines in an ecosystem, there are fewer natural resources and services to support the remaining organisms. The ecosystem is no longer as healthy, or stable, as before. Biodiversity can decline due to environmental changes, such as a drought. It can also be reduced by human activities, such as urban development and agriculture.

One example of biodiversity loss involves coffee plantations. Coffee plants grow well in the tropical, species-rich areas of the world. There are two main methods of farming coffee. Traditionally, the shrub-like coffee plants are grown in shade. They are planted among existing trees. Leaving the trees standing protects the habitat of birds. The birds eat pests that might damage the crop. The trees drop leaves that cover the ground and help prevent weed growth. Decomposition of the leaves also increases nutrient cycling.

As demand for coffee grows, the expansion of coffee plantations into deforested areas is rising. Deforestation removes all plant species from an area. Sun-grown coffee does not get the benefits provided by trees, so fertilization is necessary. Cutting down trees also increases erosion and fertilizer runoff into nearby streams and lakes. Sun-grown coffee plants must also be replaced more often than shade-grown plants. Replacing plants is an added cost for farmers.

Humans make choices about how they impact ecosystem health when they get natural resources. Scientists and engineers play an important role in these choices. They research and design ways to maintain biodiversity and ecosystem stability.

Shade-grown coffee plantations protect existing species diversity. The coffee plants produce beans for about 30 years.

Coffee plants grown in the sun produce more beans per acre. But bean quality and volume decrease after about 15 years.

9. In comparison to sun-grown coffee, shade-grown coffee needs *more / less* fertilization and *more / less* pesticide treatment. Shade-grown coffee plantations are *more / less* affected by erosion than sun-grown plantations. For these reasons, coffee grown in the *shade / sun* helps maintain biodiversity and ecosystem health.

Do the Math
Compare Costs and Benefits of Shade-Grown Coffee

10. What is the yearly profit from coffee beans grown in a shade-grown plot and a sun-grown plot?

Variable measured	Sun-grown coffee	Shade-grown coffee
Coffee beans produced per plot, per year	1,600 kg	550 kg
Diseased coffee plants per plot, per year	5	<1
Lifespan of plants	15 years	30 years
Profit per kilogram of coffee produced	$2.00	$2.50*
(*Shade-grown coffee sells at a higher price when certified as "bird friendly.")		

11. Consider the lifespan of the coffee plants. What is the total profit over the lifespan of coffee plants in a sun-grown plot? What is the total profit over the lifespan of plants in a shade-grown plot? What are some other costs and benefits of each type of plot?

Causes of Biodiversity Loss

Humans love to expand and explore. This leads to important cultural progress, but it also can cause long-term changes to ecosystems. Human activities can cause **habitat destruction**, the changing or loss of a natural ecosystem. Habitat destruction removes living space and resources needed by organisms.

Most negative impacts on ecosystems are the result of urbanization, farming, industry, or energy production. As the human population grows, resource use also increases. For example, sharks are threatened by overfishing due to demand for their fins and meat. Shark fin soup is a traditional dish in some cultures. Sharks may also be trapped by fishing nets used to catch other species. As top predators, sharks help maintain biodiversity by controlling the balance of other fish populations. Without proper planning, fishermen may destroy fish populations that provide their source of income. Human activities are the largest threat to biodiversity. Therefore, solutions need to involve changes to these activities.

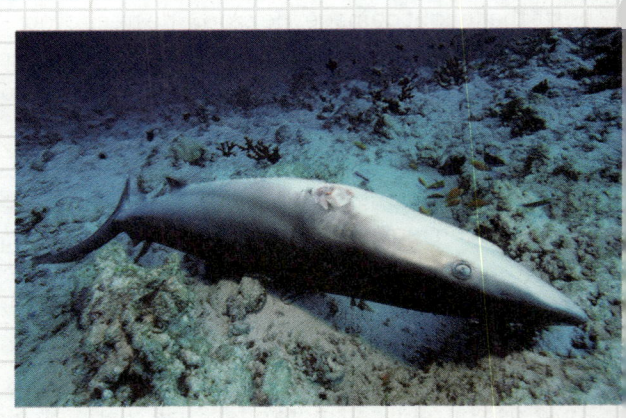

Humans kill about 100 million sharks every year. To save them, fisheries and consumers of shark products need to be part of the solution.

EVIDENCE NOTEBOOK
12. Human activities have destroyed miles of Everglade wetlands for development. How do these changes affect ecosystem health and nearby human communities? Record your evidence.

13. Changes in the health of one population can cause a cascade of effects in other populations. Consider the decline of shark populations. Sharks prey on sea turtles, which eat plants. Number the phrases to complete the cause-and-effect chain.

_____ seagrasses overgrazed

_____ loss of sharks

_____ fish nurseries destroyed

_____ sea turtles increase

Language SmArts
Evaluate Agricultural Practices

Trees and other plants may be clear-cut to make room for crops farmers grow. This displaces native species and reduces biodiversity in the ecosystem. Reservoir water used to water crops drains nutrients from the soil. The soil is poor quality and erodes easily. It travels to new locations without adding nutrients to these areas. Fertilizers and pesticides used to maintain crops pollute air, water, and soil.

Some farming practices can reduce these negative impacts. For example, providing habitat for birds that eat insects helps reduce the need for pesticides. Alternative crop types each year helps preserve soil nutrients. Planting cover plants, such as alfalfa, reduces erosion, adds nutrients to the soil, and controls weeds.

All native plants are often removed when preparing land to grow crops. The resulting loose soil erodes easily.

14. How does the clear-cutting of trees and native plants for farming affect humans? Circle all that apply.

A. Air quality decreases as wind draws dust into the air.

B. Species diversity in the community increases.

C. Water quality decreases due to increased erosion.

D. Rainwater runoff increases, which can cause erosion.

15. Consider this claim: "Removing all native plant life on land for farming is justified because it provides more space for crops. The growing human population needs more products grown by farmers, such as food crops and meat." Do you agree or disagree? Evaluate the claim and provide evidence for your argument.

Lesson 3 Engineer It: Maintaining Biodiversity and Ecosystem Services

EXPLORATION 2

Analyzing Strategies for Maintaining Biodiversity

Micronesia is an arc of more than 2,000 islands between Hawaii and the Philippines. Many of the islands are surrounded by coral reefs that are threatened by human activity. Of the 1,400 plant species on the islands, about 360 are found only on the islands. Many of these species are endangered. The islands are remote, so the people of Micronesia depend on the resources provided by the islands. Rising sea levels and human activities are depleting the islands' resources. Activities such as deforestation, overfishing, pollution, and destruction of coral reefs harm wildlife and local economies.

Conservation efforts in Micronesia are underway. They include enacting a multi-island agreement to preserve coastlines, identify coral reefs that need to be protected, and address harmful fishing practices. These efforts show that maintaining biodiversity requires collaboration among scientists, citizens, governments, and businesses.

16. Examine the coral reef photos. How does coral reef bleaching demonstrate how many small changes can weaken entire ecosystems?

Corals get their color and their food from tiny photosynthetic algae that live in the corals' tissues.

When populations of photosynthetic algae inside corals decline, the corals lose their main food source and turn white in a process called *bleaching*. The causes of bleaching include increased water temperature and pollution.

Protect Individual Species

Officials must choose where to direct limited conservation resources. Protection efforts often focus on species facing local extinction or those that most influence the success of other populations.

One cause of local extinction is overharvesting. This happens when humans reduce the population of a living resource to the point where reproduction rates are too low to restore the population. For example, Pacific bluefin tuna populations have dropped dramatically due to decades of overfishing. Most Pacific bluefin tuna caught are too young to reproduce, which leaves very few reproducing adults. The species is in danger of extinction and being considered for protection under the Endangered Species Act.

Protecting a species is also important if it is a *keystone species*. Keystone species are vital to ecosystem functioning because they affect the survival of many other species in the community. For example, sea otters are a keystone species in the North Pacific Ocean. Sea otters prey on sea urchins and other invertebrates that eat giant kelp. This helps to prevent overgrazing of kelp forests, an important marine habitat.

Two Endangered Keystone Species

Otters are a keystone species. Conservation efforts include protecting them from poachers, nets, and habitat loss.

Overfishing and illegal catching of bluefin tuna continues to threaten the species, despite conservation efforts.

Protect and Maintain Habitats

Most habitat destruction is the result of land clearing. However, other human activities add to the problems of habitat loss. For example, the Indiana bat must hibernate in cool, humid caves to survive winter. Rising temperatures due to climate change are decreasing the number of caves that bats can use. Also, disturbing hibernating bats can cause them to die of starvation. Some 50,000 bats can hibernate in just one cave. So, a single hiker may affect a large percentage of this endangered bat population.

Human activities can also cause **habitat fragmentation**, the division of an ecosystem into smaller areas by roads, housing communities, farms, or other development. Fragmentation makes it difficult for species to have enough space to live. Large predators, such as Florida panthers, need large land areas to hunt, find mates, and raise their young. Without enough space, these species might face local extinction.

Causes of habitat fragmentation include roads, factories, housing developments, farms, and recreation areas. Land bridges are one solution to reduce the effects of habitat fragmentation.

Lesson 3 Engineer It: Maintaining Biodiversity and Ecosystem Services

Hands-On Lab
Model Habitat Fragmentation

Use sheets of paper to model undisturbed and fragmented habitats and compare interior-to-edge ratios to draw conclusions about the effects of habitat fragmentation.

MATERIALS
- calculator
- ruler
- scissors
- sheets of paper (2)

Procedure and Analysis

STEP 1 Calculate and record the area of each sheet of paper by multiplying the length by the width.

STEP 2 One sheet of paper will represent an undisturbed habitat. Do not cut this paper. Model fragmentation by cutting the second sheet of paper into 5 to 10 rectangles.

STEP 3 Measure and record the perimeter of the undisturbed habitat. The perimeter is the distance around the outer edge of the paper.

STEP 4 Calculate the total perimeter of the fragmented habitat by measuring the perimeter of each piece and adding them. Record the total perimeter.

STEP 5 The perimeter of a habitat is also called the habitat's edge. Which habitat has more edge?

STEP 6 If two habitats have the same total area, is more or less edge beneficial to a species? Explain your reasoning.

STEP 7 **Do the Math** One characteristic of a habitat is its *interior-to-edge ratio*. This ratio is calculated by dividing the area of a habitat by its total perimeter. Calculate the interior-to-edge ratio for each habitat, undisturbed and fragmented.

Unit 7 Biodiversity and Ecosystem Dynamics

STEP 8 *Edge effects* are the changes to populations that happen at the boundary between two ecosystems. Edge effects can occur some distance into both ecosystems. Biologists associate a large interior-to-edge ratio with fewer edge effects. Which habitat has the greatest interior-to-edge ratio? What might this mean for the species that live in each habitat?

STEP 9 On a separate sheet of paper, draw a simple map of an ecosystem. Include human structures (roads, ranches, parks, homes) separated by natural areas (forests, grassland, mountains). What are some potential strategies to limit habitat fragmentation in this area? Draw a protected area on the map and discuss your idea with the class.

Prevent Spread of Nonnative Species

In established ecosystems, community interactions between species lead to a dynamic balance of producers, composers, and decomposers. When a new species enters the ecosystem, it can upset this balance. The nonnative species may be able to use resources in the ecosystem better than native species do. By outcompeting native species, they can cause local extinctions of native species. For example, gardeners introduced kudzu vines to the American Southeast. They believed the vine was an excellent ground cover. Farmers also used the vine to reduce soil erosion. The creeping vine grows fast, especially in open areas. It thrives in humid, warm conditions. Once planted, it began to cover existing plants, depriving them of needed sunlight. Scientists now face the difficult task of controlling kudzu growth to protect plant diversity in affected ecosystems.

Kudzu competes with native plants for light and space. It can grow over large structures such as this bulldozer.

Reduce Pollution

Pollution of soil, air, and water harms many species and their habitats. Chemical pollutants are particularly dangerous because they are usually invisible. They can also travel great distances. Chemicals can build up in the communities they enter. They can build up in the bodies of plants and animals that absorb, ingest, or inhale them.

Some pollution sources include the burning of fossil fuels, fertilizers, pesticides, medicines, and litter. Noise and light produced by humans are also forms of pollution. They disrupt the normal actions of wildlife. For example, the noise from marine oil explorations affects the feeding and mating behaviors of whales.

Pollution can harm species directly and lead to habitat destruction. For example, it can cause contaminated drinking water, acid rain, algae blooms in lakes, and ocean garbage patches.

Under water, plastic bags look like jellyfish. Young sea turtles are at high risk of dying from eating these bags.

Reduce the Impact of Synthetic Materials

The life cycle of synthetic materials can affect biodiversity in different ways. *Synthetic materials* are human-made materials produced from natural materials. Plastic bags, fertilizer, and fuel are all examples of synthetic materials.

The life cycle of synthetic materials includes obtaining the materials from which a synthetic item will be made, and production, distribution, use, and disposal of the synthetic material. For example, plastic microbeads were once common in face washes and toothpastes. These microbeads are made from ethylene, a gas made from crude oil. Obtaining and transporting oil to make ethylene can lead to habitat destruction by land clearing and pollution from oil spills and processing, which can harm plants and animals and decrease biodiversity. Plastic microbeads that enter the environment through wastewater are not biodegradable and can be toxic to fish and wildlife. Plastic microbeads have been banned in some cosmetics.

A sample from the Great Pacific Garbage Patch, a gyre in the Pacific Ocean containing a high concentration of plastic particles and other debris. This plastic is sometimes mistaken for food by sea turtles and other marine animals.

17. Laysan albatrosses in the North Pacific Ocean eat squid and sunfish, but they sometimes mistake plastic for food. Albatross chicks that eat plastic may die. How might plastic pollution affect biodiversity in this area? Select all that apply.

    A. Populations of squid may increase.
    B. Populations of squid may decrease.
    C. Populations of species eaten by sunfish may decrease.
    D. Sunfish may become a predator of squid.

Case Study: Reducing the Impact of Synthetic Fertilizers

Nitrogen-based fertilizers provide plants with nitrogen, an essential nutrient. These fertilizers improve farm productivity, but their life cycle can have negative impacts on biodiversity and ecosystems.

Production This factory produces nitrogen-based fertilizer by converting nitrogen in the air into ammonia through a chemical reaction with hydrogen from natural gas. Greenhouse gases and dust emitted from fertilizer factories can pollute air, water, and soil.

Technologies to capture and reduce emissions can help reduce the impact of fertilizer production on local ecosystems.

Use Farms like this one rely on synthetic fertilizers to produce crops. Many people also use fertilizers in their lawns and gardens. But plants use only some of the nitrogen in fertilizer. Excess nitrogen is converted into nitrous oxide, a powerful greenhouse gas that traps heat in Earth's atmosphere and causes global temperatures to rise. Excess nitrogen can also enter groundwater, where it has the potential to contaminate drinking water and alter freshwater ecosystems.

Reducing the use of fertilizers or applying only the amount needed can help to reduce these effects on biodiversity and ecosystems.

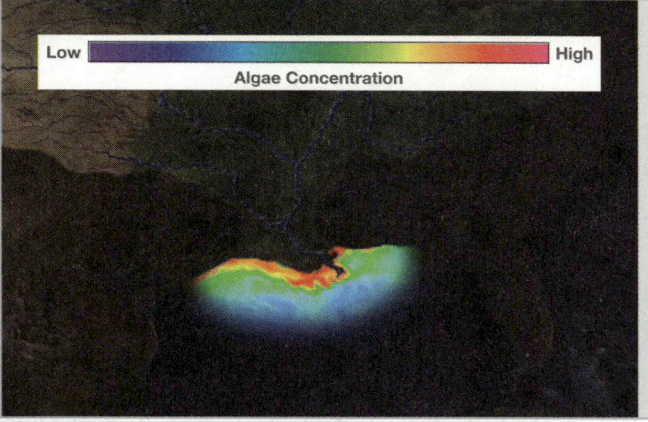

Disposal This satellite image shows the concentration of algae in the Gulf of Mexico. Fertilizer runoff from farms is carried in the Mississippi River to the Gulf, where it causes excess algal growth close to the shoreline. When the algae die, their decomposition depletes the water of oxygen, causing other marine animals to die or leave the area.

Planting cover crops such as clover to help recycle excess nutrients, using trees or shrubs on the edges of farms to filter runoff, and tilling fields less frequently can help to reduce the amount of fertilizer that enters streams and rivers.

18. Crop rotation is a method of farming in which crop types are alternated in order to preserve soil health and reduce the need for fertilizers and pesticides. Increasing crop rotation on farms near the Mississippi River would likely lead to a(n) *increase* / **decrease** in fertilizer runoff and **greater** / *less* biodiversity where the river empties into the Gulf of Mexico.

19. Think of a synthetic material you use often. What are some impacts it could have on ecosystem services in your area or in other parts of the world? How can these impacts be reduced?

Put Strategies into Action

Reducing habitat loss and pollution requires solutions that involve individuals, businesses, cities, and nations. Scientific studies of these problems can describe their effects, but the studies alone cannot determine how to fix the problems. Societies must decide on those actions. For example, individuals can help reduce pollution in many ways. They can bike instead of drive and buy environmentally safe products. They can also recycle, reduce litter at home, or volunteer at environmental cleanups. Farmers can reduce pollution by finding ways to grow crops without pesticides. Businesses can conserve resources by using less paper, water, or fuel. Cities can reduce pollution by providing low-emission mass transportation. They can also set guidelines for acceptable light and noise levels. Finally, nations can help preserve ecosystem services through policies such as funding scientific research that addresses these issues and limiting overfishing and deforestation.

Case Study: Shark Bay Ecosystem

Decreases in shark populations affect many of the ecosystem services provided by ocean communities. Tiger sharks, sea cows, sea turtles, and seagrasses live in Western Australia's Shark Bay. The sharks prey on sea cows and turtles, which in turn eat seagrasses. Fish and shellfish depend on seagrasses for shelter from predators. In areas with few sharks, sea cows and sea turtles heavily graze seagrasses. This results in less habitat for shellfish, and fewer sites for fish to lay eggs and to grow while young. If sea cow and sea turtle populations were to grow too large, seagrass populations would collapse. As a result, shellfish and fish populations would decline and fisheries would lose profits. The loss of seagrasses also means fewer ocean plants to take up and store carbon. Excess carbon cycles back into the atmosphere and contributes to climate change.

Overfishing is the greatest threat to sharks, in Shark Bay and worldwide. Fisheries capture nearly 100 million sharks each year. Sharks can take more than 10 years to mature. Females give birth to only a few offspring, and do not give birth at all some years. So it takes a long time for shark populations to recover from overfishing. Australian conservation groups say protecting sharks is a priority. Their efforts include encouraging tourism to Shark Bay, which earns more profits than shark fishing. They are also setting catch limits and creating zones where shark fishing is not allowed.

Monitoring the healthy seagrass ecosystem in Shark Bay helps scientists identify ways to help threatened communities. This shark has been fitted with a camera and biosensor. They allow scientists to observe the shark's ecosystem interactions and monitor its behavior.

20. How does the health of shark populations affect the ecosystem services in the seagrass ecosystem? Select all that apply.
   A. Sharks help carbon-capturing seagrasses thrive.
   B. Sharks threaten sea cow and dolphin populations.
   C. Sharks help protect fish populations for human use.
   D. Sharks provide ecotourism opportunities.

21. What evidence in the text about Shark Bay suggests that a reduction in the tiger shark population has a large impact on the populations of other species?

EVIDENCE NOTEBOOK
22. Restoration efforts in the Everglades include developing marshes that filter pesticides flowing into the Everglades from farms farther north. How does this strategy directly affect wetland biodiversity and ecosystem services? Record your evidence.

Analyze the Spread of a Nonnative Species

Humans can accidentally transport species between distant ecosystems. For example, the emerald ash borer is a minor pest of trees in its native habitats in eastern Asia. However, it has destroyed millions of ash trees in the United States. It was first discovered in Michigan in 2002. It is native to Asia and likely came to the United States in wooden shipping crates. Ash tree destruction leaves gaps in forest canopies. Nonnative plants can grow in these brighter-light conditions. Damage to just one tree species may have long-lasting effects on many forest species.

Larvae of the emerald ash borer beetle feed on ash trees. They disrupt water and nutrient transport in the trees.

23. Nonnative species decrease / increase biodiversity by outcompeting native species for resources. They can also upset the balance of an ecosystem by decreasing / increasing the spread of diseases.

24. What are some ideas for technologies that conservationists might use to limit the spread of the emerald ash borer beetle? What might limit the implementation of these technologies?

Lesson 3 Engineer It: Maintaining Biodiversity and Ecosystem Services **577**

EXPLORATION 3

Evaluating Solutions for Maintaining Biodiversity

The most successful solutions to biodiversity loss meet the needs of ecosystems and of people. They protect biodiversity and ecosystem services while allowing people to meet their needs and maintain their quality of life. Some of these needs might conflict, but humans also benefit from healthy ecosystems. Understanding such needs and benefits encourages better collaboration among groups that develop and implement solutions.

Creative solutions help meet the needs of both humans and the environment. For example, fresh water is used to produce bottled water, juices, and other beverages. This use of fresh water reduces a limited natural resource. Beverage companies have partnered with conservation groups in watershed-protection efforts. The conservation groups work to restore and protect freshwater supplies using money donated by the beverage companies. Water quality and ecosystems within watersheds benefit from increased conservation efforts. The beverage companies benefit from tax breaks for their donations. They also create a more caring public image for consumers.

Monitor Biodiversity and Ecosystem Services

Effective solutions begin with understanding all parts of a problem. To understand threats to biodiversity, scientists must monitor changes to wildlife and ecosystem services. Some environmental factors are better indicators of the health of species and services than others, so this process begins with identifying factors to monitor.

Scientists then evaluate the best ways to gather data. They gather the data and analyze it carefully to identify the causes of decreases in biodiversity and ecosystem services in an area. Scientists conduct research to compare past and present data collected from ecosystems. They look for changes in ecosystem populations, resources, and services.

25. When human activities threaten ecosystem services, why is monitoring needed to design successful solutions? Select all that apply.

    A. to determine the severity of the problem
    B. to provide data for fundraising efforts
    C. to correctly identify causes of declines in ecosystem services
    D. to prioritize criteria for conservation efforts

This scientist gathers data about water quality. The information will be analyzed to determine if conservation efforts are needed.

Define Criteria of the Design Problem

Maintaining biodiversity and ecosystem services can be challenging, particularly when the needs of ecosystems conflict with those of humans. Ideally, solutions to such conflicts will address human needs and ecosystem needs. For example, in California, nearly 90 percent of floodplain, river, and seasonal wetland habitats have been lost to farming and city growth. Scientists agree that urban forests can help restore some of the services, such as stormwater runoff control and water filtration, provided by these habitats. Urban forests also provide shade and visual beauty. But urban areas need open space for roads, parking lots, and playing fields, and they may have dry climates that cannot support trees that need lots of watering. Such needs and limitations must be clearly defined and carefully considered.

Volunteers plant trees on a residential street to help increase the number of urban trees in Richmond, California.

There are many ways to increase urban tree plantings, but only some of these solutions will successfully address the problem. The *criteria* are the features a potential solution must have in order to work. Defining criteria as precisely as possible helps to ensure a successful solution. In this case, the criteria may include that the trees should be native species that require little watering. Other criteria might be that the trees should not change how parks are used, or that falling leaves must not create safety hazards for pedestrians and drivers. Some of these criteria focus on meeting the needs of the ecosystem. Others aim to meet the needs of people. Identifying the solutions that best meet the criteria is the next step in solving the design problem.

Define Constraints of the Design Problem

Designing effective solutions also requires considering environmental, economic, scientific, and social factors that affect the solution. These factors help to identify any limits the solution must work within. They are called *constraints*. Solutions that do not meet all the constraints of the design problem cannot be used. For example, an exciting design solution cannot be used if it is too expensive. One constraint of the urban forest problem could be that the canopy of mature trees must be less than 9 meters (about 30 feet) wide to protect road visibility and keep paths safe. Another limit is that established tree species must be able to survive periods with little water since watering restrictions will limit the amount of extra water the trees can get during dry weather.

26. What are some examples of social factors that city planners would need to consider before agreeing on a tree planting program in an urban area?

> **EVIDENCE NOTEBOOK**
>
> 27. Restoring wetlands involves reclaiming existing ranches and farmland. What are the costs and benefits of this solution for humans and ecosystem services? Record your evidence.

Lesson 3 Engineer It: Maintaining Biodiversity and Ecosystem Services

Case Study: Mountain Meadow Restoration

When trying to maintain biodiversity and ecosystem services, decision makers evaluate how well each proposed solution meets the criteria and constraints of the design problem. This step helps them decide which solution will be the most successful.

Recently, the water levels in California's reservoirs were at historically low levels, due to a long drought. Restoring the degraded mountain meadow ecosystems in California's Sierra Nevada watersheds is one proposed solution to help retain water. Meadow plants slow the flow of rainwater and melted snow. Water can then soak into the ground. This prevents flooding and erosion. It also improves the reliability and quality of water flow to streams and reservoirs. It is a long-term drought solution.

However, there are serious barriers to the success of mountain meadow restoration programs. Ranchers living in mountain areas do not support the programs because they reduce available grazing land. Restoration requires many workers, takes many years, and needs long-term monitoring. Also, measuring the positive benefits of meadow restoration is difficult. This makes funding hard to obtain. Government leaders prefer solutions to the water shortage problem that provide immediate, measurable results.

Conservation engineers added a trail above this mountain meadow in Yosemite National Park. The trail helps protect the meadow's plant life from people.

28. Mountain meadow restoration is a chosen solution to water shortages in California. Consider each of the criteria listed in the table. Rank the criteria on a scale from 1 to 4, with 4 being the most important. Then explain your reasoning.

Criteria for Mountain Meadow Restoration Projects in the Sierra Nevada	
Criteria	Ranking
Increase native species diversity in the restored area	
Encourage growth of plants that attract birds and pollinators	
Involve volunteer organizations to lower costs and provide workers	
Include regular sampling to determine progress and success	

Explain your reasoning:

Evaluate Proposed Design Solutions

Once restored, a new mountain meadow could fail. For example, pine trees around the meadow could spread into the area. Pine trees crowd out meadow plants. They increase shade that discourages new growth. There are several solutions to the spread of pine trees into meadows.

One option is to use prescribed burns to remove the trees. Intense fires damage ecosystems by destroying plants and changing soil chemistry, but small fires do little damage, especially if the plants in the fire area are wet.

A second option is to bulldoze pine trees that sprout and remove new saplings each winter. Removing trees on top of snow minimizes the disturbance of soil. This prevents loose soil from being washed away by water. If the soil washes into reservoirs, it would take up the water space and reduce water quality.

There are other possible options to control pine tree growth. Fences could be installed. Native, dense shrubs could be planted to make a physical barrier, so that animals could not carry fertilized cones into the meadow.

29. Use the decision matrix to score the proposed solutions to remove pine trees from the meadow. Use the criteria rankings you did earlier to help you score. For example, if you gave a "4" to "increase native species diversity in the restored area," then score each proposed solution on a scale of 0–4. Base the score on how well the solution meets that criterion. For the criterion that scored a "3," proposed solutions will be scored from 0–3. Use this same process for the criteria ranked "2" and "1." When done, total the score for each solution. Identify the most successful one.

Decision Matrix: Solutions to Reduce the Spread of Pine Trees into Restored Mountain Meadows					
Proposed solutions	Increase native species	Encourage birds and pollinators	Involve volunteer organizations	Include regular sampling	Total score
1. Use prescribed burns					
2. Wintertime tree removal					
3. Use barbed-wire fencing					
4. Use native-shrub barrier					

30. Think about your top-scoring solution. What are likely cost and social constraints that might need to be met when putting the solution into action?

Solution Tradeoffs

Sometimes solution priorities conflict with one another. In this case, tradeoffs must be accepted to carry out a solution. For example, a criterion for restoring mountain meadows is to keep cost as low as possible. To meet this criterion, a lot of volunteer help is needed. Volunteers likely lack the experience of experts, so the project will likely run longer than expected. Therefore, accepting that the project will take longer to complete is a fair tradeoff to reduce costs as much as possible. Another tradeoff might include accepting the increased difficulty and cost of controlling pines in the snow rather than in spring or summer.

Some solutions might no longer work as conditions change. Sometimes, unexpected issues cause the problem to be redefined. Suppose several native shrubs that are moved to the meadow carry a disease, which spreads rapidly. This creates a new problem that needs to be solved to preserve the meadow. New criteria and constraints need to be identified. Then new solutions can be considered.

Off-road enthusiasts discover a mountain meadow. Restoration plans had to shift to address the new threat to the meadow's health.

Identify a Solution

Decision makers looking for a solution to biodiversity loss often choose solutions that optimize the balance between benefits and cost. The best solution is often the one that addresses biodiversity loss directly by enacting laws. For example, overfishing is the primary threat to tiger sharks. A solution to the decline of shark populations that involves an immediate reduction in shark fishing would likely be prioritized over solutions that involve protecting sharks' breeding areas only.

31. Conservation groups and governments have limited budgets to fund projects. Which of the following solutions is most likely to be chosen to preserve biodiversity?

   A. the one with the fewest constraints

   B. the one that provides the most benefits at the lowest cost

   C. the one that best meets criteria and constraints, regardless of cost

   D. the one that most improves biodiversity

32. Suppose ranchers near a mountain meadow lobby local officials for grazing rights. Their lobbying disrupts plans for meadow conservation. How does this show that science contributes to understanding biodiversity loss and its possible solutions, but it does not dictate decisions that society makes?

___

___

___

___

TAKE IT FURTHER

Continue Your Exploration

Name: _____ Date: _____

Check out the path below or go online to choose one of the other paths shown.

Careers in Science

- Backyard Biodiversity
- Hands-On Labs
- Propose Your Own Path

Go online to choose one of these other paths.

Ecotourism

The ecotourism industry tries to provide exciting natural experiences for travelers. Their goal is to preserve habitats and increase awareness of threats to biodiversity. However, it is a challenge to provide tours to wildlife areas without disrupting protection efforts. Ecotourism companies can maximize benefits to ecosystems by working with governments, conservation groups, scientists, and citizens to design their programs.

Case Study: Elephant Conservation in Thailand

Elephants have played an essential role in the industry and culture of Thailand for centuries. Most of these elephants were captured to work in the logging industry. Then, logging was banned. Elephant caretakers (called *mahouts*) began working with their elephants in the entertainment and tourism industries. Not all elephants and mahouts do well in this new work, as care for the elephants is inconsistent and pay for mahouts can be low.

The elephant population in Thailand now includes about 5,000 animals. Only 20% live in the wild. Many elephants live in camps run by conservation groups or by people hoping to earn money by providing interactions with elephants. The camps are popular ecotourism destinations. Yet, some of them focus on tourism more than conservation. Many fail to meet the needs of elephants or mahouts. Ecotourism to those locations may encourage elephant interactions with people that conservationists want to prevent.

Ecotourism activities, such as elephant viewing, can help conservation efforts when their impact on wildlife is minimized.

TAKE IT FURTHER

Continue Your Exploration

The Elephant Nature Park (ENP) in northern Thailand is an example of how ecotourism can help biodiversity. ENP's mission criteria include being a sanctuary for endangered species, providing rainforest restoration, preserving native culture, and providing visitor education. The park is opposed to elephant shows or rides. It is home to more than 35 elephants and has cared for 200 more, returning them to the wild. ENP is supported financially by visitors, who pay to work at the camp and to care for the elephants.

1. ENP collaborates with conservation groups, Thailand's government, and local monks. The government provides funding and lands. The monks bless trees planted by the park, which discourages illegal logging. What does this tell you about how human culture and conservation efforts influence each other?

2. Inspired by ENP, other elephant camps are changing their ways. They are getting rid of elephant shows to focus on care and conservation. How is this evidence that ENP is meeting its mission criteria?

3. When evaluating the conservation success of the Elephant Nature Park, what additional information would you like to have? Can you rely on the information provided here about elephant conservation in Thailand? Why or why not?

4. **Collaborate** Imagine there is a natural resource in your community that needs protection from heavy tourist traffic. Brainstorm ecotourism-based solutions to this problem. With your group, develop criteria and choose one solution that meets the needs of people and the ecosystem. Present your solution to the class as a brief oral report.

LESSON 3 SELF-CHECK

Can You Explain It?

Name: _____   Date: _____

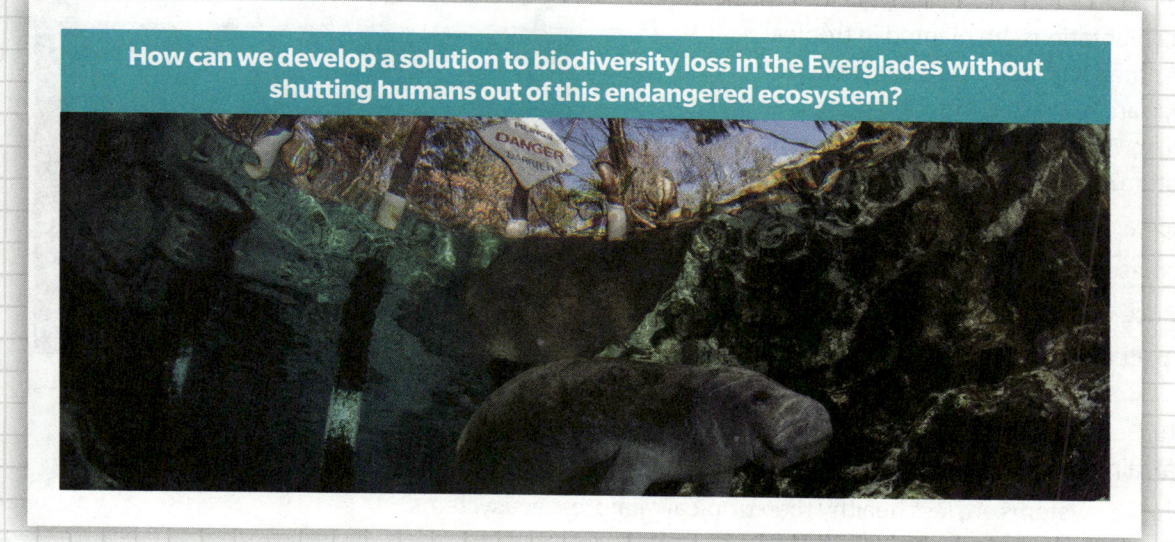

How can we develop a solution to biodiversity loss in the Everglades without shutting humans out of this endangered ecosystem?

> **EVIDENCE NOTEBOOK**
> Refer to the notes in your Evidence Notebook to help you construct an explanation for how to develop a strategy for maintaining biodiversity in the Everglades without shutting humans out.

1. State your claim. Make sure your claim fully explains what decision makers should consider and the steps engineers should take in designing a solution.

2. Summarize the evidence you have gathered to support your claim and explain your reasoning.

Lesson 3 Engineer It: Maintaining Biodiversity and Ecosystem Services

LESSON 3 SELF-CHECK

Checkpoints

Answer the following questions to check your understanding of the lesson.

Use the photo of a banana plantation to answer Question 3.

3. Banana plantations are planted in tropical forests. They displace other native plants. Bananas are harvested from the same plants year after year. What do banana plantations do in the ecosystem? Select all that apply.

   A. decrease biodiversity in the area
   B. increase natural resources
   C. reduce water pollution
   D. impact ecosystem services

4. Undisturbed polar ecosystems naturally have less biodiversity than undisturbed tropical rainforest ecosystems. Which of the following statements are true?

   A. Polar ecosystems are less healthy than tropical rainforest ecosystems.
   B. Polar ecosystems are home to fewer species than tropical rain forests.
   C. As long as they remain undisturbed, both ecosystems are equally "healthy."
   D. Polar ecosystems are less important than tropical rain forests.

5. Scientific understanding of biodiversity issues caused by overfishing *can / cannot* describe the consequences of continued overfishing. However, such knowledge *does / does not* identify the decisions society should make.

Use the photo of a protected habitat to answer Question 6.

6. Suppose people ignore a sign like this one. What might happen if they walk into the protected area? Select all that apply.

   A. increased water pollution due to littering
   B. destruction of turtle habitats
   C. increased participation in conservation efforts
   D. spread of a nonnative species

7. A wetland provides flood control services. Engineers are evaluating competing design solutions to preserve this service. What should they consider?

   A. the number of predators in the ecosystem
   B. the amount of impermeable ground cover (ground cover that does not soak up precipitation) in the ecosystem
   C. the best native plants to plant in the project area
   D. the number of pollinators in the project area

LESSON 3 SELF-CHECK

Interactive Review

Complete this page to review the main concepts of the lesson.

Humans depend on healthy ecosystems. Biodiversity is directly related to ecosystem health.

A. Explain why humans depend on healthy ecosystems for resources and services.

Strategies to maintain biodiversity include protecting habitats and individual species, reducing the impact of synthetic materials, and preventing the spread of nonnative species.

B. Explain how protecting habitats helps to maintain biodiversity.

Monitoring ecosystems allows scientists to develop solutions that help maintain biodiversity and ecosystem services. Choosing the best solution involves evaluating how well a possible solution meets the criteria and constraints of the problem.

C. When should scientists collect data about ecosystem biodiversity and services?

Lesson 3 Engineer It: Maintaining Biodiversity and Ecosystem Services 587

UNIT 7 CONNECTIONS

Choose one of the activities to explore how this unit connects to other topics.

☐ People in Science

John Paul Balmonte, Aquatic Microbial Ecologist
Born in the Philippines and raised in California, John Paul Balmonte is a member of the LGBTQ+ community and was the first person in his family to get a PhD. His studies of bacteria in aquatic ecosystems have taken him all over the world. Bacteria play many crucial roles in ecosystems as both producers and decomposers. Balmonte uses DNA sequencing to learn more about the types and functions of bacteria in lakes, rivers, and oceans.

Research a type of microorganism that is important to an aquatic ecosystem. What is its role in the ecosystem? Present your findings to the class.

☐ Engineer It

Permeable Pavers Stormwater runoff can lead to flooding and increased water pollution. Water that flows over roads, parking lots, and driveways can carry pollutants into bodies of water instead of being absorbed into soils. Permeable pavers were designed to reduce the amount of stormwater runoff.

Identify an area that has an issue with stormwater runoff. Research permeable pavers and at least two other design solutions for reducing runoff. Evaluate each solution based on the needs of your chosen area. Based on your analysis, recommend a solution and present your findings.

☐ Technology Connection

Camera Traps in Wildlife Research A camera trap takes a photo when an animal triggers its infrared sensor. Camera traps have provided important data related to wildlife conservation. Examples include evidence that Javan rhinos are breeding, a record of the first wolverine in California since 1922, and evidence that Siamese crocodiles still inhabit Cambodia. Data related to the range and size of populations are important for designing solutions to maintain biodiversity.

Research the benefits and limitations of camera traps. Investigate a case in which camera traps are being used to study a species or ecosystem. Create a pamphlet that explains how these data can help to maintain biodiversity.

A cougar caught on film by a camera trap in Wyoming.

UNIT 7 REVIEW

Name: _____ Date: _____

Complete this review to check your understanding of the unit.

Use the map to answer Questions 1 and 2.

1. Which part of the United States has the highest biodiversity of reptiles?
   A. Northwest
   B. Northeast
   C. South
   D. Midwest

2. ~~Purple / Red /~~ *Orange* regions on the map would likely be most affected by the removal of one reptile species. In general, areas with *higher* / ~~lower~~ biodiversity remain more stable, recovering *more* / ~~less~~ quickly after a disturbance.

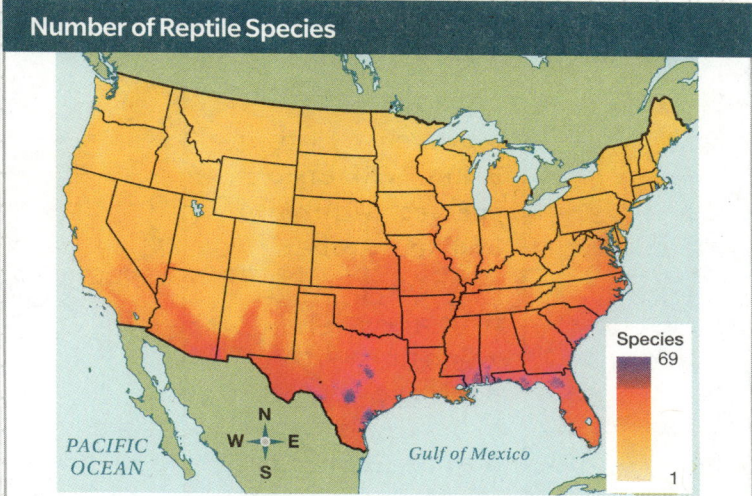

Number of Reptile Species

Credit: Adapted from "US protected lands mismatch biodiversity priorities" by Clinton N. Jenkins, et al, from *PNAS*, v. 112, no. 16, April 21, 2015. Reprinted by permission of PNAS.

3. Paclitaxel is a powerful anticancer drug that can be made from a chemical compound found in European yew trees. Paclitaxel is an example of a *natural* / ~~synthetic~~ material. Overharvesting populations of European yew trees without replenishing them would likely have a ~~positive~~ / *negative* impact on society.

Use this graph of coastal dead zones to answer Questions 4 and 5.

4. The amount of coastal dead zones *increased* / ~~decreased~~ between 1980 and 2010.

5. Biodiversity in these coastal dead zones is ~~high~~ / *low*. Therefore, the ecosystem health of these areas would be considered ~~high~~ / *low*.

Coastal Dead Zones Worldwide

Dead zones are areas in the ocean where the oxygen level in the deep water is so low that most organisms cannot live there. Fertilizer runoff is a major cause of dead zones in the ocean.

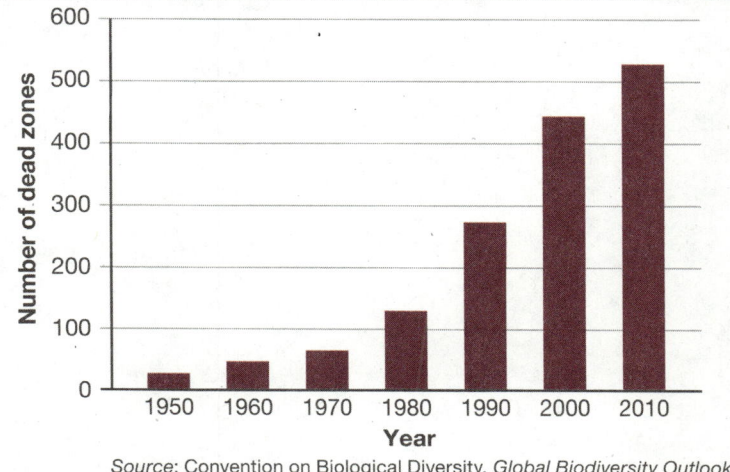

Source: Convention on Biological Diversity, *Global Biodiversity Outlook 3* (2010): 60.

Unit 7 Biodiversity and Ecosystem Dynamics

6. Complete the table by adding information about the features, stability, and impact of ecosystems with high and low biodiversity.

Ecosystem Biodiversity	Features	Stability	Impacts on Society
High Biodiversity	An ecosystem with high biodiversity has a high variety of species, in terms of the number of species and genetic variation within each species. Ecosystems with high biodiversity can generally recover relatively quickly from a disturbance.		
Low Biodiversity			

UNIT 7 REVIEW

Name: _____ Date: _____

Use the image of the farm to answer Questions 7–10.

Farm Ecosystem

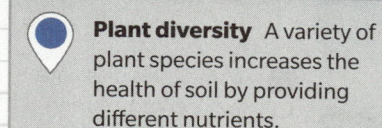

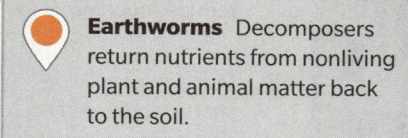

- **Plant diversity** A variety of plant species increases the health of soil by providing different nutrients.
- **Earthworms** Decomposers return nutrients from nonliving plant and animal matter back to the soil.
- **Bacteria** Some bacteria change nitrogen gas into forms of nitrogen that plants can use.
- **Fungi** Mycorrhizal fungi help provide plant roots with water and mineral nutrients.

7. Describe the ecosystem services provided by the diverse soil community shown in this farm ecosystem.

8. What might be the impacts on this farm if soil biodiversity decreased?

9. The forested area behind this farm became fragmented when the land was cleared for farming. How might this habitat fragmentation affect biodiversity in the forest?

10. In what ways could biodiversity be maintained on the farm and the surrounding ecosystems?

Unit 7 Biodiversity and Ecosystem Dynamics **591**

UNIT 7 REVIEW

Use the image of the mangroves to answer Questions 11–13.

Mangrove Trees

- Mangroves naturally filter runoff.
- Mangroves dissipate wave energy during storms, which reduces flooding.
- Mangroves provide shelter and breeding grounds for many organisms.
- Mangrove roots are well-anchored, preventing erosion.

11. What are some ways that mangrove trees promote biodiversity?

12. What are some ecosystem services that mangroves provide to humans?

13. How would this ecosystem be affected if many of the mangrove trees were removed?

592 Unit 7 Review

UNIT 7 PERFORMANCE TASK

Name: Date:

What is the best way to prevent shoreline erosion?

Humans have developed many solutions to try to prevent shoreline erosion. Compare the shorelines of these two images. In the image on the left, natural vegetation has been maintained along the lake shoreline. In the image on the right, the natural vegetation has been replaced with a stone wall. Research the strengths and weaknesses of each of these solutions, including how each solution might impact biodiversity and ecosystem services. Then make a recommendation to a homeowner on a similar lake who is considering both options. Write a report that highlights your findings.

The steps below will help guide your research and develop your recommendation.

Engineer It

1. **Define the Problem** Why is it important to prevent shoreline erosion along a lake? Define criteria and constraints of a design solution for preventing shoreline erosion. As you define the problem, consider that the lake is used for swimming, boating, fishing, and watching wildlife.

Unit 7 Biodiversity and Ecosystem Dynamics

UNIT 7 PERFORMANCE TASK

Engineer It

2. **Conduct Research** Compare and contrast the use of natural vegetation and a stone wall for preventing erosion along a shoreline. What are the strengths and weaknesses of each solution?

3. **Construct an Explanation** Explain how each solution would affect the biodiversity and ecosystem services for the lake ecosystem. How might a small change to one component of an ecosystem produce a large change in another component of the ecosystem?

4. **Recommend a Solution** Evaluate each solution based on how well they meet the criteria and constraints. Based on your evaluation, recommend one of these solutions for a homeowner who is considering both options.

5. **Communicate** Write a report that explains your evidence and reasoning for the recommended solution.

✓ Self-Check

	I defined the problem, including identifying criteria and constraints for the design solution.
	I conducted research to learn about two solutions for preventing shoreline erosion — natural vegetation and stone walls.
	I constructed an explanation for how each solution would affect biodiversity and ecosystem services in a lake ecosystem.
	I recommended a solution for a homeowner considering both options.
	I communicated the evidence and reasoning for my recommendation in a report.

Go online to access the **Interactive Glossary**. You can use this online tool to look up definitions for all the vocabulary terms in this book.

Pronunciation Key

Sound	Symbol	Example	Respelling	Sound	Symbol	Example	Respelling
ă	a	pat	PAT	ŏ	ah	bottle	BAHT'l
ā	ay	pay	PAY	ō	oh	toe	TOH
âr	air	care	KAIR	ô	aw	caught	KAWT
ä	ah	father	FAH•ther	ôr	ohr	roar	ROHR
är	ar	argue	AR•gyoo	oi	oy	noisy	NOYZ•ee
ch	ch	chase	CHAYS	o͝o	u	book	BUK
ĕ	e	pet	PET	o͞o	oo	boot	BOOT
ĕ (at end of a syllable)	eh	settee lessee	seh•TEE leh•SEE	ou	ow	pound	POWND
ĕr	ehr	merry	MEHR•ee	s	s	center	SEN•ter
ē	ee	beach	BEECH	sh	sh	cache	CASH
g	g	gas	GAS	ŭ	uh	flood	FLUHD
ĭ	i	pit	PIT	ûr	er	bird	BERD
ĭ (at end of a syllable)	ih	guitar	gih•TAR	z	z	xylophone	ZY•luh•fohn
ī	y eye (only for a complete syllable)	pie island	PY EYE•luhnd	z	z	bags	BAGZ
îr	ir	hear	HIR	zh	zh	decision	dih•SIZH•uhn
j	j	germ	JERM	ə	uh	around broken focus	uh•ROWND BROH•kuhn FOH•kuhs
k	k	kick	KIK	ər	er	winner	WIN•er
ng	ng	thing	THING	th	th	thin they	THIN THAY
ngk	ngk	bank	BANGK	w	w	one	WUHN
				wh	hw	whether	HWETH•er

R1

Index

Page numbers for key terms are in **boldface** type.
Page numbers in *italic* type indicate illustrative material, such as photographs, graphs, charts, and maps.

A

abiotic resource
  abundant, 374, *375*
  limited, 372, *372*
abrasion, in weathering process, 269, *269*, 272, 273
abundant resources
  abiotic, 374, *375*
  biotic, 374, *375*
  predicting effects of, 374–376
acetic acid, *113*, 114—115, 163
acid rain, 204, 218, *218*, 270
Act, 78, 167, 207, 349, 391
active volcano, 452, 474
  Kilauea, 455–456, *455*, *456*, 473, *473*
  Mauna Loa, Hawaii, 474–475, *475*
Adélie penguin, 523
aggregate, 10, *10*, 11, *11*, 13, *13*, 36, *36*
agricultural practices, soil impacts, 349, *349*
agriculture, ecosystem disturbances caused by, 532
Aialik Bay, Alaska, 544, *544*
air, as matter, 54
airbag, 149–150, *149*, *150*
airbag helmet, 28, *28*
air pressure, elevation changing, 97, 103
Alaska, tectonic plates in, 333, *333*
algae
  as biofuel, 257, *257*
  for biomass fuel production, 211, *211*, 213, *213*
  as biotic factor, 372
  feeding relationships, 384, 385–387, *385*
  photosynthesis in, 256
  phototrophs, 243
  producer transform sun energy into food, 236, *236*

algal bloom, 374, *374*
  effects of, 550
  in Gulf of Mexico, 575
alligator, 364, *364*, 365
Alligator Rivers region, Australia, 368, *368*
alluvial fan, 282, *282*, 432, *432*
aluminum
  extraction of, 15, *15*
  life cycle of, 9, *9*
Amazon rain forest, 565
amino acids, 251
ammonia, 154, *154*
ammonium chloride, 183, *183*, 185–186
amoeba, 366, *366*
amorphous silicon, 120, *120*
amphibolite, 297, *297*
analogy, 234
analysis
  of bicycle helmet designs, 30–31, *30–31*
  of biodiversity, 530–531
  of change of state, 88
  of chemical equations, 159–164
  of continental data, 320–323
  ecosystem energy flow, 402–406
  of habitat fragmentation, 572
  of impact of synthetic material, 500–505, *500–505*
  of interactions within Earth system, 428–431
  of molecules, 115
  natural hazard, historical data on, 450–451, *450*
  of natural resources used to create synthetic materials, 196–199
  of natural systems and chemical reactions, 138–139
  of ocean-floor data, 324–327
  of states of matter, 73–74

  of substances before and after chemical reaction changes, 146–148
  of synthetic material design, 210–212
  of thermal energy used in chemical processes, 179–183
anemone, clownfish and, 389, *389*
anglerfish, 391, *391*
animal
  as biotic factor, 372
  competition among, 393, *393*
  consumers of, 237
  decomposition of dead, 237
  feeding relationship of, 385–387, *385*, 388, 394
  impact of resource use on, 15
  plastics impact on, 516, *516*
  sunlight as energy source for, 233–234, 256–257, *256*
anole lizard, 393, *393*
Antarctica, 523
anteater, 237, *237*
apple, 235, *235*
aquifer
  contamination, synthetic material production, 502, *502*
  groundwater, 347, *347*, 352
  model recharge and withdrawal from, 353–354, *353*
Aral Sea, shrinking, 352, *352*
Arches National Park, 284, *284*
Arctic, oil drilling in, 416, *416*
arctic ecosystem
  biodiversity in, 564
  disappearing sea ice in, 50, *50*
argument
  constructing, 537
  from evidence, 36, 255, 304, 375, 387, 440, 569
  supporting, 231

R2 Index

Arizona
   Barringer Meteorite Crater, 427, *427*, 487, *487*
   meteorite crater, 427, *427*, 441, *441*
   South Coyote Buttes Wilderness area, 268, *268*

Army Corps of Engineers, 37–38, *37–38*

Art Connection
   Protein Power, 126

ash tree, 577, *577*

Asian carp, 394, *394*

aspirin, 209, *209*

Assessment
   Lesson Self-Check, 19–21, 39–41, 67–69, 81–83, 101–103, 123–125, 151–153, 171–173, 191–193, 215–217, 245–247, 263–265, 281–283, 305–307, 337–339, 357–359, 379–381, 397–398, 413–415, 441–443, 463–465, 489–491, 513–515, 541–543, 559–561, 585–587
   Unit Performance Task, 47-48, 131-132, 223-224, 313-314, 421-422, 521-522, 593-594
   Unit Review, 43–46, 127–130, 219–222, 309–312, 417–420, 517–520, 589–592

asteroid
   Barringer Meteorite Crater, Arizona, 427, *427*, 487, *487*
   biggest known Earth impacts, 488, *488*
   impact prediction, 487–488, *487–488*
   potentially hazardous asteroid (PHA), 487–488, *487–488*

Atlantic cod population, 536, *536*

atmosphere in Earth system, 429, *429*

atom
   balanced chemical equation, checking, 166
   bond to form molecule, 232, *232*
   as building blocks of matter, 231–232
   carbon as building block of living things, 251–252
   in chemical formula, 156
   in complex molecules, 115–117
   compounds of, 109–110, *109*, *110*, 125, *125*
   of elements, 108, *108*
   law of conservation of matter, 165
   mineral formation, 286
   in molecules, 112
   organisms and nonliving things made of, 104–120
   particles of matter, 107, *107*
   in simple molecules, 113
   structure affected by connections of, 119

avalanche, prediction, 468, *468*

avocado, lipids in, 252, *252*

B

bacteria
   as biotic factor, 372
   exponential growth pattern, 377, *377*
   nitrogen-fixing, 389
   photosynthesis in, 256
   phototrophs, 243
   producer transform sun energy into food, 236, *236*

baking soda and vinegar chemical reaction, 144, *144*, 163

balanced chemical equation, 165, 166–168, 169–170

bamboo, renewable source, 202, *202*

bananas, 537, 586, *586*

Banff National Park, Canada, 426, *426*

Bangladesh, *553*

Barbary macaque, 528, *528*

Barringer, Daniel Moreau, 427, *427*

Barringer Meteorite Crater, Arizona, 427, *427*, 487, *487*

basalt
   as igneous rock, 290, *290*
   metamorphic rock formation, 297, *297*

bat, 59, *59*

beach erosion, 272, *272*

bear, 56

beaver, 401, *401*, 413, *413*

bee
   biodiversity of, 530, *530*
   cross-pollination by, 390, *390*
   importance of, 549

Bezeau, Robert, 23, *23*

bicycle
   balanced equation for, 169
   helmet design, 26, *26*, 27, *27*, 29, 30–31, 41, *41*
   materials used to make, 206, *206*

bicycle helmet design, 26, *26*, 27, *27*, 29, 30–31, 41, *41*

biodiesel fuel, 212

biodiversity, 529
   of bird species, 534, *534*
   causes of loss of, 568–569
   description of, 528–531, 543
   ecosystem dynamics and, 523–594
   ecosystem health indicated by, 526–538, 587
   in ecosystem recovery, 533
   evaluating loss of, 564–569
   in Everglades, 563, *563*
   human creativity preserving, 562, *562*
   human influences on, 535–538
   loss of affecting ecosystem health, 567–569
   maintaining, 562–582
   measuring, 530–531
   monitoring and preserving, 538, 578, 587
   negative impact on, 536–537
   patterns in, 531
   protecting, 537
   solutions for maintaining, 578–582
   strategies for maintaining, 570–577
   types of, 529

biofuel, 213–214, *213*, *214*
   algae as, 257, *257*

biomass, 201, 213, 347, *347*

biomass engineer, 213–214, *213*

biomimicry, 42, *42*

bioremediation, 240, *240*

biosensor, 576

biosphere
   Earth system, 6, 429, *429*
   tabletop, 225

R3

biotic resources
   abundant, 374, 375
   limited, 372–373
bird
   biodiversity of, 534, *534*
   oil spill impact on, 205, *205*, 501, *501*
   songbird, 552
bison, 536
bleaching, 570, *570*
blizzard, 449, *449*
boiling point, 89, *89*, 98, 141
Bosch, Carl, 189–190, *189*, *190*
brainstorming, 25, *25*, 28, *28*
breccia, 292, *292*
bromine, 71, *71*, 81, *81*
Brown, Robert, 62
Brownian motion, 62
buckthorn, 536
bumblebee, 530, *530*
Burmese python, 536, *536*
burros, 532, *532*

C

calcite
   hardness of, 57
   in marble formation, 299, *299*
   as sedimentary cement, 292, *292*
calcium, 231, *231*
calcium carbonate
   limestone, 294, *294*, 295, *295*, 299, *299*
   sedimentary rock formation, 59, *59*, 294, *294*
caldera, 439, *439*, 440, *440*
California
   Clear Lake wildfire, 444, *444*
   Griffith Park in Los Angeles, 524, *524*
   mountain meadow restoration, 580–581
   Oak Woodland Regeneration, 557–558, *558*
   San Francisco Bay, 126
   Sierra Nevada, 580
   Silicon Valley, 126
   Sonoran Desert, 532, *532*
   urbanization of, 579
   water levels in, 580
   Yosemite National Park, 290, 291

canyon
   formation, 278, *278*, 285, *285*, 294, *294*, 305, *305*
   underwater, 318, *318*
Can You Explain It? 5, 19, 23, 39, *39*, 53, 67, 71, 81, 85, 101, 105, 123, 137, 155, 171, 175, 191, 195, 215, 229, 245, 249, 263, 267, 281, 285, 305, 319, 337, 341, 357, 361, 379, 383, 397, 401, 413, 427, 441, 445, 463, 467, 493, 513, 527, 545, 559, 563, 585
carbon
   as building block of living things, 251–252
   carbon-based molecules in cells, 251–252, *252*
   carbon cycle, 408, *408*
   in complex molecules, 115, *115*
   in diamonds, 106, 116, *116*, 119, *119*
   in graphite, 119, *119*
   in humans, 105, *105*, 231, *231*, 232
   in propane, 105, *105*
carbon cycle, 408, *408*
carbon dioxide
   alcoholic fermentation, 261
   in cellular respiration, 258–259, *258*
   chemosynthesis, 243
   lactic acid fermentation, 261, *261*
   molecule of, 232, *232*
   photosynthesis producing, 139, 236, *236*, 256, *256*
   plants using, 532, *532*
   removal of as ecosystem service, 7, *7*
   and water to form carbonic acid, 251, *251*
   from wood burning, 58
carbon fiber life cycle, 510
carbonic acid, 251, *251*
carbon monoxide, 113
carbon removal tower, 409, *409*
Careers in Engineering: Biomass Engineer, 213–214, *213*
Careers in Engineering: Civil Engineer, 37–38
Careers in Engineering: Materials Engineer, 511–512, *511*

Careers in Science: Ecotourism, 583–584
Careers in Science: Forensics, 99–100
Careers in Science: Restoration Ecologist, 539–540
carnivore, feeding relationships, 384, 385–387, *385*
Case Study
   Bicycle Helmet, 27, *27*
   Elephant Conservation in Thailand, 583–584
   Mountain Meadow Restoration, 580–581
   Reducing the Impact of Synthetic Fertilizers, 575
   Shark Bay Ecosystem, 576–577
cassiterite, 201, *201*
catalyst, in chemical reaction, 182, *182*
categories of matter, 55
cause and effect
   chain, 569
   constructing statements of, 527
   diagram, *376*
   relationship, 43, 359
   statement, 527
   table of, *44*, 393
cave, ecosystem of, 59, *59*
cavefish, 59, *59*
Cave of Crystals, Mexico, 52, *52*
cell of organism, 231
cell phone
   case for, 24
   design, 24, 26
   natural resources for, 6, *6*
   recycling, 504, *504*
   synthetic material life cycle example, 496–497, *496–497*, 500, *500*, 502, 506, *506*
cells
   carbon-based molecules in, 251–252, *252*
   energy production for, 248–265
   photosynthesis for energy production, 253–258

cellular respiration, 258
   for energy production, 258–260
   fermentation compared to, 261–262, *261*
   mitochondria, 258–259, *258*, *259*
   oxygen used in energy production, 258–259, *258*, *259*
cellulose, as natural resource, 197, *197*
cement, sand for, 5, *5*
cementation
   rock cycle model, 301–302, *301*
   sedimentary cement, 292, *292*, 294, *294*
ceramic, as synthetic material, 206
change of state, 86
   analyzing, 96
   classify and explain, 92, 103
   energy influences in, 86–88
   energy loss causing, 93–98
   gas to liquid, 94, *95*
   identifying, 88
   liquid to gas, 89–90
   liquid to solid, 94, *95*
   pressure affecting, 97–98
   solid to liquid, 89
Checkpoints, 20, 40, 68, 82, 102, 124, 152, 172, 192, 216, 246, 264, 282, 306, 338, 358, 380, 398, 414, 442, 464, 490, 514, 542, 560, 586
cheese, 261, *261*
chemical bond
   energy stored in molecular, 232, 250, 257
   in molecule, 232, *232*
   of molecules, 113, *113*
   photosynthetic energy storage, 256, 257
chemical cold pack design, 134, *134*, 184–188, *184*
chemical equation, 160
   analysis of, 159–164
   arrow in, 160, 162
   balanced, 160, 166–168, 169–170
   chemical reactions and, 162
   coefficient in, 160, 161, 166
   electrolysis of water, 160, *160*

   evaluate, 168
   identify, 164, *164*
   law of conservation of matter, 166–168
   to model chemical reactions, 154–173, 251, *251*, 252
   product in, 161, 251, *251*, 261
   reactant in, 251, *251*, 261
   subscript within, 160, 161, 166
chemical formulas, 156
   colored bricks as model for, 156, *156*
   using, 156–158, 160
chemical process
   chemical equations to model chemical reactions, 154–173, 251, *251*, 252
   energy analysis in, 179–183
   energy transformation through, 179–180, 181
   factors that affect thermal energy reaction rates, 182, *182*
   matter changes in chemical reactions, 136–153
   synthetic materials made from natural resources, 194–212
   thermal energy use in a device, 174–193
chemical property
   of elements, 107
   of matter, 58–59, 69, 141
   synthetic material, 209, *209*
chemical reaction, 144, 250
   in airbags, 149–150, *149*, *150*
   analysis of, 148
   balanced chemical equations, 166–168
   carbon-based molecules in cells, 251–252, *252*
   cellular respiration for energy production, 258–260
   chemical equation to model, 154–173, 251, *251*, 252
   chemistry of cells, 250–252
   energy production for cells, 248–265
   evidence of, 146, 147
   law of conservation of matter, 165–168
   matter changing identity in, 136–153

   modeling, 160, 162, 165–168, 251
   photosynthesis for energy production, 253–258
   physical change compared to, 143–145
   product, 144, 159, 250
   rate variables, 182, *182*
   reactant, 144, 159, 250
   signs of possible, 146
chemical separation of substances, 106
Chemical Vapor Disposition (CVD) diamond, 500, *500*
chemical weathering, 270, *270*
chemists, 189–190
chemosynthesis, 243
chemotrophs, 243–244, *243*
chimpanzee, 24, *24*
chloroplast
   photosynthesis, 256, *256*
chloroplasts
   electron micrograph, 257, *257*
   light energy capture in, 257, *257*
cholera, 42
circle graph
   biofuel in United States, 214
citric acid
   as synthetic material, 211
civil engineer, 37–38, *37–38*, 65–66
claim
   evaluate, 569
   stating and supporting, 19, *19*, 39, 67, 81, 101, 123, 151, 171, 191, 215, 245, 263, 281, 305, 320, 337, 357, 379, 397, 413, 441, 463, 489, 513, 541, 559, 585
climate, 449
   chemical weathering, 270, *270*
   ecosystem, 364
   freshwater distribution, 347, *347*
climate disasters, cost of, 461–462, *461*, *462*
climate hazards
   described, 448, *448*, 449, *449*, *478*
   historical data on, 478, 479
   monitoring, 480, *480*
   prediction, 477–481
   scientific understanding, 478
   worldwide data (1995–2015), 451, *451*

R5

climate regulation, as ecosystem service, 566, *566*
clownfish, 389, *389*
coal
   fossil fuel distribution, 344–345, *345*
   mining, 303–304, *303*
   as nonrenewable resource, 201
coarse-grained igneous rock, 290
coastal mangrove forest, 564, *564*
coefficient
   in balanced chemical equation, 166
   in chemical equation, 160, 161
coffee plantation, 567, *567*
coffee plants, 567–568, *567*
cold pack design, 134, *134*, 184–188, *184*
Collaborate, 18, 38, 66, 80, 100, 122, 145, 150, 170, 190, 214, 244, 262, 280, 304, 336, 356, 378, 396, 406, 412, 440, 462, 488, 512, 540, 558, 584
color
   chemical reaction to change flower petal color, 250, *250*
   as physical property of matter, 141
   as property of matter, 55, 57
colored bricks as model for chemical formulas, 156, *156*
combustion
   carbon cycle, 408, *408*
   energy produced by reactant, 181
   thermal energy and, 174, *174*
commensalism, 390
community, 365
   as level of ecosystem organization, 365
compare and contrast
   effects of disturbances, 551, *551*
   elements and compounds, *111*
   interior-to-edge ratios, 572
   performance to costs, 120
competition for natural resources, 370–373, 392–394
competitive pattern of interactions between organisms, predicting effects, 392–394
complex molecule models, 115–117
component of bicycle helmets, 27, *27*

composite material
   dental, 210, *210*
   described, 210
   fiberglass, 209, *209*
   formation of, 207
composition of matter, 118
compost, 313–314, *313*
compost bin, 238–239, *238*
compound, 109
   extended molecule structures, 116, *116*
computational thinking, 35, *35*
computer model, 34, *34*, 485
concentration in chemical reaction, 182, *182*
concrete, 6, *6*
   critical building material, 12, *12*
   production of, 10, *10*
   sand for, 5, *5*
condensation, 94, *94*, 95
   water cycle, 407, *407*
conduction, 177, *177*, 178
conductivity
   of elements, 107
   of matter, 57
   as physical property of matter, 141
coneflower, 536
conglomerate rock, 295, *295*
consequences
   long-term, 203–204
   negative, 203–204
   positive, 203–204
   short-term, 203–204
   of using natural resources, 203–205
conservation
   of elephants, 583–584
   of Everglades, 563, *563*, 568, *568*, 585, *585*
   individual species, 570–571, *571*
   in Micronesia, 570
   of natural water resources, 578
   need for, 587
constraints
   in addressing biodiversity loss, 579
   of engineering problems, 25, *25*, 26, *26*
   of fire alarms, 32, *32*
   influences of, 4, *4*

construction, sand for, 5, *5*
consumer, 237
   cellular respiration, 258
   energy pyramid, 406, *406*
consumer product, natural resources as, 12, *12*
consumer use, 12, *12*, 15, *15*
   synthetic material life cycle, 497, *497*, 503, *503*, 508, *508*
container design, cold pack, 187–188
continental data analysis, 320–323
   fossil data, 320–321, *320*, *321*
   landform data, 322, *322*
continental shelf, 322, *322*
   matching landform data across Atlantic, 320, *320*, 323
   ocean floor data, 324, *324*
contour plowing, 349, *349*
convection, 177, *177*, 178
convection current, 334
cooling in rock cycle, 301–302, *301*
copper
   distribution of, 342, *342*, 343, *343*
   electric conductivity of, 107
   as natural resource, 197, *197*, 198
   and silver nitrate chemical reaction, 155, *155*, 171, *171*
copper carbonate, 122, *122*
coral, 526, *526*, 528, 570, *570*
coral reef ecosystem, 526, *526*, 564, *564*, 570, *570*
cost versus performance, 120
cougar, 524, *524*, 588
coyote
   feeding relationships, 386–387, *386*
   population and drought, 383, 397
coyotes, 529, *529*
crime scene, 99
criteria
   in addressing biodiversity loss, 579
   of engineering problems, 25, *25*, 26, *26*
   of fire alarms, 32, *32*
   tradeoffs, 29, *29*

crop
  biodiversity lacking in, 537
  consumer use, 12, *12*
  demand on, 12, *12*
  from farming, 9, *9*
  production and distribution of, 10, *10*
  reintroducing wild genes in, 537
  resource availability, 200, *200*
  rotation of, 349, *349*, 575
cross-pollination by bees, 390, *390*
crude oil, 15, *15*
crystal, *286*
  mineral formation, 286, *287*
  model formation of, lab, 289
  time scale, igneous rock formation, 290, *290*
crystalline silicon, 120, *120*
crystals, 116, *116*
Cusatis, Ginluca, 65–66, *65*
Cynognathus, 320, *320*
cytoplasm, cellular respiration in, 258
Czech Republic, 527, *527*

D

Dalton, John, 61
dam, hydroelectric, 201, 347, 348, *348*, 352
data
  analyzing and interpreting, 35
  collecting, 538, 539
  continental data, 320–323
  fossil data, 320–321, *320*, *321*, 323
  landform data, 322, *322*, 342, *342*, 343, *343*
  from monitoring natural hazards, 469, *469*, 471, 474–475, 480
  natural hazard, 450–451, *450*
  ocean-floor data analysis, 324–327
  tornado, interpreting patterns in, 458–460
  volcanic, interpreting patterns in, 452–457
dead zone, 589, *589*
decision matrix, 581
decomposer, 237, *237*, 533

decomposition
  bioremediation, 240, *240*
  as biotic factor, 372
  carbon cycle, 408, *408*
  cycle of energy and matter, 229, 237–240, *237*, *238*, *239*
  ecosystem services of, 566, *566*
  by fungus, 236, *236*
  nitrogen cycle, 409, *409*
deep-ocean trenches, 324, *324*, 325, 327
Deepwater Horizon offshore drilling rig, 501, *501*
deer, population change in, 375, *375*
deforestation, 349, *349*, 557
  for coffee plantations, 567, *567*
delta, river, 273, *273*, 435, *435*, 517, *517*
density
  measure of mass and volume, 64
  as physical property of matter, 141
density of matter, 57
deoxyribonucleic acid (DNA), 117
deposition, 272
  agents of, 272–275
  energy driving process of, 272–278
  gravity as agent of, 274, *274*
  ice as agent of, 274, *274*
  rock cycle model, 301–302, *301*
  time scale, 278, *278*
  water as agent of, 272–275, *273–275*
  wind as agent of, 272–274, *273*
desert
  ecosystem of, 364, 528
  sand in, 36, *36*
  water supply in, 56
desert locust, 545, 559, *559*
design, of synthetic materials, 210–212
design problem. *See also* **engineering problem**
  defining constraints, 579
  defining criteria of, 579
  in real-life, 32, *32*
design process
  evaluate design solutions, 581
  identifying solutions, 2, *2*, 24, 36, 522, 582
  solution tradeoffs, 582

desire
  identifying, 26, *26*
  met by synthetic materials, 495
Devil's Tower, Wyoming, 291, *291*
diagram
  of airbag design, *150*
  of carbon-based molecules, *265*
  of carbon cycle, *408*
  cause and effect, *376*
  of cellular respiration and photosynthesis, *260*
  of chemical formulas of minerals, 158, *166*
  of chemical reaction rate variables, *182*
  of cycling of matter, *410*
  of diamond structure, *116*
  of earthquake warning system, *336*
  of elements and compounds, *111*
  of engineering design process, 25, *25*
  of fish and crab relationships, *376*
  of food chain, *403*
  of formation of polyethylene, *207*
  of landfill exposure pathways, *520*
  of molecular models, *112*, *113*
  of ocean floor, *324*, *327*
  of pencil production, *45*
  of plate boundaries and surface features, *329*
  of plate movement, *334*
  of rock cycle, *301*, *307*
  of soil formation, *344*
  Venn diagram, *551*
  of volcanic hazards, *454*
  of water molecule, *124*, *157*
  of weathering and erosion, *342*
  of web design process, *46*
  of Yellowstone Caldera area, *440*
diamond, 116, *116*, 119, *119*
  chemical formula for, 158, *158*
  synthetic, 500, *500*
digestion, chemistry of, 218
dinosaur, 230, *230*
  matching fossil data across Atlantic, 320–321, *320*, *321*
Dirzo, Rodolfo, 557–558, *557*

Discuss, 2, 6, 8, 12, 16, 24, 50, 54, 57, 75, 86, 89, 98, 118, 138, 139, 140, 143, 200, 203, 206, 226, 229, 230, 235, 241, 250, 253, 258, 271, 273, 278, 287, 288, 294, 296, 299, 301, 316, 320, 325, 342, 350, 362, 369, 374, 384, 392, 407, 424, 430, 431, 432, 446, 450, 473, 482, 495, 506, 508, 524, 546, 567

disease
  natural disasters and, 516, *516*
  as natural hazard, 448

disease control, as ecosystem service, 7, *7*

disposable glove testing, 506, *506*

disposal
  of products, 16, *16*
  synthetic material life cycle, 496, *496*, 504, *504*, 508, *508*

dissolution
  mineral formation, 286, 294, *294*
  natural resource distribution, 342–343, *343*
  sedimentary rock formation, 294, *294*
  as thermal energy reaction rate factor, 182

distribution
  impact of, 15, *15*
  synthetic material life cycle, 497, *497*, 503, *503*, 507, *507*

disturbance, 548

disturbance in ecosystem, 532–533, 541, *541*, 543, *543*, 548–550, *548*, 561

diversity, types of, 529, *529*

dodder plant, as parasite, 391, *391*

dog, 390, *390*, 391

dolerite
  as igneous rock, 290, *290*

Doppler radar
  weather data, 458, *458*, 480

dormant volcano, 452

Do the Math, 74, 168, 405, 462, 530, 572
  Analyze Eruption Data, 457, *457*
  Analyze Groundwater Use, 354
  Analyze Natural Resource Use, 199, *199*

Analyze Population Growth Data, 375, *375*
Analyze Relationships, 388, *388*
Analyze Size and Scale of Matter, 233
Analyze Temperature During a Change of State, 91
Analyze the Economics of Recycling, 505, *505*
Analyze Thermal Energy, 181
Assess Ecosystem Health, 534
Calculate Deposition, 293, *293*
Calculate Rate of Erosion, 272, *272*
Calculate Salinity, 60
Calculate the Amount of Material Needed, 28, *28*
Calculate the Rate of Sea-Floor Spreading, 326, *326*
Compare Costs and Benefits of Shade-Grown Coffee, 568
Compare Properties of Matter, 142
Compare Rates of Change, 434, *434*
Compare Rates of Renewal, 202, *202*
Compare Reactants and Products, 259
Explain Earthquake Probability, 476
Identify Factors That Change Populations, 553
Identify Ratios, 110
Interpret Natural Disaster Data, 451, *451*
Model the Scale of an Atom, 108
Reclaiming Land Using Sand in Singapore, 13, *13*
Stress-Strain Graph, 35, *35*

dragonfly, 362

Draw, 9, 95, 110, 116, 159, 187, 188, 278, 302, 319, 372, 410, 448, 499

drinking water, 12, *12*

drones (flying machine), 507, *507*

drought
  cost of, in U.S., 462, *462*
  coyote population, 383, *383*, 397
  desert locust swarms during, 545, *545*
  as natural hazard, 448, *448*
  as weather/climate hazard, 449, *449*
  worldwide data, 451, *451*

Dubai, 10, *10*

dunes, sand, 273, *273*
Dust Bowl, 349, *349*
dye, as natural resource, 197

E

eagle, 410, *410*
Earth interior, energy from, 431, *431*
earthquake
  data on U.S., 450, *450*
  deep-ocean trenches, 327, *327*
  distribution worldwide, 472, *472*
  as geographic hazard, 449, *449*, 472, *472*
  Haiti (2010), 472, *472*
  hazard areas in U.S., 450, *450*
  historic, in U.S., 450, *450*
  as natural hazard, 448, *448*
  natural hazard risk in U.S., 446, *446*
  practice drill, 424, *424*
  prediction, 475–476, *476*
  probability of major earthquake near Yellowstone National Park, 476, *476*
  tectonic plate boundaries and surface features, 329, *329*
  volcanic eruption, 452
  worldwide distribution, 472, *472*
  Yellowstone National Park, 439, *439*, 440, *440*

earthquake warning system, 335–336, *335*, *336*

Earth Science Connection
  cycling of resources, 416

Earth's system
  distribution of natural resources in, 6, 7, *7*
  subsystems of, 6

Earth surface
  continental data analysis, 320–323
  explaining changes on, 432–438
  fossil data, 320–321, *320*, *321*
  geologic processes changing, 426–443
  geologic process impacts, 426–443
  human use of synthetic materials impact on, 492–516
  large-scale geologic changes to, 432–433, *432*

R8 Index

modeling Earth's surface, 328–332
natural hazard prediction and mitigation, 466–491
natural hazards as disruptive to, 444–465
ocean-floor data analysis, 324–327
small-scale geologic changes to, 432–433, *432*
tectonic plate movement, 318–339
time scale of changes to, 433–438, *435*, *436*, *437*, *438*

Earth system, 428
analysis of interactions within, 428–431
atmosphere, 6, 429, *429*
biosphere, 6, 225, 429, *429*
cycle of energy and matter, 202, *202*, 229, 237–240, *237*, *238*, *239*, 430, *430*
cycles in, 138–139
cycling of matter in organisms, 228–247
distribution of natural resources in, 6, 7, *7*
Earth surface and plate movements, 318–339
ecosystem, 400–414
energy from Earth interior, 431, *431*
geosphere, 6, 429, *429*
human impact on, 202, 203–204
hydrosphere, 6, 429, *429*
igneous rocks related to, 288–291
inputs and outputs, 138–139
metamorphic rocks related to, 296–299
natural resource availability, 360–381
natural resource distribution, 340–359
patterns of interactions between organisms, 382–399
sedimentary rocks related to, 292–295
subsystem interactions, 429–430, *429*, *430*, *431*, *431*
time scale, 428
water on, 80

earthworm
as decomposer, 237
as food, 362, *362*

eastern gray squirrel, 551–552, *551*, *552*

ecologist, 532

ecosystem, 362, 365, **528**
abiotic factors, 362
analysis of energy flow in, 402–406
biodiversity and dynamics of, 523–594
biodiversity indicating health of, 526–538
biodiversity influencing health of, 526–538, 567–569
biotic factors, 362
carbon cycle, 408, *408*
of caves, 52, *52*, 59, *59*
changes in, 546–550
of coral reefs, 526, *526*
cycling of matter in, 407–410
distribution of, 364
disturbances in, 532–533, 541, *541*, 543, *543*, 548, 561
within Earth system, 400–414
effects of change on, 549
energy pyramid, 406, *406*
energy transfer in, 402–406
eutrophication of, 548, *548*
Florida everglades, 364, *364*, 365
food chains and food webs, 403–404, *403*, *404*, 406, *406*
forest, 363, *363*, 372, *372*
of forest floor, 546, *546*
habitat destruction of, 536, *536*
health of, 532, 564–569
human activity impact on, 535–538
human impacts on, 365
humans as part of, 535–538
humans' relying on, 564–567
impact of product disposal, 16, *16*
interactions in, 532, *532*, 573
keystone species in, 570–571
as level of ecosystem organization, 364, 365
levels of organization, 364–365, *365*
lionfish impact on local, 421–422, *421*
living environment, 362
living things and nonliving things in, 546–558, 561, *561*

maintaining, 562–582
natural resources from, 7, *7*, 14, *14*, 565, *565*
nitrogen cycle, 409, *409*
nonliving environment, 362
parts of, 362–365
pond, 402, *402*
population changes in, 551–555, 561
production and distribution disrupting, 15, *15*
rain forest, 372, *372*
recovery from disturbances, 533, 550
restoration ecologist designing solutions for, 539–540
services provided by, 566, *566*, 578
society's relationship with, 16, *16*
stability of through disturbances, 532, 533, *533*
stabilization of, 544–556
water cycle, 352, 407, *407*
water distribution in, 56, *56*
wetlands, 400, *400*

ecosystem diversity, 529, *529*
ecosystem services, 7, *7*
ecotourism, 583–584
eco-village, 23, *23*, 39, *39*
edge effect, 573
electrical energy, 120, *120*
electric conductivity of matter, 58
electromagnetic waves, 177, *177*
electronic industry, sand for, 5, *5*
electron micrograph
chloroplasts, 257, *257*
mitochondrion, 259, *259*

element, 106
in chemical formula, 156
in human body, by mass, 231, *231*
properties of, 107

elephant
as consumer, 237
preservation of, 557, 583–584
resources needed to survive, 366, *366*

Elephant Nature Park (ENP), 584
elevation
air pressure changing, 97–98, *97*
boiling point at, *98*

R9

El Niño Southern Oscillation (ENSO), 478
El Niño weather cycles, 395–396, *395, 396,* 478
Elodea, 254–255, *254, 256*
Elton, Charles, 411–412, *411*
emerald ash borer, 536, 577, *577*
emergency preparation, 483, *483,* 484
encaustic painting, 126, *126*
Endangered Species Act, 570
energy, 233
    cells, production for, 248–265
    cellular respiration for, 258–260
    chemical reactions for cellular production of, 248–265
    collecting solar energy, 9, *9*
    consumers, 237, *237*
    cycle of matter and, Earth system, 202, *202,* 229, 237–240, *237, 238, 239,* 430, *430*
    decomposer and decomposition, 229, 237–240, *237–239*
    from Earth interior, 431, *431*
    flow of in ecosystem, 532, *532*
    kinetic energy, 76–77
    law of conservation of energy, 139, 241–242, 250
    loss of causing change of state, 93–98
    in molecular chemical bonds, 232, 250, 257
    in organisms, 233–234
    in organisms, sources of, 235–240
    photosynthesis for, 253–258
    photosynthesis production of, 253–258
    producers, 236, *236*
    pyramid of, food chain, 416, *416*
    renewable, 201
    sun as source for plants and animals, 233–234, *234*
    transformation, 308, *308*
energy flow
    chemical processes analysis, 179–183
    cycle of matter and, Earth system, 202, *202,* 229, 237–240, *237, 238, 239,* 430, *430*

deposition, 272–278
drives cycling of matter in organisms, 228–247
drives the rock cycle, 284–307
drives weathering, erosion and deposition, 266–283
ecosystem analysis, 402–406
erosion, 272–278
food chain, 403, *403,* 404, *404*
food webs, 403–404, *404*
matter in organisms, 230–233
model in ecosystem, 405
weathering, 268–271
energy in molecular chemical bonds, 232, 250, 257
energy pyramid of ecosystem, 406, *406*
energy transfer
    conduction, 177, *177,* 178
    convection, 177, *177,* 178
    in ecosystem, 402–406
    radiation, 177, *177,* 178
    types of, 177–178, *177, 178*
engineer
    science practices compared to, 8, *8*
    society role of, 8
    synthetic material disposal, 508, *508*
engineering
    careers in, 37–38, 65–66, 213–214, 511–512
    distribution networks, 10, *10*
    purpose of investigations by, 33–36, *33–36*
    relationship between science, resources and, 4–21, *4–21*
    role in synthetic material life cycle, 506–509, *506–509*
    and science, 1–48
    science, technology, and, 8, *8*
    science and, 1–48
    science practices compared to, 33–36, *33–36,* 41, *41*
    solving problems and developing solutions, 33
engineering design process
    analyze and interpret data, 35, 224, 522
    ask a question, 34, 41, 521
    brainstorm solutions, 25, *25,* 28

    choose and model solutions, 25, *25*
    communicate information, 36, 48, 224, 314, 422, 522, 593
    computational thinking, 35
    conduct research, 48, 224, 314, 422, 522, 593
    consider tradeoffs, 25, *25,* 29
    construct an explanation, 422, 593
    define the problem, 25, *25,* 26, 34, 41, 47, *47,* 223, 313, 421, 593
    design solutions, 2, 24–32, 36, 522
    develop and test models, 25, *25,* 30–31, 34, 314
    develop solutions, 24–32, 33
    engage in argument from evidence, 36
    engineering problems, 26–32
    evaluate data, 48, 224
    evaluate solutions, 25, *25*
    identify and recommend solutions, 48
    identifying criteria and constraints, 25, *25*
    identifying needs or desires, 26, *26*
    identifying solutions, 2
    identify solutions, 2, 22, 48, 224
    implement solutions, 25, *25*
    iterative testing, 29, **29**
    make a recommendation, 314
    mathematical thinking, 35
    natural hazard mitigation, 486
    optimize solutions, 29, 41
    outline of, 25, *25*
    planning and carrying out investigations, 35
    recommend solutions, 2, 22, 48, 224, 422, 593
    refine solutions, 25, *25*
    solutions begin with, 24
    solve problems, 33
    test solutions, 25, *25,* 28, 29, 41
    using, 22–41
engineering model, 34
engineering problem, 29
    brainstorming solutions, 28
    constraints of, 26
    criteria of, 26
    defining, 26–27
    developing and testing solutions, 28
    identifying solutions, 2

optimizing solutions, 29
precisely wording of, 26
solutions begin with, 24
testing solutions, 29
Engineer It, 7, 11, 92, 145, 164, 211, 276, 293, 333, 354, 421, 434, 456, 593
  Analyze a Solution, 409, *409*
  Analyze the Life Cycle of Carbon Fibers, 510
  Control Population Growth, 369
  Desinging a Landslide Warning System, 471
  Evaluate Cost vs. Performance, 120
  Explore Bioremediation, 240
  Explore Uses of Algae as Biofuel, 257
  Forest Fire Control Policy, 556
  Identify Patterns in Shape and Volume, 74
  Identify the Effects of an Engineering Solution, 205
  Maintaining Biodiversity and Ecosystem Services, 562–587
  Monitor and Preserve Biodiversity, 538
  Performance Task, 47–48, 131–132, 223–224, 313–314, 421–422, 521–522, 593–594
  Permeable Pavers, 588
  Recommend a Material, 58
  Reduce Erosion, 350
  Use Competition to Control Population Size, 394
  Using the Engineering Design Process, 22–41
  Using Thermal Energy in a Device, 174–193
Enhanced Fujita Scale (EF Scale) for tornado, 459–460, *459*, *460*, 464, *464*
environment
  changes in, 567–569
  ecosystem disturbances in, 532–533
  human use impacting, 12, *12*
Environmental Science Connection
  acid rain, 218, *218*
  oil drilling in the Arctic, 416, *416*

erosion, 272
  agents of, 272–275, *273–275*
  as ecosystem service, 566, *566*
  energy driving process of, 272–278
  gravity as agent of, 274, *274*
  ice as agent of, 274, *274*
  modeling, 276–278
  natural control of, 7, *7*
  obtaining resources causing, 14, *14*
  reduction, 350
  rock cycle model, 301–302, *301*
  time scale, 278, *278*
  water as agent of, 272–275, *273–275*
  wind as agent of, 272–274, *273*
ethanol
  as synthetic fuel, 206
  as synthetic material, 211
ethylene, 574
  in polyethylene formation, 207, *207*, 210
eucalyptus leaves, as koala food, 384, *384*
Eurasian red squirrel, 551–552, *551*, *552*
European honeybee, 535, *535*
eutrophication of sediments, 548, *548*
evaporation
  of liquids, 89
  water cycle, 407, *407*
Everglades, 563, *563*, 568, *568*, 585
evidence
  analyzing, 100
  argument from, 36, *36*, 569
  forensic scientist collecting, 99
  supporting claims, 19, *19*, 39, *39*, 67, 81, 101, 123, 151, 171, 191, 215, 245, 263, 281, 305, 320, 337, 357, 379, 397, 413, 441, 463, 489, 513, 541, 559, 585
Evidence Notebook, 5, 12, 16, 19, 23, 26, 29, 34, 39, 53, 55, 60, 67, 71, 74, 76, 81, 85, 88, 91, 101, 105, 107, 109, 118, 123, 141, 146, 151, 155, 164, 167, 171, 175, 178, 180, 191, 195, 207, 210, 215, 229, 237, 241, 245, 249, 253, 260, 263, 267, 270, 275, 281, 285, 287, 295, 301, 305, 319, 327, 328, 333, 337, 341, 344, 351, 357, 361, 369, 373, 379, 383, 388, 394, 397, 401, 404, 406, 408, 413, 427, 429, 433, 435, 441,

445, 449, 454, 458, 463, 467, 469, 475, 484, 489, 493, 499, 503, 510, 513, 527, 534, 537, 541, 545, 549, 555, 559, 563, 568, 577, 579, 585
Exploration
  Analyzing Chemical Equations, 159–164
  Analyzing Continental Data, 320–323
  Analyzing Energy Flow in ecosystem, 402–406
  Analyzing Energy in Chemical Processes, 179–183
  Analyzing Feeding Relationships, 384–388
  Analyzing How Energy Influences a Change of State, 86–88
  Analyzing Human Influences on Biodiversity, 535–538
  Analyzing Interactions Within the Earth System, 428–431
  Analyzing Natural Resources, 196–199
  Analyzing Natural Systems, 138–139
  Analyzing Ocean-Floor Data, 324–327
  Analyzing Particles of Matter, 106–111
  Analyzing Parts of an Ecosystem, 362–365
  Analyzing Properties of Matter, 57–60
  Analyzing Strategies for Maintaining Biodiversity, 570–577
  Analyzing Substances Before and After a Change, 146–148
  Analyzing the Chemistry of Cells, 250–252
  Analyzing the Design of Synthetic Materials, 210–212
  Analyzing the Impact of Synthetic Materials, 500–505
  Analyzing the Life Cycle of Synthetic Materials, 494–499
  Comparing Engineering and Science Practices, 33–36
  Comparing Minerals and Rocks, 286–287

Comparing Physical Changes and Chemical Reactions, 143–145
Describing Biodiversity, 528–531
Describing Cellular Respiration, 258–260
Describing Changes in ecosystem, 546–550
Describing Matter and Energy in Organisms, 230–234
Describing Natural Hazard Mitigation, 482–486
Describing Natural Hazards and Natural Disasters, 446–451
Describing Natural Resource Use, 9–13
Describing the Cycling of Matter in ecosystem, 407–410
Describing the Impacts of Resource Use, 14–16
Designing a Cold Pack, 184–188
Developing Engineering Solutions, 24–32
Evaluating Biodiversity Loss, 564–569
Evaluating Ecosystem Health, 532–534
Evaluating How Pressure Can Affect Changes of State, 97–98
Evaluating Solutions for Maintaining Biodiversity, 578–582
Evaluating the Effects of Using Resources, 200–205
Explaining How Organisms Obtain Matter and Energy, 235–240
Explaining Human Impact on Natural Resource Distribution, 349–354
Explaining Patterns in Natural Resource Distribution, 342–348
Explaining Plate Motion, 332–334
Explaining States of Matter, 75–78
Explaining Symbiotic Relationships, 389–391
Explaining the Changes on Earth's Surface, 432–438

Exploring Agents of Erosion and Deposition, 272–275
Exploring Systems and Energy Flow, 176–178
Identifying Effects of Weathering, 268–271
Interpreting Patterns in Tornado Data, 458–460
Interpreting Patterns in Volcanic Data, 452–457
Investigating Photosynthesis, 253–257
Investigating Synthetic Materials, 206–209
Modeling Addition of Thermal Energy to a Substance, 89–92
Modeling Chemical Reactions, 165–168
Modeling Earth's Surface, 328–331
Modeling Matter, 61–64
Modeling Molecules, 112–117
Modeling Removal of Thermal Energy for a Substance, 93–96
Modeling the Rock Cycle, 300–302
Modeling Weathering, Erosion, and Deposition, 276–278
Observing Patterns in Matter, 54–56
Observing Properties of Matter, 72–74
Predicting Changes to Populations, 551–556
Predicting Effects of Abundant Resources, 374–376
Predicting Effects of Competitive Interactions, 392–394
Predicting Effects of Limited Resources, 370–373
Predicting Geologic Hazards, 472–476
Predicting Natural Hazards, 468–471
Predicting Weather and Climate Hazards, 477–481
Relating Cycling of Matter to Transfer of Energy, 241–242
Relating Engineering and the Life Cycle, 506–510

Relating Igneous Rocks to the Earth System, 288–291
Relating Metamorphic Rocks to the Earth System, 296–299
Relating Natural Resources to Science and Engineering, 6–8
Relating Resource Availability to Growth, 366–369
Relating Sedimentary Rocks to the Earth System, 292–295
Relating the Identity and Structure of Matter to Its Properties, 118–120
Using Chemical Formulas, 156–158
Using Properties to Identify Substances, 140–142

Explore First
Analyzing Food Labels, 228
Building Objects, 104
Categorizing State of Matter Changes, 84
Categorizing Substances, 194
Choosing Building Materials, 562
Classifying Events, 426
Constructing a Terrarium, 360
Constructing Puzzles, 318
Consuming Synthetics, 492
Cookie Mining, 4
Describing Properties of Objects, 52
Identifying States of Matter, 70
Investigating Changes to Matter, 266
Investigating Plants, 248
Mapping Resources, 340
Measuring Changes in Energy, 174
Modeling a Cargo Boat, 22
Modeling a Flood, 466
Modeling Ecosystem Change, 526
Modeling Rock Formation, 284
Modeling the Flow of Energy, 400
Observing Resource Use, 382
Reorganizing Materials, 136
Surviving a Natural Disaster, 444
Thinking About Changes, 544
Writing Formulas, 154

Explore ONLINE!, 24, 61, 72, 76, 86, 93, 137, 144, 149, 151, 155, 175, 179, 180, 191, 229, 250, 256, 288, 319, 328, 332, 337, 361, 379, 410, 413, 430, 452, 484, 535, 546

exponential growth of population, 377, *377*, 378, *378*

extended molecule structures, 116, *116*

extinction, 536, 570
  mass, 230

extinct volcano, 452

extrusive igneous rocks, 288

F

fabric, synthetic or natural, 194, *194*

farm
  obtaining resources, 9, *9*
  runoff from, 566, *566*, 567, 575
  synthetic fertilizer used on, 575, *575*

fat, in cells, 251–252, *252*

feeding relationship
  algae, 384, 385–387, *385*
  carnivore, 384, 385–387, *385*
  herbivore, 384, 385–387, *385*
  omnivore, 386
  pattern of interactions between organisms, 384–388
  plant, 384, 385–387, *385*
  and population size, 388
  predator and prey, 384, 385, 388, 394

fermentation, 261
  compared to cellular respiration, 261–262, *261*

fertility of soil, 344, *344*

fertilizer, 240, 503, 573

fiberglass, 209, *209*

fine-grained igneous rock, 290

fire
  alarm for, 32, *32*
  combustion, and thermal energy, 174, *174*
  non-matter, 54
  prevention, 556
  rates of energy transformation, 180

fireflies, 136

flameless heater, 175, *175*, 191, *191*

flamingo, food for, 384, *384*

flammability
  as chemical property of matter, 141
  of matter, 58

flea, as parasite, 391

flexibility of matter, 57

flood
  in Bangladesh, 553
  causes, 480, 481
  cost in U.S., 462, *462*
  ecosystem affected by, 527, *527*, 541, *541*
  Houston park improvement, 521, *521*
  model of deposition, erosion and weathering, 276–277, *277*
  as natural hazard, 448, *448*
  New Jersey, 466, *466*
  prediction of, 480–481
  protection by wetlands, 316, *316*
  river, 435, *435*
  sudden changes from, 548
  from tropical cyclone (2015), 461, *461*
  as weather/climate hazard, 449, *449*
  worldwide, 451, *451*, 480, *480*

flood maps, 481, *481*

Florida
  everglades ecosystem, 364, *364*, 365
  sinkholes in, 519, *519*

Florida panther, 571

fluorite, 340, *340*

flying squirrel, 363, *363*

food
  biodiversity lacking in crop, 537
  molecular structure of, 252, *252*
  plant, 240
  producer transform energy into food, 236, *236*
  reintroducing wild genes in crop, 537
  as synthetic material, 211

food chain
  ecosystem energy transfer, 403, *403*, 404, *404*
  limited biotic resources, 372
  pyramid of numbers, 416, *416*

food warmer, flameless, 175, *175*, 191, *191*

food web
  ecosystem, 403–404, *404*, 406, *406*
  energy pyramid, 406, *406*
  nitrogen cycle, 409, *409*

forces, collision transferring, 97

forecasting
  natural hazards, 468, *468*
  tornado, 479, *479*
  weather hazards, 479, *479*

forensic scientist, 99–100

forest
  clear-cutting, consequences of, 203
  coniferous, 360, *360*
  ecosystem of, 528, 551
  harvesting, 498, 499
  inputs or outputs in, 139, *139*
  limited resource effects, 370, *370*
  wildfire, 361, *361*, 379, *379*, 423, *423*, 431, *431*
  wildfire hazard mitigation, 484, *484*

forest ecosystem, 363, *363*, 372, *372*
  fire prevention effects on, 556

forest fire, 548–549, *549*

forest floor ecosystem, 546, *546*

formulas
  interior-to-edge ratios, 572
  percentage, 530
  salinity, 60

fossil, 321

fossil data
  continental, 320–321, *320*, *321*
  matching across Atlantic, 320–321, *320*, *321*, 323

fossil fuel
  as ancient biofuel, 257
  natural resource distribution, 344–345, *345*, 346, 350–351, *351*
  nonrenewable, 16, 201, 350–351, *351*
  pollution from, 573
  reducing need for, 12, *12*
  refining, 226, *226*
  transportation of, 15
  use of, 535, 565, *565*

fracking (hydraulic fracturing), 14, *14*, 507, *507*

R13

Fredrich Mohs, 57
freeze, cost in U.S., 462, *462*
freeze-thaw cycle
    chemical weathering, 270
    physical weathering, 269, *269*
freezing point, 94, *94*, 95
frequency, natural hazard data, 450–451, *450*
freshwater
    natural resource distribution, 346–347, *346, 347*, 352–354, *352*
    phytoplankton in ecosystem of, 249, *249*
frog, 258, *258*
fuel
    biofuel, 213–214, *213, 214*
    as synthetic material, 211, *211*
fungal disease, 537
fungus
    as biotic factor, 372
    as decomposer, 236, 237
    decomposition by, 236, *236*
    shelf fungi, 363, *363*
    soil formation, 344, *344*

G

gallium, 85, *85*, 101, *101*
game theory, 17
Garden by the Bay, Singapore, 562, *562*
gas, 74
    changing states of, 94, 95
    chemical reaction production of, 144, *144*, 146, 162, *162*, 172, *172*
    convection energy transfer, 177, *177*
gas chromatography (GC), 100, *100*
gases
    attraction of particles in, 78
    kinetic energy of, 97
    as state of matter, 55, 72, 83
    in volcanos, 49, *49*
gel electrophoresis, 131
genes, increasing variety of in crops, 537
genetic diversity, 529, *529*
    in crops, 537

geological processes
    igneous rock, 288, *288*
    metamorphic rock, 296, *296*
    sedimentary rock, 292, *292*
geologic hazard, volcanic eruption as, 452
geologic hazard prediction
    earthquake prediction, 475–476, *476*
    timing and magnitude, 472, *472*
    volcanic eruption prediction, 472, *472*, 473–475
geologic hazards
    described, 448, *448*, 449, *449*
    predicting, 472–476
geologic processes
    analysis of Earth system interactions, 428–431
    explaining changes on Earth surface, 432–438
    impacts on Earth surface, 426–443
    large-scale changes to Earth surface, 432–433, *432*
    small-scale changes to Earth surface, 432–433, *432*
    time scale of Earth surface changes, 433–438, *435, 436, 437, 438*
geosphere
    Earth system, 6, 429, *429*
    igneous rock in, 290
    metamorphic rock in, 298, *298*
    rare earth elements (REE), 355–356, *355*
    sedimentary rock in, 294, *294*
geyser, 439, *439*
Gibbons, Doug, 335–336, *335*
ginseng, 536
giraffe, 233, *233*
GIS (Graphic Information System), 485
glacier, 274, *274*, 548
glass, 6, *6*
    creating, 86, *86*
    liquid bioactive, medical, 511, *511*
    sand for, 5, *5*, 6
    as synthetic material, 206, 210, *210*
glassworker, 86, *86*
Global Positioning System (GPS), 474, *474*, 475

Glossopteris, 320, *320*
glove, testing disposable, 506, *506*
gluten-free foods, 308, *308*
gneiss, 296, *296*, 298, *298*
gold
    distribution of, 341, *341*, 342, *342*, 343, *343*
    iron pyrite compared, 140, *140*
    as nonrenewable, 351, *351*
    panning for, 278–280, *279–280*
    weathering, erosion and deposition, 278–280, *279–280*
gold particles, 62, 69, *69*
Gold Rush, 351, *351*
government, natural hazard mitigation, 483–484, *483, 484*
GPS (Global Positioning System), 474, *474*, 475
gradual changes in ecosystem, 548
graduated cylinder, 72
Grand Canyon, formation of, 285, *285*, 294, *294*, 305, *305*
granite
    as igneous rock, 290, *290*
    as natural resource, 197, 198
graph
    of bird species biodiversity, 534, *534*
    of forest coverage, 553
    Stress-Strain Graph, 35, *35*
    of temperature, 91
Graphic Information System (GIS), 485
graphic organizer
    for key concepts, 3, 51, 135, 227, 317, 425, 525
    Venn diagram, 551
graphite, 119, *119*, 197, *197*
gravel, 36, *36*
gravity
    as deposition agent, 274, *274*
    as erosion agent, 274, *274*
    tectonic plate movement, 334
    water cycle, 407, *407*
    as weathering agent, 268
gray squirrel, 551–552, *551, 552*
Great Garbage Patch, 574
Great Lakes, glacial origin of, 274
Great Salt Lake, Utah, 523, *523*
greenhouse gas, nitrous oxide, 575

greenschist, 298, *298*
Griffith Park in Los Angeles, 524, *524*
grossular, chemical formula for, 158, *158*
groundwater
  chemical weathering, 270, *270*
  contamination, synthetic material production, 502, *502*
  drilling for, 352
  filtration and treatment of, 10
  as freshwater resource, 346, *346*, 347, *347*, 352
groundwater, modeling, 562
growth, natural resource availability, 366–369
Gulf of Mexico
  Deepwater Horizon oil spill impact, 501, *501*
Gulfport, Mississippi
  Hurricane Isaac (2012), 447, *447*
gypsum crystal, 52, *52*, 286, 287
gyre, 574

H

Haber, Fritz, 189–190, *189*, *190*
Haber-Bosch reactor, 189–190, *190*
habitat
  of cougar, 524, *524*
  destruction of, 536, *536*, 568, 571
  fragmentation of, 571–572, *571*
  protecting and maintaining, 571–573
  reducing loss of, 576–577
Haiti, earthquake (2010), 472, *472*
Half Dome, Yosemite National Park, 290, 291
halite
  chemical formula for, 158, *158*
  distribution of, 343, *343*
Halls Bayou, Houston, 521, *521*
Hands-On Labs
  Analyze Visual Evidence, 436–437
  Build a Structure Using Your Own Concrete, 11
  Choose a Chemical Process, 185–186
  Design a Bicycle Helmet Model, 30–31

  Investigate a Change of State, 87–88
  Investigate Decomposition, 238–239
  Investigate Effects of Limited Resources, 371
  Investigate the Effect of Sunlight on Elodea, 254–255
  Make a Synthetic Material, 208
  Measure Biodiversity, 530–531
  Model Crystal Formation, 289
  Model Energy Flow in an Ecosystem, 405
  Model Erosion and Deposition, 277
  Model Habitat Fragmentation, 572
  Modeling Objects, 63
  Model Molecules, 114–115
  Model Recharge and Withdrawal in an Aquifer, 353–354
  Model the Movement of Continents, 330–331
  Observe a Chemical Reaction, 163
  Observe States of Matter, 73–74
  Observe Substances Before and After a Change, 147
  online, 1, 30, 63, 73, 87, 114, 147, 163, 185, 208, 238, 254, 277, 289, 330, 353, 371, 386, 405, 436, 455, 470, 509, 530, 554, 572
  Simulate Feeding Relationships, 386–387
  What Factors Influence a Population Change? 554–555
hand warmer
  energy changes in, 179, *179*
harbor seals, 377, *377*
hardness, as characteristic of matter, 55
hartebeest, at watering hole, 392, *392*
Haupt, Anna, 28, *28*
Hawaii
  Kilauea volcano, 455–456, *455*, *456*, 473, *473*
  lava flows through, 288, *288*
  lava rock formation, 438, 439
  Mauna Loa volcano eruption data, 474–475, *474*, *475*

Health Connection
  chemistry of digestion, 218, *218*
  Cholera Today, *42*
  cholera, 42
  gluten-free craze, 308, *308*
  natural disasters and disease, 516, *516*
heater, flameless, 175, *175*
heat of combustion, 58
heat pack design, 133
hematite
  chemical formula for, *158*
hematite, chemical formula for, 158
herbivore, feeding relationships, 384, 385–387, *385*, *386–387*
Himalaya mountains, 332, *332*, 432, *432*
historical data
  on hurricanes and tropical cyclones, 469, *469*
  natural hazard, 450–451, *450*
  natural hazard prediction, 469, *469*, 474, *474*
  tornado, U.S., 446, *446*, 459, *459*, 460, *460*, 478, *478*
  volcanic eruption, 474, *474*
  weather monitoring, 480
Hoover Dam, 308, *308*
hotsprings, calcium-rich, 293, *293*
Houston, Texas, 521, *521*
Huacachina Oasis, Peru, 346, *346*
human
  synthetic materials and society, 494–495, *495*
  use of synthetic materials impact on Earth surface, 492–516
human activity
  biodiversity influenced by, 535–538
  ecosystem disturbances caused by, 532–533, 543, *543*
  habitat destruction by, 568–569
  protecting biodiversity, 537, 543, *543*
human behavior, modeling, 17
human habitation
  ancient Italy, landslide or volcanic eruption, 445, *445*
  hurricane damage, 447, *447*, 482, *482*
  natural disaster risk, 447, *447*
  wildfire, 444, *444*

R15

human impacts
  on ecosystem, 365
  energy transfer in ecosystem, 402
  on fossil fuel distribution, 350–351, *351*
  on freshwater distribution, 352–354, *352*
  population and demand for natural resources, 14
  on resource quality and quantity, 368–369, *368*
  on soil distribution, 349, *349*
human population, impact of, 14
hurricane
  damage and deaths from U.S., 517, *517*
  flood maps evacuation zones, 481, *481*
  historical data on, 469, *469*
  natural hazard risk in U.S., 446, *446*
  prediction, 469, *469*
  satellite image of, 447, *447*
  as weather/climate hazard, 449
Hurricane Isaac (2012), 447, *447*
hydraulic fracturing "fracking," 14, *14*, 507, *507*
hydrochloric acid, 162, *162*, 172, *172*
hydroelectric energy, as renewable resource, 201, 347, 348, *348*
hydrogen, 61, *61*, 62
  from chemically separated water, 106
  electrolysis of water, 160, *160*
  as element, 231
  in human body, by mass, 231, *231*, 232
  in humans, 105, *105*
  in propane, 105, *105*
hydrogen chloride, 166
hydrogen peroxide, 164, *164*
hydrosphere, Earth system, 6, 429, *429*
hydrothermal vents, chemotrophs, 243–244, *243*
hyena, 373, *373*

I

ice
  as deposition agent, 274, *274*
  disappearing ecosystem of, 50
  as erosion agent, 274, *274*
  floating, 79–80
  formation of, 93
  to model energy movement, 178, *178*
  physical weathering, 269, *269*
  as solid water, 70, *70*
ice chest as thermal system, 177, *177*
ice dam, Missoula Flood, 276, *276*
Iceland, Mid-Atlantic Ridge, 318, *318*, 325, *325*
igneous rock, 288
  formation into metamorphic rock, 297, *297*, 301, *301*
  formation of, and changes to, 291, *291*
  geological processes, 288, *288*
  in geosphere, 290
  minerals in, 288, *288*, 290, *290*
  related to Earth's systems, 288–291
  time scale, 289, *289*, 438, 439
Indiana bat, 571
indigo dye, as natural resource, 197
individual
  growth and natural resource availability, 367, 368
  as level of ecosystem organization, 364, 365, *365*
infographic, 396
inputs and outputs
  Earth's system, 138–139
  system, 176
insulin, 209
interactions
  in ecosystem, 532, *532*
  feeding relationships, 384–388
  between organisms, 382–399
Interactive Review, 21, 41, 69, 83, 103, 125, 153, 173, 193, 217, 247, 265, 283, 307, 339, 359, 381, 399, 415, 443, 465, 491, 515, 543, 561, 587

interior-to-edge ratios, 572
introduced species, 536, *536*, 573, *573*, 577, *577*
intrusive igneous rock, 288, *288*, 290
investigations
  developing hypotheses, 531
  recording data, 531
  in science and engineering, 33–36
iron
  chemical weathering, 270
iron, chemical weathering, 270
iron ore
  distribution of, 343
iron ore, distribution of, 343
iron pyrite, 140, *140*, 158, *158*
island, sudden formation of, 319, *319*, 337, *337*
Italy
  ancient habitation, landslide or volcanic eruption buried, 445, *445*, 463, *463*
  eroded rock formation, 275, *275*
  Mount Vesuvius volcano, 457, *457*
iterative testing, 29

J

Japan, tsunami warnings, 469, *469*
Javan rhino, 588
jellyfish, 573
joule, 181

K

kayak, plastic, 195, *195*, 215
Kenai Fjord National Park, Alaska, 544, *544*
Kevlar©, 494, *494*
key concepts, graphic organizer for, 3, 51, 135, 227, 317, 425, 525
keystone species, 570–571, *571*
Khalili, Nadar, 42
Kilauea volcano, Hawaii, 455–456, *455*, *456*, 473, *473*
Kilhauea, 49, *49*
kinetic energy
  energy of motion, 76–77
  of gas particles, 97, *97*
  of particles, 75, 76–77, 78, 79
  thermal energy relating to, 89

kingfisher, 228, *228*
koala
   as consumer, 237
   eucalyptus leaves as food, 384, *384*
kudzu, 573, *573*
Kwolek, Stephanie, 494

L

lactic acid fermentation, 261, *261*
lahar, 453, *453*, 483, *483*
lake, ecosystem of, 528
land, biodiversity hotspots, 531, *531*
land bridges, 571, *571*
landfill
   disposal, 504, *504*
   exposure pathways, 520, *520*
landform data
   continental data analysis, 322, *322*
   mineral resource distribution, 342, *342*, 343, *343*
landforms, freshwater distribution, 347, *347*
landslide, 274, *274*
   extreme, worldwide data, 451, *451*
   as geographic hazard, 472
   as natural hazard, 448, *448*
   predicting, 470–471, *471*
landslide warning system, 471
Language Development, 3, 51, 135, 227, 317, 425, 525
Language SmArts, 9, 24, 77, 95, 148, 162, 334, 346, 552
   Analyze a Chemical Process, 183
   Analyze an Abundant Resource, 376, *376*
   Analyze Rate of Environmental Change, 550
   Categorize Matter, 55
   Cite Evidence for Conservation of Matter and Energy, 242
   Compare Tornado Data, 460
   Construct an Argument, 537
   Contrast Inquiry and Design Practices, 36
   Determine Sources and Uses of Synthetic Materials, 212
   Diagram the Cycling of Matter, 410

Evaluate Agricultural Practices, 569
Evaluate Molecule Models, 117
Examine Changes over Time, 438
Explain Evidence of Competition, 393
Find Evidence for Weathering, 271
Model the Life Cycle, 499
Model the Rock Cycle, 302
Relate Photosynthesis and Cellular Respiration, 260
Use Flood Maps, 481
large-scale geologic changes to Earth surface, 432–433, *432*
latex, in rubber production, 222, *222*
lava, 75, 96, *96*, 452
   energy from Earth interior, 431, *431*
   as hazard, 138, *138*
   igneous rock formation, 288, *288*, 290, *290*, 291, *291*
   mineral formation, 286
   rock formation, 438, 439
   sea-floor spreading, 325–326, *325*
   volcanic eruption, 452
   as volcanic hazard, 453
law of conservation of energy, 139, 241–242, 250
law of conservation of matter, 165, 250
   balanced chemical equations, 166–168
   cycling of matter and energy transfers, 241–242
   modeling chemical reactions, 165–168
   weathering, 268
law of definite proportions, 121, *121*
Laysan albatrosses, 574
lead, 121, *121*
lead iodide, 168
   lead nitrate and sodium iodide chemical reaction, *168*
lead sulfide, 121, *121*
leech, as parasite, 391

Lesson Self-Check, 19–21, 39–41, 67–69, 81–83, 101–103, 123–125, 151–153, 171–173, 191–193, 215–217, 245–247, 263–265, 281–283, 305–307, 337–339, 357–359, 379–381, 397–399, 413–415, 441–443, 463–465, 489–491, 513–515, 541–543, 559–561, 585–587
lianas vine, 236, *236*
lichen
   chemical weathering, 270
lichen, chemical weathering, 270
life cycle
   of carbon fiber, 510
   impact of resource use through, 14–16
   of products, 9–13
   synthetic material phases, 496–497, *496–497*, 500–505, *500–505*
Life Science Connection
   plastics, impact on animals, 516, *516*
lightning
   as weather/climate hazard, 449
   as weather hazard, 448
lightning bugs, 136, *136*
limestone
   marble formation, 299, *299*, 300, *300*
   rock cycle, 300, *300*
   sedimentary rock formation, 294, *294*, 295, *295*
limestone cave, 59–60, *59*
limited resources
   abiotic, 372, *372*
   biotic, 372–373
   predicting effects of, 370–373
linear sea
   formation, 325
linear sea, formation, 325
lion
   limited resources, 373, *373*
   as predator, 384, *384*
lionfish, 536
   impact on local ecosystem, 421–422, *421*

R17

lipids
   in avocado (food), 252, *252*
liquid, 74
   attraction of particles in, 78, 79
   changing states of, 89, *89, 90, 94, 95*
   convection energy transfer, 177, *177*
   gallium as, 85, 101, *101*
   as state of matter, 55, 72, 83
liquid metal, 72, *72*
litter, 573
living things
   decomposition of dead, 237
   in ecosystem, 528, *528*, 546–558, 561
   ecosystem disturbances affecting, 532
   as matter, 54, 230
   sunlight as energy source for, 233–234, *234*, 256–257, *256*
   water use of, 56
location
   chemical weathering, 270
location, chemical weathering, 270
locust, 545, *545*
logistic growth, population, 377, *377, 378, 378*
long-term consequences, of using natural resources, 204–205
Los Angeles, 524, *524*
luster, 57, *57*
Lystrosaurus, 320, *320*

M

macromolecule, 117, *117*
magma, 452
   deep-ocean trenches, 327, *327*
   energy from Earth interior, 431, *431*
   igneous rock formation, 288, *288, 290, 290, 291, 291*
   mineral formation, 286
   rock formation, 287, *287*
   sea-floor spreading, 325–326, *325*
   volcanic caldera, Yellowstone National Park, 439, *439*, 440, *440*
   volcanic eruption, 452, 453, *453*
magma chamber, metamorphic rock formation, 296, *296*

magnitude, natural hazard data, 450–451, *450*
mahouts, 583, *583*
malachite, chemical formula for, 158, *158*
malleability, as physical property of matter, 141
manatee
   conservation of, 563, *563*, 585, *585*
   as herbivore, 385, *385*
marble, formation of, 299, *299*
Marco Antinous, 126
marine debris, 574, *574*
marine ecosystem, 528, *528*
   biodiversity hotspots, 531
   biodiversity in, 536, *536*
marine ecosystem, phytoplankton in, 249, *249*
marine oil exploration, 573
Mars, 65
mass, 54
   of atoms, 108
   property of matter, 57, 83
mass extinction, 230
material
   different properties from same, 105, *105*
   recommending, 58
materials engineer, 511–512, *511*
mathematical model, 34
   of matter, 62
matter, 54, 230
   atoms as building blocks of, 231–232
   categorization of, 55
   changes in chemical reactions, 138–146
   chemical properties, 141
   chemical property of, 58–59
   condensation of, 94
   consumers, 237, *237*
   cycle of energy and, Earth system, 202, *202*, 229, 237–240, 430, *430*
   decomposer and decomposition, 229, 237–240, *237, 238, 239*
   flow of, 532, *532*
   mass and volume of, 54
   modeling, 61–64
   molecules composing, 232

   observing properties of, 72–74
   in organisms, 230–233
   in organisms, sources of, 235–240
   patterns in, 54–56, 69
   physical properties, 141
   producers, 236, *236*
   properties of, 57–60, 118–120, 140–142
   relating identity and structure to properties of, 118–120
   states of, 55, 70–78, 83, 93–96, 103
   structures of, 49–125
   as tiny, moving particles, 75
matter, changes in chemical reactions
   natural systems, analyzing, 138–139
   physical changes compared to chemical reactions, 143–145
   properties to identify substances, 140–142
   substances before and after, analyzing, 146–148
Mauna Loa, Hawaii, volcanic eruption data, 474–475, *474, 475*
meadow plant, 581
mechanical engineers, 37–38, *37*
medicine, 573
   aspirin, 209, *209*
   insulin, 211
   as synthetic material, 209, 211
melting, rock cycle model, 301–302, *301*
melting point, 89, *89*, 141
mercury, 64, *64*
Mesosaurus, 320, *320*, 321, *321*
metal
   as natural resource, 197, *197*
   thermal energy flow of hot metal in water, 176, *176*
metamorphic rock, 296
   formation of, 296, 297, *297*, 298, 299, 301, *301*
   geological processes, 296, *296*
   in geosphere, 298, *298*
   layers in, 296, *296*, 297, *297*, 298, *298*, 299, *299*
   related to Earth's systems, 296–299
   time scale, 298, *298*

metamorphism, 296
meteor, 487
meteorite
   crater in Arizona, 427, *427*, 441, *441*
   time scale of change, 433
meteorologist
   natural hazard data, 450
   tornado data, 459, *459*
methane, *113*
   balanced chemical equation, 167
Micronesia, 570
microscopes, 108
Mid-Atlantic Ridge, 324, *325*, 434, *434*
mid-ocean ridge, 324–325, *324*, *325*, 327, *327*
mineral, 286
   formation of, 286
   metamorphic rock formation, 296, *296*
   resource distribution, 342, *342*, 343, *343*
   within rock, 287, *287*
   rock compared to, 286–287
   rock formation, 287, *287*, 296, *296*
   small-scale geologic changes to Earth surface, 432–433, *432*
mineral resources, 565
   availability of, 6, *6*
   chemical formulas of, 158, *158*
   Mohs hardness scale for, 57
   as nonrenewable resource, 201, 350–351, *351*
   use of, *565*
minerals
   in igneous rocks, 288, *288*, 290, *290*
   natural resource distribution, 342–343, *342*, *343*, 350–351, *351*
   in sedimentary rock, 292, *292*
mining
   coal, 303–304, *303*
   impact on ecosystem, 14
   mountaintop removal, 205, *205*
   in United States, 7, *7*
Mississippi (state), Hurricane Isaac (2012), 447, *447*
Missoula Flood, 276, *276*
mitigation, 482
   natural hazard, 482–486

mitigation plan, natural hazard, 482, 483, 485–486, *486*
mitochondrion, cellular respiration, 258–259, *258*, *259*
model
   balanced chemical equation, 167, *167*
   chemical reactions, 160, *160*, 162, *162*, 165–168, 251
   of chemical substances, 160
   of deoxyribonucleic acid (DNA), 117, *117*
   deposition, erosion and weathering, 276–277, *267*
   developing and testing, 25, *25*, 30–31, 34
   Earth's surface, 328–332
   of ecosystem changes, 526
   of elements and compounds, *111*
   of matter, 61–64
   mitigation planning, 485
   of molecules, 112–117, *112*, 125, *125*
   of objects, 63–64
   Pangaea, 330–331, *331*
   particles of solids, liquids, and gases, 76–77, *76*
   of plastic polyvinyl chloride (PVC), 115
   removal of thermal energy, 93–96
   rock cycle, 300–302
   of scale of atom, 108, *108*
   testing solutions, 25, *25*
   of thermal energy added to substance, 89–92
   types of, 34
Mohs hardness scale, 57
mole (animal), 363, *363*
molecular structure, of food, 252, *252*
molecule
   atoms bond to form, 232, *232*
   carbon as building block of living things, 251–252
   carbon-based molecules in cells, 251–252, *252*
   chemical bonds in, 232, *232*
   chemical equations and chemical reactions, 162

chemically bonded atoms, 109, 112
chemosynthesis, 243
coefficient in chemical equation, 160
compounds of, 109–110, *109*, *110*
of deoxyribonucleic acid (DNA), 117, *117*
modeling, 112–117, *112*
particles of matter, 107, *107*
structures of, 118–120
mollusk, 528, *528*
monitoring
   earthquake warning system, 335–336, *335*, *336*
   landslide warning system, 471
   natural hazard, 469, *469*
   volcano, 474–475, *474–475*
   weather/climate hazard, 478, 480, *480*
monoxide, 118
moon in Earth system, 428
Morocco, 528, *528*
moss
   chemical weathering, 270, *270*
   resources needed to survive, 366, *366*
motion, of particles, 75, 76–77, 78, 90, *90*, 95
mountain, tectonic plate boundaries and surface features, 329, *329*
mountain ranges
   matching landform data across Atlantic, 322, *322*, 323
   volcanic, parallel to deep-ocean trenches, 327, *327*
mountaintop removal mining, 205, *205*
Mount Pinatubo volcanic eruption, 453, *453*, 472, *472*
Mount St. Helens volcanic eruption, 436–437, *436–437*, 453, *453*, 483, *483*
Mount Vesuvius volcano, Italy, 457, *457*
mudslide, lahar, 454, *454*, 483, *483*
mudstone, 292
muscle, lactic acid fermentation, 261, *261*

R19

mushroom, as decomposer, 236, 237
mutualism, as symbiotic relationship, 390

N

nail, chemical properties of, 141, *141*
National Aeronautics and Space Administration (NASA), 42, 487
National Oceanic and Atmospheric Administration (NOAA), 478, 479, *479*
National Weather Service (NWS), 478
natural disaster, 447
  climate hazards, 449, *449*
  described, 447, *447*
  geologic hazards, 448, *448*, 449, *449*, 472–475
  types of, 446, *446*, 448, *448*, 449, *449*
  weather hazards, 448, *448*, 449, *449*
  worldwide data (1995–2015), 448, *448*, 451, *451*
natural disasters
  cost of, in U.S., 461–462, *461*, *462*
  disease and, 516, *516*
natural ecosystem disturbances, 532–533
natural gas
  fossil fuel distribution, 345, *345*
  as nonrenewable resource, 201
  propane, 105, *105*
natural hazard, 446
  climate, 449, *449*
  describing risk, 446–451
  as disruptive to Earth surface, 444–465
  geologic, 448, *448*, 449, *449*, 472–475
  historical data on, 450–451, *450*
  mitigation, 482–486, *482*, *483*, *484–485*, *486*
  monitoring data on, 469, *469*, 471, 474–475, *474–475*, 480, *480*
  prediction, 468–471, *468–471*

risk in U.S., 446, *446*
  scientific understanding, 468, *468*
  tornado data, interpreting patterns in, 458–460
  types of, 446, *446*, 448, *448*, 449, *449*
  volcanic data, interpreting patterns in, 452–457
  weather, 448, *448*, 449
natural resource, 6, **196**, 340–359, 360–381
  analyzing, in creation of synthetic materials, 196–199
  availability of, 200–201, 360–381
  chemical makeup, 197, *197*
  competition for, 370–373, 392–394
  consequences of using, 203–205
  cycle of matter and energy, 202, *202*, 229, 237–240, *237*, *238*, *239*, 430, *430*
  distribution of, 6, 340–359
  ecosystem, parts of, 362–365
  evaluating the effects of using, 200–205
  factors that influence, 368–369, *368*
  fossil fuel, 344–345, *345*, 346, 350–351, *351*
  freshwater, 346–347, *346*, *347*, 352–354, *352*
  and growth, 366–369
  human impacts on, 349–354, 368–369, *368*
  life cycle of, 9–13
  limited resources, predicting effects of, 370–373
  living or nonliving, 196, 197, 202
  made from synthetic materials, 194–212
  management consequences, 203–204
  minerals, 342–343, *342*, *343*, 350–351, *351*
  nonrenewable, 16, 201, 350–351, *351*
  obtained in synthetic material life cycle, 496, *496*, 498, *498*, 501, *501*, 507, *507*

obtaining, 9, *9*
  patterns of, 342–348
  potentially renewable, 201
  predicting effects of abundant resources, 374–376
  processing of, 10
  properties of, 197, *197*
  relationship between science, engineering and, 4–21
  renewable, 201, 202, 347, *347*
  soil, 344, *344*, 349, *349*
  sources of, 6, 196
  uses of, 6, 9–13, 21, 198–199
natural resources
  from ecosystem, 565, *565*
  properties of, 60
natural system
  changes in matter and energy, 139
  inputs and outputs, 138–139
  matter and energy in, 138–139
Nebraska, tornado data collection, 458, *458*
needs
  identifying, 26, *26*
  met by synthetic materials, 494, *495*
  resource use driven by, 8
  of society, 8, 15
negative consequences, of using natural resources, 203–204 New Jersey, **flood**, 466, *466*
New Zealand, tsunami warning signs, 467, *467*, 489, *489*
Nile River, 56, *56*
nitrogen, in human body, 231, *231*
nitrogen-based fertilizer, 575, *575*
nitrogen cycle, 409, *409*
nitrogen dioxide, 110, *110*
nitrogen-fixing bacteria, 389
nitrous oxide, 110, *110*, 575, *575*
NOAA (National Oceanic and Atmospheric Administration), 478, 479, *479*
nonliving things
  in ecosystem, 528, *528*, 546–558, 561
  ecosystem disturbances affecting, 532
  as matter, 54
  observing patterns in, 52–64

R20 Index

nonliving things, as matter, 230
nonnative species, 536, *536*, 573, *573*, 577, *577*
nonrenewable resource, 16, **201**, 350–351, *351*
North Carolina, tornado risk in, 477, *477*, 478, *478*, 479, *479*
nuclear power plants, 203
nucleic acids, 251
nutrient
  in aquatic ecosystem, 550
  decomposition releasing, 546, *546*
  from forest fires, 556
NWS (National Weather Service), 478
nylon, 206, 209
  rope, 498

O

Oak Woodland Regeneration, 557–558, *558*
ocean
  chemotrophs, 243–244, *243*
ocean floor
  age estimate, 326, *326*, 327, *327*
  data analysis, 324–327
  deep-ocean trenches, 324, *324*, 325, 327, *327*
  mid-ocean ridge, 324–325, *324*, *325*, 327, *327*
  sea-floor spreading, 325–326, *325*
octopus, 366, *366*
odor, as physical property of matter, 141
off-road enthusiasts, 582
offshore oil drilling, 203, 205
Oglala Lakota Nation, 588
oil, 574
  formation of, 345–346, *346*
  fossil fuel distribution, 344–345, *345*, *346*
  plastic manufactured from, 195, *195*, 215
oil drilling
  in the Arctic, 416, *416*
  hydraulic fracturing "fracking," 14, 507, *507*
  offshore, consequences of, 203, 205
  offshore oil, 203, 205

oil spills
  bioremediation, 240, *240*
  impact of, 205, *205*, 501, *501*
OLED (organic light-emitting diode), 211, *211*
omnivore, feeding relationships, 386
online activities
  Explore ONLINE! 24, 72, 76, 86, 93, 137, 144, 149, 151, 155, 175, 179, 180, 191, 229, 250, 256, 288, 319, 328, 332, 337, 361, 379, 410, 413, 430, 452, 484, 535, 546
  Hands-On Labs, 11, 30, 63, 73, 87, 114, 147, 163, 185, 208, 238, 254, 277, 289, 330, 353, 371, 386, 405, 436, 455, 470, 509, 530, 554, 572
  Take It Further, 17, 37, 65, 79, 99, 121, 149, 169, 189, 213, 243, 261, 278, 279, 303, 335, 355, *355*, 377, 395, 411, 439, 461, 487, 511, 539, 557, 583
  Unit Project Worksheet, 2, 50, 134, 226, 316, 424, 524
  You Solve It, 1, 49, 133, 225, 315, 423, 523
ore, 343
organic light-emitting diode (OLED), 211, *211*
organic matter, soil formation, 344, *344*
organism
  atoms making, 104–120
  observing patterns in, 52–64
organisms
  chemotrophs, 243–244
  consumers, 237, *237*
  decomposer and decomposition, 229, 237–240, *237*, *238*, *239*
  energy in, 233–234
  energy sources for, 235–240
  matter in, 230–233
  matter sources for, 235–240
  phototrophs, 243, 244
  producers, 236, *236*
organisms, patterns of interactions between, 382–399
  feeding relationships, 384–388
  predicting effects of competitive, 392–394
  symbiotic relationships, 389–391

outputs
  Earth's system, 138–139
  system, 176
overharvesting, 536, 537, 570
owl, 411, *411*
oxygen
  biotic resources, 372–373, 374, 375
  in cellular respiration, 258–259, *258*, *259*
  from chemically separated water, 61, *61*, 62, 106
  chemical reaction from, 58
  in ecosystem, 528
  electrolysis of water, 160, *160*
  as element, 231
  in human body, by mass, 231, *231*
  in humans, 105, *105*
  hydrogen peroxide breakdown, 164, *164*
  molecular structure of, 118, *118*
  molecule of, 232, *232*
  as monoxide, 118
  in propane, 105, *105*
ozone, molecular structure of, 118, *118*

P

Pacific bluefin tuna, 570–571, *571*
Pacific Remote Islands Marine National Monument, 203, *203*
packing peanuts, 508
Palau, Italy, eroded rock formation, 275, *275*
Panama disease, 537
panda, as consumer, 237
Pangaea
  fossil data as support for, 320–321, *320*
  landform data to support, 322, *322*
  model, 330–331, *331*
  tectonic plate movement, 328, 331, *331*
paper, consequences of using, 203
parasitism, as symbiotic relationship, 391, *391*
parentheses, in chemical formula, 157

R21

parent rock, soil formation, 344, *344*
particle
  affecting properties of matter, 64, *64*
  density of in ice, 80
  energy of, 75–78, 83
  modeling, 63–64
  movement of, 75, 76–77, 78, 83, 90, *90*, 95
  of solids, liquids, and gases, 76–77, 90, *90*
  types of, 107
  of water, 107, *107*
particle theory of matter, 62, *62*, 69
passenger pigeon, 201, *201*
pattern
  in matter, 54–56, 57, 69
  in organisms and nonliving things, 52–64, *52*
  in resource distribution, 56, *56*
  scientist using, 56
  in shape and volume, 74
pattern of interactions between organisms, 382–399
  feeding relationships, 384–388
  predicting effects of competitive, 392–394
  symbiotic relationships, 389–391
pelican, oil spill impact on, 501, *501*
penguin, 70, *70*, 104, *104*
People in Engineering: Cusatis, Gianluca, 65
People in Engineering: Sultana, Mahmooda, 218
People in Engineering: Mensah-Biney, Robert, 516
People in Science: Alegado, Rosie, 308
People in Science: Balmonte, John Paul, 588
People in Science: Bosch, Carl, 189–190
People in Science: Dirzo, Rodolfo, 557–558
People in Science: Elton, Charles, 411–412, *411*
People in Science: Gibbons, Doug, 335–336, *335*
People in Science: Haber, Fritz, 189–190

People in Science: Hodgkin, Dorothy, 126
People in Science: Khalili, Nader, 42
People in Science: Proust, Joseph, 121–122, *121*
People in Science: Sundaram, Shrevas, 17
People in Science: Wegener, Alfred, 416, *416*
performance, cost versus, 120
permeable paver, 588, *588*
Peru, Huacachina Oasis, 346, *346*
pesticide, 573
petroleum
  as natural resource, 197
  as nonrenewable resource, 201
PHA (potentially hazardous asteroid), 487–488
phases of matter, 72
phenomena, science investigating, 33
philosophical models of matter, 62
phosphorus, in human body, 231, *231*
photosynthesis, 256
  carbon cycle, 408, *408*
  changes in matter and energy, 139, *139*
  chemical bond for energy storage, 256, 257
  chloroplasts for, 257, *257*
  as Earth system, 138–139
  for energy production, 253–258
  light energy capture in chloroplasts, 257, *257*
  modeling chemical reactions, 165, *165*
  phototrophs, 243
  of phytoplankton, 566, *566*
  producers, 253
photosynthetic algae, 570, *570*
phototrophs, 243, 244
photovoltaic cells, 120, *120*
phyllite, metamorphic rock formation, 297, *297*

physical change
  analysis of, 148
  chemical reaction compared to, 143–145
  described, 143
  law of conservation of matter, 165
physical damage, from obtaining resources, 14
physical model, 34
physical properties
  of matter, 141
  synthetic material, 209, *209*
physical properties of elements, 107
physical properties of matter, 57–58, 69
Physical Science Connection
  energy transformation, 308, *308*
physical weathering, 269, *269*
phytoplankton, 249, *249*, 566, *566*
Pinatubo volcanic eruption, 453, *453*, 472, *472*
pine marten, 552
pine tree, 581
  rates of renewal, 202
planning, natural hazard mitigation, 482, 483, 485–486, *486*
planning and carrying out investigations, 114–115
  ask questions, 132
  communicate information, 132
  conduct research, 131
  construct an explanation, 132
  develop a model, 132
plant. *See also* **photosynthesis**
  availability of crop resources, 200, *200*
  as biotic factor, 372
  consumers of, 237
  decomposition of dead, 237
  Elodea, 254–255, *254*, 256
  energy for the sun, 532, *532*
  feeding relationships, 384, 385–387, *385*
  fertilizers, 240, 503
  matching fossil data across Atlantic, 320, *320*

nitrogen cycle, 409, *409*
phototrophs, 243, 244
physical weathering, 269, *269*
producer transform sun energy into food, 236, *236*
as renewable resource, 16
sugar stored in, 252, *252*, 257
sun as energy source for, 233–234, *234*
sunlight as energy source for, 233–234, *234*, 256–257, *256*
plant material
    for biomass fuel production, 211, *211*, 213
    as natural resource, 197, *197*
plastic
    impact on animals, 516, *516*
    as synthetic material, 206, 210
plastic bag, 502, *502*, 573, *573*, 574
plastic bottle, recycling of, 23, *23*, 39, *39*, 493, *493*, 513, *513*
Plastic Bottle Village, 23, *23*, 39, *39*
plastic microbead, 574
plastic polyvinyl chloride (PVC), 115, *115*
plate tectonics, 333–334, *333–334*
platypus, as carnivore, 385, *385*
plesiosaurs, 230, *230*
pollen, 61, 62
pollination
    cross-pollination by bees, 390, *390*
    as ecosystem service, 7, 566, *566*
    from obtaining resources, 14
pollinator, role in ecosystem recovery, 533, *533*
pollution
    reducing, 573, *573*, 576–577
    from synthetic materials, 501–504
polyester, 209, *209*
polyester fabric, 493, *493*, 495, *495*, 513, *513*
polyethylene, formation of, 207, *207*, 210
polymer, 210, **210**
pond ecosystem, 402, *402*, 548, *548*

population, 365
    in community, 365
    competition, to control size, 394, *394*
    dependent on disturbances, 556
    effects of ecosystem changes on, 553–555
    exponential growth pattern, 377, *377*, *378*, *378*
    factors influencing, 554–555
    growth and natural resource availability, 367, *367*, 369, 373, *373*, 375
    as level of ecosystem organization, 365
    logistic growth pattern, 377, *377*, 378, *378*
    predicting changes in, 551–556
    size of, and feeding relationships, 388
    symbiotic relationships, predicting changes, 391, *391*
Port Campbell National Park, 267, *267*, 281, *281*
positive consequences, of using natural resources, 203–204
potentially hazardous asteroid (PHA), 487–488, *487–488*
potentially renewable resource, 201
Praia do Camilo region, Portugal, 266, *266*
prairie ecosystem, 530
precipitate
    chemical reaction production of, 146
    copper sulfate and ammonia, 154, *154*
    defined, 146
precipitation
    El Niño cycles, 395–396, *395*, *396*
    water cycle, 407, *407*
predator
    feeding relationships, 384, *384*, 385, *385*, 388, *388*, 394, *394*
    lion as, 384, *384*
    role in ecosystem recovery, 533

prediction
    asteroid impacts, 487–488, *487–488*
    of change of state, 87–88
    of climate hazards, 477–481, *477–481*
    flood, 480–481, *480–481*
    of geologic hazard, 472–476
    hurricane, 469, *469*
    of landslide, 470–471, *471*
    of natural hazard, 468–471, *468–471*, 469, *469*, 474, *474*
    of population changes, 551–556
    of volcanic eruption, 472, *472*, 473–475, *473–475*
    of weather hazard, 477–481, *477–481*
preparation, natural hazard mitigation, 483, *483*, 484
preservative, as synthetic material, 211
pressure
    affecting change of state, 97–98, 103
    to form diamonds, 119
    metamorphic rock formation, 296, 297, *297*, 298, *298*, 301, *301*
    mineral formation, 286
    rock cycle, 301, *301*
    rock cycle model, 301–302, *301*
    rock formation, 287, *287*
    sedimentary rock formation, 292, 293, *293*, 294, *294*
prey, feeding relationships, 384, 385, 388, 394, *394*
primary productivity, 253, *253*
problem, in science and engineering, 34. *See also* **engineering problem**
producer, 236, *236*
    cellular respiration, 258
    energy pyramid, 406, *406*
    photosynthesis, 253
    primary productivity, 253, *253*
product, 144
    in balanced chemical equations, 166, 167
    cellular respiration, 258, *258*
    in chemical equation, 161, 251, *251*, 261

in chemical reaction, 144, 159, 250
life cycle of, 9–13
photosynthesis, 256, *256*
synthetic material, 207
production
   impact of, 15
   processing resources, 10, 15
   synthetic material life cycle, 497, 502, *502*, 507, *507*
progesterone crystal synthesis, 133, *133*
propane, 105, *105*
properties of matter, 57–60, 69
   chemical properties, 58–59
   physical properties, 57–58
property
   of natural resources, 60
   of objects, 52
protein
   carbon-based molecules in cells, 251–252, *252*
   molecules of, 126
   in salmon (food), 252, *252*
prototype, 34
Proust, Joseph, 121–122, *121*
pumice, 290, 291
pure substance, 111, 118, 119–120, 125, *125*
P-waves, earthquake warning system, 335–336, *335*, *336*
pyramid of numbers, 416, *416*
pyroclastic flow, 452, 453, *453*

Q

quartz
   hardness of, 57
   as sedimentary cement, 292, *292*
questions
   asking questions, 34, 41, 132, 521
   in science and engineering, 34

R

rabbit, feeding relationships, 386–387, *386*
radiation
   as energy transfer, 177, *177*, 178
   nuclear power plants, 203

Rainbow Mountains, China, 295, *295*
rain forest, water supply in, 56, *56*
rain forest ecosystem, 372, *372*
rare earth elements (REE), 355–356, *355*
rates of thermal energy transformation, 180, 182
raw materials
   obtaining, 9, *9*, 14
   processing of, 10
reactant, 144
   in balanced chemical equations, 166, 167
   cellular respiration, 258, *258*
   in chemical equation, 161, 251, *251*
   in chemical reaction, 144, 159, 250
   energy produced by combustion, 181
   photosynthesis, 256, *256*
   synthetic material, 207
reactivity, of matter, *58*, 141
real-life design problem, 32
recovery, natural hazard mitigation, 484–485, *484–485*
recycling
   cell phone, 504, *504*
   disposal of synthetic materials, 504, *504*, 508, *508*
   plastic bottle into polyester fabric, 493, *493*, 513, *513*
   product disposal, 504, *504*, 508, *508*
   of products, 12, 16, 23, *23*
   resources obtained in synthetic material life cycle, 496, *496*, 498, *498*, 501, *501*, 507, *507*
   sorting machine for, 509, *509*
recycling product, 576
red clover, feeding relationships, 386–387, *386*
REE (rare earth elements), 355–356, *355*
relationship
   feeding, 384–388, *385*, *385–387*, 394
   local ecosystem and lionfish, 521–522
   science, engineering, and resources, 4–21
   society and ecosystem, 16

remora, on whale shark, 390, *390*
renewable resource, 16, **201,** 202, 347
   natural resource distribution, 347
   of natural resources, 16
resource. *See also* **natural resources**
   cycling of, 416
   discarding, reusing, or recycling, 12
   disposal of, 12, *12*
   distribution of, 10
   impact of using, 14–16, 21
   life cycle of, 9–13
   obtaining, 14–16
   relationship between science, engineering and, 4–21
respiration, carbon cycle, 408, *408*
response, natural hazard mitigation, 484, *484*, 485
restoration ecologist, 539, *539*
reusing product, 12, 16
review
   Interactive Review, 21, 41, 69, 83, 103, 125, 153, 173, 193, 217, 247, 265, 283, 307, 339, 359, 381, 399, 415, 443, 465, 491, 515, 543, 561, 587
   Unit Review, 43–46, 127–130, 219–222, 309–312, 417–420, 517–520, 589–592
rhino, 236, *236*
rift valley, formation of, 325, *325*
river
   canyon formation, 278, *278*, 285, *285*, 294, *294*, 305, *305*
   canyon underwater, 318, *318*
   delta formation, 273, *273*, 435, *435*, 517, *517*
   erosion and weathering, 273, *273*
   flood, 435, *435*
river sand, 36, *36*
road construction, 204, *204*
robin, 362, *362*
rock
   chemical weathering, 270, *270*
   formation of, 286
   igneous rocks related to Earth's systems, 288–291
   metamorphic rocks related to Earth's systems, 296–299

mineral compared to, 286–287
physical weathering, 269, *269*
sea-floor spreading based on age of, 326, *326*
sedimentary rocks related to Earth's systems, 292–295
small-scale geologic changes to Earth surface, 432–433, *432*
weathering, 268–271

rock cycle
energy flow driving process of, 284–307
modeling, 300–302

Rocky Mountains
intrusive igneous rock, 290
wildfire in, 423, *423*

roller coaster design, 24
rooftop garden, 538, *538*
root of plant, sugar stored in, 252, *252*, 257
rubber production, 222, *222*
runoff, water cycle, 407, *407*
rust
chemical property of matter and, 141
chemical weathering, 270, *270*
formation, 221, *221*
thermal energy produced by, 180, 181

S

salinity, calculating, 60
salmon, *56*
salmon (food), 363, *363*
protein in, 252, *252*
salt (table), distribution of halite, 343, *343*
salt deposits, 523
salt marsh, ecosystems of, 528
salts, sedimentary rock formation, 294, *294*
sample area, 538, *538*
sand
distribution of, 10, *10*
in hydraulic fracturing, 14, *14*
mining for, 9, *9*
as natural resource, 5, *5*, 6, *6*
rock formation, 287, *287*

sand dune, 273, 278
sandstone, 293
San Francisco Bay, 126
satellite, launch of weather, 480, *480*
satellite images
of hurricanes, 447, *447*
of Mississippi River dead zone, 575, *575*
saw mill, 199, *199*
Scablands, Missoula Flood, 276, *276*
scale. *See also* **time scale**
Enhanced Fujita Scale (EF Scale) for tornado, 459–460, *459*, *460*, 464, *464*
Volcanic Explosivity Index (VEI), 453, *453*
scale (proportion)
of atoms, 108, *108*
scanning tunneling microscope, 62
schist, 298, *298*
science, 41. *See also* **People in Science/Engineering**
analyzing and interpreting data, 35
asking questions, 33, 34, 132, 521
communicate information, 36, 48, 224, 314, 422, 522
constructing explanations, 36
defining problems, 34
developing and using models, 34
developing explanations, 33
engage in argument from evidence, 36
engineering, technology, and, 8
engineering and, 1–48
engineering practices compared to, 8, 33–36, 41
People in Science, 17–18
planning and carrying out investigations, 35
purpose of investigations by, 33–36
recognizing patterns, 56
relationship between engineering, resources and, 4–21
scientific knowledge
natural hazard mitigation, 486
scientific research
recognizing patterns, 56

scientific understanding
climate hazards, 478
natural hazards, 468, *468*
volcanic eruption, 473, *473*
weather hazards, 478
scientist
monitoring biodiversity, 578
monitoring ecosystem, 576–577, 578
society role of, 8
sea cow, 576
sea-floor spreading, 325–326, *325*
seagrass, 576
seagrass ecosystem, 576–577
sea level, rising, 570
sea otter, 570–571, *571*
season
ecosystem changes in, 547, *547*
sea star, 528, *528*
sea turtle, 573, *573*, 576
sediment, 268
buildup of, 548, *548*
erosion and deposition, 273, *273*, 274, *274*
rock formation, 287, *287*, 292, 293, *293*
soil formation, 344, *344*
sedimentary cement, 292, *292*, 294, *294*
sedimentary rock, 292
in caves, 59–60, *59*
coal as, 345, *345*
coal mining, 303–304, *303*
formation into metamorphic rock, 297, *297*, 301, *301*
formation of, and changes to, 287, *287*, 292, *292*, 293, *293*, 295, *295*
geological processes, 292, *292*
geosphere, 294, *294*
layers in, 292, *292*, 294
related to Earth's systems, 292–295
time scale, 294, *294*
seed bank, 537
seismometer
to monitor volcanoes, 474, *474*
Self-Check, 48, 132, 224, 314, 422, 522, 593, 594
sequoias, 556, *556*

R25

services, ecosystem providing, 566, *566*
shade-grown coffee, 567–568, *567*
shale, metamorphic rock formation, 296, *296,* 297, *297*
shared resource, 17
shark, 568, *568,* 576–577, *576*
sheep, 53, *53,* 67, *67*
shelf fungi, 363, *363*
shellfish, 576
Sherman, Sean, 588
shield volcano, 474, *474*
shipping, product distribution, 503, *503*
shooting stars, 487
short-term consequences, of using natural resources, 204–205
Shreyas Sundaram, 17–18, *17*
shrimp, oil spill impact on, 501, *501*
Siamese crocodile, 588
Sierra Nevada, 580
Sierra Nevada Mountains, 344, *344*
silica, 6, *6,* 36
silicon
  atoms of, 108, *108*
  in solar panels, 120, *120*
silicon dioxide, 36
silicon chips, 6, *6*
  sand for, 5, *5*
Silicon Valley, 126, *126*
silver, electric conductivity of, 107
silver nitrate, 155, *155,* 171, *171*
simple molecule models, 113
Singapore, 562, *562*
  reclaiming land, 13
sinkhole
  in Florida, 519, *519*
  as geographic hazard, 449, *449,* 472
slate, metamorphic rock formation, 297, *297*
slug, as decomposer, 237, *237*
small-scale geologic changes to Earth surface, 432–433, *432*
smoke, 58
snail, as decomposer, 246, *246*

society. *See also* **human impacts**
  demands of, 15
  ecosystem's relationship with, 16
  natural resources and, 6
  needs of, 8, 15
  role of engineers and scientists in, 8
  synthetic materials and, 494–495, *495*
sodium azide, 150, *150*
sodium chloride, 110, *110*
sodium hydroxide, 156, *156*
soil
  formation of, 344, *344*
  natural resource distribution, 344, *344,* 349, *349*
  sediment in, 268
solar energy
  collecting, 9, *9*
  as renewable resource, 16, 201, 347, 348, *348*
solar panel, 12, *12,* 120, 508, *508*
solar-powered Supertrees, 562, *562*
solid, 74
  attraction of particles in, 78
  changing states of, 89, *89,* 90
  conduction energy transfer, 177, *177*
  gallium as, 85, 101, *101*
  as state of matter, 55, 83
solubility, as physical property of matter, 141
solution
  begin with design problems, 24
  brainstorm, 25, 28
  choose and model, 25, *25*
  design, 2, 24, 36, 522
  develop, 24–32, 33
  evaluate and test, 25, *25,* 581
  for habitat loss, 576–577
  identify, 2, 22, 26, 48, 224, 582
  implement, 25, *25*
  for maintaining biodiversity, 578–582
  optimize, 29, 41
  for pollution, 576–577
  recommend, 2, 22, 48, 224, 422
  refine, 25, *25*
  to solve problems, 33
  test, 25, *25,* 28, 29, 41
  tradeoffs, 582

songbird, 552
Sonoran Desert, 532, *532*
sorting machine for recycled materials, 509, *509*
South Carolina, tropical cyclone flooding (2015), 461, *461*
South Coyote Buttes Wilderness area, Arizona, 268, *268*
space, energy transfer in, 177–178, *178*
species, 365
  extinction of, 536, *536*
  introduced, 536, *536*
  nonnative (introduced), 536, *536,* 573, *573,* 577, *577*
  overharvesting of, 536, *536*
  protecting individual, 570
species diversity, 529, *529*
Sphinx, Egypt, 278, *278*
spider, as carnivore, 385, *385*
spork, 29, *29*
squid, 574
squirrel, 551–552, *552*
  flying, 363, *363*
squirrel pox, 552
stabilization of ecosystem, 544–556
stalactite, sedimentary rock formation, 294, *294*
state change, as thermal energy reaction rate factor, 182
state of matter, thermal energy causing changes in, 84–98
states of matter, 70–78
steel, 176, *176*
steel wool, thermal energy produced by rust, 180, 181
stem of plant, sugar stored in, 252, *252,* 257
storm
  cost in U.S., 462, *462*
  as natural hazard, 448, *448*
  as weather/climate hazard, 449
  worldwide data, 451, *451*
Stress-Strain Graph, 35, *35*
structural engineer, 65
structures, of matter, 49–125

R26 Index

subscript
   in balanced chemical equation, 166
   within chemical equation, 160, *161*
   in chemical formula, 157
subsystem interactions, Earth, 429–430, *429*, *430*, 431, *431*
subunits, 116
sudden changes in ecosystem, 548–549
sugar
   carbon-based molecules in cells, 251–252, *252*
   in cellular respiration, 258–259, *258*
   molecule structure of, *116*
   plants making, 532, *532*
   producer transform sun energy into, photosynthesis, 236, *236*, 256–257, *256*
   and sulfuric acid chemical reaction, 137, *137*, 151, *151*
sugarcane, 106, *106*
sulfur, 121, *121*
   using on Mars, 65
sulfur dioxide, 110, *110*
sulfuric acid
   chemical formula for, 157
   and powdered sugar chemical reaction, 137, *137*, 151, *151*
sulfur trioxide, 110, *110*
sun, light energy capture in chloroplasts, 257, *257*
sunfish, 574
sun-grown coffee, 567–568, *567*
sunlight. *See also* **photosynthesis**
   as energy source, 532, *532*
   as energy source for plants and animals, 233–234, *234*, 256–257, *256*
   phototrophs, 243, 244
   producer transformation into food, 236
   rain forest ecosystem, 372, *372*
   as renewable resource, 16, 201, 347, 348, *348*
supercell, tornado formation, 458
Supertree, 562, *562*
surface area
   as chemical reaction rate variables, 182, *182*
   weathering, 268

S-waves, earthquake warning system, 335–336, *335*, *336*
symbiotic relationship
   commensalism, 390
   mutualism, 390
   parasitism, 391, *391*
   pattern of interactions between organisms, 389–391
   population changes, predicting, 391, *391*
symbols
   chemical formula, 156
   in parentheses, chemical formula, 157
synthetic fuels, 206
synthetic magnet, 49
synthetic material, 206
   analysis of impact of, 500–505, *500–505*
   analysis of natural resources used to make, 196–199
   analysis the design of, 210–212
   evaluating the effects of using natural resources to make, 200–205
   foods, 211
   formation of, 207, *207*
   fuel, 211, *211*
   human use impact on Earth surface, 492–516
   investigating, 206–209
   life cycle phases of, 496–497, *496–497*, 500–505, *500–505*
   materials for products, 211
   medicine, 209, 211
   natural resources used to make, 194–212
   pollution and waste, 501–504, *501–504*
   properties of, 207
   recycle as disposal of, 504, *504*, 508, *508*
   recycle for resources, 496, *496*, 498, *498*, 501, *501*, 507, *507*
   reducing impact of, 574–575
   reuse or recycle, 498
   society and, 494–495, *495*
   types of, 210–211
   uses, 209

synthetic material life cycle, 496–497, *496–497*, 500–505, *500–505*
   analysis of impact of, 500–505, *500–505*
   cell phone as example, 496–497, *496–497*, 500, *500*, 502, 506, *506*
   consumer use, 497, *497*, 503, *503*, 508, *508*
   disposal, 496, *496*, 504, *504*, 508, *508*
   distribution, 497, *497*, 503, *503*, 507, *507*
   economic impact of, 505
   engineering role in, 506–509, *506–509*
   production, 497, *497*, 502, *502*, 507, *507*
   recycle, 496, *496*, 498
   resources obtained for, 496, *496*, 498, *498*, 501, *501*, 507, *507*
system, 428. *See also* **Earth's system**
   described, 176
   energy flow in, 176–177
   inputs and outputs, 176

T

table
   of cause-and-effect, 44, *393*
   of chromatogram of evidence, *100*
   of comparing coffee plants, *568*
   of criteria and constraints, 31, 32, *580*
   decision matrix, *581*
   of electrical conductivity and reactivity of matter, *58*
   of living and nonliving things, *528*, *547*
   of observations, *73*, *87*
   of particles of solids, liquids, and gases, *77*
   of patterns, *55*
   of population changes, *554*
   of pure substances, *111*
   of salinity, *60*
   of states of matter, *83*

R27

Take It Further
  Analyzing Types of Population Growth, 377–378
  Balancing a Chemical Equation, 169–170
  Careers in Engineering: Biomass Engineer, 213–214
  Careers in Engineering: Civil Engineering, 37–38
  Careers in Engineering: Materials Engineer, 511–512
  Careers in Science: Ecotourism, 583–584
  Careers in Science: Forensics, 99–100
  Careers in Science: Restoration Ecologist, 539–540
  Chemistry and Engineering: Airbags, 149–150
  chemotrophs, 243–244
  Coal Mining, 303–304
  Cost of Natural Disasters, 461–462
  Environmental Changes and Interactions, 395–396
  Fermentation, 261–262
  Gold Rush, 279–280
  People in Engineering: Cusatis, Gianluca, 65–66
  People in Engineering: Sultana, Mahmooda, 218
  People in Engineering: Mensah-Biney, Robert, 516
  People in Science: Alegado, Rosie, 308
  People in Science: Balmonte, John Paul, 588
  People in Science: Bosch, Carl, 189–190
  People in Science: Dirzo, Rodolfo, 557–558
  People in Science: Doug, Gibbons, 335
  People in Science: Elton, Charles, 411–412
  People in Science: Gibbons, Doug, 335
  People in Science: Haber, Fritz, 189–190
  People in Science: Hodgkin, Dorothy, 126
  People in Science: Proust, Joseph, 121–122
  People in Science: Shreyas Sundaram, 17–18
  Predicting Asteroid Impacts, 487–488
  Rare Earth Elements (REE) and Technology, 355–356
  Why Does Ice Float? 79–80
  Yellowstone National Park as geologically active, 439–440
tall-grass prairie ecosystem, 530, *530*
tapeworm, as parasite, 391
technology
  development of through engineering and science, 33
  impact of on natural resources, 14, 21
  rare earth elements (REE) in, 355–356, *355*
  reducing emissions, 575, *575*
  role in natural hazard mitigation, 485–486, *486*
  science, engineering, and, 8
Technology Connection
  Biomimcry, 42
  Camera Traps in Wildlife Research, 588
  Silicon Valley, 126, *126*
tectonic plate, 328
  cause of plate movement, 334, *334*
  continental data analysis, 320–323
  earthquake and volcano distribution worldwide, 472, *472*
  Earth surface impacts, 318–339
  large-scale geologic changes to Earth surface, 432–433, *432*
  model Earth's surface, 328–332
  motion and movement, 328–334
  movement explained, 332–334
  ocean-floor data analysis, 324–327
  plate boundaries, 329, *329*, 342, *342*
  surface features, 329, *329*
  theory of plate tectonics, 333–334

temperature
  ammonium chloride and water, as chemical reaction, 183, *183*
  during changes in states of matter, 91
  changing states of matter, 84, *84*
  as chemical reaction rate variables, 182, *182*
  extreme, as weather/climate hazard, 449, *449*
  extreme, cost in U.S., 462, *462*
  extreme, worldwide data, 451, *451*
  extreme as natural hazard, 448, *448*
  to form diamonds, 119
  of lava, 96, *96*
  metamorphic rock formation, 296, 297, *297*, 301, *301*
  mineral formation, 286
  physical weathering, 269, *269*
  rock cycle, 301, *301*
  rock cycle model, 301–302, *301*
  rock formation, 287, *287*
  sedimentary rock formation, 292
  thermal energy increasing, 89, *89*
tensile strength testing, 34, *34*, 35, *35*, 41, *41*
termites, Trichonumpha mutualism, 390
Texas, Houston flooding and park improvement, 521, *521*
texture, as physical property of matter, 141
theory of plate tectonics, 333–334, *333–334*
thermal conductivity, cold pack container design, 188
thermal energy, 89
  airbags, 150
  changing states of matter, 84–98, 103
  chemical process analysis, 179–183
  cold pack design, 184–188, *184*
  energy analysis in chemical processes, 179–183
  energy transfer types, 177–178, *177, 178*
  factors that affect reaction rates, 182, *182*

Haber-Bosch reactor, 189–190, *190*
increasing particle movement, 90, *90*
modeling adding to substance, 89–92
model movement, 178, *178*
rates of energy transformation, 180, 182
systems and energy flow, exploring, 176–178
use in a device, as chemical process, 174–193
volcanic eruption as, 138, *138*

thorny devil, 414, *414*

thunderstorm
tornado formation, 458
as weather/climate hazard, 449
as weather hazard, 448

tick, 390, *390*, 391

tiger shark, 396, *396*, 574, 576–577, *576*

tiltmeter, to monitor volcanos, 474, *474*

time scale
of deposition, erosion and weathering, 271, 278, *278*
of Earth surface changes, 433–438, *435*, *436*, *437*, *438*
Earth system, 428
erosion, 278, *278*
igneous rock, 289, *289*
metamorphic rock, 298, *298*
sedimentary rock, 294, *294*
weathering, 271, 278, *278*

tool
engineers designing, 8, 24
gas chromatography (GC), 100, *100*
graduated cylinder, 72
microscopes, 108
scanning tunneling microscope, 62
scientist using, 8
technological advances of, 8
tiltmeter, 474, *474*

tornado, 548, *548*
average annual number in U.S., 459, *459*
average monthly number in U.S., 460, *460*
classification, 459, *459*
data, interpreting patterns in, 458–460, *458–460*
EF Scale (Enhanced Fujita Scale), 459–460, *459*, *460*, 464, *464*
forecasting, 479, *479*
formation, 458
hazards, 459, *459*
historical data on U.S., 446, *446*, 459, *459*, 460, *460*, 478, *478*
natural hazard risk in U.S., 446, *446*
by season in U.S., 478, *478*
warning, 477, *477*
as weather/climate hazard, 449
as weather hazard, 448
worldwide risk of, 477, *477*

Tornado Alley, U.S., 458, 459, *459*

tornado season, 458, *458*

toxicity of matter, 58

tradeoffs, 25, *25*, 29, 204

Trans-Alaska pipeline, 15

transportation system, impact of, 15, 204, *204*

tree
changes in matter and energy, 139, *139*
conservation of matter and energy, 241–242, *241*
decomposition by fungus, 236, *236*
as natural resource, 198, *198*, 199, *199*

trees
clear-cut harvesting, consequences of, 203
rates of renewal, 202

trenches, deep-ocean, 324, *324*, 325, 327, *327*

Trichonumpha, termite mutualism, 390

tropical cyclone
cost of, in U.S., 461–462, *461*, *462*
historical data on, 469, *469*

tropical storm, as weather hazard, 448

tsunami, 452
as geographic hazard, 449, *449*, 472
as natural hazard, 448
volcanic eruption, 452
warnings, Japan, 469, *469*
warning signs, 467, *467*, 489, *489*

Turkey, calcium-rich hotsprings, 293, *293*

turtle
algae on sea turtle shell, 382, *382*
competition, 370, *370*
saving sea turtle eggs, 223–224, *223*

U

United States Forestry Service, 556
United States National Park Service, 556
Unit Performance Task
How do lionfish affect relationships in local ecosystem? 421–422
Molecular Clues! 131–132
Save the Sea Turtles Eggs! 223–224
Should your school use vermicomposting? 313–314
What is the best plan to improve a park? 521–522
What is the best way to prevent shoreline erosion? 593–594
Which is the better water filtering solution for a village? 47–48

Unit Project
Design a Chemical Cold Pack, 134, 184–188
Develop a Natural Hazard Mitigation Plan, 424
Explore Disappearing Arctic Sea Ice, 50
Evaluate Biodiversity Design Solutions, 524
Investigate Fossil Fuels, 226
Relate Resource Use to Population Changes, 316
Solution Power! 2

Unit Review, 43–46, 127–130, 219–222, 309–312, 417–420, 517–520, 589–592

uplift, intrusive igneous rock, 290

uranium, as nonrenewable resource, 201

urban forest, 579

R29

V

values, met by synthetic materials, 495, *495*
vanilla, synthetic, 212
Vanuatu islands, 332, *332*
vegetable farm, 9, *9*
VEI (Volcanic Explosivity Index), 453, *453*
Venn diagram, *551*
vermicomposting, 313–314, *313*
vinegar, 144, 163
Vitava River, 527, *527*
volcanic ash
  energy from Earth interior, 431, *431*
  as hazard, 138, *138*, 452, 453, *453*
volcanic eruption, 452, 548–549, *549*
  deep-ocean trenches, 327, *327*, 332, *332*
  energy from Earth interior, 431, *431*
  as geologic hazard, 452
  hazards associated with, 454, *454*
  historical data, 474, *474*
  Mauna Loa data, 474–475, *474*, *475*
  Mount Pinatubo, 453, *453*, 472, *472*
  Mount St. Helens, 436–437, 453, *453*, 483, *483*
  as natural hazard, 448, *448*
  prediction, 472, *472*, 473–475, *473–475*
  scientific understanding, 473, *473*
  sea-floor spreading, 325–326, *325*
  tectonic plate boundaries and surface features, 329, *329*
  tectonic plate motion, 332, *332*
  volcano monitoring, 474–475, *474–475*
  Yellowstone National Park, 439–440, *439–440*
Volcanic Explosivity Index (VEI), 453, *453*
volcanic processes
  eruption, 138, *138*
  igneous rock formation, 288, *288*, 290, *290*
volcano
  caldera, 439, *439*, 440, *440*
  classification of, 452–453, *453*
  distribution worldwide, 472, *472*
  as geographic hazard, 472, *472*
  hazards, 452, 454
  hot gases and liquid molten material in, 49, *49*
  Kilauea, Hawaii, 455–456, *455*, *456*, 473, *473*
  lava from, 96, *96*
  monitoring, 474–475, *474–475*
  types of, 452
  worldwide distribution, 472, *472*
volcano data, interpreting patterns in, 452–457
  building site assessment, 455–456, *455*, *456*
  eruptions, 452–457, *452–457*
  volcanic hazards, 452, 454
  volcano classification, 452–453, *453*
volcano eruptions, data, 452–457, *452–457*
vole, as prey, 411, *411*
volume, 54
  measuring, 72
  patterns in, 74
  as property of matter, 57, 83
  of solid, liquid, and gas, 73–74
volunteer, 582

W

Wallula Gap, Missoula Flood, 276, *276*
warning
  tornado, 477, *477*
  tsunami signs, 467, *467*, 489, *489*
warning system
  earthquake, 335–336, *335*, *336*
  landslide, 471
Washington, Mount St. Helens volcanic eruption, 436–437, *436–437*, 453, *453*, 483, *483*
waste
  decomposition of, 237
  synthetic materials, 501–504, *501–504*
water
  and ammonium chloride, as chemical reaction, 183, *183*, 185–186
  carbon dioxide and, 251, *251*
  in cellular respiration, 258–259, *258*
  chemical formula for molecule of, 157, *157*
  chemical separation of, 61, *61*, 62, 106
  contamination, synthetic material production, 502, *502*
  cycle of, 138, 352, 407, *407*
  as deposition agent, 272–275, *273–275*
  distribution of, 10, 56, *56*
  drinking water extraction, 9, *9*, 565, *565*
  on Earth, 80
  electrolysis, 160, *160*
  filtering solution for, 2, 47–48, *47*
  gravity as agent of erosion, 274, *274*
  hydrogen peroxide breakdown, 164, *164*
  molecule of, 112, 232, *232*
  monitoring quality of, 578, *578*
  natural filtration of, 566, *566*
  physical weathering, 269, *269*
  pollution of, 573, 575
  producer transform sun energy into, photosynthesis, 236, *236*, 256, *256*
  purification of, 7
  states of, 75
  thermal energy flow of hot metal, 176, *176*
  as weathering agent, 268
water energy
  as renewable resource, 201, 347, 348, *348*
waterfall, 274, *274*
water molecule, *113*
watershed-protection, 578
water vapor
  condensation of, 94
  formation of, 89, *89*
waves, erosion and weathering, 273, *273*

weather, 449
   El Niño cycles, 395–396, *395*, *396*, 478
weather disasters, cost of, 461–462, *461*, *462*
weather hazards
   described, 448, *448*, 449, *449*, 477
   flood prediction, 480–481, *480–481*
   historical data on, 478, 479, 480
   monitoring, 478, 480, *480*
   prediction, 477–481, *477–481*
   scientific understanding, 478
   worldwide data (1995–2015), 451, *451*
weathering, 268
   chemical, 270, *270*
   energy driving process of, 268–271
   gravity as agent of, 268
   law of conservation of matter, 268
   modeling, 276–278
   physical, 269, *269*
   time scale, 271, 278, *278*
weather stations, 480
Wegener, Alfred, 416, *416*
Western Australia's Shark Bay, 576–577, *576*
West Mata volcano, 332, *332*
wetland
   as ecosystem, 400, *400*
   flooding protection by, 316, *316*
   natural hazard mitigation, 483, *483*
   oil drilling impact on, 501, *501*
whale, 573
whale shark, remora on, 390, *390*
White Cliffs of Dover, England, 295, *295*
WHO (World Health Organization), 42
wildebeest, 406, *406*
wildfire
   cost in U.S., 462, *462*
   extreme, worldwide data, 451, *451*
   forest, 361, *361*, 379, *379*, 423, *423*, 431, *431*
   human habitation and, 444, *444*
   as natural hazard, 448, *448*
   natural hazard mitigation, 484, *484*
wildlife corridor, 537
wildlife protection, 578

wind
   as deposition agent, 272–274, *273*
   as erosion agent, 272–274, *273*
   as renewable resource, 16, 201, 204, *204*, 347
   tornado EF Scale (Enhanced Fujita Scale), 459–460, *459*, *460*, 464, *464*
   as weathering agent, 268
wolf
   ecosystem reintroduction and beaver population, 401, *401*, 413, *413*
   population changes in, 554–555
wood
   changes in matter and energy, 139, *139*
   as matter, 54, *54*, 58, *58*
   physical change to, 143, *143*
wool, 53, *53*, 67, *67*
world biodiversity hotspots, 531, *531*
World Health Organization (WHO), 42
worldwide, natural disaster data (1995–2015), 448, *448*, 451, *451*
worms, vermicomposting, 313–314, *313*
Write, 32, 161, 370, 438, 499, 593, 594
Wyoming, Devil's Tower, 291

Y

yeast, alcoholic fermentation, 261
Yellowstone National Park
   as geologically active, 439–440, *439–440*
   probability of major earthquake near, 476, *476*
   volcanic explosivity, 453, *453*
   wolf reintroduction and beaver population, 401, *401*, 413, *413*
yogurt, lactic acid fermentation, 261
Yosemite National Park, 580
Yosemite National Park, California, 290, *291*
You Solve It, 1, 49, 133, 225, 315, 423, 523

Z

zebra, at watering hole, 392, *392*
zinc metal, 162, *162*, 172, *172*